STUDENT SOLUTIONS MANUAL

BUSINESS STATISTICS:
A Decision-Making Approach

Seventh Edition

David F. Groebner
Patrick W. Shannon
Phillip C. Fry
Kent D. Smith

PEARSON

Prentice Hall

Upper Saddle River, New Jersey 07458

VP/Editorial Director: Jeff Shelstad
Acquisitions Editor: Mark Pfaltzgraff
Assistant Editor: Kelly Loftus
Production Editor: Carol Samet
Buyer: Arnold Vila

Pearson Prentice Hall™ **is a trademark of Pearson Education, Inc.**

10 9 8 7 6 5 4 3 2 1

ISBN-13: 978-0-13-223976-9
ISBN-10:   0-13-223976-0

Table of Contents

STUDENT SOLUTIONS MANUAL

Chapter 1 Solutions

Section 1.1 Exercises

1.1 This application is primarily descriptive in nature. The owner wishes to develop a presentation. He will most likely use charts, graphs, tables and numerical measures to describe his data.

1.3 A bar chart is used whenever you want to display data that has already been categorized while a histogram is used to display data over a range of values for the factor under consideration. Another fundamental difference is that there typically are gaps between the bars on a bar chart but there are no gaps between the bars of a histogram.

1.5 Statistical inference tools are useful in situations where a decision maker needs to reach an estimate about a population based on a subset of data taken from the population. For example, a decision maker might want to know the starting annual salary of all attorneys in the United States. If it is not feasible or possible to look at the salary data for all attorneys the decision maker could look at a subset of attorneys and use statistical inference to reach a conclusion about the population of all attorneys.

1.7 Hypothesis testing is used whenever one is interested in testing claims that concern a population. Using information taken from samples, hypothesis testing evaluates the claim and makes a conclusion about the population from which the sample was taken. Estimation is used when we are interested in knowing something about all the data, but the population is too large, or the data set is too big for us to work with all the data. In estimation, no claim is being made or tested.

1.9 The major advantage of a graph is it allows a more complete representation of information in the data. Not only can a decision maker visualize the center of the data but also how spread out the data is. An average, for instance, nicely represents the center of a data set, but contains no information of how spread out the data is.

1.11 The company could use statistical inference to determine if its light bulbs last longer. Because it is not possible to examine every light bulb that could be produced the company could examine a subset of its light bulbs and compare the average life of the subset to the average life of a subset of the competitor's bulb. By using statistical inference tools the company could reach a conclusion about whether its bulbs last longer or not.

1.13 Student answers will vary depending on the periodical selected and the periodical's issue date, but should all address the three parts of the question.

1.15
  a. A commonly used measure of the center of the data is the mean or average. The executive could calculate the average age of the people in the market area and use the average as the center value.

  b. To determine a value for the percentage of people in the market area that are senior citizens, the executives would rely on estimation--a set of statistical techniques which allow one to know something about a data set by using a subset of the data whenever the data set is too large to work with all the data.

c.   The executives might want to test the hypothesis that the percentage of senior citizens in the market area is greater than the percentage of senior citizens nationwide. The executives could also test the hypothesis that the percentage of senior citizens is greater than or less than a specific value, say 27%.

Section 1.2 Exercises

1.17 A leading question is one that is designed to elicit a specific response, or one that might influence the respondent's answer by its wording. The question is posed so that the respondent believes the researcher has a specific answer in mind when the question is asked, or worded in such a way that the respondent feels obliged to provide an answer consistent with the question. For example, a question such as "Do you agree with the experts who recommend that more tax dollars be given to clean up dangerous and unhealthy pollution?" could cause respondents to provide the answer that they think will be consistent with the "experts" with whom they do not want to disagree. Leading question should be avoided in surveys because they may introduce bias.

1.19 No. The bank would most likely use a written survey or a telephone survey to collect the customer satisfaction data.

1.21
a.   Observation would be the most likely method. Observers could be located at various bike routes and observe the number of riders with and without helmets. This would likely be better than asking people if they wear a helmet since the popular response might be to say yes even when they don't always do so.
b.   A telephone survey to gas stations in the state. This could be a cost effective way of getting data from across the state. The respondent would have the information and be able to provide the correct price.
c.   A written survey of passengers. This could be given out on the plane before the plane lands and passengers could drop the surveys in a box as they de-plane. This method would likely garner higher response rates compared to sending the survey to passengers' mailing address and asking them to return the completed survey by mail.

1.23 The two types of validity mentioned in the section are internal validity and external validity. For this problem external validity is easiest to address. It simply means the sampling method chosen will be sufficient to insure the results based on the sample will be able to be generalized to the population of all students. Internal validity would involve making sure the data gathering method, for instance a questionnaire, accurately determines the respondent's attitude toward the registration process.

1.25 This data could have been collected through observation or experiment. Employees of the USDA could provide periodic reports of fire ant activity in their region. Likewise, scientists studying the spread of fire ants may have conducted experiments that indicate the rate of spread under certain conditions.

1.27 There are many potential sources of bias associated with data collection. If data is to be collected using personal interviews it will be important that the interviewer be trained so that interviewer bias, arising from the way survey questions are asked, is not injected into the survey. If the survey is conducted using either a mail survey or a telephone survey then it is important to be aware of nonresponse bias from those who do not respond to the mailing or refuse to answer your calls. You must also be careful when selecting your survey subjects so that selection bias is not a problem. In order to have useful, reliable data that is representative of the true student opinions regarding campus food service it is necessary that the data collection process be conducted in a manner that reduces or eliminates the potential for these and other sources of potential bias.

1.29 Student answers will vary. However, the issue questions should be designed to gather the desired data regarding customers' preferences for the use of the space. Demographic questions should provide data so that the responses can be broken down appropriately so that Gold's Gym managers can determine which subset of customers have what opinion about this issue. Regarding questionnaire layout, look at neatness and answer location space. Make sure questions are properly worded, used reasonable vocabulary, and are not leading questions.

1.31 The results of the survey are based on telephone interviews with 1,007 national adults, aged 18 and older (http://www.gallup.com/poll/content/?ci=18286). Students may also answer that the survey could have been conducted using personal interviews. Because telephone interviews were used to collect the survey data nonresponse biases associated with sampled adults who are not at home when phoned, or adults who refuse to participate in the survey. There is also the problem that some adults do not have a phone. If personal interviews are used to collect the data then it is important to guard against nonresponse bias from those sampled adults who refuse to be interviewed. There is also the problem of selection bias. In phone interviews we may miss the people who work evenings and nights. If personal interviews are used we must be careful to select a representative sample of the adult population, not just those who appear willing or interested in participating.

Section 1.3 Exercises

1.33
  a. Because the population is spread over a large geographical area, a cluster random sample could be selected to reduce travel costs.
  b. A stratified random sample would probably be used to keep sample size as small as possible.
  c. Most likely a convenience sample would be used since doing a statistical sample would be too difficult. It might be possible to survey every 15th customer using a systematic random sampling method.

1.35 From a numbered list of all customers who own a certificate of deposit the bank would need to randomly determine a starting point between 1 and k, where k would be equal to 25000/1000 = 25. This could be done using a random number table or by having a statistical package or a spreadsheet generate a random number between 1 and 25. Once this value is determined the bank would select that numbered customer as the first sampled customer and then select every 25th customer after that until 100 customers are sampled.

1.37 Statistical sampling techniques consist of those sampling methods that select samples based on chance. Nonstatistical sampling techniques consist of those methods of selecting samples using convenience, judgment, or other nonchance processes. In convenience sampling samples are chosen because they are easy or convenient to sample. There is no attempt to randomize the selection of the selected items. In convenience sampling not every item in the population has a random chance of being selected. Rather, items are sampled based on their convenience alone. Thus, convenience sampling is not a statistical sampling method.

1.39 A census is an enumeration of the entire set of measurements taken from the population as a whole. While in some cases, the items of interest are obtained from people such as through a survey, in many instances the items of interest come from a product or other inanimate object. For example, a study could be conducted to determine the defect rate for items made on a production line. The census would consist of all items produced on the line in a defined period of time.

1.41
     a. Stratified random sampling
     b. Simple random sampling or possibly cluster random sampling
     c. Systematic random sampling
     d. Stratified random sampling

1.43 These percentages would be parameters since it would include all U.S. colleges.

1.45
     a. Student answers will vary
     b. Cluster sampling could be used to ensure that you get all types of food. Make each cluster the area where certain foods are located (i.e., isle, row, shelf, etc.)
     c. Cluster sampling would give you a better idea of the inventory of all types of food. Simple random sampling could possibly end up with only looking at 2 or 3 food types.

1.47
     a. The population should be all users of cross-country ski lots in Colorado.
     b. Several sampling techniques could be selected. Be sure that some method of ensuring randomness is discussed. In addition, some students might give greater weight to frequent users of the lots. In which case the population would really be user days rather than individual users.
     c. Students using Excel should use the Tools – Data Analysis – Random Number Generation process. Students' answers will differ since Excel generates different streams of random numbers each time it is used. Since the application requires integer numbers, the Decrease Decimal option should be used.

Section 1.4 Exercises

1.49 Qualitative data are categories or numerical values that represent categories. Quantitative data is data that is purely numerical.

1.51.
     a. Time-series
     b. Cross-sectional
     c. Time-series
     d. Cross-sectional

1.53 Since the circles involve a ranking from best to worst, this would be ordinal data.

1.55
    a. Nominal Data
    b. Ratio Data
    c. Nominal Data
    d. Ratio Data
    e. Ratio Data
    f. Nominal Data
    g. Ratio Data

1.57

    Vehicle Name – Nominal
    Sports Car – Nominal
    Sport Utility – Nominal
    Wagon – Nominal
    Minivan – Nominal
    Pickup – Nominal
    All-Wheel Drive – Nominal
    Rear-Wheel Drive – Nominal
    Suggested Retail Price – Ratio
    Dealer Cost – Ratio
    Engine Size – Ratio
    Number of Cylinders – Ratio
    Horsepower – Ratio
    City MPG – Ratio
    Highway MPG – Ratio
    Weight – Ratio
    Wheel base – Ratio
    Length - Ratio
    Width - Ratio

End of Chapter Exercises

1.59 Nominal data or ordinal data.

1.61 Ratings are typical uses of ordinal scale data. And since ratings are based on personal opinion, even though people are using the same scale, a direct comparison between the two ratings is not possible. This is a common problem when people are asked to rate an object using an ordinal scale.

1.63 Answers will vary with the student. But a good discussion should include the following factors:
    Sampling techniques and possible problems selecting a representative sample.
    Determining how to measure confidence.
    Structuring questions to avoid bias.
    The measurement scale associated with the questions.
    The fact this poll is specifically intended to develop time-series data.

1.65 Answers will vary with the student.

1.67
 a. They would probably want to sample the cartons as they come off the assembly line at the Illinois plant for a specified time period. They would want to use a random sample. One method would be to take a systematic random sample. They could then calculate the percentage of the sample that had an unacceptable texture.

 b. The product is going to be ruined after testing it. You would not want to ruin the entire product that comes off the assembly line.

Chapter 2 Solutions

When applicable, the first few problems in each section will be done following the appropriate step by step procedures outlined in the corresponding sections of the chapter. Following problems will provide key points and the answers to the questions, but all answers can be arrived at using the appropriate steps.

Section 2.1 Exercises

2.1 Given n = 2,000, the minimum number of groups for a grouped data frequency distribution determined using the $2^k \geq n$ guideline is:

$$2^k \geq n \quad \text{or} \quad 2^{11} = 2,048 \geq 2,000 \quad \text{Thus, use k = 11 groups.}$$

2.3   Step 1: List the possible values.
The possible values for the discrete variable are 0 through 12.

    Step 2: Count the number of occurrences at each value.
The resulting frequency distribution is shown as follows:

x	Frequency
0	1
1	0
2	2
3	4
4	1
5	2
6	5
7	6
8	1
9	1
10	1
11	0
12	1
Total =	25

2.5 Note that two classes have a width of 8.05 – 7.85. Thus, the class width equals (8.05 – 7.85)/2 = 0.10. The upper class boundary equals the lower class boundary plus the class width. So, as an example, the first class boundary equals 7.85 + 0.10 = 7.95, and so on. The first class has the same relative frequency and cumulative relative frequency. The frequency is obtained by multiplying the sample size times the relative frequency. So the first class frequency equals 50(0.12) = 6. The other class frequencies follow similarly. Each cumulative relative frequency is produced by adding the respective class relative frequency to the preceding cumulative relative frequency. So the second class relative frequency is obtained as 0.48 – 0.12 = 0.36. The other calculations follow similarly yielding

Class	Frequency	Relative Frequency	Cumulative Relative Frequency
7.85 – < 7.95	6	0.12	0.12
7.95 – < 8.05	18	0.36	0.48
8.05 – < 8.15	12	0.24	0.72
8.15 – < 8.25	5	0.10	0.82
8.25 – < 8.35	9	0.18	1.00

2.7

    a. Proportion of days in which no shortages occurred = 1 – proportion of days in which shortages occurred = 1 – 0.24 = 0.76

    b. Less than \$20 off implies that overage was less than\$20 and the shortage was less than \$20 = (proportion of overages less \$20) – (proportion of shortages at most \$20) = 0.56 – 0.08 = 0.48

    c. Proportion of days with less than \$40 over or at most \$20 short = Proportion of days with less than \$40 over – proportion of days with more than \$20 short = 0.96 – 0.08 = 0.86.

2.9

    a. Step 1 and Step 2. Group the data into classes and determine the class width:

The problem asks you to group the data. Using the $2^k \geq n$ guideline we get:

$$2^k \geq 60 \text{ so } 2^6 \geq 60$$

    Class width is:

$$W = \frac{Maximum - Minumum}{\#Classes} = \frac{10 - 2}{6} = 1.33$$

    which we round up to 2.0

Step 3. Define the class boundaries:
Since the data are discrete, the classes are:

        Class
        2-3
        4-5
        6-7
        8-9
        10-i1

Step 4. Count the number of values in each class:

Class	Frequency	Relative Frequency
2-3	2	0.0333
4-5	25	0.4167
6-7	26	0.4333
8-9	6	0.1000
10-11	1	0.0167

b. The cumulative frequency distribution is:

Class	Frequency	Cumulative Frequency
2-3	2	2
4-5	25	27
6-7	26	53
8-9	6	59
10-11	1	60

c.

Class	Frequency	Relative Frequency	Cumu. Rel. Freq.
2-3	2	0.0333	0.0333
4-5	25	0.4167	0.4500
6-7	26	0.4333	0.8833
8-9	6	0.1000	0.9833
10-11	1	0.0167	1.000

The relative frequency histogram is:

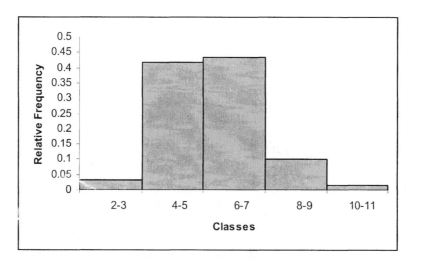

d. The ogive is a graph of the cumulative relative frequency distribution.

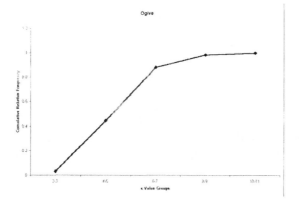

Chapter 2

2.11

a.

	Knowledge Level			
	Savvy	Experienced	Novice	Total
Online Investors	32	220	148	400
Traditional Investors	8	58	134	200
	40	278	282	600

b.

	Knowledge Level		
	Savvy	Experienced	Novice
Online Investors	0.0533	0.3667	0.2467
Traditional Investors	0.0133	0.0967	0.2233

c. The proportion that were both on-line and experienced is 0.3667.

d. The proportion of on-line investors is 0.6667

2.13

a. The turnaround times are sorted from smallest to largest to create the data array.

77	79	80	83	84	85	86
86	86	86	86	86	87	87
87	88	88	88	88	89	89
89	89	89	90	90	91	91
92	92	92	92	93	93	93
94	94	94	94	94	95	95
95	96	97	98	98	99	101

b. Five classes having equal widths are created by subtracting the smallest observed value (77) from the largest value (101) and dividing the difference by 5 to get the width for each class (4.8 rounded to 5). Five classes of width five are then constructed such that the classes are mutually exclusive and all inclusive. Identify the variable of interest. The turnaround time is the variable of interest. The number of turnaround times in each class is then counted. The frequency table is shown below.

Turnaround Time (Classes)	Frequency
77-81	3
82-86	9
87-91	16
92-96	16
97-101	5
Total =	49

c. The histogram can be created from the frequency distribution. The classes are shown on the horizontal axis and the frequency on the vertical axis. The histogram is shown below.

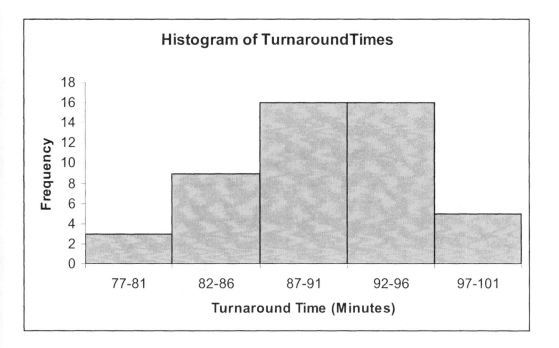

d. Convert the frequency distribution into relative frequencies and cumulative relative frequencies as shown below.

Turnaround Time (Classes)	Frequency	Relative Frequency	Cumulative Relative Frequency
77-81	3	0.0612	0.0612
82-86	9	0.1837	0.2449
87-91	16	0.3265	0.5714
92-96	16	0.3265	0.8980
97-101	5	0.1020	1.0000
Total =	49		

The percentage of sampled planes with turnaround times greater than 96 minutes is 10.20%.

2.15

a. $w = \dfrac{Largest - smallest}{number\ of\ classes} = \dfrac{214.4 - 105.0}{11} = 9.945 \rightarrow w = 10$. The classes are the first class is $(105, 105 + 10) = (105, 115)$. The frequency distribution follows

Classes Frequency		Relative Frequency	Cumulative Relative Frequency
(105 – <115)	1	0.04	0.04
(115 – <125)	1	0.04	0.08
(125 – <135)	2	0.08	0.16
(135 – <145)	1	0.04	0.20
(145 – <155)	1	0.04	0.24
(155 – <165)	7	0.28	0.52
(165 – <175)	4	0.16	0.68
(175 – <185)	3	0.12	0.80
(185 – <195)	2	0.08	0.88
(195 – <205)	0	0.00	0.88
(205 – <215)	3	0.12	1.00

b. The data shows 8 of the 25, or 0.32 of the salaries greater than 175

c. The data shows 18 of the 25, or 0.72 having salaries that are at most $205,000 and a least $135,000.

2.17

    a.

Classes	Frequency
51 - 53	7
54 - 56	15
57 - 59	28
60 - 62	16
63 - 65	21
66 - 68	9
69 - 71	2
72 - 74	2

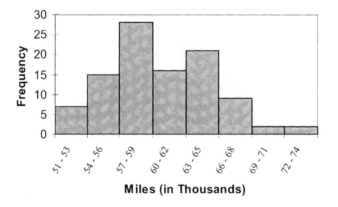

    b.   The tread life of at least 50% of the tires is 60,000 or more. The top 10% is greater than 66,000 and the longest tread tire is 74,000. Additional information will vary.

c.

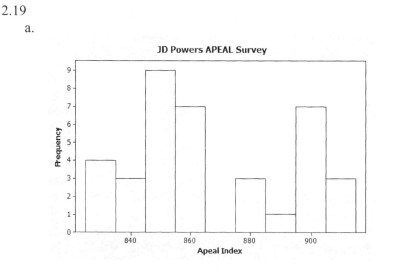

Classes	Frequency
51-52	3
53-54	9
55-56	10
57-58	22
59-60	10
61-62	12
63-64	15
65-66	10
67-68	5
69-70	2
71-72	1
73-74	1

Student will probably say that the 12 classes give better information because it allows you to see more detail about the number of miles the tires can go.

2.19

a.

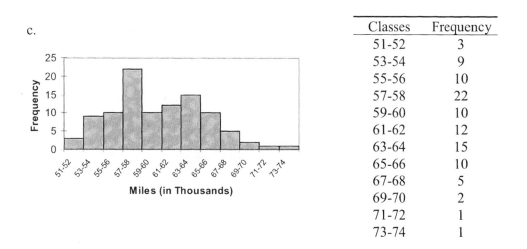

b. The 2005 average is $\bar{x} = \dfrac{32043}{37} = 866.03$ which is larger than the past industry average. This seems to indicate that the new models are more appealing to automobile customers.

c. The fifth class is vacant. This suggests that there is a distinct gap in consumers' satisfaction between the low and high rated automobiles.

2.21

a. There are n = 59 different airlines that flew into and out of Orlando in 2004. Then using the $2^k \geq n$ guideline we would need at least k = 6 classes.

b. Using k = 6 classes, the class width is determined as follows:
$$w = \frac{High - Low}{Classes} = \frac{5,398,141 - 234}{6} = \frac{5,397,907}{6} = 899,651.17$$
Rounding this up to the nearest 1,000 passengers, the class width is 900,000.

c. The frequency distribution with nine classes and a class width of 900,000 will depend on the starting point for the first class. This starting value must be at or below the minimum value of 234. Student answers will vary depending on the starting point. We have used 0 since 234 is very close to zero given the range of the data. Care should be made to make sure that the classes are mutually exclusive and all-inclusive. The following frequency distribution is developed:

Passengers	Frequency
0 - 899,999	48
900,000 - 1,799,999	7
1,800,000 - 2,699,999	1
2,700,000 - 3,599,999	1
3,600,000 - 4,499,999	1
4,500,000 - 5,399,999	1

This shows that most airlines load and unload a total of passengers under 900,000.

d. Based on the results in part c, the frequency histogram is shown as follows:

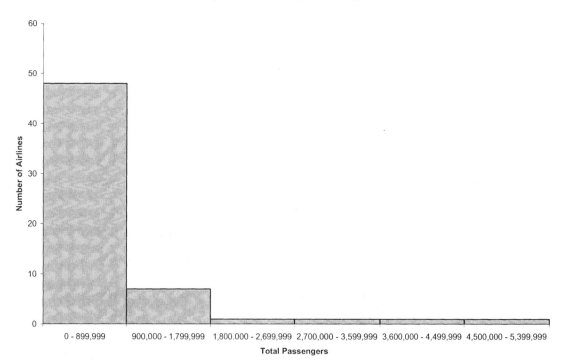

Histogram - Orlando Airport Passengers

Based on the data from the Orlando International Airport, we see that far and away more airlines have less that 900,000 passengers per year at the airport,

2.23

a. Order the observations (coffee consumption) from smallest to largest. The data array is shown below:

3.5	3.8	4.4	4.5	4.6	4.6	4.7	4.7	4.8	4.8	5.0	5.0
5.0	5.0	5.2	5.3	5.3	5.3	5.3	5.3	5.3	5.4	5.4	5.4
5.4	5.5	5.5	5.6	5.6	5.7	5.7	5.7	5.7	5.8	5.8	5.9
5.9	6.0	6.0	6.0	6.0	6.0	6.0	6.0	6.0	6.1	6.1	6.1
6.1	6.1	6.2	6.2	6.2	6.3	6.3	6.3	6.3	6.3	6.3	6.4
6.4	6.4	6.4	6.4	6.4	6.4	6.5	6.5	6.5	6.5	6.5	6.5
6.5	6.5	6.5	6.6	6.6	6.6	6.6	6.6	6.7	6.7	6.7	6.7
6.7	6.8	6.8	6.8	6.8	6.8	6.8	6.8	6.8	6.9	6.9	7.0
7.0	7.0	7.0	7.1	7.1	7.1	7.2	7.2	7.2	7.2	7.2	7.3
7.4	7.4	7.4	7.5	7.5	7.5	7.5	7.5	7.6	7.6	7.6	7.6
7.6	7.6	7.6	7.7	7.7	7.8	7.8	7.8	7.9	7.9	7.9	7.9
8.0	8.0	8.0	8.0	8.0	8.3	8.4	8.4	8.4	8.6	8.9	10.1

b. There are n = 144 observations in the data set. Using the $2^k \geq n$ guideline, the number of classes, k, would be 8. The maximum and minimum values in the data set are 10.1 and 3.5, respectively. The class width is computed to be: w = (10.1-3.5)/8 = 0.821, which is rounded to 0.8. The frequency distribution is

Coffee Consumption (kg.)	Frequency
3.5 - 4.2	2
4.3 - 5.0	12
5.1 - 5.8	21
5.9 - 6.6	45
6.7 - 7.4	31
7.5 - 8.2	26
8.3 - 9.0	6
9.1 - 9.8	0
9.9 - 10.6	1

Most observations fall in the class of 5.9 – 6.6 kg of coffee.

c. The histogram can be created from the frequency distribution. The classes are shown on the horizontal axis and the frequency on the vertical axis. The histogram is shown below.

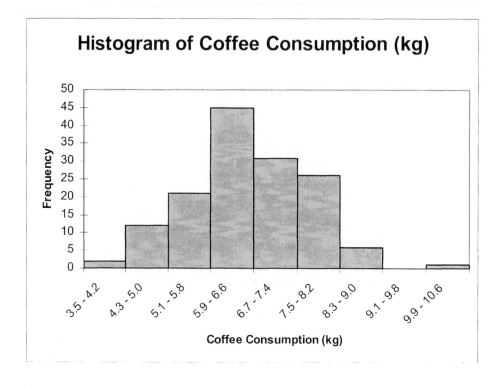

The histogram shows the shape of the distribution. This histogram is showing that fewer people consume small and large quantities and that most individuals consume between 5.1 and 8.2 kg of coffee, with the most individuals consuming between 5.9 and 6.6.

d. Convert the frequency distribution into relative frequencies and cumulative relative frequencies as shown below.

Coffee Consumption (kg.)	Frequency	Relative Frequency	Cumulative Relative Frequency
3.5 - 4.2	2	0.0139	0.0139
4.3 - 5.0	12	0.0833	0.0972
5.1 - 5.8	21	0.1458	0.2431
5.9 - 6.6	45	0.3125	0.5556
6.7 - 7.4	31	0.2153	0.7708
7.5 - 8.2	26	0.1806	0.9514
8.3 - 9.0	6	0.0417	0.9931
9.1 - 9.8	0	0.0000	0.9931
9.9 - 10.6	1	0.0069	1.0000
Total	144		

4.86% (100-95.14) of the coffee drinkers sampled consumes 8.3 kg or more annually.

Section 2-2 Exercises

2.25

    a.
    Step 1. Define the categories.
     The categories are grade level.

    Step 2. Determine the appropriate measure.
     The measure is the number of students at each grade level.

    Step 3. Develop the bar chart.

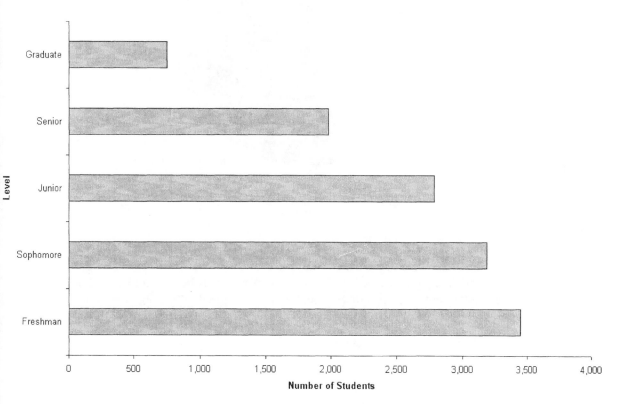

Student Distribution Bar Chart

    b.
    Step 1. Define the categories.
    The categories are grade level.

    Step 2. Determine the appropriate measure.
    The measure is the number of students at each grade level.

Step 3. Develop the pie chart.

Student Distribution Bar Chart

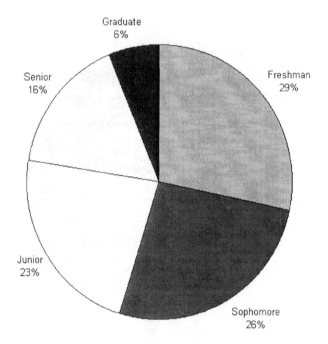

c. A case can be made for either a bar chart or pie chart. Pie charts are especially good at showing how the total is divided into parts. The bar chart is best to draw attention to specific results. In this case, a discussion might be centered on the apparent attrition that takes place in the number of students between Freshman and Senior years.

2.27.   One possible bar chart is shown as follows:

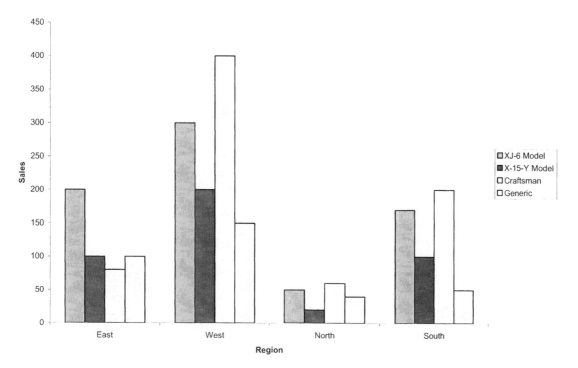

Another way to present the same data is:

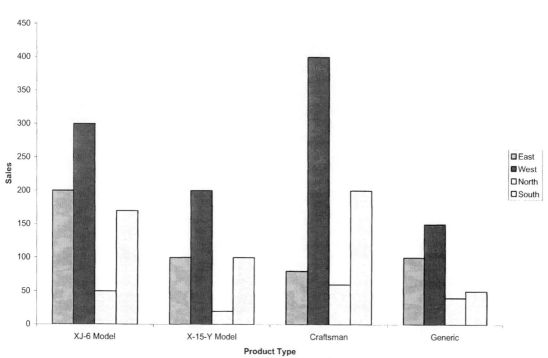

Still another possible way is called a "stacked" bar chart.

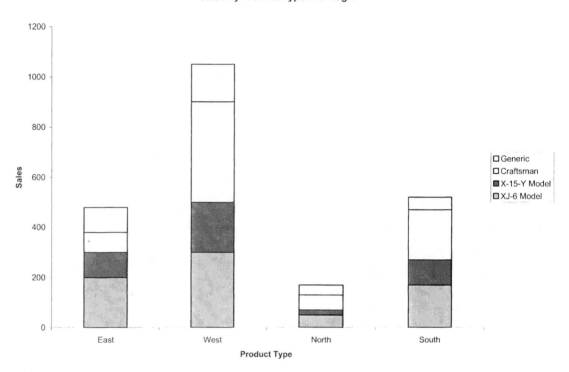

2.29

a. The pie chart showing income distribution by region is shown below. The categories are the geographic regions and the appropriate measure is the proportion of income in each region.

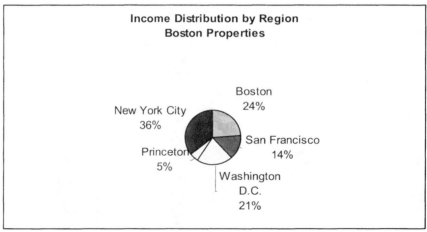

b. The bar chart displaying income distribution by region is shown below. The categories are the regions and the measure for each category is the percentage of income for that region.

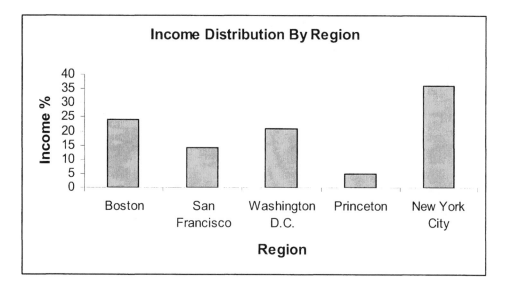

c. Both charts clearly indicate which regions produce the greatest percentage of income. The bar chart, however, makes it easier to compare percentages across regions.

2.31

a.

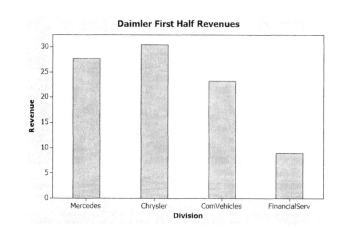

b. Proportion of Vehicle Revenue = 1 − proportion of financial services
$$= 1 - 8.9/90.3$$
$$= 1 - 0.0985 = 0.9015$$

2.33

 a. Pie charts are typically used to show how a total is divided into parts. In this case, the total of the five ratios is not a meaningful value. Thus, a pie chart showing each ratio as a fraction of the total would not be meaningful. Thus a pie chart is not the most appropriate tool. A bar chart would be appropriate.

 b

   Step 1: Define the categories.
   The categories are the five cities where the plants are located

   Step 2: Determine the appropriate measure.
   The measure of interest is the ratio of manufactured output to the number of employees at the plant

   Step 3: Develop the bar chart.
   The bar chart is shown as follows:

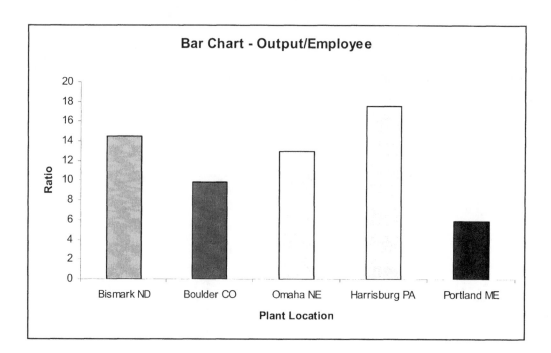

2.35 A bar chart can be used to make the comparison. Shown below are two examples of bar charts which compare North America to Other.

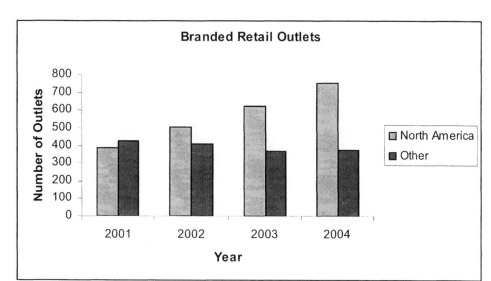

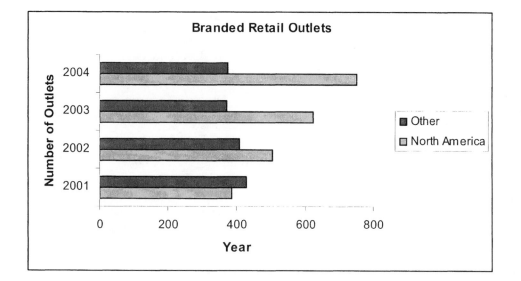

Chapter 2

2.37

a. The following stem and leaf diagram was created using PhStat. The stem unit is 10 and the leaf unit is 1.

Stem-and-Leaf Display for Drive-Thru Service (Seconds)

Stem unit: 10

```
 6 | 8
 7 | 1 3 4 6 9
 8 | 3 5 8
 9 | 0 2 3
10 | 3 5
11 | 0 6 9
12 |
13 | 0 4 8
14 | 5 6 7
15 | 6 6
16 | 2
17 | 8
18 | 1
```

b. The most frequent speed of service is between 70 and 79 seconds.

2.39

a.   The bar graph is

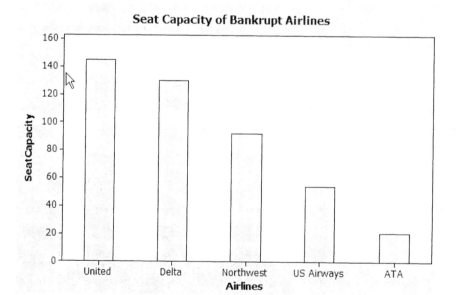

b. The percent equals the individual capacity divided by the total, e.g. United → percent = (145/858)100% = 16.90%, etc. This produces the following pie chart:

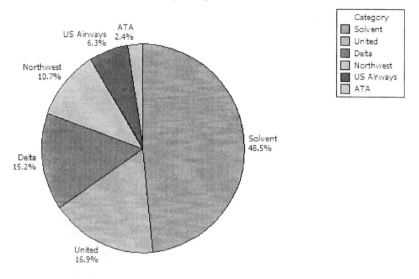

Airlines Seat Capacity

c. The percent of seat capacity of those in bankruptcy = 16.9 + 15.2 + 10.7 + 6.3 + 2.4 = 51.5%. Since this is larger than 50%, their statement was correct.

2.41

a. A bar chart is an appropriate graph since there are two categories, males and females. A pie chart could also be used to display the data.

b. The following steps are used to construct the bar chart:

Step 1: Define the categories.
The categories are the two genders, male and female

Step 2: Determine the appropriate measure.
The measure of interest is the percentage of credit card holders who are male and female.

Step 3: Develop the bar chart using computer software such as Excel or Minitab.
The bar chart is shown as follows:

Chapter 2

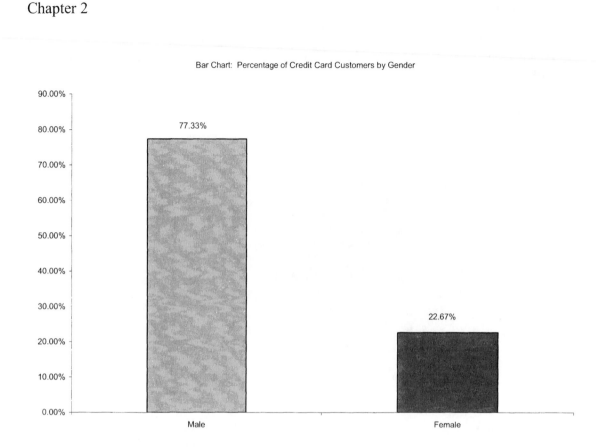

Bar Chart: Percentage of Credit Card Customers by Gender

This shows that a clear majority of credit card holders are males (77.33%)

2.43

  a.

Stem-and-Leaf Display: Days

```
Stem-and-leaf of Days  N  = 50
Leaf Unit = 1.0


   1     0   4
   2     0   7
   6     1   0344
  15     1   566677889
  23     2   00012244
 (13)    2   5666777888999
  14     3   000122344
   5     3   5669
   1     4   0
```

  b. The shape of the data is slightly skewed to the left. The center of the data appears to be between 24 and 26.

$$\bar{x} = \frac{2428}{50} = 24.28$$. This and the data indicates that the mean is larger than indicated by J.D. Power. The difference is that the data set is only a sample of the data. Each sample

will produce different results but approximately equal to the population average calculated by J.D. Power.

2.45

a. The following are the averages for each hospital computed by summing the charges and dividing b y the number of charges:

University Related	Religious Affiliated	Municipally Owned	Privately Held
$6,398	$3,591	$4,613	$5,191

b. The following steps are used to construct the bar chart:

Step 1: Define the categories.
The categories are the four hospital types

Step 2: Determine the appropriate measure.
The measure of interest is the average charge for outpatient gall bladder surgery.

Step 3: Develop the bar chart using computer software such as Excel or Minitab.
The bar chart is shown as follows:

Gall Bladder Charges

c. A pie chart is used to display the parts of a total. In this case the total charges of the four hospital types is not a meaningful number so a pie chart showing how that total is divided among the four hospital types would not be useful or appropriate.

Section 2-3 Exercises

2.47   Steps 1 and 2: Identify the two variables of interest
                    The variables are y (dependent variable) and x (independent variable)
          Step 3: Establish the scales for the vertical and horizontal axes
                    The y variable ranges from 40 to 250 and the x variable ranges from 15.9 to 35.3
          Step 4: Plot the joint values for the two variables by placing a point in the x,y space
                    shown as follows:

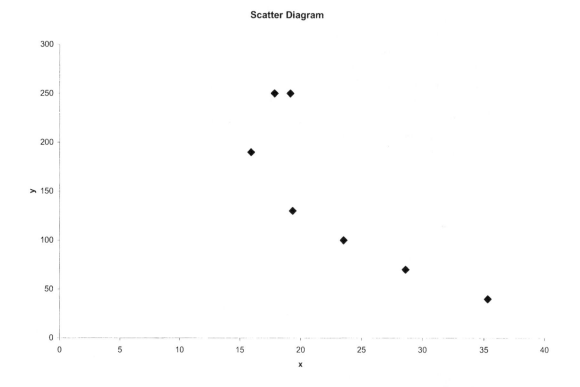

Scatter Diagram

There is negative linear relationship between the two variables.

2.49

a.

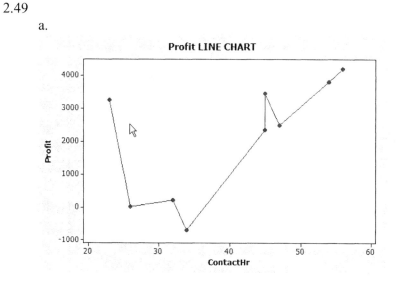

There appears to be a curvilinear relationship between the dependent and independent variables.

b.

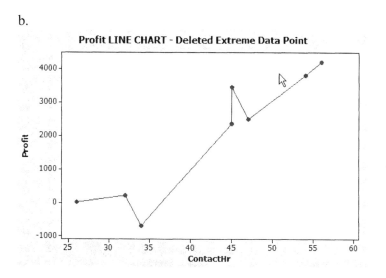

Having removed the extreme data point, the relationship between dependent and independent variables seems to be linear and positive.

2.51.

    Step 1: Identify the time-series variable
           The variable of interest is annual sales of video games in the U.S.

    Step 2: Layout the Horizontal and Vertical Axis
           The horizontal axis will be the year and the vertical axis is sales (See

    Step 3: Plot the values on the graph and connect the points

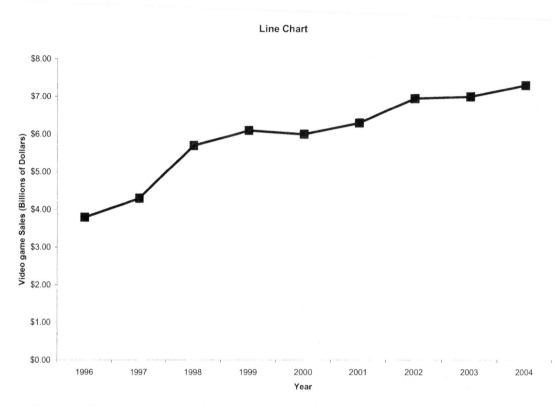

The line chart illustrates that over the nine year period between 1996 and 2004, video game sales in the U.S. have grown quite steadily from a just below $4 billion to over $7 billion.

2.53

a.

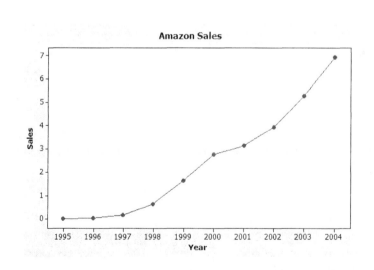

b. The relationship appears to be curvilinear.

c. The largest difference in sales occurred between 2003 and 2004. That difference was $6.9211 - 5.2637 = 1.6574$ $billions.

2.55

Steps 1 and 2: Identify the two variables of interest

In this example, there are two variables of interest, average home attendance and average road game attendance. Either one of these can be selected as the dependent variable. We will select average road game attendance.

Step 3: Establish the scales for the vertical and horizontal axes

The y variable (average road attendance) ranges from 25,906 to 37,735 and the x variable (average home attendance) ranges from 14,052 to 50,499.

Step 4: Plot the joint values for the two variables by placing a point in the x,y space shown as follows:

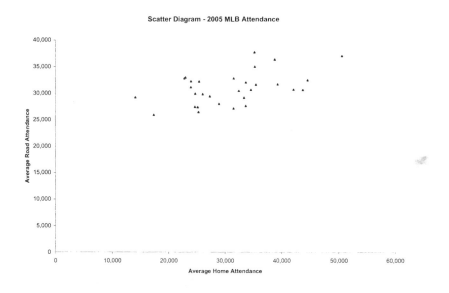

Based on the scatter diagram, it appears that there is a positive linear relationship between home and road attendance. However, the relationship is not perfect.

2.57. Steps 1 and 2: Identify the two variables of interest

In this situation, there are two variables, fuel consumption per hour, the dependent variable, and passenger capacity, the independent variable.

Step 3: Establish the scales for the vertical and horizontal axes

The y variable (fuel consumption) ranges from 631to 3,529 and the x variable (passenger capacity) ranges from 78 to 405.

Step 4: Plot the joint values for the two variables by placing a point in the x,y space shown as follows:

31

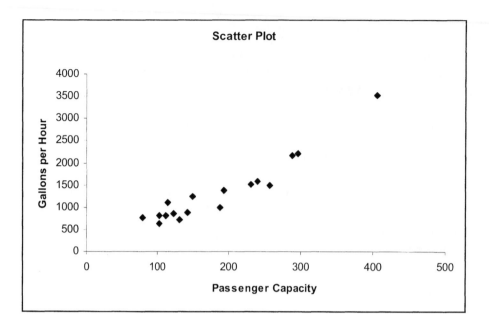

Based on the scatter diagram we see there is a strong positive linear relationship between passenger capacity and fuel consumption per hour.

2.59

    a.

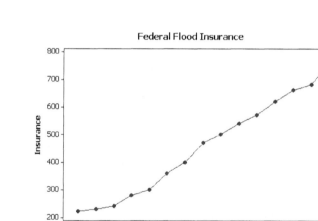

b. The relationship appears to be linear and positive.

c. The average equals the sum divided by the number of data points = 6830/15 = 455.33.

2.61

    a. Step 1: Identify the time-series variable

              The variable of interest is annual average price of gasoline in California

        Step 2: Layout the Horizontal and Vertical Axis

              The horizontal axis will be the year and the vertical axis is average price (See Step 3)

        Step 3: Plot the values on the graph and connect the points:

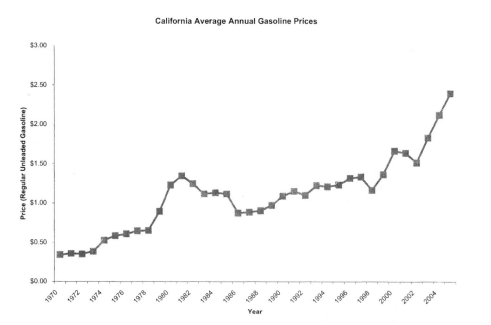

California Average Annual Gasoline Prices

Gasoline prices have trended upward over the 36 year period with some short periods of decline. However, prices rises have been very steep since 1999.

b. Adding the inflation adjusted prices to the graph does not require that we use a different scale. The results of adding the second time-series is shown as follows:

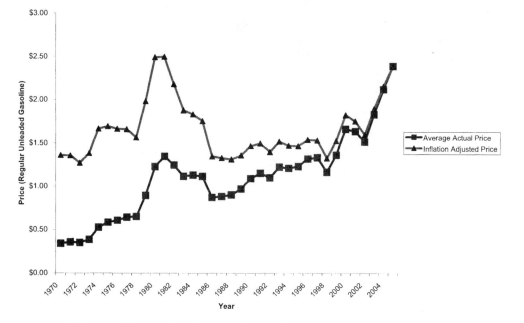

California Average Annual Gasoline Prices

c. The graph in part b. shows an interesting result. That is, although the price of gasoline has risen quite steadily since 1970, when the value of the dollar is taken into account, the overall trend has been more level. In fact, the highest prices (when the inflation index is considered) occurred in 1980 and 1981 at the equivalent of slightly more than $2.50. This exceeds the prices during the 2000-2005 years. Thus, while gasoline prices were high in California in 2005, it is not the worst that has occurred in that state.

End of Chapter Exercises

2.63 A relative frequency distribution deals with the percentage of the total observations that fall into each class rather than the number that fall into each class. Sometimes decision makers are more interested in percentages than numbers. Politicians, for instance, are often more interested in the percentage of voters that will vote for them (more than 50%) than the total number of votes they will get. Relative frequencies are also valuable when comparing distributions from two populations that have different total numbers.

2.65 Pie charts are effectively used when the data set is made up of parts of a whole, and therefore each part can be converted to a percentage. For instance, if the data involves a budget, a pie chart can represent the percentage of budget each category represents. Or, if the data involves total company sales, a pie chart can be used to represent the percentage contribution to sales for each major product line.

2.67

a.

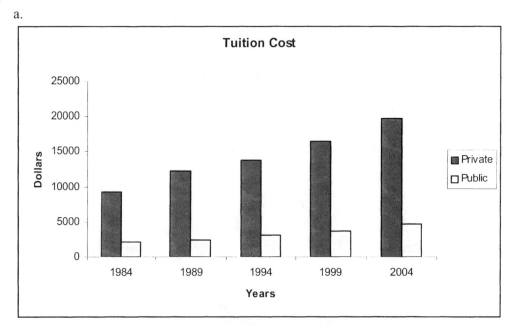

b. Student answers will vary but should include identifying that both private and public college tuition costs have more than doubled in the 20 years of data.

2.69

a.

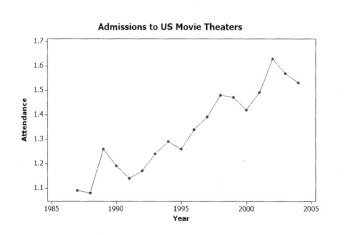

b. It appears that there is a positive linear relationship between the attendance and the year. However, there does appear to be a sharp decline in the last two years. It could be evidence of a normal cycle since a similar decline occurred in 1990/91 which was followed by a steady climb in attendance for six of the next seven years.

2.71

a. Using the $2^k \geq n$ guideline:
$$2^k \geq 48 = 2^6 \geq 48$$

To determine the class width, $(17.5 - 0.3)/6 = 2.87$ so round up to 3 to make it easier.

Classes	Frequency
0.1 to 3	27
3.1 to 6.0	9
6.1 to 9.0	6
9.1 to 12	4
12.1 to 15.0	0
15.1 to 18.0	2

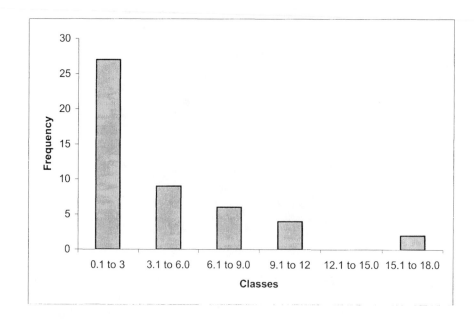

b.

Stem-and-Leaf Display			
Stem unit: 1			
0	3 4 5 7		
1	0 0 0 0 4 5 5 9		
2	0 0 0 0 0 4 5 5 5 7		
3	0 0 0 0 0 2 5 5 5 5 6		
4	0 0 0		
5			
6	4 5		
7	5		
8	3		
9	0 0 2		
10			
11	0		
12	0 0		
13			
14			
15			
16	0		
17	5		

c.

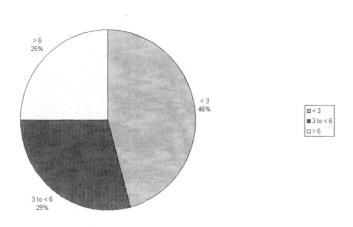

Pie Chart - Miles

d.

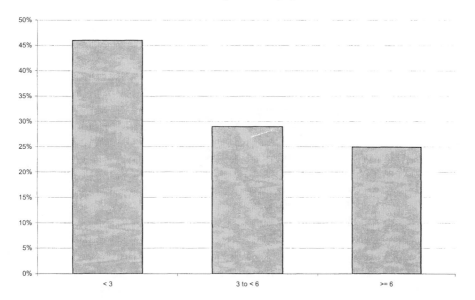

Bar Chart - Proportion of Employees

2.73

    a. The independent variable is hours and the dependent variable is sales

Scatter Plot of Hours and Sales

    b.   It appears that there is a positive linear relationship between hours worked and weekly sales. It appears that the more hours worked the greater the sales. No stores seem to be substantially different in terms of the general relationship between hours and sales.

2.75

    a.   Using the $2^k \geq n$
$$2^k \geq 100 \text{ so } 2^7 = 128$$

Determine the width = $(310495 - 70464)/7 = 34,290$ round to 35,000

Classes	Frequency
70000 - 105000	43
105001 - 140000	34
140001 - 175000	13
175001 - 210000	5
210001 - 245000	2
245001 - 280000	1
280001 - 315000	2

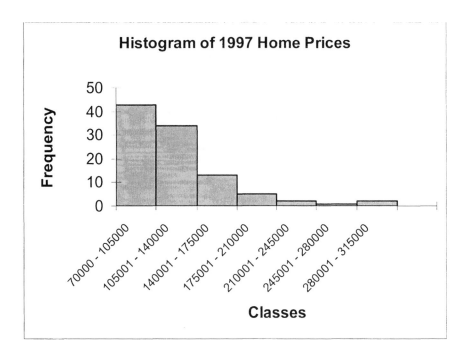

b.

	Frequency	Relative Frequency	Cumulative Relative Frequency
70000 - 105000	43	0.43	0.43
105001 - 140000	34	0.34	0.77
140001 - 175000	13	0.13	0.90
175001 - 210000	5	0.05	0.95
210001 - 245000	2	0.02	0.97
245001 - 280000	1	0.01	0.98
280001 - 315000	2	0.02	1.00

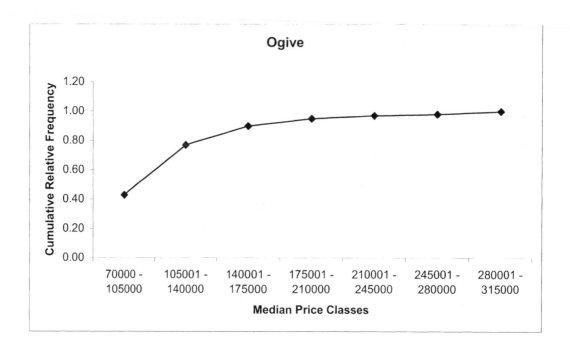

c. Using four classes

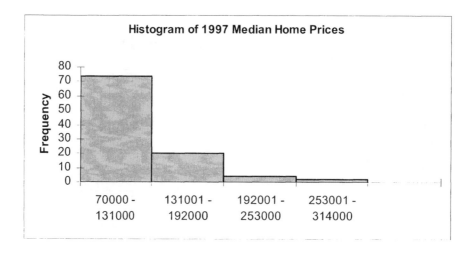

Distribution with 4 classes appears to be more skewed than when 7 classes are used. Less detail is available.

Cumulative Frequency Ogive

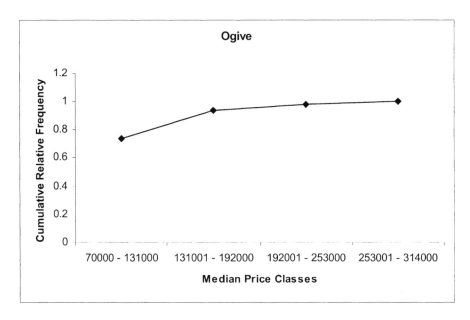

2.77

a.

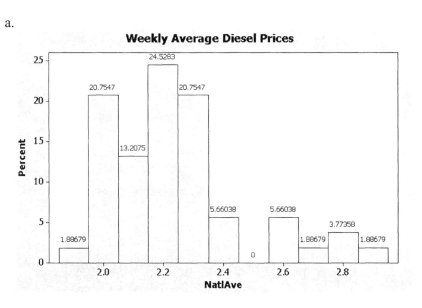

b. Notice that the class interval with no observations is the 7th class which has boundaries of $2.45 and $2.55. Since the numbers are averages taken across the United States, it is possible that the sampling technique, simply from randomness, didn't select prices in that range. Another possible explanation is that there are retailers in certain location that generally charge ten cents a gallon more. It is a commonly held belief that California retails charge more than the national average. This could be the reason. It bears further investigation.

Chapter 2

Chapter 3 Solutions

When applicable, the first few problems in each section will be done following the appropriate step-by-step procedures outlined in the corresponding sections of the chapter. Following problems will provide key points and the answers to the questions, but all answers can be arrived at using the appropriate steps.

Section 3.1 Exercises

3.1
a. The sample mean is computed using the following steps:

Step 1: Collect the sample data.
The sample data are:

3	0	2	0	1	3	5	2
5	1	3	0	0	1	3	3
4	3	1	8	4	2	4	0

Step 2: Add the values in the population:
$$\sum x = 3+0+2+....+4+0 = 58$$

Step 3: Divide the sum by the population size.

$$\mu = \frac{\sum x}{N} = \frac{58}{24} = 2.42$$

The mean number of days of remaining vacation for this sample of 24 employees is 2.42.

b. The median is computed using the following steps:

Step 1: Collect the population data.

3	0	2	0	1	3	5	2
5	1	3	0	0	1	3	3
4	3	1	8	4	2	4	0

Step 2: Sort the data from smallest to largest, forming a data array.

0	0	0	0	0	1	1	1
1	2	2	2	3	3	3	3
3	3	4	4	4	5	5	8

Step 3: Locate the middle value of the data.
The location index for the median is determined using the following equation:

$$i = \frac{1}{2}(n)$$

For $n = 24$, the index is:

$$i = \frac{1}{2}(24) = 12$$

Because the index is 12 which is an integer, the median is the average of the 12th and 13th data values going from either end. These two values are 2 and 3. This the median is:

$$M_d = \frac{2+3}{2} = 2.5$$

Half the data values fall below 2.5 and half the data values fall above 2.5.

c. To determine if there is a mode and what the value of the mode is, we use the following steps:
Step 1: Collect the population data.
See parts a. or b.

Step 2: Organize the data into a frequency distribution.

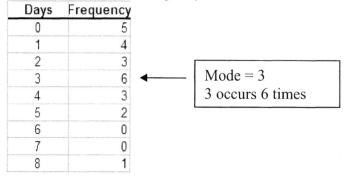

Days	Frequency
0	5
1	4
2	3
3	6
4	3
5	2
6	0
7	0
8	1

Mode = 3
3 occurs 6 times

Step 3: Determine the value that occurs most frequently.
The value 3 occurs 6 times which is the most of any value in the sample.

3.3   The sample mean is computed using the following steps:
Step 1: Collect the sample data.

Step 2: Add the values in the sample:
$$\sum x = 74349$$

Step 3: Divide the sum by the sample size.
$$\bar{x} = \frac{74349}{15} = 4956.60$$

The quartiles are found using the following steps.
Step 1: Sort the data from low to high.

4132	4188	4209	4423	4568
4573	4983	5002	5052	5176
5310	5381	5611	5736	6005

Step 2: Determine the quartile location index and find the quartile value.

To determine the location index for the 1st quartile (p=25) we do the following:
$$i = 25/100(n) = (25/100)*15 = 3.75.$$

Because the index is not an integer it is rounded up to 4. The first quartile is the fourth value in the sorted array and is equal to 4423.

The median (or second quartile) is found by sorting the data from lowest to highest (see below). The index point, i, for the median is found by $i = \frac{1}{2}(n) = \frac{1}{2}(15) = 7.5$. Because i is not an integer it is rounded up to 8. The median is located by counting 8 values into the sorted data. The median is 5002.

The location index for the 3rd quartile is:
$$75/100(n) = 75/100(15) = 11.25.$$

Because i is not an integer it is rounded up to 12. The third quartile is the 12th value in the sorted array and is equal to 5381.

3.5

Step 1: Sort the data from low to high.
The sorted data are shown below:

35	50	50	50
60	75	75	75
80	85	85	90
90	100	100	100
100	125	125	150

Step 2: Calculate the 25th percentile (Q_1), the 50th percentile (median), and the 75th percentile (Q_3).

The 25th percentile location is $(25/100)*20 = 5$. So Q_1 is the average of the values in the 5th and 6th position of the sorted array. $Q_1 = (60+75)/2 = 67.5$.

The median location is $(50/100)*20 = (1/2)*20 = 10$. Because the location point is an integer the median is the average of the values in the 10th and 11th location. Median $= (85 + 85)/2 = 85$.

The 75th percentile location is $(75/100)*20 = 15$. So Q3 is the average of the values in the 15th and 16th position of the sorted array. $Q_3 = (100 + 100)/2 = 100$.

Step 3: Draw the box so the ends correspond to Q_1 and Q_3.

Step 4: Draw a vertical line through the box at the median.

Step 5: Compute the upper and lower limits:

Lower limit = $Q_1 - 1.5(Q_3-Q_1) = 67.5 - 1.5*32.5 = 18.75$
Upper Limit = $Q_3 + 1.5(Q_3-Q_1) = 100 + 1.5*32.5 = 148.75$

Any value outside these limits will be labeled an outlier.

Step 6: Draw the whiskers.

Step 7: Plot the outliers. Outliers are typically indicated by an asterisk, *.

The box and whisker plot is shown below.

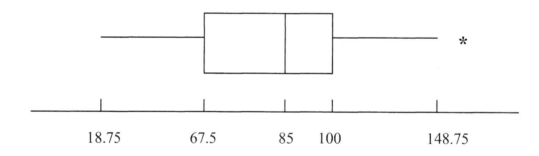

18.75	67.5	85 100	148.75

3.7
a. The index is $(p/100)n = (80/100)20 = 16$ = integer. Therefore, an 80th percentile is obtained by calculating the average of the 16th and 17th data value = $(31.2 + 32.2)/2 = 32.7$.

b. The 25th percentile: The index is $(p/100)n = (25/100)20 = 5$ = integer. Therefore, the 25th percentile is obtained by calculating the average of the 5th and 6th data value = $(12.1 + 13)/2 = 12.55$. The 75th percentile: The index is $(p/100)n = (75/100)20 = 15$ = integer. Therefore, an 75th percentile is obtained by calculating the average of the 15th and 16th data value = $(26.7 + 31.2)/2 = 28.95$.

c. The median is the 50th percentile. The index is $(p/100)n = (50/100)20 = 10$ = integer. Therefore, a 50th percentile is obtained by calculating the average of the 10th and 11th data value = $(20.8 + 22.8)/2 = 21.8$.

3.9

  a.

$$\bar{x} = \dfrac{\sum_{i=1}^{n} x_i}{n} = 456/24 = 19$$

To compute the median, rank the observations and find the average of the middle two values.

$$10\ \ 12\ \ 14\ \ 14\ \ 17\ \ 17\ \ 18\ \ 18\ \ 19\ \ 19\ \ 19\ \ 19$$
$$19\ \ 20\ \ 20\ \ 21\ \ 21\ \ 21\ \ 21\ \ 22\ \ 22\ \ 23\ \ 25\ \ 25$$

Median = (19 + 19)/2 = 19
Mode = 19

  b. This data is symmetrical since the mean = median = mode

  c.

Box-and-whisker Plot

Five-number Summary
Minimum   10
First Quartile   17
Median   19
Third Quartile   21
Maximum   25

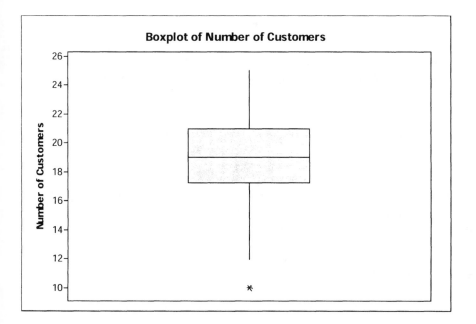

The box plot does support the idea that the distributions are symmetric although the median is not directly in the center between the Q1 and Q3.

3.11.   The sample mean is computed using the following steps:

Step 1: Collect the sample data.
         The sample data are:

31	27	29	22	24	30	28	21	29	26
22	17	17	20	38	10	38	25	27	23
23	13	17	34	25	29	22	22	14	11
29	26	29	29	37	32	27	26	18	22

Step 2: Add the values in the sample:
$$\sum x = 31 + 27 + 29 + \cdots + 18 + 22 = 989$$

Step 3: Divide the sum by the sample size.
$$\bar{x} = \frac{989}{40} = 24.73$$

The mean number of minutes for service calls for this sample of 40 calls is 24.73 minutes.

The median is computed using the following steps:

Step 1: Collect the sample data.
         See part a.

Step 2: Sort the data from smallest to largest, forming a data array.

11	12	13	15	17	17	18	18
20	22	22	22	22	23	23	24
24	25	25	26	26	26	26	27
28	28	29	30	30	30	30	30
30	31	32	32	35	38	39	39

Step 3: Locate the middle value of the data.
         The location index for the median is determined using the following equation:
$$i = \frac{1}{2}(n)$$

For $n = 40$, the index is:
$$i = \frac{1}{2}(40) = 20$$

Because the index is 12 which is an integer, the median is the average of the 20th and 21st data values going from either end. These two values are 26 and 26. This the median is:

$$M_d = \frac{26 + 26}{2} = 26$$

Half the data values fall below 26 and half the data values fall above 26.

c. To determine if there is a mode and what the value of the mode is, we use the following steps:

Step 1: Collect the sample data.
See part a.

Step 2: Organize the data into a frequency distribution.

Minutes	Frequency
10	0
11	1
12	1
13	1
14	0
15	1
16	0
17	2
18	2
19	0
20	1
21	0
22	4
23	2
24	2
25	2
26	4
27	1
28	2
29	1
30	6
31	1
32	2
33	0
34	0
35	1
36	0
37	0
38	1
39	2
40	0
41	0

Step 3: Determine the value that occurs most frequently.
The value 30 occurs 6 times which is the most of any value in the sample. Thus the mode for these sample data is 30 minutes.

In order for data to be perfectly symmetric, the mean and median must be equal. In this case, the mean is 25 while the median is 26. Thus the data are slightly left skewed.

3.13
   a. The sorted data are shown below.

68	85	110	146
71	88	116	147
73	90	119	156
74	92	130	156
76	93	134	162
79	103	138	178
83	105	145	181

The mean is 114.21 and the median is 107.50. Note the position of the median is $(1/2)(n)$ where $n = 28$. Because the median's position is 14, the average of the 14th and 15th position in the sorted array is the median, which is $(105+110)/2 = 107.50$. The mode is the most frequently occurring value and is 156.

b. Because the mean is larger than the median the data are skewed right.

c. The box and whisker plot developed using Minitab is shown below.

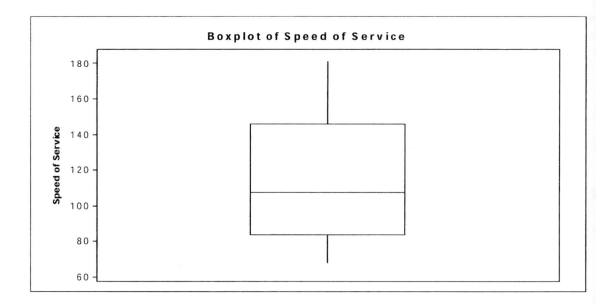

Note that the median is not in the center of the box and that the whiskers are not of equal length. The whisker going up is longer than the whisker going down which indicates that the data are skewed to the right. This supports the conclusion that the data are not symmetric, but skewed.

3.15

a. Average $= \dfrac{\Sigma x_i}{n} = \dfrac{11259.9}{20} = 562.99$

b. The 17th observation is quite larger than the rest of the data, an *outlier*. Averages, but not medians, are highly affected by outliers. Therefore, the median would be an appropriate measure for this data set. Arranged in numerical order, the data is

| 400.56 | 464.37 | 474.86 | 475.87 | 511.15 | 528.78 | 531.64 | 533.70 | 538.20 | 545.25 |
| 558.12 | 564.71 | 567.46 | 588.39 | 589.15 | 606.70 | 610.32 | 625.82 | 632.14 | 912.68 |

Calculating the index produces $(p/100)n = (50/100)20 = 10$. This is an integer. The rule says to average the 10th and 11th observation $= (545.25 + 558.12)/2 = 551.685$.

c. The outlier will have the largest effect. Deleting it, produces the average =
$\dfrac{\Sigma x_i}{n} = \dfrac{11259.9 - 912.68}{20 - 1} = 544.59$.

The observation closest to the original mean would have the least effect. That number is 564.71. Deleting it, produces the average $= \dfrac{\Sigma x_i}{n} = \dfrac{11259.9 - 564.71}{20 - 1} = 562.90$.

3.17

a. FDIC Average $= \dfrac{\Sigma x_i}{n} = \dfrac{6826804000000}{8885} = 768351603.83$

Bank of America Average $= \dfrac{\Sigma x_i}{n} = \dfrac{681570000000}{6000} = 113595000$

b. The ratio between the FDIC and BA averages is $768351603.83 / 113595000 = 6.76$. The discrepancy may be due to the use of the word "bank." The FDIC in referring to "bank" may consider a corporation such as BA to be a "bank." Whereas the BA term "banking center" refers to its branches. There may also be a small difference do to the fact that information was available for 2005 for the FDIC and for 2004 for BA.

c. The answer to this question depends upon the intent of the measurements. If they were attempting to characterize only the specified years, they would be considered to be parameters. If, however, these data were considered "typical" and were to be used to describe past, current averages, they would be considered statistics.

Chapter 3

3.19   Excel or Minitab can be used to compute the statistics shown as follows:

	White	Wheat	Multigrain	Black	Cinnamon Raisin	Sour Dough French	Light Oat
Mean	599.7727	530.4091	470.3636	383.5909	139.7272727	127.0909091	261.6364
Median	577.5	503	426	362.5	137.5	120	260
Mode	817	#N/A	#N/A	#N/A	100	104	224

The student reports will vary but should contain a discussion of the above statistics. Bar charts could be used to display the mean and median for the six bread categories.

3.21
Step 1: Sort the data from low to high.

The data, sorted by column, are:

$7,928	$16,133	$32,939	$45,044	$57,530
$8,748	$19,017	$34,553	$45,263	$58,075
$8,824	$23,381	$35,303	$46,007	$58,443
$8,858	$26,006	$35,534	$46,658	$59,233
$10,669	$26,805	$37,746	$49,427	$61,785
$11,632	$28,278	$37,986	$54,211	$62,682
$11,725	$29,786	$38,698	$54,215	$62,874
$14,136	$31,869	$38,850	$54,337	$65,878
$14,550	$31,904	$42,183	$55,807	$66,668
$15,733	$32,367	$42,961	$56,855	$66,714

Step 2: Determine the 20th percentile location index and find the 20th percentile.

To determine the location index for the 20th percentile (p=20) we do the following:

$$i = \frac{p}{100}(n) = \frac{20}{100}(50) = 10$$

Since the index, 10, is an integer, the 20th percentile is determined by finding the average of the 10th and 11th values from the lower end of the sorted data. This is:

$$Q1 = \frac{15,733 + 16,133}{2} = 15,933$$

Thus, based on these sample data, the 20th percentile is determined to be $15,933. Thus, homeowners age 65 or older with incomes at or below $15,933 will be eligible for property tax relief under the current proposal.

3.23

a. $\bar{x} = \dfrac{2448.30}{20} = 122.465$ i = (50/100)20 = 10. Therefore, use average of the 10th and 11th number: median = (123.2 + 123.7)/2 = 123.45. Since the mean < median, this suggests that the distribution is left-skewed.

b. The average monthly increase would equal the difference in the PHSI between Jan 05 and Aug 05 divided by the number of months (20). Thus, the average = (129.5 – 111)/20 = 0.925.

c. Assuming the PHSI increases by 0.925 each month, then each month's weight should be the amount of increase since Dec 04. Thus, the weights would be: w_1 = 0.925, w_2 = 2(0.925), . . ., w_8 = 8(0.925). Therefore, the weighted average is

$$\bar{x}_w = \frac{0.925(120.6) + 2(0.925)(123.2) + ... + 8(0.925)(129.5)}{0.925 + 2(0.925) + ... + 8(0.925)} = \frac{4207.825}{33.3} = 126.36$$

d. The weighted average does seem more appropriate since the PHSI continues to increase each month. We expect that the most recent observations give a better appraisal as to the current, average PHSI.

Section 3-2 Exercises

3.25

a. The range is the difference between the high value and the low value in the set of data.

Range = High – Low

Range = 8 – 0 = 8

b. The steps required to compute the sample variance are:

Step 1: Select the sample and record the data.

3	0	2	0	1	3	5	2
5	1	3	0	0	1	3	3
4	3	1	8	4	2	4	0

Step 2: Select the desired equation for computing the sample variance:

$$s^2 = \frac{\sum(x - \bar{x})^2}{n - 1}$$

Step 3: Compute the sample mean.

$$\bar{x} = \frac{\sum x}{n} = \frac{58}{24} = 2.42$$

Step 4: Determine the sum of the squared deviations of each x and $\bar{x}$.

x	$(x-\bar{x})$	$(x-\bar{x})^2$
3	0.58	0.3364
5	2.58	6.6564
4	1.58	2.4964
0	-2.42	5.8564
1	-1.42	2.0164
3	0.58	0.3364
2	-0.42	0.1764
3	0.58	0.3364
1	-1.42	2.0164
0	-2.42	5.8564
0	-2.42	5.8564
8	5.58	31.1364
1	-1.42	2.0164
0	-2.42	5.8564
4	1.58	2.4964
3	0.58	0.3364
1	-1.42	2.0164
2	-0.42	0.1764
5	2.58	6.6564
3	0.58	0.3364
4	1.58	2.4964
2	-0.42	0.1764
3	0.58	0.3364
0	-2.42	5.8564
	0	91.8

Step 5: Compute the sample variance.

$$s^2 = \frac{\sum(x-\bar{x})^2}{n-1} = \frac{91.8}{24-1} = 3.99$$

c. The sample standard deviation is the square root of the variance.

$$s = \sqrt{\frac{\sum(x-\bar{x})^2}{n-1}} = \sqrt{3.99} = 1.998$$

3.27   a. The population variance is computed using the following steps.
            Step 1: Collect the data for the population.

16	15	17	15	15	15
14	9	16	15	13	10
8	18	20	17	17	17
18	23	7	15	20	10
14	14	12	12	24	21

Step 2: Calculate the population mean.

$$\mu = \frac{\sum x}{N} = \frac{457}{30} = 15.23$$

Step 3: Compute the sum of squared deviations from the mean.

$$\sum(x-\mu)^2 = (16-15.23)^2 + (15-15.23)^2 + ...(21-15.23)^2$$
$$= 506.24$$

Step 4: Compute the population variance.

$$\sigma^2 = \frac{\sum(x-\mu)^2}{N} = \frac{506.24}{30} = 16.87$$

b. The population standard deviation is the square root of the population variance.

$$\sigma = \sqrt{\frac{\sum(x-\mu)^2}{N}} = \sqrt{\frac{506.24}{30}} = \sqrt{16.87} = 4.11$$

3.29 The sorted data is shown below.

5.4	6.6	7.5	7.8
8.5	8.9	10.3	11.5
12	12.2	13	14.4

The range is equal to the maximum value minus the minimum value = 14.4-5.4 = 9.
The first quartile's position is (25/100)*12 = 3. Therefore Q_1 is the average of the data values in the 3rd and 4th position = (7.5+7.8)/2 = 7.65.
The third quartile's position is (75/100)*12 = 9. Therefore Q_3 is the average of the data values in the 9th and 10th position = (12+12.2)/2 = 12.1.
The IQR = $Q_3 - Q_1$ = 12.1 – 7.65 = 4.45.
The variance is 7.86 and the standard deviation is 2.8.

$$\text{The variance} = \frac{\sum x^2 - \frac{(\sum x)^2}{n}}{n-1} = \frac{1,248.81-(118.1^2)/12}{12-1} = 7.86$$

The standard deviation = $\sqrt{7.86} = 2.8$

Chapter 3

3.31
    a. Range = largest – smallest = 30 – 6 = 24,

$$s^2 = \frac{\sum(x_i - \bar{x})^2}{n-1} = \frac{727.33}{14} = 51.95,\ s = \sqrt{s^2} = \sqrt{51.95} = 7.21\ ,$$

The index for Q_1 is: i = (p/100)n = (25/100)15 = 3.75. i = 4. Therefore, Q_1 = 12.
For Q_3 the index is (p/100)n = (75/100)15 = 11.25. i = 12. Therefore, Q_3 = 24. So the
IQR = $Q_3 - Q_1$ = 24 – 12 = 12

    b. Range = largest – smallest = 30 – 6 = 24,

$$\sigma^2 = \frac{\sum(x_i - \mu)^2}{N} = \frac{727.33}{15} = 48.49,\ \sigma = \sqrt{48.49} = 6.96\ ,$$

The index for Q_1 is: i = (p/100)n = (25/100)15 = 3.75. i = 4. Therefore, Q_1 = 12.
For Q_3 the index is (p/100)n = (75/100)15 = 11.25. i = 12. Therefore, Q_3 = 24. So the
IQR = $Q_1 - Q_3$ = 24 – 12 = 12

    c. σ^2 is smaller than s^2 by a factor of (N – 1)/N. σ is smaller than s by a factor of
$\sqrt{(N-1)/N}$. The range is not affected.

3.33
    a. The sorted data is shown below.

35	50	50	50
60	75	75	75
80	85	85	90
90	100	100	100
100	125	125	150

The range is equal to the maximum value minus the minimum value = 150-35 = 115.
The first quartile's position is (25/100)*20 = 5. Therefore Q_1 is the average of the data values
in the 5th and 6th position = (60+75)/2 = 67.5.
The third quartile's position is (75/100)*20 = 15. Therefore Q_3 is the average of the data
values in the 15th and 16th position = (100+100)/2 = 100.
The IQR = $Q_3 - Q_1$ = 100 – 67.5 = 32.5.
The variance is 815.79 and the standard deviation is 28.56.

$$\text{The variance} = \frac{\sum x^2 - \frac{(\sum x)^2}{n}}{n-1} = \frac{160,000 - (1.700^2)/20}{20-1} = 815.79$$

The standard deviation = $\sqrt{815.79} = 28.56$

56

b. The range is computed by taking the difference between the two extreme values in a data set. That is the difference between the maximum and the minimum. The interquartile range looks at the middle 50% of the data values by taking the difference between the 75th and the 25th percentile. Both are measures of variability but the interquartile range overcomes the susceptibility of the range to being highly influenced by extreme values.

3.35

X	$X - \bar{x}$	$(X - \bar{x})^2$
32	5.9	34.81
22	-4.1	16.81
24	-2.1	4.41
27	0.9	0.81
27	0.9	0.81
33	6.9	47.61
28	1.9	3.61
23	-3.1	9.61
24	-2.1	4.41
21	-5.1	26.01
261		148.9

a. range = 33 – 21 = 12

$$\bar{x} = \frac{\sum_{i=1}^{n} x_i}{n} = 261/10 = 26.1$$

$$s^2 = \frac{\sum_{i=1}^{n}(x - \bar{x})^2}{n-1} = 148.9/(10\text{-}1) = 16.5444$$

$$s = \sqrt{s^2} = \sqrt{16.5444} = 4.0675$$

the 1st quartile is equal to the 25th percentile

$$i = \frac{p}{100}(n) = (25/100)(10) = 2.5 \text{ or the } 3^{rd} \text{ observation} = 23$$

the 3rd quartile is equal to the 75th percentile

$$i = \frac{p}{100}(n) = (75/100)(10) = 7.5 \text{ or the 8th observation} = 28$$

Interquartile Range = 28 – 23 = 5

Chapter 3

b. Student answers will vary but they should look at the number of standard deviations the new mean is from the old mean. Old Mean (37.8) – New Mean (26.1) = 11.7 which is 11.7/4.0657 = 2.8 or almost 3 standard deviations from the old mean. Given this, although we are working with a small sample, there appears to be evidence to suggest that the ages are lower than before the campaign.

3.37

a. The range, interquartile range, variance, and standard deviation are shown below (calculated using Minitab).

```
Variable                    StDev   Variance   Range    IQR
Speed of Service            34.89   1217.14    113.00   62.25
```

The range is 113.0, the IQR is 62.25, the variance is 1217.14, and the standard deviation is 34.89.

b. No, the interquartile range looks at the middle 50% of the values so it is not affected by changes to the extreme values.

c. Adding a constant to all the data values leaves the variance unchanged.

3.39

a. 2004: $\bar{x} = \dfrac{\sum x_i}{n} = \dfrac{3.8}{9} = 0.422$.

$$s^2 = \frac{\sum (x_i - \mu)^2}{n-1} = \frac{7.992}{8} = 0.999, \ s = \sqrt{s^2} = \sqrt{0.999} = 1.000$$

For the first quartile for 2004, the index is $(p/100)n = (25/100)9 = 2.25$. The index is, therefore, 3. Therefore, $Q_1 = -0.2$. Similarly, For the third quartile, the index is $(p/100)n = (75/100)9 = 6.75$. Thus, $i = 7$. Therefore, $Q_2 = 1.5$. Therefore, the IQR is $1.5 - (-0.2) = 1.7$.

2005: $\bar{x} = \dfrac{\sum x_i}{n} = \dfrac{4.03}{4} = 1.075$.

$$s^2 = \frac{\sum (x_i - \mu)^2}{n-1} = \frac{1.188}{3} = 0.396, \ s = \sqrt{s^2} = \sqrt{0.396} = 0.629$$

For the first quartile for 2005, the index is $(p/100)n = (25/100)4 = 1$ = integer. Therefore, $Q_1 = 25^{th}$ percentile is obtained by calculating the average of the 1st and 2nd value = 0.7. Similarly, For the third quartile, the index is $(p/100)n = (75/100)4 = 3$ = integer. Therefore, $Q_2 = 75^{th}$ percentile is obtained by calculating the average of the 3rd and 4th rank = 1.45. Therefore, the IQR is $1.45 - 0.7 = 0.75$.

b. $\bar{x}_2 = 1.075$ and $\bar{x}_1 = 0.422$. The second mean is more than twice that of the first indicating that the index has risen substantially.

c.

$s_1 = 1.000$ and $s_2 = 0.629$. This indicates that the standard deviation for 2004 is approximately 60% ($1/0.629 = 1.59$) larger than that for 2005. We could say that the price indices for 2005 do not fluctuate as much as those in 2004.

3.41. The descriptive statistics can be computed using software such as Excel or Minitab. Excel's descriptive statistics option under Tools is used to provide the following results:

	Pre-MBA Salary (Average)	Post-MBA Salary (Average)	Percentage Increase in Salary	Undergraduate GPA (Average)	GMAT Score (Average)	Annual Tuition	Expected Annual Student Cost
Mean	43337.63	98902	123.29%	3.4025	631.125	15967.5	27980.75
Median	39077	82203	116.32%	3.455	635	13163.5	23169.5
Standard Deviation	12334.73	38787.1	21.75%	0.134881	48.47514	7698.981	11921.58
Sample Variance	1.52E+08	1.5E+09	4.73%	0.018193	2349.839	59274313	1.42E+08
Range	32737	97077	55.85%	0.33	139	20896	31744
Minimum	32763	68423	104.15%	3.2	553	8000	17860
Maximum	65500	165500	160.00%	3.53	692	28896	49604
Sum	346701	791216	986.28%	27.22	5049	127740	223846
Count	8	8	8	8	8	8	8

Student reports will differ but should contain a discussion of the measures of the center and the measures of the spread.

3.43. Software such as Excel or Minitab can be used to do the computations required in parts a. and b. We have used Excel's pivot table feature to provide the desired calculations.

a. The mean and standard deviation for male and female customer phone purchase prices are shown as follows:

Data	F	M
Average of Price	98	117
StdDev of Price	36.14	68.06

In this sample, males spent an average of $117 while females spent an average of $98 for their phones. The standard deviation for males was nearly twice that for females.

b. The mean and standard deviation for home and business use customer phone purchase prices are shown as follows:

Data	Business	Home
Average of Price	166.67	105.74
StdDev of Price	57.74	56.40

In this sample, business users spent an average of $166.67 on their phone while home users spent an average of $105.74. The variation in phone costs for the two groups was about equal.

3.45

a. The index is (p/100)n = (20/100)25 = 5. Therefore, the 20th percentile is obtained by calculating the average of the 5th and 6th rank = 5.5. Similarly, the 40th, 60th, and 80th percentiles are 10.5, 15.5, and 20.5, respectively.

b. Since the data represents only the ranking of the institutions for the year 2005, the measurements are parameters: $\mu_1 = \dfrac{\sum x_i}{N} = \dfrac{515279}{5} = 103056.$

$$\sigma^2 = \frac{\sum(x_i - \mu)^2}{N} = \frac{3095924785}{5} = 619184957, \ \sigma = \sqrt{\sigma^2} = \sqrt{619184957} = 24883.$$

The parameters were calculated to be:

	Top Ranked	2nd Ranked	3rd Ranked	4th Ranked	5th Ranked
μ	103056	82678	84300	87725	71047
σ^2	616184957	641965420	360030000	570233125	78214458
σ	24883	25337	18975	23880	8844

c. The ranking of the first and fifth ranked subgroup appears to coincide to their average tuition. However, the rankings of the middle three ranked subgroup seemed to be the inverse of their average tuitions. The last ranked subgroup has a significantly smaller standard deviation than do the rest of the subgroups. This reflects the fact that it has no outliers. Each of the other subgroups have at least one outlier which increases their variability.

Section 3-3 Exercises

3.47.

a. The coefficient of variation is computed at follows:

$$CV = \frac{\sigma}{\mu}(100)$$

Population 1 –

$$CV = \frac{\sigma}{\mu}(100)$$

$$CV = \frac{50}{700}(100) = 7\%$$

Population 2 –

$$CV = \frac{\sigma}{\mu}(100)$$

$$CV = \frac{5,000}{29,000}(100) = 17\%$$

b. Based on the coefficients of variation for the two populations, population 2 has a CV = 17% while population 1 has a CV = 7%. Thus, population 2 is more variable relative to the size of the population mean than is population 1.

3.49 The standardized value is computed using:

$$z = \frac{x - \mu}{\sigma}$$

Distribution A: $z = \dfrac{50,000 - 45,600}{6,333} = 0.695$

Distribution B: $z = \dfrac{40 - 33.40}{4.05} = 1.63$

The smaller the z value, the relatively closer the x value is to the mean. Thus, the 50,000 value is .6948 standard deviations from the mean of distribution A while the value 40 is 1.6296 standard deviations from the mean of distribution B. The value from distribution A is relatively closer to its mean.

3.51 a. The standardized value is computed using:

$$z = \frac{x - \mu}{\sigma}$$

For a value, x = 500, the standardized value is:

$$z = \frac{500 - 400}{50} = \frac{100}{50} = 2$$

Thus, a bulb that last 500 hours is 2 standard deviations higher than the population mean.

b. If the time distribution is bell shaped, the Empirical Rule can be used to determine the percentage of bulbs expected to last over 500 hours. The Empirical Rule states:

Approximately 95% of the data will fall with ± 2 standard deviations from the mean. This is shown as follows:

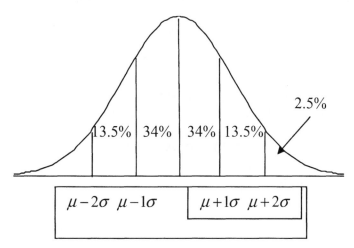

61

Thus, a bulb lasting 500 hours is two standard deviations above the mean. Only 2.5 percent of all bulbs are expected to last longer than 500 hours assuming that the distribution is approximately bell shaped.

3.53   a. The standardized value is $z = \dfrac{800 - \bar{x}}{s} = \dfrac{800 - 1000}{250} = -0.80$

b. The standardized value is $z = \dfrac{1200 - \bar{x}}{s} = \dfrac{1200 - 1000}{250} = 0.80$

c. The standardized value is $z = \dfrac{1000 - \bar{x}}{s} = \dfrac{1000 - 1000}{250} = 0.00$

3.55

a. $\bar{x} = \dfrac{1530}{30} = 51$

$s^2 = \dfrac{\sum (x_i - \bar{x})^2}{n-1} = \dfrac{14812.04}{29} = 510.76, \; s = \sqrt{s^2} = \sqrt{510.76} = 22.60.$

b.   Therefore, $\bar{x} \pm s$, $\bar{x} \pm 2s$, $\bar{x} \pm 3s$ are, respectively, 51 ± 22.60, $51 \pm 2(22.60)$, $51 \pm 3(22.60)$, i.e., (28.4, 73.6), (5.8, 96.2), and (-16.8, 118.8). There are (19/30)100% = 63.3%, of the data within (28.4, 73.6), (30/30)100% = 100%, of the data within (5.8, 96.2), (30/30)100% = 100%, of the data within (-16.8, 118.8).

c.   The Empirical indicates that the percentages should be approximately 68%, 95%, and 100% in these intervals. It does seem plausible that this data came from a bell-shaped population.

3.57
a.   The mean and standard deviation for the time to complete calls to English speaking service representatives was calculated using Excel and are shown below.

	Mean	Standard Deviation
English Speaking	111.36	22.42

b.   The mean and standard deviation for the time to complete calls to Spanish speaking service representatives was calculated using Excel and are shown below.

	Mean	Standard Deviation
Spanish Speaking	150.86	26.84

c. The coefficient of variation for the time to complete calls is shown below.

Coefficient of Variation for English Speaking = (22.42/111.36)*100% = 20.13%
Coefficient of Variation for Spanish = (26.84/150.86)*100% = 17.79%
Thus, the relative variation is greater for English Speaking than for Spanish Speaking calls.

d. A box and whisker plot for the two types of calls is shown below. Note that Spanish Speaking calls have a higher median than English speaking calls. Furthermore, the third quartile for English Speaking calls is approximately equal to the first quartile of Spanish Speaking calls. This indicates that only about 25% of the Spanish Speaking calls are completed within the time required to complete approximately 75% of the English Speaking calls. The time to complete both types of calls appears to be symmetric (medians are centered in the box), however the whisker pointing up on Spanish Speaking calls is longer than the whisker pointing down, which suggests some slight positive skewness in the time to complete Spanish Speaking calls.

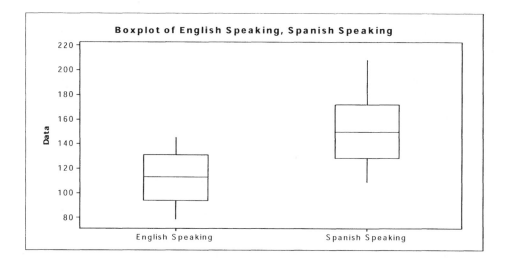

3.59 At issue is relative variability. To assess this, the proper measure is the coefficient of variation computed as follows:

$$\text{For a population:}\quad CV = \frac{\sigma}{\mu}(100)$$

$$\text{For a sample:}\quad CV = \frac{s}{\bar{x}}(100)$$

For the existing supplier, we treat the mean and standard deviation as population values giving:

$$\text{Existing Supplier:}\quad CV = \frac{\sigma}{\mu}(100)$$

$$CV = \frac{0.078}{3.75}(100) = 2.08\%$$

$$\text{New Supplier:}\quad CV = \frac{s}{\bar{x}}(100)$$

Chapter 3

We begin by computing the mean and standard deviation from the sample data giving:

$$\bar{x} = \frac{\sum x}{n} = \frac{360.586}{20} = 18.029$$

$$s = \sqrt{\frac{\sum (x-\bar{x})^2}{n-1}} = \sqrt{\frac{(18.018-18.029)^2 + (17.856-18.029)^2 + ... + (17.799-18.029)^2}{20-1}}$$

$$s = 0.135$$

Then the coefficient of variation for the new supplier is:

$$CV = \frac{s}{\bar{x}}(100)$$

$$CV = \frac{0.135}{18.029}(100) = 0.75\%$$

Student reports will differ. However, students should show the results of the coefficient of variation computations and conclude that the new supplier has the potential to produce parts with less variation than the existing supplier. The key is whether Cirus managers believe they can effectively compare the two companies when different size products are being compared. The students should point out that the purpose of the coefficient of variation is to compare variability when the means of the two groups are different.

3.61

a. The coefficient of variation measures the relative standard deviation:

Public: $CV = \frac{\sigma}{\mu}(100) = (3000/5491)100 = 54.6$.

Private: $CV = \frac{\sigma}{\mu}(100) = (10000/21235) = 47.1$.

So actually the public four-year colleges and universities have the largest relative standard deviation.

b. The Empirical Rule suggests that virtually all of the data values is contained by $\mu \pm 3\sigma = 21235 \pm 3(10000) = -8765$ to 51235.

c. It does not appear that the data values are bell shaped since about 15% [= {0 – (-8765)}/{51235 – (-8765)} = 0.146] of the range of the data is negative. Since tuition and fees are not negative, this cast doubt on the assertion that it is bell-shaped.

3.63

a. The computer calculated statistics are $\bar{x} = 1.6848$ and $s = 0.00383$.

b. Except for random variation, the diameter of the golf balls should not be smaller than 1.682. The larger the diameter the shorter the distance when driving a golf ball. So the data should be bunched around 1.682 but not smaller. This would create a right skewed distribution where as the bell shaped distribution is symmetric.

c. $\bar{x} \pm 2s = 1.6848 \pm 2(0.00383) = (1.6771, 1.6925)$ contained 43 of the data points = 96% versus Tchebysheff's stipulation, at least $(1-1/2^2)100 = 75\%$, $\bar{x} \pm 3s = 1.6848 \pm 3(0.00383) = (1.6733, 1.6963)$ contained all 45 implying 100% compared to at least $(1-1/3^2)100 = 89\%$, , $\bar{x} \pm 4s = 1.6848 \pm 4(0.00383) = (1.6695, 1.7001)$ contained all 45 implying 100% compared to at least $(1-1/4^2)100 = 93.75\%$.

3.65

a. The computer calculated statistics for the LAX/SFO flight were $\bar{x} = 336$ and $s = 162.8$; for the LAX/BCN flight $\bar{x} = 1997$ and $s = 203.4$.

b. For LAX/SFO $CV = \dfrac{s}{\bar{x}}(100) = (162.8/336)100 = 48.5\%$;

For LAX/BCN $CV = \dfrac{s}{\bar{x}}(100) = (203.4/1997)100 = 10.2\%$.

The SFO flight has a larger relative dispersion.

c. The mean and the standard deviation are multiplied by the same constant as each member of the data is multiplied. Therefore, $\bar{x} = 0.566(1997) = 1130.30$ and $s = 0.566(203.4) = 115.12$. The CV won't change since both elements of the ratio are multiplied by the same constant.

3.67 Probably the most effective way to deal with this exercise is to covert the growth rates to standardized z-values. To do this, we use:

$$z = \frac{x - \mu}{\sigma}$$

Excel or Minitab can be used to calculate the z-values. In this case, we have used Excel's STANDARDIZE function. First, we need to compute the mean and standard deviation for the growth rate in population. This is done as follows:

$$\mu = \frac{\sum x}{N} = \frac{118.8}{74} = 1.6\%$$

$$\sigma = \sqrt{\frac{\sum(x-\mu)^2}{N}} = \sqrt{\frac{(5.9-1.6)^2 + (2.3-1.6)^2 + ... + (1.5-1.6)^2}{74}}$$

$$\sigma = 1.12$$

Now we calculate the z-values for each country and sort the countries by z-value giving:

Chapter 3

Country	Country Code	2000 Population (Thousands)	1990-2000 Percent Annual Population Growth	Standardized Growth Rates z-values
Ukraine	4	50,380	-0.6	-1.96
Russia	7	147,938	-0.5	-1.88
Romania	4	20,996	-0.2	-1.61
Germany	4	85,684	-0.1	-1.52
Croatia	4	5,044	0.0	-1.43
Italy	4	57,807	0.0	-1.43
Japan	7	126,582	0.2	-1.25
Poland	4	39,010	0.2	-1.25
Spain	4	39,545	0.2	-1.25
Finland	4	5,115	0.3	-1.16
United Kingdom	4	58,894	0.3	-1.16
France	4	59,079	0.4	-1.07
Cuba	2	11,131	0.5	-0.98
Norway	4	4,461	0.5	-0.98
Greece	4	10,735	0.6	-0.89
Netherlands	4	15,893	0.6	-0.89
Sweden	4	9,052	0.6	-0.89
Jamaica	2	2,669	0.8	-0.71
Switzerland	4	7,374	0.8	-0.71
Iceland	4	280	0.9	-0.63
Taiwan	7	22,214	0.9	-0.63
China	7	1,253,438	1.0	-0.54
South Korea	7	47,351	1.0	-0.54
United States	1	274,943	1.0	-0.54
Australia	8	18,950	1.1	-0.45
Thailand	7	61,164	1.1	-0.45
Brazil	3	169,545	1.2	-0.36
Canada	1	29,989	1.2	-0.36
Sri Lanka	7	19,377	1.2	-0.36
Argentina	3	37,218	1.3	-0.27
Chile	3	14,996	1.3	-0.27
Haiti	2	6,901	1.3	-0.27
Kuwait	6	2,420	1.3	-0.27
Zimbabwe	5	11,777	1.5	-0.09
Indonesia	7	219,267	1.6	0.00
Colombia	3	39,172	1.7	0.09
India	7	1,012,909	1.7	0.09
North Korea	7	25,491	1.7	0.09
Panama	2	2,821	1.7	0.09
South Africa	5	44,018	1.7	0.09
Turkey	6	66,618	1.7	0.09
Vietnam	7	78,350	1.7	0.09
Bangladesh	7	132,081	1.8	0.18
Peru	3	26,198	1.8	0.18
Singapore	7	3,620	1.8	0.18
Mexico	2	102,912	1.9	0.27
Ecuador	3	12,360	2.0	0.36
Egypt	5	68,437	2.0	0.36
Venezuela	3	23,596	2.0	0.36
Malaysia	7	21,610	2.1	0.45
Morocco	5	32,229	2.1	0.45
Pakistan	7	141,145	2.1	0.45
Philippines	7	80,961	2.2	0.54
Tanzania	5	31,045	2.2	0.54
Algeria	5	31,788	2.3	0.63
Iran	6	71,879	2.3	0.63
Ghana	5	19,272	2.4	0.71
Kenya	5	30,490	2.4	0.71
Nepal	7	24,364	2.4	0.71
Uganda	5	21,891	2.5	0.80
Israel	6	5,852	2.6	0.89
Somalia	5	10,880	2.7	0.98
Ethiopia	5	63,514	2.8	1.07
Madagascar	5	15,295	2.8	1.07
Nicaragua	2	4,729	2.8	1.07
Cameroon	5	15,966	2.9	1.16
Iraq	6	24,731	2.9	1.16
Sudan	5	35,530	2.9	1.16
Nigeria	5	117,328	3.0	1.25
Mozambique	5	19,614	3.3	1.52
Saudi Arabia	6	22,246	3.4	1.61
Syria	6	17,759	3.4	1.61
Libya	5	6,294	3.7	1.88
Afghanistan	7	26,668	5.9	3.84

Only one country, Afghanistan, had a growth rate more than two standard deviations above the mean. This country was 3.84 standard deviations above the mean. No countries were more than 2 standard deviations below the mean. The closest was the Ukraine and z = -1.96.

End of Chapter Exercises

3.69 The first interval is $\mu \pm \sigma$. It contains 68% of the data. The remainder (100 − 68 = 32) is divided between the two tails. So a half of the area in the left hand tail is 32/2. Therefore, the lower endpoint is the 16th percentile. 68 + (32/2) of the data is to the left of the upper endpoint. It is the 84th percentile. The second interval is $\mu \pm 2\sigma$. It contains 95% of the data. The remainder (100 − 95 = 5) is divided between the two tails. So a half of the area in the left hand tail is 5/2. Therefore, the lower endpoint is the 2.5th perecentile. 95 + (5/2) of the data is to the left of the upper endpoint. It is the 97.5th percentile. The third interval is $\mu \pm 3\sigma$. It contains 100% of the data. Therefore, the lower endpoint is the 0th perecentile. The upper endpoint is the 100th percentile.

3.71 Some problems are that it does not look at total hours taken. One student could have taken one class on campus and got an A so would have a 4.0 grade point average. Another student could have taken many hours and got all A's except one or two B's and would have lower than a 4.0 grade point average and people might conclude that the first student is a better student than the second based only upon grade point average. It also does not look at the difficulty of the classes taken. Comparing across two universities has the same problems as mentioned previously along with the fact that all universities are different and the type of classes and difficulty level of classes will be completely different. None of this is accounted for in calculating a grade point average.

3.73 The mode is a useful measure of location of a set of data if the data set is large and involves nominal or ordinal data. For example, if the Labor Department is interested in the category of employment that will generate the most new jobs over the next decade, the modal class would be important. The buyer for a large department store chair would be interested in the category of shoe size most commonly bought.

3.75

a. The standardized sample data for 507 is one standard deviation from the mean.. Z = (507 − 407)/100 = 1. The Empirical Rule indicates that 68% of the data is within one standard deviation from the mean. One half of this is between 507 and 407 and 50% of the distribution is to the left of the mean, 407. Thus, the proportion of airfares less than 507 is 0.68/2 + 0.50 = 0.84.

b. Being a 25th percentile would mean than 0.25 of the area is to its left. The Empirical Rule says that 95% of the data is within one standard deviation of the mean. That means there is (100 - 68)/2 = 0.16 in each tail. Therefore, we need only produce a number less than one standard deviation below the mean: 407-1(100) = 307. So a number between 307 and 407.

c. $Z = \dfrac{X - \bar{X}}{S} = (250 - 407)/100 = -1.57$. Tchebysheff's Theorem indicates that $1 - (1/k^2) = 1 - [1/(1.57^2)] = 0.59$ of the data lies within 1.57 standard deviations from the mean. Thus, the proportion beyond 1.57 standard deviations is $1 - 0.59 = 0.41$. Since the distribution may not be symmetric, all of that proportion could be to the left of 250. Therefore, the largest percentile that could be attributed to an airfare of \$250 is the 41st percentile.

3.77

Student answers will vary but one approach would be to standardize the results for each manager

Plant 1: $(810 - 700)/200 = .55$ standard deviations
Plant 2: $(2600 - 2300)/350 = .86$ standard deviations
Plant 3: $(1320 - 1200)/30 = 4$ standard deviations

Based upon this the manager of Plant 3 performed far better than the other plants on a relative basis.

3.79

X	X - $\bar{x}$	$(X - \bar{x})^2$
229	-135.417	18,337.6736
345	-19.4167	377.0069
599	234.5833	55,029.3403
229	-135.417	18,337.6736
429	64.58333	4,171.0069
605	240.5833	57,880.3403
339	-25.4167	646.0069
339	-25.4167	646.0069
229	-135.417	18,337.6736
279	-85.4167	7,296.0069
344	-20.4167	416.8403
407	42.58333	1,813.3403
4373		183,288.9167

a. $\bar{x} = \dfrac{\sum\limits_{i=1}^{n} x_i}{n} = 4373/12 = 364.42$

b. $s^2 = \dfrac{\sum\limits_{i=1}^{n}(x - \bar{x})^2}{n-1} = 183{,}288.9167/(12\text{-}1) = 16{,}662.63$

$s = \sqrt{s^2} = \sqrt{16{,}662.6288} = 129.08$

3.81

X	X - $\bar{x}$	(X - $\bar{x}$)^2
34	-5.05556	25.55864
24	-15.0556	226.6698
43	3.944444	15.55864
56	16.94444	287.1142
74	34.94444	1221.114
20	-19.0556	363.1142
19	-20.0556	402.2253
33	-6.05556	36.66975
55	15.94444	254.2253
43	3.944444	15.55864
54	14.94444	223.3364
34	-5.05556	25.55864
27	-12.0556	145.3364
34	-5.05556	25.55864
36	-3.05556	9.33642
24	-15.0556	226.6698
54	14.94444	223.3364
39	-0.05556	0.003086
703		3726.944

a. $\bar{x} = \dfrac{\sum_{i=1}^{n} x_i}{n} = 703/18 = 39.0556$

b. To compute the median, rank the observations and average the middle two values.

19 20 24 24 27 33 34 34 34 36 39 43 43 54 54 55 56 74

Median = (34+36)/2 = 35

c. $S^2 = \dfrac{\sum_{i=1}^{n}(x - \bar{x})^2}{n-1} = 3726.944/(18\text{-}1) = 219.232$

$S = \sqrt{S^2} = \sqrt{219.232} = 14.8065$

d. Use Excel's histogram feature to create the frequency distribution.

Classes	Frequency
15 - 24	4
25 - 34	5
35 - 44	4
45 - 54	2
55 - 64	2
65 - 74	1

e. Use Excel's histogram feature to create the histogram.

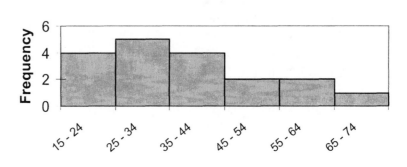

f.

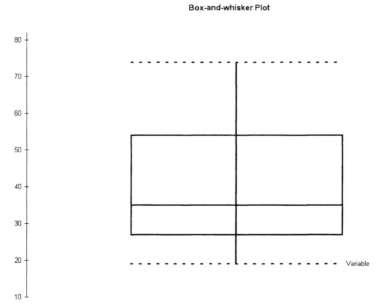

g. The 3rd quartile is equal to the 75th percentile

$i = \dfrac{p}{100}(n+1) = (75/100)(18+1) = 14.25$; Thus, the Q3 value is 25 percent of the

distance between the 14th (54) and the 15th (54) values. This is 54.

The minimum number of minutes the customer would have to wait is 54 minutes

3.83

Student answers will vary but one thing they might do is calculate the mean and standard deviation and then calculate the coefficient of variation in order to compare the data sets.

Idaho Power

X	X - $\bar{x}$	(X - $\bar{x}$)^2
100	-31.1267	968.8694
117.38	-13.7467	188.9708
97.62	-33.5067	1122.697
134.11	2.983333	8.900278
147.92	16.79333	282.016
189.73	58.60333	3434.351
786.76		6005.804

$\bar{x} = \dfrac{\sum\limits_{i=1}^{n} x_i}{n} = 786.76/6 = 131.1267$

$s^2 = \dfrac{\sum(x - \bar{x})^2}{n-1} = 6005.804/(6-1) = 1201.1608$

$s = \sqrt{s^2} = 34.6578$

S&P		
X	$\bar{x}$	(x - $\bar{x}$)^2
100	-52.563	2762.904
110.08	-42.483	1804.834
111.53	-41.033	1683.734
153.45	0.887	0.786
188.69	36.127	1305.136
251.63	99.067	9814.204
915.38		17371.599

$$\overline{x} = \frac{\sum_{i=1}^{n} x_i}{n} = 915.38 = 152.5628$$

$$s^2 = \frac{\sum (x - \overline{x})^2}{n-1} = 17371.599/(6-1) = 3474.2$$

$$s = \sqrt{s^2} = 58.943$$

EEI100

x	$x - \overline{x}$	$(x - \overline{x})^2$
100	-22.4233	502.8059
111.15	-11.2733	127.088
98.29	-24.1333	582.4178
128.78	6.356667	40.40721
130.32	7.896667	62.35734
166	43.57667	1898.926
734.54		3214.002

$$\overline{x} = \frac{\sum_{i=1}^{n} x_i}{n} = 734.54/6 = 122.4233$$

$$s^2 = \frac{\sum (x - \overline{x})^2}{n-1} = 3214.002/(6-1) = 642.8004$$

$$s = \sqrt{s^2} = 25.3535$$

Coefficient of Variation:
Idaho Power = 34.6578/131.1267 = 0.2643 or 26.43%
S&P = 58.943/152.5628 = 0.3864 or 38.64%
EEI100 = 25.3535/122.4233 = 0.2071 or 20.71%

Based strictly on the average Idaho Power has outperformed its own industry (EEI) but has underperformed with the S&P 500. Based on the coefficient of variation it is less variable than the S&P 500 but more variable than the EEI100.

3.85

a.

```
Variable     Mean   StDev
Price      22.000   3.813
```

b. $\bar{x} \pm 1s = 22 \pm (3.813) = (18.187, 25.813)$, $\bar{x} \pm 2s = (14.374, 29.626)$

$\bar{x} \pm 3s = (10.561, 33.439)$

c. The Empirical Rule indicates that 95% of the data is contained within $\bar{x} \pm 2s$. This would mean that each tail has $(1 - 0.95)/2 = 0.025$ of the data. Therefore, the costume should be priced at $14.37.

3.87

a.

```
Variable            Mean   StDev   Median
Close-Open       -0.0354  0.2615  -0.0600
```

b.   It means that the closing price for GE stock is an average of approximately four ($0.0354) cents lower than the opening price.

c.

```
Variable            Mean   StDev   Median
Open             33.947   0.503   33.980
Close-Open       -0.0354  0.2615  -0.0600
```

On the service it appears that the dispersion of the opening stock prices (0.503) is larger than that of the difference between the closing and opening stock prices (0.2615). However, the mean for the opening stock prices is approximately 959 times (33.947/0.0354) larger than that of the difference between closing and opening stock prices. The coefficient of variation should be used here.

```
Variable     CoefVar
Open            1.48
Close-Open    738.47
```

Here the relative dispersion is approximately 499 times (738.47/1.48) as large for the difference between closing and opening stock prices.

3.89

a. Use Excel's Descriptive Statistics tool to determine the sample mean and sample standard deviation for the two data sets. The results are shown below:

mileage, highway		mileage, city	
Mean	24.8333	Mean	18.4
Standard Error	0.76276	Standard Error	0.539476119
Median	24	Median	18.5
Mode	21	Mode	19
Standard Deviation	4.1778	Standard Deviation	2.954832395
Sample Variance	17.454	Sample Variance	8.731034483
Kurtosis	-1.2915	Kurtosis	0.496563717
Skewness	0.01937	Skewness	-0.25743034
Range	14	Range	13
Minimum	18	Minimum	11
Maximum	32	Maximum	24
Sum	745	Sum	552
Count	30	Count	30

Yes the data supports the premise that cars will get better mileage on the highway than around town. The mean for highway (24.8) is higher than the mean for city (18.4) but there is not a lot of difference between the standard deviations.

b. To answer this question, calculate the coefficient of variation for each variable.
Highway CV = 4.1778/24.8333 = 16.8%
City CV = 2.9548/18.4 = 16.1%
City driving has slightly less variability than highway driving.

c. Calculate how many standard deviations the mean of city driving is from the highway driving mean (24.8). The calculation is shown below:
(24.8333 – 18.4)/2.9548 = 2.17.
This is approximately 2 standard deviations away from the mean. Using the empirical rule this means that 95% of the values would be within 2 standard deviations. That means ½ of the remaining 5% would be at least 24.8333, which means 2.5%.

3.91

a. Sorting the data and determine what position 45,000 is in you can solve the percentile equation for the percentile.

$i = \dfrac{p}{100} n = (75/100)*(200) = 150$; The 75th percentile is the average of the 150th and 151st value in the data. You can use PHStat's Stack feature under Data Preparation to reorganize the data. Then sorting the data you get the following:

148	44,879
149	44,879
150	44,904
151	44,980
152	45,052
153	45,148
154	45,153
155	45,227
156	45,228
157	45,276

Thus, the 75th percentile is the average of 44,904 and 44,980, or 44,942.

b. Using Excel's Average and Median functions you can find that
Mean = 42,261
Median = 42,326

c. Using the $2^k \geq n$ guideline, the appropriate number of classes should be 8 since $2^8 = 256$: The class width is:

$$w = \frac{52,774 - 31,476}{8} = 2662.25$$

We choose to round this to 2,800 and start at 31,000 giving the following histogram:

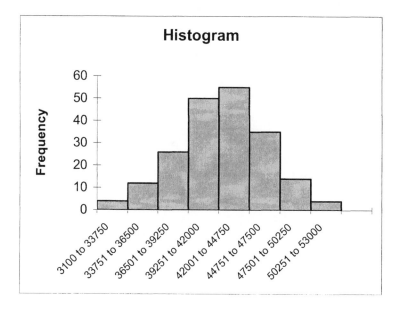

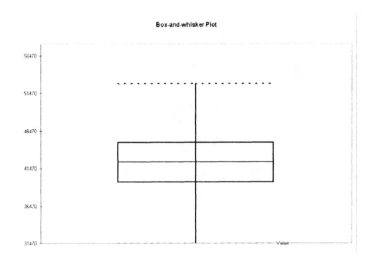

Histograms and box and whiskers plots have certain things in common. In both instances, we get an idea of how the data are distributed, where the center is, and what the shape of the distribution is and how spread out the data are. The histogram breaks the data down into classes and illustrates the actual number of values in each class where the box and whiskers plot shows the median and the inter-quartile range.

CHAPTER 1–3
SPECIAL REVIEW SOLUTIONS

SR.1   a-c. Student answers will vary but class limits should be set so that classes are mutually exclusive and all-inclusive. Class intervals should be of equal size and chosen so that observations are approximately equally distributed over the interval.

SR.3 Student reports will vary. We look for effective use of visual tools indicating trends, not just reliance on tables and numbers. Superior students might compare Intel graphs with competitors or benchmark companies.

SR.5

    a.

	Revenues	Profits	Employees
Mean	6354.71	803.43	21530.3
Median	3428	401	11000
Std Deviation	7457.66	881.812	21269.35

    b. The standardized z-values need to be computed using Equation 3-17 and can be done in either Excel or Minitab. Based on these z-values, the Mellon Bank Corporation is slightly below the average for profits ($z = -.03$) and revenues ($z = -.16$) and slightly above the average for number of employees ($z = .28$).

    c. You need to calculate the coefficient of variance for each variable.

	Revenues	**Profits**	**Employees**
Coefficient of variation	1.173564	1.097558	0.9878812

Revenues has the largest relative variation.

d.

Classes	Frequency
0.000 - 0.014	1
0.015 - 0.029	16
0.030 - 0.044	25
0.045 - 0.059	5
0.060 - 0.074	2
0.075 - 0.089	2

Profit per Employee

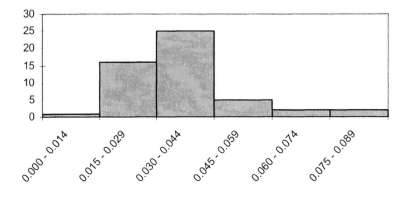

	Profits per Employee
Mean	0.0365
Median	0.0353
Standard Deviation	0.0140

Student reports will vary but should mention most of the profits per employee are between .03 and .044. The data is positively skewed.

e. two standard deviations above the mean is
$0.0365 + 2(0.0140) = 0.0645$
three banks have a profit per employee ratio above 0.0645

Chapter 4 Solutions

When applicable, selected problems in each section will be done following the appropriate step-by-step procedures outlined in the corresponding sections of the chapter. Other problems will provide key points and the answers to the questions, but all answers can be arrived at using the appropriate steps.

Section 4-1 Exercises

4.1   The sample space is listed by following these steps:

Step 1: Define the experiment
The experiment consists of asking people to express their choice among three flavors of ice cream

Step 2: Define the possible outcomes for one trial of the experiment
$$V = Vanilla$$
$$C = Chocolate$$
$$S = Strawberry$$

For two customers, the sample space is:
V, V
V, C
V, S
C, V
C, C
C, S
S, V
S, C
S, S

4.3 The concept that allows the player to know that the probability of the next spin being black is 0.5 is the concept of independent events. If events are independent, then the probability of one event occurring is not influenced by the occurrence of the other events. In this case, since the wheel is deemed to be fair, the chance of a red or a black is 0.5 for any spin regardless of what has occurred on previous spins.

4.5   a. Subjective probability based on expert opinion.

b Relative frequency based on previous customer return history

c. 1/5 = .20

Chapter 4

4.7
Step 1: Determine whether the possible outcomes are equally likely.
In this case students purchasing a meal plan are randomly assigned to one of three dining halls. Thus, any dining hall has the same probability of being assigned as any other.

Step 2: Determine the total number of possible outcomes.
There are three dining halls on campus.

Step 3: Define the event of interest.
The event of interest is the next student being assigned to the Commons dining hall.

Step 4: Determine the number of outcomes associated with the event of interest.
There is only one Commons dining hall.

Step 5: Compute the classical probability using equation 4.1.
P(Commons) = Number of Ways Commons Can Occur/Total Number of Possible Outcomes = 1/3 = 0.333333.

4.9
Probability, using the classical probability assessment method, is computed using the following steps

a. Step 1: Determine whether the outcomes are equally likely:
Since each position is chosen randomly, each outcome is equally likely. $P(e_i) = 1/16$

b. Step 2: Determine number of equally likely events:
There are 16 equally likely events: $e_1 = CM$, $e_2 = CN$, $e_3 = CD$, $e_4 = CB$, $e_5 = HM$, $e_6 = HN$, $e_7 = HD$, $e_8 = HB$, $e_9 = PM$, $e_{10} = PN$, $e_{11} = PD$, $e_{12} = PB$, $e_{13} = YM$, $e_{14} = YN$, $e_{15} = YD$, $e_{16} = YB$

c. Step 3: Determine the event of interest:
The event of interest is that both positions are filled with candidates from the Ivy League.

d. Step 4: Determine the number of outcomes associated with the event of interest:
The event of interest is comprised of e_7, e_8, e_{11}, e_{12}, e_{15}, e_{16}

e. Step 5: Compute the classical probability using Equation 4-1:

$$P(E_i) = \frac{Number\ of\ ways\ E_i\ can\ occur}{Total\ number\ of\ elementary\ events} = \frac{6}{16} = 0.375$$

4.11 Probability, using the classical probability assessment method, is computed using the following steps

a. Step 1: Determine whether the outcomes are equally likely:
   Since each decision is assumed to be equally likely, each outcome is equally likely.
   $P(e_i) = (1/2)^3 = 1/8$

b. Step 2: Determine number of outcomes:
   There are 8 equally likely events: $e_1 = BBB$, $e_2 = BBD$, $e_3 = BDB$, $e_4 = DBB$, $e_5 = BDD$, $e_6 = DBD$, $e_7 = DDB$, $e_8 = DDD$

c. Step 3: Define the events of interest:
   The events of interest are (1) only two consumers buy a HDTV (E_1), (2) at most two consumers buy HDTV's (E_2), and (3) at least two consumers buy HDTV's (E_3).

d. Step 4: Determine the number of outcomes associated with the event of interest:
   The events of interest are comprised of (1) $E_1 = \{e_2, e_3, e_4\}$, (2) $E_2 = \{e_2, e_3, e_4, e_5, e_6, e_7, e_8\}$, and $E_3 = \{e_1, e_2, e_3, e_4\}$

e. Step 5: Compute the classical probability using Equation 4-1:

$$P(E_1) = \frac{Number\ of\ ways\ E_i\ can\ occur}{Total\ number\ of\ elementary\ events} = \frac{3}{8} = 0.375,$$

4.13   The idea is to have unique assignments of three doctors. The following tree starts with Doctor 1 and shows how many unique assignments can involve Dr 1. It then moves on to Doctor 2 and so on. Finally, Doctors 4 and 5 have already been considered and so no assignments can start with them.

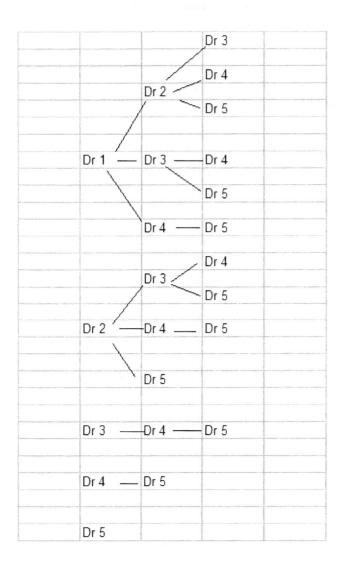

Nine weeks can be covered with this schedule.

4.15 The following steps can be used to define the sample space.

Step 1: Define the experiment.

The experiment consists of cars being sold at the dealership.

Step 2: Define the possible outcomes for one trial of the experiment.

The possible outcomes are:

B = Buick sold
C = Cadillac sold
P = Pontiac sold
U = Used car sold

For two cars sold, the sample space is:

B, B
B, C
B, P
B, U
C, C
C, B
C, P
C, U
P, P
P, B
P, C
P, U
U, U
U, B
U, C
U, P

4.17

a. The managers are using subjective assessment to arrive at the probability that sales will increase by more than 15 percent next year.

b. The closer a probability is to 0.0 or 1.0, the less uncertainty. In this case, manager 3 exhibits the least uncertainty since he/she stated the probability is 0.90.

c. Subjective probability assessments reflect the state of mind of the individual doing the assessment. As such, you could expect that different people would have different information on which to base their assessment and even with the same information, would be expected to process the information differently. Thus, we expect their assessments to differ. In this case, the assessments are widely different indicating that the individuals are very disperse in their view of the sales forecast.

4.19

a. Perkins obtained the number of large corporations that were audited, 9,560, and divided that by the number of corporations who filed tax returns for the 2004 fiscal year. This describes the relative frequency probability assessment method.

b. Since the Relative frequency of $E_i = \dfrac{Number \ of \ times \ E_i \ occurs}{N}$, then

N = (Number of times E_i occurs)/(Relative frequency of E_i) = (9560)/(1/6) = 57,360.

c. The number of large corporations that were not audited = 57,360 – 9560 = 47,800.
Then the Relative frequency of E_i =
$\dfrac{Number \ of \ times \ E_i \ occurs}{N} = \dfrac{47800}{576630}$ =0.8333 = 5/6 = 1 – (1/6).

4.21

a. Software such as Excel or Minitab could be used to assess the probability using the relative frequency assessment method. The following table from Excel's pivot table tool shows the breakdown of Caesarean versus normal births at this hospital.

Count of Delivery Method	
Delivery Method ▼	Total
Caesarean	22
Normal	28
Grand Total	50

Thus, using the relative frequency assessment method we get:
$$P(Caesarean) = \frac{22}{50} = 0.44$$
The probability of a Caesarean birth is 0.44 based on the data from past births at this hospital.

b. The concerns would be the number of births observed (50) is not very large. Second, in many cases there are specific reasons for a Caesarean delivery and not all births are alike. Thus, any new birth may not exactly match the 50 in this study.

4.23   The following joint frequency table (developed using Excel's pivot table feature) summarizes the data.

	Electrical	Mechanical	Total
Lincoln	28	39	67
Tyler	64	69	133
Total	92	108	200

a. The probability the scooter was assembled in the Tyler plant is found by dividing the row total for Tyler (133) by the overall total (200), 133/200 = 0.665.

b. The probability that a scooter breakdown was due to a mechanical failure is found by dividing the column total for Mechanical (108) by the overall total (200), 108/200 = 0.54.

c. The joint probability that a scooter with an electrical problem was assembled at the Lincoln plant is found by dividing the 28 electrical problems traced back to the Lincoln plant by the total of 200 break downs, (28/200) = 0.14.

4.25 The probabilities required to produce the answers to exercise are given by the following table:

```
Rows: Age    Columns: Preference

        Coke   Pepsi   All

17        6      6      12
18        6      6      12
19        6      5      11
20       12      7      19
21       10      6      16
22        6      8      14
23       11      5      16
All      57     43     100

Cell Contents:        Count
```

a. Relative frequency of $E_i = \dfrac{Number \ of \ times \ E_i \ occurs}{N} = \dfrac{43}{100} = 0.43$

b. Relative frequency of $E_i = \dfrac{Number \ of \ times \ E_i \ occurs}{N} = \dfrac{5+6+6}{100} = 0.17$

c. Relative frequency of $E_i = \dfrac{Number \ of \ times \ E_i \ occurs}{N}$.

For Pepsi, Probability $= \dfrac{5+6+6}{12+12+11} = \dfrac{17}{35} = 0.486$.

For Coke, Probability $= \dfrac{6+6+6}{12+12+11} = \dfrac{18}{35} = 0.514$.

d. Relative frequency of $E_i = \dfrac{Number \ of \ times \ E_i \ occurs}{N}$.

For Pepsi, Probability $= \dfrac{7+6+8+5}{19+16+14+16} = \dfrac{26}{65} = 0.4.$

For Coke, Probability $= \dfrac{12+10+6+11}{19+16+14+16} = \dfrac{39}{65} = 0.6$

Section 4-2 Exercises

4.27
  a. P(soft drink)*P(no fries) = (0.9)(1-0.5) = 0.45

  b. P(Hamburger & FF) = $P(Hamburger)P(FF|Hamburger) = (0.6)(0.8) = 0.48$

4.29
  a. P(matched) = 2/3

  b. P(both wrong) = (1/3)*(1/3) = 1/9

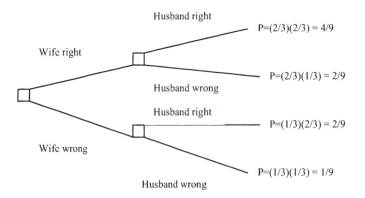

4.31
  a. Let P(H) = 0.40 be the probability of winning the hotel bid and P(O) = 0.25 be the probability of winning the office building bid. Because the two outcomes are independent Probability Rule 9 (Multiplication Rule for Independent Events) can be used to find the probability of winning both. P(H)P(O) = (0.40)(0.25) = 0.10

b. The probability of winning at least one contract can be determined by using Probability Rule 4 (Addition Rule for Any Two Events). This is equal to $P(H) + P(O) - P(H)P(O) = 0.40 + 0.25 - (0.40*0.25) = 0.55$. You could also list the possible outcomes and compute the probabilities as shown below:

Hotel	Office	Probability
Win	Win	0.40*0.25 = 0.10
Win	Lose	0.40*0.75 = 0.30
Lose	Win	0.60*0.25 = 0.15
Lose	Lose	0.60*0.75 = 0.45

The probability of winning at least one contract is $0.10 + 0.30 + 0.15 = 0.55$

c. Use the Complement Rule to determine the probability of losing the hotel contract which is $1-P(H) = 1-0.40 = 0.60$ and the probability of losing the office building contract which is $1-P(O) = 1-0.25 = 0.75$. Because the two outcomes are independent, you can use Probability Rule 9 (Multiplication Rule for Independent Events). The probability of losing both contracts is therefore $(0.60)*(0.75) = 0.45$.

4.33

a. The probability of a disk drive coming from company B can be found using the relative frequency assessment method as:

$$P(B) = \frac{number\ of\ drives\ from\ B}{total\ drives} = \frac{195}{700} = 0.28$$

b. The probability of a defective disk drive is:

$$P(Defect) = \frac{number\ of\ defective\ drives}{total\ drives} = \frac{50}{700} = 0.07$$

c. The probability of a defect *given* that company B supplied the disk drive is found using the following steps. The key word here is *given* which means that we are dealing with conditional probability.

Step 1: Define the events of interest
   The two events of interest are:
   $$E_1 = Company\ B = B$$
   $$E_2 = Defective\ Drive = Defect$$

Step 2: Define the probability statement of interest
   We are interested in the following:
   $$P(Defect|B) = ? = \text{probability of a defective drive } given \text{ company B}$$

Step 3: Convert the data to probabilities using the relative frequency assessment method

$$P(B) = \frac{number\ of\ drives\ from\ B}{total\ drives} = \frac{195}{700} = 0.28$$

$$P(Defect) = \frac{number\ of\ defective\ drives}{total\ drives} = \frac{50}{700} = 0.071$$

$$P(Defect\ and\ B) = \frac{number\ of\ defective\ drives\ from\ B}{total\ drives} = \frac{15}{700} = 0.021$$

Step 4: Use the rule for conditional probability

$$P(Defect\ |\ B) = \frac{P(Defect\ and\ B)}{P(B)} = \frac{0.02}{0.28} = 0.076$$

Note, you can also find the conditional probability from the data table by

$$P(Defect\ |\ B) = \frac{number\ of\ defective\ drives\ from\ B}{number\ of\ drives\ from\ B} = \frac{15}{195} = 0.076$$

4.35

a. Step 1: Define events of interest: Let E_1 = the driver is a woman; E_2 = the driver stops to ask for directions.

Step 2: Determine the probability of each event: $P(E_1) = 0.518$, $P(\overline{E}_1) = 1-0.518 = 0.482$, $P(E_2|E_1) = 0.61$

Step 3: Assess the joint probability: $P(E_1$ and $E_2) = P(E_2|E_1)\ P(E_1) = (0.61)(0.518) = 0.316$.

b. Step 1: as in part a.
Step 2: Determine the probability of each event: $P(E_1) = 0.518$, $P(\overline{E}_1) = 1-0.518 = 0.482$, $P(E_2|E_1) = 0.61$, $P(E_2|E_1') = 0.42$.

Step 3: Determine if the two events are mutually exclusive. Calculate the joint probabilities: If the driver is a woman and stops to ask for directions, she cannot also be a man who is stopping to ask for directions. Therefore, $(E_1$ and $E_2)$ or $(\overline{E}_1$ and $E_2)$ are mutually exclusive. $P(E_1$ and $E_2) = 0.316$ from part a., and $P(\overline{E}_1$ and $E_2) = P(E_2|\overline{E}_1)\ P(\overline{E}_1) = (0.42)(0.482) = 0.202$.

Step 4: Compute the probability using Rule 5. $P[(E_1$ and $E_2)$ or $(\overline{E}_1$ and $E_2)] = P(E_1$ and $E_2) + P(\overline{E}_1$ and $E_2) = 0.316 + (0.42)(0.482) = 0.316 + 0.202 = 0.518$.

c. $P(\overline{E}_1|E_2) = P(\overline{E}_1$ and $E_2)/P(E_2) = 0.202/0.518 = 0.39$

4.37   If they purchase 4 black-and-white copiers, their probability of being able to provide a color copy is 0.0. Their probability of being able to provide a black-and-white copy on demand is $1 - [(0.1)(0.1)(0.1)(0.1)] = 0.9999$. If they buy all color copiers the probability of providing a black-and-white copy is the same as providing a color copy since color copiers can make black-and-white copies. This probability is $1 - [(0.2)(0.2)(0.2)(0.2)] = 0.9984$. They cannot get to 99.9% on color copies regardless of the configuration.

4.39   The probability of 3 consecutive 9's assuming each number is equally likely is $(1/10)(1/10)(1/10)$ but since only 30% are eligible for free gas the probability is $(1/10)(1/10)(1/10)(.3) = 0.0003$

4.41

a. The probability of interest is found using the addition rule for mutually exclusive events:

$$P(> 7 days) = P(8 \text{ to } 30) + P(over 30)$$

There are a total of 2,020 homes in the study. Of these, 830 required 8-30 days and 340 took more than 30 days to sell. Thus:

$$P(8-30) = \frac{830}{2,020} = 0.41$$

$$P(over\ 30) = \frac{340}{2,020} = 0.17$$

Then:

$$P(> 7\ days) = 0.41 + 0.17 = 0.58$$

There is 0.58 chance that a home will take more than 7 days to sell.

b. In order for two events to be independent the following must hold:

$$P(1-7\ and\ \$200 - \$500) = P(1-7)\ x\ P(\$200 - \$500)$$

First, the joint probability of 1-7 days and a price between $200 - $500 is found by taking the joint frequency over the total number of houses in the study. This is:

$$P(1-7\ and\ \$200 - \$500) = \frac{200}{2,020} = 0.099$$

Now:

$$P(1-7) = \frac{850}{2,020} = 0.42$$

$$P(\$200 - \$500) = \frac{450}{2,020} = 0.22$$

Check for Independence:

Does $\qquad P(1-7 \text{ and } \$200-\$500) = P(1-7) \text{ } x \text{ } P(\$200-\$500)$??

$$P(1-7) \text{ } x \text{ } P(\$200-\$500) = 0.42 \text{ } x \text{ } 0.22 = 0.09 \neq 0.099$$

Thus, the two events are not independent.

c. We are interested in the conditional probability that a home would sell in a given price range *given* that it was on the marker for 1-7 days. For instance:

$$P(under \text{ } \$200|1-7 \text{ } days) = \frac{125}{850} = 0.15$$

Likewise:

$$P(\$200-\$500|1-7 \text{ } days) = \frac{200}{850} = 0.24$$

$$P(\$501-\$1,000|1-7 \text{ } days) = \frac{400}{850} = 0.47$$

$$P(over \text{ } \$1,000|1-7 \text{ } days) = \frac{125}{850} = 0.15$$

Note, the four probabilities have a sum slightly different from 1.0 due to rounding.

Thus, given that the house sold in 1-7 days, it most likely was in $501 - $1,000 price range at a 0.47 probability.

4.43 We want to determine the probability that at least one overseas plant will be included in the performance evaluation. This is the probability that one or more overseas plants are randomly selected. Another way to view this is to find the probability that no overseas plants are selected and subtract that probability from 1.0. The probability that no overseas plants are selected is equal to the probability that all four randomly selected plants are domestic. There are 7 domestic plants. The probability that only domestic plants are randomly selected is equal to $(7/11)*(6/10)*(5/9)*(4/8) = 0.1061$. This is also the probability that no overseas plants are selected. Therefore, the probability of one or more overseas plants being selected is $1-0.1061 = 0.8939$.

4.45 $P(\text{Line 1}) = 0.4$
$P(\text{Line 2}) = 0.35$
$P(\text{Line 3}) = 0.25$

$P(\text{Defective}|\text{Line 1}) = 0.05$
$P(\text{Defective}|\text{Line 2}) = 0.10$
$P(\text{Defective}|\text{Line 3}) = 0.07$

You need to calculate the probability of each line given you know the cases are defective. Use Bayes' Rule to calculate this.

P(Defective) = P(Defective|Line1)P(Line1) + P(Defective|Line2)P(Line2) + P(Defective|Line3)P(Line3) = (0.05)(0.4) + (0.1)(0.35)+(0.07)(0.25) = 0.0725

P(Line1|Defective) = (0.05)(0.4)/0.0725 = 0.2759
P(Line2|Defective) = (0.10)(0.35)/0.0725 = 0.4828
P(Line3|Defecitve) = (0.07)(0.25)/0.0725 = 0.2413

The unsealed cans probably came from Line 2

4.47   Let D = defective
            F = Franklin
            W = Wilson
            E = Evergreen
            S = Scott

The event of interest is:
$$P(F|D) = ?$$

This is a conditional probability and we would find the probability using the rule for conditional probability:
$$P(F|D) = \frac{P(F\ and\ D)}{P(D)}$$

The problem is that we don't have the information given directly for determining $P(D)$. However, we can use Bayes' theorem to determine the probability of interest. This is:

$$P(F|D) = \frac{P(F)P(d|F)}{P(F)P(d|F) + P(W)P(d|W) + P(E)P(d|E) + P(S)P(d|S)}$$

$$P(F|D) = \frac{(0.40)(0.03)}{(0.40)(0.03) + (0.30)(0.06) + (0.20)(0.02) + (0.10)(0.08)}$$

$$P(F|D) = 0.29$$

Thus, given a defective light string has been discovered, the probability that it came from Franklin is 0.29

4.49

a. Let B = voted for Pres. Bush, V = voted in the election, R = registered to vote. P(B and V) = P(B|V)P(V) = 0.508(0.607) = 0.308.

Step 1: Define events of interest:
Let E_1 = an individual voted for Pres. Bush; E_2 = an individual voted in the election.

Step 2: Determine the probability of each event:
$P(E_2) = 0.607$, $P(E_1|E_2) = 0.508$.

Step 3: Determine if the two events are independent:
Since $P(E_1|E_2) = 0.508$ and $P(E_1|\overline{E}_2) = 0$, E_1 and E_2 are not independent.

Step 4: Compute the probability using Rule 8.
$P(E_1 \text{ and } E_2) = P(E_1|E_2)P(E_2) = 0.508(0.607) = 0.308$.

b. Since one cannot vote without registering $P(V) = P(V \text{ and } R) = 0.607$. Since $P(V|R) = P(V \text{ and } R)/P(R)$, $P(R) = P(V \text{ and } R)/P(V|R) = 0.607/0.853 = 0.712$.

Step 1: Define events of interest:
Let E_1 and E_2 be defined as in part a. Let E_3 = an individual registered to vote.

Step 2: Determine the probability of each event:
$P(E_2) = 0.607$, $P(E_1|E_2) = 0.508$. Since one cannot vote without registering $P(E_2) = P(E_2 \text{ and } E_3) = 0.607$. $P(E_1|E_3) = 0.853$

Step 3: Determine if the two events are independent:
Since $P(E_1|E_3) = 0.853$ and $P(E_1|\overline{E}_3) = 0$, E_1 and E_3 are not independent.

Step 4: Compute the probability using Rule 8.
Since $P(E_1|E_3) = P(E_1 \text{ and } E_3)/P(E_3)$, $P(E_3) = P(E_1 \text{ and } E_3)/P(E_1|E_3) = 0.607/0.853 = 0.712$

4.51 Student can use Excel's pivot table feature to answer this question.

a. P(neither on business) = 1 - (27/62)(26/61) = 1 - 0.1856 = 0.81454

Type of Trip	Total
Business	27
Pleasure	26
Combination	9
Grand Total	62

b. P(business or no hotel problem) = 27/62 + 48/62 − 17/62 = 58/62 = 0.936

Type of Trip	Any Problems Problems	No Problems	Grand Total
Business	10	17	27
Pleasure	3	23	26
Combination	1	8	9
Grand Total	14	48	62

c. P(pleasure and in-state area code) = 2/62 = 0.0323

	Phone			
Type of Trip	No Response	In-State	Out-State	Grand Total
Business	3	2	22	27
Pleasure	9	2	15	26
Combination	1	1	7	9
Grand Total	13	5	44	62

4.53   The probabilities required to produce the answers to exercise are given by the following
        table:

```
              Rows: Response   Columns: Age Group

          15-25   26-35   36-45   46-55   56-65   66-75      All

   1         53      52      53      51      45      29      283
          26.37   25.37   27.04   25.00   24.46   29.59    26.01
          4.871   4.779   4.871   4.688   4.136   2.665   26.011

   2         39      39      41      47      36      16      218
          19.40   19.02   20.92   23.04   19.57   16.33    20.04
          3.585   3.585   3.768   4.320   3.309   1.471   20.037

   3         19      25      24      21      29      13      131
           9.45   12.20   12.24   10.29   15.76   13.27    12.04
          1.746   2.298   2.206   1.930   2.665   1.195   12.040

   4         13      19      16      16      11       1       76
           6.47    9.27    8.16    7.84    5.98    1.02     6.99
          1.195   1.746   1.471   1.471   1.011   0.092    6.985

   5         13      15       9      12       8       8       65
           6.47    7.32    4.59    5.88    4.35    8.16     5.97
          1.195   1.379   0.827   1.103   0.735   0.735    5.974

   6         64      55      53      57      55      31      315
          31.84   26.83   27.04   27.94   29.89   31.63    28.95
          5.882   5.055   4.871   5.239   5.055   2.849   28.952

 All        201     205     196     204     184      98     1088
         100.00  100.00  100.00  100.00  100.00  100.00   100.00
         18.474  18.842  18.015  18.750  16.912   9.007  100.000

 Cell Contents:      Count
                   % of Column
                   % of Total
```

a. Let E_1 = the respondents 36 or older; E_2 = would not use a wireless phone exclusive
    because of some type of difficulty in placing and receiving calls. $P(E_2|E_1) = P(E_1$ and
    $E_2)/P(E_1) = (16+16+11+1+9+12+8+8)/1088]/[(196+204+184+98)]/1088 = 0.074/0.627$
    $= 0.119$

b. For ease of typing, let not E_1 be the compliment of E_1. Then: $P(E_2|$ not $E_1) = P($ not E_1 and $E_2)/P(E_2) = (13+19+13+15)/1088]/[(201+205)]/1088 = 0.55/0.373 = 0.148$

c. Let A_i = the ith respondent stated that the most important reason for not using a wireless exclusively was that they need a line for Net access. P(at least one) = 1 – P(none) = 1 – P(not A_1 and not A_2 and not A_3) = 1 - P(not A_1)P(not A_2) P(not A_3) = 1 - [1- P(A_1)][1- P(A_2)] [1- P(A_3)] = 1 – (1 – 0.148)(1 – 0.148) (1 – 0.148) = 1 – 0.6186 = 0.3814

4.55 The following joint frequency table (developed using Excel's pivot table feature) summarizes the data.

	Electrical	Mechanical	Total
Lincoln	28	39	67
Tyler	64	69	133
Total	92	108	200

a. This is the conditional probability of an electrical problem given the scooter was assembled in Tyler. P(Electrical\Tyler) = P(Electrical and Tyler)/P(Tyler) = (64/200)/(133/200) = 0.4812.

b. The probability of a scooter having a mechanical failure is independent of the scooter being assembled at the Lincoln plant if P(Mechanical) = P(Mechanical given Lincoln). Because P(Mechanical) = 108/200 = 0.54 does not equal P(Mechanical given Lincoln) = P(Mechanical and Lincoln)/P(Lincoln) = (39/200)/(67/200) = 0.5821, the two events are not independent; they are dependent. The probability of a mechanical problem is not independent of the plant where the scooter was assembled.

c. P(Electrical and Tyler) = 64/200 = 0.32. P(Mechanical and Tyler) = 69/200 = 0.3450. P(Electrical and Lincoln) = 28/200 = 0.14. P(Mechanical and Lincoln) = 0.1950. These probabilities can be used to assign costs for each plant next year if 500 scooters are expected to be returned.
P(Electrical and Tyler) * 500 Scooters * $100 = $16,000
P(Mechanical and Tyler)* 500 Scooters * $75 = $12,937.50
P(Electrical and Lincoln)* 500 Scooters * $100 = $7,000
P(Mechanical and Lincoln)*500 Scooters * $75 = $7,312.50

Total budgeted expense would be $43,250. Of this total $28,937.50 would be assigned to Tyler and $14,312.50 would be assigned to Lincoln.

End of Chapter Exercises

4.57   The relative frequency assessment approach takes the number of times the item of interest occurred and divides it by the total number of times the event or activity was done. An example of this might be that a health insurance company is interested in the number of errors that occur in claims. They could look at a sample of claims and count the number of times errors occurred divided by the sample size that they reviewed.

4.59   Classical probability assessment, sometimes referred to as *a priori* probability, is the method of determining probability based on the ratio of the number of ways the event of interest can occur to the total number of ways any event can occur when the individual elementary events are equally likely. In most business situations, it is often not possible for the decision-maker to enumerate all the possible ways an event can occur. Furthermore, it is unlikely that the individual elementary events are equally likely. Therefore, classical probability assessment is rarely applied

4.61

a. $P(A) = 500/2000 = 0.25$, $P(\overline{A}) = 1 - P(A) = 1 - 0.25 = 0.75$.

$P(A|B) = P(A \text{ and } B)/P(B) = (200/2000)/[(200 + 800)/2000] = 0.20$,

$P(\overline{A}|B) = P(\overline{A} \text{ and } B)/P(B) = (800/2000)/[(200 + 800)/2000] = 0.80$,

$P(A|\overline{B}) = P(A \text{ and } B')/P(\overline{B}) = (300/2000)/[(300 + 700)/2000] = 0.30$,

and $P(\overline{A}|) = P(\overline{A} \text{ and } \overline{B})/P(\overline{B}) = (700/2000)/[(300 + 700)/2000] = 0.70$.

b.   So (1) $P(A|B) = 0.20 \neq 0.25 = P(A)$ and A and B are dependent,

(2) $P(\overline{A}|B) = 0.80 \neq 0.75 = P(\overline{A})$ and $\overline{A}$ and B are dependent,

(3) $P(A|\overline{B}) = 0.30 \neq 0.25 = P(A)$ and A and $\overline{B}$ are dependent,

(4) $P(\overline{A}|\overline{B}) = 0.70 \neq 0.75 = P(\overline{A})$ and A and B are dependent.

c. $P(A) = 0.25 = P(A|B)$ if A and B are independent. This says that 25% of the sample space and 25% of B's 1000 elementary events must be A's. This means that 25% of B's elementary events must also be A's. A similar argument for $\overline{A}$ yields 750 elementary events in ($\overline{A}$ and B) and in ($\overline{A}$ and $\overline{B}$). So the table becomes

	A	$\overline{A}$	Totals
B	250	750	1000
B'	250	750	1000
Totals	500	1500	2000

And the relevant probabilities become $P(A|B) = P(A \text{ and } B)/P(B) = (250/2000)/[(250 + 750)/2000] = 0.25 = P(A)$. A and B are independent, $P(\overline{A}|B) = P(\overline{A} \text{ and } B)/P(B) = (750/2000)/[(250 + 750)/2000] = 0.75 = P(\overline{A})$. $\overline{A}$ and B are independent, $P(A|\overline{B}) = P(A \text{ and } B')/P(\overline{B}) = (250/2000)/[(250 + 750)/2000] = 0.25 = P(A)$. A and $\overline{B}$ are independent. And $P(\overline{A}|\overline{B}) = P(\overline{A} \text{ and } \overline{B})/P(\overline{B}) = (750/2000)/[(250 + 750)/2000] = 0.75 = P(\overline{A})$. $\overline{A}$ and $\overline{B}$ are independent.

4.63   The probability of correctly guessing on any one question is .25. The questions are independent.

a.   P(C and C and C) = .25 x .25 x .25 = 0.0156

b.   Sample space is:

$$P(C \text{ and } C \text{ and } C) = .25 \text{ x } .25 \text{ x } .25 = 0.0156$$
Or
$$P(C \text{ and } C \text{ and } W) = .25 \text{ x } .25 \text{ x } .75 = 0.0469$$
Or
$$P(C \text{ and } W \text{ and } C) = .25 \text{ x } .75 \text{ x } .25 = 0.0469$$
Or
$$P(W \text{ and } C \text{ and } C) = .75 \text{ x } .25 \text{ x } .25 = 0.0469$$

The probability of interest is found by summing these probabilities:
P(Passing) = .0156 + .0469 + .0469 + .0469 = 0.1563

Thus, the chances of passing a three question multiple choice exam if two or more correct answers are required is only 0.1563. Moral of the story is that you had better plan on studying.

c.   For a. P(C and C and C) = .5 x .5 x .5 = 0.125

For b. Sample space is:

$$P(C \text{ and } C \text{ and } C) = .5 \text{ x } .5 \text{ x } .5 = 0.125$$
Or
$$P(C \text{ and } C \text{ and } W) = .5 \text{ x } .5 \text{ x } .5 = 0.125$$
Or
$$P(C \text{ and } W \text{ and } C) = .5 \text{ x } .5 \text{ x } .5 = 0.125$$
Or
$$P(W \text{ and } C \text{ and } C) = .5 \text{ x } .5 \text{ x } .5 = 0.125$$

The probability of interest is found by summing these probabilities:
P(Passing) = .0125 + .125 + .125 + .125 = 0.50

Thus, the chances of passing a three question multiple choice exam if two or more correct answers are required is increased to 0.50. Moral of the story is that you still better plan on studying on a more regular basis.

4.65

a.   Let E_1 = a randomly selected wealthy individual is audited. $P(E_1) = 1/63 = 0.016$ and $P(E_1') = 1 - P(E_1) = 1 - 0.016 = 0.984$. P(at least one) = $1 - P(\text{none}) = 1 - P(E_1' \text{ and } E_1'$ and . . . and $E_1') = 1 - P(E_1')P(E_1') \ldots P(E_1') = 1 - (0.984)(0.984) \ldots (0.984) = 1 - 0.851 = 0.149$

b. Let E_2 = a randomly selected corporation with assets of at least \$250 million would be audited. $P(E_2) = 0.44$ and $P(E_2') = 1 - P(E_2) = 1 - 0.44 = 0.56$. P(at least one) = $1 -$ P(none) = $1 - P(E_2'$ and E_2' and . . . and $E_2') = 1 - P(E_2')P(E_2') . . . P(E_2') = 1 - (0.56)($ $0.56) . . . (0.56) = 1 - 0.003 = 0.997$

c. $P(E_1$ or $E_2) = P(E_1) + P(E_2) - P(E_1$ and $E_2) = P(E_1) + P(E_2) - P(E_1)P(E_2) = 0.016 +$ $0.44 - (0.016)(0.44) = 0.449$.

4.67

$P(\text{Plant A}) = 0.5$
$P(\text{Plant B}) = 0.3$
$P(\text{Plant C}) = 0.2$
$P(\text{Incorrect Mix}|\text{Plant A}) = 0.1$
$P(\text{Incorrect Mix}|\text{Plant B}) = 0.05$
$P(\text{Incorrect Mix}|\text{Plant C}) = 0.20$

You need to calculate the probability of each plant given you know the paint was incorrectly mixed. Use Bayes' Rule to calculate this

$P(\text{Incorrect Mix}) = P(\text{Incorrect Mix}|\text{Plant A})P(\text{Plant A}) +$ $P(\text{Incorrect Mix}|\text{Plant B})P(\text{Plant B}) + P(\text{Incorrect Mix}|\text{Plant C}) = (0.1)(0.5) +$ $(0.05)(0.3) + (0.2)(0.2) = 0.105$

$P(\text{Plant A}|\text{Incorrect Mix}) = (0.1)(0.5)/0.105 = 0.4762$
$P(\text{Plant B}|\text{Incorrect Mix}) = (0.05)(0.3)/0.105 = 0.1429$
$P(\text{Plant C}|\text{Incorrect Mix}) = (0.2)(0.2)/0.105 = 0.3809$

Cost to Plant A = (0.4762)(\$10,000) = \$4,762
Cost to Plant B = (0.1429)(\$10,000) = \$1,429
Cost to Plant C = (0.3809)(\$10,000) = \$3,809

4.69

$P(\text{Clerk 1}) = 0.4$
$P(\text{Clerk 2}) = 0.3$
$P(\text{Clerk 3}) = 0.3$
$P(\text{Defective}|\text{Clerk 1}) = 0.02$
$P(\text{Defective}|\text{Clerk 2}) = 0.025$
$P(\text{Defective}|\text{Clerk 3}) = 0.015$

You need to calculate the probability of each clerk given you know the chocolates are defective. Use Bayes' Rule to calculate this

$P(\text{Defective}) = P(\text{Defective}|\text{Clerk 1})P(\text{Clerk 1}) + P(\text{Defective}|\text{Clerk 2})P(\text{Clerk 2}) +$ $P(\text{Defective}|\text{Clerk 3})P(\text{Clerk 3}) = (0.02)(0.4) + (0.025)(0.3) + (0.015)(0.3) = 0.02$

$P(\text{Clerk 1}|\text{Defective}) = (0.02)(0.4)/0.02 = 0.4$
$P(\text{Clerk 2}|\text{Defective}) = (0.025)(0.3)/0.02 = 0.375$
$P(\text{Clerk 3}|\text{Defective}) = (0.015)(0.3)/0.02 = 0.225$

Clerk 1 is most likely responsible for the boxes that raised the complaints.

Chapter 4

4.71   Students can use Excel's pivot table feature to answer these questions.

   a.   P(Salt Lake) = 24/110 = 0.2182

Manufacturing Plant	Total
Boise	78
Salt Lake	24
Toronto	8
Grand Total	110

   b.   P(Wiring) = 23/110 = 0.2091

Complaint Code	Total
Corrosion	35
Cracked Lens	45
Wiring	23
Sound	7
Grand Total	110

   c.   P(Salt Lake and Wiring) = 8/110 = 0.0727

	Manufacturing Plant			
Complaint Code	Boise	Salt Lake	Toronto	Grand Total
Corrosion	30	3	2	35
Cracked Lens	31	11	3	45
Wiring	13	8	2	23
Sound	4	2	1	7
Grand Total	78	24	8	110

   d.   P(Day Shift and Salt Lake and Cracked Lens) = 8/110 = 0.0727

	Manufacturing Plant Shift		
	Salt Lake		
Complaint Code	Day	Swing	Graveyard
Corrosion	1	1	1
Cracked Lens	8	2	1
Wiring	5	2	1
Sound	2		
Grand Total	16	5	3

e. The most likely profile would be the largest number which would be the Boise day shift for cracked lens

	Manufacturing Plant							
	Boise			Salt Lake			Toronto	
Complaint Code	Day	Swing	Grave-yard	Day	Swing	Grave-yard	Day	Swing
Corrosion	20	10		1	1	1	2	
Cracked Lens	21	10		8	2	1	3	
Wiring	10	1	2	5	2	1	1	1
Sound	2	2		2				1
Grand Total	53	23	2	16	5	3	6	2

4.73 The following table can be used to answer the questions.

```
Rows: Type    Columns: Location

             MW        NE        SE        SW         W       All

  C           24        18        13        17        28       100
            32.00     36.00     52.00     34.00     28.00     33.33
            8.000     6.000     4.333     5.667     9.333    33.333

  E           15        15         5        10        30        75
            20.00     30.00     20.00     20.00     30.00     25.00
            5.000     5.000     1.667     3.333    10.000    25.000

  F           21        12         4        15        23        75
            28.00     24.00     16.00     30.00     23.00     25.00
            7.000     4.000     1.333     5.000     7.667    25.000

  M           15         5         3         8        19        50
            20.00     10.00     12.00     16.00     19.00     16.67
            5.000     1.667     1.000     2.667     6.333    16.667

  All         75        50        25        50       100       300
           100.00    100.00    100.00    100.00    100.00    100.00
           25.000    16.667     8.333    16.667    33.333   100.000

Cell Contents:      Count
                    % of Column
                    % of Total
```

a. Relative frequency of W = $\dfrac{Number\ of\ times\ W\ occurs}{N} = \dfrac{100}{300} = 0.33$

b. Relative frequency of (W and E) = $\dfrac{Number\ of\ times\ W\ \&\ E\ occurs}{N} = \dfrac{30}{300} =$ 0.10

c. Note: East = NE + SE. Relative frequency of East =
$\dfrac{Number\ of\ times\ NE\ +\ SE\ occurs}{N} = \dfrac{50+25}{300} = 0.25$

Relative frequency of C = $\dfrac{Number\ of\ times\ C\ occurs}{N} = \dfrac{100}{300} = 0.333.$

Relative frequency of (East and C) = $\dfrac{Number\ of\ times\ East\ +\ C\ occurs}{N} =$

$\dfrac{18+13}{300} = 0.103.$

Therefore, P(East or C) = P(East) + P(C) – P(East and C) = 0.25 + 0.333- 0.103 = 0.48.

d. P(C|East) = P(C and East)/P(East) = 0.103/0.25 = 0.41

4.75

a.

```
                Boomer    GenX    GenY   Silent

email               13      13      10      10
                 13.00   13.00   10.00   10.00
                 3.250   3.250   2.500   2.500

Face-to-face        39      38      52      39
                 39.00   38.00   52.00   39.00
                 9.750   9.500  13.000   9.750

Gp Meeting          41      42      36      40
                 41.00   42.00   36.00   40.00
                10.250  10.500   9.000  10.000

Other                7       7       2      11
                  7.00    7.00    2.00   11.00
                 1.750   1.750   0.500   2.750

All                100     100     100     100
                100.00  100.00  100.00  100.00
                25.000  25.000  25.000  25.000

Cell Contents:     Count
                   % of Column
                   % of Total
```

b. Let E_1 = a member of the silent generation, E_2 = boomer generation, E_3 = X generation, E_4 = Y generation, and B = prefers face-to-face communication.
$P(E_1)P(B|E_1) + P(E_2)P(B|E_2) + ... + P(E_4)P(B|E_4) = 0.39(0.075) + 0.39(0.42) + 0.38(0.295) + 0.52(0.21) = 0.4144.$

c. $P(E_1|B) = \dfrac{P(E_i)P(B|E_i)}{P(E_1)P(B|E_1) + P(E_2)P(B|E_2) + ... + P(E_k)P(B|E_k)} =$

For Silent Generation:

$$\frac{(0.39)(0.075)}{(0.39)(0.075) + (0.39)(0.42) + (0.38)(0.295) + 0.52(0.21)} = \frac{0.0281}{0.4144} = 0.0678$$

For Baby Boomers:

$$\frac{(0.39)(0.42)}{(0.39)(0.075) + (0.39)(0.42) + (0.38)(0.295) + 0.52(0.21)} = \frac{1638}{0.4144} = 0.3953$$

For X generation:

$$\frac{(0.38)(0.295)}{(0.39)(0.075) + (0.39)(0.42) + (0.38)(0.295) + 0.52(0.21)} = \frac{0.1121}{0.4144} = 0.2705$$

For Y generation:

$$\frac{(0.52)(0.21)}{(0.39)(0.075) + (0.39)(0.42) + (0.38)(0.295) + 0.52(0.21)} = \frac{0.1092}{0.4144} = 0.2635$$

The most likely generation of which the individual is a member is the Baby Boomers.

Chapter 5 Solutions

When applicable, selected problems in each section will be done following the appropriate step-by-step procedures outlined in the corresponding sections of the chapter. Other problems will provide key points and the answers to the questions, but all answers can be arrived at using the appropriate steps.

Section 5-1 Exercises

5.1

  a. The variable, x, is a discrete random variable because x can take on only specific integer values.

  b. The possible values for x are:
      $x = \{0, 1, 2, 3, 4, 5, 6\}$

5.3   The random variable is the sum of two number selected randomly from the list of five numbers. One approach to determining the probability distribution is to list the sample space showing all possible outcomes when two items are selected. The sample space can be developed using a tree diagram as follows:

Draw 1	Draw 2	Total
	2	4
2	4	6
	6	8
	8	10
	2	4
2	4	6
	6	8
	8	10
	2	6
4	2	6
	6	10
	8	12
	2	8
6	4	10
	2	8
	8	14
	2	10
8	4	12
	6	14
	2	10

The random variable, x, and the frequency and relative frequency distributions are shown as follows:

Total	Frequency	Rel. Freq.
4	2	0.1
6	4	0.2
8	4	0.2
10	6	0.3
12	2	0.1
14	2	0.1
	20	

The relative frequencies form the probabilities of each outcome for the random variable. The graph of the probability distribution is shown as follows:

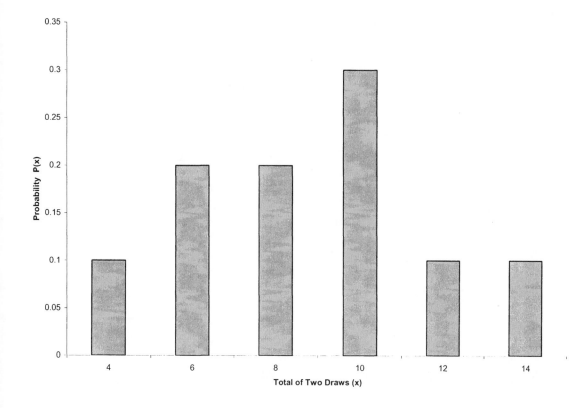

5.5

a. The expected value of x is calculated using equation 5-1, $E(x) = \sum xP(x)$.
$E(x) = (100)(0.25) + (125)(0.30) + (150)(0.45) = 130$.

b. The variance of x is calculated using the following equation, $\sum[x-E(x)]^2P(x)$. The calculations are shown below

x	P(x)	xP(x)	[x-E(x)]	[x-E(x)]²P(x)
100	0.25	25	-30	225
125	0.3	37.5	-5	7.5
150	0.45	67.5	20	180

The variance of x is equal to $225 + 7.5 + 180 = 412.50$.

c. The standard deviation is computed using equation 5-2. The standard deviation is the positive square root of the variance calculated in (b) above. $\sigma_x = \sqrt{412.50} = 20.31$

105

5.7 a. The expected value of x is calculated using equation 5-1, $E(x) = \sum xP(x)$. The expected value of the sum of two randomly rolled dice is equal to $(2)(1/36) + (3)(2/36) + (4)(3/36) + (5)(4/36) + (6)(5/36) + (7)(6/36) + (8)(5/36) + (9)(4/36) + (10)(3/36) + (11)(2/36) + (12)(1/36) = 7$.

b. The variance of the random variable x is computed using the following equation, $\sum[x-E(x)]^2 P(x)$. The calculations are shown below (Note: the probabilities for the various outcomes of the random variable x were entered into Excel as 1/36, 2/36, etc)

x	P(x)	xP(x)	[x-E(x)]	$[x-E(x)]^2 P(x)$
2	0.0278	0.056	-5	0.694
3	0.0556	0.167	-4	0.889
4	0.0833	0.333	-3	0.750
5	0.1111	0.556	-2	0.444
6	0.1389	0.833	-1	0.139
7	0.1667	1.167	0	0.000
8	0.1389	1.111	1	0.139
9	0.1111	1.000	2	0.444
10	0.0833	0.833	3	0.750
11	0.0556	0.611	4	0.889
12	0.0278	0.333	5	0.694

The variance is equal to $\sum[x-E(x)]^2 P(x) = 5.833$.

c. The standard deviation is computed using equation 5-2. The standard deviation is the positive square root of the variance calculated in (b) above. Thus, $\sigma_x = \sqrt{5.833} = 2.415$

5.9 $E(x) = \sum xP(x) = 3(0.13) + \ldots + 12(0.60) = 9.66$.

$$\sigma^2 = \sum(x - E(x))^2 P(x) = (-6.99)^2(0.13) + \ldots + 2.34^2(0.60) = 10.7247,$$

$$\sigma = \sqrt{\sigma^2} = \sqrt{10.7247} = 3.2749.$$

a. The probability distribution of y is

y	P(y)
10	0.13
13	0.12
16	0.15
19	0.60

$E(y) = \Sigma y P(y) = 10(0.13) + \ldots + 19(0.60) = 16.66.$

$\sigma^2 = \Sigma(y - E(y))^2 \, P(y) = (-6.66)^2(0.13) + \ldots + 2.34^2(0.60) = 10.7247,$

$\sigma = \sqrt{\sigma^2} = \sqrt{10.7247} = 3.2749.$

b. The probability distribution of z is

z	P(z)
21	0.13
42	0.12
63	0.15
84	0.60

$E(z) = \Sigma z P(z) = 21(0.13) + \ldots + 84(0.60) = 67.62 = 7(9.66).$

$\sigma^2 = \Sigma(z - E(z))^2 \, P(z) = (-46.62)^2(0.13) + \ldots + 16.38^2(0.60) = 525.51 = 7^2(10.7247),$

$\sigma = \sqrt{\sigma^2} = \sqrt{525.51} = 22.924 = 7(3.2749).$

c. Neither the variance nor the standard deviation is affected by adding a constant to each value of the random variable.

d. When each of the values of the random variable is multiplied by a constant, the variance is increased by a multiple equal to the constant squared. The standard deviation is increased by a multiple equal to the constant.

5.11

a. $E(X) = \Sigma x P(x) = 2(0.27) + \ldots + 7(0.03) = 3.51.$

b. $\sigma^2 = \Sigma(x - E(x))^2 \, P(x) = (-1.51)^2(0.27) + \ldots + 3.49^2(0.03) = 1.6499,$

$\sigma = \sqrt{\sigma^2} = \sqrt{1.6499} = 1.2845.$

5.13 The expected value of a discrete probability distribution is determined using:

$$E(x) = \sum x P(x)$$

The calculations are shown as follows:

Number of minutes (x)	Probability P(x)	xP(x)
60	0.05	3
70	0.15	10.5
80	0.2	16
90	0.45	40.5
100	0.1	10
110	0.05	5.5
Sum =		85.5

The average number of minutes spent in the Bittercreek Grille is 85.5.
The variance for a discrete random variable is computed using the following equation:

$$\sigma^2 = \sum [x - E(x)]^2 P(x)$$

The variance is computed as follows:

Number of minutes (x)	Probability P(x)	xP(x)	[x - E(x)]	[x - E(x)]²	[x - E(x)]²P(x)
60	0.05	3	-25.5	650.25	32.51
70	0.15	10.5	-15.5	240.25	36.04
80	0.2	16	-5.5	30.25	6.05
90	0.45	40.5	4.5	20.25	9.11
100	0.1	10	14.5	210.25	21.03
110	0.05	5.5	24.5	600.25	30.01
Sum =		85.5			134.75

The variance is 134.75 minutes squared. The standard deviation is the square root of the variance as follows:

$$\sigma = \sqrt{\sum [x - E(x)]^2 P(x)}$$

$$\sigma = \sqrt{134.75} = 11.61$$

The standard deviation is 11.61 minutes.

5.15

a. The average lead time can be computed using equation 5-1, $E(x) = \sum xP(x) =$
$(2)(0.15) + (3)(0.45) + (4)(0.30) + (5)(0.075) + (6)(0.025) = 3.375$ days. It takes slightly more than 3 days on average for the component to be received after it is ordered.

b. The coefficient of variation is the ratio of the standard deviation to the average, expressed as a percentage. The standard deviation of the lead time is calculated using equation 5-2. The results are shown below:

x	$P(x)$	$xP(x)$	$[x-E(x)]$	$[x-E(x)]^2P(x)$
2	0.15	0.3	-1.375	0.28359375
3	0.45	1.35	-0.375	0.06328125
4	0.3	1.2	0.625	0.1171875
5	0.075	0.375	1.625	0.198046875
6	0.025	0.15	2.625	0.172265625

The standard deviation is equal to $\sqrt{\sum[x - E(x)]^2 P(x)} = \sqrt{0.834375} = 0.913441$ days. The expected value was found in (a) above. Therefore the coefficient of variation = $(0.913441/3.375)*100\% = 27.065\%$

c. There is a relationship among lead times, customer service, safety stock and inventory costs. By reducing lead times the company can reduce the amount of inventory in its pipeline. By reducing lead time variability the manufacturing firm can reduce the amount of safety stock it must carry. By knowing its average lead time and its standard deviation the firm can better plan its ordering and inventory requirements.

5.17

a. Let x = the number of Ivy League graduates that fill these positions. Let I_1 = CEO is selected from an Ivy League university; I_2 = CFO is selected from an Ivy League university.

$P(x = 0) = P(\bar{I}_1 \text{ and } \bar{I}_2) = P(\bar{I}_1)P(\bar{I}_2) = (1/4)(2/4),\ P(x =1) =$

$P(I_1 \text{ and } \bar{I}_2) + P(\bar{I}_1 \text{ and } I_2) = P(I_1)P(\bar{I}_2) + P(\bar{I}_1)P(I_2) = (3/4)(2/4) + (1/4)(2/4)$

$=1/2,\ P(x = 2) = P(I_1 \text{ and } I_2) = P(I_1)P(I_2) = (3/4)(2/4) = 3/8.$

x	0	1	2
P(x)	1/8 = 0.125	1/2 = 0.5	3/8 = 0.375

b. P(both from Ivy League) = P(2) = 0.375. This is a substantial probability. Therefore, it would not be surprising.

c. $E(x) = \Sigma x P(x) = 0(0.125) + 1(0.5) + 2(0.375) = 1.25$.

$\sigma^2 = \Sigma(x - E(x))^2 P(x) = (-1.25)^2(0.125) + (-.25)^2(0.5) + .75^2(0.375) = 0.7187$,

$\sigma = \sqrt{\sigma^2} = \sqrt{0.7187} = 0.8478$.

5.19

a. Step 1: Convert the frequency distribution into a probability distribution using the relative frequency of occurrence method.
The frequency distribution is:

Months	Count	Percent
14	1	0.80
15	3	2.40
16	8	6.40
17	6	4.80
18	23	18.40
19	27	21.60
20	30	24.00
21	16	12.80
22	9	7.20
23	2	1.60
N=	125	

x	14	15	16	17	18	19	20	21	22	23
P(x)	0.008	0.024	0.064	0.048	0.184	0.216	0.240	0.128	0.072	0.016

b. Step 2: Compute the expected value using Equation 5-1.
$E(X) = \Sigma x P(x) = 14(0.008) + 15(0.024) + \ldots + 23(0.016) = 19.168$.

Step 3: Compute the standard deviation using 5-2.
$\sigma^2 = \Sigma(x - E(X))^2 P(x) = (-4.168)^2(0.008) + (-3.168)^2(0.024) + \ldots +$
$3.832(0.016) = 3.1634$, (2) $\sigma = \sqrt{\sigma^2} = \sqrt{3.1634} = 1.7787$.

c. For the majority of the covers to last longer than 19 months, the median would have to be at most 19. Here, $P(X \le 19) = = 0.544 > 0.50$ and $P(X \ge 19) = 0.672 > 1 - 0.50$. Therefore, the median is 19 and the quality control department is incorrect.

5.21

a. Step 1: Convert the frequency distribution into a probability distribution using the relative frequency of occurrence method.

Days	Count	Percent
25	1	0.50
27	3	1.50
28	24	12.00
29	51	25.50
30	53	26.50
31	37	18.50
32	24	12.00
33	7	3.50
N=	200	

x	25	26	27	28	29	30	31	32	33
P(x)	0.005	0.0	0.015	0.120	0.255	0.265	0.185	0.120	0.035

b. Step 2: Compute the expected value using Equation 5-1.
$E(X) = \Sigma xP(x) = 25(0.005) + 26(0.0) + \ldots + 33(0.035) = 29.965$.

Step 3: Compute the standard deviation using 5-2.
$\sigma^2 = \Sigma(x - E(X))^2 P(x) = (-4.965)^2(0) + (-3.965)^2(0.0) + \ldots + 3.035^2(0.035) = 1.973$, $\sigma = \sqrt{\sigma^2} = \sqrt{1.973} = 1.405$.

c. The marketing department is most likely trying to discover what the 10th percentile for this data might be. Using equation 3-5, $i = \dfrac{p}{100} n = \dfrac{10}{100} 200 = 20$.
Since i is an integer, then the 10th percentile is the average of the 20 and 21st ordered numbers = $(28 + 28)/2 = 28$. So 90% of the cast remain protected for 18 days.

Section 5-2 Exercises

5.23

a. The answer to this question can be found using the following steps:
Step 1: Define the characteristics of the binomial distribution.
  $n = 15, p = .20, x = 4$

Step 2: Go to the binomial table in Appendix B. Locate the appropriate section of the table for a sample size of $n = 15$ and the column headed $p = 0.20$. This is:

X	p = 0.15	p = 0.20	p = 0.25	p = 0.30	p = 0.35	p = 0.40	p = 0.45	p = 0.50	n-X
0	0.0874	0.0352	0.0134	0.0047	0.0016	0.0005	0.0001	0.0000	15
1	0.2312	0.1319	0.0668	0.0305	0.0126	0.0047	0.0016	0.0005	14
2	0.2856	0.2309	0.1559	0.0916	0.0476	0.0219	0.0090	0.0032	13
3	0.2184	0.2501	0.2252	0.1700	0.1110	0.0634	0.0318	0.0139	12
4	0.1156	0.1876	0.2252	0.2186	0.1792	0.1268	0.0780	0.0417	11
5	0.0449	0.1032	0.1651	0.2061	0.2123	0.1859	0.1404	0.0916	10
6	0.0132	0.0430	0.0917	0.1472	0.1906	0.2066	0.1914	0.1527	9
7	0.0030	0.0138	0.0393	0.0811	0.1319	0.1771	0.2013	0.1964	8
8	0.0005	0.0035	0.0131	0.0348	0.0710	0.1181	0.1647	0.1964	7
9	0.0001	0.0007	0.0034	0.0116	0.0298	0.0612	0.1048	0.1527	6
10	0.0000	0.0001	0.0007	0.0030	0.0096	0.0245	0.0515	0.0916	5
11	0.0000	0.0000	0.0001	0.0006	0.0024	0.0074	0.0191	0.0417	4
12	0.0000	0.0000	0.0000	0.0001	0.0004	0.0016	0.0052	0.0139	3
13	0.0000	0.0000	0.0000	0.0000	0.0001	0.0003	0.0010	0.0032	2
14	0.0000	0.0000	0.0000	0.0000	0.0000	0.0000	0.0001	0.0005	1
15	0.0000	0.0000	0.0000	0.0000	0.0000	0.0000	0.0000	0.0000	0
	q = 0.85	q = 0.80	q = 0.75	q = 0.70	q = 0.65	q = 0.60	q = 0.55	q = 0.50	

Step 3: Define the event of interest and obtain the desired probabilities from the binomial table.
The event of interest is:
$P(x = 4) = 0.1876$

Thus, the probability of exactly four people in the sample of n = 15 having a credit card balance at the limit of the credit card is 0.1876.

b. The answer to this question can be found using the following steps:

Step 1: Define the characteristics of the binomial distribution.
$n = 15, p = .20, x \leq 4$

Step 2: Go to the binomial table in Appendix B. Locate the appropriate section of the table for a sample size of n = 15 and the column headed p = 0.20. This is was shown in part a.

Step 3: Define the event of interest and obtain the desired probabilities from the binomial table.
The event of interest is:
$P(x \leq 4) = P(x = 4) + P(x = 3) + ... + P(x = 0)$
$P(x \leq 4) = 0.1876 + 0.2501 + 0.2309 + 0.1319 + 0.0352$
$P(x \leq 4) = 0.8358$

Thus, the probability of four or fewer people in the sample of n = 15 having a credit card balance at the limit of the credit card is 0.8358.

5.25

The following steps are used to solve this problem.
Step 1: Define the characteristics of the binomial distribution.

$n = 20, p = .40, x \leq 2$

Step 2: Go to the binomial table in Appendix B. Locate the appropriate section
of the table for a sample size of $n = 20$ and the column headed $p = 0.40$.

Step 3: Define the event of interest and obtain the desired probabilities from the
binomial table.

The event of interest is:

$P(x \leq 2) = P(x = 2) + P(x = 1) + P(x = 0)$

$P(x \leq 2) = 0.0031 + 0.0005 + 0.0000$

$P(x \leq 2) = 0.0036$

The probability of 2 or fewer home owners remodeling within 5 years is 0.0036 or
just slightly over 3 chances in 1000. This is a very low probability. It suggests
that the original assumption about $p = 0.4$ may be wrong.

5.27

This problem can be solved using the following steps:
Step 1: Define the characteristics of the binomial distribution.

$n = 10, p = .70, x = 5$

Step 2: Go to the binomial table in Appendix B. Locate the appropriate section
of the table for a sample size of $n = 10$ and the column with $q = 0.70$ at
the bottom. This is:

X	p = 0.15	p = 0.20	p = 0.25	p = 0.30	p = 0.35	p = 0.40	p = 0.45	p = 0.50	n-X
0	0.1969	0.1074	0.0563	0.0282	0.0135	0.0060	0.0025	0.0010	10
1	0.3474	0.2684	0.1877	0.1211	0.0725	0.0403	0.0207	0.0098	9
2	0.2759	0.3020	0.2816	0.2335	0.1757	0.1209	0.0763	0.0439	8
3	0.1298	0.2013	0.2503	0.2668	0.2522	0.2150	0.1665	0.1172	7
4	0.0401	0.0881	0.1460	0.2001	0.2377	0.2508	0.2384	0.2051	6
5	0.0085	0.0264	0.0584	0.1029	0.1536	0.2007	0.2340	0.2461	5
6	0.0012	0.0055	0.0162	0.0368	0.0689	0.1115	0.1596	0.2051	4
7	0.0001	0.0008	0.0031	0.0090	0.0212	0.0425	0.0746	0.1172	3
8	0.0000	0.0001	0.0004	0.0014	0.0043	0.0106	0.0229	0.0439	2
9	0.0000	0.0000	0.0000	0.0001	0.0005	0.0016	0.0042	0.0098	1
10	0.0000	0.0000	0.0000	0.0000	0.0000	0.0001	0.0003	0.0010	0
	q = 0.85	q = 0.80	q = 0.75	q = 0.70	q = 0.65	q = 0.60	q = 0.55	q = 0.50	

Step 3: Define the event of interest and obtain the desired probabilities from the binomial table.
The event of interest is:
$P(x = 5) = 0.1029$

Hint: The value of x is found on the right side of the table when you are getting the probability of a success from the bottom of the column.

There is a 0.1029 probability that exactly five successes will be observed in a sample of 10 items if the probability of a success is 0.70.

5.29

a. Step 1: Define the characteristics of the binomial distribution.
In this case the characteristics are n = 11, p = 0.45, and q = 1-p = 0.55.

Step 2; Go the binomial table in Appendix B. Locate the appropriate column for p = 0.45 and the appropriate section in the table for the sample size n = 11.

Step 3: Define the event of interest and obtain the probability from the binomial distribution.
We are interested in the probability of exactly 1 success. $P(x = 1) = 0.0125$.

b. Steps 1 and 2 are identical to (a) above. Step 3: the event of interest is the probability of four or fewer successes. $P(x \leq 4) = P(0) + P(1) + P(2) + P(3) + P(4)$ = 0.0014 + 0.0125 + 0.0513 + 0.1259 + 0.2060 = 0.3971.

c. Steps 1 and 2 are identical to (a) above. Step 3: the event of interest is the probability of at least 8 successes, which is $P(x \geq 8) = P(8) + P(9) + P(10) + P(11) = 0.0462 + 0.0126 + 0.0021 + 0.0002 = 0.0611$.

5.31

a.
Step 1: Define the characteristics of the binomial distribution.
In this case the characteristics are n = 7, p = 0.65, and q = 1-p = 0.35.

Step 2; Go the binomial table in Appendix B. Locate the appropriate column for p = 0.65 and the appropriate section in the table for the sample size n = 7.

Step 3: Define the event of interest and obtain the probability from the binomial distribution.
We are interested in the probability of exactly 3 successes. $P(x = 3) = 0.1442$.

b. Steps 1 and 2 are identical to (a) above. Step 3: the event of interest is the probability of four or more successes. $P(x \geq 4) = P(4) + P(5) + P(6) + P(7) = 0.2679 + 0.2985 + 0.1848 + 0.0490 = 0.8002$.

c. Steps 1 and 2 are identical to (a) above. Step 3: the event of interest is the probability of exactly 7 successes. $P(x = 7) = 0.0490$.

d. The expected value of the random variable can be found using the equation 5-5, $E(x) = np = (7)(0.65) = 4.55$

5.33

   a. $E(x) = np = 8(0.40) = 3.2$

   b. $\sigma = \sqrt{npq} = \sqrt{8(0.4)(1 - 0.4)} = \sqrt{1.92} = 1.386$

   c. $P(x > 3.2) = P(x \geq 4) = P(x = 4) + P(x = 5) + P(x = 6) + P(x = 7) + P(x = 8) = 0.2322 + 0.1239 + 0.0413 + 0.0079 + 0.0007 = 0.4060$.

   d. $P(\mu - 2\sigma \leq x \leq \mu + 2\sigma) = P[3.2 - 2(1.386) \leq x \leq 3.2 - 2(1.386)] = P(0.428 \leq x \leq 5.972) = P(1 \leq x \leq 5) = P(x = 1) + P(x = 2) + P(x = 3) + P(x = 4) + P(x = 5) = 0.0896 + 0.2090 + 0.2787 + 0.2322 + 0.1239 = 0.9334$.

5.35

   a. Step 1: Define the characteristics of the binomial distribution:

   $n = 10$, $p = 0.308$, $q = 1 - p = 1 - 0.308 = 0.692$.

   Step 2: Use equation 5-4 to find the expected value:

   $\mu_X = E(X) = np = 10(0.308) = 3.08$

   b. Step 1: Define the characteristics of the binomial distribution:

   $n = 10$, $p = 0.607$, $q = 1 - p = 1 - 0.607 = 0.393$.

   Step 2: Determine the probability of x successes in n trials using the binomial formula, Equation 5-4:

   $P(X = 10) = \binom{10}{10} 0.607^{10} (0.393)^{10-10} = 0.0068$

c. Step 1: Define the characteristics of the binomial distribution:
$n = 10$, $p = 0.308$, $q = 1 - p = 1 - 0.308 = 0.692$.

Step 2: Determine the probability of x successes in n trials using the binomial formula, Equation 5-4:

$$P(X \geq 8) = P(X = 8) + P(X = 9) + P(X = 10) = \binom{10}{8} 0.308^8 (0.692)^{10-8} +$$

$$\binom{10}{9} 0.308^9 (0.692)^{10-9} + \binom{10}{10} 0.308^{10} (0.692)^{10-10} = \frac{10!}{8!(10-8)!} 0.308^8 0.692^2 +$$

$$\frac{10!}{9!(10-9)!} 0.308^9 0.692^1 + \frac{10!}{10!(10-10)!} 0.308^{10} 0.692^0 = 0.0017 + 0.0002 + 0.0000$$

$$= 0.0019.$$

d. It is quite unlikely that the employees followed the national trend. The probability of such an occurrence is very small, for voting only .0068, and for voting for President Bush, only 0.0019, assuming they were following the national trend.

5.37

a. To find the expected value of the binomial distribution, you can use the following steps:

Step 1: Describe the characteristics of the discrete distribution.

The situation described in the problem satisfies the characteristics of a binomial distribution with:
$$n = 20; \ p = 0.80; \ q = 1 - 0.80 = 0.20$$

Step 2: Compute the expected value for the binomial distribution.

The general equation for the expected value of a discrete probability distribution is:
$$E(x) = \sum xP(x)$$

However, because the discrete distribution possesses the characteristics of a binomial distribution, the expected value is computed using:
$$E(x) = np = (20)(0.80) = 16$$

Thus, the McNeal executives would expect at least 16 of the 20 people sampled to be able to recall the name of the company in the commercial one-hour after viewing it.

b. To find the desired probability, you can use the following steps:

Step 1: Define the characteristics of the binomial distribution.

The characteristics are:
$$n = 20; \ p = 0.80; \ q = 1 - p = 0.20$$

Step 2: Go to the appropriate section of the binomial table for the desired sample size.
The sample size in this case is n = 20.

Step 3: Determine the appropriate column in the binomial table to locate the probabilities.
In this case the probability of a success is p = 0.80. Since p = 0.80 is greater than 0.50, we need to look to the bottom of the columns in the binomial table for q = 0.80 and then get the values of x from the right most column. This gives the following section of the binomial table:

p = 0.15	p = 0.20	p = 0.25	p = 0.30	p = 0.35	p = 0.40	p = 0.45	p = 0.50	n-X
0.0388	0.0115	0.0032	0.0008	0.0002	0.0000	0.0000	0.0000	20
0.1368	0.0576	0.0211	0.0068	0.0020	0.0005	0.0001	0.0000	19
0.2293	0.1369	0.0669	0.0278	0.0100	0.0031	0.0008	0.0002	18
0.2428	0.2054	0.1339	0.0716	0.0323	0.0123	0.0040	0.0011	17
0.1821	0.2182	0.1897	0.1304	0.0738	0.0350	0.0139	0.0046	16
0.1028	0.1746	0.2023	0.1789	0.1272	0.0746	0.0365	0.0148	15
0.0454	0.1091	0.1686	0.1916	0.1712	0.1244	0.0746	0.0370	14
0.0160	0.0545	0.1124	0.1643	0.1844	0.1659	0.1221	0.0739	13
0.0046	0.0222	0.0609	0.1144	0.1614	0.1797	0.1623	0.1201	12
0.0011	0.0074	0.0271	0.0654	0.1158	0.1597	0.1771	0.1602	11
0.0002	0.0020	0.0099	0.0308	0.0686	0.1171	0.1593	0.1762	10
0.0000	0.0005	0.0030	0.0120	0.0336	0.0710	0.1185	0.1602	9
0.0000	0.0001	0.0008	0.0039	0.0136	0.0355	0.0727	0.1201	8
0.0000	0.0000	0.0002	0.0010	0.0045	0.0146	0.0366	0.0739	7
0.0000	0.0000	0.0000	0.0002	0.0012	0.0049	0.0150	0.0370	6
0.0000	0.0000	0.0000	0.0000	0.0003	0.0013	0.0049	0.0148	5
0.0000	0.0000	0.0000	0.0000	0.0000	0.0003	0.0013	0.0046	4
0.0000	0.0000	0.0000	0.0000	0.0000	0.0000	0.0002	0.0011	3
0.0000	0.0000	0.0000	0.0000	0.0000	0.0000	0.0000	0.0002	2
q = 0.85	q = 0.80	q = 0.75	q = 0.70	q = 0.65	q = 0.60	q = 0.55	q = 0.50	

Step 4: Define the event of interest.
We are interested in knowing:

$$P(x \leq 11) = P(x = 11) + P(x = 10) + \ldots + P(x = 0)$$

Step 5: Locate the desired probabilities in the binomial table.

$$P(x \leq 11) = 0.0074 + 0.0020 + \ldots 0.0000$$
$$P(x \leq 11) = 0.0100$$

The probability of 11 or fewer people being able to identify the name of the company in the commercial is 0.01 or 1 chance in 100.

c. The expected number of people being able to identify the company in the commercial is 16 as computed in part a. The actual number observed in the sample is x = 11. The probability of 11 or fewer was computed in part b. to be 0.01. Given this very small chance of 11 or fewer happening if 80 percent in the population would be able to identify, we would conclude that the 80 percent figure is too high. If so, then by the McNeal executives' definition, the advertising campaign will not be successful.

5.39

n=8, p=0.37

a. Expected number = $8(0.37) = 2.96$

b. Variance = $8(0.37)(0.63) = 1.8648$, standard deviation = 1.3656

c. $P(x \leq 2) = 0.0248 + 0.1166 + 0.2397 = 0.3811$

5.41

a. The characteristics of the binomial distribution are p = 0.15, q = 1-p = 0.85, n = 20 and the event of interest is P(x = 5). From the binomial table in Appendix B we find the probability that x = 5 for p = 0.15 = 0.1028.

b. The expected value of a binomial distribution is equal to E(x) = np = (20)(0.15) = 3.0.

c. The process produces 15% defective items. Therefore, 85% (1-0.15 = 0.85) of the items produced are nondefective. The probability that there will be 15 or more nondefective items occurring by chance alone is $P(x \geq 15)$ given that the probability of success is 0.85. From the binomial table we find P(15) = 0.1028 + P(16) = 0.1821 + P(17) = 0.2428 + P(18) = 0.2293 + P(19) = 0.1368 + P(20) = 0.0388 = 0.9326. With an 85% success rate the probability, by chance alone, of observing 15 or more good items out of a sample of 20 is 0.9326.

5.43

a. If 5 confirmed guests do not show then no guests will be sent to another hotel. Therefore, we find the probability of exactly 5 successes, where a success is defined as a confirmed reservation that does not show. In this case n = 25, p = 0.15 and x = number of no shows. The P(x = 5) = 0.156378 is found using Excel.

b. The probability that exactly two confirmed guests will be sent to another hotel is the probability of there being exactly 3 successes. That is there are 3 no shows from the 25 confirmed reservations leaving 22 guests for only 20 rooms. The probability is found to be P(x = 3) = 0.2174.

c. The probability that three or more guests will be sent to another hotel means that there are two or fewer no shows. If x = number of no shows is defined as a success then x = 0 implies that 5 guests must be sent to another hotel. If x = 1 then four guests must be sent to another hotel. If x = 2 then three guests must be sent to another hotel. Thus, we find P(x=0) + P(x=1) + P(x=2) = 0.01720 + 0.07587 + 0.16067 = 0.25374.

5.45

a. $\bar{x}_w = \dfrac{\sum w_i x_i}{\sum w_i} = \dfrac{30(0.50) + 10(0.10) + 50(0.35)}{30 + 10 + 50} = 0.372$.

If Vericours is correct (i.e., that 40% don't redeem their rebates) this would suggest that 60% do redeem their rebates. It appears that TCA Fulfillment's redemption rate is much smaller that indicated by Vericours.

b. Step 1: Define the characteristics of the binomial distribution:
n = 20, p = 0.60, q = 1 − p = 1 − 0.60 = 0.40.

Step 2: Use equation 5-4 to find the expected value:
μ_x = E(x) = np = 20(0.60) = 12.

Given that the average obtained in is 12, 4 seems to be extremely small. It would seem that Vericours' estimate may be too high.

c. Step 1: Define the characteristics of the binomial distribution:
n = 20, p = 0.372, q = 1 − p = 1 − 0.372 = 0.628.

Step 2: Determine the probability of x successes in n trials using the binomial formula, Equation 5-4:

P(x ≤ 4) = P(x = 0) + P(x = 1) + P(x = 2) + P(x = 3) + P(x = 4) =

$\binom{20}{0} 0.372^0 (0.628)^{20-0} + \binom{20}{1} 0.372^1 (0.628)^{20-1} + \binom{20}{2} 0.372^2 (0.628)^{20-2} +$

$\binom{20}{3} 0.372^3 (0.628)^{20-3} + \binom{20}{4} 0.372^4 (0.628)^{20-4} = \dfrac{20!}{0!(20-0)!} 0.372^0 0.628^{20} +$

$\dfrac{20!}{1!(20-1)!} 0.372^1 0.628^{20-1} + \dfrac{20!}{2!(20-2)!} 0.372^2 0.628^{20-2} +$

$\dfrac{20!}{3!(20-3)!} 0.372^3 0.628^{20-3} + \dfrac{20!}{4!(20-4)!} 0.372^4 0.628^{20-4} = 0.0001 + 0.0011 +$

0.0061 + 0.0216 + 0.0543 = 0.0832.

d. Substituting p = 0.60 for 0.372 in the calculations for part c., the resulting answer for Vericours is 0.0003.

e. Given the probabilities in part c. and d., it would seem that the redemption rate is lower than either Vericours or TCA Fulfillment estimate.

5.47

    a. Minitab output:

        Columns: Returned

        0   1   All

        112   13   125
        89.60 10.40 100.00

        Cell Contents: Count
                  % of Row

    So the number of pairs of wrong size shoes that were delivered to customers is 13.

    b. Minitab output:

        Binomial with n = 125 and p = 0.05

        x $P(X \leq 12)$
        12   0.989994

        $P(x \geq 13) = 1 - P(x \leq 12) = 1 - 0.989994 = 0.010006$

    c. As the probability shows, it is very unusual to obtain 13 or more successes in 125 trials if the proportion of successes is 0.05. Since a "success" in this experiment is that the shoe size delivered was different than that ordered, Zappos does not seem to have achieved its goal.

    d. E(x) = np = 5000000(13/125). This indicates that the E(Cost) = 520000(4.75) = $2,470,000.

5.49

    a. Minitab output
       Tabulated statistics: Male-Female

          Columns: Male-Female (M-F > 0) = "0" (M-F ≤ 0) = "1"

          0   1   All

          113   37   150
          75.33 24.67 100.00

          Cell Contents: Count
                     % of Row

    b. $E(x) = np = 135(0.325) = 43.875$.

    c. Minitab output
       Cumulative Distribution Function

       Binomial with $n = 135$ and $p = 0.325$

          $P(x \leq 36) = 0.086047$
          $P(x \geq 37) = 1 - P(x \leq 36) = 1 - 0.086047 = 0.913953$.

    d. Since there is a very large probability that the outcome we observed or
       something larger would occur, it seems quite plausible that the California
       percentage agrees with that obtained by the Bureau of Labor Statistics.

Section 5-3 Exercises

5.51

    To determine the desired probability, you can use the following steps.
    Step 1: Define the segment unit.
          Because the mean was stated to be 1.5 errors per page, the segment unit is
          1 page.

    Step 2: Determine the mean of the random variable.
          The mean is $\lambda = 1.5$

    Step 3: Determine the segment size, t.
          The issue in the problem asks for the probability of more than 3 errors in 3
          pages so $t = 3$. $\lambda t = (1.5)(3) = 4.5$

Step 4: Define the event of interest and use the Poisson table to find the desired probability.

We are asked to calculate the probability that more than 3 errors will be discovered. The event of interest is:

$$P(x > 3) = P(x = 4) + P(x = 5) + \ldots\ldots$$

or

$$P(x > 3) = 1 - P(x \le 3)$$
$$P(x > 3) = 1 - [P(x = 3) + P(x = 2) + P(x = 1) + P(x = 0)]$$

To use the Poisson table, go to the column headed $\lambda t = 4.5$. Then find the values of x from the left hand column. The desired probability is:

$$P(x > 3) = 1 - [0.1687 + 0.1125 + 0.0500 + .0111]$$
$$P(x > 3) = 1 - 0.3423 = 0.6577$$

5.53

To determine this probability we recognize that because the sampling is without replacement and the sample size is large relative to the size of the population, the hypergeometric distribution applies. The following steps can be used:

Step 1: Define the population size and the combined sample size.

The population size is N = 14 and the combined sample size is n = 5

Step 2: Define the event of interest.

We are interested in the event described by getting

$$P(x_1 = 3 \, Fords; x_2 = 2 \, GM; x_3 = 0 \, Toyotas) = ?$$

Step 3: Determine the number of each category in the population and the number in category in the sample.

$$X_1 = 5 \, Fords \, x_1 = 3$$
$$X_1 = 4 \, GM \, x_1 = 2$$
$$X_1 = 5 \, Fords \, x_1 = 0$$

Step 4: Compute the desired probability using the hypergeometric distribution.

$$P(x_1 = 3, x_2 = 2, x_3 = 0) = \frac{C_{x_1}^{X_1} \Box C_{x_2}^{X_2} \Box C_{x_3}^{X_3}}{C_n^N} = \frac{C_3^5 \Box C_2^4 \Box C_0^5}{C_5^{14}} = \frac{(10)(6)(1)}{2,002} = \frac{60}{2,002} = 0.03$$

5.55

    a. Step 1: Determine the population size, N, and the sample size, n. The population size, N, is the number of manufacturing plants and is equal to 11. The sample size, n, is the number of plants selected for a performance evaluation and is equal to 4.

Step 2: Define the event of interest. The event of interest is the probability that exactly four plants outside the United States are included in the performance evaluation $P(x = 4)$

Step 3: Determine the number of successes in the population and the number of successes in the sample. In this case the number of successes in the population is the number of plants located outside the United States, which is 4. Therefore $X = 4$. The number of successes in the sample is the number of plants outside the United States included in the performance evaluation and is equal to 1. Therefore, $x = 1$.

Step 4: Compute the desired probability using the following equation:

$$P(x) = \frac{C_{n-x}^{N-X} * C_x^X}{C_n^N} = P(x = 1) = \frac{C_{4-1}^{11-4} * C_1^4}{C_4^{11}} = 0.4242$$

    b. Step 1: Determine the population size, N, and the sample size, n. The population size, N, is the number of manufacturing plants and is equal to 11. The sample size, n, is the number of plants selected for a performance evaluation and is equal to 4.

Step 2: Define the event of interest. The event of interest is the probability that exactly three plants in the United States are included in the performance evaluation $P(x = 3)$

Step 3: Determine the number of successes in the population and the number of successes in the sample. In this case the number of successes in the population is the number of plants located in the United States, which is 7. Therefore $X = 7$. The number of successes in the sample is the number of plants in the United States included in the performance evaluation and is equal to 3. Therefore, $x = 3$.

Step 4: Compute the desired probability using the following equation:

$$P(x) = \frac{C_{n-x}^{N-X} * C_x^X}{C_n^N} = P(x = 3) = \frac{C_{4-3}^{11-7} * C_3^7}{C_4^{11}} = 0.4242$$

c. Step 1: Determine the population size, N, and the sample size, n. The population size, N, is the number of manufacturing plants and is equal to 11. The sample size, n, is the number of plants selected for a performance evaluation and is equal to 4.

Step 2: Define the event of interest. The event of interest is the probability that two or more plants outside the United States are included in the performance evaluation $P(x \geq 2)$

Step 3: Determine the number of successes in the population and the number of successes in the sample. In this case the number of successes in the population is the number of plants located outside the United States, which is 4. Therefore X = 4. The number of successes in the sample is the number of plants outside the United States included in the performance evaluation and is equal to 2 or more. Therefore, $x \geq 2$.

Step 4: Compute the desired probability using the following equation:

$P(x \geq 2) = P(x = 2) + P(x = 3) + P(x = 4)$, where

$$P(x) = \frac{C_{n-x}^{N-X} * C_x^X}{C_n^N}$$

$$P(x = 2) = \frac{C_{4-2}^{11-4} * C_2^4}{C_4^{11}} = 0.3818$$

$$P(x = 3) = \frac{C_{4-3}^{11-4} * C_3^4}{C_4^{11}} = 0.0848$$

$$P(x = 4) = \frac{C_{4-4}^{11-4} * C_4^4}{C_4^{11}} = 0.0030$$

Therefore, the $P(x \geq 2) = 0.4696$

5.57

(Using the tables in Appendix C)
a. $P(x \leq 3) = P(x = 0) + P(x = 1) + P(x = 2) + P(x = 3) = 0.0498 + 0.1494 + 0.2240 + 0.2240 = 0.6472$.

b. $P(x > 3) = P(x \geq 4) = 1 - P(x \leq 3) = 1 - 0.6472 = 0.3528$.

c. $P(2 < x \le 5) = P(x = 3) + P(x = 4) + P(x = 5) = 0.2240 + 0.1680 + 0.1008 = 0.4928$.

d. From part a. $P(x \le 3) = 0.6472$, and $P(x \le 2) = 0.4232$. Therefore, x' = 3 is the smallest x' so that $P(x \le x') > 0.50$.

5.59

Step 1: Define the segment unit.
The problem is made easiest if the segment unit is defined in minutes.

Step 2: Determine the mean of the random variable.
The mean of the random variable, which is the number of electronic transfer requests during the busiest periods is 170 per ten minute period.

Step 3: Determine the segment size t.
The segment size t is one minute. Therefore t = 1/10 =(1 minute/10 minutes) = 0.10. So $\lambda t = 0.10(170) = 17$.

Step 4: Define the event of interest.
The event of interest is the probability that there are more transfer requests than capacity. In one minute the transfer capacity is 25. The probability that there would be more requests than capacity is $P(x > 25) = P(x \ge 26) = P(26) + P(27) + P(28) + \ldots$. Using the Poisson Table in Appendix C for $\lambda t = 17$ we find, P(26) = 0.0101, P(27) = 0.0063, P(28) = 0.0038, P(29) = 0.0023, P(30) = 0.0013, P(31) = 0.0007, P(32) = 0.0004, P(33) = 0.0002, P(34) = 0.0001, P(35) = 0.0000 and all subsequent probabilities are essentially 0 above P(35). The sum of these individual probabilities is the $P(x \ge 26) = 0.0252$.

5.61

This is a situation in which the sampling will be performed without replacement from a finite population when the sample size is large relative to the population size. As such, the desired probability can be computed using the hypergeometric distribution. The event of interest is:

$$P(x_1 = 7, x_2 = 0, x_3 = 0) = \frac{C_{x_1}^{X_1} C_{x_2}^{X_2} C_{x_3}^{X_3}}{C_n^N} = \frac{C_7^{10} C_0^5 C_0^5}{C_7^{20}} = \frac{(120)(1)(1)}{77,520} = \frac{120}{77,520} = 0.0015$$

The probability of all seven stocks being "large caps" is 0.0015. This means that in only 15 chances in ten thousand would this happen due to chance so it is very likely that the sampling was not done using random selection as directed by the customer.

Chapter 5

5.63

$$\lambda = 3/400 = 0.0075; \, t = 1200; \, \lambda t = 9$$

a. $P(x=0) = 0.000123$

b. $P(x>14) = P(x\geq15) = 1 - P(x\leq14) = 1 - 0.9585 = 0.0415$

c. $P(x<9) = P(x\leq8) = 0.4557$

d. There is only a 4.15% chance of finding 15 or more errors if the claim is actually true. Students will probably conclude that the error rate is probably higher than 3 per 400.

5.65

This problem requires that the hypergeometric probability distribution be used. Using the hypergeometric probability distribution the probability of 2 defectives is computed to be 0.21672. The probability of 3 defectives is computed as 0.03096, and the probability of 4 defectives is 0.001032. Therefore the probability of rejecting the box of fasteners is $0.21672 + 0.03096 + 0.001032 = 0.24871$. The probability of accepting the shipment is equal to the probability of 1 or fewer defective in the sample. Therefore, the probability of accepting the shipment is $P(0) = 0.28173 + P(1) = 0.46956 = 0.7513$.

5.67

a. Step 1: Determine the population size and the combined sample size.
The population size and sample size are
$N = 20$ and $n = 5$.

Step 2: Define the event of interest.
The Geek Squad technician needs to determine
$P(x = 4)$.

Step 3: Determine the number of successes in the population and the number of successes in the sample.
In this situation, a success is the event that the technician selects a non-defective processor. There are $20 - 4 = 16 \, (= X)$ successes in the population and $4 \, (5 - 1 = x)$ in the sample.

Step 4: Compute the desired probabilities using Equation 5-9.

$$P(x = 4) = \frac{C_{n-x}^{N-X} C_{x}^{SX}}{C_{n}^{N}} = \frac{C_{5-4}^{20-16} C_{4}^{16}}{C_{5}^{20}} = \frac{4(1820)}{15504} = 0.4696$$

126

b. $P(x = 3) = \dfrac{C_{n-x}^{N-X} C_x^X}{C_n^N} = \dfrac{C_{5-3}^{20-16} C_3^{16}}{C_5^{20}} = \dfrac{6(560)}{15504} = 0.2167$

c. The technician will have enough processors if he selects 3 or more non-defective processors. Thus, noting that

$$P(x = 5) = \dfrac{C_{5-5}^{20-16} C_5^{16}}{C_5^{20}} = \dfrac{1(4368)}{15504} = 0.2817$$

The probability is

$P(x \geq 3) = 0.4696 + 0.2167 + P(X = 5) = 0.6863 + 0.2817 = 0.9680$

5.69

a. $P(x_1, x_2, x_3) = \dfrac{C_{x_1}^{S_1} C_{x_2}^{S_2} C_{x_3}^{S_3}}{C_n^N} = \dfrac{C_5^{15} C_3^{26} C_2^9}{C_{10}^{50}} = \dfrac{3003(2600)(36)}{10272278170} = 0.0274$

b. $P(10,0,0) = \dfrac{C_{x_1}^{S_1} C_{x_2}^{S_2} C_{x_3}^{S_3}}{C_n^N} = \dfrac{C_{10}^{15} C_0^{26} C_0^9}{C_{10}^{50}} = \dfrac{3003(1)(1)}{10272278170} = 0.0000$

c. $P(6,0,4) = \dfrac{C_{x_1}^{S_1} C_{x_2}^{S_2} C_{x_3}^{S_3}}{C_n^N} = \dfrac{C_6^{15} C_0^{26} C_4^9}{C_{10}^{50}} = \dfrac{5005(1)(126)}{10272278170} = 0.0001$

5.71

a. Minitab output
   Sum of Scratches

   Sum of Scratches = 8

b. Step 1: Define the segment unit. Since the company's goal is to have no more than an average of one scratch per set of pocket billiard balls and that sixteen balls are in a set, the segment unit is 16 balls.

   Step 2: Determine the mean of the random variable. One scratch per set of balls is the company's goal. Therefore, the mean will be $\lambda = 1$.

Step 3: Determine the segment size t. Since there are 16 balls per set, the 48 balls were that were selected is the same as 3 (48/16) sets of balls. So t = 3. So the average number per set would be $\lambda t = 1(3) = 3$.

c. Step 4: Define the event of interest and use the Poisson formula or the Poisson tables to find the probability.

Here 8 scratches were observed. Since the 8 exceeds the expected number ($\lambda t = 1(3) = 3$), Cliff would want to find $P(X \geq 8)$ which we will obtain from Minitab: Cumulative Distribution Function

Poisson with mean = 3

```
x        P( X <= x )
7        0.988095
```

$P(X \geq 8) = 1 - P(X \leq 7) = 1 - 0.9881 = 0.0119$.

d. It is very unlikely that as many or more than 8 scratches would occur in 48 balls if the company's goal had been met. Therefore, we believe that the goal has not been met.

End of Chapter Exercises

5.73

Both the binomial and Poisson distributions are discrete distributions. There are several differences in the two distributions. In the binomial distribution you must be able to count the number of success and number of failures. In the Poisson distribution the outcomes of interest are rare relative to the possible outcomes.

5.75

a. Let S_i = a success is obtained on the ith trial and F_i = a failure is obtained on the ith trial. $P(S_2|S_1) = \frac{1}{2}$. $P(S_2|F_1) = 2/2 = 1$. Thus, the probability of getting a success on the second trial depends upon what occurs on the first trial. This means the trials are dependent.

b. $P(S_1) = 2/3$.

$P(S_2) = P[(S_1 \text{ and } S_2) \text{ or } (F_1 \text{ and } S2)] = P(S_1 \text{ and } S_2) + P(F_1 \text{ and } S2) = P(S_2|S_1)P(S_1) + P(S_2|F_1)P(F_1) = (1/2)(2/3) + (2/2)(1/3) = 2/3$, and

$P(S_3) = P[(S_3 \text{ and } S_2 \text{ and } F_1) \text{ or } P(S_3 \text{ and } F_2 \text{ and } S_1)] = P(S_3 \text{ and } S_2 \text{ and } F_1) + P(S_3 \text{ and } F_2 \text{ and } S_1) = P(S_3| F_2 \text{ and } S_1)P(F_2 \text{ and } S_1) + P(S_3| S_2 \text{ and } F_1)P(S_2 \text{ and } F_1) = P(S_3| F_2 \text{ and } S_1)P(F_2| S_1)P(S_1) + P(S_3| S_2 \text{ and } F_1)P(S_2| F_1)P(F_1) = (1/1)(1/2)(2/3) + (1/1)(2/2)(1/3) = 2/3$.

Therefore, the probability of a success is the same (2/3) for all three trials. This indicates that the probability of a success being constant does not imply that the trials are independent.

5.77

n = 9 cans; p = .50 (if in control)

P(x = 9) = 0 .0020

Thus, there is a 0.002 chance that this sample result would occur from a process that is in control. Because this is such a small probability, we would likely conclude that the process is not in control. The filling process tends to overfill.

5.79

n = 10 parts; p = .05 (defect rate) ; binomial

If x $\leq$ 2 defects, keep the shipment.

a. P(x $\leq$ 2) = .0746 + .3151 + .5987 = .9884

b. Suppose p = .10

P(x $\leq$ 2) = .1937 + .3874 + .3487 = .9298

c. While the sampling plan is very good (prob = .9884) at keeping shipments that actually contain .05 defects, the sampling plan also keeps most (prob = .9298) of the shipments which contain twice (p = .10) as many defects as allowed. Thus the plan is one-sided. It favors the supplier.

5.81

Use the Hypergeometric distribution with: $P(x) = \dfrac{C_{n-x}^{N-X} \bullet C_x^X}{C_n^N}$

Then with N = 20; n = 4; X = 4; x = 0

$P(x \geq 1) = 1 - P(x = 0). \quad P(0) = \dfrac{C_{4-0}^{20-4} \bullet C_0^4}{C_4^{20}} = \dfrac{1,820 \bullet 1}{4,845} = .3756.$

1-0.3756 =0.6244.

5.83

X	P(x)	xP(x)	x-E(x)	[x-E(x)]^2	[x-E(x)]^{2}P(x)
0	0.3	0	-1.1	1.21	0.363
1	0.4	0.4	-0.1	0.01	0.004
2	0.2	0.4	0.9	0.81	0.162
3	0.1	0.3	1.9	3.61	0.361
		1.1			0.89

a. Expected number of packages = 1.1

b. Var. = 0.89, Standard Deviation = 0.9434

c. The production cost would be $3(3) = $9; remember all packages are produced regardless of how many are purchased. Students should set the expected cost equal to the expected revenue.

$$9 = 0.99 + 1.1x$$
$$8.01 = 1.1x$$

x = $7.282 per package so round to $7.29 per package in order to break even.

5.85

x	P(x)	xP(x)
0	0.2	0
1	0.2	0.2
2	0.2	0.4
3	0.2	0.6
4	0.2	0.8
		2.0

a. The expected number of defectives is equal to 2. This means that on the average of several shipments Bentfield should expect the number of defectives to be 2. It does not mean that each shipment will have exactly 2 defects.

b.

X	P(x)	xP(x)	x-E(x)	[x-E(x)]^2	[x-E(x)]^{2}P(x)
0	0.2	0	-2	4	0.8
1	0.2	0.2	-1	1	0.2
2	0.2	0.4	0	0	0
3	0.2	0.6	1	1	0.2
4	0.2	0.8	2	4	0.8
		2			2

The standard deviation is equal to 1.4142. This is the square root of the average squared deviation from the mean. It is a measure of average deviation from the mean number of defective products based on the probability distribution.

c. This probability distribution is called a Uniform Distribution since the probability of each outcome is equally likely (0.2). Often times if there is no estimate or past history to base the probability on people will use the uniform distribution.

5.87

a. Let x = the number of non-smoking rooms given to the tour guide.

$$P(x = 6) = \frac{C_{10-6}^{20-12} C_6^{12}}{C_{10}^{20}} = \frac{70(924)}{184756} = 0.3501$$

b. $P(x \leq 5) = 1 - P(x \geq 6) = 1 - P(x = 6) - P(x = 7) - PxX = 8) - P(X = 9) -$

$$P(x = 10) = 1 - 0.3501 - \frac{C_{10-7}^{20-12} C_7^{12}}{C_{10}^{20}} - \frac{C_{10-8}^{20-12} C_8^{12}}{C_{10}^{20}} - \frac{C_{10-9}^{20-12} C_9^{12}}{C_{10}^{20}} - \frac{C_{10-10}^{20-12} C_{10}^{12}}{C_{10}^{20}} = 1$$

$- 0.3501 - 0.2400 - 0.075 - 0.0095 - 0.0004 = 0.3250.$

5.89

a. Minitab output:
Sum of Defectives

Sum of Defectives = 38

So then proportion of defectives is 38/[20(90)] = 0.02.

b. $E(X) = \mu = np = 20(0.02) = 0.4; \sigma = \sqrt{npq} = \sqrt{20(0.02)(1 - 0.02)} = 0.6261.$

c. $\mu \pm \sigma = 0.4 \pm 3(0.6261) = (-1.4783, 2.2783)$. Since it is impossible to have a negative number here the limits are (0, 2.2783)

d. $P(0 \leq X \leq 2.2783) = P(0 \leq X \leq 2)$. So the probability that the number of defectives is beyond the control limits equals $1 - P(X \leq 2)$.

Using Minitab:
Cumulative Distribution Function

Binomial with n = 20 and p = 0.02

x P(X <= x)
2   0.992931

So $1 - P(X \leq 2) = 1 - 0.9929 = 0.0071$.

Chapter 6 Solutions

When applicable, selected problems in each section will be done following the appropriate step-by-step procedures outlined in the corresponding sections of the chapter. Other problems will provide key points and the answers to the questions, but all answers can be arrived at using the appropriate steps.

Section 6-1 Exercises

6.1

The following steps are used to compute the desired probabilities

Step 1: Determine the mean and standard deviation

Step 2: Determine the event of interest.

Step 3: Convert the random variable to a standardized z-value using: with

$$z = \frac{x - \mu}{\sigma}$$

Step 4: Find the probability associated the z-value from the standard normal distribution table (Appendix D)

a. We are given the mean and standard deviation as follows: $\mu = 100$ and $\sigma = 20$
The event of interest is $P(x > 130) = ?$

We find the z-value using: $z = \frac{x - \mu}{\sigma} = \frac{130 - 100}{20} = \frac{30}{20} = 1.50$

The probability from the standard normal table associated with z = 1.50 is 0.4332. This corresponds to the area between z = 1.50 and the mean. To desired probability is found by subtracting 0.4332 from 0.5000 giving 0.0668. This is illustrated in the following graph.

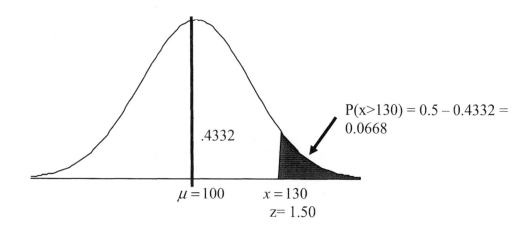

$P(x>130) = 0.5 - 0.4332 = 0.0668$

.4332

$\mu = 100$ $x = 130$
                 $z = 1.50$

b. We are given the mean and standard deviation as follows: $\mu = 100$ and $\sigma = 20$
The event of interest is $P(x < 90) = ?$

We find the z-value using: $z = \dfrac{x - \mu}{\sigma} = \dfrac{90 - 100}{20} = \dfrac{-10}{20} = -0.50$

The probability from the standard normal table associated with z = -.50 is 0.1915. This corresponds to the area between z = -.50 and the mean. To desired probability is found by subtracting 0.1915 from 0.5000 giving 0.3085. This is illustrated in the following graph.

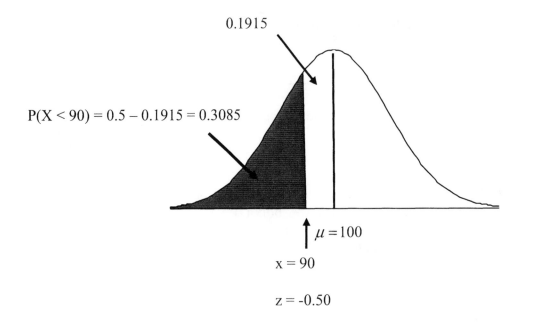

0.1915

$P(X < 90) = 0.5 - 0.1915 = 0.3085$

$\mu = 100$

x = 90

z = -0.50

c. We are given the mean and standard deviation as follows: $\mu = 100$ and $\sigma = 20$
The event of interest is $P(90 \le x \le 130) = ?$

We find the z-value using: $z = \dfrac{x - \mu}{\sigma} = \dfrac{90 - 100}{20} = \dfrac{-10}{20} = -0.50$

and $z = \dfrac{x - \mu}{\sigma} = \dfrac{130 - 100}{20} = \dfrac{30}{20} = 1.50$

The probability from the standard normal table associated with z = -.50 is 0.1915. The probability associated with z = 1.50 is .4332. These corresponds to the areas between z = -.50 and the mean and z = 1.50 and the mean. To desired probability is found by adding the two probabilities:

$P(90 \le x \le 130) = 0.1915 + 0.4332 = 0.6247$

6.3

The following steps are used to compute the z-values

Step 1: Determine the mean and standard deviation

Step 2: Determine the event of interest.

Step 3: Convert the random variable to a standardized z-value using:

$$z = \frac{x - \mu}{\sigma}$$

a. We are given the mean and standard deviation as follows: $\mu = 200$ and $\sigma = 20$

The event of interest is x = 225

We find the z-value using: $z = \frac{x - \mu}{\sigma} = \frac{225 - 200}{20} = \frac{25}{20} = 1.25$

b. We are given the mean and standard deviation as follows: $\mu = 200$ and $\sigma = 20$

The event of interest is x = 190

We find the z-value using: $z = \frac{x - \mu}{\sigma} = \frac{190 - 200}{20} = \frac{-10}{20} = -0.50$

c. We are given the mean and standard deviation as follows: $\mu = 200$ and $\sigma = 20$

The event of interest is x = 240

We find the z-value using: $z = \frac{x - \mu}{\sigma} = \frac{240 - 200}{20} = \frac{40}{20} = 2.00$

6.5

a. The following steps are used to compute the desired value of x

Step 1: Determine the mean and standard deviation

The mean and standard deviation are $\mu = 5.5$ and $\sigma = .50$

Step 2: Determine the event of interest.

We are interested in determining the value of x such that the probability of a value exceeding x is at most 0.10.

Step 3: Determine the z-value corresponding to the known probability.
The area in the upper tail of the distribution above x is defined to be 0.10. That means that the area between x and the population mean of 5.5 is 0.40. In Appendix D, we go to the inside of the table and locate the value 0.40 or just larger and determine the z-value associated with this probability. The closest probability is 0.4015. The z-value corresponding to this probability is z = 1.29.

Step 4: Solve for x using the following equation:

$$z = \frac{x - \mu}{\sigma}$$

We now solve for x as follows:

$$1.29 = \frac{x - 5.5}{.50}$$
$$x = 1.29(.50) + 5.5 = 6.145$$

Thus, the desired value is x = 6.145.

b. We are asked to determine what the population mean must be if we want the following:
$$P(x > 6.145) \le 0.05$$

The following steps can be used to solve for the new population mean:
Step 1: Determine the z-value that corresponds to an upper tail area equal to 0.05. From the standard normal distribution table, we look for a probability on the inside of the table equal to 0.45 (or slightly larger) and determine the corresponding z-value. The closest probability is .4505. The z-value corresponding to this probability is 1.65. (Note, students could interpolate between 0.4495 and 0.4505 giving a z=1.645.)

Step 2: Solve for the population mean using the following equation:
$$z = \frac{x - \mu}{\sigma}$$
Solve for μ as follows:
$$1.65 = \frac{6.145 - \mu}{.50}$$
$$\mu = 6.145 - (1.65)(.50) = 5.32$$
Thus, the population mean must be reduced from 5.5 to 5.32 in order for the probability of a value exceeding 6.145 to be reduced from 0.10 to 0.05.

6.7

a.

Step 1: The mean and standard deviation of the random variable are 1,500
and $\sqrt{324} = 18$, respectively.

Step 2: The event of interest is $P(x > 1,550)$

Step 3: Convert the random variable to a standardized value using Equation 6-2.
$$z = \frac{1550 - 1500}{18} = 2.78$$

Step 4: Find the probability associated with the z-value in the standard normal
distribution table.
$P(z > 2.78) = 0.5 - 0.4973 = 0.0027$
therefore, $P(x > 1,550) = 0.0027$

b.

Step 1: The mean and standard deviation of the random variable are 1,500
and $\sqrt{324} = 18$, respectively.

Step 2: The event of interest is $P(x < 1,485)$

Step 3: Convert the random variable to a standardized value using Equation 6-2.
$$z = \frac{1485 - 1500}{18} = -0.83$$

Step 4: Find the probability associated with the z-value in the standard normal
distribution table.

$P(z < -0.83) = 0.5 - 0.2967 = 0.2033$
therefore, $P(x < 1,485) = 0.2033$

c.

Step 1: The mean and standard deviation of the random variable are 1,500
and $\sqrt{324} = 18$, respectively.

Step 2: The event of interest is $P(x < 1,475 \text{ or } x > 1,535)$

Step 3: Convert the random variables to standardized values using Equation 6-2.
$$z = \frac{1475 - 1500}{18} = -1.39 \qquad z = \frac{1535 - 1500}{18} = 1.94$$

Step 4: Find the probabilities associated with the z-values in the standard normal distribution table.

$P(z < -1.39) = 0.5 - 0.4177 = 0.0823$

$P(z > 1.94) = 0.5 - 0.4738 = 0.0262$

$P(x < 1,475 \text{ or } x > 1,535) = 0.0823 + 0.0262 = 0.1085$

6.9

a.

Step 1: The mean and standard deviation of the random variable are 60 and 9, respectively.

Step 2: The event of interest is $P(x < 46.5)$

Step 3: Convert the random variable to a standardized value using Equation 6-2.

$$z = \frac{46.5 - 60}{9} = -1.5$$

Step 4: Find the probability associated with the z-value in the standard normal distribution table.

$P(z < -1.5) = 0.5 - 0.4332 = 0.0668$

therefore, $P(x < 46.5) = 0.0668$

b.

Step 1: The mean and standard deviation of the random variable are 60 and 9, respectively.

Step 2: The event of interest is $P(x > 78)$

Step 3: Convert the random variable to a standardized value using Equation 6-2.

$$z = \frac{70 - 60}{9} = 1.11$$

Step 4: Find the probability associated with the z-value in the standard normal distribution table.

$P(z > 1.11) = 0.5 - 0.3665 = 0.1335$

therefore, $P(x > 78) = 0.1335$

c.

Step 1: The mean and standard deviation of the random variable are 60 and 9, respectively.

Step 2: The event of interest is $P(51 < x < 73.5)$

Step 3: Convert the random variable to a standardized value using Equation 6-2.

$$\frac{51-60}{9} < z < \frac{73.5-60}{9} = -1 < z < 1.5$$

Step 4: Find the probability associated with the z-value in the standard normal distribution table.

$P(-1 < z < 1.5) = 0.3413 + 0.4332 = 0.7745$

therefore, $P(51 < x < 73.5) = 0.7745$

6.11

a. $P(0 < z < 1.96) = 0.4750$.

b. $P(z > 1.645) = \dfrac{0.4495 + 0.4505}{2} = 0.4500$.

c. $P(1.28 < z \le 2.33) = P(0 < z \le 2.33) - P(0 < z \le 1.28) = 0.4901 - 0.3997 = 0.0904$

d. $P(-2 \le z \le 3) = P(-2 < z \le 0) + P(0 < z \le 3) = P(0 < z \le 2) + P(0 < z \le 3) = 0.4772 + 0.49865 = 0.97585$.

e. $P(z > -1) = P(-1 < z \le 0) + P(Z \ge 0) = P(0 < z \le 1) + P(z \ge 0) = 0.3413 + 0.5000 = 0.8513$.

6.13

a. $P(z > 1.645) = 0.05$. $x_o = \mu + z_o\sigma$; so $x_o = 13.6 + 1.645(2.90) = 18.37$.

b. $P(0 \le z \le 1.96) = 0.4750$. So $P(z \le 1.96) = 0.05 + 0.475$. $x_o = \mu + z_o\sigma$; so $x_o = 13.6 + 1.96(2.90) = 19.284$.

c. $P(0 \le z \le 1.96) = 0.4750$. So $P(-1.96 \le z \le 1.96) = 0.4750 + 0.4750 = 0.95$. $x_o = \mu + z_o\sigma$; so $\mu - x_o = z_o\sigma = 1.96(2.90) = 5.684$. Therefore, $x_o = \mu - 5.684 = 13.6 - 5.684 = 7.916$.

6.15

a.

Step 1: Determine the mean, μ, and the standard deviation, σ.

$\mu = 3$ and $\sigma = 0.3$

Step 2: Define the event of interest.

$P(X > 3.5)$

Step 3: Convert the normal distribution to the standard normal distribution using Equation 6 – 2.

$$z = \frac{x - \mu}{\sigma} = \frac{3.5 - 3}{0.3} = 1.67$$

Step 4: Use the standard normal table to find the probabilities associated with each z-value.

$$P(0 \leq Z \leq 1.67) = 0.4525$$

Step 5: Determine the desired probability for the event of interest.
Since $P(0 \leq z \leq 1.67) = 0.4525$, $P(z \geq 1.67) = P(z > 1.67) = 0.5 - 0.4525 = 0.0475 = P(x > 3.5)$.

b.
Step 1: Determine the mean, μ, and the standard deviation, σ.
$\mu = 3$ and $\sigma = 0.3$

Step 2: Define the event of interest.
$P(x > 2.75)$

Step 3: Convert the normal distribution to the standard normal distribution using Equation 6 – 12.

$$z = \frac{x - \mu}{\sigma} = \frac{2.75 - 3}{0.3} = -0.83$$

Step 4: Use the standard normal table to find the probabilities associated with each z-value.

$$P(-0.83 \leq z \leq 0) = P(0 \leq z \leq 0.83) = 0.2967$$

Step 5: Determine the desired probability for the event of interest.
Since $P(-0.83 \leq z \leq 0) = 0.2967$, $P(z > -0.83) = P(-0.83 \leq z \leq 0) + 0.5$ $P(z > -0.83) = 0.2967 + 0.5 = 0.7967$.

c.
Step 1: Determine the mean, μ, and the standard deviation, σ.
$\mu = 3$ and $\sigma = 0.3$

Step 2: Define the event of interest.
We wish to calculate x_0, so that $P(x > x_0) = 0.10$.

Step 3: Express the event of interest in terms of a standard normal distribution.
We must find z_0 so that $P(z > z_0) = 0.10$.

Step 4: Use the standard normal table to find the z-value, z_0, associated with the probability of interest.

> If $P(z > z_0) = 0.10$, then $P(0 < z < z_0) = 0.5 - 0.10 = 0.40$. From the standard normal table, $P(0 < z < 1.28) = 0.40$. So $z_0 = 1.28$.

Step 5: Determine the desired value, x_0, of the normal random variable.

> Since $x_0 = \mu + z_0\sigma$, $x_0 = 3 + 1.28(0.3) = 3.384$ years. Therefore, the length of life values for the ten percent of the watches' batteries that last the longest are those greater than 3.384 years.

6.17

The mean and standard deviation of the random variable are 50 and 1.25, respectively.

a. $P(x < 49.5) = P(z < (49.5 - 50)/1.25 = P(z < -0.40) = 0.5 - 0.1554 = 0.3446$

b. $P(48.5 < z < 51) = P((48.5 - 50)/1.25 < z < (51 - 50)/1.25) = P(-1.2 < z < 0.8) = 0.3849 + 0.2881 = 0.6730$

c. You want 15% in the upper tail of the standard normal distribution. Go to the body of the standard normal table and find the probability as close to 0.35 (0.5 - .15) as possible. This is 0.3508, therefore, z=1.04.

Substituting known values into Formula 6.2 gives

$$1.04 = \frac{x - 50}{1.25}$$

Solving for x,

$$x = 50 + 1.04(1.25) = 51.30$$

Therefore, the minimum weight a bag of dog food could be and remain in the top 15% of all bags filled is 51.3 kilograms.

d. You want 2% in the upper tail of the standard normal distribution. Go to the body of the standard normal table and find the probability as close to 0.48 (0.5 - .02) as possible. This is essentially between 0.4798 and 0.4803, therefore, z is approximately 2.055.

Substituting known values into Formula 6.2 gives

$$2.055 = \frac{52 - 50}{\sigma}$$

Solving for σ,

$$\sigma = (52-50)/2.055 = 0.9732$$

Therefore, the standard deviation would need to be approximately 0.9732.

Chapter 6

6.19

a. The z score such that 97.5% of the area is under the normal curve is 1.96. The retailer will need to stock μ + zσ units where, μ = 2,500 and σ = 300. Thus, 2,500 + 1.96(300) = 2,500 + 588 = 3,088 toys.

b. $P(x > 2,750) = P(z) > \dfrac{2750 - 2500}{300} = P(z > 0.8333)$. Rounding gives P(z > 0.83)

= 0.5 − 0.2967 = 0.2033 (from table). If you solve using Excel with a z value equal to 0.8333 the answer will be 0.2023.

c. From part (a), when σ = 300, the retailer had to stock 3,088 to limit the probability of being out of stock to 97.5%. If σ = 500, the retailer will need to stock 2,500 + 1.96(500) = 2,500 + 980 = 3,480 toys. This is an increase of 3,480-3,088 = 392 toys over the case where the standard deviation of demand was 300 per week.

6.21

The first thing to do here is to establish the time associated with an $85.00 bid. Since A-1 gets $75 for the first 30 minutes and $2 for each additional minute, an $85 bid would correspond to a work time of 35 minutes. If the distribution of work time on the disposal jobs is normally distributed with $\mu = 47$ minutes and $\sigma = 12$ minutes, we wish to find:
$$P(x > 35) = ?$$

Then, we convert x = 35 to the corresponding z-value using:
$$z = \frac{x - \mu}{\sigma} = \frac{35 - 47}{12} = \frac{-12}{12} = -1.00$$

Next, we find the probability associated with z = -1.00 from the standard normal table. This is 0.3413. Note, this is the probability of a value between z = -1.00 and the mean. To find the desired probability, we must add this probability to the probability of exceeding the population mean which is 0.5000. This gives:
$$P(x > 35) = 0.3413 + 0.5000 = 0.8413$$

Thus, if A-1 bids $85, they will not meeting their desired billing level over 84% of the time. Thus, they will have to get faster at doing this job or recognize that their desired billing rates cannot be achieved on this job if they are to charge the going rate of $85.00.

6.23

At issue here is the need to determine the probability of a loan having a balance less that $170,000. Students should then multiply this probability by the 100 loans in the sample to get the expected proportion of loans with balances under $170,000.

The following steps are used to compute the desired probabilities

Step 1: Determine the mean and standard deviation
The population parameters are $\mu = \$155,600$ and $\sigma = \$33,050$

Step 2: Determine the event of interest.
We are interested in
$$P(x < \$170,000) = ?$$

Step 3: Convert the random variable to a standardized z-value using:
$$z = \frac{x - \mu}{\sigma} = \frac{170,000 - 155,600}{33,050} = 0.44$$

Step 4: Find the probability associated the z-value from the standard normal distribution table (Appendix D)

The Probability associated with a z-value = 0.44 from the standard normal table is 0.1700. As shown in the graph below, this probability is added to 0.5000 to get the desired probability as follows:

$$P(x < \$170,000) = 0.1700 + 0.5000 = 0.6700$$

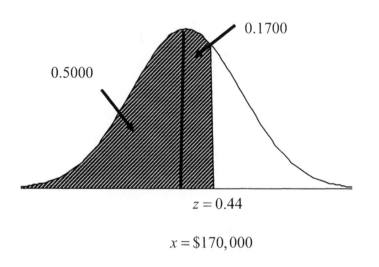

0.1700

0.5000

$z = 0.44$

$x = \$170,000$

Thus, there is a .67 probability that a loan selected at random from the Wells Fargo real estate portfolio will have a balance less than $170,000.

Now to get the expected proportion of loans in the sample of 100 loans with balances under $170,000, we multiply 0.6700 times 100 loans giving 67 loans. The actual number of such loans in the sample was 80 which is quite high relative to the expected number of 67. Student reports should outline their calculations and conclude that the loans tend to overstate the loans with smaller loan balances under $170,000.

6.25

a. $P(x > 1500) = P\left(z > \dfrac{1500 - 1200}{350}\right) = P(z > 0.86) = 0.50 - P(0 \le z \le 0.86) = 0.5 -$

0.3051= 0.1949.

b. $\mu \pm 2\sigma = 1200 \pm 2(350) = (500, 1900).$ $P(500 \le x \le 1900) =$

$P\left(\dfrac{500 - 1200}{350} \le z \le \dfrac{1900 - 1200}{350}\right) = P(-2 \le z \le 2) = P(-2 \le z \le 0) + P(0 \le z \le 2) =$

$2\,P(0 \le z \le 2) = 2(0.4772) = 0.9544$

c. The median is the value, x_0, such that $P(x \le x_0) = 0.5$. For a symmetric distribution such as the normal, this is also the characteristic of the mean. That is to say, that the mean and the median are the same for a normal distribution. Here the mean is $1,200 and so is the median.

6.27

a. At issue is the need to determine the probability that a can will contain between 11.98 and 12.02 ounces given the filling process in use by the Aberdeen Coca-Cola Bottling Company. The following steps can be used to compute this probability:

Step 1: Determine the mean and standard deviation
The population parameters are $\mu = 12.0$ and $\sigma = 0.035$

Step 2: Determine the event of interest.
We are interested in
$$P(11.98 \le x \le 12.02) = ?$$

Step 3: Convert the random variable to a standardized z-value.
We have to values to convert as follows
$$z = \frac{x - \mu}{\sigma} = \frac{11.98 - 12.0}{.035} = -0.57$$
and
$$z = \frac{x - \mu}{\sigma} = \frac{12.02 - 12.0}{.035} = 0.57$$

Step 4:   Find the probability associated the z-value from the standard normal distribution table (Appendix D)

The probability associated with a z-value = 0.57 from the standard normal table is 0.2157. Likewise, the probability associated with a z-value of -0.57 is 0.2157. These two probabilities are added to get the desired probability as follows:

$$P(11.98 \leq x \leq 12.02) = 0.2157 + 0.2157 = 0.4314$$

Thus, there is slightly more than a .43 chance that a can will contain a fill volume within the desired level.

b. Referring to the answer to part a., we see that since the probability associated with z = 0.57 is 0.2157. This is the probability between z = -.57 and the mean. Therefore, the probability that a can will contain less than 11.98 ounces is 0.5000 – 0.2157 = 0.2843. The manager is also concerned about the probability that a can will contain less than 11.97 ounces, the cut-point used by the NC Department of Weights and Measures. We find this probability by first converting 11.97 ounces to a corresponding z-value as follows:

$$z = \frac{x - \mu}{\sigma} = \frac{11.97 - 12.0}{.035} = -0.86$$

From the standard normal table, the probability associated with z = -.86 is 0.3051. Therefore:

$$P(x < 11.97) = 0.5000 - 0.3051 = 0.1949$$

Thus, as it currently stands, there is a .1949 chance that the company would get reprimanded by the NC Weights and Measures. The manager wants no more than a 0.05 chance of this happening. At issue, is what should the mean fill adjustment be set at? To determine this we first determine the z-value that is associated with a lower tail area equal to 0.05. This would be the same z-value associated with an area between z and the mean equal to .5000 – 0.05 = 0.45. Going to the inside of the standard normal table, we find the z-value to be -1.65 (if you wish to interpolate, then use z = -1.645.)

Next we solve for μ as follows:

$$z = \frac{x - \mu}{\sigma}$$

$$-1.65 = \frac{11.97 - \mu}{0.035}$$

$$\mu = 11.97 + (1.65)(0.035) = 12.03$$

Thus, the manager should adjust the fill setting to 12.03 ounces. For one or a few cans, this increase in fill volume is not an issue for the company. But if they fill tens of thousands of cans per week, the extra Coke product dispensed will impact the bottom line of the company. Instead of adjusting the mean, the company would be better served by figuring out a way of reducing the standard deviation to make the fill volume more consistent.

6.29

a.

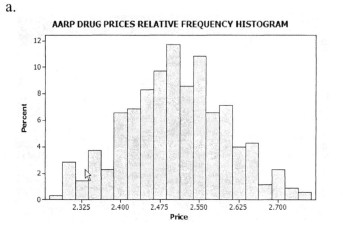

Although the distribution is not perfectly "mound shaped," the histogram appears to be approximately so. Sampling error could easily account for the imperfection.

b.

Descriptive Statistics: Price

```
Variable    Mean    StDev
Price      2.5052   0.0961
```

c. $P(x \leq 2.12) = P\left(z \leq \dfrac{2.12 - 2.51}{0.0961}\right) = P(z \leq -4.06)$.

Since $P(0 \leq z \leq 3.09) = 0.4990$, then $P(z > 3.09) = P(-3.09 < z) = 0.5 - 0.4990 = 0.0010$.

Since $P(z \leq -4.06) < P(-3.09 < z) = 0.0010$, $P(z \leq -4.06) < 0.0010 \approx 0$.

6.31

a.

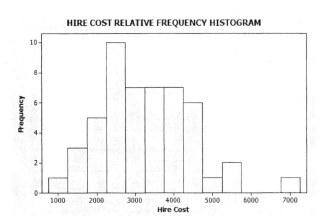

The histogram seems to be "bell shaped" with the exception of three or four observations. These could be due to sampling error.

b.

Descriptive Statistics: Hire Cost

```
Variable    Mean   StDev
Hire Cost   3270   1181
```

c. The $P(2000 < x < 3000) = P\left(\dfrac{2000 - 3270}{1181} < z < \dfrac{3000 - 3270}{1181} \right) =$

$P(-1.08 < z < -0.23) = P(-1.08 \le z \le 0) - P(-0.23 \le z < 0) =$
$P(0 \le z < 1.08) - P(0 \le z \le 0.23) = 0.3599 - 0.0910 = 0.2689.$

d. We wish to find the $P(x > 2500 | 2000 < x < 3000)$.

Using conditional probability, we have

$$\frac{P[(x > 2500) \text{ and } (2000 < x < 3000)]}{P(2000 < x < 3000)} = \frac{P(2500 < x < 3000)}{P(2000 < x < 3000)}.$$

We obtain $P(2500 < x < 3000) = P\left(\dfrac{2500 \cdot 3270}{1181} < z < \dfrac{3000 - 3270}{1181}\right) =$

$P(-0.65 < z < -0.23) = P(-0.65 \le z \le 0) - P(-0.23 \le z < 0) =$
$P(0 \le z < 0.65) - P(0 \le z \le 0.23) = 0.2422 - 0.0910 = 0.1512.$

Then $P(x > 2500 | 2000 < x < 3000) = \dfrac{P(2500 < x < 3000)}{P(2000 < x < 3000)} = \dfrac{0.1512}{0.2689} = 0.5623.$

Section 6-2 Exercises

6.33

a. Step 1: Define the probability density function.

$$f(x) = \frac{1}{b-a} = \frac{1}{9-5} = 0.25 .$$

Step 2: Define the event of interest.
We wish to find $P(5.5 \le x \le 8)$.

Step 3: Calculate the probability.
$P(c \le x \le d) = f(x)(d - c) = 0.25(8 - 5.5) = 0.625.$

b. Step 1: Define the probability density function.

$$f(x) = \frac{1}{b-a} = \frac{1}{9-5} = 0.25 .$$

Step 2: Define the event of interest.
We wish to find $P(x > 7)$.

Step 3: Calculate the probability.
Since x's upper limit is 9, $P(x > 7) = P(7 < x \le 9) = f(x)(d - c) =$
$0.25(9 - 7) = 0.50.$

c. $\mu = \dfrac{b+a}{2} = \dfrac{9+5}{2} = 7 \quad \sigma = \sqrt{\dfrac{(b-a)^2}{12}} = \sqrt{\dfrac{(9-5)^2}{12}} = \sqrt{1.333} = 1.155$

d. $(\mu \pm 2\sigma) = [7 \pm 2(1.155)] = 7 \pm 2.31 = (4.69, 9.31)$. Since the distributions limits are 5 and 9, $P(4.69 \le x \le 9.31) = 1$ or 100%.

6.35

a. Lambda is equal to 1/mean, so $\lambda = 1/1.5 = 0.6667$. The probability that the time between the next two calls is 45 seconds or less is computed by converting the 45 seconds to minutes $(45/60) = 0.75$. Therefore, $a = 0.75$. Probability $(x \le 0.75) = 1 - e^{-(0.6667)(0.75)} = 1 - 0.6065 = 0.3935$

b. In this case $a = 112.5$ seconds which is $112.5/60 = 1.875$ minutes. Probability $(x \ge 112.5 \text{ seconds}) = e^{-\lambda a} = e^{-(0.0.6667)(1.875)} = e^{-1.25} = 0.2865$.

6.37

a. $f(x) = \dfrac{1}{b-a} = \dfrac{1}{30-10} = 0.05$. $P(10 \le x \le 20) = f(x)(d - c) = 0.05(20 - 10) = 0.5$
and $P(15 \le x \le 25) = f(x)(d - c) = 0.05(25 - 15) = 0.5$

Using the Addition Rule for two events $P[(10 \le x \le 20) \text{ or } (15 \le x \le 25)] = P(10 \le x \le 20) + P(15 \le x \le 25) - P[(10 \le x \le 20) \text{ and } (15 \le x \le 25)] = P(10 \le x \le 20) + P(15 \le x \le 25) - P[(15 \le x \le 20)] = 0.5 + 0.5 - 0.05(20 - 15) = 0.75$.

b. $f(x) = \dfrac{1}{b-a} = \dfrac{1}{20-4} = 0.0625$.

For the first quartile
$.0625(Q_1 - 4) = .25$
$Q_1 = 4.25/.0625 = 8$

For the second quartile
$.0625(Q_2 - 4) = .50$
$Q_2 = 4.50/.0625 = 12$

For the third quartile
$.0625(Q_3 - 4) = .75$
$Q_3 = 4.75/.0625 = 16$

c. The mean time between events equals $1/\lambda$. $P(0 \le x \le a) = 1 - e^{-\lambda a}$, so the median (Q_2) is derived from $0.50 = 1 - e^{-\lambda Q_2} = 1 - e^{-\lambda 10}$. Therefore $\lambda = [\ln(1 - 0.50)]/(-10) = 0.069$. So the mean time between events equals $1/\lambda = 1/0.069 = 14.43$.

d. The mean time between events $= 1/\lambda = 0.4$. Therefore, $\lambda = 1/0.4 = 2.5$. The 90th percentile is such that $0.90 = 1 - e^{-2.5x}$. Therefore $x = [\ln(1 - 0.90)]/(-2.5) = 0.92$.

Chapter 6

6.39
Students can use Excel's EXPONDIST function to solve this problem.

a. $\lambda = 1/4000 = .00025$; $P(x<2100) = $ EXPONDIST(2100,0.00025,true) = 0.4084;
    Yes because this is a pretty high probability of a failure at less than 2100.

b. 100,000(0.4084) = 40,840

6.41
a. If buses stop every 20 minutes then the time you will have to wait can be
    described by a uniform distribution with a = 0 and b = 20. To find the
    probability that you will have to wait for 10 minutes or more

$$f(x) = \frac{1}{b-a} = \frac{1}{20-0} = 0.05$$

$P(x > 10) = 1\text{-}P(x \leq 10) = 1 - 0.05(10\text{-}0) = 0.50.$

b. $P(x \leq 6) = 0.05(6\text{-}0) = 0.30$

c. $P\ (8 \leq x \leq 15) = 0.05(15\text{-}8) = 0.35.$

6.43
a. If 15 arrive every 20 minutes on average then 15/20 = 0.75 arrivals per minute.
    $P(x \leq 3) = 1\text{-}\ e^{-\lambda a} = 1\text{-}\ e^{-0.75(3)} = 0.1054.$

b. $P(x \geq 12) = e^{-\lambda a} = e^{-0.75(12)} = 0.00012.$

c. $P(4 \leq x \leq 6) = e^{-0.75(4)} - e^{-0.75(6)} = 0.0498 - 0.0111 = 0.0387.$

6.45
a. In minutes, $f(x) = \dfrac{1}{b-a} = \dfrac{1}{350-320} = 0.033$. More than 10 minutes late would
    mean that the flight time would be more that 337 + 10 = 347 minutes. Therefore,
    we calculate $P(347 \leq x \leq 350) = f(x)(d\text{- }c) = 0.033(350 - 347) = 0.099.$

b. Five minutes early would mean that the flight took 337 – 5 = 332 minutes. So we
    calculate $P(320 \leq x \leq 332) = f(x)(d\text{- }c) = 0.033(332 - 320) = 0.396$

c. $\mu = \dfrac{b+a}{2} = \dfrac{350+320}{2} = 335$.

d. $\sigma^2 = \dfrac{(b-a)^2}{12} = \dfrac{(350-320)^2}{12} = 75$.

6.47

a. The average amount spent $= 1/\lambda = 1{,}250$. Therefore, $\lambda = 1/1250 = 0.0008 =$
   Since $P(0 \le x \le a) = 1 - e^{-\lambda a}$, $P(x > 5{,}000) = 1 - P(0 \le x \le 5{,}000) =$
   $1 - [1 - e^{-0.0008(5000)}] = 0.0183$

b. $P(x > 1{,}250) = 1 - P(0 \le x \le 1{,}250) = 1 - [1 - e^{-0.0008(1250)}] = 0.3679$.

c. For the exponential distribution the average = standard deviation $= 1/\lambda$. Therefore, one standard deviation below the mean $= 1{,}250 - 1{,}250 = 0$. So this exercise is requiring $P(x > 0) = 1$.

6.49

a. Minitab output

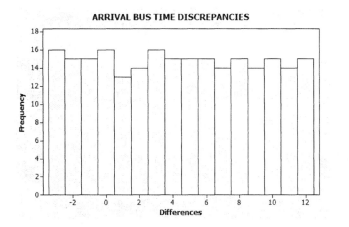

The frequency for each difference seems to be very close to the same, a characteristic of a uniform distribution. Sampling error could account for differences in this sample.

b. The range of values are from -3 to 6. In minutes,

$$f(x) = \dfrac{1}{b-a} = \dfrac{1}{12-(-3)} = 0.067.$$

c. For the students to be late the bus would have to arrive later than 9:05. The discrepancy would then be 9:05 – 8:54 = 11. Therefore, we need to calculate $P(11 < X \leq 12) = f(x)(d - c) = 0.067(12 – 11) = 0.067$.

d. The median and the mean are the same for a continuous uniform distribution. Therefore, the median $= \mu = \dfrac{b+a}{2} = \dfrac{12+(-3)}{2} = 4.5$.

End of Chapter Exercises

6.51

The exponential distribution is defined by a sample parameter, its mean. It is not a symmetric distribution. Example will vary by student.

6.53

A discrete distribution allows you to list the individual outcomes. A continuous distribution can take on any value over some range of values. It is impossible to list these values. One variable of interest that may be considered either continuous or discrete would be dollar values.

6.55

a. The average $= 1/\lambda = 0.5$. Therefore, $\lambda = 1/(0.5) = 2$. Since $P(0 \leq X \leq a) = 1 – e^{-\lambda a}$. $P(X > 1) = 1 - P(0 \leq X \leq 1) = 1 – [1 – e^{-2(1)}] = e^{-2} = 0.1353$.

b. This is a conditional probability $P(X > 1 + 2 | X > 2) =$
$$\dfrac{P[(X > 3) \text{ and } (X > 2)]}{P(X > 2)} = \dfrac{P(X > 3)}{P(X > 2)} = \dfrac{1 - [1 - e^{-2(3)}]}{1 - [1 - e^{-2(2)}]} = \dfrac{e^{-2(3)}}{e^{-2(2)}} = e^{-2} = 0.1353.$$ So we see that the exponential distribution does have a "memoryless" property.

6.57

Machine #1: $P(11.9 \leq x \leq 12.0) = P\left(\dfrac{11.9 - 11.9}{0.07} \leq z \leq \dfrac{12.0 - 11.9}{0.07}\right) =$

$P(0 \leq z \leq 1.43) = 0.4236$.

Machine #2: $P(11.9 \leq x \leq 12.0) = P\left(\dfrac{11.9 - 12.0}{0.05} \leq z \leq \dfrac{12.0 - 12.0}{0.05}\right) =$

$P(-2 \leq z \leq 0) = P(0 \leq z \leq 2) = 0.4772$.

There is a larger probability of producing acceptable amounts of dispensed liquid with Machine #2. It should be selected.

6.59

   a. The range is $0.25 \pm 0.10 = (0.15, 0.35)$. We calculate $f(x) = 1/(b - a) = 1/(0.35 - 0.15) = 5$.

   b. "More than 0.05 of an inch below the mean" means less than 0.20. Therefore, $P(0.15 \le x \le 0.20) = f(x)(d - c) = 5(0.20 - 0.15) = 0.25$.

   c. "More than 0.075 above the mean" means more than $0.25 + 0.075 = 0.325$. Therefore, $P(x > 0.325) = P(0.325 \le x \le 0.35) = f(x)(d - c) = 5(0.35 - 0.325) = 0.125$.

   d. $P(x > 0.325 | x > 0.2) =$
$$\frac{P[(x > 0.325) \text{ and } (x > 0.2)]}{P(x > 0.2)} = \frac{P(x > 0.325)}{P(x > 0.2)} = \frac{0.125}{0.75} = 0.167$$

6.61

   $\lambda = 12/\text{hour} = 0.2$ per minutes; $P(x<4) = 1 - e^{-(.2)(4)} = 1 - 0.4493 = 0.5507$

6.63

   a. $P(5.85 < x < 6.15) = P[(5.85 - 6)/0.1 < z < (6.15 - 6)/0.1] = P(-1.5 < z < 1.5) = 2(0.4332) = 0.8664$; since this is less than 99% Bryce Brothers should not purchase this machine.

   b. for 99% chance z would be ± 2.575
      $2.575 = (6.15 - 6)/\text{standard deviation}$; standard deviation = 0.058 inch

6.65

   a. $P(x < 10) = P(z < (10 - 14.25)/2.92) = P(z < -1.46) = 0.5 - 0.4279 = 0.0721$

   b. Since the core is 3" you need to make sure that this is not more than 32% of the diameter of the log. To determine this $3/0.32 = 9.375$. This allows you to have a log with a diameter of 9.375

      $P(x < 9.375) = P(z < (9.375 - 14.25)/2.92) = P(z < -1.67) = 0.5 - 0.4525 = 0.0475$

6.67

   a. Minitab output

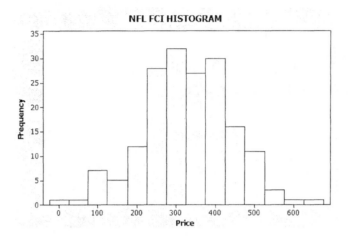

The histogram seems to be "bell shaped" with the exception of a few observations. These could be due to sampling error.

   b. Minitab output:

Descriptive Statistics: Price

```
Variable    Mean    StDev
Price     329.82   112.41
```

   c. Minitab output:

Inverse Cumulative Distribution Function

```
Normal with mean = 329.82 and standard deviation = 112.41

P( X <= x )        x
       0.9   473.879
```

   d. Minitab output:

Cumulative Distribution Function

```
Normal with mean = 329.82 and standard deviation = 112.41

  x    P( X <= x )
347       0.560735
```

So 347 is the 56th percentile.

6.69

a.

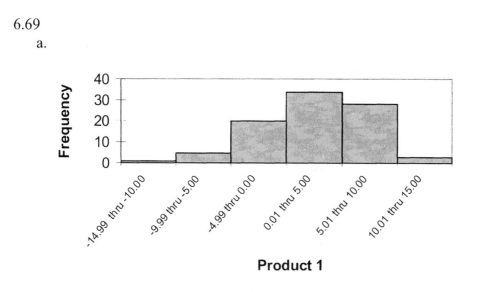

Product 1

It does appear that the distribution is approximately normally distributed.

b. Students can use Excel's descriptive statistics to determine the mean and standard deviation.

Product # 1	
Mean	2.452747253
Standard Error	0.500820671
Median	2.6
Mode	0.9
Standard Deviation	4.777524711
Sample Variance	22.82474237
Kurtosis	1.325755364
Skewness	-0.643107821
Range	29.2
Minimum	-15.5
Maximum	13.7
Sum	223.2
Count	91

c. Remember that positive values indicate weight gain so students need to determine the Probability that the weight loss is more than negative 12.

$$P(x<-12) = P(z < (-12 - 2.4527)/4.7775) = P(z < -3.03) = 0.5 - 0.4988 = 0.0012$$

d. No, this would not be an appropriate claim. The probability of losing 12 or more pounds is only 0.12%. In fact the average for this plan in a weight gain of 2.45 pounds.

Chapter 6

6.71

Using Excel to find the descriptive statistics:

Garbage Truck Weights	
Mean	42260.64
Standard Error	278.2153265
Median	42325.5
Mode	40010
Standard Deviation	3934.55888
Sample Variance	15480753.58

a. $P(x > 46,000) = P(z > (46000 - 42260.64)/3934.55888) = P(z > 0.95) = 0.5 - 0.3289 = 0.1711$

b. In the sample 35 of 200 weighed over 46,000 which is 0.175; this implies that the distribution is nearly normally distributed.

c. $P(x < 38,000) = P(z < ((38,000 - 42,260.64)/3934.56) = P(z < -1.08) = .50 - .3599 = .1401$

Chapter 7 Solutions

When applicable, selected problems in each section will be done following the appropriate step-by-step procedures outlined in the corresponding sections of the chapter. Other problems will provide key points and the answers to the questions, but all answers can be arrived at using the appropriate steps.

Section 7-1 Exercises

7.1

The following steps can be used to determine the sampling error:

Step 1: Determine the population mean.

The population mean is computed as follows:

$$\mu = \frac{\sum x}{N} = \frac{273}{24} = 11.38$$

Step 2: Compute the sample mean.

$$\bar{x} = \frac{\sum x}{n} = \frac{61}{6} = 10.17$$

Step 3: Compute the sampling error.

$$\text{Sampling error} = \bar{x} - \mu = 10.17 - 11.38 = -1.21$$

7.3

Step 1: The population mean of 125 is given

Step 2: Compute the sample mean using Equation 7-3

$$\bar{x} = (103 + 123 + 99 + 107 + 121 + 100 + 100 + 99)/8 = 852/8 = 106.5$$

Step 3: Compute the sampling error using Equation 7-1

$$\text{Sampling Error} = \bar{x} - \mu = 106.5 - 125 = -18.50$$

The sample of eight has a sampling error of -18.50. The sample has a smaller mean than the population as a whole.

7.5

a. Step 1: Determine the population mean using Equation 7-2:

$$\mu = \frac{\sum x_i}{N} = \frac{375}{15} = 25.$$

Step 2: Compute the sample mean using Equation 7-3:

$$\bar{x} = \frac{\sum x_i}{n} = \frac{196}{8} = 24.5.$$

Step 3: Compute the sampling error using Equation 7-1:
Sampling error = $\bar{x} - \mu$ = 24.5 – 25 = -0.5.

b. The 8 largest observations are

| 24 | 26 | 29 | 29 | 32 | 34 | 35 | 38 |

The mean of these data points is $\bar{x} = \dfrac{\sum x_i}{n} = \dfrac{247}{8} = 30.875.$

This produces a sampling error of $\bar{x} - \mu$ = 30.875 – 25 = 5.875.

c. The 8 Smallest observations are

| 13 | 17 | 17 | 17 | 18 | 22 | 24 | 24 |

The mean of these data points is $\bar{x} = \dfrac{\sum x_i}{n} = \dfrac{152}{8} = 19.$

This produces a sampling error of $\bar{x} - \mu$ = 19 – 25 = -6.

7.7

a.

Step 1: Compute the population mean using Equation 7-2.

μ= 10+14+32+9+34+19+31+24+33+11+14+30+6+27+33+32+28+30+
10+31+19+13+6+35)/24 = 531/24 = 22.125

Step 2: Compute the sample mean using Equation 7-3

$\bar{x}$ = (32+19+6+11+10+19+28+9+13+33)/10 = 180/10 = 18

Step 3: Compute the sampling error using Equation 7-1

Sampling Error = $\bar{x} - \mu = 18 - 22.125 = -4.125$

The sample of ten has a sampling error of -4.125. The sample has a smaller mean than the population as a whole.

For parts (b) and (c), the population rank order is shown below.

6	6	9	10	10	11	13	14
14	19	19	24	27	28	30	30
31	31	32	32	33	33	34	35

b. In order to calculate the extreme sampling error, the data needs to be rank-ordered from lowest to highest. Use the rank-order table shown above. Calculate the sample mean for the 6 smallest values and the 6 largest values. Compute the sampling error for each.

Lowest Possible Sample Mean = $(6+6+9+10+10+11)/6 = 52/6 = 8.667$

The population mean is 22.125 from part (a).

Sampling Error = $8.667 - 22.125 = -13.458$

Highest Possible Sample Mean = $(32+32+33+33+34+35)/6 = 199/6 = 33.167$

Sampling Error = $33.167 - 22.125 = 11.042$

The range of extreme sampling error for a sample of size n = 6 is -13.458 to 11.042.

c. In order to calculate the extreme sampling error, the data needs to be rank-ordered from lowest to highest. Use the rank-order table shown above. Calculate the sample mean for the 12 smallest values and the 12 largest values. Compute the sampling error for each.

Lowest Possible Sample Mean = $(6+6+9+10+10+11+13+14+14+19+19+24)/12 = 155/12 = 12.917$

The population mean is 22.125 from part (a).

Sampling Error = $12.917 - 22.125 = -9.208$

Highest Possible Sample Mean =
(27+28+30+30+31+31+32+32+33+33+34+35)/12 = 376/12 = 31.333

Sampling Error = 31.333 – 22.125 = 9.208

The range of extreme sampling error for a sample of size n = 12 is –9.208 to 9.208.

As the sample size increases, the range of sampling error decreases.

7.9

a. μ = 35,802/25 = 1,432.08

b. $\bar{x}$ = 7,596/5 = 1,591.2
Sampling error = 1,591.2 – 1,432.08 = 87.12

c. The population rank-order is shown below

1093	1134	1216	1291	1347
1350	1362	1362	1365	1371
1378	1410	1446	1447	1453
1480	1500	1522	1532	1534
1552	1575	1601	1647	1834

Lowest Possible Sample Mean = 8,793/7 = 1,256.143

Sampling Error = 1,256.143 – 1,432.08 = -175.937

Highest Possible Sample Mean = 11,275/7 = 1,610.714

Sampling Error = 1,610.714 – 1,432.08 = 178.634

The range of extreme sampling error for a sample of size n = 7 is -175.937 to 178.634.

7.11

$$\mu = \frac{\sum x}{N} = \frac{18{,}430}{30} = 614.33$$

a. The smallest 6 values are:

395 400 405 415 450 455

$$\bar{x} = \frac{\sum x}{n} = \frac{2{,}520}{6} = 420.0$$

The sampling error = 420.0 - 614.33 = -194.33

The largest 6 values are:

995 905 800 780 780 780

$$\bar{x} = \frac{\sum x}{n} = \frac{5{,}040}{6} = 840.0$$

The sampling error = 840.0 – 614.33 = 225.67

The range in sampling error for a sample of size 6 is –194.33 to 225.67.

b. The smallest 10 values are:

395 400 405 415 450 455 490 495 495 500

$$\bar{x} = \frac{\sum x}{n} = \frac{4{,}500}{10} = 450$$

The sampling error = 450 – 614.33 = -164.33

The largest 10 values are:

995 905 800 780 780 780 750 750 700 690

$$\bar{x} = \frac{\sum x}{n} = \frac{7,930}{10} = 793$$

The sampling error = $793 - 614.33 = 178.67$

The range in sampling error for a sample of size 10 is -164.33 to 178.67

Larger sample sizes will yield a lower range in the potential sampling error.

7.13

Step 1: Determine the population mean:
$\mu = 6.16$ (from CDC)

Step 2: Compute the sample mean using Equation 7-3:
$$\bar{x} = \frac{\sum x_i}{n} = \frac{340}{50} = 6.8.$$

Step 3: Compute the sampling error using Equation 7-1:
Sampling error = $\bar{x} - \mu = 6.8 - 6.16 = 0.64$.

7.15

The following steps can be used to determine the sampling error:
Step 1: Determine the population mean.
The population mean is computed as follows:

$$\mu = \frac{\sum x}{N} = \frac{178}{24} = 7.4$$

Step 2: Compute the sample mean.

$$\bar{x} = \frac{\sum x}{n} = \frac{26.2}{5} = 5.24$$

Step 3: Compute the sampling error.
Sampling error = $\bar{x} - \mu = 5.24 - 7.4 = -2.16$

The sample mean is 2.16 lower than the population mean of 7.4 percent. Thus, if the advisor uses this sample of clients to try the investment program, he must realize that the historical average for these clients has been less than the historical average for the population of 24 clients. This might adversely affect the trial of the new program.

7.17

   a. The population mean closing value of the Dow is:

$$\mu = \frac{\sum x}{N} = \frac{13,364.664}{1,345} = 9,936.55$$

   b. Student answers will vary depending the sample selected. For example using Excel, students can go to *Tools-Data Analysis-Sampling*. Next, define the input range (F2-F1346) Then select *Random* and specify the number of samples as 50. Designate an output location. One possible result gives the following sample values:

10578.24	10427.67	8433.71	9750.95	10472.84
11164.84	9487	10803.16	9624.64	10326.48
8432.61	9586.29	10170.5	8862.57	8358.95
10676.45	9997.49	9653.39	9389.48	10064.75
10668.72	11238.78	10205.2	10416.25	10867.01
10481.47	8602.61	8274.09	10238.8	9200.05
8842.62	9763.96	10609.62	8494.27	10435.16
10676.45	9985.18	9471.55	8197.94	10151.13
9862.12	7986.02	11032.99	10479.57	7837.86
8862.57	9972.83	8571.6	9791.09	9687.84

The sample mean for this sample of n = 50 closing values is:

$$\bar{x} = \frac{\sum x}{n} = \frac{487,167.4}{50} = 9,743.34$$

Based on this particular sample, the sampling error is:

$$\text{Sampling error} = \bar{x} - \mu = 9,743.34 - 9,936.55 = -193.21$$

c. Again student responses are going to different because each one will select a different sample. Suppose the following sample of n =100 closing prices is selected.

10539.06	10412.49	8601.69	11055.64	9517.26
8473.41	10219.52	10093.67	10485.18	11055.64
9659.13	10525.37	10472.84	10345.95	10213.22
10379.58	9397.51	9412.45	10810.05	9605.85
10550.24	10690.13	10216.08	10478.16	10314
10216.73	10649.81	10626.85	9310.56	8312.69
10229.5	9981.58	10963.8	10847.37	9624.64
10284.46	7945.13	10584.37	8191.29	10241.26
10142.98	8531.57	7859.71	10511.17	10334.73
10543.22	8265.45	10635.25	9747.64	10098.63
9894.45	9240.86	10272.27	10310.95	10377.95
10443.81	9645.4	9711.86	10252.68	9706.12
8013.29	9930.82	10881.2	7717.19	9177.15
10481.47	10693.71	7524.06	10549.57	10345.95
10456.96	10469.84	10549.57	10469.84	10212.97
10812.75	10957.42	10868.76	9608	10592.21
9925.25	8659.97	9811.15	11114.27	8283.7
10229.15	10416.67	8919.01	9862.12	8337.65
10085.14	10635.56	10422.27	10276.9	10461.2
11119.86	10054.39	9709.79	8306.35	10241.12

The sample mean for this sample of n = 100 closing values is:

$$\bar{x} = \frac{\sum x}{n} = \frac{995,245.1}{100} = 9,952.45$$

Based on this particular sample, the sampling error is:

$$\text{Sampling error} = \bar{x} - \mu = 9,952.45 - 9,936.55 = 15.90$$

d. Student answers will vary depending on the sample selected. Suppose our sample of n = 10 closing prices contained the values:

11233.23
10219.34
10248.08
10495.55
10866.98
10803.16
10470.23
10912.62
9954.55
10629.66

The sample mean for this sample of n = 100 closing values is:

$$\bar{x} = \frac{\sum x}{n} = \frac{105,833.4}{10} = 10,583.4$$

Based on this particular sample, the sampling error is:

Sampling error = $\bar{x} - \mu = 10,583.4 - 9,936.55 = 646.85$

e. Student reports will vary depending on individual results. For the samples we selected, we find that the sampling error was greater when the sample size was smallest and the sampling error was smallest when the largest sample size was used. This is consistent with what we would expect to occur in the long run.

7.19

a. The first step is compute the sample mean based on the data in the file called Badke, Either Excel or Minitab can be used to get:

$$\bar{x} = \frac{\sum x}{n} = \frac{\$2,629}{166} = \$15.84$$

Because the consultant claimed that the mean would be $20.00, we use that as the population mean. If that number is correct, then this sample has a sampling error of:

Sampling error = $\bar{x} - \mu = \$15.84 - \$20.00 = -\$4.16$

b. It is possible that this sample constitutes a random sample. However, there is no was to be assured of that. We don't have anyway of knowing if the people who contributed are a random selection of all those who would eventually contribute. We don't know what process was used to distribute the letter and materials in the first place. However, that being said, the computation of sampling error does not depend on whether the sample is a random sample. Random and non-random samples can produce sampling error and the error is computed the same way.

7.21

a. Either Excel or Minitab could be used to compute the sample mean potential value for each log diameter. We have used Excel's pivot table feature to get the following:

Diameter	Mean Value
6	$7.90
7	$11.13
8	$16.55
9	$21.54
10	$28.87
11	$35.40
12	$41.80
13	$48.54
14	$58.86
15	$65.97
16	$76.48
17	$85.33
18	$93.63
19	$105.01
20	$109.89
21	$120.31

b. Assuming that the sample means calculated in part a. are based on a random sample from the population of all logs to be used by the company, there is no way to predict with any certainty what the sampling error is. To do so would require that we know the true population mean. Also, we cannot predict with accuracy whether the sample means are higher or lower than the true population mean.

Section 7-2 Exercises

7.23

Because the population is normally distributed, the sampling distribution for the mean will also be normally distributed. Thus, the following steps can be used to answer this question:

Step 1: Determine the sample mean.
    The sample mean is given to be $\bar{x} = 2,100$

Step 2: Define the sampling distribution.
    The sampling distribution will be normally distributed and will have
    $\mu_{\bar{x}} = \mu = 2000$ and a standard deviation equal to $\sigma_{\bar{x}} = \dfrac{\sigma}{\sqrt{n}} = \dfrac{230}{\sqrt{8}} = 81.32$

Step 3: Define the event of interest.
    We are interested in the following:
    $P(\bar{x} > 2,100) = ?$

Step 4: Convert the sample mean to a standardized z value.

$$z = \frac{\bar{x} - \mu}{\frac{\sigma}{\sqrt{n}}} = \frac{2,100 - 2,000}{\frac{230}{\sqrt{8}}} = \frac{100}{81.32} = 1.23$$

Step 5: Use the standard normal distribution to find the desired probability. The probability associated with a z-value of 1.23 from the standard normal table is 0.3907. Then
$$P(\bar{x} > 2,100) = 0.5000 - 0.3907 = 0.1093$$

Thus, there is slightly more than a 0.10 chance that a sample mean exceeding 2,100 would come from this population if a sample size of n = 8 is selected.

7.25

Step 1: Compute the sample mean. The sample mean is given as 1325.

Step 2: Define the sampling distribution. Although the population is not normally distributed the sample size is sufficiently large therefore the sampling distribution will be approximately normal with

$$\mu_{\bar{x}} = \mu = 1,250 \text{ and } \sigma_{\bar{x}} = \frac{\sigma}{\sqrt{n}} = \frac{400}{\sqrt{64}} = 50$$

Step 3: Define the event of interest.
    The event of interest is: $P(\bar{x} < 1325)$

Step 4: Use the standard normal distribution to find the probability of interest. Convert the sample mean to a corresponding z-value:

$$z = \frac{\bar{x} - \mu}{\frac{\sigma}{\sqrt{n}}} = \frac{1325 - 1250}{\frac{400}{\sqrt{64}}} = 1.5 \,.$$

From the standard normal table the probability associated with z = 1.50 = 0.4332. Therefore, $P(\bar{x} < 1325) = P(z < 1.5) = 0.5 + 0.4332 = 0.9332$.

7.27

Step 1: Compute the sample mean. The sample mean is $\bar{x} = \dfrac{\Sigma x}{n} = \dfrac{855}{9} = 95$

Step 2: Define the sampling distribution. The population is normally distributed with a mean of 100 and a standard deviation of 20. Therefore, the sampling distribution is also normally distributed with

$$\mu_{\bar{x}} = \mu = 100 \text{ and } \sigma_{\bar{x}} = \dfrac{\sigma}{\sqrt{n}} = \dfrac{20}{\sqrt{9}} = 6.6667$$

Step 3: Define the event of interest.

The event of interest is: $P(\bar{x} < 95)$

Step 4: Use the standard normal distribution to find the probability of interest. Convert the sample mean to a corresponding z-value:

$$z = \dfrac{\bar{x} - \mu}{\dfrac{\sigma}{\sqrt{n}}} = \dfrac{95 - 100}{\dfrac{20}{\sqrt{9}}} = -0.75 .$$

From the standard normal table the probability associated with z = -0.75 = 0.2734. Therefore, $P(\bar{x} < 95) = P(z < -0.75) = 0.5 - 0.2734 = 0.2266$.

7.29

a. $P(\bar{x} > \bar{x}_o) = P\left(z > \dfrac{\bar{x}_o - \mu}{\sigma / \sqrt{n}} \right)$. So $P(\bar{x} > 37) = P\left(z > \dfrac{37 - 40}{13 / \sqrt{49}} \right) = P(z > -1.62) =$

$0.5 + P(0 \le z \le 1.62) = 0.5 + 0.4474 = 0.9474.$

b. $P(\bar{x} \le 43) = P\left(z \le \dfrac{43 - 40}{13 / \sqrt{49}} \right) = P(z \le 1.62) = 0.5 + P(0 \le z \le 1.62) = 0.5 + 0.4474$

$= 0.9474.$

c. $P(37 < \bar{x} < 43) = P\left(\dfrac{37 - 40}{13 / \sqrt{49}} \le z \le \dfrac{43 - 40}{13 / \sqrt{49}}\right) = P(-1.62 \le z \le 1.62) =$

$2P(0 \le z \le 1.62) = 2(0.4474) = 0.8948.$

d. $P(43 < \bar{x} < 45) = P\left(\dfrac{43 - 40}{13 / \sqrt{49}} \le z \le \dfrac{45 - 40}{13 / \sqrt{49}}\right) = P(1.62 \le z \le 2.69) =$

$P(0 \le z \le 2.69) - P(0 \le z \le 1.62) = 0.4964 - 0.4474 = 0.0490.$

e. $P(\bar{x} \le 35) = P\left(z \le \dfrac{35 - 40}{13 / \sqrt{49}}\right) = P(z \le -2.69) = 0.5 - P(0 \le z \le 2.69) = 0.5 -$

$0.4964 = 0.0036.$

7.31

a. Step 1: Compute the sample mean. In this case there are two sample means: $\bar{x} = 70$ and $\bar{x} = 80$.

Step 2: Define the sampling distribution. The population is approximately normally distributed with a mean of 75 and a standard deviation of 10. Therefore, the sampling distribution is also approximately normally distributed with

$$\mu_{\bar{x}} = \mu = 75 \text{ and } \sigma_{\bar{x}} = \frac{\sigma}{\sqrt{n}} = \frac{10}{\sqrt{1}} = 10.$$

Step 3: Define the event of interest.

The event of interest is: $P(70 \le \bar{x} \le 80)$

Step 4: Use the standard normal distribution to find the probability of interest. Convert the sample means to corresponding z-values:

$$z = \frac{\bar{x} - \mu}{\dfrac{\sigma}{\sqrt{n}}} = \frac{70 - 75}{\dfrac{10}{\sqrt{1}}} = -0.50, \text{ and } \frac{\bar{x} - \mu}{\dfrac{\sigma}{\sqrt{n}}} = \frac{80 - 75}{\dfrac{10}{\sqrt{1}}} = 0.50.$$

From the standard normal table the probability associated with z = -0.50 = 0.1915 and the probability associated with z = 0.50 = 0.1915.

Therefore, $P(70 \leq \bar{x} \leq 80) = P(-0.50 \leq z \leq 0.50) = 0.1915 + 0.1915 = 0.3830$.

b. Step 1: Compute the sample mean. In this case there are two sample means: $\bar{x} = 70$ and $\bar{x} = 80$.

Step 2: Define the sampling distribution.
   The population is approximately normally distributed with a mean of 75 and a standard deviation of 10. Therefore, the sampling distribution is also approximately normally distributed with

$$\mu_{\bar{x}} = \mu = 75 \text{ and } \sigma_{\bar{x}} = \frac{\sigma}{\sqrt{n}} = \frac{10}{\sqrt{16}} = 2.5.$$

Step 3: Define the event of interest.
   The event of interest is: $P(70 \leq \bar{x} \leq 80)$

Step 4: Use the standard normal distribution to find the probability of interest. Convert the sample means to corresponding z-values:

$$z = \frac{\bar{x} - \mu}{\dfrac{\sigma}{\sqrt{n}}} = \frac{70 - 75}{\dfrac{10}{\sqrt{16}}} = -2.00, \text{ and } \frac{\bar{x} - \mu}{\dfrac{\sigma}{\sqrt{n}}} = \frac{80 - 75}{\dfrac{10}{\sqrt{16}}} = 2.00.$$

From the standard normal table the probability associated with z = -2.00 = 0.4772 and the probability associated with z = 2.00 = 0.4772.

Therefore, $P(70 \leq \bar{x} \leq 80) = P(-2.00 \leq z \leq 2.00) = 0.4722 + 0.4722 = 0.9444$.

c. Step 1: Compute the sample mean. In this case there are two sample means: $\bar{x} = 70$ and $\bar{x} = 80$.

Step 2: Define the sampling distribution.

The population is approximately normally distributed with a mean of 75 and a standard deviation of 9. Therefore, the sampling distribution is also approximately normally distributed with

$$\mu_{\bar{x}} = \mu = 75 \text{ and } \sigma_{\bar{x}} = \frac{\sigma}{\sqrt{n}} = \frac{9}{\sqrt{16}} = 2.25.$$

Step 3: Define the event of interest.

The event of interest is: $P(70 \le \bar{x} \le 80)$

Step 4: Use the standard normal distribution to find the probability of interest. Convert the sample means to corresponding z-values:

$$z = \frac{\bar{x} - \mu}{\frac{\sigma}{\sqrt{n}}} = \frac{70 - 75}{\frac{9}{\sqrt{16}}} = -2.22, \text{ and } \frac{\bar{x} - \mu}{\frac{\sigma}{\sqrt{n}}} = \frac{80 - 75}{\frac{9}{\sqrt{16}}} = 2.22.$$

From the standard normal table the probability associated with z = -2.22 = 0.4868 and the probability associated with z = 2.22 = 0.4868.

Therefore, $P(70 \le \bar{x} \le 80) = P(-2.22 \le z \le 2.22) = 0.4868 + 0.4868 = 0.9736$.

7.33   a.

Step 1:   Compute the sample mean. The sample mean is $\bar{x} = \frac{\Sigma x}{n} = \frac{450}{36} = 12.5$.

Step 2:   Define the sampling distribution.
If the population is approximately normally distributed with a mean of 12 and a standard deviation of 3, the sampling distribution is also approximately normally distributed with

$$\mu_{\bar{x}} = \mu = 12 \text{ and } \sigma_{\bar{x}} = \frac{\sigma}{\sqrt{n}} = \frac{3}{\sqrt{36}} = 0.50.$$

Step 3: Define the event of interest.
The event of interest is: $P(\bar{x} \le 12.5)$

Step 4: Use the standard normal distribution to find the probability of interest. Convert the sample means to corresponding z-values:

$$z = \frac{\bar{x} - \mu}{\frac{\sigma}{\sqrt{n}}} = \frac{12.5 - 12}{\frac{3}{\sqrt{36}}} = 1.00.$$

From the standard normal table the probability associated with z = 1.00 = 0.3413.

Therefore, $P(\bar{x} \leq 12.5) = P(z \leq 1.00) = 0.50 + 0.3413 = 0.8413$.

b.
Step 1: Compute the sample mean.
The sample mean is $\bar{x} = \frac{\Sigma x}{n} = \frac{450}{36} = 12.5$.

Step 2: Define the sampling distribution.
If the population is approximately normally distributed with a mean of 12 and a standard deviation of 3, the sampling distribution is also approximately normally distributed with

$$\mu_{\bar{x}} = \mu = 12 \text{ and } \sigma_{\bar{x}} = \frac{\sigma}{\sqrt{n}} = \frac{3}{\sqrt{36}} = 0.50.$$

Step 3: Define the event of interest.
The event of interest is: $P(\bar{x} > 12.5)$

Step 4: Use the standard normal distribution to find the probability of interest. Convert the sample means to corresponding z-values:

$$z = \frac{\bar{x} - \mu}{\frac{\sigma}{\sqrt{n}}} = \frac{12.5 - 12}{\frac{3}{\sqrt{36}}} = 1.00.$$

From the standard normal table the probability associated with z = 1.00 = 0.3413.

Therefore, $P(\bar{x} > 12.5) = P(z > 1.00) = 0.50 - 0.3413 = 0.1587$.

c. Although the population of returns processed daily is not normally distributed, the sample size is sufficiently large so that the sampling distribution of $\bar{x}$ is normally distributed. In other words, the Central Limit Theorem applies here because the sample size, n=36, is sufficiently large so that the distribution of sample means $\bar{x}$ will be approximately normally distributed.

7.35

The following steps can be used to answer this question:
Step 1: Determine the sample mean.
      The sample mean was calculated to be 4.2 minutes

Step 2: Define the sampling distribution.
      The sampling distribution will be normally distributed and will have $\mu_{\bar{x}} = \mu = 3.5$ and a standard deviation equal to

$$\sigma_x = \frac{\sigma}{\sqrt{n}} = \frac{1.0}{\sqrt{25}} = 0.2$$

Step 3: Define the event of interest.
      We are interested in the following:
$$P(\bar{x} > 4.2) = ?$$

Step 4: Convert the sample mean to a standardized z value.

$$z = \frac{\bar{x} - \mu}{\dfrac{\sigma}{\sqrt{n}}} = \frac{4.2 - 3.5}{\dfrac{1}{\sqrt{25}}} = \frac{0.7}{0.2} = 3.5$$

Step 5: Use the standard normal distribution to find the desired probability.
      The probability associated with a z-value of 3.5 from the standard normal table is approximately 0.4989. Then

$$P(\bar{x} \geq 4.2) = 0.5000 - 0.4989 = 0.0011$$

Thus, there virtually no chance that a random sample of size 25 could produce a sample mean equal to 4.2 or greater if the sample came from a population with mean equal to 3.5 and standard deviation equal to 1.0. Either sample was not randomly selected, or the population parameters are misstated. The manager should be concerned that the waiting time has increased.

7.37

a. Step 1: Compute the mean for this sample.

$$\bar{x} = \frac{\sum x_i}{n} = \frac{1570}{100} = 15.7.$$

Step 2: Define the sampling distribution:
Theorems 7-1 and 7-2 indicate the distribution is normally distributed with

$$\mu_{\bar{x}} = \mu = 14.3 \text{ and } \sigma_{\bar{x}} = \frac{\sigma}{\sqrt{n}} = \frac{5}{\sqrt{100}} = 0.5$$

Step 3: Define the event of interest.
$$\bar{x} \geq 15.7$$

Step 4: Convert the sample mean to a standardized z-value, using Equation 7-4.

$$z = \frac{\bar{x} - \mu}{\frac{\sigma}{\sqrt{n}}} = \frac{15.7 - 14.3}{\frac{5}{\sqrt{100}}} = 2.80$$

Step 5: Use the standard normal distribution table to determine the desired probability.

$$P(\bar{x} \geq 15.7) = P(z \geq 2.80) = 0.5 - P(0 \leq z \leq 2.80) = 0.5 - 0.4974 = 0.0026.$$

b. Step 1: Compute the mean for this sample.
$$\bar{x} = 16.8 \text{ by specification.}$$

Step 2: Define the sampling distribution:
Theorem 7-1 indicates that the distribution is normally distributed with

$$\mu_{\bar{x}} = \mu = 14.3 \text{ and } \sigma_{\bar{x}} = \frac{\sigma}{\sqrt{n}} = \frac{5}{\sqrt{100}} = 0.5$$

Step 3: Define the event of interest.
$$\bar{x} > 16.8$$

Step 4: Convert the sample mean to a standardized z-value, using Equation 7-4.
$$z = \frac{\bar{x} - \mu}{\frac{\sigma}{\sqrt{n}}} = \frac{16.8 - 14.3}{\frac{5}{\sqrt{100}}} = 5.0$$

Step 5: Use the standard normal distribution table to determine the desired probability.
The standard normal distribution table in Appendix D does not show z-values as high as 5.00. This implies that $P(Z \geq 5.00) = 0$. Therefore, $P(\bar{x} \geq 15.7) = P(z \geq 5.00) = 0$.

c. Step 1: Compute the mean for this sample.
The forecast using the present system estimates that the 2008 F-150 will average 16.8 mpg. A reduction of 10 to 20% would indicate that the average would be somewhere between 15.12 [= 16.8 – 0.10(16.8) = 16.8(0.90)] and 13.44 [= 16.8(0.80)].

Step 2: Define the sampling distribution:
Theorems 7-1 and 7-2 indicate the distribution is normally distributed with

$$\mu_{\bar{x}} = \mu = 14.3 \text{ and } \sigma_{\bar{x}} = \frac{\sigma}{\sqrt{n}} = \frac{5}{\sqrt{100}} = 0.5$$

Step 3: Define the event of interest.
$13.44 \leq \bar{x} \leq 15.12$

Step 4: Convert the sample mean to a standardized z-value, using Equation 7-4.

$$z = \frac{\bar{x} - \mu}{\frac{\sigma}{\sqrt{n}}} = \frac{15.12 - 14.3}{\frac{5}{\sqrt{100}}} = 1.64 \text{ and } z = \frac{\bar{x} - \mu}{\frac{\sigma}{\sqrt{n}}} = \frac{13.44 - 14.3}{\frac{5}{\sqrt{100}}} = -1.72$$

Step 5: Use the standard normal distribution table to determine the desired probability.

$P(13.44 \leq \bar{x} \leq 15.12) = P(-1.72 \leq z \leq 1.64) = P(0 \leq z \leq 1.72) + P(0 \leq z \leq 1.64) = 0.4573 + 0.4495 = 0.9068$.

7.39

The sample mean computed from the 60 fill volumes is:

$$\bar{x} = \frac{\sum x}{n} = \frac{718.39}{60} = 11.97$$

The sample mean is 11.97 ounces. Now we want to find:

$$P(\bar{x} \leq 11.97) = ?$$

To do this, we standardize as follows:

$$z = \frac{\bar{x} - \mu}{\frac{\sigma}{\sqrt{n}}} = \frac{11.97 - 12}{\frac{0.05}{\sqrt{60}}} = -4.65$$

Thus, the sample mean is 4.65 standard errors below the desired 12 ounce population mean. From the standard normal distribution table, the probability associated with z=-4.65 is approximately 0.5000. Thus:

$$P(\bar{x} \leq 11.97) = 0.5000 - 0.5000 = 0.0$$

Therefore, there is essentially no chance that a sample mean of 11.97 ounces or less would occur if the population mean is 12 ounces and the population standard deviation is 0.05 ounces.

7.41

a. We can use Excel's *Tools –Data Analysis- Descriptive Statistics* option to find the population parameters shown as follows:

Age	
Mean	55.68
Standard Error	0.30
Median	56
Mode	56
Standard Deviation	6.75
Sample Variance	45.52
Kurtosis	0.43
Skewness	0.20
Range	42
Minimum	39
Maximum	81
Sum	27617
Count	496

Thus, the population mean is 55.68 years with a population standard deviation equal to 6.75 years.

b. Student answers will vary depending on what sample is selected. One possible sample of 12 ages is the following:

63
61
55
59
55
57
52
46
49
51
47
60

The sample mean for this sample is:

$$\bar{x} = \frac{\sum x}{n} = \frac{655}{12} = 54.58$$

The sampling error for this sample is:

$$\bar{x} - \mu = 54.58 - 55.68 = -1.10$$

c. We are asked to find the probability of a sample mean as large or larger than the one we found. This is:

$$P(\bar{x} \geq 54.58) = ?$$

To find this probability, we standardize as follows:

$$z = \frac{\bar{x} - \mu}{\frac{\sigma}{\sqrt{n}}} = \frac{54.58 - 55.68}{\frac{6.75}{\sqrt{12}}} = -0.56$$

From the standard normal distribution table, the probability associated with z = -0.56 is 0.2123. Thus:

$$P(\bar{x} \geq 54.58)0.2123 + 0.5000 = 0.7123$$

Student answers to parts b. and c. will vary depending on the sample selected but the methodology should follow that displayed in this solution.

7.43

a. Minitab output:

Median of HD Costs   **Mean of HD Costs**

Median of HD Costs = 144.89   Mean of HD Costs = 141.99

The box plot indicates that the median is somewhat larger than the sample mean. This indicates that the sample is negatively skewed. The upper whisker appears to be longer than the lower whisker suggesting a positive skewness of the sample. These two would seem to offset each other and allow that the population from which the sample was drawn could, in fact, be normally distributed.

b. More than $5 away from the obtained sample mean would be beyond $141.99 − $5 = $136.99 and beyond $141.99 + $5 = $146.99. We first calculate the standard deviation of the sample means:

$$\sigma_{\bar{x}} = \frac{\sigma}{\sqrt{n}} = \frac{50}{\sqrt{150}} = 4.082$$

$$P(\bar{x} < 136.99) = P(z < \frac{136.99 - 150}{4.082}) = P(z < -3.19) \cong 0$$

$$P(\bar{x} > 146.99) = P(z > \frac{146.99 - 150}{4.082}) = P(z > -0.74) = 0.5000 + 0.2704 = 0.7704$$

c. The box plot presents differing evidence indicating both positive and negative skewness. This could very well signal either sampling error or a non-normal distribution of the population. However, since the sample size is considerably larger than 30, there is not a requirement that the population is normally distributed in order to make these procedures valid.

Section 7-3 Exercises

7.45

Step 1: The population proportion has been given as $\pi = 0.30$.

Step 2: The sample proportion has been given as p = 0.27

Step 3: Determine the mean and standard deviation of the sampling distribution:
$$\mu_p = \pi = 0.30$$

$$\sigma_p = \sqrt{\frac{\pi(1-\pi)}{n}} = \sqrt{\frac{0.30(1-0.30)}{200}} = 0.0324$$

Step 4: Define the event of interest.
$$P(p \leq 0.27) = ?$$

Step 5: If $n\pi$ and $n(1-\pi)$ are both ≥ 5, then convert p to a standardized z-value.
Checking we get $200(0.30) = 60 \geq 5$ and $200(1-0.30) = 140 \geq 5$
Then we convert, p to a standardized z-value using

$$z = \frac{p - \pi}{\sigma_p} = \frac{0.27 - 0.30}{0.0324} = -0.93$$

Step 6: Use the standard normal distribution table in Appendix D to determine the probability for the even of interest.
We want

$$P(p \leq 0.27) \text{ or } P(z \leq -0.93) = 0.5 - 0.3238 = 0.1762$$

7.47

a.

Step 1: The population proportion has been given as $\pi = 0.20$.

Step 2: In this case there are two sample proportions, p = 0.18 and p = 0.23.

Step 3: Determine the mean and standard deviation of the sampling distribution:
$$\mu_p = \pi = 0.20$$

$$\sigma_p = \sqrt{\frac{\pi(1-\pi)}{n}} = \sqrt{\frac{0.20(1-0.20)}{500}} = 0.0179$$

Step 4: Define the event of interest.
$$P(0.18 \le p \le 0.23) = ?$$

Step 5: If $n\pi$ and $n(1-\pi)$ are both ≥ 5, then convert p to a standardized z-value. Checking we get $500(0.20) = 100 \ge 5$ and $500(1-0.20) = 400 \ge 5$. Then we convert, p to a standardized z-value using

$$z = \frac{p-\pi}{\sigma_p} = \frac{0.18-0.20}{0.0179} = -1.12$$

$$z = \frac{p-\pi}{\sigma_p} = \frac{0.23-0.20}{0.0179} = 1.68$$

Step 6: Use the standard normal distribution table in Appendix D to determine the probability for the even of interest. We want

$$P(0.18 \le p \le 0.23) \text{ or } P(-1.12 \le z \le 1.68) = 0.3686 + 0.4535 = 0.8221$$

b.
Step 1: The population proportion has been given as $\pi = 0.20$.

Step 2: In this case there are two sample proportions, $p = 0.18$ and $p = 0.23$.

Step 3: Determine the mean and standard deviation of the sampling distribution:
$$\mu_p = \pi = 0.20$$

$$\sigma_p = \sqrt{\frac{\pi(1-\pi)}{n}} = \sqrt{\frac{0.20(1-0.20)}{200}} = 0.0283$$

Step 4: Define the event of interest.

$$P(0.18 \le p \le 0.23) = ?$$

Step 5: If $n\pi$ and $n(1-\pi)$ are both ≥ 5, then convert p to a standardized z-value.
Checking we get $200(0.20) = 40 \geq 5$ and $200(1-0.20) = 160 \geq 5$
Then we convert, p to a standardized z-value using

$$z = \frac{p - \pi}{\sigma_p} = \frac{0.18 - 0.20}{0.0283} = -0.71$$

$$z = \frac{p - \pi}{\sigma_p} = \frac{0.23 - 0.20}{0.0283} = 1.06$$

Step 6: Use the standard normal distribution table in Appendix D to determine the probability for the even of interest.
We want

$$P(0.18 \leq p \leq 0.23) \text{ or } P(-0.71 \leq z \leq 1.06) = 0.2611 + 0.3554 = 0.6165$$

7.49

a. The sampling error is computed as follows:
Sampling error $= p - \pi = 0.65 - 0.70 = -0.05$

b. To find the probability that the sample proportion will be 0.65 or less, we rely on the fact that the sampling distribution for the sample proportion will be approximately normal so long as both $n\pi \geq 5$ and $n(1-\pi) \geq 5$ which are satisfied in this situation. We can use the following steps:

Step 1: Determine the population proportion.
The population proportion is $\pi = 0.70$

Step 2: Calculate the sample proportion.
The sample proportion is calculated using $p = \frac{x}{n}$. In this case, we are given $p = 0.65$.

Step 3: Determine the mean and standard deviation of the sampling distribution.
The mean is $\mu_p = \pi = 0.70$ and the standard deviation of the sampling distribution is $\sigma_p = \sqrt{\frac{\pi(1-\pi)}{n}} = \sqrt{\frac{0.70(1-0.70)}{100}} = 0.046$

Step 4: Define the event of interest.
We are interested in finding:
$$P(p \leq 0.65) = ?$$

Step 5: Convert the sample proportion to a standardized z-value.

$$z = \frac{p - \pi}{\sqrt{\dfrac{\pi(1-\pi)}{n}}} = \frac{0.65 - 0.70}{\sqrt{\dfrac{0.70(1-0.70)}{100}}} = \frac{-0.05}{0.046} = -1.09$$

Step 6: Use the standard normal distribution table to determine the probability for the event of interest.
The probability associated with z = -1.09 is 0.3621. This, the desired probability is:
$$P(p \leq 0.65) = 0.5000 - 0.3621 = 0.1379$$

Thus, there is nearly a .14 chance that the sample proportion would be 0.70 or less.

7.51

a. The sample proportion is computed using:

$$p = \frac{x}{n}$$

where x is the number of "YES" responses in the sample and n is the sample size. We get:

$$p = \frac{x}{n} = \frac{27}{60} = 0.45$$

b. To find the probability of a sample proportion as extreme or more extreme than that found in part a. we can use the following steps:

Step 1: Determine the population proportion.
The population proportion is $\pi = 0.40$

Step 2: Calculate the sample proportion.
The sample proportion is calculated using $p = \dfrac{x}{n}$. This was found in part a. to be

$$p = \frac{x}{n} = \frac{27}{60} = 0.45$$

Step 3: Determine the mean and standard deviation of the sampling distribution. The mean is $\mu_p = \pi = 0.40$ and the standard deviation of the sampling distribution is $\sigma_p = \sqrt{\dfrac{\pi(1-\pi)}{n}} = \sqrt{\dfrac{0.40(1-0.40)}{60}} = 0.063$

Step 4: Define the event of interest. We are interested in finding:
$$P(p \geq 0.45) = ?$$

Step 5: Convert the sample proportion to a standardized z-value.

$$z = \frac{p - \pi}{\sqrt{\dfrac{\pi(1-\pi)}{n}}} = \frac{0.45 - 0.40}{\sqrt{\dfrac{0.40(1-0.40)}{60}}} = \frac{0.05}{0.063} = 0.79$$

Step 6: Use the standard normal distribution table to determine the probability for the event of interest. The probability associated with $z = 0.79$ is 0.2852.

Thus, the desired probability is:
$$P(p \geq .45) = 0.5000 - 0.2852 = 0.2148$$

7.53

a.

Step 1: Determine the population proportion, π. The population proportion was stipulated to be 0.30.

Step 2: Calculate the sample proportion. The sample proportion was given as 0.35

Step 3: Determine the mean and standard deviation of the sampling distribution. The mean of the sampling distribution is equal to π, the population proportion. So $\mu_p = 0.30$.
The standard deviation of the sampling distribution for π is computed using:

$$\sigma_p = \sqrt{\frac{\pi(1-\pi)}{n}} = \sqrt{\frac{0.30(1-0.30)}{100}} = \sqrt{0.0021} = 0.0458$$

Step 4: Define the event of interest.
$$p \leq 0.35$$

Step 5: If $n\pi$ and $n(1 - \pi)$ are both ≥ 5. then convert p to a standardized z-value. Checking, we get

$n\pi = 100(0.30) = 30 > 5$ and $n(1 - \pi) = 100(0.70) = 0.70 > 5$ then we convert p to a standardized z-value

$$z = \frac{p - \pi}{\sqrt{\dfrac{\pi(1 - \pi)}{n}}} = \frac{0.35 - 0.30}{\sqrt{\dfrac{0.30(1 - 0.30)}{100}}} = 1.09$$

Step 6: Use the standard normal distribution table in Appendix D to determine the probability for the event of interest.
We want

$$P(p \leq 0.35) \text{ or } P(z \leq 1.09) = 0.50 + 0.3621. = 0.8621$$

b. Using the same steps outlined above:

   (1) $\pi = 0.30$,

   (2) $p = 0.40$,

   (3) $\mu_p = 0.30$, $\sigma_p = \sqrt{\dfrac{0.30(1 - 0.30)}{100}} = 0.0458$,

   (4) $p \leq 0.40$,

   (5) $n\pi = 100(0.30) = 30 > 5$ and $n(1 - \pi) = 100(0.70) = 0.70 > 5$ then

$$z = \frac{0.40 - 0.30}{\sqrt{\dfrac{0.30(1 - 0.30)}{100}}} = 2.18,$$

   (6) $P(p > 0.40)$ or $P(z > 2.18) = 0.50 - 0.4854 = 0.0146$.

c.   (1) $\pi = 0.30$,

   (2) $0.25 \leq p \leq 0.40$,

   (3) $\mu_p = 0.30$, $\sigma_p = \sqrt{\dfrac{0.30(1 - 0.30)}{100}} = 0.0458$,

   (4) $0.25 \leq p \leq 0.40$,

(5) $n\pi = 100(0.30) = 30 > 5$ and $n(1 - \pi) = 100(0.70) = 0.70 > 5$ then

$$z = \frac{0.25 - 0.30}{\sqrt{\dfrac{0.30(1 - 0.30)}{100}}} = -1.09,$$

(6) $P(0.25 \leq p \leq 0.40)$ or $P(-1.09 \leq z \leq 2.18) = 0.3621 + 0.4854 = 0.8475$.

d.   (1) $\pi = 0.30$,

    (2) $p = 0.27$,

    (3) $\mu_p = 0.30$, $\sigma_p = \sqrt{\dfrac{0.30(1 - 0.30)}{100}} = 0.0458$,

    (4) $p \geq 0.27$,

    (5) $n\pi = 100(0.30) = 30 > 5$ and $n(1 - \pi) = 100(0.70) = 0.70 > 5$ then

$$z = \frac{0.27 - 0.30}{\sqrt{\dfrac{0.30(1 - 0.30)}{100}}} = -0.65,$$

    (6) $P(p \geq 0.27)$ or $P(z \geq -0.65) = 0.50 + 0.2422 = 0.7422$.

7.55

The following steps can be used to answer the question posed in this problem.
Step 1: Define the Population of Interest and the Population Proportion
The population consists of N = 40,000 sprinkler valves. The variable of interest is the proportion of defect-free valves in the population. The contract calls for the population proportion to be $\pi = 0.97$ or more.

Step 2: Select a Simple Random Sample from the Population and Compute the Sample Proportion
The managers tested a simple random sample of n = 200 sprinkler valves from the population and found x = 190 defect-free valves.
    The sample proportion is:

$$p = \frac{x}{n} = \frac{190}{200} = 0.95$$

This is less than the required 0.97 for the population.

Step 3: Define the Sampling Distribution for the Sample Proportion
Because both $n\pi \geq 5$ and $n(1-\pi) \geq 5$, the sampling distribution for the sample proportion is approximately normally distributed with:

$$\mu_p = \pi = 0.97$$

and

$$\sigma_p = \sqrt{\frac{\pi(1-\pi)}{n}} = \sqrt{\frac{0.97(1-0.97)}{200}} = 0.012$$

The sampling distribution for the sample proportion is shown below:

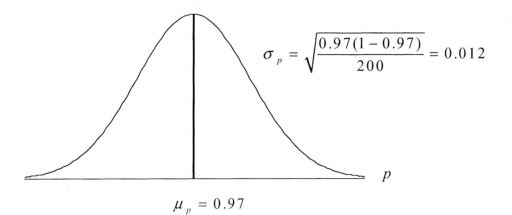

$$\sigma_p = \sqrt{\frac{0.97(1-0.97)}{200}} = 0.012$$

$$\mu_p = 0.97$$

Step 4: Determine the Probability of the Sample Result
The sample proportion found in Step 3 is $p = 0.95$. The managers are interested in determining P($p \leq 0.95$), if $\pi = .97$. This is done using the usual method for finding probabilities for a normal distribution, shown as follows:

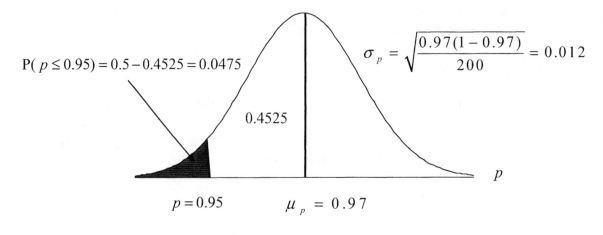

$$P(p \leq 0.95) = 0.5 - 0.4525 = 0.0475$$

$$\sigma_p = \sqrt{\frac{0.97(1-0.97)}{200}} = 0.012$$

0.4525

$$p = 0.95 \qquad \mu_p = 0.97$$

$$z = \frac{p - \mu_p}{\sigma_p} = \frac{0.95 - 0.97}{0.012} = -1.67$$

From the standard normal distribution table in Appendix D, the probability associated with z = -1.67 is 0.4525. Therefore P($p \leq 0.95$) = 0.5 - 0.4525 = 0.0475.

The probability that the sample proportion will be less than or equal to .95, if the population has .97 defect-free sprinkler valves, is 0.0475. This indicates that this result, or a worse sample result, will occur by chance in less than 5% of all samples of size 200. United Manufacturing and Supply should be concerned that its product may not meet the contract requirements.

7.57

a.

Step 1: Determine the population proportion, π.
The population proportion was stipulated to be 0.43.

Step 2: Calculate the sample proportion.
The sample proportion was given as 12/20 = 0.60

Step 3: Determine the mean and standard deviation of the sampling distribution.
The mean of the sampling distribution is equal to π, the population proportion. So $\mu_p = 0.43$
The standard deviation of the sampling distribution for π is computed using:

$$\sigma_p = \sqrt{\frac{\pi(1-\pi)}{n}} = \sqrt{\frac{0.43(1-0.43)}{20}} = \sqrt{0.0123} = 0.1107$$

Step 4: Define the event of interest.
$p \geq 0.60$

Step 5: If $n\pi$ and $n(1 - \pi)$ are both ≥ 5. then convert p to a standardized z-value.
Checking, we get
$n\pi = 20(0.43) = 8.6 > 5$ and $n(1 - \pi) = 20(0.57) = 11.4 > 5$ then we convert p to a standardized z-value

$$z = \frac{p - \pi}{\sqrt{\frac{\pi(1-\pi)}{n}}} = \frac{0.60 - 0.43}{\sqrt{\frac{0.43(1-0.43)}{20}}} = 1.54$$

Step 6: Use the standard normal distribution table in Appendix D to determine the probability for the event of interest.
We want P(p $\geq$ 0.60) or P(z $\geq$ 1.54) = 0.50 - 0.4382 = 0.0618.

b. Step 1: $\pi = 0.53$,

Step 2: $p = 0.60$,

Step 3 $\mu_p = 0.53$, $\sigma_p = \sqrt{\dfrac{0.53(1-0.53)}{20}} = 0.1116$,

Step 4 $p \geq 0.60$,

Step 5: $n\pi = 20(0.53) = 10.6 > 5$ and $n(1-\pi) = 20(0.47) = 9.4 > 5$ then

$$z = \frac{0.60 - 0.53}{\sqrt{\dfrac{0.53(1-0.53)}{20}}} = 0.6272,$$

Step 6: $P(p \geq 0.60)$ or $P(z \geq 0.63) = 0.50 - 0.2357 = 0.2643$

c. Step 1: $\pi = 0.43$,

Step 2: $p = 8/20 = 0.40$ and $p = 12/20 = 0.60$,

Step 3: $\mu_p = 0.43$, $\sigma_p = \sqrt{\dfrac{0.43(1-0.43)}{20}} = 0.1107$,

Step 4: $0.40 \leq p \leq 0.60$,

Step 5: $n\pi = 20(0.43) = 8.6 > 5$ and

$n(1-\pi) = 20(0.57) = 11.4 > 5$ then $z = \dfrac{0.40 - 0.43}{\sqrt{\dfrac{0.43(1-0.43)}{20}}} = -0.2710$

$$z = \frac{0.60 - 0.43}{\sqrt{\dfrac{0.43(1-0.43)}{20}}} = 1.5356,$$

Step 6: $P(0.40 \leq p \leq 0.60)$ or $P(-0.27 \leq z \leq 1.54) = 0.1064 + 0.4382 = 0.5446$

7.59

a. Step 1: $\pi = 0.33$,

   Step 2: $p = 0.25$,

   Step 3: $\mu_p = 0.33$, $\sigma_p = \sqrt{\dfrac{0.33(1 - 0.33)}{75}} = 0.0543$,

   Step 4: $p \geq 0.25$,

   Step 5: $n\pi = 75(0.33) = 25 > 5$ and $n(1 - \pi) = 75(0.67) = 50 > 5$ then

   $$z = \frac{0.25 - 0.33}{\sqrt{\dfrac{0.33(1 - 0.33)}{75}}} = -1.473,$$

   Step 6: $P(p \geq 0.25)$ or $P(z \geq -1.47) = 0.50 + 0.4292 = 0.9292$.

b. Step 1: $\pi = 0.33$,

   Step 2: $p = 0.45$,

   Step 3: $\mu_p = 0.33$, $\sigma_p = \sqrt{\dfrac{0.33(1 - 0.33)}{75}} = 0.0543$,

   Step 4: $p \geq 0.50$,

   Step 5: $n\pi = 75(0.33) = 25 > 5$ and $n(1 - \pi) = 75(0.67) = 50 > 5$ then

   $$z = \frac{0.45 - 0.33}{\sqrt{\dfrac{0.33(1 - 0.33)}{75}}} = 2.21,$$

   Step 6: $P(p \geq 0.400)$ or $P(z \geq 2.21) = 0.5000 - 0.4864 = 0.0136$. One would conclude that it is highly implausible for a sample of size 75 to yield a sample proportion of 0.50 or more from a population with a proportion equal to 0.33.

c. Step 1: $\pi = 0.33$,

   Step 2; $p = 25/90 = 0.278$ and $p = 35/90 = 0.389$,

Step 3: $\mu_p = 0.33$, $\sigma_p = \sqrt{\dfrac{0.33(1-0.33)}{90}} = 0.0496$,

Step 4: $0.278 \le p \le 0.389$,

Step 5: $n\pi = 90(0.278) > 5$ and $n(1 - \pi) = 90(0.722) > 5$ then

$z = \dfrac{0.278 - 0.33}{\sqrt{\dfrac{0.33(1-0.33)}{90}}} = -1.05$ $z = \dfrac{0.389 - 0.33}{\sqrt{\dfrac{0.33(1-0.33)}{90}}} = 1.19$,

Step 6: $P(0.278 \le p \le 0.389)$ or $P(-1.05 \le z \le 1.19) = 0.3531 + 0.3830 = 0.7361$.

7.61

a. There are 131 1's which means 131 sampled subscribers have annual incomes over $100,000 and 65 0's which means 65 sampled subscribers have incomes of $100,000 or less.

b. $p = 131/196 = 0.668$

c. $P(p > 0.668) = P\left(z > \dfrac{0.668 - 0.65}{\sqrt{\dfrac{0.65(1-0.65)}{196}}} = 0.53\right) = 0.5 - 0.2019 = 0.2981$

d, It would be a judgment call. The sample proportion of 0.668 is higher than the claimed population proportion of 0.65. But because the chance of getting a sample proportion of 0.668 or higher if the true proportion is 0.65 is about almost 30%, the value seen could be due to sampling error.

7.63

a. Minitab output
   Tally for Discrete Variables: Yes/No

Yes/No	Count	Percent
no	56	28.00
yes	144	72.00
N=	200	

   The sample proportion = 0.72,

b. The sampling error = $p - \pi = 0.72 - 0.66 = 0.06$.

c. To obtain the required probability, the mean and the standard error for the sampling distribution must be obtained. The mean was obtained in part a.: 0.50.

The standard error is given by $\sigma_p = \sqrt{\dfrac{\pi(1-\pi)}{n}} = \sqrt{\dfrac{0.66(1-0.66)}{200}} = \sqrt{0.00112} = 0.0335$.

Minitab output:
Cumulative Distribution Function

```
Normal with mean = 0.66 and standard deviation = 0.033496

    x    P( X <= x )
 0.72      0.963374
```

So $P(p \geq 0.72) = 1 - P(p \leq 0.72) = 1 - 0.963374 = 0.0366$.

d. It is very unlikely (0.0366) that a sample proportion of 0.72 or more would be obtained from a population whose proportion was 0.66. It, therefore, is apparent that the proportion of P&G workers who participate in 401(k) plans is larger than that for the nation as a whole.

End of Chapter Exercises

7.65

The sample means are measures of central location and would therefore, measure the centers of the samples. These averages cannot be as extreme as the values upon which they are based and, therefore, would be less variable than the population. Examples will vary.

7.67

The finite correction factor should be used if the sample size is greater than 5 percent of the population size and sampling is performed without replacement.

7.69

The standard deviation and the standard error both measure the dispersion or spread of data sets or variables. The difference between them is that the standard error measures the spread of the sampling distribution of a statistic. That statistic is a function of the data sets or variables whose spread is measured by a standard deviation. So a data set or variable's spread is measured by a standard deviation. However, the spread of a function of those same data sets or variables is measured by a standard error. As an example, the spread of the data set $x_1, x_2 \ldots x_N$ is measured by σ: the sample standard deviation. However, $\bar{x} = \dfrac{\sum x_i}{n}$. It is a function of $x_1, x_2. \ldots x_N$. Thus, $\bar{x}$'s spread is measured by $\dfrac{\sigma}{\sqrt{n}}$ which is its standard error.

7.71

A sample size of 1 would be sufficient since the population itself is normal. Large samples would also produce normally distributed sampling distributions.

7.73

$\pi = 0.30$, p = 66/200 = 0.33

$$P(p \geq 0.33) = P\left(z \geq \frac{0.33 - 0.30}{\sqrt{\dfrac{0.30(1-0.30)}{200}}}\right) = P(z \geq 0.93) = 0.5 - 0.3238 = 0.1762$$

7.75

a. For a continuous uniformly distributed random variable the mean, $\mu = \dfrac{a+b}{2}$, where a is the lower limit and b is the upper limit. In this case, $\mu = \dfrac{3+6}{2} = 4.5$. The standard deviation for a continuous uniformly distributed random variable is $\sigma = \sqrt{\dfrac{(b-a)^2}{12}} = \sqrt{\dfrac{(6-3)^2}{12}} = 0.8660$

b. Step 1: Compute the sample mean. Here the sample mean is given: $\bar{x} = 4.25$.

   Step 2: Define the sampling distribution. The population is uniformly distributed with a mean of 4.5 and a standard deviation of 0.8660. However, because the sample size, n = 49, is sufficiently large, the distribution of sample means is approximately normally distributed with

$$\mu_{\bar{x}} = \mu = 4.5 \text{ and } \sigma_{\bar{x}} = \frac{\sigma}{\sqrt{n}} = \frac{0.8660}{\sqrt{49}} = 0.1237.$$

   Step 3: Define the event of interest. The event of interest is: $P(\bar{x} \geq 4.25)$

Step 4: Use the standard normal distribution to find the probability of interest. Convert the sample means to corresponding z-values:

$$z = \frac{\bar{x} - \mu}{\frac{\sigma}{\sqrt{n}}} = \frac{4.25 - 4.5}{\frac{0.8660}{\sqrt{49}}} = -2.02.$$

From the standard normal table the probability associated with z = -2.02 is 0.4783. Therefore, $P(\bar{x} \geq 4.25) = P(z \geq -2.02) = 0.4783 + 0.50 = 0.9783$.

c. Although the population of service times is not normally distributed, but uniformly distributed, the sample size is sufficiently large so that the sampling distribution of $\bar{x}$ is normally distributed. In other words, the Central Limit Theorem applies here because the sample size, n=49, is sufficiently large so that the distribution of sample means $\bar{x}$ will be approximately normally distributed even though the original population is uniformly distributed.

7.77

$$P = 14/100 = 0.14$$

a. $P(p > 0.14) = P(z > (0.14 - .10)/ \sqrt{[0.10(1 - 0.10)]/100}) = P(z > 1.33) = 0.5 - 0.4082 = 0.0918$. The probability of getting 14 or more requests if the average is really 10% is 0.0918. This is a reasonably small probability. Since you did get 14 requests, it probably indicates the percentage that want these drives is greater than 10%.

b. $P(p > 0.14) = P(z > (0.14 - .10)/ \sqrt{[0.10(1 - 0.10)]/200}) = P(z > 1.89) = 0.5 - 0.4706 = 0.0294$

Now the evidence is even more compelling to suggest that the proportion of customers wanting hard drives with 40 mega bytes or less exceeds 10%.

7.79

a. $P(\bar{x} > 50) = P(z > (50 - 45)/ [(5/\sqrt{16})]) = P(z > 4) = 0$
It is virtually impossible for this to happen if the mean for the population is 45 minutes

b. Yes, since the probability of a sample of size 16 having a mean of 50 or more is essentially 0. Since the sample average baking time was 50 minutes it appears that the ovens may not be working properly.

Chapter 7

7.81

Note, because of the small population, the finite correction factor is used.

a. $P(\bar{x} \le 5.9) = P(z \le (5.9 - 6.2)/ [(3/\sqrt{100})\sqrt{(300-100)/(300-1)}] = P(z \le -1.22) = 0.5 - 0.3888 = 0.1112$

b. Based on this low probability either the mean or the standard deviation or both may have changed.

c. $P(\bar{x} \le 5.9) = P(z \le (5.9 - 6.2)/ [(3/\sqrt{40})\sqrt{(300-40)/(300-1)}] = P(z \le -0.68) = 0.5 - 0.2517 = 0.2483$

d. The probabilities differ because the spread of the sampling distribution is smaller for the larger sample. For a large sample, the distribution is more tightly grouped and the probability of observing an extreme value is smaller.

7.83

a. $P(\bar{x} \le 88626) = P\left(\dfrac{88626 - 92500}{40000 / \sqrt{5829}} \le z \right) = P(-7.39 \le z) = 0.$

b. A sample mean of at most \$88,626 from a population with a mean of \$92500 is highly unlikely, i.e., has a probability that is essentially 0. Therefore, the two years' means are highly unlikely to be equal to each other.

c. Let X = the number of graduates who receive an annual base salary of at least \$92,500. X has a binomial distribution with n = 5 and p = 0.50 since the mean and median have the same value in a Normal distribution. Therefore, we capture $P(x \ge 5/2) = P(x \ge 3) = P(x = 3) + P(x = 4) = P(x = 5) =$
$\binom{5}{3}0.5^3(1-0.5)^{5-3} + \binom{5}{4}0.5^4(1-0.5)^{5-4} + \binom{5}{5}0.5^5(1-0.5)^{5-5} = 0.3125 + 0.1562 + 0.0312 = 0.4999.$

7.85

a.

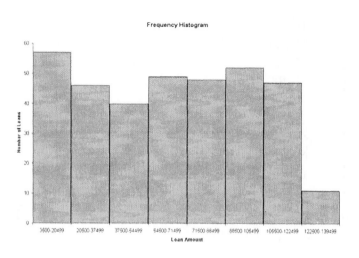

Based upon this distribution, the data do not appear to be normally distributed.

b. Using Excel's average function the mean = 63,668.57

c. Using Excel's STDEVP function the standard deviation = 35938.16

d. Student answers will vary depending upon the sample selected. Students should remember that the Central Limit Theorem shows that the sampling distribution will be approximately normally distributed as long as the sample size is greater than 30 even though the distribution of the underlying parent population is unknown.

7.87

Students can use Excel's pivot table feature to group data by sex.

a. $\pi = 67/138 = 0.4855$

F	70
M	67
U	1
Grand Total	138

$P(p<0.4855) = P(z < (0.4855 - 0.70)/ \sqrt{[0.70(1-0.70)]/138}) = P(z < -5.50) = 0$

Because there is essentially no chance of getting a sample proportion of .4855 if the true proportion of males is .70, then you can only conclude that the population proportion of males patients must be less than 70%.

Students can use Excel's pivot table feature to group by Medicare.

b. P(Medicare) = 116/138 = 0.8406

BC	5
CAID	7
CARE	116
HMO	1
INS	3
OGVT	1
OTHR	4
SELF	1
Grand Total	138

$P(p > 0.8406) = P(z > (0.8406 - 0.80)/ \sqrt{[0.80(1-0.80)]/138}) = P(z > 1.19)$
$= 0.5 - 0.383 = 0.117$

Since the probability of finding a sample with a proportion of .8406 or greater if the true proportion is .80 is only 11.7% then you may reasonably assume that the proportion of people on Medicare is actually greater than 80%.

7.89

a. Minitab output

Tally for Discrete Variables: Online

```
Online   Count   Percent
   No       42     20.79
   Yes     160     79.21
   N=      202
```

So then the proportion of adults who connect onto the internet using a computer is 0.79.

b. The sampling error = $p - \pi = 0.79 - 0.74 = 0.05$.

The standard error of the sample's proportion equals

$$\sqrt{\frac{\pi(1-\pi)}{n}} = \sqrt{\frac{0.74(1-0.74)}{202}} = 0.031 \text{ and the mean proportion equals } 0.74.$$

c. If 0.05 is the maximum sampling error, the sample values would have to be between .69 and .79. We need to find:

$$P(0.69 < p < 0.79) = P(\frac{0.69 - 0.76}{0.031} < z < \frac{0.79 - 0.74}{0.031}) = P(-1.61 < z < 1.61) =$$
$$0.4463 + 0.4463 = 0.8926$$

d. The standard error of the sample's proportion equals

$$\sqrt{\frac{\pi(1-\pi)}{n}} = \sqrt{\frac{0.74(1-0.74)}{2022}} = 0.0098 \text{ and the mean proportion equals 0.74.}$$

To be at most as far away as the ONLINE's sample proportion from that of the Harris Poll would be to be within $0.74 \pm 0.02 = (0.72, 0.76)$.

Minitab output:

Cumulative Distribution Function

```
Normal with mean = 0.74 and standard deviation = 0.0098

    x    P( X <= x )
0.72       0.020635
0.76       0.979365
```

So $P(0.72 \le p \le 0.76) = 0.9794 - 0.0206 = 0.9588$.

Chapter 7

Chapter 8 Solutions

When applicable, selected problems in each section will be done following the appropriate step-by-step procedures outlined in the corresponding sections of the chapter. Other problems will provide key points and the answers to the questions, but all answers can be arrived at using the appropriate steps.

Section 8-1 Exercises

8.1

Since the population standard deviation is known, the following steps can be used to develop the desired confidence interval estimate.

Step 1: Define the population of interest and select a simple random sample.
The population of interest is the collection of all items of interest. A simple random sample of size n = 250 will be collected.

Step 2: Specify the confidence level.
The desired confidence level is 95%.

Step 3: Compute the sample mean.
The sample mean is given to be $\bar{x} = 300$.

Step 4: Determine the standard error of the sampling distribution.
The population standard deviation is known to be $\sigma = 55$. The standard error of the sampling distribution is:

$$\sigma_{\bar{x}} = \frac{\sigma}{\sqrt{n}} = \frac{55}{\sqrt{250}} = 3.48$$

Step 5: Determine the critical value, z, from the standard normal distribution table.
The z value is 1.96.

Step 6: Compute the confidence interval estimate.
The 95% confidence interval estimate for the population mean is:

$$\bar{x} \pm z \frac{\sigma}{\sqrt{n}}$$

The critical value for 95% confidence from the standard normal distribution table is $z = 1.96$. Therefore the confidence interval is:

$$300 \pm 1.96 \frac{55}{\sqrt{250}}$$

$$300 \pm 6.82$$

293.18 -------------------------------- 306.82

8.3

Since the population standard deviation is known, the following steps can be used to develop the desired confidence interval estimate.

Step 1: Define the population of interest and select a simple random sample.
The population of interest is the collection of all items of interest. A simple random sample of size $n = 65$ will be collected.

Step 2: Specify the confidence level.
The desired confidence level is 90%.

Step 3: Compute the sample mean.
The sample mean is given as 70.

Step 4: Determine the standard error of the sampling distribution.
The population standard deviation is known to be 15. The standard error of the sampling distribution is:

$$\sigma_{\bar{x}} = \frac{\sigma}{\sqrt{n}} = \frac{15}{\sqrt{65}} = 1.86$$

Step 5: Determine the critical value, z, from the standard normal distribution table.
The z value is 1.645.

Step 6: Compute the confidence interval estimate.
The 90% confidence interval estimate for the population mean is:

$$\bar{x} \pm z \frac{\sigma}{\sqrt{n}}$$

The critical value for 90% confidence from the standard normal distribution table is $z = 1.645$. Therefore the confidence interval is:

$$70 \pm 1.645(1.86)$$

$$70 \pm 3.06$$

66.94 -------------------------------73.06

8.5

a. Since the population standard deviation is unknown, the following steps can be used to compute the confidence interval estimate.

Step 1: Define the population of interest and select a simple random sample. The population of interest is the collection of all items of interest. A simple random sample of size n = 10 has been collected with the following results:

2	8	0	2	3
5	3	1	4	2

Step 2: Specify the confidence level. The desired confidence level is 90%.

Step 3: Compute the sample mean and the sample standard deviation. The sample mean and sample standard deviation are computed as follows:

$$\bar{x} = \frac{\sum x}{n} = \frac{30}{10} = 3 \quad \text{and} \quad s = \sqrt{\frac{\sum (x - \bar{x})^2}{n-1}} = 2.26$$

Step 4: Determine the standard error of the sampling distribution. The sample standard deviation is computed to be $s = 2.26$. The standard error of the sampling distribution is:

$$\sigma_{\bar{x}} \approx \frac{s}{\sqrt{n}} = \frac{2.26}{\sqrt{10}} = 0.71$$

Step 5: Determine the critical value for the desired confidence level. The critical value for 90% confidence from the student t-distribution table with degrees of freedom equal to n – 1 = 9 is $t = 1.8331$.

Step 6: Compute the confidence interval estimate. The 90% confidence interval estimate for the population mean is:

$$\bar{x} \pm t \frac{s}{\sqrt{n}}$$

Therefore the confidence interval is:
$$3 \pm 1.8331 \frac{2.26}{\sqrt{10}}$$
$$3 \pm 1.31$$
1.69 ------------------------------- 4.31

b. If the confidence level is increased to 95%, the critical t from the t-distribution will change from 1.8331 to 2.2622. This will result in a wider confidence interval as follows:

$$3 \pm 2.2622 \frac{2.26}{\sqrt{10}}$$

$$3 \pm 1.62$$

$$1.38 \text{ -------------------------------- } 4.62$$

For a higher confidence interval, the margin of error is greater causing the interval to be wider (less precise).

8.7

Step 1: Define the population of interest and select a simple random sample.
The population of interest is not precisely stated here. A simple random sample of n = 100 is selected.

Step 2: Specify the confidence level.
A 90% confidence interval estimate is to be constructed.

Step 3: Compute the sample mean.
The sample mean, $\bar{x}$, is given as being equal to 1,200.

Step 4: Determine the standard error of the sampling distribution.
The standard error of the sampling distribution is $\dfrac{\sigma}{\sqrt{n}} = \dfrac{121}{\sqrt{100}} = 12.1$

Step 5: Determine the critical value, z, from the standard normal table.
Because the sample size is large the sampling distribution will be normally distributed and the critical value will be a z-value from the standard normal distribution. Because a 90% confidence interval estimate is desired the z-value is 1.645.

Step 6: Compute the confidence interval estimate.
The 90% confidence interval estimate for the population mean is

$$\bar{x} \pm z \frac{\sigma}{\sqrt{n}} = 1200 \pm 1.645 \frac{121}{\sqrt{100}} = 1200 \pm 19.90$$

$$1180.10 \text{ ------------- } 1219.90.$$

8.9

Step 1: Define the population of interest and select a simple random sample.
The population of interest is not precisely stated here. A simple random sample of n = 9 is selected.

Step 2: Specify the confidence level.
A 90% confidence interval estimate is to be constructed.

Step 3: Compute the sample mean.
The sample mean, $\bar{x}$, is computed using $\dfrac{\sum x}{n} = \dfrac{450}{9} = 50$.

Step 4: Determine the standard error of the sampling distribution.
Since the population variance is given, the standard error of the sampling distribution is $\dfrac{\sigma}{\sqrt{n}} = \dfrac{5}{\sqrt{9}} = 1.67$

Step 5: Determine the critical value, z, from the standard normal table.
Even though the sample size is small, the problem states the population is normally distributed and the population variance is given, therefore, the sampling distribution will be normally distributed and the critical value will be a z-value from the standard normal distribution. Because a 90% confidence interval estimate is desired the z-value is 1.645.

Step 6: Compute the confidence interval estimate.
The 90% confidence interval estimate for the population mean is

$$\bar{x} \pm z \dfrac{\sigma}{\sqrt{n}} = 50 \pm 1.645 \dfrac{5}{\sqrt{9}} = 50 \pm 2.74 = 47.26 \text{ ------------- } 52.74.$$

8.11

a.

Step 1: Define the population of interest and select a simple random sample of size n.
The population has a normal distribution whose mean is unknown.

Step 2: Specify the confidence level.
A 90% confidence is to be constructed. Therefore, 90% of all possible intervals will contain the population mean.

Step 3: Compute the sample mean and standard deviation.
$$\bar{x} = \dfrac{\sum x_i}{n} = \dfrac{134}{10} = 13.4 \text{ and } s = 3.1.$$

Step 4: Determine the standard error of the sampling distribution.

$$s_{\bar{x}} = \frac{s}{\sqrt{n}} = \frac{3.1}{\sqrt{10}} = 0.9804$$

Step 5: Determine the critical value for the desired level of confidence.
Since the population standard deviation is unknown and the sample size is small, the critical value will come from the t-distribution. The critical value for 90% confidence and $10 - 1 = 9$ degrees of freedom is found in the t-distribution table to be 1.8331.

Step 6: Compute the confidence interval estimate.
The 90% confidence interval estimate for the population mean is

$$\bar{x} \pm t\frac{s}{\sqrt{n}} = 13.4 \pm 1.8331(0.9804) = 13.4 \pm 1.7972 =$$

$$(11.6028,\ 15.1972)$$

b. Using the same steps as part a:

$$\bar{x} = \frac{\sum x_i}{n} = \frac{3744}{120} = 31.2 \text{ and } s = 8.2.$$

$$s_{\bar{x}} = \frac{s}{\sqrt{n}} = \frac{8.2}{\sqrt{120}} = 0.7486.$$

The population has a normal distribution. However, the population standard deviation is unknown. Therefore, the critical value will come from the t-distribution. Using Excel, the critical value for 90% confidence is 1.6578. The 90% confidence interval estimate for the population mean is

$$\bar{x} \pm t\frac{s}{\sqrt{n}} = 31.2 \pm 1.6578(0.7486) = 31.2 \pm 1.241 = (29.9590,\ 32.4410)$$

c. The population has a normal distribution whose mean is unknown but standard deviation is known.

$$\bar{x} = \frac{\sum x_i}{n} = \frac{40.5}{9} = 4.5 \text{ and } \sigma = 2.9.$$

$$\sigma_{\bar{x}} = \frac{\sigma}{\sqrt{n}} = \frac{2.9}{\sqrt{9}} = 0.9667.$$

The critical value will come from the standard normal distribution. The critical value for a 90% confidence interval is 1.645. The 90% confidence interval estimate for the population mean is

$$\bar{x} \pm z\frac{s}{\sqrt{n}} = 4.5 \pm 1.645(0.9667) = 4.5 \pm 1.5902 = (2.9098, \ 6.0902)$$

d. The population has a normal distribution whose mean and standard deviation are unknown.

$$\bar{x} = \frac{\sum x_i}{n} = \frac{585.9}{27} = 21.7$$

$$s = \sqrt{\frac{\sum x^2 - \dfrac{(\sum x)^2}{n}}{n-1}} = \sqrt{\frac{15472.37 - \dfrac{(585.9)^2}{27}}{26}} = 10.3.$$

$$s_{\bar{x}} = \frac{s}{\sqrt{n}} = \frac{10.3}{\sqrt{27}} = 1.9822.$$

The population standard deviation is unknown, the sample size is less than 30, and the sample came from a population that is normally distributed. Therefore, the critical value will come from the t-distribution. The critical value for 90% confidence and 27 -1 = 26 degrees of freedom is 1.7056. The 90% confidence interval estimate for the population mean is

$$\bar{x} \pm t\frac{s}{\sqrt{n}} = 21.7 \pm 1.7056(1.9822) = 21.7 \pm 3.3808 = (18.3192, \ 25.0808)$$

Chapter 8

8.13
    a. point estimate = $\bar{x}$ = $1.875

    b. The population will have to be a normal distribution in this situation. The critical value can then come from the t-distribution.

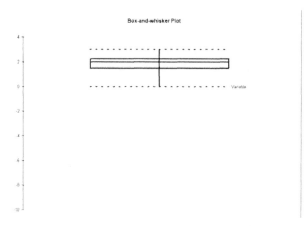

    c. The population must be normally distributed.
    Based on the box and whiskers plot there is reason to believe that the data may come from a population that is approximately normally distributed.

    d. $1.875 \pm 1.7959(.735/\sqrt{12})$; $1.875 \pm .3810$; 1.494 ----------- 2.256

8.15
    a. $\bar{x} \pm z\dfrac{s}{\sqrt{n}} = 5000 \pm 1.96(\dfrac{1500}{\sqrt{179}}) = 5000 \pm 219.75 = (4780.25, 5219.75)$

    b. The margin of error is $z\dfrac{s}{\sqrt{n}} = 1.96(\dfrac{1500}{\sqrt{179}}) = 219.75$.

    c. Reducing the margin of error by 50 percent would produce a margin of error = $219.75/2 = 109.875$. So $z\dfrac{s}{\sqrt{n}} = 1.96(\dfrac{1500}{\sqrt{n}}) = 109.875$.

    Solving n = $\left(\dfrac{1.96(1500)}{109.875}\right)^2 = 715.97 \approx 716$.

8.17

a. Since the population standard deviation is unknown, the following steps can be used to compute the confidence interval estimate.

Step 1: Define the population of interest and select a simple random sample. The population of interest consists of all hotel bookings in which there was a difference between the quoted rate and the negotiated rate. A random sample of n = 30 differences between quoted and negotiated rates were obtained with the following results.

$15.45	$5.23	-$5.72	$30.86	$6.31	$14.00	$2.09	$18.91	$20.73	$12.72
-$17.34	$23.60	$12.48	$6.02	$15.84	$3.48	$0.93	$5.72	$8.29	$3.00
$6.64	$24.81	$4.57	$11.61	$9.25	-$4.85	$25.60	-$4.56	$7.14	$12.45

Step 2: Specify the confidence level.
The desired confidence level is 95%.

Step 3: Compute the sample mean and the sample standard deviation.
The sample mean and sample standard deviation are computed as follows:

$$\bar{x} = \frac{\sum x}{n} = \frac{275.28}{30} = 9.18 \quad \text{and} \quad s = \sqrt{\frac{\sum (x - \bar{x})^2}{n-1}} = 10.41$$

Step 4: Determine the standard error of the sampling distribution.
The sample standard deviation is computed to be $s = \$10.41$. The standard error of the sampling distribution is:

$$\sigma_{\bar{x}} \approx \frac{s}{\sqrt{n}} = \frac{\$10.41}{\sqrt{30}} = \$1.90$$

Step 5: Determine the critical value for the desired confidence level.
The critical value for 95% confidence from the student t-distribution table with degrees of freedom equal to n – 1 = 29 is $t = 2.0452$.

Step 6: Compute the confidence interval estimate.
The 95% confidence interval estimate for the population mean is:

$$\bar{x} \pm t \frac{s}{\sqrt{n}}$$

Therefore the confidence interval is:

$$\$9.18 \pm 2.0452 \frac{\$10.41}{\sqrt{30}}$$

$9.18 ± 3.89

$5.29 ---------------------------- $13.07

Based on the sample data, with 95% confidence, we can state that the true population mean error in hotel charges is between $5.29 and $13.07.

b. The interval includes the $11.35 mean value determined in the American Express study. Therefore, these sample data do not dispute the American Express study. Any value in the confidence interval computed in part a. is equally likely to be the true population mean.

8.19

a. The best estimate of the true mean is the sample mean.

$$\bar{x} = \frac{\sum x}{n} = \frac{630}{36} = \$17.50.$$

b. Because the population standard deviation is unknown, the z-distribution cannot be used. However, because the sample size is large (≥ 30), the t-distribution is used. Because the population standard deviation is unknown, the standard error of the sampling distribution is estimated using $\frac{s}{\sqrt{n}}$. The sample standard deviation is computed using the formula:

$$s = \sqrt{\frac{\sum (x - \bar{x})^2}{n-1}} = 7.52.$$

The standard error $= \dfrac{7.52}{\sqrt{36}} = 1.25.$

Using Excel, the degrees of freedom = 36-1 = 35.

The t-value = 2.03.

The 95% confidence level is

$$\bar{x} \pm t \frac{s}{\sqrt{n}} = 17.50 \pm 2.03 \frac{7.52}{\sqrt{36}} = 17.50 \pm 2.54 = 14.96 \text{------------} 20.04.$$

c. Yes. While the sample mean of $17.50 is less than the average of $19.00 stated by the manager, the sample mean is subject to sampling error. One would not expect a specific $\bar{x}$ to equal the true mean. However, the 95% confidence interval has limits of $14.96 and $20.04, which contain the $19.00 stated by the manager. Therefore, the statement made by the concessions manager is consistent with the results found in part (b).

8.21

a. The point estimate for a population mean is the sample mean. Excel has been used to compute the six sample means as follows:

Company A – Passenger Car: $\bar{x} = 60.2$
Company B – Passenger Car: $\bar{x} = 65.4$
Company C – Passenger Car: $\bar{x} = 76.8$
Company A – SUV: $\bar{x} = 97.2$
Company B – SUV: $\bar{x} = 92.6$
Company C – SUV: $\bar{x} = 101.0$

b. If we assume that the populations are normally distributed, then the t-distribution is used to provide the critical value for constructing the confidence interval estimates for the mean. The critical t-value for n-1 = 4 degrees of freedom and 95% confidence is 2.7765.

The following confidence interval estimates are constructed based on the sample data:

Company A – Passenger Car: $60.2 \pm 2.7765 \dfrac{12.7}{\sqrt{5}}$

60.2 ± 15.8
44.4 ------------------76.0

Company B – Passenger Car: $65.4 \pm 2.7765 \dfrac{11.3}{\sqrt{5}}$

65.4 ± 14.0
51.4 ------------------79.4

Company C – Passenger Car: $76.8 \pm 2.7765 \dfrac{9.0}{\sqrt{5}}$

76.8 ± 11.2
65.6 ------------------88.0

Company A – SUV: $97.2 \pm 2.7765 \dfrac{18.7}{\sqrt{5}}$

97.2 ± 23.2
74.0 ------------------120.4

Company B – SUV: $92.6 \pm 2.7765 \dfrac{5.4}{\sqrt{5}}$

92.6 ± 6.7

85.9 ------------------99.3

Company C – SUV: $101 \pm 2.7765 \dfrac{14.1}{\sqrt{5}}$

101 ± 17.5

83.5 ------------------118.5

c. Given the confidence intervals computed in part b., since any value in the interval is equally likely to be the true population mean, in order to conclude that a difference exists, the intervals cannot overlap. We see that Company B and C SUV brake installation time means exceed the mean time for passenger cars for Company A and B. Company A's SUV mean time overlaps the mean time for passenger cars from all companies.

8.23

a. The sample mean, $\bar{x}$ = 167.52. The population standard deviation is not known. The sample standard deviation, s, is used to estimate the population standard deviation. The sample standard deviation, s = 28.5179 . The critical value for a confidence interval when the population standard deviation is not known is the t-distribution. Here the sample size, n, is 196. The degrees of freedom are 196-1 = 195. The t-value for 95% level of confidence is 1.9722. The confidence interval is calculated as follows:

$\bar{x} \pm t \dfrac{s}{\sqrt{n}} = 167.52 \pm 1.9722 \dfrac{28.5179}{\sqrt{196}} = 167.52 \pm 4.0174 = 163.5026$ --------------
171.5374

b. The margin of error can be reduced by increasing the sample size, or by decreasing the level of confidence. The margin of error can also be reduced if the standard deviation can be reduced but this is not an option available to the study's authors in this case.

8.25

   a. Minitab results:

Descriptive Statistics: ChickWt

```
Variable    Mean   StDev
ChickWt    86.71   24.90
```

   b. Minitab results:

One-Sample Z: ChickWt

```
The assumed standard deviation = 24.9


Variable    N     Mean    StDev  SE Mean        99% CI
ChickWt   200  86.7100  24.8989   1.7607  (82.1747, 91.2453)
```

   c. If the trend continued, the per capita consumption of chicken in 2006 would be 88 (1.3 + 86.7) pounds. The 99% confidence interval indicates that the plausible values for the 2006 per capita consumption of chicken are between 82.2 and 91.2 pounds. Since 88 is contained in this interval it is one of the plausible values and the trend seems to be continuing.

Section 8-2 Exercises

8.27

The sample size can be determined using the following steps.

Step 1: Specify the desired margin of error.

        The margin of error is given to be $e = 44$.

Step 2: Determine the population standard deviation.

        The population standard deviation is thought to be 680.

Step 3: Determine the critical value for the desired level of confidence.

        The confidence level is 95 percent. The critical value from the standard normal distribution table is $z = 1.96$.

Step 4: Compute the required sample size.

        The equation for sample size is:

$$n = \frac{z^2\sigma^2}{e^2} = \left(\frac{z\sigma}{e}\right)^2 = \left(\frac{(1.96)(680)}{44}\right)^2 = 917.54 \approx 918$$

The required sample size is 918 items from the population.

8.29

Step 1: Specify the desired margin of error.
The advertising company wants the estimate to be within $\pm$ \$2,500 of the true mean, so the margin of error is e = 2500.

Step 2: Determine the population standard deviation.
Based on previous studies or other knowledge, the population standard is known. Therefore, σ = 27,500.

Step 3: Determine the critical value for the desired level of confidence.
The critical value will be a z-value from the standard normal table for 90% confidence. This is z = 1.645.

Step 4: Compute the required sample size using Equation 8-6.

The required sample size is n = $\dfrac{z^2\sigma^2}{e^2} = \dfrac{1.645^2 27500^2}{2500^2} = 327.43 = 328$

8.31

Step 1: Specify the desired margin of error.
The estimate is to be within $\pm$ 50 of the true mean, so the margin of error is e = 50.

Step 2: Determine the population standard deviation.
Based on previous studies or other knowledge, the population variance is known to be 122500. Therefore, the population standard is
$\sigma = \sqrt{122500} = 350$.

Step 3: Determine the critical value for the desired level of confidence.
The critical value will be a z-value from the standard normal table for 95% confidence. This is z = 1.96.

Step 4: Compute the required sample size using Equation 8-6.
The required sample size is n = $\dfrac{z^2\sigma^2}{e^2} = \dfrac{1.96^2 350^2}{50^2} = 188.24 = 189$

8.33

a. Step 1: Specify the desired margin of error.
    e = 4.

    Step 2: Determine the population standard deviation.
    σ = 16

Step 3: Determine the critical value for the desired level of confidence.
$z = 1.96$

Step 4: Compute the required sample size using Equation 8-8.

$$n = \frac{z^2\sigma^2}{e^2} = \frac{1.96^2(16)^2}{4^2} = 61.47, n = 62.$$

b. Using the same steps as in part a. (1) $e = 0.5$, (2) $\sigma = 23$, (3) $z = 1.645$, (4)

$$n = \frac{1.645^2(23)^2}{0.5^2} = 5725.95, n = 5726.$$

c. (1) $e = 1$, (2) $\sigma = 0.5$, (3) $z = 2.575$, (4) $n = \frac{2.575^2(0.5)^2}{1^2} = 1.658, n = 2.$

d. (1) $e = 0.2$, (2) $\sigma = 1.5$, (3) $z = 2.33$, (4) $n = \frac{2.33^2(1.5)^2}{0.2^2} = 305.38, n = 306.$

e. (1) $e = 4$, (2) $\sigma = 16$, (3) $z = 1.96$, (4) $n = \frac{1.96^2(16)^2}{4^2} = 61.47, n = 62.$

8.35

Step 1: Specify the desired margin of error.
The research group wants the estimate to be within ± 100 seconds of the true mean, so the margin of error is $e = 100$.

Step 2: Determine the population standard deviation.
Based on the pilot study the standard deviation is found to be $1,225. Therefore, σ is assumed to be 1,225.

Step 3: Determine the critical value for the desired level of confidence.
The critical value will be a z-value from the standard normal table for 90% confidence. This is $z = 1.645$.

Step 4: Compute the required sample size using Equation 8-6.
The required sample size is n =

$$\frac{z^2\sigma^2}{e^2} = \frac{1.645^2 1225^2}{100^2} = 406.07 = 407 \text{ samples must be taken.}$$

8.37

a. The sample size can be determined using the following steps.

Step 1: Specify the desired margin of error.
The margin of error is given to be $e = 0.25$.

Step 2: Determine the population standard deviation.
The population standard deviation is not known so it must be estimated using the pilot sample. The following sample data were recorded:

35	33	37	33	36	40	34	40	39	40
39	41	35	42	43	46	34	41	38	44

The sample standard deviation is computed using:

$$s = \sqrt{\frac{\sum(x-\bar{x})^2}{n-1}}$$

where:

$$\bar{x} = \frac{\sum x}{n} = \frac{770}{20} = 38.5$$

Then:

$$\sigma \approx s = \sqrt{\frac{\sum(x-\bar{x})^2}{n-1}} = 3.71 \quad \sigma \cong s = \sqrt{\frac{(x-\bar{x})}{n-1}} = 3.79$$

Step 3: Determine the critical value for the desired level of confidence.
The confidence level is 95%. The critical value from the standard normal distribution table is $z = 1.96$.

Step 4: Compute the required sample size.
The equation for sample size is:

$$n = \frac{z^2\sigma^2}{e^2} = \left(\frac{z\sigma}{e}\right)^2 = \left(\frac{(1.96)(3.79)}{.25}\right)^2 = 882.898 \cong 883$$

The required sample size is 883 bags from the population. However, the 20 items in the pilot sample can be used so the net required sample is $883 - 20 = 863$.

b. If sampling an additional 863 bags is thought to be too much, the airline has the following general options for reducing the required sample size:
1. Reduce the confidence level to something less than 95 percent
2. Increase the margin of error beyond 0.25 pounds.
3. Some combination of decreasing the confidence level and increasing the margin of error.

Note, decreasing the deviation would also result in a lower required sample size but it is doubtful that the airlines can do anything about the standard deviation.

8.39

a. The sample size can be determined using the following steps.

Step 1:   Specify the desired margin of error.
The margin of error is given to be $e = 0.2$.

Step 2:   Determine the population standard deviation.
The population standard deviation is not known so it must be estimated using the pilot sample.
The sample standard deviation was computed using:

$$\sigma \approx s = \sqrt{\frac{\sum (x - \bar{x})^2}{n - 1}} = 1.4$$

Step 3:   Determine the critical value for the desired level of confidence.
The confidence level is 99 percent. The critical value from the standard normal distribution table is $z = 2.575$.

Step 4:   Compute the required sample size.
The equation for sample size is:

$$n = \frac{z^2 \sigma^2}{e^2} = \left(\frac{z\sigma}{e} \right)^2 = \left(\frac{(2.575)(1.4)}{.2} \right) = 324.9 \cong 325$$

The required sample size is 325 customers from the population. However, the 50 items in the pilot sample can be used so the net required sample is $325 - 50 = 275$.

8.41

a.

Step 1:   Specify the desired margin of error.
The restaurant managers want the estimate to be within ± 10 seconds of the true mean, so the margin of error is $e = 10$.

Step 2:   Determine the population standard deviation.
Based on previous studies or other knowledge, the population standard is known to be 30 seconds. Therefore, $\sigma = 30$.

Step 3: Determine the critical value for the desired level of confidence. The critical value will be a z-value from the standard normal table for 99% confidence. This is z = 2.575.

Step 4: Compute the required sample size using Equation 8-6.

The required sample size is n = $\dfrac{z^2\sigma^2}{e^2} = \dfrac{2.575^2 30^2}{10^2} = 59.68 = 60$ samples must be taken.

b. With a margin of error, e = 5, the required sample size is

n = $\dfrac{z^2\sigma^2}{e^2} = \dfrac{2.575^2 30^2}{5^2} = 238.70 = 239$. The manager is incorrect the required sample size has nearly quadrupled.

8.43
  a. The margin of error equals 1.25 = e. Therefore,

n = $\dfrac{z^2\sigma^2}{e^2} = \dfrac{1.96^2 10^2}{(1.25)^2} = 245.86$, n = 246.

  b. Step 1: Specify the desired margin of error. Decreasing the margin of error by a dollar would imply that the margin of error = 1.25 -1 = 0.25.

Step 2: Determine the population standard deviation: σ = 10.

Step 3: Determine the critical value for the desired level of confidence. z = 1.96

Step 4: Compute the required sample size using Equation 8-6.

n = $\dfrac{z^2\sigma^2}{e^2} = \dfrac{1.96^2 10^2}{(0.25)^2} = 6146.56$, n = 6147.

b. For n = 1,500, σ = 10, 1.96, $e = \dfrac{z\sigma}{\sqrt{n}} = \dfrac{1.96(10)}{\sqrt{1500}} = 0.5061$

For n = 2,000, σ = 10, 1.96, $e = \dfrac{z\sigma}{\sqrt{n}} = \dfrac{1.96(10)}{\sqrt{2000}} = 0.4383$.

So the range of values for the margin of error is from \$0.44 to \$0.51.

8.45

a. The sample size can be determined using the following steps.

Step 1: Specify the desired margin of error.
            The margin of error is given to be $e = 0.15$.

Step 2: Determine the population standard deviation.
            The population standard deviation is not known so it must be estimated
            using the pilot sample.   The sample standard deviation was
            computed using Excel's STDEV function:

$$\sigma \approx s = \sqrt{\dfrac{\sum (x - \bar{x})^2}{n-1}} = 3.2$$

Step 3: Determine the critical value for the desired level of confidence.
            The confidence level is 95 percent. The critical value from the standard
            normal distribution table is z = 1.96.

Step 4: Compute the required sample size.
            The equation for sample size is:

$$n = \dfrac{z^2 \sigma^2}{e^2} = \left(\dfrac{z\sigma}{e}\right)^2 = \left(\dfrac{(1.96)(3.2)}{0.15}\right)^2 = 1,748.35 \approx 1,749$$

The required sample size is 1,749 customers from the population. However, the
150 calls in the pilot sample can be used so the net required sample is 1,749 – 150
= 1,599.

b. If an additional sample size of 1,599 is considered to be too many, the
company has the option to reduce the confidence level (lowers the z-value) or
increase the margin of error or some combination of the two.

8.47

a. Using Excel

Paychecks	
Mean	36.161
Standard Error	0.508
Median	36.370
Mode	39.690
Standard Deviation	6.223
Sample Variance	38.731
Kurtosis	-0.103
Skewness	0.033
Range	32.110
Minimum	20.880
Maximum	52.990
Sum	5424.210
Count	150
Confidence Level(98.0%)	1.195

The margin of error is the Confidence Level in the output = 1.195.
The confidence interval is: $36.616 \pm 1.195 = 35.421$ to 37.811.

b. $n = \dfrac{z^2 \sigma^2}{e^2} = \left(\dfrac{z\sigma}{e}\right)^2 = \left(\dfrac{(2.33)(6.22)}{1.4}\right) = 107.16 \cong 108$

c. The 98% confidence interval, (35.421 to 37.811), is considerably below the mean hourly compensation below \$44.82. It, therefore, seems as though the average for the state and local workers' average hourly compensation is less than that of the federal government workers.

Section 8-3 Exercises

8.49

The following steps can be used in determining the confidence interval estimate for π.

Step 1: Define the population and the variable of interest.
    The population consists of all people living in the county

Step 2: Determine the sample size.
    The sample size is stated to be n = 240.

Step 3: Determine the level of confidence and the critical z value using the standard normal distribution.
The desired confidence level is 95%. The z-value for 95% confidence is z = 1.96.

Step 4: Compute the point estimate based on the sample data.
The point estimate is:

$$p = \frac{x}{n} = \frac{66}{240} = 0.28$$

Step 5: Compute the confidence interval.
The format for the confidence interval is:

$$p \pm z\sqrt{\frac{p(1-p)}{n}}$$

$$0.28 \pm 1.96\sqrt{\frac{0.28(1-0.28)}{240}}$$

$$0.28 \pm 0.056$$

0.224 ------------------------------- 0.336

Based on the sample data, with 95% confidence, we believe that the true population proportion of people that do not have health coverage is between 0.224 and 0.336.

8.51

Step 1: Define the population and variable of interest.
The problem does not specify a particular population or variable of interest. The problem requires finding a confidence interval estimate for the population proportion.

Step 2: Determine the sample size.
The sample size is given as n = 100.

Step 3: Specify the desired level of confidence and determine the critical value.
A 90% confidence level is desired. The critical value from the standard normal distribution table is z = 1.645.

Step 4: Compute the point estimate based on the sample data.
The point estimate is the sample proportion, p, which is equal to 0.40.

Step 5: Compute the confidence interval using Equation 8-10

$$p \pm z\sqrt{\frac{p(1-p)}{n}} = 0.4 \pm 1.645\sqrt{\frac{0.4(1-0.4)}{100}} = 0.4 \pm 0.0806$$

0.3194 --------- 0.4806

8.53

a. The point estimate for the population proportion for all items having the attribute of interest is, p, the sample proportion, computed using Equation 8-7.

$$p = \frac{x}{n} = \frac{144}{200} = 0.72, \text{ where } x = \text{the number of items in the sample having the}$$

attribute of interest and n = the sample size.

b.
Step 1: Define the population and variable of interest.
The problem does not specify a particular population or variable of interest. The problem requires finding a confidence interval estimate for the population proportion.

Step 2: Determine the sample size.
The sample size is given as n = 200.

Step 3: Specify the desired level of confidence and determine the critical value.
A 95% confidence level is desired. The critical value from the standard normal distribution table is z = 1.95.

Step 4: Compute the point estimate based on the sample data.
The point estimate was determined in part (a) and is equal to 0.72.

Step 5: Compute the confidence interval using Equation 8-10

$$p \pm z\sqrt{\frac{p(1-p)}{n}} = 0.72 \pm 1.96\sqrt{\frac{0.72(1-0.72)}{200}} = 0.72 \pm 0.0622$$

0.6578 --------- 0.7822

8.55

a. $p = \frac{x}{n} = \frac{7}{40} = 0.175$

b.
Step 1: Define the population and the variable of interest.
The population is all of the TV viewers in the U.S., and the variable of interest is the proportion of individuals who said they watched the current week's epsisode of "Lost."

Step 2: Determine the sample size.
The sample size was n = 40. np = 40(7/40) = 7 and n(1-p) = 40[1 – (7/40)] = 33 > 5. Therefore, the sampling distribution of p can be justifiably approximately by a normal distribution.

Step 3: Specify the desired level of confidence and determine the critical value
For a 95% confidence level, the critical value from the standard normal distribution table is z = 1.96.

Step 4: Compute the point estimate based on the sample data.

$$p = \frac{x}{n} = \frac{7}{40} = 0.175$$

Step 5: Compute the confidence interval using Equation 8-10.

$$p \pm z\sqrt{\frac{p(1-p)}{n}} = 0.175 + 1.96\sqrt{\frac{0.175(1-0.175)}{40}} = 0.175 \pm 0.118 =$$
(0.057, 0. 293)

c. The equation to calculate the required sample size is

$$n = \frac{z^2 p(1-p)}{e^2} = \frac{1.96^2(0.175)(1-0.175)}{(0.025)^2} = 887.4, n = 888.$$

8.57

The following steps can be used in determining the confidence interval estimate for π.
Step 1: Define the population and the variable of interest.
The population consists of all people in North America who drive.

Step 2: Determine the sample size.
The sample size is stated to be n = 1,100.

Step 3: Determine the level of confidence and the critical z value using the standard normal distribution.
The desired confidence level is 95%. The z-value for 95% confidence is z = 1.96.

Step 4: Compute the point estimate based on the sample data.
The point estimate is:

$$p = \frac{x}{n} = 0.33$$

Step 5: Compute the confidence interval.
The format for the confidence interval is:

$$p \pm z\sqrt{\frac{p(1-p)}{n}}$$

$$0.33 \pm 1.96\sqrt{\frac{0.33(1-0.33)}{1,100}}$$

$$0.33 \pm 0.028$$

0.302 ---------------------------------- 0.358

Based on the sample data, with 95% confidence, we believe that the true population proportion of drivers who are annoyed by cell phone users is between 0.302 and 0.358.

8.59

Assuming that the sampling by *Allure* magazine was done using random sampling methods, the confidence interval estimate can be developed using the following steps.

Step 1: Define the population and the variable of interest.
The population consists of all women in the United States.

Step 2: Determine the sample size.
The sample size is stated to be n = 1,000.

Step 3: Determine the level of confidence and the critical z value using the standard normal distribution.
The desired confidence level is 90%. The z-value for 90% confidence is z = 1.645.

Step 4: Compute the point estimate based on the sample data.
The point estimate is:

$$p = \frac{x}{n} = 0.91$$

Step 5: Compute the confidence interval.
The format for the confidence interval is:

$$p \pm z\sqrt{\frac{p(1-p)}{n}}$$

$$0.91 \pm 1.645\sqrt{\frac{0.91(1-0.91)}{1,000}}$$

$$0.91 \pm 0.015$$

0.895 ---------------------------------- 0.925

Based on the sample data, with 95% confidence, Nike can conclude that the true proportion of women who are satisfied with their bodies is between 0.895 and 0.925. However, because Nike's target population is not "all" women, they should be careful in how they use the results of this survey. The proportions may overstate the true proportion of younger women who have a positive view of their bodies.

8.61

a.

Step 1: Define the population and variable of interest.
The population of interest is adults in Albuquerque between the ages of 25 and 35. The variable of interest is the number of these adults that have a college degree in a high-technology field.

Step 2: Determine the level of confidence and find the critical z-value using the standard normal distribution.
The desired level of confidence is 95%. The z-value for the 95% confidence level is 1.96.

Step 3: Determine the desired margin of error.
The Chamber of Commerce wants the estimate to be within $\pm\, 0.03$ percentage points of the true proportion. Therefore, the margin of error is e = 0.03.

Step 4: Arrive at the value to use for the population proportion, π.
Because the Chamber has no information concerning the proportion of adults with the variable of interest a conservative estimate is used. Therefore, $\pi = 0.5$ is assumed.

Step 5: Compute the sample size required using Equation 8-12.

$$n = \frac{z^2\pi(1-\pi)}{e^2} = \frac{1.96^2\ 0.5(1-0.5)}{0.03^2} = 1{,}067.22 \ or \ 1068.$$

The required sample size is 1,068

b.

Step 1: Define the population and variable of interest.
The population of interest is adults in Albuquerque between the ages of 25 and 35. The variable of interest is the number of these adults that have a college degree in a high-technology field.

Step 2: Determine the level of confidence and find the critical z-value using the standard normal distribution.
The desired level of confidence is 95%. The z-value for the 95% confidence level is 1.96.

Step 3: Determine the desired margin of error.
The Chamber of Commerce wants the estimate to be within ± 0.03 percentage points of the true proportion. Therefore, the margin of error is e = 0.03.

Step 4: Arrive at the value to use for the population proportion, π.
A pilot study indicates that the sample proportion of the population having the variable of interest is $p = \dfrac{x}{n} = \dfrac{28}{200} = 0.14$. Therefore, p = 0.14 is used for π.

Step 5: Compute the sample size required using Equation 8-12.
$$n = \frac{z^2 \pi(1-\pi)}{e^2} = \frac{1.96^2 \ 0.14(1-0.14)}{0.03^2} = 513.92 \ or \ 514 \ .$$

The required sample size is 514. The Chamber can use the 200 from the pilot study, which results in an additional 514-200 = 314 samples needed.

8.63

a. The desired level of confidence is 90%. The z-value for the 90% confidence level is 1.645. The estimate is to be within ± 0.03 percentage points of the true proportion. Therefore, the margin of error is e = 0.03. The company performed a pilot study to determine an estimate for the population proportion. The sample proportion is 14/100 = 0.14, therefore the estimate for the population proportion, π, is 0.14. Compute the sample size required using Equation 8-12.

$$n = \frac{z^2 \pi(1-\pi)}{e^2} = \frac{1.645^2 \ 0.14(1-0.14)}{0.03^2} = 362.006 = 363.$$ The company will need to randomly sample an additional 363 – 100 = 263 employees.

b. The point estimate for the population proportion is calculated from the sample information as 50/363 = 0.1377, where the sample size of 363 was determined in part (a). A 90% confidence level is desired. The critical value from the standard normal distribution table is z = 1.645. Compute the confidence interval using Equation 8-10

$$p \pm z\sqrt{\frac{p(1-p)}{n}} = 0.1377 \pm 1.645\sqrt{\frac{0.1377(1-0.1377)}{363}} = 0.1377 \pm 0.0298 =$$

0.1079 --------- 0.1675.

8.65

a. The confidence interval is given by $p \pm z\sqrt{\frac{p(1-p)}{n}} = p \pm e = 0.66 \pm 0.05 = (0.61,$

0.71).

b. The equation to calculate the required sample size for Seniors is

$$n = \frac{z^2 p(1-p)}{e^2} = \frac{1.96^2 0.66(1-0.66)}{(0.05)^2} = 344.82 , n = 345.$$

For Baby Boomers

$$n = \frac{z^2 p(1-p)}{e^2} = \frac{1.96^2 0.61(1-0.61)}{(0.05)^2} = 365.57 , n = 366.$$

For Generation X

$$n = \frac{z^2 p(1-p)}{e^2} = \frac{1.96^2 0.58(1-0.58)}{(0.05)^2} = 374.33 , n = 375.$$

8.67

a. Use Excel to count the number of working adults in Atlanta between the ages of 35 and 44 who own a 401(k) type retirement plan. The number is 56; therefore, the point estimate for the population proportion is calculated from the sample information as 56/144 = 0.3889. The sample size is 144. A 95% confidence level is desired. The critical value from the standard normal distribution table is z = 1.96. Compute the confidence interval using Equation 8-10

$$p \pm z\sqrt{\frac{p(1-p)}{n}} = 0.3889 \pm 1.96\sqrt{\frac{0.3889(1-0.3889)}{144}} = 0.3889 \pm 0.0796 =$$

0.3093 --------- 0.4685.

b. No, the Atlanta Chamber of Commerce should not advertise that a greater proportion of working adults in Atlanta between the ages of 35 and 44 have 401(k) type retirement plans in 2002 than in the nation as a whole. The sample proportion for Atlanta, p = 0.3889, is higher than the national proportion of 0.34 but the estimated Atlanta proportion is subject to sampling error. When the confidence interval is calculated we find that the national average of 0.34 falls within the confidence interval limits. Therefore, it would not be correct to advertise that Atlanta has a greater proportion of its 35-44 year old adults participating than the nation as a whole.

8.69

a. Minitab output:

Test and CI for One Proportion: Referrals

```
Test of p = 0.5 vs p not = 0.5

Event = referral


Variable     X    N  Sample p          95% CI          Z-Value  P-Value
Referrals  291  502  0.579681  (0.536502, 0.622861)     3.57    0.000
```

The margin of error is half the distance between the upper and lower control limits. Therefore, the margin of error = (0.6229 – 0.5365)/2 = 0.0432.

b. The confidence interval is provided by the Minitab output in part a., (0.5365, 0.6229).

c. To "decrease the margin of error by 25%" would result in a margin of error = 0.75(0.0432) = 0.0324 = e. The required sample size is

$$n = \frac{z^2 p(1-p)}{e^2} = \frac{1.96^2 0.58(1-0.58)}{(0.0324)^2} = 891.45 \,, \, n = 892$$

End of Chapter Exercises

8.71

The "double whammy" is that you must use the sample standard deviation as an estimate for the population standard deviation and that you must use the t-distribution instead of the normal distribution. The t will be greater than z for a given confidence level and $s/\sqrt{n}$ will be a larger value when n is small.

8.73

This is not correct. The average number of miles people commute is a single value. Therefore it has no probability. What the confidence interval is telling you is that if you want to produce all the possible confidence intervals using each possible sample mean from the population, 95% of these intervals would contain the population mean.

8.75

a. $n = (1.96)^2(200)^2/(50)^2 = 61.4656$ or 62 so you would need to sample 62-40 = 22 more

b. cost of pilot with the 22 additional sampled = (62)($10) = $620
without pilot:
$n = (1.96)^2(300)^2/(50)^2 = 138.29$ or 139 @ $10 = $1390;
so savings of $1390 - $620 = $770

8.77

a. $0.76 \pm 1.645(\sqrt{[(0.76)(1-0.76]/441}\,)$; 0.7265 ----- 0.7935

b. 0.7265(35,000) ----- 0.7935(35,000); 25,427.50 ----- 27,772.50

8.79

a. $\bar{x} = \dfrac{\sum x_i}{n} = \dfrac{250,000}{48,000} = 5.21$

b. $n = \dfrac{z^2\sigma^2}{e^2} = \dfrac{1.645^2 1.5^2}{(1/8)^2} = 389.67$, n = 390

c. $e = \dfrac{z\sigma}{\sqrt{n}} = \dfrac{1.645(1.5)}{\sqrt{100}} = 0.25$ work days = 2.00 work hours.

8.81

Using Excel's average and stdev functions the mean = 11.9991; standard deviation = 0.2002

$11.9991 \pm 1.96(0.2002/\sqrt{5000})$; 11.9936 ----- 12.0046

The confidence interval does include the 12 ounces. However, it barely includes the 12 ounces and if you consider any weight for the can itself they may actually determine that the mean fluid in the can is not 12 ounces.

8.83

a. $p = 404/548 = 0.7372$

Count of Current Cable Subscriber	
Current Cable Subscriber	Total
No	144
Yes	404
Grand Total	548

$0.7372 \pm 1.96(\sqrt{[(0.7372)(1-0.7372]/548})$; 0.7372 ± 0.0369; 0.7003 ----- 0.7741

b.

Household Annual Income	
Mean	32801.09489
Standard Error	266.1365661
Median	31000
Mode	30000
Standard Deviation	6230.097282
Sample Variance	38814112.14
Kurtosis	3.044243192
Skewness	1.481126946
Range	41000
Minimum	20000
Maximum	61000
Sum	17975000
Count	548

$32801.095 \pm 1.96(6230.097/\sqrt{548})$; 32,279.4674 ----- 33,322.7227

Based on the sample data, with 95% confidence the company can conclude that the mean income is between $32,279 and $33,323.

8.85

a. The population mean = 9987.44

b.

Classes	Frequency
5001 - 6000	0
6001 - 7000	1
7001 - 8000	4
8001 - 9000	24
9001 - 10000	100
10001 - 11000	79
11001 - 12000	40
12001 - 13000	2

Histogram

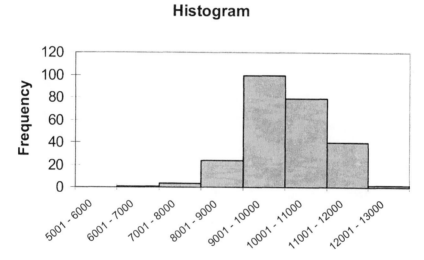

c.

Count of Sales	
Region	Total
East	39.60%
Midwest	17.60%
South	31.60%
West	11.20%
Grand Total	100.00%

d. e, and f. Student answers for d-f will vary depending upon the sample selected.

Chapter 8

Chapter 9 Solutions

When applicable, selected problems in each section will be done following the appropriate step-by-step procedures outlined in the corresponding sections of the chapter. Other problems will provide key points and the answers to the questions, but all answers can be arrived at using the appropriate steps.

Section 9-1 Exercises

9.1

    a. $z = 1.96$

    b. $t = -1.6991$

    c. $t = \pm 2.4033$

    d. $z = \pm 1.645$

9.3

    a. This is a one-tailed test of the population mean with σ unknown. Therefore, the decision rule is: reject the null hypothesis if the calculated value of the test statistic, t, is less than the critical value of -2.0639. Otherwise, do not reject.

    b. $t = (20-23)/(8/\sqrt{25}) = -1.875$

    c. Because the computed value of $t = -1.875$ is not less than the critical value of $t = -2.0639$, do not reject the null hypothesis and conclude that the mean is not less than 23.

9.5

    a. This is a two-tailed test of the population mean with σ unknown. Therefore, the decision rule is: reject the null hypothesis if the calculated value of the test statistic, t, is less than -2.1448 or greater than 2.1448. Otherwise, do not reject.

    b. $t = (62.2-60.5)/(7.5/\sqrt{15}) = .878$

    c. Because the computed value of $t = .878$ is not less than -2.1448 and not greater than 2.1448, do not reject the null hypothesis.

9.7

a. p-value $= P(z > 1.34) = 0.5000 - 0.4099 = 0.0901$

b. p-value $= P(z > 2.09) = 0.5000 - 0.4817 = 0.0183$

c. p-value $= P(z < -1.55) = 0.5000 - 0.4394 = 0.0606$

9.9

a. This is a one tailed test with the population standard deviation known so a z value can be calculated:

$$z = \frac{\overline{x} - \mu}{\frac{\sigma}{\sqrt{n}}} = \frac{58.4 - 58}{\frac{0.8}{\sqrt{16}}} = 2,$$

Using the standard normal distribution table, the p-value $= 0.5 - 0.4772 = 0.0228$

b. This is a two tailed test with the population standard deviation unknown so a t value is determined:

$$t = \frac{\overline{x} - \mu}{\frac{s}{\sqrt{n}}} = \frac{58.4 - 45}{\frac{35.407}{\sqrt{41}}} = 2.4233,$$

Using the t-distribution table with 40 degrees of freedom, the p-value $= 2(0.01) = 0.02$

c. This is a two tailed test, like b., but now the population standard deviation is known so a z value can be calculated:

$$z = \frac{\overline{x} - \mu}{\frac{\sigma}{\sqrt{n}}} = \frac{58.4 - 45}{\frac{35.407}{\sqrt{41}}} = 2.4233$$

Using the standard normal distribution table, the p-value $= 2(0.5 - 0.4922) = 0.0156$.

d. This is a one tailed test with the population standard deviation unknown so a t value is determined after the sample standard deviation is calculated:

$$s = \sqrt{\frac{\sum(x-\bar{x})^2}{n-1}} = \sqrt{\frac{130.48}{4}} = \sqrt{32.62}$$

$$t = \frac{\bar{x}-\mu}{\frac{s}{\sqrt{n}}} = \frac{58.4-69}{\frac{5.7114}{\sqrt{5}}} = -4.15,$$

The calculated t value falls between the 0.005 and 0.01 columns in the t-distribution table, so the p-value is in this range. [p-value = 0.0071 found using Excel]

9.11

a. If the null hypothesis is rejected a Type I error would be committed.

b. If the null hypothesis is not true a Type II error would be committed.

c. If the null hypothesis is true a Type I error would be committed.

d. No error is made.

e. If the null hypothesis is not rejected a Type II error would be committed.

f. No error is made.

9.13

Step 1: Specify the population value of interest.
The association is interested in the average initiation fee, μ.

Step 2: Formulate the null and alternative hypotheses.
　　Ho: $\mu \le 33757$
　　H$_A$: $\mu > 33757$

Step 3. Specify the significance level.
　　$\alpha = 0.05$

Step 4: Construct the rejection region.
With d.f. = 9 – 1 = 8, reject Ho if t is greater than 1.8595. Otherwise, do not reject.

Step 5. Compute the test statistic.
With n = 9, s = 3877.34, and $\bar{x}$ =35091.56.

$$t = \frac{35091.56 - 33757}{\frac{3877.34}{\sqrt{9}}} = 1.0326.$$

Step 6. Reach a decision.
Because $t = 1.0326$ is less than 1.8595, do not reject Ho.

Step 7. Draw a conclusion.
Initiation fees for U.S. country-club memberships have not increased over the 2004 average.

9.15

a. H_o: $\mu = 24$ ounces
     H_a: $\mu \neq 24$ ounces

b. $t = (24.32 - 24)/(0.7/\sqrt{16}) = 1.83$

     $t_{.05/2} = \pm 2.1315$
     Since $-2.1315 < 1.83 < 2.1315$ do not reject H_o and conclude that the filling machine remains all right to operate.

c.   Because the production control manager does not want the boxes under-filled or over-filled.

d.   Using Excel's TDIST function, p-value = 0.0872 > 0.025; therefore do not reject H_o

e.   Since the null hypothesis was "accepted", a Type II error may have been committed.

9.17

a.

$$H_o : \mu \geq 55$$
$$H_A : \mu < 55$$

b. Since the population standard deviation is unknown, the t-distribution should be used to conduct this test as long as you are willing to assume that the population is approximately normal.

The sample provides the following statistics:

$$\bar{x} = \frac{\sum x}{n} = \frac{1,562}{30} = 52.07 \quad \text{and} \quad s = \sqrt{\frac{\sum(x - \bar{x})^2}{n-1}} = 17.19$$

The test statistic is:

$$t = \frac{\bar{x} - \mu}{\frac{s}{\sqrt{n}}} = \frac{52.07 - 55}{\frac{17.19}{\sqrt{30}}} = -0.93$$

From the t-distribution table for alpha = 0.01 and df = 29, the critical t-value for a one tail test is −2.4620. Because t = -0.93 > -2.4620, the null hypothesis is not rejected. Thus, based on these sample data, we are unable to reject the null hypothesis. Thus, the statement that the mean age of millionaires in the United States is less than 55 years old is not supported by the data

9.19

Step 1: Specify the population value of interest.
The population value of interest is the average past due amount, μ.

Step 2: Formulate the null and alternative hypotheses.

$$H_o : \mu \le \$20.00$$
$$H_A : \mu > \$20.00$$

Step 3. Specify the significance level.

$$\alpha = 0.10.$$

Step 4. Compute the test statistic.
Because the population standard deviation, σ, is assumed known with a value of $60.00, the standard normal distribution can be used to conduct the hypothesis test. We can use software such as Excel or Minitab to compute the sample mean past due amount from the data in the file. Using Excel's *AVERAGE* function, we get:

$$\bar{x} = 24.84$$
$$z = \frac{\bar{x} - \mu}{\frac{\sigma}{\sqrt{n}}} = \frac{24.84 - 20}{\frac{60}{\sqrt{67}}} = 0.66$$

Step 5: Calculate the p-value.

$$\text{p-value} = P(z > 0.66)$$
$$= 0.50 - 0.2454 = 0.2546$$

Step 6. Reach a decision.

Because p-value = 0.2546 > alpha = 0.10, we do not reject the null hypothesis.

Step 7. Draw a conclusion.

The sample data do not provide sufficient evidence to reject the call center manager's statement that the mean past due amount is $20.00 or less.

9.21

a. H_O: $\mu = 66$

H_A: $\mu \neq 66$

reject H_O if $|t| > 2.8073$

$\bar{x} = 66.3126$ s = 0.6976

$$t = \frac{\bar{x} - \mu}{\frac{s}{\sqrt{n}}} = \frac{66.3126 - 66}{\frac{0.6976}{\sqrt{24}}} = 2.1953,$$

Since t = 2.1953 < 2.8073 do not reject H_O. There is not sufficient evidence to conclude that the average height of the plastic tees is different from 66 mm.

b. The null hypothesis, the specification is being met, was rejected when in fact it was being met, this is a Type I error.

Section 9-2 Exercises

9.23

a. $z = 1.96$

b. $z = -1.645$

c. $z = \pm 2.33$

d. $z = \pm 1.645$

9.25

a. This is a one-tailed test of the population proportion. The decision rule is: reject the null hypothesis if the calculated value of the test statistic, z, is less than the critical value of the test statistic z = -1.96. Otherwise, do not reject.

b. $z = (0.66-0.75)/ (\sqrt{0.75*(1-0.75)/100})=-2.0785$

c. Because the computed value of z= -2.0785 is less than the critical value of z = -1.96, reject the null hypothesis and conclude that the population proportion is less than 0.75.

9.27

Begin by computing the sample proportion as:

$$p = \frac{x}{n} = \frac{105}{200} = 0.525$$

The z-test statistic is computed as follows:

$$z = \frac{p - \pi}{\sqrt{\dfrac{\pi(1-\pi)}{n}}} = \frac{0.525 - 0.60}{\sqrt{\dfrac{(0.60)(0.40)}{200}}} = -2.17$$

From the standard normal table, the critical z-values for a one-tailed test with alpha = .05 is z = -2.33 Since -2.17 > -2.33, the null hypothesis is not rejected.

9.29

a. $z = \dfrac{0.12-0.30}{\sqrt{\dfrac{0.3(0.7)}{25}}} = -1.964$

p-value = $2[P(z \le -1.964)] = 2(.5 - 0.475) = 0.05$

b. $z = \dfrac{0.35 - 0.30}{\sqrt{\dfrac{0.3(0.7)}{25}}} = .5454$

p-value $= 2[P(z \geq 0.5454)] = 2(.5 - 0.2054) = 0.5892$

c. $z = \dfrac{0.42 - 0.30}{\sqrt{\dfrac{0.3(0.7)}{25}}} = 1.3093$

p-value $= 2[P(z \geq 1.3093)] = 2(.5 - 0.4049) = 0.1902$

d. $z = \dfrac{0.50 - 0.30}{\sqrt{\dfrac{0.3(0.7)}{25}}} = 2.1822$

p-value $= 2[P(z \geq 2.1822)] = 2(.5 - 0.4854) = 0.0292$

9.31

Step 1: Specify the population value of interest.
The value of interest is the population proportion, π.

Step 2: Formulate the null and alternative hypotheses.
Ho: $\pi \geq 0.65$
H_A: $\pi < 0.65$

Step 3. Specify the significance level.
$\alpha = 0.02$

Step 4: Construct the rejection region.
If z is less than -2.055, reject Ho. Otherwise, do not reject.

Step 5. Compute the test statistic.
x= the number preferring stocks = 900-360 = 540

p = x/n = 540/900 =0.60

$$z = \frac{0.60 - 0.65}{\sqrt{\frac{0.65*(1-0.65)}{900}}} = -3.145$$

Step 6. Reach a decision.
Because z = -3.145 is less than -2.055, reject Ho.

Step 7. Draw a conclusion.
A lower proportion of investors prefer stocks today than 10 years ago.

9.33

a. The appropriate null and alternative hypotheses are:

$$H_o : \pi = 0.69$$
$$H_A : \pi \neq 0.69$$

b. The first step is to compute the sample proportion:

$$p = \frac{x}{n} = \frac{105}{180} = 0.58$$

The z-test statistic is computed as follows:

$$z = \frac{p - \pi}{\sqrt{\frac{\pi(1-\pi)}{n}}} = \frac{0.58 - 0.69}{\sqrt{\frac{(0.69)(0.31)}{180}}} = -3.19$$

The z-critical values from the standard normal table for a two-tailed test with alpha = 0.05 are z = 1.96 and z = -1.96. Since z = -3.19 < -1.96, we reject the null hypothesis. Thus, based on these sample data, we believe that the accuracy rate is actually lower than the 0.69 rate quoted in the *Detroit Free Press* article.

9.35

    a. The null and alternative hypotheses are:

$$H_o : \pi \leq 0.40$$
$$H_A : \pi > 0.40$$

    b. The sample proportion is:

$$p = \frac{x}{n} = \frac{174}{400} = 0.435$$

    The z-test statistic is computed as follows:

$$z = \frac{p - \pi}{\sqrt{\dfrac{\pi(1-\pi)}{n}}} = \frac{0.435 - 0.40}{\sqrt{\dfrac{(0.40)(0.60)}{400}}} = 1.43$$

The critical z-value from the standard normal table for a one-tailed test with alpha = 0.05 is 1.645. Since z = 1.43 < 1.645, we do not reject the null hypothesis. Therefore, the statement that population proportion exceeds .40 is not statistically supported by these sample data.

9.37

a.

Step 1: Specify the population value of interest.
       The value of interest is the population proportion, π.

Step 2: Formulate the null and alternative hypotheses.
       $H_O: \pi \leq 0.70$
       $H_A: \pi > 0.70$

Step 3. Specify the significance level.
       $\alpha = 0.025$

Step 4: Construct the rejection region.
       Reject H_O if p-value < 0.025

Step 5. Compute the test statistic.

$$z = \frac{p - \pi}{\sqrt{\dfrac{\pi(1-\pi)}{n}}} = \frac{0.73 - 0.70}{\sqrt{\dfrac{0.70(0.30)}{1000}}} = 2.0702$$

p-value = 0.5 - 0.4808 = 0.0192

Step 6. Reach a decision.
Since the p-value = 0.0192 is less than $\alpha = 0.025$, reject H_O.

Step 7. Draw a conclusion.
There is sufficient evidence to conclude that more than 70% of adults prefer seeing movies in their homes.

b.   A Type II error involves failing to reject H_0 when H_A is true . Here a Type II error would be concluding that the poll does not indicate that more than 70% of adults prefer seeing movies in their homes when, in fact, they do.

9.39

a. H_o: $\pi \geq 0.01$
     H_a: $\pi < 0.01$

p = 6/800 = 0.0075

z = (0.0075 – 0.01)/ $\sqrt{(0.01)(1-0.01)/800}$ = -0.7107

Decision Rule:
If z < -1.645 reject H_o, otherwise do not reject

Since z = -0.7107 > -1.645 do not reject and conclude that the percentage of lost luggage is 1% or more.

b. 0.0075 $\pm$ 1.96($\sqrt{(0.0075)(1-0.0075)/800}$); .0075 $\pm$ .006 ; 0.0015 ----- 0.0135

Chapter 9

9.41

Step 1: Specify the population value of interest.
The value of interest is the population proportion, π.

Step 2: Formulate the null and alternative hypotheses.
Ho: $\pi \geq 0.21$
H_A: $\pi < 0.21$

Step 3. Specify the significance level.
$\alpha = 0.025$

Step 4: Construct the rejection region.
Decision Rule: If z is less than -1.96 reject Ho. Otherwise, do not reject.

Step 5. Compute the test statistic.
x =30

$p = x/n = 30/198 = 0.1515$

$$z = \frac{0.1515 - 0.21}{\sqrt{\frac{0.21*(1-0.21)}{198}}} = -2.021$$

Step 6. Reach a decision.
Because z = -2.021 is less than -1.96, reject Ho.

Step 7. Draw a conclusion.
A smaller percentage of the employees are receiving more spam that a year ago.

9.43   a. The appropriate null and alternative hypotheses are:

$$H_o : \pi = 0.50$$
$$H_A : \pi \neq 0.50$$

b. We have set this up as a two-tailed test because the statement made was exactly 50 percent of cell phones are registered to females. The sample data contain data for 50 individuals of which 20 are female

Next, we compute the sample proportion as:

$$p = \frac{x}{n} = \frac{20}{50} = 0.40$$

The z-test statistic is computed as follows:

$$z = \frac{p - \pi}{\sqrt{\dfrac{\pi(1-\pi)}{n}}} = \frac{0.40 - 0.50}{\sqrt{\dfrac{(0.50)(0.50)}{50}}} = -1.41$$

The z-critical values from the standard normal table for a two-tailed test with alpha = 0.05 are z = 1.96 and z = -1.96. Since z = -1.41 > -1.645, we do not reject the null hypothesis. Thus, based on these sample data, there is insufficient evidence to conclude that the 0.50 rate of female cell phone ownership is wrong.

9.45

a. The appropriate null and alternative hypotheses are:

$$H_o : \pi \geq 0.95$$
$$H_A : \pi < 0.95$$

Note, the hypothesis is tested as a one tail test as Seadoo would only be interested in rejecting the hypothesis if the sample proportion of highly satisfied customers is too low.

b. Based on the sample data in the file called Seadoo, a total of 638 customers in the sample of 700 were highly satisfied.

Next, we compute the sample proportion as:

$$p = \frac{x}{n} = \frac{638}{700} = 0.91$$

The z-test statistic is computed as follows:

$$z = \frac{p - \pi}{\sqrt{\dfrac{\pi(1-\pi)}{n}}} = \frac{0.91 - 0.95}{\sqrt{\dfrac{(0.95)(0.05)}{700}}} = -4.85$$

The z-critical values from the standard normal table for a one-tailed test with alpha = 0.05 is z = -1.645. Since z = -4.85 < -1.645, we reject the null hypothesis. Thus, based on these sample data, there is sufficient evidence to reject the null hypothesis and conclude that less than 95 percent of Seadoo's customers are "Highly Satisfied"

Section 9-3 Exercises

9.47

    a. $\bar{x}_\alpha = 4{,}350 - 1.645(200/\sqrt{100}\,)$; $\bar{x}_\alpha = 4{,}317.10$

        $P(z > (4317.10 - 4345)/(200/\sqrt{100}\,)$; $= P(z > -1.40) = 0.5 + 0.4192 = 0.9192$

    b. Power $= 1 - \text{Beta} = 1 - 0.9192 = 0.0808$

    c. The power increases, and beta decreases, as the sample size increases. We could also increase alpha since alpha and beta are inversely related.

    d. If $\bar{x} < 4{,}317.10$, reject the null hypothesis
        Otherwise, do not reject the null hypothesis
            Since $\bar{x} = 4{,}337.5 > 4{,}317.1$, do not reject the null hypothesis.

9.49

Given $\alpha = 0.10$ for a two-tailed test $z = \pm 1.645$

$200 + 1.645 * (24/\sqrt{36}\,) = 206.58$; $200 - 1.645 * (24/\sqrt{36}\,) = 193.42$

Type II Error $= \text{Prob}((193.42 - 197)/(24/\sqrt{36}\,) \le z \le (206.58 - 197)/(24/\sqrt{36}\,))$
Type II Error $= \text{Prob}(-0.895 \le z \le 2.395) \approx 0.3146 + 0.4917 = 0.8063$

9.51

Given the one-tailed hypothesis test with alpha $= 0.05$, the critical z-value from the standard normal table is $z = 1.645$

Next, we compute the critical value which marks the cut-off for the rejection region as follows:

$$\bar{x}_\alpha = \mu + z_\alpha \frac{\sigma}{\sqrt{n}}$$

$$\bar{x}_\alpha = 100 + 1.645\frac{10}{\sqrt{49}} = 102.35$$

Next, we calculate the z-value associated with the "true" population mean as follows:

$$z = \frac{102.35 - 103}{\frac{10}{\sqrt{49}}} = -0.46$$

The probability from the standard normal table for a z-value of -0.46 is 0.1772. Then beta = 0.5000 – 0.1772 = 0.3228. Thus, there is over a 0.32 chance that a type II error will be made.

9.53

a. $H_0: \mu = 30$
    $H_A: \mu \neq 30$

$\alpha = 0.05$

$\pm z_{\alpha/2} = \pm 1.96$

$$\bar{x}_{L/U} = \mu \pm z_{\alpha/2} \frac{\sigma}{\sqrt{n}} = 30 \pm 1.96 \frac{13}{\sqrt{50}}, \text{ so:}$$

$\bar{x}_L = 26.3966$ and $\bar{x}_U = 33.6034$

For $\mu = 22$, $z = \dfrac{\bar{x}_L - \mu}{\frac{\sigma}{\sqrt{n}}} = \dfrac{26.3966 - 22}{\frac{13}{\sqrt{50}}} = 2.3914$

and $z = \dfrac{\bar{x}_U - \mu}{\frac{\sigma}{\sqrt{n}}} = \dfrac{33.6034 - 22}{\frac{13}{\sqrt{50}}}$

$\beta = P(2.39 < z < 6.31) = 0.5 - 0.4916 = 0.0084$

b. $\alpha = 0.05$

$\pm z_{\alpha/2} = \pm 1.96$

$\bar{x}_{L/U} = \mu \pm z_{\alpha/2} \dfrac{\sigma}{\sqrt{n}} = 30 \pm 1.96 \dfrac{13}{\sqrt{50}}$, so

$\bar{x}_L = 26.3966$ and $\bar{x}_U = 33.6034$

For $\mu = 25$, $z = \dfrac{\overline{x_L} - \mu}{\dfrac{\sigma}{\sqrt{n}}} = \dfrac{26.3966 - 25}{\dfrac{13}{\sqrt{50}}} = 0.7596$ and

$z = \dfrac{\overline{x_U} - \mu}{\dfrac{\sigma}{\sqrt{n}}} = \dfrac{33.6034 - 25}{\dfrac{13}{\sqrt{50}}} = 4.6796$

$\beta = P(0.76 < z < 4.68) = 0.5 - 0.2764 = 0.2236$

c. $\alpha = 0.05$

$\pm z_{\alpha/2} = \pm 1.96$

$\bar{x}_{L/U} = \mu \pm z_{\alpha/2} \dfrac{\sigma}{\sqrt{n}} = 30 \pm 1.96 \dfrac{13}{\sqrt{50}}$ so

$\bar{x}_L = 26.3966$ and $\bar{x}_U = 33.6034$

For $\mu = 29$, $z = \dfrac{\overline{x_L} - \mu}{\dfrac{\sigma}{\sqrt{n}}} = \dfrac{26.3966 - 29}{\dfrac{13}{\sqrt{50}}} = -1.4161$ and

$z = \dfrac{\overline{x_U} - \mu}{\dfrac{\sigma}{\sqrt{n}}} = \dfrac{33.6034 - 29}{\dfrac{13}{\sqrt{50}}} = 2.5039$

$\beta = P(-1.42 \leq z \leq 2.50) = 0.4222 + 0.4938 = 0.9160$

9.55

a. Given the one-tailed hypothesis test with $\alpha = 0.01$, the critical z-value from the standard normal table is $z = -2.33$

Next, we compute the critical value which marks the cut-off for the rejection region as follows:

$$p_\alpha = \pi + z_\alpha \sqrt{\frac{\pi(1-\pi)}{n}} = 0.35 - 2.33 \sqrt{\frac{0.35(1-0.35)}{400}}$$

$p_\alpha = 0.294$

Next, we calculate the z-value associated with the "true" population mean as follows:

$$z = \frac{0.294 - 0.32}{\sqrt{\dfrac{0.32(1-0.32)}{400}}} = -1.11$$

The probability from the standard normal table for a z-value of -1.11 is 0.3665. Then $\beta = 0.5000 + 0.3665 = 0.8665$. We then solve for the power as:

Power $= 1 - \beta$

$= 1 - 0.8665 = 0.1335$

Thus, there is only about a 13% chance that the hypothesis test will reject that the population mean is 0.35 or more if the true mean is actually 0.32.

b. Done like a. with different true π and critical z values.

$$p_\alpha = \pi + z_\alpha \sqrt{\frac{\pi(1-\pi)}{n}} = 0.35 - 1.96 \sqrt{\frac{0.35(1-0.35)}{400}}$$

$p_\alpha = 0.303$

Next, we calculate the z-value associated with the "true" population mean as follows:

$$z = \frac{0.303 - 0.33}{\sqrt{\dfrac{0.33(1-0.33)}{400}}} = -1.15$$

The probability from the standard normal table for a z-value of -1.15 is 0.3749. Then $\beta = 0.5000 + 0.3749 = 0.8749$. We then solve for the power as:

$$Power = 1 - \beta$$

$$= 1 - 0.8749 = 0.1251$$

c. Done like a. with different true π and critical z values.

$$p_\alpha = \pi + z_\alpha \sqrt{\frac{\pi(1-\pi)}{n}} = 0.35 - 1.645\sqrt{\frac{0.35(1-0.35)}{400}}$$

$$p_\alpha = 0.311$$

Next, we calculate the z-value associated with the "true" population mean as follows:

$$z = \frac{0.311 - 0.34}{\sqrt{\dfrac{0.34(1-0.34)}{400}}} = -1.22$$

The probability from the standard normal table for a z-value of -1.22 is 0.3888. Then $\beta = 0.5000 + 0.3888 = 0.8888$. We then solve for the power as:

$$Power = 1 - \beta$$

$$= 1 - 0.8888 = 0.1122$$

9.57

a. The appropriate null and alternative hypotheses are:

$$H_o : \mu \geq 15$$
$$H_a : \mu < 15$$

b. Given the one-tailed hypothesis test with alpha = 0.01, the critical z-value from the standard normal table is z = -2.33

Next, we compute the critical value which marks the cut-off for the rejection region as follows:

$$\bar{x}_\alpha = \mu + z_\alpha \frac{\sigma}{\sqrt{n}}$$

$$\bar{x}_\alpha = 15 - 2.33 \frac{2}{\sqrt{60}} = 14.40$$

Next, we calculate the z-value associated with the "true" population mean as follows:

$$z = \frac{14.40 - 14}{\frac{2}{\sqrt{60}}} = 1.55$$

The probability from the standard normal table for a z-value of 1.55 is 0.4394. Then beta = 0.5000 – 0.4394 = 0.0606. Thus, there is just over a 6 percent chance that a type II error will be made.

9.59

a. The appropriate null and alternative hypotheses are:

$$H_o : \mu \geq \$41,000$$
$$H_a : \mu < \$41,000$$

b. Given the one-tailed hypothesis test with alpha = 0.01, the critical z-value from the standard normal table is z = -2.33

Next, we compute the critical value which marks the cut-off for the rejection region as follows:

$$\bar{x}_\alpha = \mu + z_\alpha \frac{\sigma}{\sqrt{n}}$$

$$\bar{x}_\alpha = 41,000 - 2.33 \frac{4,600}{\sqrt{200}} = 40,242.12$$

Next, we calculate the z-value associated with the "true" population mean as follows:

$$z = \frac{40,242.12 - 40,000}{\frac{4,600}{\sqrt{200}}} = 0.74$$

The probability from the standard normal table for a z-value of 0.74 is 0.2704. Then beta = 0.5000 - 0.2704 = 0.2296. Thus, there is just under a 23 percent chance that a type II error will be made.

9.61

Step 1: Formulate the null and alternative hypotheses.

$H_0: \mu \geq 85$
$H_A: \mu < 85$

Step 2. Specify the significance level.

$\alpha = 0.05$

Step 3: Determine the critical statistical value from the appropriate distribution.

$-z_\alpha = -1.645$

Step 4. Calculate the critical value.
For the original hypothesis:

$$\bar{x}_\alpha = \mu - z_\alpha \frac{\sigma}{\sqrt{n}} = 85 - 1.645 \frac{50}{\sqrt{1097}} = 82.5167,$$

Step 5. Specify the stipulated value for μ.
Asssume the true value of $\mu = 81$ with the above critical value of x.

Step 6. Compute the test statistic based on the stipulated population mean.

$$z = \frac{\bar{x}_\alpha - \mu}{\frac{\sigma}{\sqrt{n}}} = \frac{82.5167 - 81}{\frac{50}{\sqrt{1097}}} = 1.0047$$

Step 7. Determine β.
$\beta = P(z > 1.0047) = 0.5 - 0.3413 = 0.1587$

9.63

Step 1: Formulate the null and alternative hypotheses.

Step 2. Specify the significance level.

Step 3: Determine the critical statistical value from the appropriate distribution.

Step 4. Calculate the critical value.

Step 5. Specify the stipulated value for μ.

Step 6. Compute the test statistic based on the stipulated population mean.

Step 7. Determine β.

$H_0: \mu \geq 21.6$

$H_A: \mu < 21.6$

$\alpha = 0.01$

This is a one tailed test with a critical value $-z_\alpha = -2.33$, the critical value of x is

$$\bar{x}_\alpha = \mu - z_\alpha \frac{\sigma}{\sqrt{n}} = 21.6 - 2.33 \frac{40}{\sqrt{1500}} = 19.1936$$

Assuming the true value of $\mu = 21.6 - 0.10(21.6) = 19.44$, power can be determine as follows:

$$z = \frac{\bar{x}_\alpha - \mu}{\frac{\sigma}{\sqrt{n}}} = \frac{19.1936 - 19.44}{\frac{40}{\sqrt{1500}}} = -0.2386$$

So $\beta = P(z > -0.2386) = 0.5 + 0.0948 = 0.5948$

Power $= 1 - \beta = 1 - 0.5948 = 0.4052$

9.65

Step 1: Formulate the null and alternative hypotheses.
H_0: $\mu = 1800/7 = 257.14$
$H_{A:}$ $\mu \neq 257.14$

Step 2. Specify the significance level.
$\alpha = 0.05$

Step 3: Determine the critical statistical value from the appropriate distribution. Since this is an equal to hypothesis, we perform a two tailed test, $\pm z_{\alpha/2} = \pm 1.96$.

Step 4. Calculate the critical value.
Performing the appropriate calculations:

$$\bar{x}_{L/U} = \mu \pm z_{\alpha/2}\frac{\sigma}{\sqrt{n}} = 257.14 \pm 1.96\frac{100}{\sqrt{41}}$$

gives

$$\bar{x}_L = 226.53; \quad \bar{x}_U = 287.75$$

Step 5. Specify the stipulated value for μ.
Assume the true value of $\mu = 300$

Step 6. Compute the test statistic based on the stipulated population mean. Since this is a two sided test we need to find two values:

$$z = \frac{\bar{x}_U - \mu}{\dfrac{\sigma}{\sqrt{n}}} = \frac{287.75 - 300}{\dfrac{100}{\sqrt{41}}} = -0.7842$$

$$z = \frac{\bar{x}_L - \mu}{\dfrac{\sigma}{\sqrt{n}}} = \frac{226.53 - 300}{\dfrac{100}{\sqrt{41}}} = -4.7042$$

Step 7. Determine β.
$\beta = \text{Prob}(-4.7042 < z < -0.7842) = 0.5 - 0.2823 = 0.2177$

End of Chapter Exercises

9.67

A Type I error occurs when the decision maker rejects a true null hypothesis. A Type II error occurs when a false null hypothesis is accepted. Business examples of these two types of error will vary.

9.69

The critical value is the cut-off point or demarcation between acceptance and rejection regions in a hypothesis test. It may be expressed in terms of a value of the sample mean, as a z value of as a nnn alpha value.

9.71

The probability of committing a Type I error is denoted by alpha (α) and is usually specified by the decision maker. The choice of alpha reflects the cost of making a Type I error. If the cost is high, alpha will be set at a lower value than if the cost of committing the error is low.

9.73

You use the population proportion to calculate the standard error. If you were testing that the population proportion were 0 then the standard error would be 0. This would make it impossible to make a logical calculation.

9.75

a. z (Standard normal) test statistic, $z = \dfrac{\overline{x} - \mu}{\dfrac{\sigma}{\sqrt{n}}}$

b. t (Student's t) test statistic, $t = \dfrac{\overline{x} - \mu}{\dfrac{s}{\sqrt{n}}}$

c. z (standard normal) test statistic, $z = \dfrac{p - \pi}{\sqrt{\dfrac{\pi(1-\pi)}{n}}}$, should not be used since

n(1-p) < 5.

d. A hypothesis test using a small (< 30) sample from a skewed distribution cannot be conducted using procedures in this text.

9.77

   a. If α is decreased, the rejection region is smaller making it easier to accept H_0, so β is increased.

   b. If n is increased, the test statistic is also increased making it harder to accept H_0, so β is decreased.

   c. If n is increased, the test statistic is also increased making it harder to accept H_0, so β is decreased and power is increased.

   d. If α is decreased, the rejection region is smaller making it easier to accept H_0, so β is increased and power is decreased.

9.79

   a. H_o: $\mu \geq 100$
        H_a: $\mu < 100$

$$t = (114 - 100)/(50/\sqrt{50}) = 1.98$$

$t_{.10} = 1.2991$ (using Excel)

Since $z = 1.98 > 1.2991$ reject H_o and conclude that the sample data do refute the director's claim.

   b. $1.2991 = (\bar{x} - 100)/50/\sqrt{50}$); $\bar{x} = 109.186$

9.81

   a. H_o: $\pi \geq 0.70$
        H_a: $\pi < 0.70$

$p = 63/100 = 0.63$

$$z = (0.63 - 0.70)/\sqrt{(0.70)(1 - 0.70)/100} = -1.5275$$

Decision Rule:
If $z < -1.645$ reject H_o, otherwise do not reject

Since $z = -1.5275 > -1.645$ do not reject and conclude that the difficulty of the test seems to be appropriate

b. A Type II error in this problem would mean that the proportion of students passing the test is actually less than 0.70 but the sample results lead the administrators to believe that it is actually 70% or better. This would mean that a test that must be too difficult would continue to be administered.

9.83

a. $n\pi = 883(0.21) = 185.43 > 5$ and $n(1-\pi) = 883(1-0.21) = 697.57 > 5$. The normal approximation to the binomial is warranted.

b. H_O: $\pi \geq 0.21$
H_A: $\pi < 0.21$
$\alpha = 0.05$

reject H_O if $z < -z_\alpha = -1.645$ (5) $p = \dfrac{168}{883} = 0.1903$

$$z = \dfrac{p - \pi}{\sqrt{\dfrac{\pi(1-\pi)}{n}}} = \dfrac{0.1903 - 0.21}{\sqrt{\dfrac{0.21(0.79)}{883}}} = -1.4401$$

Since $z = -1.4401 > -1.645$ do not reject H_O., There is not sufficient evidence to conclude that the proportion of adults who find Overstock.com's ads to be very effective is smaller than the Harris Ad Track average.

9.85

H_o: $\mu \geq 18.0$
H_a: $\mu < 18.0$

a. $\bar{x}_\alpha = 18 - 1.88(2.4/\sqrt{60})$; $\bar{x}_\alpha = 17.4175$

$P(z > (17.4175 - 16.5)/ (2.4/\sqrt{60})) = P(z > 2.96) = 0.5 - 0.4985 = 0.0015$

b. $P(z > (17.4175 - 17.3)/ (2.4/\sqrt{60})) = P(z > .38) = .50 - .1480 = .352$

As the mean selected from H_A moves closer to the mean specified in H_0, the harder it is for the hypothesis test to distinguish and thus, the larger β becomes and the smaller the Power becomes.

c. The probability of a Type II error would be smaller.
As the mean selected from H_A moves farther from the mean specified in H_0, the easier it is for the hypothesis test to distinguish and thus, the smaller β becomes and the larger the Power becomes.

d. The probabilities of Type II errors would be reduced for larger sample sizes.

9.87

a. The research hypothesis is that the parts do not have an average diameter of 6 inches.
H_o: $\mu = 6$ inches
H_a: $\mu \neq 6$ inches

b. Reject H_o if $z > 2.58$ or $z < -2.58$; otherwise do not reject H_o

$$\bar{x}_{\alpha/2} = 6 \pm 2.58(.10/\sqrt{200}) = 5.9818 \text{ and } 6.0182$$

If $\bar{x} < 5.9818$, reject the null hypothesis
If $\bar{x} > 6.0182$, reject the null hypothesis
Otherwise, do not reject

c. Since $\bar{x} = 6.03 > 6.0182$, reject the null hypothesis. Thus, the average diameter appears to be higher than 6 inches.

9.89

a. $n\pi = 2500(0.75) = 1875 > 5$; $n(1-\pi) = 625 > 5$
The normal approximation to the binomial is warranted.

b. H_O: $\pi \geq 0.75$
H_A: $\pi < 0.75$

$\alpha = 0.025$, reject H_O if $z < -z_\alpha = -1.96$

$$z = \frac{p - \pi}{\sqrt{\dfrac{\pi(1-\pi)}{n}}} = \frac{0.74 - 0.75}{\sqrt{\dfrac{0.75(0.25)}{2500}}} = -1.1547$$

Since $z = -1.1547 > -1.96$ do not reject H_O. There is not sufficient evidence to conclude that less than 75% of new mortgages had a loan amount at least 5% above the original mortgage balance.

9.91

    a. "Keeping pace of average balance" becomes a research hypothesis:
        H_O: $\mu = 61,000$
        H_A: $\mu \neq 61,000$
        $\alpha = 0.025$

        Since σ is known, we can use a z test statistic and reject H_O if $z > 2.24$ or $z < -2.24$.

$$z = \frac{\overline{x} - \mu}{\dfrac{\sigma}{\sqrt{n}}} = \frac{61834.12 - 61000}{\dfrac{1734.23}{\sqrt{55}}} = 3.567$$

        Because $z = 3.567 > 2.24$ we reject H_O. There is sufficient evidence to conclude that GM's workers average balance in 401(k) accounts is, in fact, exceeding that of other workers.

    b. The statement ". . .average balance in which you have 90% confidence" implies a confidence interval.

$$\overline{x} \pm z_{\alpha/2} \frac{\sigma}{n}; \text{ at the 90% confidence level}$$

$$\overline{x} \pm z_{\alpha/2} \frac{\sigma}{\sqrt{n}} = 61834.12 \pm 1.645 \frac{1734.23}{\sqrt{55}} = 61834.12 \pm 384.67 \text{ (61449.45,}$$
62218.79).

        The largest plausible average balance in the GM workers' 401(k) in which you could have 90% confidence = \$62218.79.

9.93

    a. H_o: $\mu \leq 7.4$
        H_a: $\mu > 7.4$

Whenever possible, we want to place the research hypothesis in the alternative since if the sample data leads to rejecting the null, there is statistical evidence to support the alternative. It is likely that the standard is set at a level lower than that which would cause a health risk and we only want to signal a problem if there is very likely to be a problem.

b. Students can use Excel's AVERAGE and STDEV functions to determine the sample mean and standard deviation.

$\bar{x} = 7.6306 \quad s = 0.2218$

$t = (7.6306 - 7.4)/(0.2218/\sqrt{95}) = 10.1335$

$t_{.05} = 1.6612$ using Excel or between 1.6602 and 1.6620 using the tables in the book.

Since $t = 10.1335 > 1.6612$ reject H_o and conclude that the average pH level is higher than 7.4

9.95

a. H_o: $\pi \geq 0.30$

   H_a: $\pi < 0.30$

Count of Club Status	
Club Status	Total
Copy	26.87%
Original	73.13%
Grand Total	100.00%

$z = (0.2687 - 0.30)/\sqrt{(0.30)(1 - 0.30)/294} = -1.1711$

Decision Rule:

If $z < -1.645$ reject H_o, otherwise do not reject

Since $z = -1.1711 > -1.645$ do not reject and conclude that the speaker is incorrect and that "knock-offs" is greater than or equal to 30%

b. In this case, a Type II error may have been committed. From the manufacturers' viewpoint, "accepting" the null hypothesis when it is false means that they think that the problem is worse than it is. That is probably not as serious as a Type I error which would mean that they would be understating the problem.

c. As long as the sample size is sufficiently large such that np and n(1-p) are both greater than 5, you are justified in using the standard normal when estimating a population proportion. In this case, we have .2687(67) > 5 and (1-.2687)(5) > 5 so we are okay.

d. Use Excel's Pivot Table – use percent of rows option and group handicaps as shown below. Note there are 67 golfers with handicaps of 20 or more.

Count of Club Status	Club Status		
USGA Handicap	Copy	Original	Grand Total
0-19.99	27.31%	72.69%	100.00%
20.00-39.98	25.37%	74.63%	100.00%
Grand Total	26.87%	73.13%	100.00%

H_o: $\pi \geq 0.30$
H_a: $\pi < 0.30$

$z = (0.2537 - 0.30)/\sqrt{(0.30)(1-0.30)/67} = -1.8047$

Decision Rule:

If $z < -1.645$ reject H_o, otherwise do not reject

Since $z = -1.8047 < -1.645$ reject H_o and conclude that the "knock-offs" is less than 30% in the high handicap players.

9.97

a. H_o: $\mu \geq 40$
H_a: $\mu < 40$

b. Students can use Excel's AVERAGE and STDEV functions to determine the sample mean and standard deviation.

$\bar{x} = 38.52$ $s = 12.9965$

$t = (38.52 - 40)/(12.9965/\sqrt{50}) = -0.8052$

$t_{.10} = -1.2991$ (using Excel or Minitab)

Since $z = -0.8052 > -1.2991$ do not reject H_o and conclude that the average age is not less than 40.

c. Type II error. There is very little chance of ever being able to determine if the error has been made as that would require the company to know the age of every customer (ie. know the true population mean.)

d. $\bar{x}_\alpha = 40 - 1.2991(12.9965/\sqrt{50})$; $\bar{x}_\alpha = 37.6123$

Chapter 9

e. Since $\overline{x}_\alpha = 37.6123$ is associated with a significance level of 0.10, we know that the p-value for $\overline{x} = 38.52$ must be greater than 0.10. If the p-value is greater than alpha we do not reject the null. Alternatively, using the sample average in part b, $t = -0.8052$. Using Excel's TDIST function, the p-value = 0.2122 which is greater than 0.10.

f. Age denoted to the nearest year is a discrete variable. Thus the age variable cannot be an exact normal distribution but if the values x can take are large enough it might be approximated by a continuous distribution which could be approximately a normal distribution. Given a sample size of n = 50, the sampling distribution for $\overline{x}$ will be approximately normal based on the Central Limit Theorem. Thus, the use of the distribution to find the critical t value and the p-value is appropriate.

9.99

a. Wanting to prove the machines can be paid for we hypothesize as:
H_O: $\mu \leq 750$
H_A: $\mu > 750$

$\alpha = 0.05$

Since σ is unknown we use a t test statistic with d.f. = 24 – 1. Reject H_O if p-value is less than 0.05.

From the data: $\overline{x} = \dfrac{\Sigma x}{n} = \dfrac{18671.74}{24} = 777.989$

$$s = \sqrt{\dfrac{\sum(x-\overline{x})^2}{n-1}} = \sqrt{\dfrac{174323.20}{23}} = \sqrt{7579.27} = 87.059,$$

$$t = \dfrac{\overline{x}-\mu}{\dfrac{s}{\sqrt{n}}} = \dfrac{777.989-750}{\dfrac{87.059}{\sqrt{24}}} = 1.5750$$

The p-value = Prob(t ≥ 1.575). Using Excel's TDIST option this probability is 0.0644. ;Since the p-value is greater than α we do not reject H_O. There is not sufficient evidence to conclude that an average monthly income of more than $750 can be obtained.

260

b. Trial has two outcomes: average monthly income of at least $ 750 or not with a fixed number of trials. But the probability on the second try depends on what happens on the first. We have a hypergeometric distribution. Using Equation 5-9 we find:

$$P(x \geq 2) = 1 - P(x \leq 1) = 1 - \left[\frac{C_4^6 \times C_0^4}{C_4^{10}} + \frac{C_3^6 \times C_1^4}{C_4^{10}} \right] = 1 - 95/210$$

$$= 1 - 0.4524 = 0.5476$$

Chapter 10 Solutions

When applicable, selected problems in each section will be done following the appropriate step-by-step procedures outlined in the corresponding sections of the chapter. Other problems will provide key points and the answers to the questions, but all answers can be arrived at using the appropriate steps.

Section 10-1 Exercises

10.1

Step 1: Define the population value of interest:
The objective here is to estimate the difference between two population means. The parameter of interest is $\mu_1 - \mu_2$.

Step 2: Select independent samples from the two populations, verify that the assumptions are satisfied and compute the point estimate.
Independent random samples of size $n_1 = 24$ and $n_2 = 28$ have been taken. We are told that the populations from which the samples are taken are normally distributed with equal variances.

Step 3: Compute the point estimate.
The point estimate is $\bar{x}_1 - \bar{x}_2 = 130 - 125 = 5$.

Step 4: Specify the desired confidence level and determine the critical value.
We are asked to determine a 95% confidence interval estimate. Because the sample sizes are small and taken from normally distributed populations with equal variances the critical value is a t-value from the normal distribution with degrees of freedom $= n_1 + n_2 - 2 = 24 + 28 - 2 = 50$. The critical value of t for a 95% confidence interval estimate with 50 degrees of freedom is 2.0086.

Step 5: Develop a confidence interval using equation 10-4.

$$(\bar{x}_1 - \bar{x}_2) \pm ts_p \sqrt{\frac{1}{n_1} + \frac{1}{n_2}}$$

$$s_p = \sqrt{\frac{(n_1 - 1)s_1^2 + (n_2 - 1)s_2^2}{n_1 + n_2 - 2}} = \sqrt{\frac{(24 - 1)19^2 + (28 - 1)17.5^2}{24 + 28 - 2}} = 18.21$$

Then the interval estimate is

$$5 \pm 2.0086(18.21)\sqrt{\frac{1}{24} + \frac{1}{28}} = 5 \pm 10.17 = -5.17 \leq (\mu_1 - \mu_2) \leq 15.17$$

10.3

The confidence interval estimate for the difference between two population means when the population standard deviations are known can be developed using the following steps:

Step 1: Define the population value of interest.
We are interested in the difference between the two population means, $\mu_1 - \mu_2$.

Step 2: Specify the desired confidence level and determine the critical value.
The desired confidence level is 95 percent. Because the population standard deviations are assumed to be known, the critical value is a z-value from the standard normal distribution. The critical value is $z = 1.96$.

Step 3: Select independent samples from the two populations and compute the point estimate.
Samples of size 50 and 80 have been selected from populations 1 and 2 respectively. The point estimate is:
$$\bar{x}_1 - \bar{x}_2 = 355 - 320 = 35$$

Step 4: Develop the confidence interval estimate.
Given that the population standard deviations are know, the confidence interval estimate is developed using:

$$(\bar{x}_1 - \bar{x}_2) \pm z \sqrt{\frac{\sigma_1^2}{n_1} + \frac{\sigma_2^2}{n_2}}$$

Then, the 95 percent confidence interval estimate is:

$$(355 - 320) \pm 1.96 \sqrt{\frac{34^2}{50} + \frac{40^2}{80}}$$

$$35 \pm 12.87$$

$$22.13 \leq \mu_1 - \mu_2 \leq 47.87$$

10.5

The following steps can be used to construct the desired confidence interval estimate.

Step 1: Define the population value of interest.
We are interested in the difference between the two population means, $\mu_1 - \mu_2$.

Step 2: Select independent samples from the two populations.
Independent samples of size 12 were selected from each population with the following statistics computed from the samples

$$\overline{x}_1 = \frac{\sum x}{n_1} = \frac{4,808}{12} = 400.67 \quad \text{and} \quad \overline{x}_2 = \frac{\sum x}{n_2} = \frac{4,504}{12} = 375.33$$

$$s_1 = 42.5 \quad \text{and} \quad s_2 = 41.9$$

Step 3: Compute the point estimate.
The point estimate is the difference between the two sample means:
$$\text{Point estimate} = \overline{x}_1 - \overline{x}_2 = 400.67 - 375.33 = 25.34$$

Step 4: Specify the desired confidence level and determine the critical value.
The desired confidence level is 95 percent. Since we are unable to assume that the population variances are equal, we must first calculate the degrees of freedom for the t-distribution. This is done as follows:

$$df = \frac{\left(\frac{s_1^2}{n_1} + \frac{s_2^2}{n_2}\right)^2}{\left[\frac{\left(\frac{s_1^2}{n_1}\right)^2}{n_1 - 1} + \frac{\left(\frac{s_2^2}{n_2}\right)^2}{n_2 - 1}\right]} = \frac{\left(\frac{42.5^2}{12} + \frac{41.9^2}{12}\right)^2}{\left[\frac{\left(\frac{42.5^2}{12}\right)^2}{11} + \frac{\left(\frac{41.9^2}{12}\right)^2}{11}\right]} = \frac{88,103}{4,004.68} = 22$$

Thus, the degrees of freedom will be 22. For 95% confidence, using the t-distribution table the approximate t value is 2.0739

Step 5: Develop the confidence interval estimate.
The confidence interval estimate is computed using:

$$\left(\bar{x}_1 - \bar{x}_2\right) \pm t \sqrt{\frac{s_1^2 + s_2^2}{n_1 + n_2}}$$

Then the interval estimate is:

$$\left(400.67 - 375.33\right) \pm 2.0739 \sqrt{\frac{42.5^2 + 41.9^2}{12 + 12}}$$

$$25.34 \pm 25.27$$

$$0.07 \le \left(\mu_1 - \mu_2\right) \le 50.61$$

10.7

    a.

Point estimate for the difference between the two population means is $\bar{x}_1 - \bar{x}_2 =$ 24.96 − 25.01 = -0.05

    b.

Step 1: Define the population value of interest:
The objective here is to estimate the difference between the population means for the two production lines. The parameter of interest is $\mu_1 - \mu_2$.

Step 2: Select independent samples from the two populations, verify that the assumptions are satisfied and compute the point estimate.
Independent random samples of size $n_1 = 19$ and $n_2 = 23$ have been taken. We are told that the populations from which the samples are taken are normally distributed with equal variances.

Step 3: Compute the point estimate.
The point estimate was determined in part (a) to be -0.05.

Step 4: Specify the desired confidence level and determine the critical value.
Management wants a 95% confidence interval estimate. Because the sample sizes are small and taken from normally distributed populations with equal variances the critical value is a t-value from the normal distribution with degrees of freedom = $n_1 + n_2 - 2 = 19 + 23 - 2 = 40$. The critical value of t for a 95% confidence interval estimate with 40 degrees of freedom is 2.0211.

Step 5: Develop a confidence interval using equation 10-4.

$$(\bar{x}_1 - \bar{x}_2) \pm ts_p \sqrt{\frac{1}{n_1} + \frac{1}{n_2}}$$

$$s_p = \sqrt{\frac{(n_1-1)s_1^2 + (n_2-1)s_2^2}{n_1 + n_2 - 2}} = \sqrt{\frac{(19-1)0.07^2 + (23-1)0.08^2}{19+23-2}} = 0.0757$$

Then the interval estimate is

$$-0.05 \pm 2.0211(0.0757)\sqrt{\frac{1}{19} + \frac{1}{23}} = -0.05 \pm 0.0474 =$$

$$-0.0974 \le (\mu_1 - \mu_2) \le -0.0026$$

c.

Since the interval does not contain zero, the managers can conclude the two lines do not fill bags with equal average amounts. However, the difference is at most about 0.1 lbs.

10.9

The following steps are used to construct a confidence interval estimate when the samples are selected from normally distributed populations with equal variances and when the population variances are unknown:

Step 1: Define the population value of interest.
We are interested in the difference between the two population means, $\mu_1 - \mu_2$ for the length of time it takes to make a part from start to finish at the two facilities.

Step 2: Compute the point estimate.
The point estimate is the difference between the two sample means. The two sample means are:

$$\bar{x}_1 = \frac{\sum x}{n_1} = 56.7 \qquad \text{and} \quad \bar{x}_2 = \frac{\sum x}{n_2} = 70.4$$

The point estimate is: $\bar{x}_1 - \bar{x}_2 = 56.7 - 70.4 = -13.7 \; hours$

Step 3: Specify the desired confidence level and determine the critical value. The desired confidence level is 95 percent. The critical value comes from a t-distribution with $df = n_1 + n_2 - 2$. The degrees of freedom is $15 + 15 - 2 = 28$. The critical value from the t-distribution table is 2.0484.

Step 4: Compute the confidence interval estimate.
When the population variances are assumed to be equal, the confidence interval estimate is computed using:

$$(\bar{x}_1 - \bar{x}_2) \pm t s_p \sqrt{\frac{1}{n_1} + \frac{1}{n_2}}$$

where:

$$s_p = \sqrt{\frac{(n_1 - 1)s_1^2 + (n_2 - 1)s_2^2}{n_1 + n_2 - 2}} = \sqrt{\frac{(15-1)7.1^2 + (15-1)8.3^2}{15+15-2}} = 7.72$$

Then

$$-13.7 \pm 2.0484(7.72)\sqrt{\frac{1}{15} + \frac{1}{15}}$$

$$-13.7 \pm 5.77$$

$$-19.47 \leq \mu_1 - \mu_2 \leq -7.93$$

Based on the sample data with 95% confidence the manager can conclude that the Denton Texas facility produces parts on average between 7.93 and 19.47 hours faster than the Lincoln plant. This may be due to the automation or some other factor such as plant layout.

10.11

Excel or Minitab could be used to find an exact value for t. However, we will use the table in the book and use the t value for the nearest degrees of freedom less than that for the problem.

$$s_p = \sqrt{\frac{(n_1 - 1)s_1^2 + (n_2 - 1)s_2^2}{n_1 + n_2 - 2}} = \sqrt{\frac{(200-1)3.6^2 + (200-1)5^2}{200+200-2}} = 4.36$$

a. $(41.5 - 39) \pm 1.9695(4.36)\sqrt{(1/200)+(1/200)}$; 1.6413 ----- 3.3587; yes because the interval does not contain the value 0 which would indicated no difference.

b. Company A:

$-1.6602 = (\bar{x} - 41.5)/(3.6/\sqrt{200})$; $\bar{x} = 41.0774$

Company B:

$-1.6602 = (\bar{x} - 39)/(5/\sqrt{200})$; $\bar{x} = 38.4130$

10.13

a. The ratio between the two variances is 200. It seems highly unlikely that sample variances that are so different would come from populations with the same variance.

b. Since it seems unlikely that the population variances are equal to each other, the appropriate alternative to the confidence interval must be made.

Step 1: Define the population value of interest.

The measure of interest is $\mu_1 - \mu_2$.

Step 2: Select independent samples from the two populations, verify that the assumptions are satisfied and compute the point estimate.

We have already surmised that the two population variances differ. Since raw data does not exist, we must assume the populations have normal distributions. $\overline{x_1} = 38.9$ $\overline{x_2} = 2$

Step 3: Compute the point estimate.

$(\overline{x_1} - \overline{x_2}) = 38.9 - 2 = 36.9$

Step 4: Specify the confidence level and determine the critical value.

The confidence level equals 99%. The degrees of freedom are derived as

$$df = \frac{(s_1^2/n_1 + s_2^2/n_2)^2}{\left(\dfrac{\left(s_1^2/n_1\right)^2}{n_1-1} + \dfrac{\left(s_2^2/n_2\right)^2}{n_2-1}\right)} = \frac{(64/1442 + 0.36/1442)^2}{\left(\dfrac{(64/1442)^2}{1442-1} + \dfrac{(0.36/1442)^2}{1442-1}\right)} =$$

$1457.2 \approx 1457$. Therefore, the critical value $= 2.5792$.

Step 5: Develop the confidence interval estimate using Equation 10-6.

$$(\bar{x}_1 - \bar{x}_2) \pm t_{\alpha/2}\sqrt{\frac{s_1^2}{n_1} + \frac{s_2^2}{n_1}} = (38.9 - 2) \pm 2.5792\sqrt{\frac{64}{1442} + \frac{0.36}{1442}} = 36.9 \pm$$

$0.5449 = (36.3551, 37.4449)$

c. The confidence interval expresses the plausible values for the difference in the average number of job applications between 2002 and 2005. Since both 36.5 and 37 are in this interval, this indicates that both values are plausible values for the difference in the average number of job applications. This is not a contradiction. All values contained in the interval are plausible values for the difference in the means. Sampling error produces the uncertainty.

10.15

The confidence interval estimate can be computed using software such as Excel or Minitab. Using Excel's pivot table feature, we compute the following from the sample data:

Data	Men	Women
Average of % increase	7.44%	5.71%
StdDev of % increase	7.50%	2.85%
Count of % increase	15	25

Based on the population assumptions of normality and equal variances, we can use the t-distribution to obtain the critical value and the interval estimate is computed as follows:

$$(\bar{x}_1 - \bar{x}_2) \pm ts_p \sqrt{\frac{1}{n_1} + \frac{1}{n_2}}$$

where:

$$s_p = \sqrt{\frac{(n_1-1)s_1^2 + (n_2-1)s_2^2}{n_1+n_2-2}} = \sqrt{\frac{(15-1)7.5^2 + (25-1)2.85^2}{15+25-2}} = 5.08$$

The degrees of freedom for the t-distribution is $15 + 25 - 2 = 38$

Because df = 38 is not in the table, we can use Excel's TINV function as:

$$=\text{TINV}(0.05,38) = 2.0244$$

Then

$$(7.44 - 5.71) \pm 2.0244(5.08)\sqrt{\frac{1}{15} + \frac{1}{25}}$$

1.73 ± 3.36

$-1.63 \le \mu_1 - \mu_2 \le 5.09$

This confidence interval indicates that based on the sample data with 95 percent confidence, the difference in mean percentage raise for males could be anywhere from 5.09 higher than females to 1.63 lower than females. These results should make the manager feel a bit more at ease since based on these data there is no conclusive evidence to suggest that the two groups differ with respect to mean raise percentage.

10.17

a. Minitab output:

```
              N    Mean   StDev   SE Mean
INCOME01    100   72400   12879      1288
INCOME04    100   70700   14678      1468
```

```
Difference = mu (INCOME01) - mu (INCOME04)
Estimate for difference:  1699.75
```

The percentage decline is $= \dfrac{72400 - 70700}{72400} 100\% = 2.35\%.$

b. Minitab output:

Two-Sample T-Test and CI: INCOME01, INCOME0‹

```
Two-sample T for INCOME01 vs INCOME04
```

```
              N    Mean   StDev   SE Mean
INCOME01    100   72400   12879      1288
INCOME04    100   70700   14678      1468
```

```
Difference = mu (INCOME01) - mu (INCOME04)
Estimate for difference:  1699.75
90% CI for difference:  (-1527.32, 4926.82)
```

c. Since the confidence interval defines the plausible values for the difference in the average family incomes, one of the plausible values for this difference is 0. Indicating that is plausible that there is no difference.

d. The measure this exercise alludes to is the margin of error. The margin of error for the two-sampled t is equal to the width of the confidence interval divided by 2.

Therefore, the margin of error $= \dfrac{4926.82 - (-1527.32)}{2} = 3227$

Section 10-2 Exercises

10.19

The following steps can be used to test the null hypothesis.

Step 1: Specify the population value of interest.
The population value of interest is the difference in population means, $\mu_1 - \mu_2$.

Step 2: Formulate the null and alternative hypotheses.
The null and alternative hypotheses are:
$$H_0 : \mu_1 \leq \mu_2$$
$$H_A : \mu_1 > \mu_2$$

This will be a one tail, upper tail test. The entire rejection region will be in the upper tail of the sampling distribution.

Step 3: Specify the significance level for the test.
The test will be conducted using an alpha level equal to 0.05.

Step 4: Compute the test statistic
Since the population standard deviations are assumed to be known, the test statistic will be a z-value computed as follows:

$$z = \frac{(\bar{x}_1 - \bar{x}_2) - (\mu_1 - \mu_2)}{\sqrt{\dfrac{\sigma_1^2}{n_1} + \dfrac{\sigma_2^2}{n_2}}}$$

Substituting we get:

$$z = \frac{(144 - 129) - 0}{\sqrt{\dfrac{11^2}{40} + \dfrac{16^2}{50}}} = 5.26$$

Step 5:   Determine the rejection region and state the decision rule:
The rejection region is in the upper tail of the normal distribution corresponding to an alpha = 0.05 level. From the standard normal distribution the critical z is:

$$z_{0.05} = 1.645$$

Therefore, the decision rule is:
If z > 1.645, reject the null hypothesis.

Since z = 5.26 > 1.645, we reject and conclude that the mean for population 1 exceeds the mean for population 2.

10.21

The following steps can be used to test the null hypothesis for the difference between two population means when the populations are assumed to be normally distributed with equal variances.

Step 1:   Specify the population value of interest.
The population value of interest is the difference in population means, $\mu_1 - \mu_2$.

Step 2:   Formulate the null and alternative hypotheses.
The null and alternative hypotheses are:
$$H_0 : \mu_1 - \mu_2 = 0$$
$$H_A : \mu_1 - \mu_2 \neq 0$$
This will be a two-tail test. The rejection region will be split evenly between the upper and lower tails of the sampling distribution.

Step 3:   Specify the significance level for the test.
The test will be conducted using an alpha level equal to 0.05.

Step 4: Compute the test statistic

Since the population standard deviations are unknown and must be estimated from the sample data, the test statistic will be a t-value from the t distribution.

$$t = \frac{(\bar{x}_1 - \bar{x}_2) - (\mu_1 - \mu_2)}{s_p\sqrt{\dfrac{1}{n_1} + \dfrac{1}{n_2}}}$$

where:

$$s_p = \sqrt{\frac{(n_1 - 1)s_1^2 + (n_2 - 1)s_2^2}{n_1 + n_2 - 2}}$$

and

$$s = \sqrt{\frac{\sum(x - \bar{x})^2}{n - 1}}$$

Then

$$\bar{x}_1 = \frac{\sum x}{n_1} = \frac{312}{9} = 34.67 \qquad\qquad \bar{x}_2 = \frac{\sum x}{n_2} = \frac{400}{9} = 44.44$$

and

$$s_1 = 5.2 \quad \text{and} \quad s_1 = 3.2$$

and

$$s_p = \sqrt{\frac{(n_1 - 1)s_1^2 + (n_2 - 1)s_2^2}{n_1 + n_2 - 2}} = \sqrt{\frac{(9 - 1)5.2^2 + (9 - 1)3.2^2}{9 + 9 - 2}} = 4.32$$

Substituting we get:

$$t = \frac{(34.67 - 44.44) - 0}{4.32\sqrt{\dfrac{1}{9} + \dfrac{1}{9}}} = -4.80$$

Step 5: Determine the rejection region and state the decision rule:
The rejection region is split between the two tails of the t-distribution with 0.025 in each tail and the degrees of freedom ae $(9 + 9 - 2 = 16)$. From the t-distribution for 16 degrees of freedom and one-tail = 0.025 (or two tails = 0.05), the critical t-value is 2.1199.
Therefore, the decision rule is:
If the test statistics, $t > 2.1199$, reject the null hypothesis.
If the test statistics, $t < -2.1199$, reject the null hypothesis
Otherwise, do not reject

Since $t = -4.80 < -2.1199$, we reject and conclude that the mean for population 1 is not equal to the mean for population 2.

10.23

a.
Step 1: Specify the population value of interest.
You performing a hypothesis test on the difference between two populations' means, $\mu_1 - \mu_2$

Step 2: Formulate the appropriate null and alternative hypotheses.
H_O: $\mu_1 - \mu_2 \geq -4$
H_A: $\mu_1 - \mu_2 < -4$

Step 3: Specify the significance for the test.
The significance level $= \alpha = 0.01$.

Step 4: Construct the rejection region.
Since the population standard deviations are not known, we must assume that the populations have normal distributions and that the two population standard deviations equal each other. The critical value will, therefore, be obtained from a t-distribution with $n_1 - n_2 - 2 = 41 + 51 - 2 = 90$. From the t-table, the critical value is $t = 2.3685$. The rejection region is any test statistic < -2.3685.

Step 5: Compute the test statistic using Equation 10-8.

$$s_P = \sqrt{\frac{(n_1-1)s_1^2 + (n_2-1)s_2^2}{n_1 + n_2 - 2}} = \sqrt{\frac{(41-1)(5.6)^2 + (51-1)(7.4)^2}{41+51-2}} = 6.6603$$

$$t = \frac{(\bar{x}_1 - \bar{x}_2) - (\mu_1 - \mu_2)}{s_P\sqrt{\frac{1}{n_1} + \frac{1}{n_2}}} = \frac{(25.4 - 33.2) - (-4)}{6.6603\sqrt{\frac{1}{41} + \frac{1}{51}}} = -2.7200$$

Step 6: Reach a decision.
Because t = -2.7200< -2.3685, the null hypothesis is rejected.

Step 7: Draw a conclusion.
a. Based on these sample data, there is sufficient evidence to conclude that the difference of the two population means is less than -4.

b. The p-value = $P(\overline{x_1} - \overline{x_2} \leq 25.4 - 33.2) = P(t \leq -2.7200) < 0.005$.

c. Since the null hypothesis was rejected, the only statistical error that could have been made would be a Type I error = reject H_O given that H_O is true.

10.25

Step 1: Specify the population value of interest.
We are testing whether the average speed of play in 2005 is different from the average speed of play in 2006 at Shadow Pines Golf Club.

Step 2: Formulate the appropriate null and alternative hypotheses.
The following null and alternative hypotheses are specified:
$$H_o : \mu_1 = \mu_2$$
$$H_A : \mu_1 \neq \mu_2$$

Step 3: Specify the significance level for the test.
The test will be conducted using $\alpha = 0.10$.

Step 4: Compute the test statistic using equation 10-8.
When the population standard deviations are unknown, the critical value is a t-value from the t-distribution if the populations are assumed to be normally distributed and the population variances are assumed to be equal. The test statistic is

$$t = \frac{(\overline{x_1} - \overline{x_2}) - (\mu_1 - \mu_2)}{s_p \sqrt{\dfrac{1}{n_1} + \dfrac{1}{n_2}}}$$

The pooled standard deviation is

$$s_p = \sqrt{\frac{(n_1 - 1)s_1^2 + (n_2 - 1)s_2^2}{n_1 + n_2 - 2}}$$

$$s_p = \sqrt{\frac{(36-1)20.25^2 + (31-1)21.70^2}{36+31-2}} = 20.932$$

Then the t-statistic is

$$t = \frac{(225 - 219) - (0)}{20.932\sqrt{\frac{1}{36} + \frac{1}{31}}} = 1.17$$

Step 5: Construct the rejection region.
Based on a two-tailed test with $\alpha = 0.10$, the critical value is a t-value from the t-distribution with $36 + 31 - 2 = 65$ degrees of freedom. From Excel, the critical t-value is $t = \pm 1.6686$. The decision rule is

If t calculated > 1.6686 or t calculated < -1.6686, reject the null hypothesis;

Otherwise do not reject the null hypothesis.

Step 6: Reach a decision.
Because the calculated value of $t = 1.17$ is neither less than the lower tail critical value of $t = -1.6686$, nor greater than the upper tail critical value of $t = 1.6686$, do not reject the null hypothesis.

Step 7: Draw a conclusion.
Based on these sample data, at the $\alpha = 0.10$ level of significance there is not sufficient evidence to conclude that the average speed of play is different in 2006 than in 2005.

10.27

The following steps can be used to test the null hypothesis for the difference between two population means if the populations are assumed to be normally distributed with equal variances.

Step 1: Specify the population value of interest.
The population value of interest is the difference in population means, $\mu_1 - \mu_2$.

Step 2: Formulate the null and alternative hypotheses.
The null and alternative hypotheses are:
$$H_0 : \mu_1 - \mu_2 \leq 0$$
$$H_A : \mu_1 - \mu_2 > 0$$

This will be a one-tail test. The rejection region will be entirely in the upper tail of the sampling distribution because the only way the null hypothesis can be rejected is if the sample mean from population 2 (the new paint product) is substantially less the sample mean from population 1 (the existing paint).

Step 3: Specify the significance level for the test.
The test will be conducted using an alpha level equal to 0.01.

Step 4: Compute the test statistic
Since the population standard deviations are unknown and must be estimated from the sample data, the test statistic will be a t-value from the t distribution.

$$t = \frac{(\bar{x}_1 - \bar{x}_2) - (\mu_1 - \mu_2)}{s_p\sqrt{\dfrac{1}{n_1} + \dfrac{1}{n_2}}}$$

where:

$$s_p = \sqrt{\frac{(n_1 - 1)s_1^2 + (n_2 - 1)s_2^2}{n_1 + n_2 - 2}} = \sqrt{\frac{(25-1)22.4^2 + (15-1)16.8^2}{25 + 15 - 2}} = 20.52$$

Substituting we get:

$$t = \frac{(423 - 406) - 0}{20.32\sqrt{\dfrac{1}{25} + \dfrac{1}{15}}} = 2.56$$

Step 5: Determine the rejection region and state the decision rule:
The rejection region is entirely in the upper tail of the t-distribution with 0.01 probability in the rejection region and the degrees of freedom is (25 + 15 − 2 = 38). From the t-distribution for 38 degrees of freedom and one-tail = 0.01 can be approximated from the t-distribution table using df = 40. This critical t is 2.4233.

Note, students can use Excel's TINV function to get the precise value of t as =TINV(0.02,38)= 2.4286. Therefore, the decision rule is:
      If the test statistic, t > 2.4233, reject the null hypothesis.
      Otherwise, do not reject

Since t = 2.56 > 2.4233, we reject the null hypothesis and conclude that the mean for population 1 exceeds the mean for population 2. This means that the mean coverage for the new paint is less than the mean for the existing paint product. This was what the R & D managers were afraid of finding, but based on the sample data, that is what the conclusion must be.

10.29

The following steps can be used to test the null hypothesis for the difference between two population means if the populations are assumed to be normally distributed with equal variances.

Step 1: Specify the population value of interest.
The population value of interest is the difference in population means, $\mu_1 - \mu_2$.

Step 2: Formulate the null and alternative hypotheses.
The null and alternative hypotheses are:
$$H_0 : \mu_1 - \mu_2 \geq 0$$
$$H_A : \mu_1 - \mu_2 < 0$$

This will be a one-tail test. The rejection region will be entirely in the lower tail of the sampling distribution because the only way the null hypothesis can be rejected is if the sample mean from population 2 (the traditional) is substantially more the sample mean from population 1 (the self service method).

Step 3: Specify the significance level for the test.
The test will be conducted using an alpha level equal to 0.05.

Step 4: Compute the test statistic
Since the population standard deviations are unknown and must be estimated from the sample data, the test statistic will be a t-value from the t distribution.

$$t = \frac{(\bar{x}_1 - \bar{x}_2) - (\mu_1 - \mu_2)}{s_p\sqrt{\dfrac{1}{n_1} + \dfrac{1}{n_2}}}$$

where:

$$s_p = \sqrt{\frac{(n_1 - 1)s_1^2 + (n_2 - 1)s_2^2}{n_1 + n_2 - 2}} = \sqrt{\frac{(125-1)58.20^2 + (125-1)62.45^2}{125 + 125 - 2}} = 60.36$$

Substituting we get:

$$t = \frac{(45.68 - 78.49) - 0}{60.36\sqrt{\dfrac{1}{125} + \dfrac{1}{125}}} = -4.30$$

Step 5: Determine the rejection region and state the decision rule:

The rejection region is entirely in the lower tail of the t-distribution with 0.05 probability in the rejection region and the degrees of freedom is (125 + 125 – 2 = 248). From the t-distribution for 248 degrees of freedom and one-tail = 0.05 can be approximated from the t-distribution table using df = 250. This critical t is 1.6510. (Note, students can use Excel's TINV function to get the precise value of t as =TINV(0.10,248)= 1.65102. Therefore, the decision rule is:

> If the test statistic, t < - 1.6510, reject the null hypothesis.
> Otherwise, do not reject

Since t = -4.30 < -1.6510, we reject the null hypothesis and conclude that the mean for population 2 exceeds the mean for population 1. This means that the mean transaction at the self checkout is less than the mean transaction at the traditional checkout. If this has resulted in the overall decline in sales volume, there would be cause for concern.

10.31

a. The ratio of these two standard deviations is 2084/2050 = 1.02. This, quite conceivably, could indicate that the population standard deviations are equal to each other.

b. Step 1: $\mu_1 - \mu_2$,

Step 2: H_O: $\mu_1 - \mu_2 \geq 12,500$
H_A: $\mu_1 - \mu_2 < 12,500$,

Step 3: $\alpha = 0.01$,

Step 4: Reject H_O if p-value $< \alpha = 0.01$,

Step 5: $s_P = \sqrt{\dfrac{(n_1 - 1)s_1^2 + (n_2 - 1)s_2^2}{n_1 + n_2 - 2}}$

$= \sqrt{\dfrac{(75 - 1)(2050)^2 + (205 - 1)(2084)^2}{75 + 205 - 2}} = 2075.004$

$t = \dfrac{(\bar{x}_1 - \bar{x}_2) - (\mu_1 - \mu_2)}{s_P\sqrt{\dfrac{1}{n_1} + \dfrac{1}{n_2}}} = \dfrac{(24200 - 10600) - (12500)}{2075.004\sqrt{\dfrac{1}{75} + \dfrac{1}{205}}} = 3.93.$

$n_1 - n_2 - 2 = 75 + 205 - 2 = 278$. Therefore, the p-value = $P(t \leq 3.93) \cong 1.00$ (from t-table).

Step 6: Because p-value = $P(t \leq 3.93) \cong 1.00$, the null hypothesis is not rejected.

Step 7: Based on these sample data, there is evidence to conclude that the average college debt for bachelor of arts degree recipients is at least $12,500 more for graduates from private than for public college graduates.

10.33

Software such as Excel of Minitab can be used to aid in answering this question. We have used Excel.

a. The null and alternative hypotheses are:

$$H_0 : \mu_1 - \mu_2 = 0$$
$$H_A : \mu_1 - \mu_2 \neq 0$$

b. Using Excel's Data Analysis tool for testing two means when we assume equal variances, the following output is generated:

t-Test: Two-Sample Assuming Unequal
Variances

	Fairfield Inn	Residence Inn
Mean	3.04	3.52
Variance	2.7459	4.1107
Observations	100	100
Hypothesized Mean Difference	0	
df	190	
t Stat	-1.8331	
P(T<=t) one-tail	0.0342	
t Critical one-tail	1.6529	
P(T<=t) two-tail	0.0684	
t Critical two-tail	1.9725	

We have two options for reaching a conclusion based on the calculations from the sample data. First, we can compare the calculated t statistic to the critical t value for a two tailed test. We get the following:

Test statistic $= t = -1.833$

Critical t from the t-distribution with 198 degrees of freedom for a two-tailed test with alpha $= 0.05$ is $t = 1.9725$ or $t = -1.9725$
Because $t = -1.833 > -1.9725$, we do not reject the null hypothesis.

The second approach is the p-value approach. For a two-tail test, we compare the calculated p-value to the alpha $= 0.05$ level. The calculated p-value for a two-tailed test is 0.068. Then, because p-value $= 0.068 >$ alpha $= 0.05$, we do not reject the null hypothesis. This is the same conclusion reached using the test statistic approach.

Thus, the intern should report that based on the sample data there is not reason to believe that a difference exists in the mean length of stay at the two hotels.

10.35

a. Minitab output:

Two-Sample T-Test and CI: 05Fares, 06Fares

```
Two-sample T for 05Fares vs 06Fares

           N    Mean   StDev   SE Mean
05Fares   75   110.3   19.0      2.2
06Fares   75   117.7   20.5      2.4


Difference = mu (05Fares) - mu (06Fares)
Estimate for difference:  -7.3820
95% CI for difference:  (-13.7640, -1.0000)
```

Since μ_2 represents the average for fares in 2006, a difference of -10 or more would indicate that Neeleman has been able to meet his goal. Since -10 is contained in this interval it is plausible to conjecture that he has met his goal.

b. H_0: μ(06 fares) - μ(05 fares) $\geq$ \$10.00
   H_A: μ(06 fares) - μ(05 fares) < \$10.00

t-Test: Two-Sample Assuming Equal Variances

	06Fares	05Fares
Mean	117.6776	110.2956
Variance	420.0532	362.205
Observations	75	75
Pooled Variance	391.1291	
Hypothesized Mean Difference	10	
df	148	
t Stat	-0.81063	
P(T<=t) one-tail	0.209439	
t Critical one-tail	1.976123	
P(T<=t) two-tail	0.418877	
t Critical two-tail	2.264433	

Since the p-value is greater than 0.025, we do not reject the null hypothesis.

c. You should be able to reach the same conclusion using either a confidence interval estimate of a hypothesis test. You have to be careful about how you formulate your null hypothesis however. In this problem, if the null had been an increase of \$9.00 or less, you would not have rejected that hypothesis and seemingly reached a different conclusion.

Section 10-3 Exercises

10.37

Step 1: Define the population value of interest.
The population value of interest is μ_d, the mean paired difference.

Step 2: Specify the desired confidence level and determine the appropriate critical value.
For a 95% confidence interval, the critical value is a t-value from the t-distribution with n-1 = 11-1 = 10 degrees of freedom. From the t-table, we get t = 2.2281.

Step 3: Collect the sample data and compute the point estimate, $\overline{d}$, and the standard deviation, s_d.
The sample data, paired differences, are shown as follows.

Sample 1	Sample 2	d
22	31	-9
25	24	1
27	25	2
26	32	-6
22	25	-3
21	27	-6
23	31	-8
25	27	-2
28	31	-3
27	31	-4
23	26	-3

The point estimate is computed using Equation 10-12.

$$\overline{d} = \frac{\sum d}{n} = \frac{-41}{11} = -3.727$$

The standard deviation for the paired differences is computed using Equation 10-13.

$$s_d = \sqrt{\frac{\sum(d-\overline{d})^2}{n-1}} = 3.409$$

Step 4: Compute the confidence interval estimate using Equation 10-14.

$$\bar{d} \pm t \frac{s_d}{\sqrt{n}}$$

$$-3.727 \pm 2.2281 \frac{3.409}{\sqrt{11}}$$

$$-3.727 \pm 2.29$$

$$-6.017 \le \mu_d \le -1.437$$

10.39

The following steps can be taken to answer this question involving two paired samples.

Step 1: Specify the population value of interest.
We are interested in the mean paired difference for the two populations. This is μ_d. We will assume that the paired differences are normally distributed.

Step 2: Formulate the null and alternative hypotheses.
The hypotheses are:
$$H_0 : \mu_d = 0$$
$$H_A : \mu_d \ne 0$$

Step 3: Specify the significance level for the test.
The hypothesis test is to be conducted using an alpha = 0.05 level.

Step 4: Compute the test statistic.

The test statistic is computed using:

$$t = \frac{\bar{d} - \mu_d}{\frac{s_d}{\sqrt{n}}}$$

The following statistics have been computed

$$\bar{d} = \frac{\sum d}{n} = 12.45$$

and

$$s_d = \sqrt{\frac{\sum (d - \bar{d})^2}{n-1}} = 11$$

Then we compute the test statistic as

$$t = \frac{\bar{d} - \mu_d}{\frac{s_d}{\sqrt{n}}} = \frac{12.45 - 0}{\frac{11}{\sqrt{20}}} = 5.06$$

Step 5: Construct the rejection region.
This is a two-tailed test with an alpha = 0.05. We split the rejection region (and alpha) into the two tails equally. The critical t value from the t-distribution with df = 20-1 = 19 and a one-tail area equal to 0.025 is t = 2.0930. The decision rule is:

If the test statistic t > 2.0930, reject the null hypothesis
If the test statistic t < - 2.0930, reject the null hypothesis
Otherwise, do not reject.

Step 6: Reach a decision.
Because t = 5.06 > 2.0930, reject the null hypothesis.

Step 7: Draw a conclusion.
Based on the sample data we are able to conclude that a difference exists between the two population means based on the paired samples.

10.41

a.
Step 1: Specify the population value of interest.
Of interest is the difference in the population means, μ_d.

Step 2: Specify the desired confidence level and determine the appropriate critical value.
For a 90% confidence interval, the critical value is a t-value from the t-distribution with n-1 = 6 − 1 = 5. From the t-table , t = 2.015.

Step 3: Collect the sample data and compute the point estimate, $\bar{x}_d$, and the standard deviation, s_d

$$\bar{d} = \frac{\sum\limits_{i=1}^{n} d_i}{n} = \frac{63.2}{6} = 10.5333$$

$$s_d = \sqrt{\frac{\sum\limits_{i=1}^{n}(d-\bar{d})^2}{n-1}} = \sqrt{\frac{62.5733}{6-1}} = 3.5376$$

Step 4: Compute the confidence interval using Equation 10-14.

$$\bar{x}_d \pm t\frac{s_d}{\sqrt{n}} = 10.5333 \pm 2.015\frac{3.5376}{\sqrt{6}} =$$

$$10.5333 \pm 2.9101 = (7.6232, 13.4434)$$

b.
Step 1: Specify the population value of interest.
Of interest is difference in the population means, μ_d, observed at two different time periods.

Step 2: Formulate the appropriate null and alternative hypotheses.
$$H_O: \mu_d \le 10$$
$$H_A: \mu_d > 10$$

Step 3: Specify the significance for the test.
The significance level $= \alpha = 0.10$.

Step 4: Construct the rejection region.
Since the population standard deviation is not known, we must assume that the population has normal distribution. The critical value will, therefore, be obtained from a t-distribution with $n - 1 = 6 - 1 = 5$. From the t-table, the critical value is $t = 1.4759$. The rejection region is any test statistic > 1.4759.

Step 5: Compute the test statistic using Equation 10-15.

$$t = \frac{\bar{d} - \mu_d}{\frac{s_d}{\sqrt{n}}} = \frac{10.5333 - 10.0}{\frac{3.5376}{\sqrt{6}}} = 0.37$$

Step 6: Reach a decision.
Because t = 0.37< 1.459, the null hypothesis can not be rejected.

Step 7: Draw a conclusion.
Based on these sample data, there is not sufficient evidence to conclude that the difference of the two population means is more than 10.

10.43

Step 1: Specify the population value of interest.
In this case we will form paired differences by subtracting the After output from the Before output. It is assumed that the paired differences are normally distributed.

Step 2: Formulate the null and alternative hypotheses.
If modifications to the line (after layout) increases worker productivity then differences computed by subtracting the After output values from the Before output values should generally be negative. The null and alternative hypotheses are therefore:

$$H_o: \mu_d \geq 0$$
$$H_A: \mu_d < 0$$

Step 3: Specify the significance level for the test:
The test will be conducted using $\alpha = 0.05$.

Step 4: Construct the rejection region.
The critical value is a t-value from the t-distribution, with $\alpha = 0.05$ and 12-1=11 degrees of freedom. The critical value is t = -1.7959. The decision rule is
        If t calculated < -1.7959, reject the null hypothesis
            Otherwise, do not reject the null hypothesis

Step 5: Compute the test statistic.
A random sample of 12 employees' output Before and After the line was modified was selected. The following data and paired differences were observed:

Employee	1	2	3	4	5	6	7	8	9	10	11	12
Before	49	45	43	44	48	42	46	46	49	42	46	44
After	49	46	48	50	46	50	45	46	47	51	51	49
D	0	-1	-5	-6	2	-8	1	0	2	-9	-5	-5

The mean paired difference is

$$\bar{x}_d = \frac{\sum d}{n} = \frac{-34}{12} = -2.833$$

The standard deviation for the paired differences is

$$s_d = \sqrt{\frac{\sum (d - \bar{x}_d)}{n-1}} = 3.927$$

The test statistic is calculated using Equation 10-15.

$$t = \frac{\bar{x}_d - \mu_d}{\frac{s_d}{\sqrt{n}}} = t = \frac{-2.833 - 0.0}{\frac{3.927}{\sqrt{12}}} = -2.499$$

Step 6: Reach a decision.
Because the calculated t = -2.499 is less than the critical t = -1.7959, reject the null hypothesis.

Step 7: Draw a conclusion.
Based on these sample data, there is sufficient evidence to conclude that the modified line yields a higher output than the line before modification.

10.45

a. This study was set up as a paired sample experiment. The reason is to control the outside influences due to driver and car differences. For example, we would not want to randomly assign a majority of drivers who have a "heavy foot" and low mileage cars to the Acetone product (or vice-versa) thus unduly influencing the results due to driver behavior or car type. By pairing the samples, we are able to control from these outside influences that may adversely affect the results.

b. The following steps can be taken to answer this question involving two paired samples.

Step 1: Specify the population value of interest.
We are interested in the mean paired difference for the two populations. This is μ_d. We will assumed that the paired differences are normally distributed. We will compute the paired differences by subtracting the mpg with Acetone from the mpg without Acetone.

Step 2: Formulate the null and alternative hypotheses.

Because the article claims that the Acetone additive will result in increased mileage, we might want to place the burden of proof on this claim and formulate the null and alternative hypothesis as a one-tailed test.

The hypotheses are:

$H_0 : \mu_d \geq 0$ (using no additive will provide at least as high mean mpg)

$H_A : \mu_d < 0$ (Acetone additive is associated with higher mean mpg.)

Step 3: Specify the significance level for the test.

The hypothesis test is to be conducted using $\alpha = 0.05$.

Step 4: Compute the test statistic.

The test statistic is computed using:

$$t = \frac{\overline{x}_d - \mu_d}{\dfrac{s_d}{\sqrt{n}}}$$

We begin by computing the paired differences, d, for each sample as follows:

Driver	MPG: No Additive	MPG: Acetone Added	d
1	18.4	19	-0.6
2	23.5	22.8	0.7
3	31.4	30.9	0.5
4	26.5	26.9	-0.4
5	27.2	28.4	-1.2
6	16.3	18.2	-1.9
7	19.4	19.2	0.2
8	20.1	21.4	-1.3
9	14.2	16.1	-1.9
10	22.1	21.5	0.6

Next, we compute the sample mean paired difference and the standard deviation for the sample paired differences:

$$\overline{x}_d = \frac{\sum d}{n} = \frac{-5.3}{10} = -.53$$

and

$$s_d = \sqrt{\frac{\sum (d - \overline{x}_d)^2}{n-1}} = 1.01$$

Then we compute the test statistic as

$$t = \frac{\bar{x}_d - \mu_d}{\frac{s_d}{\sqrt{n}}} = \frac{-0.53 - 0}{\frac{1.01}{\sqrt{10}}} = -1.66$$

Step 5: Construct the rejection region.
This is a one-tailed test with $\alpha = 0.05$. The entire rejection region is placed in one tail (lower tail). The critical t value from the t-distribution with df = 10-1 = 9 and a one-tail area equal to 0.05 is t = -1.8331.

The decision rule is:
      If the test statistic t < - 1.8331, reject the null hypothesis
      Otherwise, do not reject.

Step 6: Reach a decision.
Because t = -1.66 > 1.8331, do not reject the null hypothesis.

Step 7: Draw a conclusion.
Based on the sample data we are unable to conclude that a difference exists between the two population means based on the paired samples. Thus, the claim that is being made in the article about Acetone's ability to improve fuel efficiency is not supported by this study.

10.47
a. Step 1: Specify the population value of interest.
    μ_d,

   Step 2: Formulate the null and alternative hypotheses.
      H_O: $\mu_d = 0$ H_A: $\mu_d \neq 0$,

   Step 3: Specify the significance level for the test:
      $\alpha = 0.02$,

   Step 4: Construct the rejection region.
      n - 1 = 23 - 1 = 22.
    So t = 2.5083. Reject H_O if t < -2.5083 or t > 2.5083.

Step 5: Compute the test statistic.

$$\bar{x}_d = \frac{\sum_{i=1}^{n} d_i}{n} = \frac{-28.3}{23} = -1.2304 \qquad s_d = \sqrt{\frac{\sum_{i=1}^{n}\left(d - \bar{x}_d\right)^2}{n-1}} = \sqrt{\frac{8.97}{23-1}} = 0.63849$$

$$t = \frac{-1.2304 - 0}{\frac{0.63849}{\sqrt{23}}} = -9.24$$

Step 6: Reach a decision.
Because $t = -9.24 < -2.3646$ the null hypothesis is rejected.

Step 7: Draw a conclusion.
The average measured cardiac output by the two evaluators differ.

b. $\displaystyle s_1 = \sqrt{\frac{\sum(x-\bar{x})^2}{n-1}} = \sqrt{\frac{61.66}{22}} = 1.6741.$ $\displaystyle s_2 = \sqrt{\frac{70.87}{22}} = 1.7948.$

$$s_P = \sqrt{\frac{(n_1-1)s_1^2 + (n_2-1)s_2^2}{n_1 + n_2 - 2}} = \sqrt{\frac{(23-1)(1.6741)^2 + (23-1)(1.7948)^2}{23+23-2}} =$$
1.7355

$$s_P\sqrt{\frac{1}{n_1}+\frac{1}{n_2}} = 1.7355\sqrt{\frac{1}{23}+\frac{1}{23}} = 0.5118, \quad \frac{s_d}{\sqrt{n}} = \frac{0.63849}{\sqrt{23}} = 0.13313.$$

The ratio of the two standard errors is 3.84 (= 0.5118/0.13313). Since the standard error is in the denominator of the t-statistic, a smaller standard error means that the test can detect smaller differences in the population means.

10.49
  a. The data obtained by the National Association of Home Builders consists of both the average and median selling prices for the same houses. Knowing that the average selling price in 2004 was $274,500, say, makes it more likely that the median selling price would be in this neighborhood. Therefore, the samples are dependent.

b. Minitab output:

Paired T-Test and CI: 95AV04, 95M04

```
Paired T for 95AV04 - 95M04

               N     Mean    StDev   SE Mean
95AV04        10   204850    36899    11668
95M04         10   168120    27274     8625
Difference    10  36730.0   9808.1    3101.6


90% CI for mean difference: (31044.5, 42415.5)
```

c. It is plausible to assert that the mean of the average selling prices for houses during the period 1995 to 2004 is more than mean of the median selling prices during this period. Since the confidence interval provides the range of plausible values for the difference and the confidence interval only contains positive numbers, this indicates that it is plausible to assert that the mean of the average selling prices is larger than the mean of the median selling prices.

d. Minitab output:

Paired T-Test and CI: 95AV04, 95M04

```
Paired T for 95AV04 - 95M04

               N     Mean    StDev   SE Mean
95AV04        10   204850    36899    11668
95M04         10   168120    27274     8625
Difference    10  36730.0   9808.1    3101.6


95% lower bound for mean difference: 31044.5
T-Test of mean difference = 30000 (vs > 30000): T-Value = 2.17   P-Value = 0.029
```

Since the p-value $= 0.029 < 0.05 = \alpha$, it is plausible to assert that the mean of the average selling prices for houses during the period 1995 to 2004 is more than $30,000 larger than the mean of the median selling prices during this period.

Section 10-4 Exercises

10.51

Step 1: Specify the population value of interest.
We are interested in knowing if the two population proportions are different or not.

Step 2: Formulate the appropriate null and alternative hypotheses.
The null and alternative hypotheses are

$$H_o : \pi_1 = \pi_2$$
$$H_A : \pi_1 \neq \pi_2$$

Step 3: Specify the significance level.
The test will be conducted using an $\alpha = 0.10$.

Step 4: Construct the rejection region.
For a two-tailed test, the critical values are z = 1.645 and z = -1.645. The decision rule based on the z-statistic is:
 If z calculated < -1.645 or z calculated > 1.645, reject the null hypothesis;
                Otherwise, do not reject.

Because we are using the p-value approach our decision rule will be reject Ho if the p-value is < α. Therefore, we will reject the null hypothesis is the p-value is < 0.10.

Step 5: Compute the z test statistic using Equation 10-18 and apply it to the decision rule.
The sample proportions are

$$p_1 = \frac{42}{120} = 0.35 \text{ and } p_2 = \frac{57}{150} = 0.38$$

The test statistic is calculated using Equation 10-18

$$z = \frac{(p_1 - p_2) - (\pi_1 - \pi_2)}{\sqrt{\overline{p}(1 - \overline{p})(\frac{1}{n_1} + \frac{1}{n_2})}}$$

where, using Equation 10-17:

$$\overline{p} = \frac{n_1 p_1 + n_2 p_2}{n_1 + n_2} = \frac{120(0.35) + 150(0.38)}{120 + 150} = 0.367$$

Then:

$$z = \frac{(0.35 - 0.38) - (0)}{\sqrt{0.367(1 - 0.367)(\frac{1}{120} + \frac{1}{150})}} = -0.508$$

Step 6: Reach a decision.
The probability of finding a z-value this small or smaller when the null hypothesis is true is approximately 0.5- 0.1950 =0.3050. Because this is a two-tailed test the p-value is twice this amount. Therefore, the p-value is 2*0.3050 = 0.61. There is evidence to reject the null hypothesis when the p-value is smaller than α. Here, because the p-value is greater than α, we do not reject the null hypothesis.

Step 7: Draw a conclusion.
Conclude there is no difference in the two population proportions.

10.53

a. A rule of thumb for sufficiently large is that np and n(1-p) are greater than or equal to 5 for both samples.

For sample 1, we have $p_1 = \dfrac{40}{200} = 0.20$. Thus, np = 200(.2) = 40 and n(1-p) = 200(1-.20) = 160.

For sample 2, we have $p2 = \dfrac{27}{150} = 0.18$. Thus, np = 150(.18) = 27 and n(1-p) = 150(1-.18) = 123. Therefore, we conclude that the sample sizes are sufficiently large.

b. The confidence interval estimate can be calculated using Equation 10-16.

$$(p_1 - p_2) \pm z \sqrt{\dfrac{(p_1)(1 - p_1)}{n_1} + \dfrac{(p_2)(1 - p_2)}{n_2}}$$

For a 95% confidence interval the critical value of z = 1.96. The confidence interval is therefore

$$(0.20 - 0.18) \pm 1.96 \sqrt{\dfrac{(0.20)(1 - 0.20)}{200} + \dfrac{(0.18)(1 - 0.18)}{150}} =$$

$$0.02 \pm 0.083$$

$$-0.063 \le (\pi_1 - \pi_2) \le 0.103$$

10.55

a.

Step 1: Specify the population value of interest.

$\pi_1 - \pi_2$

Step 2: Formulate the appropriate null and alternative hypotheses.

$H_O: \pi_1 - \pi_2 = 0$

$H_A: \pi_1 - \pi_2 \neq 0$

Step 3: Specify the significance level.

$\alpha = 0.05.$

Step 4: Construct the rejection region.

Since $\alpha = 0.05$, the critical values are ± 1.96. Reject H_O if $z < -1.96$ or $z > 1.96$.

Step 5: Compute the z test statistic using Equation 10-18 and apply it to the decision rule:

$$p = \frac{x_1 + x_2}{n_1 + n_2} = \frac{35 + 35}{50 + 75} = \frac{70}{125} = 0.56$$

$$z = \frac{p_1 - p_2 - (\pi_1 - \pi_2)}{\sqrt{pq(\frac{1}{n_1} + \frac{1}{n_2})}} = \frac{0.70 - 0.47 - (0)}{\sqrt{0.56(0.44)(\frac{1}{50} + \frac{1}{75})}} = 2.538$$

Step 6: Reach a decision.

Since $z = 2.538 > 1.96$, reject H_O

Step 7: Draw a conclusion.

There is sufficient evidence to conclude that $\pi_1 - \pi_2 \neq 0$.

b. .Using the same steps found in part a, indicated in ( ). (1). $\pi_1 - \pi_2$, (2) $H_O: \pi_1 - \pi_2 \geq 0$ vs. $H_A: \pi_1 - \pi_2 < 0$, (3) $\alpha = 0.05$, (4) the critical value is - 1.645, Reject H_O if z < -1.645, (5) $z = 2.538$, (6) Since $z = 2.538 > -1.645$, fail to reject H_O, (7) There is not sufficient evidence to conclude that $\pi_1 - \pi_2 < 0$.

c. Using the same steps found in part a, indicated in ( ). (1). $\pi_1 - \pi_2$, (2) $H_O: \pi_1 - \pi_2 = 0$ vs. $H_A: \pi_1 - \pi_2 > 0$, (3) $\alpha = 0.025$, (4) the critical value is 1.96, Reject H_O if $z > 1.96$, (5) $z = 2.538$, (6) Since $z = 2.538 > 1.96$, reject H_O, (7) There is sufficient evidence to conclude that $\pi_1 - \pi_2 > 0$.

d. Using the same steps found in part a, indicated in ( ). (1). $\pi_1 - \pi_2$, (2) H_O: $\pi_1 - \pi_2$ = 0.05 vs. H_A: $\pi_1 - \pi_2 \neq 0.05$, (3) $\alpha = 0.02$, (4) the critical values are ± 2.33, Reject H_O if z < -2.33 or z > 2.33, (5)

$$z = \frac{p_1 - p_2 - (\pi_1 - \pi_2)}{\sqrt{\dfrac{p_1 q_1}{n_1} + \dfrac{p_2 q_2}{n_2}}} = \frac{0.70 - 0.47 - (0.05)}{\sqrt{\dfrac{0.70(0.30)}{50} + \dfrac{0.47(0.53)}{75}}} = 2.08,$$

(6) Since z = 2.08 < 2.33, fail to reject H_O, (7) There is not sufficient evidence to conclude that $\pi_1 - \pi_2 \neq 0.05$.

10.57

$$H_o : \pi_S = \pi_M$$
$$H_A : \pi_S \neq \pi_M$$

Using an $\alpha = 0.01$, the critical value is $z = \pm 2.575$. The decision rule based on the z-statistic is: If z calculated < -2.575 or z calculated > 2.575, reject the null hypothesis; Otherwise, do not reject.

$$p_S = \frac{66}{200} = 0.33 \text{ and } p_M = \frac{63}{180} = 0.35$$

Using Equation 10-17:

$$\bar{p} = \frac{n_1 p_1 + n_2 p_2}{n_1 + n_2} = \frac{200(0.33) + 180(0.35)}{200 + 180} = 0.3395$$

Using Equation 10-18

$$z = \frac{(p_1 - p_2) - (\pi_1 - \pi_2)}{\sqrt{\bar{p}(1 - \bar{p})(\dfrac{1}{n_1} + \dfrac{1}{n_2})}} = \frac{(0.33 - 0.35) - (0)}{\sqrt{0.3395(1 - 0.3395)(\dfrac{1}{200} + \dfrac{1}{180})}} = -0.4111$$

Since the test statistic, -0.4111, is not less than the critical value of -2.575, do not reject the null hypothesis and conclude that there is no difference between the population proportions of adults between the ages of 27 and 35 in the two cities with college degrees.

Chapter 10

10.59

a. Step 1: $\pi_1 - \pi_2$

Step 2: H_O: $\pi_1 - \pi_2 \le 0.04$ vs. H_A: $\pi_1 - \pi_2 > 0.04$

Step 3: $\alpha = 0.05$

Step 4: Reject H_O if p-value > 0.05

Step 5: $z = \dfrac{p_1 - p_2 - (\pi_1 - \pi_2)}{\sqrt{\dfrac{p_1 q_1}{n_1} + \dfrac{p_2 q_2}{n_2}}} = \dfrac{0.149 - 0.103 - (0.04)}{\sqrt{\dfrac{0.149(0.851)}{23601} + \dfrac{0.103(0.897)}{23601}}} = 1.97,$

p-value $= P(z > 1.97) = 0.5 - 0.4756 = 0.0244$

Step 6: Since p-value $= 0.0244 < 0.05$ reject H_O

Step 7: There is sufficient evidence to conclude that there has been more than a 0.04 increase in the proportion of students that indicate they have been diagnosed with depression.

b. The margin of error is given by $\pm z \sqrt{\dfrac{p_1 q_1}{n_1} + \dfrac{p_2 q_2}{n_2}} =$

$\pm 1.96 \sqrt{\dfrac{0.149(0.851)}{23601} + \dfrac{0.103(0.897)}{23601}} = 0.00597.$

c. This is testing to see if the student understand what the margin of error represents. As such, the smallest difference equals the margin of error $= 0.00597$.

10.61

$H_o : \pi_U = \pi_R$

$H_A : \pi_U \ne \pi_R$

Using an $\alpha = 0.01$, the critical value is $z = \pm 2.575$. The decision rule based on the z-statistic is: If z calculated < -2.575 or z calculated > 2.575, reject the null hypothesis; Otherwise, do not reject.

$p_U = \dfrac{42}{150} = 0.28$ and $p_R = \dfrac{52}{150} = 0.3467$

Using Equation 10-17:

$\overline{p} = \dfrac{n_1 p_1 + n_2 p_2}{n_1 + n_2} = \dfrac{150(0.28) + 150(0.3467)}{150 + 150} = 0.3133$

Using Equation 10-18

$$z = \frac{(p_1 - p_2) - (\pi_1 - \pi_2)}{\sqrt{\bar{p}(1-\bar{p})(\frac{1}{n_1} + \frac{1}{n_2})}} = \frac{(0.28 - 0.3467) - (0)}{\sqrt{0.3133(1 - 0.3133)(\frac{1}{150} + \frac{1}{150})}} = -1.2454$$

Since the test statistic, -1.2454, is not less than the critical value of -2.575, do not reject the null hypothesis and conclude that there is no difference between the proportion of urban households and rural households that use the Internet to download computer games.

10.63

a. $n_1 p_1 = 147(72/147) = 72 > 5$, $n_1 q_1 = 147(75/147) = 75 > 5$; $n_2 p_2 = 120(48/120) = 48 > 5$, $n_2 q_2 = 120(72/120) = 72 > 5$. There was no test that failed. Therefore, the sampling distribution can be approximated with a normal distribution.

b. Minitab output:

Test and CI for Two Proportions: UpperIncome, LowIncome

```
Event = Male


Variable      X    N   Sample p
UpperIncome   72   147  0.489796
LowIncome     48   120  0.400000


Difference = p (UpperIncome) - p (LowIncome)
Estimate for difference:  0.0897959
99% lower bound for difference:  -0.0517098
Test for difference = 0.01 (vs > 0.01):  Z = 1.31  P-Value = 0.095
```

Since the p-value = 0.095 > 0.01. The null hypothesis is not rejected. There is not sufficient evidence to indicate that the proportion of male undergraduates in the upper income category is more than 1% greater than that of the low income category.

c. The difference, $p_1 - p_2 = 0.49 - 0.40 = 0.09$, is greater than the hypothesized value 0.01. However, the difference "0.09" is the difference between the sample proportions. The hypothesis test is testing the difference between the population proportions. Given the sample sizes, the difference, 0.09, is not large enough to support the assertion that the difference in the population proportions is more than 0.01. Incidentally, the sample sizes cannot support an assertion that the population proportion are not equal to each other. Larger sample sizes would be required to detect a difference in the two population proportions.

End of Chapter Exercises

10.65

When dealing with one sample, where the population standard deviation is not known, an additional cause of variation is introduced in the analysis. Therefore, the t distribution is used instead of the z distribution, since the t distribution is always larger than the z. In means, for instance, a confidence interval is wider to adjust for the additional uncertainty. When two sample are used, and the two population variances can not be assumed to be equal yet another course of uncertainty is introduced and degrees of freedom need to be adjusted to give, for instance, a wider interval.

10.67

a.

$$s_p = \sqrt{\frac{(n_1 - 1)s_1^2 + (n_2 - 1)s_2^2}{n_1 + n_2 - 2}} = \sqrt{\frac{(15 - 1)(3)^2 + (10 - 1)(4)^2}{15 + 10 - 2}}$$

$$s_p = 3.4262, \quad (\bar{x}_1 - \bar{x}_2) \pm t_{\alpha/2} \, s_p \sqrt{\frac{1}{n_1} + \frac{1}{n_2}} = (12 - 7) \pm$$

$$(2.0687)(3.4262)\sqrt{\left(\frac{1}{15} + \frac{1}{10}\right)} = 5 \pm 2.8936 = (2.1064, 7.8936).$$

b. $$t = \frac{(\bar{x}_1 - \bar{x}_2) - (\mu_1 - \mu_2)}{s_p \sqrt{\frac{1}{n_1} + \frac{1}{n_2}}} = \frac{(12 - 7) - (7.8936)}{3.4262\sqrt{\frac{1}{15} + \frac{1}{10}}} . = -2.0687$$

Any value specified in H_O larger than the upper confidence limit would result in a test statistic smaller than the lower critical value and a rejection of H_O

c. $$t = \frac{(\bar{x}_1 - \bar{x}_2) - (\mu_1 - \mu_2)}{s_p \sqrt{\frac{1}{n_1} + \frac{1}{n_2}}} = \frac{(12 - 7) - (2.1064)}{3.4262\sqrt{\frac{1}{15} + \frac{1}{10}}} . = 2.0687$$

Any value specified in H_O smaller than the lower confidence limit would result in a test statistic larger than the upper critical value and a rejection of H_O

d. To conduct a two-tailed hypothesis test using a confidence interval, simply compare the value stated in H_O. If that value is contained in the confidence interval, do not reject H_O. If that value is not contained in the confidence interval, reject H_O.

10.69

The following steps are used to construct a confidence interval estimate when the samples are selected from normally distributed populations with equal variances and when the population variances are unknown:

Step 1: Define the population value of interest.
We are interested in the difference between the two population means, $\mu_1 - \mu_2$, the difference between mean time that males have been customers with the company versus females.

Step 2: Compute the point estimate.
The point estimate is the difference between the two sample means. The two sample means are:

$$\text{Males} = \bar{x}_1 = \frac{\sum x}{n_1} = \frac{128}{13} = 9.85 \quad \text{and} \quad \text{Females} = \bar{x}_2 = \frac{\sum x}{n_2} = \frac{69}{13} = 5.31$$

The point estimate is: $\bar{x}_1 - \bar{x}_2 = 9.85 - 5.31 = 4.54$

Step 3: Specify the desired confidence level and determine the critical value.
The desired confidence level is 90 percent. The critical value comes from a t-distribution with $df = n_1 + n_2 - 2$. The degrees of freedom is $13 + 13 - 2 = 24$. The critical value from the t-distribution table is 1.7109.

Step 4: Compute the confidence interval estimate.
When the population variances are assumed to be equal, the confidence interval estimate is computed using:

$$(\bar{x}_1 - \bar{x}_2) \pm ts_p \sqrt{\frac{1}{n_1} + \frac{1}{n_2}}$$

where:

$$s_p = \sqrt{\frac{(n_1 - 1)s_1^2 + (n_2 - 1)s_2^2}{n_1 + n_2 - 2}} = \sqrt{\frac{(13-1)3.6^2 + (13-1)2.9^2}{13 + 13 - 2}} = 3.27$$

Then

$$4.54 \pm 1.7109(3.27)\sqrt{\frac{1}{13} + \frac{1}{13}}$$

$$4.54 \pm 2.19$$

$$2.35 \leq \mu_1 - \mu_2 \leq 6.73$$

Thus, based on the sample data with 90 percent confidence the manager can conclude that male customers have a longer average duration with the company by anywhere from 2.35 years to 6.73 years than do female customers.

10.71

Step 1: Specify the population value of interest.
In this case we will form paired differences by subtracting the Internet textbook price from the Campus textbook price. It is assumed that the paired differences are normally distributed.

Step 2: Formulate the null and alternative hypotheses.
The null and alternative hypotheses are:
$$Ho: \mu_d = 0$$
$$H_A: \mu_d \neq 0$$

Step 3: Specify the significance level for the test:
The test will be conducted using $\alpha = 0.01$.

Step 4: Construct the rejection region.
The critical value is a t-value from the t-distribution, with $\alpha = 0.01$ and 10-1=9 degrees of freedom. The critical value is $t = \pm 3.2498$. The decision rule is
    If t calculated < -3.2498, of if t calculated > 3.2498, reject the null hypothesis
                Otherwise, do not reject the null hypothesis

Step 5: Compute the test statistic.
A random sample of 10 textbooks was taken from the campus bookstore and an Internet retailer. The following price data and paired differences were observed:

Textbook	Physics	Chemistry	Spanish	Accounting	Calculus	Economics	Art	Biology	History	English
Campus	108	114	114	110	118	108	119	115	119	114
Internet	124	120	107	112	122	123	125	108	117	119
d	-16	-6	7	-2	-4	-15	-6	7	2	-5

The mean paired difference is

$$\bar{d} = \frac{\sum d}{n} = \frac{-38}{10} = -3.8$$

The standard deviation for the paired differences is

$$s_d = \sqrt{\frac{\sum(d-\bar{d})}{n-1}} = 7.857$$

The test statistic is calculated using Equation 10-15.

$$t = \frac{\bar{d}-\mu_d}{\frac{s_d}{\sqrt{n}}} = t = \frac{-3.8-0.0}{\frac{7.857}{\sqrt{10}}} = -1.529$$

Step 6: Reach a decision.
Because the calculated t = -1.529 is not less than the critical t = -3.2498, nor > 3.2498, do not reject the null hypothesis.

Step 7: Draw a conclusion.
Based on these sample data, there is insufficient evidence to conclude that there is a difference in average textbook prices between the Campus and Internet retailer.

10.73
a. If the populations are assumed to have normal distributions, the mean = the median. Therefore, the test will be:
Step 1: Define the population value of interest.
$\mu_1 - \mu_2$,

Step 2: Formulate the appropriate null and alternative hypotheses:
$H_O: \mu_1 - \mu_2 \le 10{,}000$ $H_A: \mu_1 - \mu_2 > 10{,}000$,

Step 3: Specify the significance level for the test:
$\alpha = 0.05$,

Step 4: Determine the rejection region and state the decision rule.
$n_1 + n_2 - 2 = 500$ So t = 1.6479. Reject H_O if t > 1.6479,

Step 5: Compute the test statistic.

$$s_p = \sqrt{\frac{(n_1-1)s_1^2 + (n_2-1)s_2^2}{n_1+n_2-2}} =$$

$$\sqrt{\frac{(200-1)(10000)^2 + (302-1)(9000)^2}{200+302-2}} = 9410.9385$$

$$t = \frac{(\bar{x}_1 - \bar{x}_2) - (\mu_1 - \mu_2)}{s_p\sqrt{\frac{1}{n_1} + \frac{1}{n_2}}} = \frac{(58939 - 47315) - (10000)}{9410.9385\sqrt{\frac{1}{200} + \frac{1}{302}}} = 1.89.$$

Step 6: Reach a decision.
Because t = 1.89 > 1.6479 , the null hypothesis is rejected.

Step 7: Draw a conclusion.
Based on these sample data, there is sufficient evidence to conclude that the median income for men buying homes is more than $10,000 larger than that of women.

b. The required assumptions are the three listed on page 445.

10.75

a. The "gap" between private and public 4-year colleges for the 1980 – 81 academic year in 2005 dollars was $8,180 - $1,818 = $6362. Doubling this would yield 2(6362) = 12724.

$$H_0: \mu(2005\text{-}2006) - \mu(1980\text{-}19811) \leq 12724$$
$$H_A: \mu(2005\text{-}2006) - \mu(1980\text{-}19811) > 12724$$

t-Test: Two-Sample Assuming Equal Variances

	Private05	Public05
Mean	21234.59	5490.938
Variance	23168591	3601780
Observations	81	81
Pooled Variance	13385186	
Hypothesized Mean Difference	12724	
df	160	
t Stat	5.252578	
P(T<=t) one-tail	2.36E-07	
t Critical one-tail	2.34988	
P(T<=t) two-tail	4.72E-07	
t Critical two-tail	2.606903	

The critical values for the one tailed test is 2.3499. the calculated t value is 5.25. The null hypothesis is rejected. The gap between the average tuition and fees at private and public colleges has more than doubled.

b. Since the null hypothesis was rejected, the only statistical error that could have been made is a type I error = rejecting H_O when in fact H_O was true.

10.77

a.

$H_o : \mu_{H} \geq \mu_{A}$

$H_A : \mu_{H} < \mu_{A}$

Using Excel's data analysis tool for t-Test: Two-Sample Assuming Equal Variance, the following information is obtained:

t-Test: Two-Sample Assuming Equal Variances

	Hispanic	Asian-American
Mean	18659.18152	20002.53845
Variance	22090351.66	33727253.02
Observations	92	110
Pooled Variance	28432462.9	
Hypothesized Mean Difference	0	
df	200	
t Stat	-1.783194648	
P(T<=t) one-tail	0.038035584	
t Critical one-tail	2.345137058	

Since the test statistic of -1.7832 is not less than the critical value for a one-tail lower tail test of -2.345, do not reject the null hypothesis and conclude the mean undergraduate debt for Hispanic students is not less than the mean undergraduate debt for Asian-American students.

b. Using the Excel information from part (a), the P(T<=t) one-tail value of 0.038 is the p-value which means that for all alpha values greater than 0.038 would change your decision.

c.

$$H_o : \mu_{H} \geq \mu_{A}$$
$$H_A : \mu_{H} < \mu_{A}$$

Using Excel's data analysis tool for t-Test: Two-Sample Assuming Unequal Variance, the following information is obtained:

t-Test: Two-Sample Assuming Unequal Variances

	Hispanic	Asian-American
Mean	18659.18152	20002.53845
Variance	22090351.66	33727253.02
Observations	92	110
Hypothesized Mean Difference	0	
df	200	
t Stat	-1.816801114	
P(T<=t) one-tail	0.035372237	

For any alpha values less than 0.0354 you would not reject the null hypothesis and conclude the mean undergraduate debt for Hispanic students is not less than the mean undergraduate debt for Asian-American students. For any alpha values greater than 0.0354 you would reject the null hypothesis and conclude the mean undergraduate debt for Hispanic students is less than the mean undergraduate debt for Asian-American students.

Chapter 10

Chapter 11 Solutions

When applicable, selected problems in each section will be done following the appropriate step-by-step procedures outlined in the corresponding sections of the chapter. Other problems will provide key points and the answers to the questions, but all answers can be arrived at using the appropriate steps.

Section 11-1 Exercises

11.1

The following steps can be used to conduct the hypothesis test.

Step 1: Specify the population values of interest.
We are interested in testing about the population standard deviation. However, we must state this in terms of the population variance so the population value of interest is the population variance.

Step 2: State the null and alternative hypotheses.
The manager wishes to determine whether the standard deviation has dropped below 130. In variance terms, she is interested in whether the population variance has dropped below $\sigma^2 = 130^2 = 16,900$. This will be a one tailed, lower tail test with the null and alternative hypotheses shown as follows:

$$H_0 : \sigma^2 \geq 16,900$$
$$H_A : \sigma^2 < 16,900$$

Step 3: Specify the significance level.
The significance level will be 0.05.

Step 4: Construct the rejection region.
This is a one-tailed test with the entire rejection region in the lower tail. The critical value from the chi-square distribution with df = 20 − 1 = 19 and alpha = 0.05 in the lower tail is 10.1170. Note, because this is a lower tail test, the table value in Appendix G is found for an area to the right of the critical value equal to $1 - 0.05 = 0.95$. The decision rule is:

If $\chi^2 < 10.1170$, reject the null hypothesis
Otherwise, do not reject the null hypothesis

Step 5: Compute the test statistic.
The random sample of n = 20 items provided a sample standard deviation equal to 105. Thus, $s^2 = 11,025$. The test statistic is:

$$\chi^2 = \frac{(n-1)s^2}{\sigma^2} = \frac{(20-1)11,025}{16,900} = 12.39$$

Step 6. Reach a decision.
Since $\chi^2 = 12.39 > 10.1170$, do not reject the null hypothesis.

Step 7: Draw a conclusion.
Based on the test results, the data do not present sufficient evidence to justify concluding that the population standard deviation has dropped below 130.

11.3

No statistical method exists for developing a confidence interval estimate for a population standard deviation directly. Instead we must first convert to variances. This, we get a sample variance equal to $s^2 = 360^2 = 129,600$.

Now we compute the interval estimate using:

$$\frac{(n-1)s^2}{\chi_U^2} \leq \sigma^2 \leq \frac{(n-1)s^2}{\chi_L^2}$$

where

$s^2 =$ sample variance
$n =$ sample size
$\chi_L^2 =$ Lower Critical Value
$\chi_U^2 =$ Upper Critical Value

The denominators come from the chi-square distribution with n -1 degrees of freedom. In an application in which the sample size is n = 20 and the desired confidence level is 95%, from the chi-square table in Appendix G we get the critical value

$$\chi_U^2 = \chi_{0.025}^2 = 32.8523$$

Likewise, we get:

$$\chi_L^2 = \chi_{0.975}^2 = 8.9065$$

Now given that the sample variance computed from the sample of n = 20 values is $s^2 = 360^2 = 129,600$. Then, we construct the 95% confidence interval as follows:

$$\frac{(20-1)129,600}{32.8523} \leq \sigma^2 \leq \frac{(20-1)129,600}{8.9065}$$

$$74,953.7 \leq \sigma^2 \leq 276,472.2$$

Thus, at the 95% confidence level, we conclude that the population variance will fall in the range 79,953.7 to 276.472. By taking the square root, you can convert to an interval estimate of the population standard deviation as the interval .732.78 to 525.81.

11.5

a.

Step 1: Specify the population value of interest.
We are interested in testing the population variance.

Step 2: Specify the null and alternative hypotheses.
The null and alternative hypotheses are stated in terms of the population variance. This is a two-tailed test.

Step 3: Specify the significance level.
The significance level is $\alpha = 0.10$.

Step 4: Construct the rejection region and define the decision rule.
Because this is a two tail test, two critical values from the chi-square distribution in Appendix G, one for the upper (right) tail and one for the lower (left) tail are required. The alpha will be split evenly between the two tails with $\alpha/2 = 0.05$ in each tail. The degrees of freedom for the chi-square distribution is $n-1 = 12 -1 = 11$. The upper tail critical value is found by locating the column headed 0.05 and going to the row for degrees of freedom equal to 11. This gives $\chi^2_{0.05} = 19.6752$. The lower critical level test statistic is found by going to the column headed 0.95 and to the row for 11 degrees of freedom. This gives $\chi^2_{0.95} = 4.5748$. Thus, the decision rule is:

If the test statistic, $\chi^2 > \chi^2_{0.05} = 19.6752$, reject the null hypothesis

If the test statistic, $\chi^2 < \chi^2_{0.95} = 4.5748$, reject the null hypothesis
Otherwise, do not reject the null hypothesis

Step 5: Compute the test statistic.
The random sample consists of $n = 12$ observations. The sample variance is $s^2 = 9^2 = 81$. The test statistic is

$$\chi^2 = \frac{(n-1)s^2}{\sigma^2} = \frac{(12-1)81}{50} = 17.82$$

Step 6: Reach a decision.

Because $\chi^2 = 17.82 < \chi^2_{0.05} = 19.6752$ and because

$\chi^2 = 17.82 > \chi^2_{0.95} = 4.5748$ do not reject the null hypothesis based on these sample data.

Step 7: Draw a conclusion.

Based on the sample data and the hypothesis test conducted we do not reject the null hypothesis at the $\alpha = 0.10$ level of significance and we conclude the population variance is not different from 50.

b.

Step 1: Specify the population value of interest.

We are interested in testing the population variance.

Step 2: Specify the null and alternative hypotheses.

The null and alternative hypotheses are stated in terms of the population variance. This is a two-tailed test.

Step 3: Specify the significance level.

The significance level is $\alpha = 0.05$.

Step 4: Construct the rejection region and define the decision rule.

Because this is a two tail test, two critical values from the chi-square distribution in Appendix G, one for the upper (right) tail and one for the lower (left) tail are required. The alpha will be split evenly between the two tails with $\alpha/2 = 0.025$ in each tail. The degrees of freedom for the chi-square distribution is n-1 = 19 -1 = 18. The upper tail critical value is found by locating the column headed 0.025 and going to the row for degrees of freedom equal to 18. This gives $\chi^2_{0.025} =$ 31.5264. The lower critical level is found by going to the column headed 0.975 and to the row for 18 degrees of freedom. This gives $\chi^2_{0.975} = 8.2307$. Thus, the decision rule is:

If the test statistic, $\chi^2 > \chi^2_{0.25} = 31.5264$, reject the null hypothesis

If the test statistic, $\chi^2 < \chi^2_{0.975} = 8.2307$, reject the null hypothesis

Otherwise, do not reject the null hypothesis

Step 5: Compute the test statistic.

The random sample consists of n = 19 observations. The sample variance is $s^2 = 6^2 = 36$. The test statistic is

$$\chi^2 = \frac{(n-1)s^2}{\sigma^2} = \frac{(19-1)36}{50} = 12.96$$

Step 6: Reach a decision.

Because $\chi^2 = 12.96 < \chi^2_{0.025} = 31.5264$ and because

$\chi^2 = 12.96 > \chi^2_{0.975} = 8.2307$ we do not reject the null hypothesis.

Step 7: Draw a conclusion.

Based on the sample data and the hypothesis test conducted we do not reject the null hypothesis at the $\alpha = 0.05$ level of significance and conclude the population variance is not different from 50.

11.7

a.

Step 1: Specify the population value of interest.

The parameter of interest is the population variance, σ^2.

Step 2: Specify the null and alternative hypotheses.

It is required to determine if the variance has increased. Historically, $\sigma^2 = (6.3)^2 = 39.69$. Therefore, the hypotheses are

H_O: $\sigma^2 \leq 39.69$

H_A: $\sigma^2 > 39.69$

Step 3: Specify the significance level.

$\alpha = 0.05$.

Step 4: Compute the p-value.

Since $\chi^2 = \dfrac{(n-1)s^2}{\sigma^2} = \dfrac{(28-1)66.2}{(6.3)^2} = 45.03$,

p-value = $P(\chi^2 \geq 45.03)$. Therefore, $0.01 <$ p-value < 0.025.

Step 5: Compare the p-value to the significance level.

$0.01 <$ p-value $< 0.1 = \alpha$

Step 6: Reach a decision.

Since p-value $< \alpha$, reject H_O.

Step 7: Draw a conclusion.

Conclude that the variance has increased.

b. Using the same seven steps as in part a.:
Step 1: The parameter of interest is the population variance, σ^2,

Step 2: H_O: $\sigma^2 \geq 39.69$ H_A: $\sigma^2 < 39.69$,

Step 3: $\alpha = 0.025$,

Step 4: $\chi^2 = \dfrac{(n-1)s^2}{\sigma^2} = \dfrac{(8-1)9.02}{(6.3)^2} = 1.591$,

Step 5: The critical value is obtained from a χ^2 distribution with n – 1 = 7 degrees of freedom, i.e., 1.6899,

Step 6: Since the test statistic = 1.591 < the χ^2 critical value = 1.6899, reject the null hypothesis,

Step 7: Conclude that the variance has decreased.

c. Using the same seven steps as in part a.
Step 1: The parameter of interest is the population variance, σ^2

Step 2: H_O: $\sigma^2 \geq 39.69$ H_A: $\sigma^2 < 39.69$.

Step 3: $\alpha = 0.025$

Step 4: Since $\chi^2 = \dfrac{(n-1)s^2}{\sigma^2} = \dfrac{(18-1)62.9}{(6.3)^2} = 26.94$,

p-value = $P(s^2 \geq 62.9) = P(\chi^2 \geq 26.94)$.

Step 5: $\alpha = 0.10 < $ p-value $= 0.94$

From Minitab:

Cumulative Distribution Function
Chi-Square with 17 DF

x P(X <= x)
26.94   0.941046

Step 6: Fail to reject H$_O$,

Step 7: Conclude that there is not enough evidence to conclude that the variance has decreased.

11.9

a. We are asked to conduct a hypothesis test for a single population mean. Recalling the concepts covered in Chapter 9, we will use the following steps to perform the hypothesis test when the population is assumed to be normally distributed with an unknown population standard deviation.

Step 1: Specify the population value of interest.
We are interested in the mean downtime per occurrence at this machine center.

Step 2: Formulate the appropriate null and alternative hypothesis.
The assumption in the simulation model is that the population mean downtime is 30 minutes so the following null and alternative hypotheses will be used:
$$H_0 : \mu = 30$$
$$H_A : \mu \neq 30$$
Thus, the test will be a two-tailed test.

Step 3: Specify the desired level of significance.
The test will be conducted using an alpha = 0.05 level.

Step 4: Construct the rejection region and specify the decision rule:
The test will be a two-tailed test so the alpha will be split into the two tails evenly. Because we assume that the population is normally distributed, the critical value will come from the t-distribution with degrees of freedom equal to n – 1. From the t-table, for 9 degrees of freedom and a one tailed area equal to 0.025, we get t = 2.2622. Thus, the decision rule is:
>   If the test statistic, t > 2.2622, reject the null hypothesis
>   If the test statistic, t < -2.2622, reject the null hypothesis
>   Otherwise, do not reject

Step 5: Compute the test statistic.
First we compute the sample mean and sample standard deviation as follows:

$$\bar{x} = \frac{\sqrt{x}}{n} = \frac{311}{10} = 31.1$$

And

$$s = \sqrt{\frac{(x-\bar{x})}{n-1}} = 18.44$$

The test statistic is:

$$t = \frac{\bar{x}-\mu}{\frac{s}{\sqrt{n}}} = \frac{31.1-30}{\frac{18.44}{\sqrt{10}}} = 0.19 \quad t = \frac{\bar{x}-\mu}{\frac{s}{\sqrt{n}}} = \frac{31.2-30}{\frac{18.5}{\sqrt{10}}} = 0.21$$

Step 6: Reach a decision.
Because the test statistic, t = 0.19 < t = 2.2622, do not reject the null hypothesis.

Step 7: Draw a conclusion.
Based on these sample data, the consultants have no reason to conclude that the mean downtime is not equal to 30 minutes per occurrence.

b. The consultants are also interested in testing whether the population standard deviation is equal to 10 minutes. There is no test procedure that allows us to test directly about a population standard deviation so we must first convert to a variance and test. The following steps can be used:

Step 1: Specify the population value of interest.
We are interested in the population standard deviation (and likewise the population variance.)

Step 2: Specify the null and alternative hypothesis.
The assumption is made by the consultants that the population standard deviation is 10 minutes. This means they are also assuming that the population variance is $\sigma^2 = 100$. Thus, we form the null and alternative hypotheses as follows:

$$H_0 : \sigma^2 = 100$$
$$H_0 : \sigma^2 \neq 100$$

Step 3: Specify the significance level.
The test will be conducted using an alpha = 0.05 level.

Step 4: Construct the rejection region.
This will be a two-tailed test. The rejection region will be split into two the tails evenly with $\frac{\alpha}{2} = \frac{0.05}{2} = 0.025$ in each tail. The critical values will be from the chi-square distribution with n – 1 degrees of freedom. The upper tail critical value from the chi-square distribution with 9 degrees of freedom is $\chi^2 = 19.0228$. The lower tail critical value from the chi-square distribution is found by using the 1 – 0.025 = 0.975 to the right of the chi-square value. The lower tail critical value is $\chi^2 = 2.7004$. Thus, the decision rule is:

If the test statistic, $\chi^2 > 19.0228$, reject the null hypothesis
If the test statistic, $\chi^2 < 2.7004$, reject the null hypothesis
Otherwise, do not reject the null hypothesis

Step 5: Compute the test statistic.
Recall in part a., we computed the sample standard deviation to be $s = 18.5$. Then the sample variance is $s^2 = 18.5^2 = 342.25$. The test statistic is a chi-square value computed as follows:

$$\chi^2 = \frac{(n-1)s^2}{\sigma^2} = \frac{(10-1)342.25}{100} = 30.8$$

Step 6: Reach a decision.
Because $\chi^2 = 30.8 > 19.0228$, we reject the null hypothesis

Step 7: Draw a conclusion.
Because the null hypothesis was rejected, we conclude that the population variance is not equal to 100. Thus, we also conclude that the population standard deviation is not equal to 10 minutes.

c. Based on the results in parts a. and b., the consultants are justified in using a mean of 30 minutes for the downtime per occurrence at this machine center, but they are going to want to modify their standard deviation. It appears that the population standard deviation exceeds 10 minutes. They will need to estimate the population standard deviation from sample data from the machine center.

11.11

The confidence interval estimate for the population variance, σ^2 is computed using Equation 11-2 shown below:

$$\frac{(n-1)s^2}{\chi_U^2} \le \sigma^2 \le \frac{(n-1)s^2}{\chi_L^2}$$

Where s^2 = the sample variance, n = the sample size, and α = 1-confidence interval. For a 95% confidence interval we find the following values for χ_L^2 and χ_U^2 with n-1 = 14-1 = 13 degrees of freedom:

$$\chi_{0.975}^2 = 5.0087 \quad \text{and} \quad \chi_{0.025}^2 = 24.7356.$$

The sample variance is found to be: $s^2 = 672.39$

The confidence interval is calculated using Equation 11-2:

$$\frac{(14-1)672.39}{24.7356} \le \sigma^2 \le \frac{(14-1)672.39}{5.0087} = 353.38 \le \sigma^2 \le 1745.18$$

11.13

    a. H_o: $\mu \leq 10$

        H_a: $\mu > 10$

    b. Using Excel's AVERAGE and STDEV functions

        $\bar{x} = 11$ $s = 2.5820$

        $t = (11-10)/(2.5820/\sqrt{10}) = 1.2247$

        $t_{.10} = 1.383$

        Since 1.2247 < 1.383 do not reject H_o and conclude that the mean time may be 10 minutes or less.

    c. H_o: $\sigma^2 \leq 16$

        H_a: $\sigma^2 > 16$

        $\chi^2 = [(10-1)(2.5820)^2]/16 = 3.75$

        Decision Rule:

        If $\chi^2 > 14.6837$, reject H_o, otherwise do not reject H_o

        Since 3.75 < 14.6837 do not reject Ho and conclude that the population variance is less than or equal to 16

11.15

    a. Hartford's wage average is 19 + 0.38(19) = \$26.22 and Brownsville's is 19 − 0.30(19) = \$13.30. Therefore, the range of values is 26.22 − 13.30 = 12.92. The relationship between a normal distribution's range and standard deviation is $\sigma \approx \dfrac{R}{6} = \dfrac{12.92}{6} = 2.153$. Therefore, $\sigma^2 = 4.637$.

    b. There are two hypothesis tests called for here. First we perform the test to determine if the standard deviation is smaller in San Antonio. Using the seven steps outlined in the chapter:

        Step 1: The parameter of interest is the population variance, σ^2,

        Step 2: H_O: $\sigma^2 \geq 4.637$ H_A: $\sigma^2 < 4.637$,

        Step 3: $\alpha = 0.05$,

        Step 4: $\chi^2 = \dfrac{(n-1)s^2}{\sigma^2} = \dfrac{(25-1)(1.46)^2}{(4.637)} = 11.03$,

        Step 5: The critical value is obtained from a χ^2 distribution with n − 1 = 24 degrees of freedom, i.e., 13.8484.

        Step 6: Since the test statistic = 11.03 < the χ^2 critical value = 13.8484, reject the null hypothesis,

Step 7: Conclude that the variance of the construction workers in San Antonio is less than the variance of the nation construction workers as a whole.

Since the variance for wages of the construction workers in San Antonio is (smaller than the nation as a whole but) unknown, a test of hypothesis utilizing the t-distribution is appropriate.

The second part of the problem involves testing a hypothesis about the population mean, μ,

H_O: $\mu \geq 19$

H_A: $\mu < 19$

$\alpha = 0.05$,

Since σ is unknown, we use a t test statistic

$$t = \frac{\bar{x} - \mu}{\frac{s}{\sqrt{n}}} = \frac{13.87 - 19}{\frac{1.46}{\sqrt{25}}} = -17.57 \text{, with } 25 - 1 = 24 \text{ degrees of freedom.}$$

We reject H_O if t < -1.7109.

Since t = -17.57 < -1.7109 , reject H_O. There is sufficient evidence to conclude that the construction workers average wage is smaller than that of the national construction workers as whole.

11.17

a. Using Excel's CHIINV option, the critical value is 156.714

Minitab output:

Test and CI for One Variance: HomeHeat

```
Test of sigma squared = 10000 vs > 10000


Chi-Square Method (Normal Distribution)

                        95%
                      Lower
Variable    N  Variance  Bound  Chi-Square      P
HomeHeat  125    12894  10589      159.88  0.017
```

Since the calculated value is greater than the critical value and p-value = 0.017 < 0.025 the null hypothesis is rejected. Therefore, there is sufficient evidence to conclude that the variability in heating costs in the winter of 2006 was larger than that indicated by historical data

b. Minitab output:

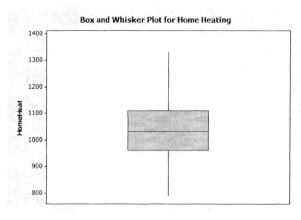

The major requirement that must be met is that the population has a normal distribution. Here the upper whisker seems to be longer than the lower whisker and the median seems to be to the left of the center of the box. However, you must remember that you are asking the following question: Could this sample data have come from a normal distribution? You cannot expect the sample data to be an exact replica of the population. You must expect some deviation in the sample. The two minor deviations do not seem large enough to convince us that the population is not normal. Therefore, the analysis in part a. seems valid.

Section 10-2 Exercises

11.19

   a. Using the F distribution in Appendix H, $F = 3.619$

   b. Using the F distribution in Appendix H, $F = 3.106$

   c. Using the F distribution in Appendix H, $F = 3.051$

11.21

   a. Using Appendix H: If the calculated $F > 2.278$, reject H_0, otherwise do not reject H_0

   b.

   c. $F = 1450/1320 = 1.0985$
      Since $1.0985 < 2.278$ do not reject H_0

11.23

    a. Using the seven step procedure from the chapter:

        Step 1: σ^2,

        Step 2: H_O: $\sigma_1^2 \le \sigma_2^2$, H_A: $\sigma_1^2 > \sigma_2^2$,

        Step 3: $\alpha = 0.05$,

        Step 4: $s_1^2 = \dfrac{7.028}{4} = 1.757$ $s_2^2 = \dfrac{\sum(x - \bar{x})^2}{n-1} = \dfrac{8.108}{4} = 2.027$.

        The test statistic is $F = \dfrac{s_2^2}{s_1^2} = \dfrac{2.027}{1.757} = 1.154$,

        Step 5: The critical value is obtained from the F-distribution. $F = 6.388$. Reject H_O if $F > 6.388$.

        Step 6: Since $F = 1.154 < 6.388 = F_{0.05}$, fail to reject H_O.

        Step 7: Based on these sample data, there is not sufficient evidence to conclude that population one's variance is larger than population two's variance.

    b. P-value $= P(F \ge 1.154)$. Using the F-table $P(F \ge 6.388) = 0.05 \rightarrow$ p-value > 0.05. Using Excel, p-value $= 0.4465$.

    c. If the two population variances were equal, the probability that the ratio of the two sample variances being larger than 1.154 is 0.4465.

11.25

    H_0: $\sigma_m^2 \le \sigma_f^2$
    H_A: $\sigma_m^2 > \sigma_f^2$

    Using Appendix H with $D_1 = 24$ and $D_2 = 24$: If the calculated $F > 1.984$, reject H_0, otherwise do not reject H_0

    $F = 2.5^2/1.34^2 = 3.4807$

    Since $3.4807 > 1.984$ reject H_0 and conclude that there is more variability in male donations than in female donations.

11.27

   a. H_0: $\sigma_A{}^2 \leq \sigma_T{}^2$
       H_A: $\sigma_A{}^2 > \sigma_T{}^2$
       If the calculated F > 2.534, reject H_0, otherwise do not reject H_0
          $F = 0.202^2/0.14^2 = 2.0818$
       Since 2.0818 < 2.534 do not reject H_0 and conclude that the Trenton plant is not less variable than the Atlanta plant.

   b. You would have rejected a true null hypothesis, which is a Type I, error. You could decrease the alpha level to decrease the probability of a Type I error or you could increase the sample sizes.

11.29

   a. Using the seven steps outlined in the chapter:

   Step 1: σ^2,

   Step 2: H_O: $\sigma_1^2 \leq \sigma_2^2$ H_A: $\sigma_1^2 > \sigma_2^2$,

   Step 3: $\alpha = 0.05$,

   Step 4: The test statistic is $F = \dfrac{s_1^2}{s_2^2} = \dfrac{(2636)^2}{(1513)^2} = 3.035$,

   Step 5: The critical value is obtained from the F-distribution. F = 2.526. Reject H_O if F > 2.526.

   Step 6: Since F = 3.035 > 2.526 = $F_{0.05}$, reject H_O.

   Step 7: Based on these sample data, there is sufficient evidence to conclude that the starting salary in accounting is larger than that in business administration.

   b. $P(X < 39448) = P\left(z = \dfrac{39448 - 43809}{2636}\right) = P(z < -1.65) = 0.5000 - 0.4505 =$ 0.0495. So only about 5% of accounting majors would end up making less than the average business administration major.

11.31

Sales Plan	Data	Total
Basic Plan	Count of Cell Phone Minutes	52.000
	StdDev of Cell Phone Minutes	34.434
Business Plan	Count of Cell Phone Minutes	148.0000
	StdDev of Cell Phone Minutes	29.9187

H_0: $\sigma_{Basic}^2 \leq \sigma_{Bus.}^2$
H_A: $\sigma_{Basic}^2 > \sigma_{Bus}^2$

Using either Excel of Minitab to find the critical value the decision rule becomes:
If the calculated F > 1.4341, reject H_0, otherwise do not reject H_0
$F = 34.434^2/29.9187^2 = 1.3246$

Since 1.3246 < 1.4341 do not reject H_0 and conclude that the standard deviation in minutes used by the Business Plan is not less than the Basic Plan

11.33

a. Minitab output

Test for Equal Variances: 04Salary, 94Salary

```
95% Bonferroni confidence intervals for standard deviations

              N    Lower    StDev    Upper
04Salary    100  7.36764  8.54544  10.1500
94Salary    100  1.26546  1.46776   1.7434


F-Test (normal distribution)
Test statistic = 33.90, p-value = 0.000


Levene's Test (any continuous distribution)
Test statistic = 83.55, p-value = 0.000
```

Since the populations are assumed to be normally distributed, the F-test approach is the appropriate test to determine equality of variances.

b. Minitab output:

Descriptive Statistics: 94Salary, 04Salary

```
Variable   Mean   StDev
94Salary   1.398  1.468
04Salary   9.603  8.545
```

$$P(X > 1.398) = P\left(z = \frac{1.398 - 9.603}{8.545}\right) = P(z > -0.96) = 0.5000 + 0.3315 = 0.8315.$$

End of Chapter Exercises

11.35

Answers will vary, but any examples involving manufacturing, service or scheduling would be appropriate.

11.37

Student answers will vary with the article.

11.39

The interval estimate is completed using:

$$\frac{(n-1)s^2}{\chi_U^2} \le \sigma^2 \le \frac{(n-1)s^2}{\chi_L^2}$$

where

s^2 = sample variance

n = sample size

χ_L^2 = Lower Critical Value

χ_U^2 = Upper Critical Value

For the 95% interval, with 24 degrees of freedom, we get the critical value

$$\chi_U^2 = \chi_{0.025}^2 = 39.3641$$

Likewise, we get:

$$\chi_L^2 = \chi_{0.975}^2 = 12.4011$$

The 95% confidence interval becomes:

$$\frac{(25-1)47^2}{39.3641} \le \sigma^2 \le \frac{(25-1)47^2}{12.4011}$$

$$1{,}346.8 \le \sigma^2 \le 4{,}275.1$$

By taking the square root, you can convert to an interval estimate of the population standard deviation as the interval 36.7 to 65.38 seconds. For the 90% interval we get the critical value

$$\chi_U^2 = \chi_{0.05}^2 = 36.4150$$

Likewise, we get:

$$\chi_L^2 = \chi_{0.95}^2 = 13.8484$$

The 90% confidence interval becomes:

$$\frac{(25-1)47^2}{36.4150} \le \sigma^2 \le \frac{(25-1)47^2}{13.8484}$$

$$1{,}455.89 \le \sigma^2 \le 3{,}828.31$$

By taking the square root, you can convert to an interval estimate of the population standard deviation as the interval 38.16 to 61.87 seconds.

11.41

The interval estimate is completed using:

$$\frac{(n-1)s^2}{\chi_U^2} \le \sigma^2 \le \frac{(n-1)s^2}{\chi_L^2}$$

where

s^2 = sample variance
n = sample size
χ_L^2 = Lower Critical Value
χ_U^2 = Upper Critical Value

For the 98% interval, with 26 degrees of freedom, we get the critical value

$$\chi_U^2 = \chi_{0.01}^2 = 45.6416$$

Likewise, we get:

$$\chi_L^2 = \chi_{0.99}^2 = 12.1982$$

The 98% confidence interval becomes:

$$\frac{(27-1)1.15^2}{45.6416} \le \sigma^2 \le \frac{(27-1)1.15^2}{12.1982}$$

$$0.753 \le \sigma^2 \le 2.819$$

By taking the square root, you can convert to an interval estimate of the population standard deviation as the interval 0.868 to 1.679 degrees.

11.43

    a. H_O: $\sigma^2 = (0.05)^2$
        H_A: $\sigma^2 \ne 0.0025$
        $\alpha = 0.10$

        Reject H_O if $\chi^2 < \chi_L^2 = 10.1170$ or $\chi^2 > \chi_U^2 = 30.1435$

$$\chi^2 = \frac{(n-1)s^2}{\sigma^2} = \frac{(20-1)(0.07)^2}{0.0025} = 37.24$$

        Since $\chi^2 = 37.24 > \chi_U^2 = 30.1435 \to$ reject H_O. There is enough evidence to conclude that the standard deviation of the amount of Coke in the cans differs from the standard deviation specified by the quality control division.

    b. From part a, random sampling with indicate the process is not meeting specifications 10% of the time when it is meeting specifications ($\alpha = 0.10$). The trial has two outcomes: meet specifications or not. There were seven trials. If we assume the trials were random and independent we have a binomial distribution where we are looking for the probability of three or more with n = 7. From the binomial table with p = α = 0.10:
        $P(x \ge 3) = 0.0230 + 0.0026 + 0.0002 = 0.0256$.

11.45

a. Step 1: Specify the population value of interest.

$$\sigma^2$$

Step 2: Formulate the appropriate null and alternative hypotheses.

$$H_O: \sigma_1^2 \neq \sigma_2^2,$$
$$H_A: \sigma_1^2 = \sigma_2^2$$

Step 3: Specify the level of significance.
$$\alpha = 0.05$$

Step 4: Construct the rejection region.
The critical value is obtained from the F-distribution. F = 1.752. Reject H_O if F > 1.752.

Step 5: Compute the test statistic:
$$s_1^2 = 295^2 = 87,025 \text{ and } s_2^2 = 151^2 = 22,801.$$

The test statistic is $F = \dfrac{s_1^2}{s_2^2} = \dfrac{87025}{22801} = 3.817$

Step 6: Reach a decision:
Since F = 3.817 > 1.752 = $F_{0.025}$, reject H_O.

Step 7: Draw a conclusion:
Based on these sample data, there is sufficient evidence to conclude that the two population variances are not equal to each other. The two-sample t could not be used.

b. Regardless of the test to be used in this situation, it would be necessary to determine if the populations' distributions had normal distributions.

11.47

$$H_o: \sigma^2 \leq 3,900^2$$
$$H_a: \sigma^2 > 3,900^2$$

$\alpha = 0.10$ s = 3,934.5589   n = 200   df = 200 - 1 = 199

$$\chi^2 = \frac{(n-1)s^2}{\sigma^2} = \frac{(200-1)3,934.5589^2}{3,900^2} = 202.5424$$

Since the table in the book does not contain df = 199, use Excel's CHIINV function to find the critical value. If $\chi^2 > 224.9568$, reject the null hypothesis.

Since 202.5424 < 224.9568, do not reject the null hypothesis and conclude that the manager is correct in the consistency of the current routes so he does not need to reroute trucks.

11.49

H_o: $\sigma^2_M \le \sigma^2_F$
H_a: $\sigma^2_M > \sigma^2_F$
$\alpha = 0.05$

$n_F = 70$ $s_F = 3,694.5429$ $n_M = 67$ $s_M = 5,303.8555$

$$F = = \frac{5,303.8555^2}{3,694.5429^2} = 2.0609$$

If F > 1.4953, reject the null hypothesis
Since 2.0609 > 1.4953, reject the null hypothesis and conclude that the negotiator's concern is valid and that the variability of total charges for male patients is greater than the variability of total charges for female patients.

11.51
  a. Minitab output:

Test for Equal Variances: INCOME01, INCOME04

```
95% Bonferroni confidence intervals for standard deviations

            N    Lower    StDev    Upper
INCOME01   100   11104.2  12879.4  15297.7
INCOME04   100   12654.8  14677.9  17433.9


F-Test (normal distribution)
Test statistic = 0.77, p-value = 0.195
```

Since the p-value = 0.195 > 0.05 = α = 0.05, fail to reject the null hypothesis. Conclude that there is not enough evidence to determine that the income of families in the USA in 2001 to 2004 had different standard deviations.

  b. It would be appropriate to use the two-sample t since the two population variances were determined to be equal to each other. One other requirement must be met: the populations must have normal distributions.

Chapter 12 Solutions

When applicable, selected problems in each section will be done following the appropriate step-by-step procedures outlined in the corresponding sections of the chapter. Other problems will provide key points and the answers to the questions, but all answers can be arrived at using the appropriate steps.

Section 12-1 Exercises

12.1
  a. The calculations for the completed ANOVA table below are:

   Between groups df = k-1 where k is the number of magazines = 3-1 = 2

   Within groups df = n_t –k, where n_t = 25 subscribers * 3 magazines = 75;
       75 – 3 = 72

   SSW = SST-SSB = 9,271,678,090 – 2,949,085,157 = 6,322,592,933

   MSB = 2,949,085,157/2 = 1,474,542,579

   MSW = 6,322,592,933/72 = 87,813,791

   F = 1,474,542,579/87,813,791 = 16.79

ANOVA

Source of Variation	SS	df	MS	F
Between Groups	2,949,085,157	2	1,474,542,579	16.79
Within Groups	6,322,592,933	72	87,813,791	
Total	9,271,678,090	74		

  b.
  Step 1: Specify the parameter(s) of interest. The parameter of interest is the mean household incomes of subscribers of three different magazines.

  Step 2: Formulate the null and alternative hypotheses. The appropriate null and alternative hypotheses are:
    H_o: $\mu_1 = \mu_2 = \mu_3$
    H_A: Not all populations have the same mean

  Step 3: Specify the significance level (α) for testing the hypothesis. The test will be conducted using an $\alpha = 0.10$.

Step 4: Select independent simple random samples from each population. There are three magazines. Simple random samples of subscribers from each magazine have been selected: 25 subscribers from each magazine for a total of 75 subscribers.

Step 5: Check to see that normality and equal variance assumptions have been satisfied. The problem stated in part (b) that these assumptions have been satisfied.

Step 6: Construct the rejection region. The F critical value can be found using Excel's FINV function or Minitab's Calc > Probability Distributions command. Using Excel the F critical value for $\alpha = 0.10$, and 2 and 72 degrees of freedom is 2.3778. The decision rule is
>   If F > 2.3778, reject the null hypothesis
>   Otherwise, do not reject the null hypothesis

Step 7: Compute the test statistic. $F = MSB/MSW = 1{,}474{,}542{,}579/87{,}813{,}791 = 16.79$

Step 8: Reach a decision. Because the F test statistic $= 16.79 > F_\alpha = 2.3778$, we do reject the null hypothesis based on these sample data.

Step 9: Draw a conclusion. We are able to detect a difference in the mean household income per subscriber by magazine.

12.3

The following steps can be used to conduct the hypothesis test.

Step 1: Specify the parameter of interest.
>   The parameter of interest is the population mean for each of the four

Step 2: Formulate the null and alternative hypotheses.
>   The null and alternative hypotheses are:
$$H_0 : \mu_1 = \mu_2 = \mu_3 = \mu_4$$
$$H_A : \text{not all } \mu_j \text{ are equal}$$

Step 3: Specify the significance level.
>   The test will be conducted using a 0.05 significance level.

Step 4: Select independent samples from the populations and compute the sample means and the grand mean.

The following sample data were obtained:

Sample 1	Sample 2	Sample 3	Sample 4
9	12	8	17
6	16	8	15
11	16	12	17
14	12	7	16
14	9	10	13

The means for each sample are:

$$\bar{x}_1 = 10.8 \qquad \bar{x}_2 = 13 \qquad \bar{x}_3 = 9 \qquad \bar{x}_4 = 15.6$$

The grand mean is $\bar{\bar{x}} = 12.1$

Step 5: Check to see if the assumptions are satisfied.

The samples are independent and the data level is ratio. Because the sample sizes are equal, the ANOVA test is robust to the normality and equal variance assumptions. The Hartley's F max test can be used to check the equal variance assumption. The samples are too small to check the normality assumption.

$$H_0 : \sigma_1^2 = \sigma_2^2 = \sigma_3^2 = \sigma_4^2$$
$$H_A : \text{not all population variances are equal}$$

The sample variances are:

$$s_1^2 = 11.7 \qquad s_2^2 = 9 \qquad s_3^2 = 4 \qquad s_4^2 = 2.8$$

The test statistic for the F max test is:

$$F = \frac{s_{max}^2}{s_{min}^2} = \frac{11.7}{2.8} = 4.18$$

The critical value from the F max table with c = 4 and v = 4 degrees of freedom for $\alpha = 0.05$ is 20.6.
Because F = 4.18 < 20.6, do not reject the null hypothesis
Thus, there is no evidence to suggest that population variances are not equal.

Step 6: Construct the rejection region.

The F critical value from the F- distribution for $\alpha = 0.05$ and with $D_1 = 3$ and $D_2 = 16$ degrees of freedom is 3.239. Thus, the decision rule is:

If the test statistic F > 3.239, reject the null hypothesis
Otherwise do not reject

Step 7: Compute the test statistic.

The required calculations can be computed manually using equations 12-3, 12-4, and 12-5 or by using Excel or Minitab. We get the following:

Anova: Single Factor						
SUMMARY						
Groups	Count	Sum	Average	Variance		
Sample 1	5	54	10.8	11.7		
Sample 2	5	65	13	9		
Sample 3	5	45	9	4		
Sample 4	5	78	15.6	2.8		
ANOVA						
Source of Variation	SS	df	MS	F	P-value	F crit
Between Groups	121.8	3	40.6	5.905455	0.006523	3.238867
Within Groups	110	16	6.875			
Total	231.8	19				

Step 8: Reach a decision.

Since the test statistic = F = 5.905 > 3.239, reject the null hypothesis. Also, using the p-value approach, because p-value = 0.0065 < 0.05, we reject the null hypothesis.

Step 9: Draw a conclusion.

Since the null hypothesis is rejected, we conclude that the populations do not all have equal means.

12.5

a. $df_B = 3 = k - 1 \rightarrow k = 4$ = number of populations.

b.

Source	SS	df	MS	F
Between Samples	483	3	161	11.1309
Within Samples	405	28	14.464	
Total	888	31		

c. H_0: $\mu_1 = \mu_2 = \mu_3 = \mu_4$
     H_A: At least two population means are different

d.   F critical = 2.9467 (Minitab); from text table use $F_{3,\,24} = 3.009$
     Since 11.1309 > 2.9467 reject H_0 and conclude that at least two populations
     means are different.

12.7

a.

Step 1: Specify the parameter(s) of interest.
The parameters of interest are the means of the three populations.

Step 2: Formulate the appropriate null and alternative hypotheses.
H_O: $\mu_1 = \mu_2 = \mu_3$
H_A: At least two population means are different.

Step 3: Specify the significance for the test.
The significance level = $\alpha = 0.05$.

Step 4: Select independent simple random samples from each population.

Step 5: Check to see that the normality and equal-variance assumptions have been
satisfied.
Because of the small sample sizes, the box and whisker diagram is used.

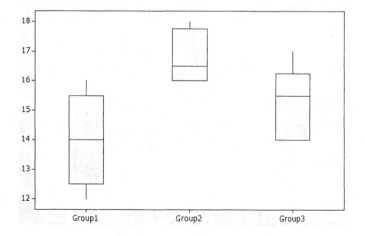

The box plots indicate some skewness in the samples. However, if we assume that the populations are normally distributed, Harley's F_{max} test can be used to test whether the three populations have equal variances. The sample variances are s_1^2

$$= \frac{\sum(x-\bar{x})^2}{n-1} = \frac{10}{5-1} = 2.50, \; s_2^2 = 0.916, \text{ and } s_3^2 = 1.467 \text{ test statistic is } F_{max} =$$

$$\frac{s_{max}^2}{s_{min}^2} = \frac{2.50}{0.916} = 2.729.$$

From Appendix I, the critical value for alpha $= 0.05$, $k = 3$, and $\bar{n} - 1 = 4$ is 15.5. Because $2.729 < 15.5$, we conclude that the population variances could be equal.

Step 6: Use Excel or Minitab to construct the ANOVA table

One-way ANOVA: Group1, Group2, Group3

```
Source   DF     SS     MS      F      P
Factor    2   16.85   8.43   5.03   0.026
Error    12   20.08   1.67
Total    14   36.93

S = 1.294    R-Sq = 45.62%    R-Sq(adj) = 36.56%


                               Individual 95% CIs For Mean Based on
                               Pooled StDev
Level    N     Mean   StDev    -----+---------+---------+---------+----
Group1   5   14.000   1.581    (-------*--------)
Group2   4   16.750   0.957                       (---------*--------)
Group3   6   15.333   1.211                (------*-------)
                               -----+---------+---------+---------+----
                               13.5      15.0      16.5      18.0

Pooled StDev = 1.294
```

Step 7: Determine the decision rule.
    Because $k - 1 = 2$ and $n_T - k = 12$, $F_{0.05} = 3.885$. The decision rule is if the calculated $F > F_{0.05} = 3.885$, reject H_O, or if the p-value $< \alpha = 0.05$, reject H_O; otherwise, do not reject H_O.

Step 8: Reach a decision.
    Since $F = 5.03 > 3.885$, we reject H_O.

Step 9: Draw a conclusion.
    We conclude there is sufficient evidence to indicate that at least two of the population means differ.

b. Step 10: Use the Tukey-Kramer test to determine which populations have different means.

Using Equation 12-7 to construct the critical ranges:

$$q_{1-\alpha}\sqrt{\frac{MSW}{2}\left(\frac{1}{n_i}+\frac{1}{n_j}\right)}$$

For $n_1 = 5$ and $n_2 = 4$, critical range $= 3.77\sqrt{\frac{1.67}{2}\left(\frac{1}{5}+\frac{1}{4}\right)} = 2.311$;

for $n_1 = 5$ and $n_3 = 6$, critical range $= 3.77\sqrt{\frac{1.67}{2}\left(\frac{1}{5}+\frac{1}{6}\right)} = 2.086$;

and for $n_2 = 4$ and $n_3 = 6$, critical range $= 3.77\sqrt{\frac{1.67}{2}\left(\frac{1}{4}+\frac{1}{6}\right)} = 2.224$

The contrast are $|\bar{x}_1 - \bar{x}_2| = |14 - 16.75| = 2.75 > 2.311$,

$|\bar{x}_1 - \bar{x}_3| = |14 - 15.33| = 1.33 < 2.086$, and

$|\bar{x}_2 - \bar{x}_3| = |16.75 - 15.33| = 1.42 < 2.224$

Therefore, we can infer that population 1 and population 2 have different means. However, no other differences are supported by these sample data.

12.9

a.

Step 1: Specify the parameter(s) of interest.
The parameters of interest are the mean compressive strength of the three types of Portland cement from the three populations.

Step 2: Formulate the appropriate null and alternative hypotheses.
H_O: $\mu_1 = \mu_2 = \mu_3$
H_A: At least two population means are different.

Step 3: Specify the significance for the test.
The significance level $= \alpha = 0.01$.

Step 4: Select independent simple random samples from each population.

Step 5: Check to see that the normality and equal-variance assumptions have been satisfied.

Because of the small sample sizes, the box and whisker diagram is used.

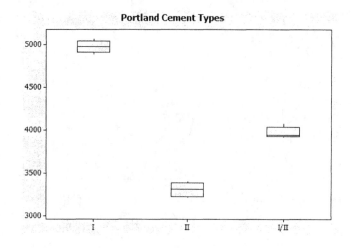

The box plots indicate some skewness in the "I/II" sample. However, if we assume that the populations are normally distributed, Harley's F_{max} test can be used to test whether the three populations have equal variances. The sample variances are $s_1{}^2 = \dfrac{\sum (x - \bar{x})^2}{n-1} = \dfrac{15208}{4-1} = 5069$, $s_2{}^2 = 6939$, and $s_3{}^2 = 4747$ test statistic is $F_{max} = \dfrac{s^2_{max}}{s^2_{min}} = \dfrac{6939}{4747} = 1.462.$

From Appendix I, the critical value for alpha = 0.01, k = 3, and $\bar{n}$ - 1 = 3 is 85. Because 1.462 < 85, we conclude that the population variances could be equal.

Step 6: Use Excel or Minitab to construct the ANOVA table

One-way ANOVA: I, II, I/II

```
Source   DF       SS        MS        F       P
Factor    2   5637128   2818564   504.88   0.000
Error     9     50244      5583
Total    11   5687372

S = 74.72    R-Sq = 99.12%    R-Sq(adj) = 98.92%


                              Individual 95% CIs For Mean Based on
                              Pooled StDev
Level  N    Mean   StDev   -----+---------+---------+---------+----
I      4  4976.8   71.2                                       (-*)
II     4  3309.8   83.3    (*-)
I/II   4  3970.8   68.9                      (*-)
                           -----+---------+---------+---------+----
                            3500      4000      4500      5000

Pooled StDev = 74.7
```

Step 7: Determine the decision rule.

Because $k - 1 = 2$ and $n_T - k = 9$, $F_{0.01} = 8.022$. The decision rule is f the calculated $F > F_{0.01} = 8.022$, reject H_O, or if the p-value $< \alpha = 0.05$, reject H_O; otherwise, do not reject H_O.

Step 8: Reach a decision.

Since $F = 504.88 > 8.022$, we reject H_O.

Step 9: Draw a conclusion.

We conclude there is sufficient evidence to indicate that at least two of the population means differ.

b. Step 10: Use the Tukey-Kramer test to determine which populations have different means.

Using Equation 12-7 to construct the critical ranges:

$$q_{1-\alpha}\sqrt{\frac{MSW}{2}\left(\frac{1}{n_i}+\frac{1}{n_j}\right)}$$

For $n_1 = n_2 = n_3 = 4$, critical range $= 5.43\sqrt{\frac{5583}{2}\left(\frac{1}{4}+\frac{1}{4}\right)} = 202.86;$

The contrast are $|\bar{x}_1 - \bar{x}_2| = |4976.8 - 3309.8| = 1667 > 202.86,$

$|\bar{x}_1 - \bar{x}_3| = |4976.8 - 3970.8| = 1006 > 202.86,$ and

$|\bar{x}_2 - \bar{x}_3| = |3309.8 - 3970.8| = 661 > 202.86$

Therefore, we can infer that the mean compression strengths differ among the three types of Portland cement.

12.11

a. Step 1. The parameters of interest are the mean fire points of the three types of dielectric fluid.

Step 2. H_O: $\mu_1 = \mu_2 = \mu_3$,

H_A: At least two population means are different.

Step 3. The significance level is $\alpha = 0.05$.

Step 4. The selected samples are specified in the heading of this exercise.

Step 5. Because of the small sample sizes, the box and whisker diagram is used.

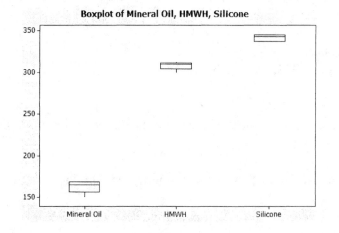

Boxplot of Mineral Oil, HMWH, Silicone

The box plots indicate some skewness but not sufficient to deny normality. If we assume that the populations are normally distributed, Harley's F_{max} test can be used to test whether the three populations have equal variances. The sample variances are $s_1^2 = \dfrac{\sum(x - \bar{x})^2}{n-1} = \dfrac{210}{5-1} = 52.5$, $s_2^2 = 23.2$, and $s_3^2 = 16.8$ test

statistic is $F_{max} = \dfrac{s_{max}^2}{s_{min}^2} = \dfrac{52.5}{16.8} = 3.125.$

From Appendix I, the critical value for alpha = 0.05, k = 3, and $\bar{n} - 1 = 4$ is 15.5. Because 3.125 < 15.5, we conclude that the population variances could be equal.

Step 6.

One-way ANOVA: Mineral Oil, HMWH, Silicone

```
Source   DF       SS        MS         F      P
Factor    2   90019.7   45009.9   1459.78  0.000
Error    12     370.0      30.8
Total    14   90389.7

S = 5.553   R-Sq = 99.59%   R-Sq(adj) = 99.52%


                          Individual 95% CIs For Mean Based on
                          Pooled StDev
Level          N    Mean   StDev  --------+---------+---------+---------+-
Mineral Oil    5  163.00    7.25  (*)
HMWH           5  308.20    4.82                           (*)
Silicone       5  341.40    4.10                                    (*)
                                  --------+---------+---------+---------+-
                                        200       250       300       350
```

Step 7. Because k − 1 = 2 and $n_T - k = 12$, $F_{0.05} = 3.885$. The decision rule is if the calculated $F > F_{0.05} = 3.885$, reject H_O, or if the p-value $< \alpha = 0.05$, reject H_O; otherwise, do not reject H_O.

Step 8. Since F = 1459.78 > 3.885, we reject H_O.

Step 9.   We conclude there is sufficient evidence to indicate that at least two of the population means differ.

b. Using Equation 12-7 to construct the critical ranges:

$$q_{1-\alpha}\sqrt{\frac{MSW}{2}\left(\frac{1}{n_i} + \frac{1}{n_j}\right)}$$

For $n_1 = n_2 = n_3 = 5$, critical range $= 3.77\sqrt{\frac{30.8}{2}\left(\frac{1}{5} + \frac{1}{5}\right)} = 9.36$;

The contrast are $|\bar{x}_1 - \bar{x}_2| = |163 - 308.2| = 145.2 > 9.36$,

$\qquad |\bar{x}_1 - \bar{x}_3| = |163 - 341.4| = 178.4 > 9.36$, and

$\qquad |\bar{x}_2 - \bar{x}_3| = |308.2 - 341.4| = 33.2 > 9.36$

Therefore, we can infer that the mean fire points differ among the three types of dielectic fluids.

12.13

a. $H_0: \mu_1 = \mu_2 = \mu_3 = \mu_4$
    H_A: At least two population means are different

Anova: OneW ay

SUMMARY

Groups	Count	Sum	Average	Variance
Type A	4	4417	1104.25	11576.25
Type B	4	5343	1335.75	4257.583
Type C	4	4634	1158.5	1845.667
Type D	4	4114	1028.5	8393

ANOVA

rce of Varia	SS	df	MS	F	P-value	F crit
Between G	204993.5	3	68331.17	10.48326	0.001137	5.952529
Within Gro	78217.5	12	6518.125			
Total	283211	15				

Since $10.48326 > 5.9525$ reject H_0 and conclude that at least two populations means are different.

b. Using a value of 0.01 we can construct the following table:

	Absolute Difference	Critical Range	Significant?
Type A - Type B	231.5	222.02	Yes
Type A - Type C	54.25	222.02	No
Type A - Type D	75.75	222.02	No
Type B - Type C	177.25	222.02	No
Type B - Type D	307.25	222.02	Yes
Type C - Type D	130.00	222.02	No

Based on the Tukey-Kramer test you can eliminate Type D and A since the mean life is less than B.

12.15

a. H_0: $\mu_1 = \mu_2 = \mu_3$
   H_A: At least two population means are different

Anova: Single Factor

SUMMARY

Groups	Count	Sum	Average	Variance
Car 1	5	68	13.6	0.345
Car 2	3	38.9	12.96667	0.263333
Car 3	4	59.1	14.775	0.515833

ANOVA

Source of Variation	SS	df	MS	F	P-value	F crit
Between Groups	6.0725	2	3.03625	7.911098	0.010407	4.256492
Within Groups	3.454167	9	0.383796			
Total	9.526667	11				

Since $0.01 < 0.05$ reject H_0 and conclude that at least two populations means are different.

b. Using a value of 0.05 we can construct the following table:

	Absolute Differences	Critical Range	Significant?
Car 1 - Car 2	0.633	1.264	no
Car 1 - Car 3	1.175	1.161	yes
Car 2 - Car 3	1.808	1.322	yes

Student reports will vary but they should recommend either Car 1 or Car 2 since there is no statistically significance difference between them..

c. The confidence interval is constructed around the difference between the largest sample value and the smallest sample value. The pooled estimator of the population standard deviation is found by taking the square root of the mean square within.

$(14.775 - 12.967) \pm 1.7959(0.6197)\sqrt{(1/3)+(1/4)}$; 0.978 ----- 2.678 range for cents per mile so the maximum and minimum difference in average savings per year would be

($0.00978)(30,000) ----- ($0.02678)(30,000); $293.40 ----- $803.40

12.17
a. Minitab output:

One-way ANOVA: Life versus Manufacturer

```
Source         DF      SS      MS      F      P
Manufacturer    2  2218.2  1109.1  22.05  0.000
Error         132  6640.8    50.3
Total         134  8859.0

S = 7.093   R-Sq = 25.04%   R-Sq(adj) = 23.90%


                                Individual 95% CIs For Mean Based on
                                Pooled StDev
Level      N    Mean   StDev   ---+---------+---------+---------+------
Delphi    15  36.933   3.654   (------*------)
Exide     45  47.911   8.146                         (---*---)
Johnson   75  50.253   6.911                              (---*--)
                                ---+---------+---------+---------+------
                                35.0      40.0      45.0      50.0
```

The p-value = 0.000 < α = 0.05. Therefore, there appears to be sufficient evidence to indicate that there is a difference in the average length of life among the batteries from the different manufacturers.

b. Minitab output:

```
Tukey 95% Simultaneous Confidence Intervals
All Pairwise Comparisons among Levels of Manufacturer

Individual confidence level = 98.07%


Manufacturer = Delphi subtracted from:

Manufacturer  Lower  Center   Upper  ---------+---------+---------+---------+
Exide         5.968  10.978  15.987                      (-------*--------)
Johnson       8.568  13.320  18.072                         (-------*-------)
                                     ---------+---------+---------+---------+
                                          0.0       6.0      12.0      18.0


Manufacturer = Exide subtracted from:

Manufacturer  Lower  Center   Upper  ---------+---------+---------+---------+
Johnson      -0.826   2.342   5.510        (----*----)
                                     ---------+---------+---------+---------+
                                          0.0       6.0      12.0      18.0
```

The confidence intervals by Minitab indicate that there is no significant difference in the means if the confidence interval contains 0. The confidence intervals indicate that there is sufficient evidence to conclude that the average length of life differs between Delphi and Exide and also between Delphi and Johnson. There is, however, not enough evidence to indicate that the average lifetime for batteries made by Exide and Johnson differ.

Section 12-2 Exercises

12.19

a. The calculations for the completed ANOVA table below are:
Textbooks (blocks) df = b-1 = 12-1 = 11
Retailer df = k-1 = 3-1 = 2
Error df = (k-1)(b-1) = 11(2) = 22
Total df = n_t -1, where n_t = (12 textbooks) * (3 retailers) = 36
= 36 – 1 = 35
SSW (error) = SST-SSBL-SSB = 17,477.6 – 16,624 – 2.4 = 851.2
MSBL (Textbooks) = 16,624/11 = 1,511.3
MSB (Retailer) = 2.4/2 = 1.2
MSW (error) = 851.2/22 = 38.7
F (textbooks) = 1,511.3/38.7 = 39.05
F (Retailer) = 1.2/38.7 = 0.031

ANOVA

Source of Variation	SS	df	MS	F
Textbooks	16,624	11	1511.3	39.05
Retailer	2.4	2	1.2	0.031
Error	851.2	22	38.7	
Total	17477.6	35		

b.

Step 1: Specify the parameter of interest and formulate the appropriate null and alternative hypothesis. The parameter of interest is the mean textbook price at different retail outlets, and the question is whether there is a difference between the mean prices at the three different retail outlets. The appropriate null and alternative hypotheses are:
H_o: $\mu_{On} = \mu_{Off} = \mu_I$
H_A: Not all populations have the same mean
In this case, they want to control for variation in prices due to the discipline of the textbook by having the same textbooks priced at each of the types of retail outlets. Here the textbooks are the blocks.

Step 2: Select simple random samples from each population, check the normality and equal variance assumptions. Twelve textbooks across disciplines are selected and the prices are checked at each of the three types of retail outlets. The problem stated that normality and equal variance assumptions had been met.

Step 3: Complete the ANOVA table. This was completed in part (a) above.

Step 4: Specify the level of significance for conducting the tests. The tests will be conducted using $\alpha = 0.10$.

Step 5: Test to determine whether blocking is effective. Twelve textbooks were used to evaluate the prices at the three types of retail outlets. These constitute the blocks. The null and alternative hypotheses are:

H_o: $\mu_1 = \mu_2 = \mu_3 = \ldots = \mu_{12}$
H_A: Not all block means are equal.

As shown in the ANOVA table from part (a), the F test statistic for this hypothesis test is the F for blocks (textbooks) = 39.05.

Using Excel's FINV function with $\alpha = 0.10$ and 11 and 22 degrees of freedom, $F_{\alpha=0.10} = 1.88$. Since $F = 39.05 > F_{\alpha=0.10} = 1.88$, reject the null hypothesis. This means that based on these sample data we can conclude that blocking is effective.

c.

Step 6: Conduct the main hypothesis test to determine whether the types of retail outlets have equal means.
We have three types of retail outlets (on-campus, off-campus, and Internet). The appropriate null and alternative hypotheses are:

H_o: $\mu_{On} = \mu_{Off} = \mu_I$
H_A: Not all populations have the same mean

As shown in the ANOVA table from part (a), the F test statistic for this null hypothesis is 0.031.

Using Excel's FINV function with $\alpha = 0.10$ and 2 and 22 degrees of freedom, $F_{\alpha=0.10} = 2.56$. Since $F = 0.031 < F_{\alpha=0.10} = 2.56$, do not reject the null hypothesis. Thus, based on these sample data we cannot conclude that there is a difference in textbook prices at the three different types of retail outlets.

12.21

The hypothesis test can be performed using the following steps.

Step 1: Specify the parameter of interest and formulate the appropriate null and alternative hypothesis.
The parameter of interest is the population mean for each of the three populations.
The primary null and alternative hypotheses are:

$$H_0 : \mu_1 = \mu_2 = \mu_3$$
$$H_A : not\ all\ \mu_j\ are\ equal$$

Step 2: Collect the sample data.
The sample data are:

Block	Sample 1	Sample 2	Sample 3
1	30	40	40
2	50	70	50
3	60	40	70
4	40	40	30
5	80	70	90
6	20	10	10

Step 3: Compute the sums of squares and complete the ANOVA table.
The following sums of squares values are computed:

$$SST = 9,000 \quad SSB = 33.33 \quad SSBL = 7,866.67 \quad SSW = 1,100$$

The completed ANOVA table is:

ANOVA						
Source of Variation	SS	df	MS	F	P-value	F crit
Rows (Blocks)	7866.667	5	1573.333	14.30303	0.000277	3.325837
Columns (Populations)	33.33333	2	16.66667	0.151515	0.861341	4.102816
Error (Within)	1100	10	110			
Total	9000	17				

Step 4: Specify the significance level.
The hypothesis tests are to be conducted using an alpha = 0.05 level.

Step 5: Test to determine if blocking was effective.
The hypothesis to be tested is:

$$H_0 : \mu_1 = \mu_2 = \mu_3 = \mu_4 = \mu_5 = \mu_6 \quad \text{(blocking is not effective)}$$
$$H_A : not\ all\ \mu_j\ are\ equal \quad \text{(blocking is effective)}$$

The hypothesis is tested by computing the test statistic F ratio as follows:

$$F = \frac{MSBL}{MSW} = \frac{1,573.33}{110} = 14.3$$

The critical F value from the F-distribution for alpha = 0.05 and degrees of freedom $D_1 = 5 \; and \; D_2 = 10$ is 3.326. Therefore the decision rule is:

If test statistic F > critical F = 3.326, reject the null hypothesis
Otherwise, do not reject the null hypothesis

Because F = 14.3 > critical F = 3.326, we reject the null hypothesis and conclude that blocking is effective.

Step 6: Conduct the main hypothesis test to determine whether the treatments have different means.
Recall that the main hypothesis is:

$$H_0 : \mu_1 = \mu_2 = \mu_3$$
$$H_A : not \; all \; \mu_j \; are \; equal$$

This hypothesis is tested using an F test with the test statistic computed as follows:

$$F = \frac{MSB}{MSW} = \frac{16.67}{110} = 0.1515$$

The critical F value from the F-distribution for alpha = 0.05 and degrees of freedom $D_1 = 2 \; and \; D_2 = 10$ is 4.103. Therefore the decision rule is:

If test statistic F > critical F = 4.103, reject the null hypothesis
Otherwise, do not reject the null hypothesis

Because F = 0.1515 < critical F = 4.103, we do not reject the null hypothesis and conclude that the three populations may have the same mean value.

12.23
a. Step 1: H$_0$: $\mu_1 = \mu_2 = \mu_3 = \mu_4$,
            H$_A$: at least two SARs have different means

Step 2: SAR (blocks): $\bar{x}_1 = 106.50$, $\bar{x}_2 = 161.50$, $\bar{x}_3 = 144.00$, and $\bar{x}_4 = 144.50$.

Types of lettuce: $\bar{x}_1 = 134.80$, $\bar{x}_2 = 143.50$. $\bar{\bar{x}} = \frac{\sum n_i \bar{x}_i}{n_T} = 139.15$,

Step 3: $SSB = \sum(n_i)(\bar{x}_i - \bar{\bar{x}})^2 = 153.13$, $SSBL = \sum k(\bar{x}_j - \bar{\bar{x}})^2 = 3235.37$, SST $= 3524.88$, SSW = SST – (SSB + SSBL) = 3524.88 – (153.13 + 3235.37) = 136.38. MSBL = SSBL/((b – 1) = 3235.37/(4 – 1) = 1078.46 MSB = SSB/(k – 1) = 153.13/1 = 153.13 MSW = SSW/(k -1)(b – 1) = 136.38/3(1) = 45.46

Source	SS	df	MS	F-ratio
Between Blocks	3235.37	3	1078.46	23.72
Between Samples	153.13	1	153.13	3.37
Within samples	136.38	3	45.46	
Total	3524.88	7		

Step 4: $\alpha = 0.05$, (5) F = MSBL/MSW = 1078.46/45.46 = 23.72 $F_{0.05} = 9.277$. Since F = 23.72 > $F_{0.05}$ = 9.277, reject H_O. Conclude that blocking was effective.

b.
H_O: $\mu_1 = \mu_2$,
H_A: the two types of lettuce don't have equal means

F = MSBL/MSW = 153.13/45.46 = 3.37 $F_{0.05}$ = 10.128. Since F = 3.37 < $F_{0.05}$ = 10.126, fail to reject H_O. Conclude that the two types of lettuce may have equal means

c. Step 1: $LSD = t_{\alpha/2}\sqrt{MSW}\sqrt{\frac{2}{b}} = 3.1824\sqrt{45.46}\sqrt{\frac{2}{2}} = 21.457$

Step 2:

Source	$\bar{x}_1$	$\bar{x}_2$	$\bar{x}_3$	$\bar{x}_4$
Between	106.50	161.50	144.00	144.50

Step 3:
$|\bar{x}_1 - \bar{x}_2| = |106.50 - 161.50| = 55.00 > 21.457,$
$|\bar{x}_1 - \bar{x}_3| = |106.50 - 144.00| = 37.50 > 21.457,$
$|\bar{x}_1 - \bar{x}_4| = |106.50 - 144.50| = 38.00 > 21.457,$
$|\bar{x}_2 - \bar{x}_3| = |161.50 - 144.00| = 17.50 < 21.457,$
$|\bar{x}_2 - \bar{x}_4| = |161.50 - 144.50| = 17.00 < 21.457,$
$|\bar{x}_3 - \bar{x}_4| = |144.00 - 144.50| = 0.50 < 21.457,$

this indicates that $\mu_2 > \mu_1$ and $\mu_3 > \mu_1$, and $\mu_4 > \mu_1$. Thus, the SAR level of 3, produced the smallest average number of lettuce heads.

12.25

Using Excel's ANOVA Two-Factor without Replication Data Analysis tool with an $\alpha = 0.01$, the following ANOVA table was generated. Use this information to answer parts (a and b).

Anova: Two-Factor
Without Replication

SUMMARY	Count	Sum	Average	Variance
Product 1	3	24831	8277	221673
Product 2	3	25595	8531.667	708756.3
Product 3	3	27885	9295	14491
Product 4	3	17519	5839.667	30190.33
Rail	4	31810	7952.5	2035434
Plane	4	30834	7708.5	1965691
Truck	4	33186	8296.5	3118892

ANOVA

Source of Variation	SS	df	MS	F	P-value	F crit
Rows (blocks)	20107982	3	6702661	32.11967	0.000431	9.779538
Columns (carrier)	698154.7	2	349077.3	1.672805	0.264625	10.92477
Error	1252067	6	208677.8			
Total	22058204	11				

a. Test to determine whether blocking is effective. Four products were examined. These constitute the blocks. The null and alternative hypotheses are:

H_o: $\mu_1 = \mu_2 = \mu_3 = \mu_4$
H_A: Not all populations have the same mean

As shown in the ANOVA table above, the rows represent blocking (products). The F test statistic for this null hypothesis is 32.12.
$F_{\alpha=0.01} = 9.78$ is obtained from the ANOVA table above. Because F = 32.12 > $F_{\alpha=0.01} = 9.78$, reject the null hypothesis. Thus, based on these sample data we conclude that blocking is effective.

b. Conduct the main hypothesis test to determine whether there is a difference due to carrier type. The appropriate null and alternative hypotheses are:

H_o: $\mu_R = \mu_P = \mu_T$
H_A: Not all populations have the same mean

As shown in the ANOVA table above, the columns represent the main test (carrier type). The F test statistic for this null hypothesis is 1.673.
$F_{\alpha=0.01} = 10.925$ is obtained from the ANOVA table above. Because $F = 1.673 < F_{\alpha=0.01} = 10.925$, do not reject the null hypothesis. This means that based on these sample data we cannot conclude average dollar breakage per shipment is different among the three carrier types.

12.27

a. The local news station is interested in determining which store has the lowest prices. They designed the experiment the way they did because they wanted to use a variety of items rather than letting specific items affect the outcome of the experiment. If someone designed a specific list they could inadvertently select items that were in fact lower priced at one store or higher priced at another store. It was attempting to remove the effect of items selected.

b.

H_0: $\mu_1 = \mu_2 = \mu_3 \ldots = \mu_{20}$
H_A: At least two blocks have different means

ANOVA

Source of Variation	SS	df	MS	F	P-value	F crit
Shopper (Blocks)	86099.68	19	4531.562	952.6155	4.92E-45	1.867331
Stores	395.8113	2	197.9056	41.60331	2.68E-10	3.244821
Error	180.7648	38	4.756969			
Total	86676.26	59				

Since $952.6155 > 1.8673$ reject H_0 and conclude that there is an indication that blocking was effective.

c. H_0: $\mu_1 = \mu_2 = \mu_3$
H_A: At least two population means are different
Using the ANOVA table shown in part b, since the p-value of 2.68E-10 < 0.05 reject H_0 and conclude that at least two means are different

d. $LSD = t_{.025}\sqrt{MSW}\sqrt{\dfrac{2}{b}}$

$LSD = 2.024\sqrt{4.75}\sqrt{\dfrac{2}{20}} = 1.396$

Least Significant Difference (LSD)   1.3962405

	Mean Difference	Absolute Mean Difference	Significant?
D1 - D2	-6.29	6.29	YES
D1 - D3	-3.032	3.032	YES
D2 - D3	3.258	3.258	YES

Store 2 has the highest average prices.

12.29
a.   Minitab output:
b.

Two-way ANOVA: Revenue versus Restaurant, Week

```
Source       DF      SS       MS      F      P
Restaurant    2   26.234  13.1168  11.61  0.004
Week          4  110.123  27.5307  24.36  0.000
Error         8    9.040   1.1300
Total        14  145.396

S = 1.063   R-Sq = 93.78%   R-Sq(adj) = 89.12%
```

The p-value = 0.000 < α = 0.05. This indicates that inserting the week on which the testing was done was necessary.

b.   The p-value = 0.004 < α = 0.05. This indicates that we should reject the null hypothesis and conclude that there exists a difference in the average revenue among the three restaurants.

c. If you did conclude that there was a difference in the average revenue, use Fisher's LSD approach to determine which restaurant should be closed.

Source	$\bar{x}_1$	$\bar{x}_2$	$\bar{x}_3$
Between	9.06	8.24	11.37

We calculate LSD = $t_{\alpha/2}\sqrt{MSW}\sqrt{\dfrac{2}{b}} = 2.3060\sqrt{1.13}\sqrt{\dfrac{2}{5}} = 1.550$.

Since $|\bar{x}_1 - \bar{x}_2| = |9.06 - 8.24| = 0.82 < 1.550$,

$\quad\quad |\bar{x}_1 - \bar{x}_3| = |9.06 - 11.37| = 2.31 > 1.550$,

$\quad\quad |\bar{x}_2 - \bar{x}_3| = |8.24 - 11.37| = 3.13 > 1.550$,

$\quad\quad\quad \mu_1 < \mu_3$ and $\mu_2 < \mu_3$.

This indicates that Restaurant 3 has the highest average revenue while there is no evidence of a difference between Restaurant 1's and 2's average revenues.

Section 12-3 Exercises

12.31

a. H_0: Factors A and B do not interact
   H_A: Factors A and B do interact

ANOVA

Source of Variation	SS	df	MS	F	P-value	F crit
Factor B	150.2222	1	150.2222	5.753191	0.033605	4.747221
Factor A	124.1111	2	62.05556	2.376596	0.135052	3.88529
Interaction	24.11111	2	12.05556	0.461702	0.640953	3.88529
Within	313.3333	12	26.11111			
Total	611.7778	17				

Since $0.4617 < 3.8853$ do not reject H_0 and conclude that Factors A and B do not interact.

b. H_0: $\mu_{\alpha 1} = \mu_{\alpha 2} = \mu_{\alpha 3}$
   H_A: Not all means are equal
   Since $2.3766 < 3.8853$ do not reject H_0 and conclude that all means are equal

c. H_0: $\mu_{\beta 1} = \mu_{\beta 2}$
   H_A: Not all means are equal
   Since $5.7532 > 4.7472$ reject H_0 and conclude that not all means are equal.

12.33

Minitab output:

General Linear Model: Response versus Factor A, Factor B

```
Factor    Type   Levels  Values
Factor A  fixed       3  1, 2, 3
Factor B  fixed       2  1, 2
```

Analysis of Variance for Response, using Adjusted SS for Tests

```
Source             DF   Seq SS   Adj SS   Adj MS      F      P
Factor A            2  1020.50  1020.50   510.25  47.10  0.000
Factor B            1    75.00    75.00    75.00   6.92  0.039
Factor A*Factor B   2     3.50     3.50     1.75   0.16  0.854
Error               6    65.00    65.00    10.83
Total              11  1164.00
```

S = 3.29140   R-Sq = 94.42%   R-Sq(adj) = 89.76%

a. H_O: $\mu_{AB1} = \mu_{AB2}$,
   H_A: the interaction terms have different response averages.
   P-value = 0.854 > α = 0.05. Therefore, fail to reject H_O. Conclude that there is not sufficient evidence to determine that there is interaction between Factor A and Factor B.

b. H_O: $\mu_{A1} = \mu_{A2} = \mu_{A3}$,
   H_A: at least two levels have different mean response
   F = MSA/MSW = 47.10 $F_{0.05}$ = 5.143. Since F = 47.10 > $F_{0.05}$ = 5.143, reject H_O. Conclude that there is sufficient evidence to indicate that at least two of the Factor A response variable averages differ.

c. H_O: $\mu_{B1} = \mu_{B2}$,
   H_A: the two levels of Factor B have different response averages.
   P-value = 0.039 < α = 0.05. Therefore, reject H_O. Conclude that there is sufficient evidence to determine that the two mean responses of Factor B differ

12.35
a. Minitab output:

Two-way ANOVA: Response versus Factor A, Factor B

Source	DF	SS	MS	F	P
Factor A	2	11133.4	5566.72	53.61	0.000
Factor B	2	10836.8	5418.39	52.18	0.000
Interaction	4	16459.6	4114.89	39.63	0.000
Error	9	934.5	103.83		
Total	17	39364.3			

S = 10.19   R-Sq = 97.63%   R-Sq(adj) = 95.52%

H_O: AB interaction does not exist,
H_A: AB interaction does exist

F = MSAB/MSW = 39.63 $F_{0.05}$ = 3.633.

Since F = 39.63 > $F_{0.05}$ = 3.633, reject H_O. Conclude that there is sufficient evidence to indicate that interaction exists between Factors A and B.

b. Since interaction exists, it is futile to conduct inference on the response means associated with the levels of Factor A and Factor B. Therefore, a one-way analysis of variance using only those values for Factor A associated with level one of Factor B.

Minitab output:

One-way ANOVA: ResponseB1 versus Factor A B1

Source	DF	SS	MS	F	P
Factor A B1	2	276.3	138.2	2.90	0.199
Error	3	143.0	47.7		
Total	5	419.3			

S = 6.904   R-Sq = 65.90%   R-Sq(adj) = 43.16%

H_O: $\mu_{A1} = \mu_{A2} = \mu_{A3}$ @ Level 1 of Factor B,
H_A: at least two levels of Factor A have different mean responses @ Level 1 of Factor B

F = MSA$_{B1}$/MSW = 2.90 $F_{0.05}$ = 9.552.

Since F = 2.90 < $F_{0.05}$ = 9.552, fail to reject H_O. Conclude that there is not sufficient evidence to indicate that at least two levels of Factor A have different mean responses @ Level 1 of Factor B.

c. Minitab output with Factor B at level 2:

One-way ANOVA: ResponseB2 versus Factor A B2

```
Source        DF    SS     MS     F      P
Factor A B2    2   202.3  101.2  3.49   0.165
Error          3    87.0   29.0
Total          5   289.3
```

```
S = 5.385   R-Sq = 69.93%   R-Sq(adj) = 49.88%
```

H_O: $\mu_{A1} = \mu_{A2} = \mu_{A3}$ @ Level 2 of Factor B,
H_A: at least two levels of Factor A have different mean responses @ Level 2 of Factor B

$F = MSA_{B2}/MSW = 3.49$ $F_{0.05} = 9.552$.

Since $F = 3.49 < F_{0.05} = 9.552$, fail to reject H_O. Conclude that there is not sufficient evidence to indicate that at least two levels of Factor A have different mean responses @ Level 2 of Factor B.

Minitab output with Factor B at level 3:

One-way ANOVA: Respose B3 versus Factor A B3

```
Source        DF    SS     MS      F      P
Factor A B3    2   27114  13557  57.73   0.004
Error          3    705    235
Total          5   27819
```

```
S = 15.32   R-Sq = 97.47%   R-Sq(adj) = 95.78%
```

```
                          Individual 95% CIs For Mean Based on
                          Pooled StDev
Level  N    Mean   StDev  ----+---------+---------+---------+-----
1      2   313.00  15.56  (-----*-----)
2      2   470.00  21.21                              (----*-----)
3      2   348.50   3.54        (-----*-----)
                          ----+---------+---------+---------+-----
                            300       360       420       480
```

```
Pooled StDev = 15.32
```

H_O: $\mu_{A1} = \mu_{A2} = \mu_{A3}$ @ Level 3 of Factor B,
H_A: at least two levels of Factor A have different mean responses @ Level 3 of Factor B

$F = MSA_{B3}/MSW = 57.73$ $F_{0.05} = 9.552$.

Since $F = 57.73 > F_{0.05} = 9.552$, reject H_O. Conclude that there is sufficient evidence to indicate that at least two levels of Factor A have different mean responses @ Level 2 of Factor B.

12.37

Using Excel's ANOVA Two-Factor with Replication Data Analysis tool with an $\alpha = 0.1$, the following ANOVA table was generated. Use this information to answer parts (a-c).

ANOVA

Source of Variation	SS	df	MS	F	P-value	F crit
Height	95.51111	2	47.75556	0.322092	0.726698	2.456346
Location	10497.64	2	5248.822	35.40123	0.00000	2.456346
Interaction	99.68889	4	24.92222	0.168091	0.95324	2.107896
Within	5337.6	36	148.2667			
Total	16030.44	44				

a. Test to determine whether there is an interaction effect between the height of the product's placement and the location in the store. The null and alternative hypotheses are:

H_o: Height and location do not interact to affect mean sales
H_A: Height and location do interact

The F test statistic for this null hypothesis is 0.168.

$F_{\alpha=0.10} = 2.108$ is obtained from the ANOVA table above. Because $F = 0.168 < F_{\alpha=0.10} = 2.108$, do not reject the null hypothesis. Based on these sample data we conclude that there is no interaction between the variables height and location.

b. To test whether there is a difference in mean sales due to the height of the product's placement, the appropriate null and alternative hypotheses are:

H_o: $\mu_L = \mu_M = \mu_H$
H_A: Not all populations have the same mean

The F test statistic for this null hypothesis is 0.322.

$F_{\alpha=0.10} = 2.456$ is obtained from the ANOVA table above. Because $F = 0.322 < F_{\alpha=0.10} = 2.456$, do not reject the null hypothesis. Based on these sample data we conclude that there are no differences in the average sales due to the height of the product's placement.

c. To test whether there is a difference in mean sales due to location in the store, the appropriate null and alternative hypotheses are:

H_o: $\mu_F = \mu_M = \mu_R$
H_A: Not all populations have the same mean

The F test statistic for this null hypothesis is 35.401.

$F_{\alpha=0.10} = 2.456$ is obtained from the ANOVA table above. Because $F = 35.401 > F_{\alpha=0.10} = 2.456$, reject the null hypothesis. Based on these sample data we conclude that there are differences in mean sales due to the location of the product in the store.

12.39
a.

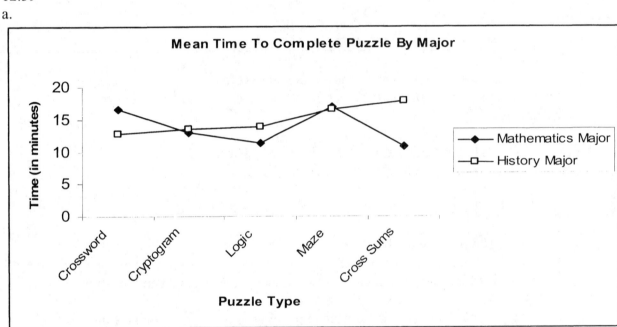

Based on the plot of average times we see that there is an interaction effect indicated by the fact that the effect due to puzzle type is not uniform across the type of major.

Using Excel's ANOVA Two-Factor with Replication Data Analysis tool with $\alpha = 0.05$, the following ANOVA table was generated. Use this information to answer parts (b and c).

Anova: Two-Factor With Replication

SUMMARY	Crossword	Cryptogram	Logic	Maze	Cross Sums	Total
Mathematics Major						
Count	5	5	5	5	5	25
Sum	83	65	57	85	54	344
Average	16.6	13	11.4	17	10.8	13.76
Variance	2.8	1	0.8	1.5	0.7	8.106667
History Major						
Count	5	5	5	5	5	25
Sum	64	68	69	83	89	373
Average	12.8	13.6	13.8	16.6	17.8	14.92
Variance	5.2	0.8	0.2	0.3	1.7	5.243333
Total						
Count	10	10	10	10	10	
Sum	147	133	126	168	143	
Average	14.7	13.3	12.6	16.8	14.3	
Variance	7.566667	0.9	2.044444	0.844444	14.6777778	

ANOVA

Source of Variation	SS	df	MS	F	P-value	F crit
Sample	16.820	1	16.820	11.21333	0.00178	4.08475
Columns	102.920	4	25.730	17.15333	0.00000	2.60597
Interaction	157.480	4	39.370	26.24667	0.00000	2.60597
Within	60.000	40	1.500			
Total	337.220	49				

b. Test to determine whether interaction exists between type of major and type of puzzle. The null and alternative hypotheses are:

H_o: Type of major and type of puzzle do not interact to affect the mean time

H_A: Type of major and type of puzzle do interact

The F test statistic for this null hypothesis is 26.247.

$F_{\alpha=0.05} = 2.606$ is obtained from the ANOVA table above. Because $F = 26.247 > F_{\alpha=0.05} = 2.606$, reject the null hypothesis. Thus, based on these sample data we conclude that there is interaction between type of major and type of puzzle.

c. You will need to run two one-way ANOVA for this problem. A one-way ANOVA on puzzles for only History majors and one on puzzles for only Mathematics majors.

History Majors:

One-Way ANOVA History Major

Source of Variation	SS	df	MS	F	P-value	F crit
Between Groups	93.04	4	23.26	14.18293	0.00001	2.866081
Within Groups	32.8	20	1.64			
Total	125.84	24				

The appropriate null and alternative hypotheses are:

H_o: $\mu_1 = \mu_2 = \mu_3 = \mu_4 = \mu_5$
H_A: Not all populations have the same mean

The F test statistic for this null hypothesis is 14.183.
$F_{\alpha=0.05} = 2.866$ is obtained from the ANOVA table above. Because $F = 14.183 > F_{\alpha=0.05} = 2.866$, reject the null hypothesis. Based on these sample data we conclude that for history majors, the mean time to complete a puzzle depends on the type of puzzle.

Mathematic Majors:

One-Way ANOVA Math Major

Source of Variation	SS	df	MS	F	P-value	F crit
Between Groups	167.36	4	41.84	30.76471	0.00000	2.866081
Within Groups	27.2	20	1.36			
Total	194.56	24				

The appropriate null and alternative hypotheses are:

H_o: $\mu_1 = \mu_2 = \mu_3 = \mu_4 = \mu_5$
H_A: Not all populations have the same mean

The F test statistic for this null hypothesis is 30.765.
$F_{\alpha=0.05} = 2.866$ is obtained from the ANOVA table above. Because $F = 30.765 > F_{\alpha=0.05} = 2.866$, reject the null hypothesis. Based on these sample data we conclude that the mean time for mathematics majors to complete a puzzle depends on the type of puzzle.

12.41

a. Minitab output:

Two-way ANOVA: Fat versus Formula, Plant

Source	DF	SS	MS	F	P
Formula	4	324.68	81.1700	15.61	0.000
Plant	4	66.08	16.5200	3.18	0.031
Interaction	16	50.52	3.1575	0.61	0.849
Error	25	130.00	5.2000		
Total	49	571.28			

S = 2.280   R-Sq = 77.24%   R-Sq(adj) = 55.40%

H_O: Interaction between Factor A and Factor B does not exist,
H_A: Interaction between Factor A and Factor B does exist,

$\alpha = 0.025 <$ p-value $= 0.849$. Therefore, fail to reject H_O.

Conclude that there is not sufficient evidence to indicate interaction between the Eukanuba formulas and plant site where they are produced.

b. H_O: $\mu_{A1} = \mu_{A2} = \mu_{A3} = \mu_{A4} = \mu_{A5}$,
   H_A: at least two plant sites have different averages of percent of crude fat,

$\alpha = 0.025$, $F = $ MSA/MSW $= 15.61$ $F_{0.025} = 3.353$. Since $F = 15.61 > F_{0.025} = 3.353$, reject H_O.

Conclude that there is sufficient evidence to indicate that at least two formulas have different averages of percent of crude fat.

c. H_O: $\mu_{B1} = \mu_{B2} = \mu_{B3} = \mu_{B4} = \mu_{B5}$,
   H_A: at least two plant sites have different averages of percent of crude fat,

$\alpha = 0.025$, $F = $ MSB/MSW $= 15.61$ $F_{0.025} = 3.353$. Since $F = 3.18 < F_{0.025} = 3.353$, do not reject H_O.

Conclude that there is not sufficient evidence to indicate that at least two plant sites have different averages of percent of crude fat.

d. In order to provide the answer for this question, you must conduct the test of hypothesis

H_O: $\mu_{A4} = 9$,

H_A: $\mu_{A4} \neq 9$, $\alpha = 0.05$.

This is conducted using a one-sample t-test with a standard error of $\sqrt{MSE/n} = \sqrt{5.200/10} = 0.7211$.

Minitab output:

One-Sample T

Test of mu = 9 vs not = 9

N	Mean	StDev	SE Mean	T
10	8.50000	2.28035	0.72111	-0.69

The critical value for this test is obtained from a t-distribution with degrees of freedom equal to the degrees of freedom for error in the ANOVA table = 25. This says the critical values are ± 2.0595. Since $-2.0595 < t = -0.69 < 2.0595$. Fail to reject H_O and conclude that the average percent of crude fat for the "Reduced Fat" formula is equal to the advertised nine percent.

End of Chapter Exercises

12.43

Answers will vary with the student.

12.45

If the null hypothesis is not rejected we conclude that there is no difference in population means. In this case we would expect that the Tukey-Kramer procedure for multiple comparisons would show no significant difference in any pairwise comparison.

12.47

In the two-sample t-test for a difference between any two means, the estimate of the population variances only includes data from the two specific samples under consideration. For ANOVA situations where there are three or more groups, we would be disregarding some of the information available to estimate the common population variance. To overcome this problem we base our confidence intervals using as our estimate of the pooled standard deviation the square root of the mean square within (MSW) value. The MSW is the weighted average of all sample variances in the problem under consideration. This is preferred to the two-sample t-test procedure because we are assuming that each of the sample variances is an estimate of the common population variance. Using the MSW enables us to incorporate all the information related to the estimate of the common population variance not just some of it as would be the case with the two-sample t-test approach.

12.49

a. H_0: $\mu_1 = \mu_2 = \mu_3 = \mu_4$
H_A: At least two population means are different

Anova: Single Factor						
SUMMARY						
Groups	Count	Sum	Average	Variance		
Supplier A	4	2017	504.25	11576.25		
Supplier B	4	2923	730.75	5234.25		
Supplier C	4	2234	558.5	1845.667		
Supplier D	4	1714	428.5	8393		
ANOVA						
Source of Variation	SS	df	MS	F	P-value	F crit
Between Groups	197908.5	3	65969.5	9.755495	0.001536	5.952529
Within Groups	81147.5	12	6762.292			
Total	279056	15				

Since 9.7555 > 5.9525 reject H_0 and conclude that at least two populations means are different.

b.

$$CriticalRange = q_{1-\alpha}\sqrt{\frac{MSW}{2}\left(\frac{1}{n_i}+\frac{1}{n_j}\right)} = 5.5\sqrt{\frac{6762.29}{2}\left(\frac{1}{4}+\frac{1}{4}\right)} = 226.23$$

	Absolute Difference	Critical Range	Significant?
Supplier A-Supplier B	226.5	226.23	Yes
Supplier A-Supplier C	54.25	226.23	No
Supplier A-Supplier D	75.75	226.23	No
Supplier B-Supplier C	172.25	226.23	No
Supplier B-Supplier D	302.25	226.23	Yes
Supplier C-Supplier D	130	226.23	No

Based on the Tukey-Kramer test you can eliminate Type D and A since the mean life is less than B.

12.51

a. Using the steps outlined in the chapter:

Step 1: The parameters of interest are the average percentage gains accrued by the analyst's customers among the mutual fund types.

Step 2: H_O: $\mu_1 = \mu_2 = ... = \mu_8$,
H_A: At least two population means are different.

Step 3: The significance level is $\alpha = 0.05$.

Step 4: The selected samples are specified in the heading of this exercise.

Step 5: Because of the small sample sizes, the box and whisker diagram is used.

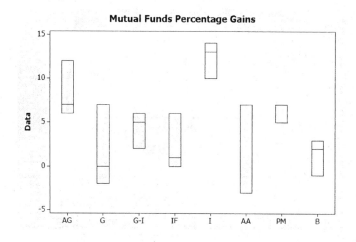

The box plots indicate some skewness but not sufficient to deny normality. If we assume that the populations are normally distributed, Harley's F_{max} test can be used to test whether the three populations have equal variances. The sample

variances are $s_1^2 = \dfrac{\sum (x - \bar{x})^2}{n - 1} = \dfrac{20.66}{2} = 10.33$, $s_2^2 = 22.33$, and $s_3^2 = 4.33$,

$s_4^2 = 10.33$, $s_5^2 = 4.33$, $s_6^2 = 33.33$, $s_7^2 = 1.333$, $s_8^2 = 4.33$, test statistic is $F_{max} =$

$$\frac{s_{max}^2}{s_{min}^2} = \frac{33.33}{1.333} = 25.004.$$

From Appendix I, the critical value for alpha = 0.05, k = 8, and n - 1 = 2 is 403. Because 25.004 < 403, we conclude that the population variances could be equal.

Step 6:

Anova: Single Factor

SUMMARY

Groups	Count	Sum	Average	Variance
AG	3	25	8.333	10.333
G	3	5	1.667	22.333
G-I	3	13	4.333	4.333
IF	3	7	2.333	10.333
I	3	37	12.333	4.333
AA	3	11	3.667	33.333
PM	3	17	5.667	1.333
B	3	4	1.333	4.333

ANOVA

Source of Variation	SS	df	MS	F	P-value	F crit
Between Groups	297.625	7	42.518	3.752	0.014	2.657
Within Groups	181.333	16	11.333			
Total	478.958	23				

Step 7: Because $k - 1 = 7$ and $n_T - k = 16$, $F_{0.05} = 2.657$. The decision rule is if the calculated $F > F_{0.05} = 2.657$, reject H_O, or if the p-value $< \alpha = 0.05$, reject H_O; otherwise, do not reject H_O.

Step 8: Since $F = 3.752 > 2.657$, we reject H_O.

Step 9: We conclude there is sufficient evidence to indicate that there is a difference in the average percentage gains accrued by his customers among the mutual fund types

b. Using Equation 12-7 to construct the critical ranges:

$$q_{1-\alpha}\sqrt{\frac{MSW}{2}\left(\frac{1}{n_i}+\frac{1}{n_j}\right)}$$

For $n_1 = n_2 = \ldots = n_8 = 3$, critical range $= 4.90\sqrt{\frac{11.3}{2}\left(\frac{1}{3}+\frac{1}{3}\right)} = 9.5099$;

Minitab has a procedure to construct Tukey-Kramer comparisons. They look different than the tables produced in the chapter but present the same information. If you want to compare your answers with those that follow, compare the absolute values of the differences found in the following output with the critical range calculated above.

```
Tukey 95% Simultaneous Confidence Intervals
All Pairwise Comparisons

Individual confidence level = 99.68%

AG subtracted from:

         Lower   Center   Upper    -------+---------+---------+---------+--
G      -16.191   -6.667   2.857        (-------*-------)
G-I    -13.524   -4.000   5.524           (-------*-------)
IF     -15.524   -6.000   3.524        (-------*-------)
I       -5.524    4.000  13.524                (-------*-------)
AA     -14.191   -4.667   4.857        (-------*-------)
PM     -12.191   -2.667   6.857          (-------*-------)
B      -16.524   -7.000   2.524       (-------*-------)
                                     -------+---------+---------+---------+--
                                          -12        0        12       24

G subtracted from:

         Lower   Center   Upper    -------+---------+---------+---------+--
G-I     -6.857    2.667  12.191           (-------*-------)
IF      -8.857    0.667  10.191         (-------*------)
I        1.143   10.667  20.191                   (-------*-------)
AA      -7.524    2.000  11.524         (-------*-------)
PM      -5.524    4.000  13.524          (-------*-------)
B       -9.857   -0.333   9.191        (-------*-------)
                                     -------+---------+---------+---------+--
                                          -12        0        12       24
```

```
G-I subtracted from:

        Lower   Center   Upper    -------+---------+---------+---------+--
IF    -11.524   -2.000   7.524        (-------*-------)
I      -1.524    8.000  17.524              (-------*-------)
AA    -10.191   -0.667   8.857         (------*-------)
PM     -8.191    1.333  10.857          (-------*-------)
B     -12.524   -3.000   6.524         (-------*------)
                                      -------+---------+---------+---------+--
                                           -12        0        12        24

IF subtracted from:

        Lower   Center   Upper    -------+---------+---------+---------+--
I       0.476   10.000  19.524              (-------*-------)
AA     -8.191    1.333  10.857         (-------*-------)
PM     -6.191    3.333  12.857          (-------*-------)
B     -10.524   -1.000   8.524        (-------*-------)
                                      -------+---------+---------+---------+--
                                           -12        0        12        24

I subtracted from:

        Lower   Center   Upper    -------+---------+---------+---------+--
AA    -18.191   -8.667   0.857     (-------*-------)
PM    -16.191   -6.667   2.857      (------*-------)
B     -20.524  -11.000  -1.476    (-------*-------)
                                      -------+---------+---------+---------+--
                                           -12        0        12        24


AA subtracted from:

        Lower   Center   Upper    -------+---------+---------+---------+--
PM     -7.524    2.000  11.524          (-------*-------)
B     -11.857   -2.333   7.191        (-------*-------)
                                      -------+---------+---------+---------+--
                                           -12        0        12        24

PM subtracted from:

        Lower   Center   Upper    -------+---------+---------+---------+--
B     -13.857   -4.333   5.191        (-------*-------)
                                      -------+---------+---------+---------+--
                                           -12        0        12        24
```

Tukey-Kramer, therefore, indicates that $\mu_I > \mu_B$, $\mu_I > \mu_{IF}$, and $\mu_I > \mu_G$. Other pairwise comparison were deemed to be equal.

12.53

a. H_0: Factors A and B do not interact
    H_A: Factors A and B do interact
        Students can select desired critical level. Assuming alpha = .05:

ANOVA

Source of Variation	SS	df	MS	F	P-value	F crit
Driver	411.5139	2	205.7569	0.74628	0.476117	3.064756
Golf Balls	897.8542	3	299.2847	1.085505	0.357631	2.673218
Interaction	978.5417	6	163.0903	0.591528	0.736642	2.167951
Within	36393.75	132	275.7102			
Total	38681.66	143				

Since 0.59153 < 2.16795 do not reject H_0 and conclude that there is no interaction between drives and type of golf balls.

b. H_0: $\mu_{\beta 1} = \mu_{\beta 2} = \mu_{\beta 3}$
    H_A: Not all means are equal
    Assuming alpha = .05:
    Since 0.74628 < 3.0648 do not reject H_0 and conclude that there is no significant effect due to the type of driver used.

c. It could be used by Gordon to keep them from making a claim that was not true which would affect public perception.

12.55

a. H_0: $\mu_1 = \mu_2 = \mu_3 = \mu_4$
    H_A: At least two population means are different

Anova: Single Factor					
SUMMARY					
Groups	Count	Sum	Average	Variance	
Little Rock	33	5523389	167375.4	4894622	
Wichita	33	5332859	161601.8	6368664	
Tulsa	33	5561588	168533	5019125	
Memphis	33	5620136	170307.2	6399072	
ANOVA					
Source of Variation	SS	df	MS	F	P-value	F crit
Between Groups	1.4E+09	3	4.68E+08	82.56392	8.74E-30	2.675385
Within Groups	7.26E+08	128	5670371			
Total	2.13E+09	131				

Since the p-value = 8.74E-30 < 0.05 reject H_0 and conclude that at least two of the means are different.

b. The Tukey-Kramer critical range is computed using:

$$CR = q_{.95} \sqrt{\frac{MSW}{2} \left(\frac{1}{n_i} + \frac{1}{n_j}\right)}$$

$$CR = 3.63 \sqrt{\frac{5,670,370.5}{2} \left(\frac{1}{33} + \frac{1}{33}\right)} = 1,504.72$$

	Absolute Difference	Critical Range	Significant?
Little Rock - Wichita	5773.6	1504.72	yes
Little Rock - Tulsa	1157.6	1504.72	no
Little Rock - Memphis	2931.8	1504.72	yes
Wichita - Tulsa	6931.2	1504.72	yes
Wichita - Memphis	8705.4	1504.72	yes
Tulsa - Memphis	1774.2	1504.72	yes

c. $n = 1.96^2(6368664)/500^2 = 97.8634$ or 98

12.57

a. Minitab output:

Two-way ANOVA: Nitrogen versus Corn Yield, Plant

```
Source         DF       SS       MS       F       P
Corn Yield      4   35843.2  8960.80  541.98   0.000
Plant           2    7337.6  3668.80  221.90   0.000
Interaction     8     710.4    88.80    5.37   0.003
Error          15     248.0    16.53
Total          29   44139.2


S = 4.066    R-Sq = 99.44%    R-Sq(adj) = 98.91%
```

H_O: interaction does not exist,
H_A: interaction does exist
$F = MSAB/MSW = 5.37$ $F_{0.05} = 3.682$.

Since $F = 5.37 > F_{0.05} = 3.682$, reject H_O. Conclude that there is sufficient evidence to indicate that interaction exists between the yield levels of corn and the crop that had been previously planted in the field.

b. Since interaction exists, it is futile to conduct inference on the major effects. Therefore, a one-way analysis of variance using only those levels associated with the specific crop that had been previously planted will be presented. Minitab output:

One-way ANOVA: NitroCorn versus Yield Corn

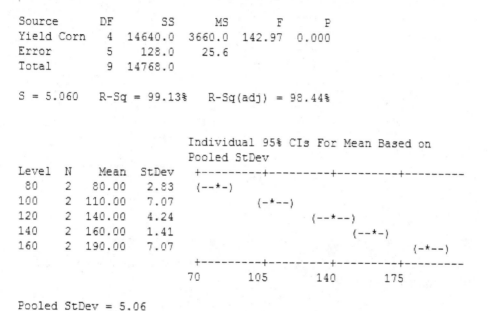

```
Source       DF       SS       MS       F       P
Yield Corn    4   14640.0   3660.0   142.97   0.000
Error         5     128.0     25.6
Total         9   14768.0

S = 5.060    R-Sq = 99.13%    R-Sq(adj) = 98.44%


                                Individual 95% CIs For Mean Based on
                                Pooled StDev
Level   N    Mean   StDev    +---------+---------+---------+---------
  80    2   80.00    2.83    (--*-)
 100    2  110.00    7.07             (-*--)
 120    2  140.00    4.24                     (--*--)
 140    2  160.00    1.41                         (--*-)
 160    2  190.00    7.07                                 (-*--)
                             +---------+---------+---------+---------
                             70       105       140       175

Pooled StDev = 5.06
```

H_O: $\mu_{A1} = \mu_{A2} = \mu_{A3} = \mu_{A4}$ with corn as previous crop,
H_A: at least two levels of corn yields require different amounts of nitrogen with corn as previous crop

$F = MSA_{B1}/MSW = 142.97 \quad F_{0.05} = 5.192$.

Since $F = 142.97 > F_{0.05} = 5.192$, reject H_O. Conclude that there is sufficient evidence to indicate that at least two levels of corn yields require different amounts of nitrogen with corn as previous crop.

c. Minitab output with soybeans as the previous crop:

One-way ANOVA: NitroSoy versus Yield Soy

```
Source      DF     SS      MS      F       P
Yield Soy    4  9353.6  2338.4  129.91  0.000
Error        5    90.0    18.0
Total        9  9443.6

S = 4.243   R-Sq = 99.05%   R-Sq(adj) = 98.28%
```

```
                            Individual 95% CIs For Mean Based on
                            Pooled StDev
Level  N    Mean   StDev  -+---------+---------+---------+--------
 80    2   80.00   1.41   (--*--)
100    2   80.00   7.07   (--*--)
120    2  114.00   1.41                  (--*--)
140    2  130.00   4.24                        (--*--)
160    2  160.00   4.24                                    (--*--)
                          -+---------+---------+---------+--------
                          75        100       125       150
```

H_0: $\mu_{A1} = \mu_{A2} = \mu_{A3} = \mu_{A4}$ with soybeans as previous crop,
H_A: at least two levels of corn yields require different amounts of nitrogen with soy beans as previous crop

$F = MSA_{B2}/MSW = 129.91$ $F_{0.05} = 5.192$.

Since $F = 129.91 > F_{0.05} = 5.192$, reject H_0. Conclude that there is sufficient evidence to indicate that at least two levels of corn yields require different amounts of nitrogen with soy beans as previous crop.

Minitab output with sod grass as previous crop:

One-way ANOVA: Nitro Gras versus Yield Gras

```
Source       DF       SS       MS       F       P
Yield Gras    4  12560.00  3140.00  523.33  0.000
Error         5     30.00     6.00
Total         9  12590.00

S = 2.449   R-Sq = 99.76%   R-Sq(adj) = 99.57%


                               Individual 95% CIs For Mean Based on
                               Pooled StDev
Level  N    Mean   StDev  -----+---------+---------+---------+----
  80   2   50.00    4.24  (-*)
 100   2   70.00    1.41        (*-)
 120   2  100.00    1.41                  (*-)
 140   2  120.00    2.83                          (*)
 160   2  150.00    0.00                                   (*)
                           -----+---------+---------+---------+----
                               60        90       120       150
```

H_O: $\mu_{A1} = \mu_{A2} = \mu_{A3} = \mu_{A4}$ with sod grass as previous crop,

H_A: at least two levels of corn yields require different amounts of nitrogen with sod grass as previous crop

$F = MSA_{B3}/MSW = 129.91$ $F_{0.05} = 5.192$.

Since $F = 523.33 > F_{0.05} = 5.192$, reject H_O. Conclude that there is sufficient evidence to indicate that at least two levels of corn yields require different amounts of nitrogen with soy beans as previous crop.

Chapter 12

CHAPTER 8-12
SPECIAL REVIEW SOLUTIONS

SR.1

Conditions: (1) Parameter of concern: average, (2) sample size = 50 > 30 ==> Use a large sample hypothesis test for the mean of a population. Research hypothesis: average of new starter units is greater than 1000 ==>

H_0: $\mu \leq 1000$

H_A: $\mu > 1000$

$\alpha = 0.05$

$$z = \frac{\overline{x} - \mu}{\frac{s}{\sqrt{n}}} = \frac{1010 - 1000}{\frac{48}{\sqrt{50}}} = 1.4731$$

Rejection region: z > 1.645

Decision: z = 1.4731 < 1645 = z_α ==> do not reject H_0

Conclusion: The average cycles for the new starter unit is not greater than that of the old starter unit. Do not recommend changing suppliers.

SR.3

Conditions: (1) Parameter of concern: difference between two proportions, (2)

$n_1 \overline{p}_1 = 800(.05) = 40 > 5$; $n_1(1 - \overline{p}_1) = 800(.95) = 760 > 5$;

$n_2 \overline{p}_2 = 900(.09) = 81 > 5$; $n_2(1 - \overline{p}_2) = 900(.91) = 819 > 5$ ==> use a normal approximation ==> Use a large sample hypothesis test for the difference between two proportions. Research hypothesis: There is a difference in the turnover rates for the two trial policies. ==>

H_0: $p_1 - p_2 = 0$

H_A: $p_1 - p_2 \neq 0$

$\alpha = 0.05$ $\qquad \overline{p} = \frac{\overline{p}_1 n_1 + \overline{p}_2 n_2}{n_1 + n_2} = \frac{40 + 81}{800 + 900} = .0712$

$$z = \frac{\overline{p}_1 - \overline{p}_2 - (p_1 - p_2)}{\sqrt{\overline{p}(1 - \overline{p})\left(\frac{1}{n_1} + \frac{1}{n_2}\right)}} = \frac{.05 - (.09) - 0}{\sqrt{.0712(.9288)\left(\frac{1}{800} + \frac{1}{900}\right)}} = -3.2011$$

Rejection region: z < -1.96 or z > 1.96

Decision: z = -3.2011 < -1.96 = $-z_{\alpha/2}$ ==> reject H_0

Conclusion: There is a difference in the turnover rates for the two trial policies.

SR.5

Conditions: (1) Parameter of concern: population variances, (2) assume population is normally distributed ==> Use a hypothesis test for the equality of two variances. Research hypothesis: There is no difference in variability of attendance between downtown and suburban theaters.

$H_0: \sigma_1^2 = \sigma_2^2$

$H_A: \sigma_1^2 \neq \sigma_2^2$

$\alpha = 0.05$

$$F = \frac{s_1^2}{s_2^2} = \frac{1684}{1439} = 1.1703$$

Rejection region: $F > 3.137$

Decision: $F_\alpha = 3.137 > 1.1703 = F$ ==> do not reject H_0

Conclusion: There is no difference in variability of attendance between downtown and suburban theaters.

Conditions: (1) Parameter of concern: population means, (2) sample sizes < 30, (3) population variances unknown, (4) population variances equal, and (5) assume population is normally distributed ==> Use a hypothesis test for the equality of two means. Research hypothesis: There is no difference in mean attendance between downtown and suburban theaters.

$H_0: \mu_1 = \mu_2$

$H_A: \mu_1 \neq \mu_2$

$\alpha = 0.05$ $\qquad s_p = \sqrt{\dfrac{(11-1)1684 + (10-1)(1439)}{11 + 10 - 2}} = 39.5973$

$$t = \frac{\bar{x}_1 - \bar{x}_2 - (\mu_1 - \mu_2)}{s_p \sqrt{\dfrac{1}{n_1} + \dfrac{1}{n_2}}} = \frac{855 - 750}{39.5973 \sqrt{\dfrac{1}{11} + \dfrac{1}{10}}} = 6.0689$$

Rejection region: $t < -2.0930$ or $t > 2.0930$

Decision: $t_{\alpha/2} = 2.0930 < 6.0689 = t$ ==> reject H_0

Conclusion: There is a difference in the average attendance between downtown and suburban theaters.

SR.7

Conditions: (1) Parameter of concern: differences among three population means, (2) population variances unknown, (3) samples are independent, and (4) assume population is normally distributed ==> Use an analysis of variance for the difference between population means. Research hypothesis: There is no difference in mean strength of the three types of shocks after 20,000 miles.

The equality of the populations' variances must be verified first.

Conditions: (1) Parameter of concern: population variances, (2) assume population is normally distributed ==> Use a hypothesis test for the equality of population variances. Research hypothesis: There is no difference in variability among the strength of the three types of shocks after 20,000 miles.

H_0: $\sigma_1^2 = \sigma_2^2 = \sigma_3^2$

H_A: at least two σ_i^2 differ

$\alpha = 0.05$

$$F = \frac{s_{max}^2}{s_{min}^2} = \frac{4.0280}{3.0695} = 1.3123$$

Rejection region: $F_H > 10.8$

Decision: $F_H = 10.8 > 1.3123 = F$ ==> do not reject H_0

Conclusion: There is no difference in variability of the strength of the three types of shocks after 20,000 miles.

H_0: $\mu_1 = \mu_2 = \mu_3$

H_A: at least two μ_i differ

$\alpha = 0.05$

Anova: Single Factor

SUMMARY

Groups	Count	Sum	Average	Variance
Manufacturer	6	64.3	10.71667	3.069667
Competitor 1	6	61.8	10.3	3.304
Competitor 2	6	64.3	10.71667	4.029667

ANOVA

Source of Variation	SS	df	MS	F	P-value	F crit
Between Groups	0.694444	2	0.347222	0.100128	0.905321	3.682317
Within Groups	52.01667	15	3.467778			
Total	52.71111	17				

Rejection region: $F > 3.682$

Decision: $F_\alpha = 3.682 > 0.10 = F$ ==> do not reject H_0

Conclusion: There is no difference in average strength of the three types of shocks after 20,000 miles.

SR.9

Conditions: (1) Parameter of concern: differences among three population means, (2) treatment effects for Phosphor type are different for different levels of the glass type → interaction, (3) samples are independent, and (4) assume population is normally distributed ==> Use a two factor analysis of variance for the difference between population means. Research hypothesis: There is no difference in brightness of the monitors for the three Phosphor types. There is no difference in brightness of the monitors for glass types. There is no interaction between the glass type and relationship between the Phosphor type and the brightness of the monitor types.

Two-way ANOVA: Brightness versus GlassType, PhosType

```
Analysis of Variance for Brightne
Source         DF      SS      MS       F        P
GlassTyp       1      7896    7896    33.11    0.000
PhosType       2       181      90     0.38    0.692
Interaction    2      1650     825     3.46    0.065
Error         12      2861     238
Total         17     12588
```

Test for Interaction:
p-value = 0.692 > 0.05 = α. Therefore, do not reject the null hypothesis that interaction does not exist.

Test for Factor 1: Glass type
p-value = 0.065 > 0.05 = α. Therefore, do not reject the null hypothesis that the average brightness of the monitors is not different between the glass types.

Test for Factor 2: Phosphor type
p-value = 0.000 < 0.05 = α. Therefore, reject the null hypothesis that the average brightness of the monitors is not different among the Phosphor types

SR.11

Conditions: (1) Parameter of concern: difference between two proportions, (2)

$$n_1 p_1 = 250\left(\frac{9}{250}\right) = 9 > 5; \; n_1(1-p_1) = 250\left(\frac{241}{250}\right) = 241 > 5 \; ;$$

$$n_2 p_2 = 250\left(\frac{16}{250}\right) = 16 > 5; \; n_2(1-p_2) = 250\left(\frac{234}{250}\right) = 234 > 5 \Longrightarrow \text{use a normal}$$

approximation. Requires range of possible values ==> Use a large sample confidence interval for the difference between two proportions.

==>

$$p_1 - p_2 \pm z_{\alpha/2}\sqrt{\frac{p_1(1-p_1)}{n_1} + \frac{p_2(1-p_2)}{n_2}} = (\frac{16}{250} - \frac{9}{250}) \pm 1.96\sqrt{\frac{0.064(0.936)}{250} + \frac{0.036(0.964)}{250}}$$

$$= 0.028 \pm 0.0381 =$$

$(0.019, 0.0781)$

Using a 95% confidence level, it is estimated that the percentage of the blenders returned with the old switch is somewhere between 0% and 7% greater than the percentage of blenders returned with the new switch. Therefore the claim that the difference is somewhere between 3% and 6% seems quite plausible.

Chapter 13 Solutions

When applicable, selected problems in each section will be done following the appropriate step-by-step procedures outlined in the corresponding sections of the chapter. Other problems will provide key points and the answers to the questions, but all answers can be arrived at using the appropriate steps.

Section 13-1 Exercises

13.1

Step 1: Formulate the appropriate null and alternative hypotheses.
If the die is fair each outcome should have the same frequency of occurrence. That is the outcomes would be uniformly distributed. The following null and alternative hypotheses are formed:

H_0: Distribution of die outcomes is uniformly distributed.
H_A: Distribution of die outcomes is not uniformly distributed.

Step 2: Specify the significance level.
The test will be conducted using $\alpha = 0.05$.

Step 3: Collect the sample data and compute the chi-square test statistic.
Data were collected for 2,400 tosses of the die. The following represent the observed frequency for each die outcome:

Outcome	1	2	3	4	5	6
Frequency	352	418	434	480	341	375

A total of 2,400 tosses were performed. Under the null hypothesis of a uniform distribution, 1/6, or 400, of the total tosses should be a "1", 400 should be a "2", etc. Equation 13-1 is used to form the test statistic on these sample data.

$$\chi^2 = \sum \frac{(o-e)^2}{e} =$$

$$\frac{(352-400)^2}{400} + \frac{(418-400)^2}{400} + \frac{(434-400)^2}{400} + \frac{(480-400)^2}{400} + \frac{(341-400)^2}{400} + \frac{(375-400)^2}{400}$$

$$= 5.76 + 0.81 + 2.89 + 16 + 8.7025 + 1.5625 = 35.725.$$

Step 4: Determine the critical value.

The critical value for the goodness-of-fit test is a chi-square value from the chi-square distribution, with k-1 = 6-1=5 degrees of freedom and $\alpha = 0.05$ is 11.0705.

Step 5: Reach a decision.

The decision rule is:

If $\chi^2 > 11.0705$, reject Ho;
Otherwise, do not reject Ho.

Because $\chi^2 = 35.725 > 11.0705$, reject the null hypothesis.

Step 6: Draw a conclusion.

We conclude, based on the sample information and the results of the goodness-of-fit test that the die is not fair. The distributions of outcomes for this die are not uniformly distributed.

13.3

Step 1: Formulate the appropriate null and alternative hypotheses.

The following null and alternative hypotheses are formed:

H_0: Distribution of battery defects is binomial, with n = 50 and p =0.02.

H_A: Distribution of battery defects follows another distribution.

Step 2: Specify the significance level.

The test will be conducted using $\alpha = 0.01$.

Step 3: Collect the sample data and compute the chi-square test statistic.

The company selected a random sample of 400 battery packs, with each pack consisting of 50 batteries. The number of defective batteries in each package was recorded. The number of defective batteries per package for the random sample of 400 packages that was observed is shown below:

# of Defective Batteries Per Package	Frequency of Occurrence
0	165
1	133
2	65
3	28
4 or more	9

The following table shows the computations for the chi-square statistic.

# of Defective Batteries Per Package	Observed (o)	Binomial Probability n=50, p = 0.02	Expected Frequency (e)	$(o_i-e_i)^2/e_i$
0	165	0.36417	145.668	2.5656
1	133	0.37160	148.641	1.6458
2	65	0.18580	74.320	1.1688
3	28	0.06067	24.268	0.5740
4 or more	9	0.01776	7.103	0.5065
Total	400			6.4607

The calculated chi-square test statistic is $\chi^2 = 6.4607$.

Step 4: Determine the critical value.
The critical value for the goodness-of-fit test is a chi-square value from the chi-square distribution, with k-1 = 5-1=4 degrees of freedom and $\alpha = 0.01$ is 13.2767.

Step 5: Reach a decision.
The decision rule is:

If $\chi^2 > 13.2767$, reject Ho;
Otherwise, do not reject Ho.

Because $\chi^2 = 6.4607 < 13.2767$, do not reject the null hypothesis.

Step 6: Draw a conclusion.
We conclude, based on the sample information and the results of the goodness-of-fit test that the binomial distribution with n = 50 and p = 0.02 is an appropriate distribution for describing the company's sampling plan.

13.5

Step 1: State the appropriate null and alternative hypothesis.
In this case, the null and alternative hypotheses are:
Ho: Distribution of successes is binomial, with n = 18 and p = 0.15
HA: Distribution is not binomial, with n = 18 and p = 0.15

Step 2: Specify the level of significance.
The test will be conducted using $\alpha = 0.01$.

Step 3: Collect the sample data and compute the chi-square test statistic using Equation 13-1.

Note that the expected frequency for 5 successes is $= np_5 = 200(0.18453) = 3.6906 < 5$. Therefore, the number of successes 4 and 5 were combined.

Successes	o Observed Successes	Binomial Probability n = 18, p = 0.15	e Expected Frequency	$\dfrac{(o_i - e_i)^2}{e_i}$
0	80	0.050328	10.0657	485.894
1	75	0.205889	41.1778	27.780
2	39	0.336909	67.3819	11.955
3	6	0.275653	55.1306	43.784
4 - 5	0	0.131220	26.2440	26.244
Total	200	1	200	595.657

The calculated chi-square test statistic is $\chi^2 = 595.657$.

Step 4: Determine the critical value.

The degrees of freedom equals $k - 1 = 5 - 1 = 4$. The critical chi-square value found in Appendix G is 13.2767.

Step 5: Reach a decision.

Because the calculated value of $595.657 > 13.2767$, we do not reject H_O.

Step 6: Draw a conclusion.

There is sufficient evidence to reject that the binomial distribution with n = 18 and p = 0.15 is the appropriate distribution to describe the distribution of the number of successes.

13.7

The following steps can be used to conduct the hypothesis test.

Step 1: State the appropriate null and alternative hypotheses

The null and alternative hypotheses are:

H_0 : The population distribution of errors per page is Poisson distributed with mean equal to 0.2 per page.

H_A : The population distribution is not distributed as a Poisson distribution with mean equal to 0.2 per page.

Step 2: Specify the level of significance

The hypothesis test will be conducted using an alpha level equal to 0.01.

Step 3: Collect the sample data and compute the chi-square test statistic using equation 13-1.

A random sample of 400 pages was selected. The observed frequencies based on the sample data are shown as follows:

Errors	Frequency
0	335
1	56
2	7
3	2
Total	400

Now in order to compute the chi-square test statistic you next determine the expected frequencies. You start by determining the probability for each number of typographical errors based on the hypothesized distribution (Poisson with $\lambda t = 0.2$.) The expected frequencies are calculated by multiplying the probability by the total observed frequency of 400. These results are shown as follows:

Errors	o Frequency	Poisson Probabilities	e Frequency
0	335	0.8187308	327.49
1	56	0.1637462	65.50
2 or more	9	0.0174662	6.99
	400		

Now we can compute the chi-square test statistic using equation 13-1 as follows:

$$\chi^2 = \sum \frac{(o-e)^2}{e} = \frac{(335-327.49)^2}{327.49} + \frac{(56-65.50)^2}{65.50} + \cdots + \frac{(9-6.99)^2}{6.99} = 2.1229$$

Step 4: Determine the critical value.

The critical value depends on the level of significance and the number of degrees of freedom. The degrees of freedom is equal to k – 1, where k is the number of categories. In this case, after collapsing the categories to get the expected frequencies to at least 5, we have 3 categories. Thus, the degrees of freedom for the chi-square critical value is 3-1 = 2 with alpha equal 0.01. From table G we get a critical value of $\chi^2 = 9.2104$. Thus the decision rule is:

If $\chi^2 > 9.2104$, reject the null hypothesis
Otherwise, do not reject

Chapter 13

Step 5: Reach a decision.
Because $\chi^2 = 2.1229 < 9.2104$, we do not reject the null hypothesis.

Step 6: Draw a conclusion.
Thus, based on these sample data there is insufficient evidence to conclude that the error rate on published pages is not Poisson distributed with a mean equal to 0.2 errors per page. It appears that the publisher continues to meet the standards for typographical errors.

13.9

Step 1: State the appropriate null and alternative hypothesis.
In this case, the null and alternative hypotheses are:
H_O: Distribution of loan applicant arrivals is Poisson, with $\lambda = 3.5$
H_A: Distribution is not Poisson, with $\lambda = 3.5$

Step 2: Specify the level of significance.
The test will be conducted using $\alpha = 0.025$.

Step 3: Collect the sample data and compute the chi-square test statistic using Equation 13-1.
Note that the expected frequency for 0 successes is $= np_1 = 52(0.030197) = 1.5703 < 5$. Therefore, the number of successes 0 and 1 were combined.

Successes	o Observed Successes	Binomial Probability n = 200, p = 0.15	e Expected Frequency	$\frac{(o_i - e_i)^2}{e_i}$
≤1	3	0.135888	6.9622	2.25487
2	9	0.184959	9.6179	0.03969
3	11	0.215785	11.2208	0.00435
4	14	0.188812	9.8182	1.78109
5	6	0.132169	6.8728	0.11083
≥6	9	0.144387	7.5081	0.29644
Total	52	1	52	4.48727

The calculated chi-square test statistic is $\chi^2 = 4.48727$

Step 4: Determine the critical value.
The degrees of freedom equals $k - 1 = 6 - 1 = 5$. The critical chi-square value found in Appendix G is 12.8345.

Step 5: Reach a decision.

Because the calculated value of 4.48727 is less than the critical value of 12.8345, we do not reject H_O.

Step 6: Draw a conclusion.

There is not sufficient evidence to conclude that the distribution of loan applicant arrivals is not Poisson, with $\lambda = 3.5$.

13.11

a. The appropriate null and alternative hypotheses are:

H_0 : distribution of dollars spent per person is normally distributed

H_A : distribution of dollars spent is not normally distributed

b. We are asked to organize the data into six classes. We start by determining the class width. From Chapter 2 we know that the class width is found by:

$$w = \frac{\max imum - \min imum}{\# \ of \ classes} = \frac{193 - 14}{6} = 29.83$$

We round this up to $30.00 as the class width. The frequency distribution is:

Amount Spent	Frequency
under $44	24
$44 < $74	108
$74 < $104	224
$104 < $134	172
$134 < $164	65
$164 < $194	7
	600

c. We can now determine the expected frequencies in each class by using the normal distribution to first find the probability that a value for a normal distribution will fall within each class. We will then multiply these normal probabilities by 600 to obtain the expected frequencies. To get the normal probabilities, we must compute the sample mean and sample standard deviation as follows:

$$\bar{x} = \frac{\sum x}{n} = \frac{\$58,120}{600} = \$96.87 \quad \text{and} \quad s = \sqrt{\frac{\sum (x - \bar{x})^2}{n-1}} = \$30.21$$

For instance, the z-value for the first class is:

$$z = \frac{43.99 - 96.87}{30.21} = -1.75$$

Then $P(z \leq -1.75) = 0.5000 - 0.4599 = 0.0401$

The rest of the normal probabilities and the expected frequencies are shown as follows:

Amount Spent	o Frequency	z-value	Normal Probability	e Expected Frequency
under $44	24	-1.75	0.0401	24.06
$44 < $74	108	-0.76	0.1835	110.1
$74 < $104	224	0.24	0.3712	222.72
$104 < $134	172	1.23	0.2959	177.54
$134 < $164	65	2.22	0.0961	57.66
$164 < $194	7	3.21	0.0132	7.92
	600		1.0000	

Note, all of the expected frequencies exceed 5 so there is no need to collapse any of the categories together.

d. The chi-square test statistic is computed as:

$$\chi^2 = \sum \frac{(o-e)^2}{e} = 1.26$$

The critical chi-square from the chi-square distribution with alpha = 0.05 and degrees of freedom equal to k – 3 = 3 is $\chi^2 = 7.8147$. Note, we lose two additional degrees of freedom due to the fact that we must estimate the population mean and population standard deviation – they were not hypothesized.

The decision rule is:

If the test statistic > $\chi^2 = 7.8147$, reject the null hypothesis
Otherwise, do not reject the null hypothesis

Because $\chi^2 = 1.26 < 7.8147$, do not reject the null hypothesis.

This means that based on the sample data, there is no reason to conclude that the distribution of money spent per capita by visitors to Disney World is not normally distributed. The Disney managers can proceed with their confidence interval estimation using the t-distribution.

13.13

H_0: The arrival distribution is Poisson distributed

H_A: The arrival distribution is not Poisson distributed

The sample mean is 2.30. This will be used to determine the Poisson probabilities since no mean is specified in the null hypothesis.

x	Observed	Poisson	Expected
0	4	0.100259	3.007765
1	6	0.230595	6.91786
2	6	0.265185	7.955539
3	10	0.203308	6.099247
4	3	0.116902	3.507067
5	0	0.053775	1.613251
6	0	0.020614	0.618413
7	0	0.006773	0.203193
8	0	0.001947	0.058418
9	1	0.000498	0.014929
	30		30.00

We combine cells to make the expected cell frequencies 5 or greater.

x	observed	Poisson	expected	$(o-e)^2/e$
less than 2	10	0.3309	9.927	0.0005
2	6	0.2652	7.956	0.4809
3	10	0.2033	6.099	2.4951
greater than 3	4	0.2007	6.021	0.6784
				3.6549

The critical Chi-Square value with an $\alpha = .025$ and $k-1-1 = 2$ degrees of freedom is 7.3778, The calculated Chi-Square is 3.6549 which is less than 7.3778 so do not reject H_0 and thus conclude that the arrival distribution may be Poisson distributed. Note, one extra degree of freedom is lost since we had to estimate the mean from the sample data.

13.15

a. Using the steps outlined in the chapter:

Step 1: In this case, the null and alternative hypotheses are

H_0: Distribution of successes is binomial, with $n = 15$ and $\pi = 0.50$

H_A: Distribution is not binomial, with $n = 15$ and $\pi = 0.50$

Step 2: $\alpha = 0.05$

Step 3: Note that expected values of less than 5 required that the values less than 5 and those greater than 10, respectively, required that categories be combined.

Chi-Square Goodness-of-Fit Test for Observed Counts in Variable: FasTrak

Using category names in FasTrak11

Category	Observed	Historical Counts	Test Proportion	Expected	Contribution to Chi-Sq
<5	5	0.059235	0.059235	5.3311	0.02057
5	7	0.091644	0.091644	8.2480	0.18883
6	13	0.152740	0.152740	13.7466	0.04055
7	21	0.196381	0.196381	17.6742	0.62580
8	18	0.196381	0.196381	17.6742	0.00600
9	14	0.152740	0.152740	13.7466	0.00467
10	9	0.091644	0.091644	8.2480	0.06857
>10	3	0.059235	0.059235	5.3311	1.01934

N	DF	Chi-Sq	P-Value
90	7	1.97433	0.961

The calculated chi-square test statistic is $\chi^2 = 1.97433$.

Step 4: The degrees of freedom equals $k - 1 = 8 - 1 = 7$. The critical chi-square value found in Appendix G is 14.0671.

Step 5: Because the calculated value of 1.97433 is less than the critical value of 14.0671, we do not reject H_O.

Step 6: There is not sufficient evidence to conclude the distribution of the number of FasTrak users could not be described as a binomial distribution with $n = 15$ and a population proportion equal to 0.50

b. Step 1: π is the parameter of interest

Step 2: H_O: $\pi \leq 0.70$, H_A: $\pi > 0.70$

Step 3: $\alpha = 0.05$.

Step 4: From the data set in 90 days 1350 cars were observed. A total of 673 used the electronic payment system.

$$p = 673/1350 = .488$$

$$z = \frac{p - \pi}{\sqrt{\dfrac{\pi(1-\pi)}{n}}} = \frac{.499 - .7}{\sqrt{\dfrac{.7(.3)}{90}}} = \frac{-0.201}{0.0483} = -4.16$$

Step 5: Since $\alpha = 0.05$, the critical value is 1.645. Reject H_O if $z > 1.645$,

Step 6: Since $z = -4.16 < 1.645$, reject H_O.

Step 7: There is not sufficient evidence to conclude that the percent of tolls paid electronically has increased to more than 70% since March 2006

Section 13-2 Exercises

13.17

Step 1: Formulate the appropriate null and alternative hypotheses. The following null and alternative hypotheses are formed:
H_0: Age of the customer is independent of the payment method used.
H_A: Age of the customer and the payment method are not independent.

Step 2: Specify the significance level. The test will be conducted using $\alpha = 0.01$.

Step 3: Collect the sample data and compute the chi-square test statistic using Equation 13-2. The following contingency table shows the results of the sampling with a total column and total row added.

Payment Method	Age of Customer				
	20-30	31-40	41-50	Over 50	Total
In Person	8	12	11	13	44
By Mail	29	67	72	50	218
By Credit Card	26	19	5	7	57
By Funds Transfer	23	35	17	6	81
Total	86	133	105	76	400

The expected cell frequencies are determined by multiplying the row total by the column total and dividing by the overall sample size. For example, for the cell corresponding to In Person and 20-30 Age, we get:

$$\text{Expected} = \frac{86 \times 44}{400} = 9.46$$

The expected cell values for all cells are

Payment Method	Age of Customer			
	20-30	31-40	41-50	Over 50
In Person	9.46	14.63	11.55	8.36
By Mail	46.87	72.485	57.225	41.42
By Credit Card	12.255	18.9525	14.9625	10.83
By Funds Transfer	17.415	26.9325	21.2625	15.39

The test statistic is computed using Equation 13-2.

$$\chi^2 = \sum_{i=1}^{r} \sum_{j=1}^{c} \frac{(o_{ij} - e_{ij})^2}{e_{ij}} =$$

$$\frac{(8-9.46)^2}{9.46} + \frac{(12-14.63)^2}{14.63} + \frac{(11-11.55)^2}{11.55} + \frac{(13-8.36)^2}{8.36} + \frac{(29-46.87)^2}{46.87} + \frac{(67-72.485)^2}{72.485} + \frac{(72-57.225)^2}{57.225} + \frac{(50-41.42)^2}{41.42}$$

$$+ \frac{(26-12.255)^2}{12.255} + \frac{(19-18.9525)^2}{18.9525} + \frac{(5-14.9625)^2}{14.9625} + \frac{(7-10.83)^2}{10.83} + \frac{(23-17.415)^2}{17.415} + \frac{(35-26.9325)^2}{26.9325} + \frac{(17-21.2625)^2}{21.2625}$$

$$+ \frac{(6-15.39)^2}{15.39} = 50.3155$$

Step 4: Determine the critical value. The critical value for this test will be the chi-square value, with $(r-1)(c-1) = (4-1)*(4-1) = 9$ degrees of freedom with an $\alpha = 0.01$. From Appendix G, the critical value is $= 21.666$.

Step 5: Reach a decision. Because $\chi^2 = 50.3115 > 21.666$, reject the null hypothesis.

Step 6: Draw a conclusion. Based on the sample data conclude that age and type of payment are not independent.

13.19

Step 1: Formulate the appropriate null and alternative hypotheses. The following null and alternative hypotheses are formed:

H_0: Age of the individual is independent of the individual's preferred source for news.

H_A: Age of the individual and the individual's preferred source for news are not independent.

Step 2: Specify the significance level. The test will be conducted using $\alpha = 0.01$.

Step 3: Collect the sample data and compute the chi-square test statistic using Equation 13-2. The following contingency table shows the results of the sampling with a total column and total row added.

Age of Respondent

Preferred News Source	20-30	31-40	41-50	Over 50	Total
Newspaper	19	62	95	147	323
Radio/TV	27	125	168	88	408
Internet	104	113	37	15	269
	150	300	300	250	1000

The expected cell frequencies are determined by multiplying the row total by the column and dividing by the overall sample size. For example, for the cell corresponding to Newspaper and 20-30 Age, we get:

$$\text{Expected} = \frac{150 \, x \, 323}{1000} = 48.45$$

The expected cell values for all cells are

Age of Respondent

Preferred News Source	20-30	31-40	41-50	Over 50
Newspaper	48.45	96.9	96.9	80.75
Radio/TV	61.2	122.4	122.4	102
Internet	40.35	80.7	80.7	67.25

The test statistic is computed using Equation 13-2.

$$\chi^2 = \sum_{i=1}^{r} \sum_{j=1}^{c} \frac{\left(o_{ij} - e_{ij}\right)^2}{e_{ij}} =$$

$$\frac{(19-48.45)^2}{48.45} + \frac{(62-96.9)^2}{96.9} + \frac{(95-96.9)^2}{96.9} + \frac{(147-80.75)^2}{80.75} + \frac{(27-61.2)^2}{61.2} + \frac{(125-122.4)^2}{122.4}$$
$$+ \frac{(168-122.4)^2}{122.4} + \frac{(88-102)^2}{102} + \frac{(104-40.35)^2}{40.35} + \frac{(113-80.7)^2}{80.7} + \frac{(37-80.7)^2}{80.7} + \frac{(15-67.25)^2}{67.25} =$$
$$300.531$$

Step 4: Determine the critical value. The critical value for this test will be the chi-square value, with $(r-1)(c-1) = (4-1)*(3-1) = 6$ degrees of freedom with an $\alpha = 0.01$. From Appendix G, the critical value is $= 16.8119$.

Step 5: Reach a decision. Because $\chi2 = 300.531 > 16.8119$, reject the null hypothesis.

Step 6: Draw a conclusion. Based on the sample data conclude that age of the individual and the individual's preferred source for news are not independent.

13.21

The following steps can be used to test the required hypothesis.

Step 1: Specify the null and alternative hypothesis
H_0: The grade a student receives in the class is independent of the seat location in the class.
H_A: The grade received is not independent of seat location

Step 2: Determine the significance level
The hypothesis will be conducted using an alpha = 0.05 level.

Step 3: Collect the sample data and compute the chi-square test statistic.
We start by computing the expected cell frequencies using:

$$Expected = \frac{Row\ Total\ x\ Column\ Total}{Sample\ Size}$$

The contingency table with expected frequencies included is:

	A	B	C	D	F	Total
Front	18	55	30	3	0	106
	7.42	29.68	60.685	7.42	0.795	
Middle	7	42	95	11	1	156
	10.92	43.68	89.31	10.92	1.17	
Back	3	15	104	14	2	138
	9.66	38.64	79.005	9.66	1.035	
Total	28	112	229	28	3	400

We have some expected cell frequencies that are smaller than 5. Before collapsing categories, we will see if the null hypothesis is rejected. If not, then we need not worry about the small expected frequencies.

Then the test statistic is:

$$\chi^2 = \sum\sum \frac{(o-e)^2}{e} = 87.3$$

Step 4: Determine the critical value.
The critical value from the chi-square table with alpha = 0.05 and degrees of freedom equal to (r-1)(c-1) = (3-1)(5-1) = 8 is 15.507

Step 5: Reach a decision.

Because $\chi^2 = \sum\sum \frac{(o-e)^2}{e} = 87.3 > 15.507$ we would reject the null

hypothesis. Because we reject, we need to take care of the small expected frequencies. We will do this by combining the D and F grades with the revised contingency table as follows:

	A	B	C	D&F	Total
Front	18	55	30	3	106
	7.42	29.68	60.685	8.22	
Middle	7	42	95	12	156
	10.92	43.68	89.31	12.09	
Back	3	15	104	16	138
	9.66	38.64	79.005	10.7	
Total	28	112	229	31	

The revised test statistic is:

$$\chi^2 = \sum\sum \frac{(o-e)^2}{e} = 86.9$$

and the revised critical value now has (3-1)(4-1) = 6 degrees of freedom and is 12.5916. Therefore,

Because $\chi^2 = \sum\sum \frac{(o-e)^2}{e} = 86.9 > 12.5916$, we reject the null hypothesis.

Step 6: Draw a conclusion.
The instructor should conclude that course grade is related to seating location.

13.23

H_0: Account balance and model of washer purchased are independent.

H_A: Account balance and model of washer purchased are not independent.

$\alpha = 0.025$.

		Observed Frequencies				
		Washer Model Purchased				
		Standard	Deluxe	Superior	XLT	Total
Credit Balance	Under $200	10	16	40	5	71
	$200-800	8	12	24	15	59
	Over $800	16	12	16	30	74
	Total	34	40	80	50	204

		Expected Frequencies				
		Washer Model Purchased				
		Standard	Deluxe	Superior	XLT	Total
Credit Balance	Under $200	11.8333	13.9216	27.8431	17.4020	71
	$200-800	9.8333	11.5686	23.1373	14.4608	59
	Over $800	12.3333	14.5098	29.0196	18.1373	74
	Total	34	40	80	50	204

$$\chi^2 = \sum\sum \frac{(o-e)^2}{e} = \frac{(10-11.83)^2}{11.83} + \frac{(16-13.92)^2}{13.92} + \cdots + \frac{(30-18.13)^2}{18.13} = 30.2753$$

The p-value for a chi-square value of 30.2753 and 6 d.f. is 0.00003484. Since the p-value is less than $\alpha = 0.02$, we reject the null hypothesis and conclude that account balance and model of washer purchased are not independent.

13.25

a.

Step 1: Specify the null and alternative hypotheses.

H_0: The number of lettuce heads harvested for the two lettuce types is independent of the levels of sodium absorption ratios (SAR).

H_A: The number of lettuce heads harvested for the two lettuce types is not independent of the levels of sodium absorption ratios (SAR).

Step 2: Determine the significance level.
  $\alpha = 0.025$.

Step 3: Collect the sample data and compute the chi-square test statistic using Equation 13.2.

The following contingency table shows the results of the sampling

SAR	Salinas	Sniper	Total
3	104	109	213
5	160	163	323
7	142	146	288
10	133	156	289
Total	539	574	1113

The expected cell frequencies are determined by

$$e_{ij} = \frac{(\text{row total})(\text{column total})}{\text{grand total}}$$

As an example $e_{11} = \dfrac{213(539)}{1113} = 103.151$. The expected cell values for all cells are

SAR	Salinas	Sniper	Total
3	103.15	109.85	213
5	156.42	166.58	323
7	139.47	148.53	288
10	139.96	149.04	289
Total	539	574	1113

The test statistic is computed using Equation 13.2

$$\chi^2 = \sum\sum \frac{(o_{ij} - e_{ij})^2}{e_{ij}} = \frac{(104 - 103.15)^2}{103.151} + \ldots + \frac{(156 - 149.04)^2}{149.04} = 0.932$$

Step 4: Determine the critical value.
  The critical value for this test will be the chi-square value with $(r-1)(c-1) = (4-1)(2-1) = 3$ degrees of freedom with $\alpha = 0.025$. From Appendix G, the critical value is 9.3484. Since $\chi^2_{0.025} = 9.3484 > \chi^2 = 0.932$, then p-value > 0.025.

Step 5: Reach a decision.
  Because p-value > 0.025 = α, do not reject H_O.

Step 6: Draw a conclusion.

The number of lettuce heads harvested for the two lettuce types is independent of the levels of sodium absorption ratios (SAR).

b. Examine the average number of heads per SAR level for Salinas and Sniper:

$$\bar{x}_1 = \frac{\sum x_i}{n} = \frac{539}{4} = 134.75 \text{ and } \bar{x}_2 = \frac{\sum x_i}{n} = \frac{574}{4} = 143.50.$$

Since H_O was not rejected in part a. even thought a difference exists, it could be due to sampling error. A decision could be made for other reasons, like cost.

13.27

This hypothesis test can be conducted using the following steps:

Step 1: Specify the null and alternative hypothesis

H_0 : The plan to stay at the hotel again is independent of whether or not this is the first time the customer has stayed at the hotel.

H_A : The plan to stay again is not independent of whether the customer has stayed at the hotel before

Step 2: Determine the significance level

The hypothesis will be conducted using an alpha = 0.05 level.

Step 3: Collect the sample data and compute the chi-square test statistic.

We start by computing the expected cell frequencies using:

$$Expected = \frac{Row\ Total\ x\ Column\ Total}{Sample\ Size}$$

The contingency table with expected frequencies included is:

| | | First Stay? | | |
		Yes	No	Total
	Definitely Will	9	12	21
		14.90	6.10	
	Probably Will	18	2	20
Stay Again?		14.19	5.81	
	Maybe	15	3	18
		12.77	5.23	
	Probably Not	2	1	3
		2.13	0.87	
	Total	44	18	62

We have some expected cell frequencies that are smaller than 5. Before collapsing categories, we will see if the null hypothesis is rejected. If not, then we need not worry about the small expected frequencies.

Then the test statistic is:

$$\chi^2 = \sum\sum \frac{(o-e)^2}{e} = 12.9$$

Step 4: Determine the critical value.
The critical value from the chi-square table with alpha = 0.05 and degrees of freedom equal to (r-1)(c-1) = (4-1)(2-1) = 3 is 7.8147

Step 5: Make a decision.

Because $\chi^2 = \sum\sum \frac{(o-e)^2}{e} = 12.9 > 7.8147$ we would reject the null hypothesis.

Thus, we need to take care of the small expected frequencies. We will do this by combining the "Maybe" and the "Probably not" categories on the stay again variable with the revised contingency table as follows:

| | | First Stay? | | |
		Yes	No	Total
	Definitely Will	9	12	21
		14.90	6.10	
	Probably Will	18	2	20
Stay Again?		14.19	5.81	
	Maybe or	17	4	21
	Probably Not	14.90	6.10	
	Total	44	18	62

The revised test statistic is:

$$\chi^2 = \sum\sum \frac{(o-e)^2}{e} = 11.6$$

and the revised critical value now has (3-1)(2-1) = 2 degrees of freedom and is 5.9915. Therefore,

Because $\chi^2 = \sum\sum \frac{(o-e)^2}{e} = 11.6 > 5.9915$, we reject the null hypothesis.

Step 6: Draw a conclusion.
The company can conclude that whether someone is staying for the first time or not is not independent of plans to stay again. In general, people who have stayed before are more likely to say that they will stay again.

13.29

a. Minitab output:

Tabulated statistics: Severity, Emotions

```
Rows: Severity   Columns: Emotions

              Anger  Hostility  Irritability   All

A little        166        151           367   684
Extreme         110         55           113   278
Moderate        101         70           189   360
Quite a bit      81         55           131   267
All             458        331           800  1589

Cell Contents:      Count
```

b. Step 1: H_O: The type of emotion felt by patients just before they were injured is independent of the severity of that emotion, H_A: The type of emotion felt by patients just before they were injured is not independent of the severity of that emotion.

Step 2: $\alpha = 0.05$

Step 3: The expected cell frequencies are determined by

$e_{ij} = \dfrac{(\text{row total})(\text{column total})}{\text{grand total}}$. The results are obtained in the following Minitab output:

Tabulated statistics: Severity, Emotions

Rows: Severity   Columns: Emotions

	Anger	Hostility	Irritability	All
A little	166	151	367	684
	197.2	142.5	344.4	684.0
Extreme	110	55	113	278
	80.1	57.9	140.0	278.0
Moderate	101	70	189	360
	103.8	75.0	181.2	360.0
Quite a bit	81	55	131	267
	77.0	55.6	134.4	267.0
All	458	331	800	1589
	458.0	331.0	800.0	1589.0

Cell Contents: Count
                    Expected count

Pearson Chi-Square = 24.439, DF = 6, P-Value = 0.000

Step 4: The critical value for this test will be the chi-square value with $(r-1)(c-1)$ = $(4-1)(3-1) = 6$ degrees of freedom with $\alpha = 0.05$. From Appendix G, the critical value is 12.5916.

Step 5: Because $\chi^2 = 24.439 > 12.5916$, reject the null hypothesis.

Step 6: Conclude that there is sufficient evidence to conclude that the type of emotion felt by patients just before they were injured is not independent of the severity of that emotion.

13.31

H_0: Type of warranty problem and shift are independent.
H_A: The of warranty problem and shift are not independent

Expected Frequencies	Plant			
Type of Complaint	Day	Swing	Graveyard	Total
Corrosion	23.8636364	9.545454545	1.59090909	35
Cracked Lens	30.6818182	12.27272727	2.04545455	45
Wiring	15.6818182	6.272727273	1.04545455	23
Sound	4.77272727	1.909090909	0.31818182	7
Total	75	30	5	110

Since several of the expected frequencies are less than 5 we need to combine swing and graveyard and combine wiring and sound.

Observed Frequencies:	Shift		
Type of Complaint	Day	Swing and Graveyard	Total
Corrosion	23	12	35
Cracked Lens	32	13	45
Wiring & Sound	20	10	30
Total	75	35	110

Expected Frequencies:	Shift		
Type of Complaint	Day	Swing and Graveyard	Total
Corrosion	23.86364	11.13636364	35
Cracked Lens	30.68182	14.31818182	45
Wiring & Sound	20.45455	9.545454545	30
Total	75	35	110

Chi-Square Calculation	Shift	
Type of Complaint	Day	Swing and Graveyard
Corrosion	0.031255	0.066975881
Cracked Lens	0.056633	0.121356421
Wiring & Sound	0.010101	0.021645022

Chi-Square Critical	5.991476
Chi-Square Calculated	0.307967
p-value	0.857286

Since $0.307967 < 5.9915$ do not reject H_0 and conclude there is not sufficient evidence to conclude the type of warranty problem and shift are not independent.

End of Chapter Exercises

13.33

Student answers will vary depending upon the marketing research book selected and what is included in the book.

13.35

The hypothesis test procedure allows the researcher to conduct a one-tail test to determine if one proportion is larger than the other while the contingency analysis establishes independence/dependence (equal proportions/unequal proportions). The second advantage is that the test of proportions allows the test the difference between the two proportions to be something other than zero while the contingency analysis only tests the equality of the proportions.

13.37

H_0: The length is normally distributed with a mean of 3.05 and a standard deviation of 0.015.

H_A: The length is not normally distributed with a mean of 3.05 and a standard deviation of 0.015.

Length (inches)	Observed Frequency	Normal Distribution Probability	Expected Frequency	(O-E)2/E
Under 3.030	5	0.0912	9.1211282	1.862017
3.030 and under 3.035	16	0.0674	6.74439778	12.70183
3.035 and under 3.040	7	0.0938	9.38372076	0.60553
3.040 and under 3.050	20	0.2475	24.7507532	0.911878
3.050 and under 3.060	36	0.2475	24.7507533	5.112796
3.060 and under 3.065	8	0.0938	9.38372076	0.204043
Over 3.065	8	0.1587	15.865526	3.899429
				25.29752

Chi-Square Critical	16.811872
Chi-Square Calculated	25.29752
p-value	0.0003007

Since 25.2975 > 16.8118, reject H_0 and conclude that the length is not normally distributed with a mean of 3.05 and a standard deviation of 0.015.

13.39

a. Students will need to collapse rows to make the expected cell frequencies reach 5 or more.

Readmissions Last Year	Observed Frequency	Poisson Probability Distribution	Expected Frequency
0	139	0.3012	90.3583
1	87	0.3614	108.4299
2	48	0.2169	65.0579
3	14	0.0867	26.0232
4 or more	12	0.0338	10.1400

b. H_0: The distribution of patient readmissions is Poisson distributed with mean of 1.2

H_A: The distribution of patient readmission is not Poisson distributed with mean of 1.2

$\alpha = .05$

Readmissions Last Year	Observed Frequency	Poisson Probability Distribution	Expected Frequency	(O-E)2/E
0	139	0.3012	90.3583	26.18486
1	87	0.3614	108.4299	4.235375
2	48	0.2169	65.0579	4.47253
3	14	0.0867	26.0232	5.554927
4 or more	12	0.0338	10.1400	0.341183
				40.78888

Chi-Square Critical	9.4877
Chi-Square Calculated	40.7889

Since 40.7889 > 9.4877 reject H_0 and conclude that the distribution of patient readmission is not Poisson distributed with mean of 1.2

13.41

Step 1: H_O: the type of preferred outdoor activity is not dependent on the year,
H_A: the type of preferred outdoor activity is dependent on the year.

Step 2: $\alpha = 0.05$

Step 3: The observed data were

	Bicycling	Swimming	Baseball	Fishing	Touch football	Total
1995	68	60	29	25	16	198
2004	47	42	22	18	10	139
Total	115	102	51	43	26	337

The expected cell frequencies are determined by

$$e_{ij} = \frac{(\text{row total})(\text{column total})}{\text{grand total}}$$

As an example $e_{11} = \dfrac{198(115)}{337} = 67.5668$. The expected cell values for all cells
are

	Bicycling	Swimming	Baseball	Fishing	Touch football	Total
1995	67.5668	59.9288	29.9644	25.2641	15.2760	198
2004	47.4332	42.0712	21.0356	17.7359	10.7240	139
Total	115	102	51	43	26	337

The test statistic is computed using Equation 13.2

$$\chi^2 = \sum\sum \frac{(o_{ij} - e_{ij})^2}{e_{ij}} = \frac{(68 - 67.5668)^2}{67.5668} + \ldots + \frac{(10 - 10.7240)^2}{10.7240} = 0.172$$

Step 4: The critical value for this test will be the chi-square value with $(r-1)(c-1)$
$= (2-1)(5-1) = 4$ degrees of freedom with $\alpha = 0.05$. From Appendix G, we see that
$P(\chi^2 > 0.2070) = 0.995$. Therefore, p-value $= P(\chi^2 = 0.172) > 0.995 > \alpha = 0.05$.

Step 5: Because p-value > 0.995 > $\alpha = 0.05$, reject the null hypothesis.

Step 6: There is not sufficient evidence to conclude that the type of preferred outdoor activity is dependent on the year of this survey.

13.43

a. H_0: Blood pressure loss is normally distributed with $\mu = 10$ and $\sigma = 4$.
   H_A: Blood pressure loss is not normally distributed with $\mu = 10$ and $\sigma = 4$.

There is no one right way to break these data into classes to perform the goodness of fit test. Below is one possible method. If students use different groupings, they will get a different Chi-Square. However, they should reach the same conclusion with respect to the null hypothesis. This is a good place to discuss issues associated with defining classes.

Classes	Observed Frequency	Normal Distribution Probability	Expected Frequency	$(O-E)^2/E$
less than 4	1	0.0668	6.6807229	4.8304073
4 and under 8	9	0.2417	24.17303	9.523871827
8 and under 12	25	0.3829	38.292493	4.614230005
12 and under 16	32	0.2417	24.17303	2.534289635
16 and over	33	0.0668	6.6806942	103.6877063
				125.190505

The calculated $\chi 2$ value of 125.1905 is greater than the critical value of 9.4877 so reject Ho and conclude that blood pressure loss is not normally distributed with $\mu = 10$ and $\sigma = 4$.

b. H_0: $\sigma^2 = 16$
   H_A: $\sigma^2 \neq 16$
   s = 4.34

$\chi^2 = (100-1)(4.34)^2/16 = 116.55$

Use Excel's CHINV function to get χ^2 critical $= 117.4069$
Since $116.55 < 117.4069$ do not reject H_0 and conclude that the standard deviation could equal 4.0

c. Yes it is appropriate to construct a confidence interval for the mean since the confidence interval is based upon $\bar{x}$ and the standard deviation and we have established that the standard deviation could be equal to 4.

d. $13.839 \pm 2.575(4/\sqrt{100}\,)$; 12.81 ----- 14.87; no since the 99% confidence interval estimate for the true mean is between 12.81 and 14.87. This does not include the value of 10. Thus, an average diastolic loss of 10 mm does not seem reasonable.

13.45

a.   Minitab output:

Tabulated statistics: Invest, Race

```
Rows: Invest   Columns: Race

                AfricanAmerican  White     All

Don't Invest              175       90     265
                        132.5    132.5   265.0

Invest                    325      410     735
                        367.5    367.5   735.0

All                       500      500    1000
                        500.0    500.0  1000.0

Cell Contents:      Count
                    Expected count
```

b. Step 1: H_O: The proportion of African-Americans does not differ from the proportion of white Americans who invest in stocks in 2005.
H_A: The proportion of African-Americans differs from the proportion of white Americans who invest in stocks.

Step 2: $\alpha = 0.05$

Step 3: The expected cell frequencies are determined by

$$e_{ij} = \frac{(\text{row total})(\text{column total})}{\text{grand total}}$$. The results are obtained in the following Minitab output:

Tabulated statistics: Invest, Race

```
Rows: Invest    Columns: Race

                AfricanAmerican  White     All

Don't Invest                175     90     265
                          132.5  132.5   265.0

Invest                      325    410     735
                          367.5  367.5   735.0

All                         500    500    1000
                          500.0  500.0  1000.0


Cell Contents:      Count
                    Expected count


Pearson Chi-Square = 37.094, DF = 1, P-Value = 0.000
Likelihood Ratio Chi-Square = 37.604, DF = 1, P-Value = 0.000
```

Step 4: The critical value for this test will be the chi-square value with $(r-1)(c-1)$ = $(2-1)(2-1) = 1$ degrees of freedom with $\alpha = 0.05$. From Appendix G, the critical value is 3.8415.

Step 5: Because $\chi^2 = 37.094 > 3.8415$, reject the null hypothesis.

Step 6: Conclude there is sufficient evidence to conclude that the proportion of African-Americans differs from the proportion of white Americans who invest in stocks.

Chapter 14 Solutions

When applicable, selected problems in each section will be done following the appropriate step-by-step procedures outlined in the corresponding sections of the chapter. Other problems will provide key points and the answers to the questions, but all answers can be arrived at using the appropriate steps.

Section 14-1 Exercises

14.1

a. The scatter plot is shown below:

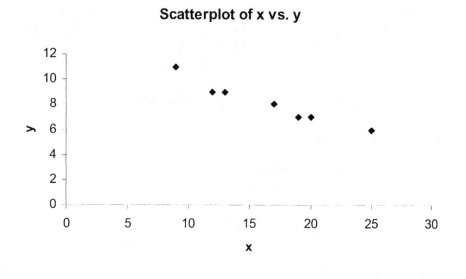

Scatterplot of x vs. y

From the scatter plot it appears that a negative linear relationship exists between the two variables x and y.

b. Using Equation 14-1, we get a correlation coefficient of

$$r = \frac{\sum (x-\bar{x})(y-\bar{y})}{\sqrt{\left[\sum (x-\bar{x})^2\right]\left[\sum (y-\bar{y})^2\right]}} = -0.9707$$

c.

Step 1: Specify the population value of interest.
We wish to determine whether there is a negative correlation between x and y.

Step 2: Formulate the appropriate null and alternative hypotheses.
Because we are interested in a negative relationship between x and y, the test will be one-tailed as follows:

Ho: $\rho \geq 0$
H_A: $\rho < 0$

Step 3: Specify the level of significance.
A significance level of 0.05 is given.

Step 4: Construct the rejection region and decision rule.
For an alpha level equal to 0.05, the one-tailed, lower-tail, critical value for n-2 = 8-2 = 6 degrees of freedom is t = -1.9432. The decision rule is
    If t < -1.9432, reject the null hypothesis;
    Otherwise, do not reject the null hypothesis.

Step 5: Compute the correlation coefficient and the test statistic.
From part (b), the correlation coefficient is -0.9707. Compute the test statistic using Equation 14-3

$$t = \frac{r}{\sqrt{\frac{1-r^2}{n-2}}} = \frac{-0.9707}{\sqrt{\frac{1-(-0.9707)^2}{8-2}}} = -9.895.$$

Step 6: Reach a decision.
Because t = -9.895 < -1.9432, reject the null hypothesis

Step 7: Draw a conclusion.
Because the null hypothesis is rejected, the sample data does support the hypothesis that there is a negative linear relationship between x and y.

14.3

The hypothesis test can be completed using the following steps:
Step 1: Specify the population value of interest.
    We are interested in the population correlation coefficient between units sold and marketing expenses.

Step 2: Formulate the appropriate null and alternative hypotheses:
$$H_0 : \rho \leq 0.0$$
$$H_A : \rho > 0.0$$

Step 3: Specify the level of significance.
The test is to be conducted using $\alpha = 0.05$

Step 4: Construct the rejection region and form the decision rule.
This is a one-tailed test in the upper tail of the t-distribution. The critical t for 15-2 = 13 degrees of freedom and $\alpha = 0.05$ is t = 1.7709.
The decision rule is:
If the test statistic t > 1.7709, reject the null hypothesis.
Otherwise do not reject

Step 5: Compute the correlation coefficient and the test statistic.
The correlation coefficient is r = 0.57. The test statistic is computed as follows:

$$t = \frac{r}{\sqrt{\dfrac{1-r^2}{n-2}}} = \frac{0.57}{\sqrt{\dfrac{1-0.57^2}{15-2}}} = 2.50$$

Step 6: Reach a decision.
Because t = 2.50 > 1.7709, reject the null hypothesis

Step 7: Draw a conclusion
There is sufficient evidence to conclude there is a positive linear relationship between sales units and marketing expense for companies in this industry.

14.5

a. Minitab output produces the following correlation coefficient:

Correlations: Xi, Yi

```
Pearson correlation of Xi and Yi = 0.206
P-Value = 0.569
```

b.
Step 1: Specify the population value of interest.
The parameter of interest is the population correlation coefficient.

Step 2: State the appropriate null and alternative hypothesis.
In this case, the null and alternative hypotheses are
H_O: $\rho = 0$
H_A: $\rho \neq 0$

Step 3: Specify the level of significance.
  The test will be conducted using $\alpha = 0.10$.

Step 4: Compute the correlation coefficient and the test statistic.
  Compute the sample correlation coefficient using Equation 14-1, 14-2, or software such as Excel or Minitab.
  The following sample data were obtained:

x_i	29	48	28	22	28	42	33	26	48	44
y_i	16	46	34	26	49	11	41	13	47	16

Using Equation 14-1, we obtain:

$$r = \frac{\Sigma(x - \bar{x})(y - \bar{y})}{\sqrt{[\Sigma(x - \bar{x})^2][\Sigma(y - \bar{y})^2]}} = 0.206$$

Compute the t test statistic using Equation 14-3

$$t = \frac{r}{\sqrt{\dfrac{1 - r^2}{n - 2}}} = \frac{0.206}{\sqrt{\dfrac{1 - 0.206^2}{10 - 2}}} = 0.59$$

Step 5: Construct the rejection region.
  For an alpha level equal to 0.10, the two-tailed, upper-tail, critical value for $n - 2 = 10 - 2 = 8$ degrees of freedom is $t = 1.8595$. The decision rule is

  If $t < -1.8595$ or $t > 1.8595$ reject H_O;
  Otherwise, do not reject the null hypothesis

Step 6: Reach a decision.
  Because $-1.8595 < t = 0.59 < 1.8595$, we do not reject H_O.

Step 7: Draw a conclusion.
  There is not sufficient evidence to conclude that there is a correlation between the two population variables.

14.7

a. There appears to be a fairly strong positive correlation between the standardized mathematics examination and the standardized English examination at this Seattle high school.

b.
Step 1: Specify the population value of interest.
We wish to determine whether there is a positive correlation between the standardized mathematics examination and the standardized English examination at this Seattle high school.

Step 2: Formulate the appropriate null and alternative hypotheses.
Because we are interested in a positive relationship between the standardized mathematics examination and the standardized English examination at this Seattle high school, the test will be one-tailed as follows:

$H_0: \rho \leq 0$
$H_A: \rho > 0$

Step 3: Specify the level of significance.
A significance level of 0.01 is given.

Step 4: Construct the rejection region and decision rule.
Using Excel and an alpha level equal to 0.01, the one-tailed, upper-tail, critical value for n-2 = 50-2 = 48 degrees of freedom is t = 2.4066. The decision rule is

If t > 2.4066, reject the null hypothesis;
Otherwise, do not reject the null hypothesis.

Step 5: Compute the correlation coefficient and the test statistic.
The correlation coefficient is 0.75. Compute the test statistic using Equation 14-3

$$t = \frac{r}{\sqrt{\dfrac{1-r^2}{n-2}}} = \frac{0.75}{\sqrt{\dfrac{1-(0.75)^2}{50-2}}} = 7.856$$

Step 6: Reach a decision.
Because t = 7.856 > 2.4066, reject the null hypothesis

Step 7: Draw a conclusion.
Because the null hypothesis is rejected, the sample data does support the hypothesis that there is a positive linear relationship between the standardized mathematics examination and the standardized English examination at this Seattle high school.

14.9

a. The dependent variable will be the variable for which the analysis are interested in explaining or predicting. That would be the average credit card balance. The independent variable is the variable that the analysts will use in an attempt to explain the variation in the dependent variable or to predict the value of the dependent variable. That would be the income variable.

b. The scatter plot for these two variables is:

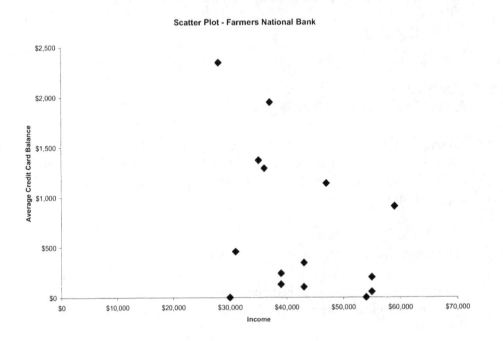

Based on this scatter plot there does not appear to be a strong relationship of any kind between income and credit card balance. If anything, the relationship is negative – as income rises, there is a tendency for credit card balances to be lower.

c. The correlation coefficient can be computed using the following equation:

$$r = \frac{\sum(x-\bar{x})(y-\bar{y})}{\sqrt{[\sum(x-\bar{x})^2][\sum(y-\bar{y})^2]}}$$

or we can use the algebraic equivalent equation:

$$r = \frac{n\sum xy - \sum x \sum y}{\sqrt{[n\sum(x^2)-(\sum x)^2][n\sum(y^2)-(\sum y)^2]}}$$

Using either of these two, we get r = -0.397

The hypothesis test can be completed using the following steps:
Step 1: Specify the population value of interest.
We are interested in the population correlation coefficient between income and credit card balance.

Step 2: Formulate the appropriate null and alternative hypotheses:
$$H_0 : \rho = 0.0$$
$$H_A : \rho \neq 0.0$$
This formulation reflects our interest in testing to determine whether there is a significant correlation. No direction is predicted so the test is two-tailed.

Step 3: Specify the level of significance.
The test is to be conducted using $\alpha = 0.05$

Step 4: Construct the rejection region and form the decision rule.
This is a two tailed test of the t-distribution. The critical t for 15-2 = 13 degrees of freedom and $\alpha = 0.05$ for a two-tailed test is t = ±2.1604. The decision rule is:

If the test statistic t > 2.1604, reject the null hypothesis.
If the test statistic t < - 2.1604, reject the null
Otherwise do not reject

Step 5: Compute the correlation coefficient and the test statistic.
The correlation coefficient is r = -0.397. The test statistic is computed as follows:

$$t = \frac{r}{\sqrt{\frac{1-r^2}{n-2}}} = \frac{-0.397}{\sqrt{\frac{1--0.397^2}{15-2}}} = -1.56$$

Step 6: Reach a decision.
Because t = -1.56 > -1.7709, do not reject the null hypothesis

Step 7: Draw a conclusion
Based on these sample data we have no basis for concluding that the population correlation is different from zero. This means that we can not state that there is a linear relationship between income and credit card balance.

14.11

   a. Minitab output:

Correlations: Network, Cable

Pearson correlation of Network and Cable = 0.979

   b. Using the steps outline in the chapter:

      Step 1: The parameter of interest is the population correlation coefficient.

      Step 2: $H_O: \rho \leq 0$, $H_A: \rho > 0$

      Step 3: $\alpha = 0.05$

      Step 4: r = 0.979, using Equation 14-3.

$$t = \frac{r}{\sqrt{\dfrac{1-r^2}{n-2}}} = \frac{0.979}{\sqrt{\dfrac{1-(0.979)^2}{4-2}}} = 6.791$$

      Step 5: The degrees of freedom with n -2 = 4 – 2 = 2 degrees of freedom, t = 2.9200. The decision rule is if $t > 2.9200$ reject H_O, otherwise, do not reject the null hypothesis.

      Step 6: Because $6.791 > t = 2.9200$, we reject H_O.

      Step 7: There is sufficient evidence to conclude that a positive correlation exists between the average non-program minutes in an hour of prime-time between network and cable television.

14.13

a. Either Excel or Minitab can be used to generate the scatter plot shown as follows:

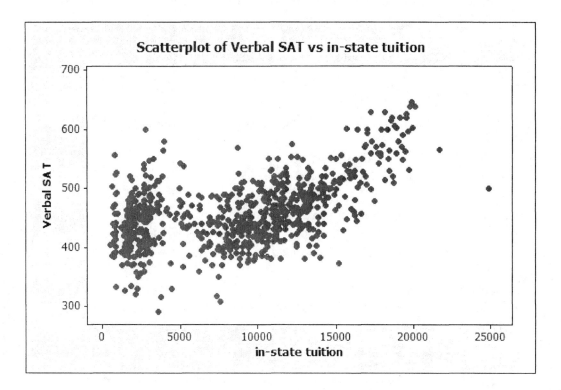

Based on this scatter plot it appears that there is a positive linear relationship between verbal SAT scores and in-state tuition. However, the relationship is far from a perfect one.

b. The sample correlation coefficient is computed using either Excel of Minitab giving the following:

	Verbal SAT
Verbal SAT	1
in-state tuition	0.510141

the sample correlation coefficient is 0.51.

c. The hypothesis test can be completed using the following steps:

Step 1: Specify the population value of interest.
We are interested in the population correlation coefficient between verbal SAT scores and In-State Tuition.

Step 2: Formulate the appropriate null and alternative hypotheses:
$$H_0 : \rho \leq 0.0$$
$$H_A : \rho > 0.0$$
We are predicting that there will be a positive linear relationship.

Step 3: Specify the level of significance.
The test is to be conducted using $\alpha = 0.05$

Step 4: Construct the rejection region and form the decision rule.
This is a one-tailed test in the upper tail of the t-distribution. The critical t for 718-2 = 716 degrees of freedom and $\alpha = 0.05$ is t = 1.647.

The decision rule is:
If the test statistic t > 1.647, reject the null hypothesis.
Otherwise do not reject

Step 5: Compute the correlation coefficient and the test statistic.
The correlation coefficient is r = 0.57. The test statistic is computed as follows:

$$t = \frac{r}{\sqrt{\dfrac{1-r^2}{n-2}}} = \frac{0.51}{\sqrt{\dfrac{1-0.51^2}{718-2}}} = 15.87$$

Step 6: Reach a decision.
Because t = 15.87 > 1.647, reject the null hypothesis

Step 7: Draw a conclusion
There is a positive linear relationship between verbal SAT scores and the price of in-state tuition at US Colleges and Universities.

14.15

  a. Minitab scatter plot:

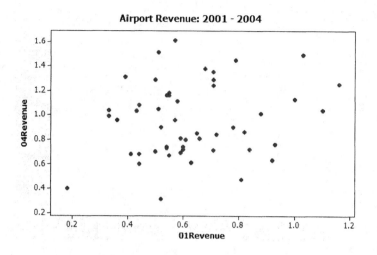

    It appears that as 2001 revenue increases there is an increase in the 2004 revenue which can be seen as the upward "tilt" of the scatter plot.

  b. Minitab output:

Scatterplot of 04Revenue vs 01Revenue

Correlations: 04Revenue, 01Revenue

Pearson correlation of 04Revenue and 01Revenue = 0.186

This correlation coefficient indicates there is a very weak positive linear relationship between per-person airport spending in 2004 versus 2001. Given this weak relationship, one could not project that the 2004 revenue would increase in response to an increase in 2001 revenue.

  c. Step 1: The parameter of interest is the population correlation coefficient

      Step 2: $H_O: \rho \leq 0$, $H_A: \rho > 0$

      Step 3: $\alpha = 0.05$

      Step 4: r = 0.186, using Equation 14-3.

$$t = \frac{r}{\sqrt{\dfrac{1-r^2}{n-2}}} = \frac{0.186}{\sqrt{\dfrac{1-(0.186)^2}{51-2}}} = 1.325$$

Step 5: The degrees of freedom with n -2 = 51 – 2 = 49 degrees of freedom, t = 1.67655 (from Minitab). The decision rule is if t > 1.67655 reject H_O, otherwise, do not reject the null hypothesis.

Step 6: Because 1.325 < t = 1.67655, we reject do not reject H_O.

Step 7: There is insufficient evidence to conclude that a positive correlation exists between the per-person spending in 2001 and that in 2004.

Section 14-2 Exercises

14.17

a. The following steps can be used to obtain the regression equation based on these sample data:

Step 1: Specify the independent and dependent variables.
The x and y variables are specified in the problem data labels.

Step 2: Compute the regression equation.
The least squares slope coefficient is manually computed using:

$$b_1 = \frac{\sum xy - \dfrac{\sum x \sum y}{n}}{\sum x^2 - \dfrac{(\sum x)^2}{n}}$$

The interim calculations are:

	X	y	xy	x^2	y^2
	10	120	1200	100	14400
	14	130	1820	196	16900
	16	170	2720	256	28900
	12	150	1800	144	22500
	20	200	4000	400	40000
	18	180	3240	324	32400
	16	190	3040	256	36100
	14	150	2100	196	22500
	16	160	2560	256	25600
	18	200	3600	324	40000
Sums=	154	1650	26080	2452	279300

Then we substitute into the equation as follows:

$$b_1 = \frac{\sum xy - \frac{\sum x \sum y}{n}}{\sum x^2 - \frac{(\sum x)^2}{n}} = \frac{26,080 - \frac{(154)(1,650)}{10}}{2,452 - \frac{154^2}{10}} = 8.33$$

The intercept is computed using:

$$b_0 = \bar{y} - b_1 \bar{x}$$

Then we get:

$$b_0 = \bar{y} - b_1 \bar{x} = \frac{1,650}{10} - (8.33)\frac{154}{10} = 36.7$$

The regression equation is:

$$\hat{y} = 36.7 + 8.33x$$

b. The sum of squared residuals is:

$$SSE = \sum (y - \hat{y})^2$$

We first determine the predicted values based on the regression equation by substituting the values of x into the equation. We then find the difference between each predicted value and the actual value and then square these differences:

x	y	xy	x^2	y^2	$\hat{y}$	$y - \hat{y}$	$(y - \hat{y})^2$
10	120	1200	100	14400	120	0	0
14	130	1820	196	16900	153.32	-23.32	543.8
16	170	2720	256	28900	169.98	0.02	0.0
12	150	1800	144	22500	136.66	13.34	178.0
20	200	4000	400	40000	203.3	-3.3	10.9
18	180	3240	324	32400	186.64	-6.64	44.1
16	190	3040	256	36100	169.98	20.02	400.8
14	150	2100	196	22500	153.32	-3.32	11.0
16	160	2560	256	25600	169.98	-9.98	99.6
18	200	3600	324	40000	186.64	13.36	178.5
154	1650	26080	2452	279300		0	1467

SSE = 1,467

The total sum of squares is calculated using:

$$SST = \sum (y - \bar{y})^2$$

The interim calculations are:

x	y	xy	x^2	y^2	$\hat{y}$	$y - \hat{y}$	$(y - \hat{y})^2$	$(y - \bar{y})^2$
10	120	1200	100	14400	120	0	0	2025
14	130	1820	196	16900	153.32	-23.32	543.8	1225
16	170	2720	256	28900	169.98	0.02	0.0	25
12	150	1800	144	22500	136.66	13.34	178.0	225
20	200	4000	400	40000	203.3	-3.3	10.9	1225
18	180	3240	324	32400	186.64	-6.64	44.1	225
16	190	3040	256	36100	169.98	20.02	400.8	625
14	150	2100	196	22500	153.32	-3.32	11.0	225
16	160	2560	256	25600	169.98	-9.98	99.6	25
18	200	3600	324	40000	186.64	13.36	178.5	1225
154	1650	26080	2452	279300		0	1467	7050

SST = 7,050

Then the coefficient of determination is computed using:

$$R^2 = \frac{SSR}{SST} = 1 - \frac{SSE}{SST} = 1 - \frac{1,467}{7,050} = 0.79$$

Thus, 79 percent of the variation in the y variable is explained by knowing the x variable.

c. The standard error of the estimate is computed using:

$$S_e = \sqrt{\frac{SSE}{n-2}} = \sqrt{\frac{1,467}{8}} = 13.54$$

d. The standard deviation of the regression slope is:

$$s_{b_1} = \frac{S_e}{\sqrt{\sum x^2 - \frac{(\sum x)^2}{n}}} = \frac{13.54}{\sqrt{2,452 - \frac{154^2}{10}}} = 1.51$$

e. The hypothesis test is conducted as follows:

$$H_0 : B_1 = 0.0$$
$$H_A : B_1 \neq 0.0$$

$$\alpha = 0.02$$

The test statistic is:

$$t = \frac{b_1 - B_1}{s_{b_1}} = \frac{8.33 - 0}{1.51} = 5.52$$

The t-value from the t-distribution with n -2 = 8 degrees of freedom is t = 2.8965 Because t = 5.52 > 2.8965, we reject the null hypothesis and conclude that the regression slope is significantly different than zero.

14.19

a. The slope of the regression equation is given by

$$b_1 = \frac{\Sigma(x - \bar{x})(y - \bar{y})}{\Sigma(x - \bar{x})^2} = \frac{-269.613}{547.66} = -0.4923 .$$

The y-intercept = b_0 = $\bar{y}$ - $b_1\bar{x}$ = 19.175 – (–0.4923)(15.55) = 26.830. So the regression equation is $\hat{y}$ = 26.830 – 0.4923x

b. When x = 10, $\hat{y}$ = 26.830 – 0.4923(10) = 21.907.

c. The slope of the equation indicates the change in the average value of y when the x variable increases by 1 unit. Therefore, what is being sought here is ten times the slope = 10(-0.4923) = - 4.923 (a decrease of 4.923 units).

d. The test is to determine if the regression slope is negative. This will be done using the steps outlined in the chapter.

Step 1: Define the independent (x) and dependent (y) variables.
    The independent variable is denoted as x and the dependent variable as y.

Step 2: Develop a scatter plot of y and x

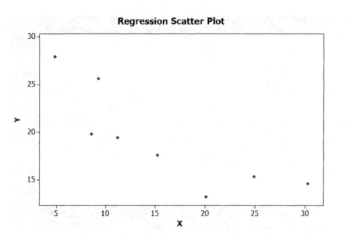

Step 3: Compute the correlation coefficient for the sample data

$$r = \frac{\Sigma(x - \bar{x})(y - \bar{y})}{\sqrt{[\Sigma(x - \bar{x})^2][\Sigma(y - \bar{y})^2]}} = \frac{-269.613}{\sqrt{547.66(191.975)}} = -0.8315$$

Step 4: Calculate the least squares regression line for the sample data and the simple coefficient of determination.
The slope of the regression equation is given by

$$b_1 = \frac{\Sigma(x - \bar{x})(y - \bar{y})}{\Sigma(x - \bar{x})^2} = \frac{-269.613}{547.66} = -0.4923.$$

The y-intercept $= b_0 = \bar{y} - b_1\bar{x} = 19.175 - (-0.4923)(15.55) = 26.830$.

So the regression equation is $\hat{y} = 26.830 - 0.4923x$

The coefficient of determination is

$$R^2 = r^2 = (-0.8315)^2 = 0.691$$

Step 5: Conduct a test to determine whether the regression model is statistically significant (or whether the population slope is < zero for this problem).

H_O: $\beta_1 \geq 0$, H_A: $\beta_1 < 0$; $\alpha = 0.025$, the test statistic is

$$t = \frac{b_1 - \beta_1}{S_{b_1}} = \frac{-0.4923 - 0}{0.1343} = -3.67,$$

the degrees of freedom = $n - 2 = 8 - 2 = 6$ and the critical value is $t_{0.025}$ = - 2.4469

Step 6: Reach a decision
The t test statistic of -3.67 is less than the t-critical value of -2.4469. Reject the null hypothesis.

Step 7: Draw a conclusion
There is sufficient evidence to conclude the regression slope coefficient is less than zero.

14.21

a. The scatter plot is shown below:

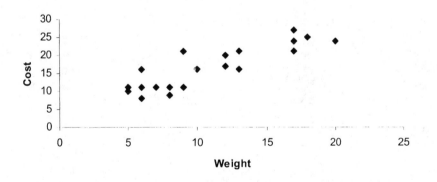

There appears to be a positive linear relationship between x and y.

b. Using equation 14-7,

$$b_1 = \frac{\sum xy - \frac{\sum x \sum y}{n}}{\sum x^2 - \frac{(\sum x)^2}{n}} = \frac{4{,}079 - \frac{(218)(330)}{20}}{2{,}814 - \frac{218^2}{20}} = 1.101$$

$$\bar{y} = \frac{\sum y}{n} = \frac{330}{20} = 16.5 \qquad \bar{x} = \frac{\sum x}{n} = \frac{218}{20} = 10.9$$

$$b_0 = \bar{y} - b_1 \bar{x} = 16.5 - (1.101)(10.9) = 4.50$$

$$\hat{y} = 4.5 + 1.101(x)$$

The b_0 value of 4.5 would be the cost if weight were 0; b_1 of 1.101 means that for every one unit increase in weight, cost will increase 1.101.

c. Conduct a test to determine whether the regression model is statistically significant (or whether the population correlation is equal to 0). The null and alternative hypotheses to test the correlation coefficient are:

Ho: $\rho = 0$
H_A: $\rho \neq 0$

Using Excel, the correlation coefficient is:

	Weight (x)	Cost (y)
Weight (x)	1	
Cost (y)	0.8763	1

The test statistic is

$$t = \frac{r}{\sqrt{\frac{1 - r^2}{n - 2}}} = \frac{0.8763}{\sqrt{\frac{1 - (0.8763)^2}{20 - 2}}} = 7.7171$$

The critical t for a significant level of 0.05 and 18 degrees of freedom = 2.1009. Because t = 7.7171 > 2.1009, reject H_o and conclude that the overall model is significant. We could also have conducted an F-test to determine whether ρ^2 is significantly different from zero, or a t-test to determine whether the slope coefficient is significantly different from zero. The three tests are equivalent in the simple linear regression model and only one needs to be conducted.

d. Using Excel, the results of the regression analysis are shown below:

SUMMARY
OUTPUT

Regression Statistics	
Multiple R	0.8763
R Square	0.7680
Adjusted R Square	0.7551
Standard Error	2.9846
Observations	20

The percentage of the total variation in shipment cost that can be explained by variation in the weight of the packages is equal to R^2, which is 0.7680. Therefore, approximately 77% of the total variation is explained by the independent variable. The R^2 value could also have been calculated from the ANOVA table (not shown but would be part of the computer output) by dividing the sum of squares for regression (SSR, the explained variation) by the total sum of squares (SST).

14.23

a. Using the steps outlined in the chapter:
Step 1: Define the independent (x) and dependent (y) variables.
The independent variable is the average public college tuition; the dependent variable is the average private college tuition.

Step 2: Develop a scatter plot of y and x

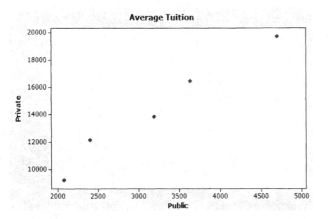

Step 3: Compute the correlation coefficient for the sample data
From Minitab:

Correlations: Private, Public

```
Pearson correlation of Private and Public = 0.985
```

Step 4: Calculate the least squares regression line for the sample data and the simple coefficient of determination.
Minitab output:

Regression Analysis: Private versus Public

```
The regression equation is
Private = 2109 + 3.80 Public


Predictor     Coef  SE Coef    T     P
Constant      2109     1303  1.62  0.204
Public      3.8048   0.3913  9.72  0.002


S = 814.684   R-Sq = 96.9%   R-Sq(adj) = 95.9%
```

The resulting regression equation is $\hat{y} = 2109 + 3.80x$. The coefficient of determination is 96.9%.

Step 5: Conduct a test to determine whether the regression model is statistically significant (or whether the population slope is equal to zero).

H_O: $\beta_1 = 0$,
H_A: $\beta_1 \neq 0$;

$\alpha = 0.10$,

The test statistic as given by Minitab in Step 4 is $t = 9.72$, the degrees of freedom $= n - 2 = 5 - 2 = 3$ and the critical value is 2.3534

Step 6: Reach a decision
The t test statistic of 9.72 is greater than the upper t-critical value of 2.3534.

Step 7: Draw a conclusion
The regression slope coefficient is not zero.

b. An increase of the average public college tuition of $1 would accompany and increase in the average private college tuition of $3.80 (which is the slope of the regression equation). Therefore, an increase in the average public college tuition of $100 would accompany and increase in the average private college tuition of $3.80(100) = $380.

c. This is just asking what the predicted y value will be when x equals 7500 = $\hat{y}$ = 2109 + 3.80(7500) = $30,609.

14.25

The completed regression output is shown as follows:

SUMMARY OUTPUT					
Regression Statistics					
Multiple R	0.198732547				
R Square	0.0395				
Adjusted R Square	0.007477779				
Standard Error	8693.34				
Observations	32				
ANOVA					
	df	SS	MS	F	Significance F
Regression	1	93224985.89	93224986	1.233558	0.275539149
Residual	30	2267222428	75574081		
Total	31	2360447414			
	Coefficients	Standard Error	t Stat	P-value	Lower 95%	Upper 95%
Intercept	63260.5323	3993.499925	15.84087	4.08E-16	55104.7258	71416.33881
Wins	511.7303371	460.7458564	1.110656	0.275539	-429.2372656	1452.69794

a. The R-square value for the regression model is 0.0395 which can be computed as follows:

$$R^2 = \frac{SSR}{SST} = \frac{93,223,985.89}{2,360,447,414} = 0.0395$$

So approximately 4% of the variation in average home attendance can be explained by knowing the number of games won.

b. The standard error or the estimate is computed as follows:

$$s_e = \sqrt{\frac{SSE}{n-2}} = \sqrt{\frac{2,267,222,428}{30}} = 8,693.34$$

The standard error is the measure of variation between the fitted regression values and the actual y values.

c. The hypothesis test is conducted as follows:

$$H_0 : \beta_1 = 0.0$$
$$H_0 : \beta_1 \neq 0.0$$

$$\alpha = 0.05$$

The test statistic is:

$$t = \frac{b_1 - \beta_1}{s_{b_1}} = \frac{511.73 - 0}{460.75} = 1.11$$

The critical value from the t-distribution for $\alpha = 0.05$ and 30 degrees of freedom is 2.0423. Because $t = 1.11 < 2.0423$, do not reject the null hypothesis. This means that the number of wins in the season does not explain a significant proportion of the variation in average home attendance.

d. After analyzing the regression model it is clear that using the number of wins in the season to predict average home attendance is not effective. The low R-square (0.0395) indicates just under 4 percent of the attendance variation is explained by the number of wins. The slope coefficient is insignificant. The staff at the NFL office should look for other variables to predict average attendance.

14.27

a. Minitab scatter plot

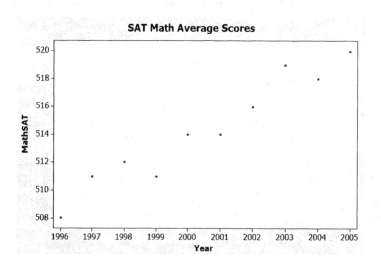

b. Minitab output:

Regression Analysis: MathSAT versus Years

```
The regression equation is
MathSAT = - 1995 + 1.25 Years


Predictor      Coef  SE Coef      T      P
Constant   -1995.4    223.7  -8.92  0.000
Years       1.2545   0.1118  11.22  0.000


S = 1.01578   R-Sq = 94.0%   R-Sq(adj) = 93.3%


Analysis of Variance

Source           DF       SS       MS       F      P
Regression        1   129.85   129.85  125.84  0.000
Residual Error    8     8.25     1.03
Total             9   138.10
```

Minitab produced the equation $\hat{y} = -1995 + 1.25x$

c. The research hypothesis to determine if the the College Board's assertion concerning the improvement in SAT average math test scores over the last 10 years is overly optimistic would be that the slope of the population regression equation is less than average SAT scores divided by 10 years ($14/10 = 1.4$). The test follows, using the steps outlined in the chapter:

1: The independent variable is the year the SAT test was taken; the dependent variable is the average SAT math score of all students taking the exam.

2: The scatter plot is in the solution to part a.

3: From Minitab:

Correlations: MathSAT, Years

```
Pearson correlation of MathSAT and Years = 0.970
```

4: The regression equation is $\hat{y} = -1995 + 1.2545x$ and the coefficient of determination was given in part b. as $R^2 = 94.0\%$

5: H_O: $\beta_1 \geq 1.4$, H_A: $\beta_1 < 1.4$; $\alpha = 0.05$, the test statistic is

$$t = \frac{b_1 - \beta_1}{S_{b_1}} = \frac{1.2545 - 1.4}{0.1118} = -1.301$$

the degrees of freedom = $n - 2 = 10 - 2 = 8$ and the critical value is $t_{0.05} = -1.8595$. (Note, the significance level was not specified in the problem, students may choose a different value, giving a different critical value.)

6: The t test statistic of -1.301 is greater than the t-critical value of -1.8595. Therefore, do not reject the null hypothesis.

7: There does not exist enough evidence to indicate that the Average Math SAT score increases less than 1.4 points per year over the last ten years.

14.29

a. Minitab provides the following regression equation:

$$\hat{y} = 145,000,000 + 1.3220x$$

b. Step 1: The independent variable is the gambling revenue of the Las Vegas Strip; the dependent variable is the gambling revenue for all of Clark County.

Step 2: The scatter plot is

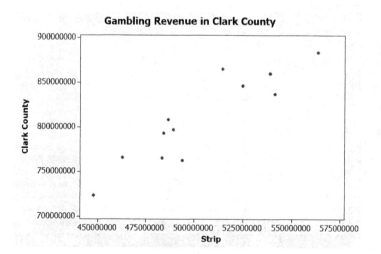

Step 3: From Minitab:

Correlations: Clark County, Strip

Pearson correlation of Clark County and Strip = 0.912

Step 4: Minitab output:

Regression Analysis: Clark County versus Strip

```
The regression equation is
Clark County = 1.45E+08 + 1.32 Strip


Predictor       Coef    SE Coef      T      P
Constant    144671002   94901882   1.52   0.158
Strip          1.3220     0.1884   7.02   0.000


S = 21438796   R-Sq = 83.1%   R-Sq(adj) = 81.4%


Analysis of Variance

Source           DF          SS          MS       F      P
Regression        1   2.26267E+16  2.26267E+16  49.23  0.000
Residual Error   10   4.59622E+15  4.59622E+14
Total            11   2.72230E+16
```

The regression equation is $\hat{y} = 145{,}000{,}000 + 1.3220x$ and the coefficient of determination is $R^2 = 83.1\%$

Step 5: $H_O: \beta_1 = 0,$
$H_A: \beta_1 \neq 0;$
$\alpha = 0.05,$
the test statistic is $t = \dfrac{b_1 - \beta_1}{S_{b_1}} = 7.02$

the degrees of freedom $= n - 2 = 12 - 2 = 10$ and the upper critical value is $t_{0.025} = 2.2281$. (Note, the significance level was not specified in the problem, students may choose a different value, giving a different critical value.)

Step 6: The t test statistic of 7.02 is greater than the t-critical value of 2.2281. Therefore, reject the null hypothesis.

Step 7: There does exist enough evidence to indicate that the Las Vegas Strip gambling revenue can be used to predict the gambling revenue for all of Clark County

c. Determining the increase gambling revenue that would accrue to all of Clark County if the gambling revenue on the Las Vegas Strip were to increase by a million dollars would require that we estimate $1,000,000 \hat{y} = 1000000(1.322) = \$1,322,000$.

Section 14-3 Exercises

14.31

The interval estimate for the slope coefficient is developed using:

$$b_1 \pm ts_{b_1}$$

For 90% confidence and n-1 = 73 degrees of freedom, the critical t is approximately equal to 1.67. Then:

$$0.0943 \pm 1.67(0.107)$$
$$0.0943 \pm 0.179$$

-0.0847   ---------------------------------   +0.2733

Thus, based on the sample data, with 90% confidence, a one unit increase in x will be associated with an average change in y of anywhere between -0.0847 and 0a +0.2733. The fact the interval contains zero means the true population regression slope may be zero. Thus, it is possible that there is no relationship between the two variables in this study.

14.33

a.

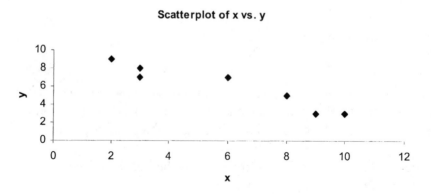

b. Using equation 14-7,

$$b_1 = \frac{\sum xy - \frac{\sum x \sum y}{n}}{\sum x^2 - \frac{(\sum x)^2}{n}} = \frac{202 - \frac{(41)(42)}{7}}{303 - \frac{41^2}{7}} = -0.7$$

$$\bar{y} = \frac{\sum y}{n} = \frac{42}{7} = 6 \qquad\qquad \bar{x} = \frac{\sum x}{n} = \frac{41}{7} = 5.857$$

$$b_0 = \bar{y} - b_1\bar{x} = 6 - (-0.7)(5.857) = 10.1$$

$$\hat{y} = 10.1 + (-0.7)(x)$$

c.

Step 1: Define the y (dependent) and x (independent) variables:
In this case the dependent variable is called y and the independent variable is called x.

Step 2: Obtain the sample data.
The sample data is given above for 7 observations.

Step 3: Compute the regression equation and standard error of the slope coefficient.
The regression equation was calculated in Part (b) and the slope coefficient is -0.7. The standard error of the slope coefficient can be calculated using equation 14-20 or by using Excel. Using Excel, the standard error of the slope coefficient is 0.1009.

Step 4: Construct and interpret the confidence interval estimate for the regression slope using Equation 14-22.
The confidence interval estimate is
$b_1 \pm t\, s_{b1}$
where the degrees of freedom for the critical t is $7 - 2 = 5$. The critical t for a 95% confidence interval estimate are 2.5706, and the interval estimate is
$-0.7 \pm 2.5706\,(0.1009)$
-0.7 ± 0.2594
-0.9594 -------------- -0.4406

So, for a one-unit increase in x, y will decrease by an average of between -0.9469 and -0.4531.

d. Using the equation determined in part (b) the point estimate of the predicted y for a given $x_p = 7$,

$$\hat{y} = 10.1 + (-0.7)(7) = 5.2$$

To determine the 95% prediction interval estimate for a particular y, given x_p, use Equation 14-24

$$\hat{y} \pm t s_e \sqrt{1 + \frac{1}{n} + \frac{(x_p - \bar{x})^2}{\sum(x - \bar{x})^2}}$$

Because this equation can be tedious to use, the results of the calculation using PhStat are shown below:

Confidence Interval Estimate

Data	
X Value	7
Confidence Level	95%

Intermediate Calculations	
Sample Size	7
Degrees of Freedom	5
t Value	2.570582
Sample Mean	5.857143
Sum of Squared Difference	62.85714
Standard Error of the Estimate	0.8
h Statistic	0.163636
Predicted Y (YHat)	5.2

For Average Y	
Interval Half Width	0.831881
Confidence Interval Lower Limit	4.368119
Confidence Interval Upper Limit	6.031881

For Individual Response Y	
Interval Half Width	2.21835
Prediction Interval Lower Limit	2.98165
Prediction Interval Upper Limit	7.41835

The prediction interval for an individual response is
2.98165 ------ 7.41835

14.35

The least square regression model can be developed manually or through the use of software such as Excel or Minitab. The resulting output based on these sample data is:

SUMMARY OUTPUT						
Regression Statistics						
Multiple R	0.706					
R Square	0.498					
Adjusted R Square	0.465					
Standard Error	15991.444					
Observations	17					
ANOVA						
	df	SS	MS	F	Significance F	
Regression	1	3810861239	3.81E+09	14.90	0.00154	
Residual	15	3835894055	2.56E+08			
Total	16	7646755294				
	Coefficients	Standard Error	t Stat	P-value	Lower 95%	Upper 95%
Intercept	58766.11	8193.92	7.17	3.22E-06	41301.2	76231.0
Weeks on the Market	943.58	244.43	3.86	0.001541	422.6	1464.6

The regression equation is:

$$\hat{y} = \$58,766.11 + \$943.58(x)$$

b. The hypothesis test is conducted as follows:

$$H_0 : \beta_1 = 0.0$$
$$H_0 : \beta_1 \neq 0.0$$

$$\alpha = 0.05$$

The test statistic is:

$$t = \frac{b_1 - \beta_1}{s_{b_1}} = \frac{943.58 - 0}{244.43} = 3.86$$

The critical value from the t-distribution for alpha = 0.05 and 15 degrees of freedom is 2.1315. Because t = 3.86 > 2.1315, reject the null hypothesis. This means that the number of days a condo is on the market is a significant variable in explaining the variation in the selling prices for condos in the Tempe, Arizona area.

c. A confidence interval estimate for the regression slope coefficient is computed using the following steps:

Step 1: Define the y (dependent) and x (independent) variables.
The y variable is the sales price and the x variable is the number of weeks the condo is on the market.

Step 2: Obtain the sample data.
The sample data were collected on 17 condos that have sold recently. Both selling price and number of weeks on the market was recorded for each condo.

Step 3: Compute the regression equation and standard error of the slope coefficient.
The regression model results are displayed in part a. The model is:

$$\hat{y} = \$58,766.11 + \$943.58$$

The standard error of the slope is:

$$s_{b_1} = \frac{s_e}{\sqrt{\sum(x-\bar{x})^2}} = 244.43$$

Step 4: Construct and interpret the confidence interval estimate for the regression slope.

$$b_1 \pm t s_{b_1}$$

For 95% confidence and n-1 = 15 degrees of freedom, the critical t = 2.1315. Then:

$$\$943.58 \pm 2.1315(\$244.43)$$
$$\$943.58 \pm \$521$$

$422.58 -------------------------------- $1,464.58

Thus, based on the sample data, with 95% confidence, for a one week increase in time that a condo is on the market the mean change in selling price is increased by somewhere between $422.58 and $1,464.58. Note, this interpretation is valid only for the relevant range of data in the study.

14.37

a. $b_1 = \dfrac{\Sigma(x - \bar{x})(y - \bar{y})}{\Sigma(x - \bar{x})^2} = \dfrac{156.4}{173.5} = 0.9014$.

The y-intercept $= b_0 = \bar{y} - b_1\bar{x} = 56.4 - (0.9014)(13.4) = 44.3207$.

So the regression equation is
$\hat{y} = 44.3207 + 0.9014x$

b. To determine if there is a linear relationship we must test the hypotheses:
$H_O: \beta_1 = 0, H_A: \beta_1 \neq 0, \alpha = 0.05$,

$$s_\varepsilon = \sqrt{\dfrac{SSE}{n - k - 1}} = \sqrt{\dfrac{40.621}{15 - 1 - 1}} = 1.7677 \, ,$$

$$s_{b_1} = \dfrac{s_\varepsilon}{\sqrt{\Sigma(x_i - \bar{x})^2}} = \dfrac{1.7677}{\sqrt{173.5}} = 0.1342$$

$$t = \dfrac{b_1 - \beta_1}{s_{b_1}} = \dfrac{0.9014 - 0}{0.1342} = 6.717 \, ,$$

the degrees of freedom $= n - 2 = 15 - 2 = 13$. Therefore, the p-value < 0.05 (6.717 is greater than any value for 13 degrees of freedom shown in the table) and the null hypothesis is rejected. There is sufficient evidence to indicate that there is a linear relationship between the dependent and independent variable.

c. This part is asking you to produce a confidence interval for the slope of the regression model.
Step 1: Define the y (dependent) and x (independent) variables:
Y is the dependent and x is the independent variable.

Step 2: Obtain the sample data.
The heading of the exercise specifies the summary statistics from the sample data.

Step 3: Compute the regression equation and the standard error of the slope coefficient.
The regression equation ($\hat{y} = 44.3207 + 0.9014x$) and the standard error (0.1342) were produced in part b.

Step 4: Construct and interpret the confidence interval estimate for the regression slope using Equation 14-22.
The degrees of freedom are n – 2 – 15 – 2 = 13. The critical value is then 1.7709. The confidence interval is calculated as $b_1 \pm t s_{b_1} = 0.9014 \pm 1.7709(0.1342) = (0.6637, 1.1391)$. At the 90% confidence level, the dependent variable will increase somewhere between 0.6637 and 1.1391 units for every unit the independent variable increases.

14.39

a. Minitab output:

Regression Analysis: Condo/Co-op versus Single Family

```
The regression equation is
Condo/Co-op = - 372 + 0.205 Single Family


Predictor           Coef  SE Coef      T      P
Constant          -371.9    243.1  -1.53  0.154
Single Family    0.20470  0.03968   5.16  0.000


S = 24.3061    R-Sq = 70.8%    R-Sq(adj) = 68.1%


Analysis of Variance

Source           DF     SS     MS      F      P
Regression        1  15726  15726  26.62  0.000
Residual Error   11   6499    591
Total            12  22225
```

b. Using the steps outlined in the chapter:
Step 1: The independent variable is the Single Family Sales; the dependent variable is the Condo/Co-op Sales.

Step 2: The scatter plot is

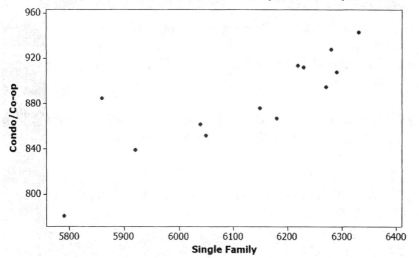

SINGLE FAMILY - CONDO/CO-OP SALES, April 2005 - April 2006

Step 3: From Minitab:

Correlations: Condo/Co-op, Single Family

Pearson correlation of Condo/Co-op and Single Family = 0.841

Step 4: Minitab output:

Regression Analysis: Condo/Co-op versus Single Family

```
The regression equation is
Condo/Co-op = - 372 + 0.205 Single Family

Predictor          Coef  SE Coef      T      P
Constant         -371.9    243.1  -1.53  0.154
Single Family   0.20470  0.03968   5.16  0.000

S = 24.3061   R-Sq = 70.8%   R-Sq(adj) = 68.1%

Analysis of Variance

Source           DF     SS     MS      F      P
Regression        1  15726  15726  26.62  0.000
Residual Error   11   6499    591
Total            12  22225
```

The regression equation is $\hat{y} = -372 + 0.205x$ and the coefficient of determination is $R^2 = 70.8\%$

Step 5: H_O: $\beta_1 \geq 0$, H_A: $\beta_1 < 0$; $\alpha = 0.05$.
The critical value for this lower tail test is -1.7959 and the decision rule is:

If the calculated $t < -1.7959$ reject H_0, otherwise do not reject.

Step 6: From the Minitab output, $t = 5.16$. Therefore, fail to reject the null hypothesis.

Step 7: There does not exist enough evidence to indicate that the Condo/CO-op sales will decrease as Single Family Sales increase.

c. Using the equation determined in part (b) the point estimate of the predicted y for a given $x_p = 6000$,

$$\hat{y} = -371.9 + .2047(6000) = 856.30$$

To determine the 95% prediction interval estimate for a particular y, given x_p, use Equation 14-24

$$\hat{y} \pm t s_e \sqrt{1 + \frac{1}{n} + \frac{(x_p - \bar{x})^2}{\sum(x - \bar{x})^2}}$$

Because this equation can be tedious to use, the results of the calculation using PhStat are shown below:

Confidence Interval Estimate

Data	
X Value	6000
Confidence Level	95%

Intermediate Calculations	
Sample Size	13
Degrees of Freedom	11
t Value	2.200986
Sample Mean	6123.846
Sum of Squared Difference	375307.7
Standard Error of the Estimate	24.30607
h Statistic	0.117791
Predicted Y (YHat)	856.341

For Average Y	
Interval Half Width	18.36061
Confidence Interval Lower Limit	837.9804
Confidence Interval Upper Limit	874.7016

For Individual Response Y	
Interval Half Width	56.56037
Prediction Interval Lower Limit	799.7807
Prediction Interval Upper Limit	912.9014

The prediction interval for an individual response is:
799.87 to 912.1

Chapter 14

14.41

    a.   Minitab scatter plot:

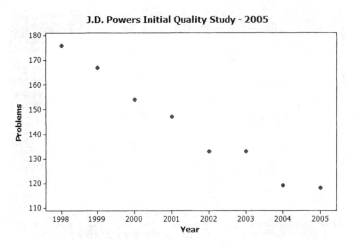

    b.   Minitab output:

Step 1: The independent variable is the year for the period 2000-2005; the dependent variable is the average number of reported problems per 100 vehicles over that same period.

Step 2: The scatter plot is in the solution to part a.

Step 3: From Minitab:

Correlations: Problems, Year

Pearson correlation of Problems and Year = -0.986

Step 4: Minitab output:

Regression Analysis: Problems versus Year

```
The regression equation is
Problems = 17371 - 8.61 Year


Predictor     Coef  SE Coef      T      P
Constant     17371     1199  14.49  0.000
Year       -8.6071   0.5989 -14.37  0.000


S = 3.88143   R-Sq = 97.2%   R-Sq(adj) = 96.7%


Analysis of Variance

Source         DF      SS      MS       F      P
Regression      1  3111.5  3111.5  206.53  0.000
Residual Error  6    90.4    15.1
Total           7  3201.9
```

The regression equation is $\hat{y} = 17371 - 8.61x$ and the coefficient of determination is $R^2 = 97.2\%$

Step 5: H_O: $\beta_1 \geq 0$, H_A: $\beta_1 < 0$; $\alpha = 0.01$, p-value is 0.000.

Step 6: The p-value = $0.000 < \alpha = 0.01$. Therefore, reject the null hypothesis.

Step 7: There does exist enough evidence to indicate that the average number of reported problems per 100 vehicles declines from year to year

c.   Minitab output:

```
Predicted Values for New Observations

New
Obs    Fit  SE Fit      95% CI           95% PI
  1  70.21    5.27  (57.31, 83.12)  (54.19, 86.23)XX

XX denotes a point that is an extreme outlier in the predictors.


Values of Predictors for New Observations

New
Obs  Year
  1  2010
```

The 95% prediction interval for the initial quality industry average of the number of reported problems per 100 vehicles for 2010 is (54.19, 86.23).

14.43
   a. Minitab scatter plot:

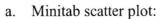

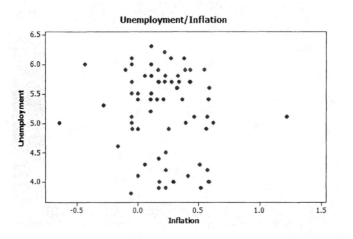

If anything, the relationship may be linear with a slightly negative slope.

   b. The maximum inflation rate is 1/223.

Confidence Interval Estimate

Data	
X Value	1.223
Confidence Level	95%

Intermediate Calculations	
Sample Size	72
Degrees of Freedom	70
t Value	1.994435
Sample Mean	0.220139
Sum of Squared Difference	5.401291
Standard Error of the Estimate	0.729999
h Statistic	0.200091
Predicted Y (YHat)	4.837578

For Average Y	
Interval Half Width	0.651262
Confidence Interval Lower Limit	4.186316
Confidence Interval Upper Limit	5.488839

For Individual Response Y	
Interval Half Width	1.594958
Prediction Interval Lower Limit	3.24262
Prediction Interval Upper Limit	6.432535

The prediction interval is (3.2426, 6.4325).

c.

Confidence Interval Estimate

Data	
X Value	0
Confidence Level	95%

Intermediate Calculations	
Sample Size	72
Degrees of Freedom	70
t Value	1.994435
Sample Mean	0.220139
Sum of Squared Difference	5.401291
Standard Error of the Estimate	0.729999
h Statistic	0.022861
Predicted Y (YHat)	5.252455

For Average Y	
Interval Half Width	0.220135
Confidence Interval Lower Limit	5.03232
Confidence Interval Upper Limit	5.472591

For Individual Response Y	
Interval Half Width	1.472484
Prediction Interval Lower Limit	3.779972
Prediction Interval Upper Limit	6.724939

The prediction interval is (3.78 to 6.5).

d. The equation for the prediction interval is $\hat{y} \pm t_{\alpha/2} s_e \sqrt{1 + \dfrac{1}{n} + \dfrac{(x_p - \bar{x})^2}{\sum(x - \bar{x})^2}}$.

Of this $t_{\alpha/2} s_e \sqrt{1 + \dfrac{1}{n} + \dfrac{(x_p - \bar{x})^2}{\sum(x - \bar{x})^2}}$ is the margin of error for the prediction

interval. The width of the prediction interval is calculated as

$$\hat{y} + t_{\alpha/2} s_e \sqrt{1 + \dfrac{1}{n} + \dfrac{(x_p - \bar{x})^2}{\sum(x - \bar{x})^2}} - \hat{y} - t_{\alpha/2} s_e \sqrt{1 + \dfrac{1}{n} + \dfrac{(x_p - \bar{x})^2}{\sum(x - \bar{x})^2}} =$$

$$2 t_{\alpha/2} s_e \sqrt{1 + \dfrac{1}{n} + \dfrac{(x_p - \bar{x})^2}{\sum(x - \bar{x})^2}} \text{ which is 2 times the margin of error.}$$

For this example the margin of error = $(6.7249 - 3.7800)/2 = 1.4724$ when x_p = 0. It equals $(6.4325 - 3.2426)/2 = 1.5950$ when $x_p = 1.223$. Thus, the former case has the larger margin of error. The difference between the margin of error for part b. and c. is the specific value of the term $\left(x_p - \bar{x}\right)^2$. The former prediction interval has the largest margin of error since its x_p (= 1.223) is further away from $\bar{x}$ (= 0.2201) than is the other x_p (= 0).

End of Chapter Exercises

14.45

No. The correlation coefficient measures the strength of the linear relationship between two variables. If we conclude that the population correlation coefficient may be zero, then we can say there is no linear relationship between the two variables. However, there may be a very clearly defined nonlinear relationship between the two variables that we have not quantified.

14.47

The correlation is a quantitative measure of the strength of the linear relationship between two variables. The correlation coefficient may range in value between – 1.00 and + 1.00. If the correlation coefficient equals –1.00, then the two variables are said to be perfectly negatively   correlated, with increases in one variable associated with uniform decreases in the other. If the correlation coefficient equals +1.00, then the two variables are said to be perfectly positively correlated, meaning that the two variables move in the same direction. The value of 0.45 would indicate a relatively weak positive correlation.

14.49

a. No you cannot assume this because correlation does not assume cause and effect. Two unconnected variables could be highly correlated.

b. On the basis of the correlation coefficient case you can still not assume cause and effect, although an increase in the common dividends may well cause an increase in the stock price. Stock prices are based on expected future value. Individuals will assume that if a company is raising their dividends they must expect future growth. Companies do not raise dividends in one year if they expect to have to decrease dividends in the next year.

14.51

The answer will vary depending on the article the students select. We have started considering not only how complete the analysis is, but also the quality of the article selected.

14.53

a.

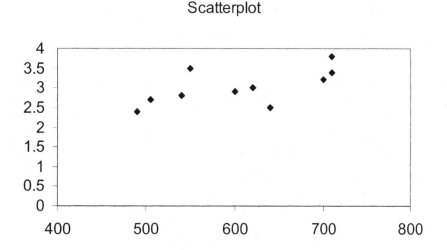

Scatterplot

There appears to be a weak positive linear relationship.

b. (1) r = 0.6239

(2) H_0: $\rho = 0$
H_A: $\rho \neq 0$
d.f. = 10-2 = 8

Decision Rule:
If t > 3.3554 or t < -3.3554, Reject H_0, otherwise do not reject H_0

$$t = 0.6239 / \sqrt{(1 - 0.6239)^2) / (10 - 2)} = 2.2581$$

Since 2.2580 < 3.3554 do not reject H_0 and conclude that there is not a correlation between SAT scores and final GPA.

c. (1). $\hat{y} = 0.9772 + 0.0034(x)$

(2). The y-intercept would indicate the average university GPA of all students who received an SAT score of 0. Such a situation seems highly unlikely. Therefore, the y-intercept has no interpretation in this case. The slope indicates that the average university GPA increases by 0.0034 for each increase of 1 unit in the SAT score.

14.55

a. Minitab output:

Regression Analysis: Private versus Public

```
The regression equation is
Private = 2109 + 3.80 Public


Predictor     Coef   SE Coef      T       P
Constant      2109      1303   1.62   0.204
Public      3.8048    0.3913   9.72   0.002


S = 814.684   R-Sq = 96.9%   R-Sq(adj) = 95.9%
```

The regression equation is $\hat{y} = 2109 + 3.80x$.

b. To determine if there is a linear tendency for the average college tuition for private colleges to increase when the average college tuition for public colleges increases we must test the hypotheses:

H_O: $\beta_1 \le 0$, H_A: $\beta_1 > 0$, $\alpha = 0.05$,

$$s_\varepsilon = \sqrt{\frac{SSE}{n-2}} = \sqrt{\frac{1991132}{5-2}} = 814.684,$$

$$s_{b_1} = \frac{s_\varepsilon}{\sqrt{\sum(x_i - \bar{x})^2}} = \frac{814.684}{\sqrt{4334702.734}} = 0.3913$$

$$t = \frac{b_1 - \beta_1}{s_{b_1}} = \frac{3.8048 - 0}{0.3913} = 9.72,$$ the degrees of freedom = n − 2 = 5 − 2 = 3.

Therefore, the p-value < 0.001 < 0.05 = α and the null hypothesis is rejected. There is sufficient evidence to indicate that there is a linear tendency for the average college tuition for private colleges to increase when the average college tuition for public colleges increases.

c. Minitab output:

```
Predicted Values for New Observations

New
Obs    Fit  SE Fit       95% CI           95% PI
  1  21133     794  (18605, 23660)  (17512, 24754)
```

The 95% confidence interval is ($18,605, $23,660).

d. Since the 95% confidence interval is ($18,605, $23,660), this suggests that the largest the average college tuition for private colleges would expect to be is $23,660. Since $25,000 is larger than $23,660, it does not seem to be a plausible value.

14.57

    a. Minitab scatter plot:

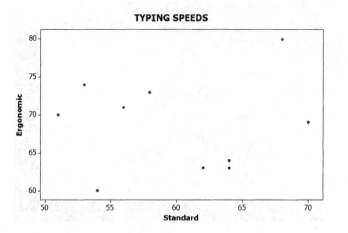

Examining the scatter plot there seems to be a random pattern in the relationship between the typing speed using the standard and ergonomic keyboards since an increase in the standard user's typing speed at times is associated with an increase in the ergonomic user's typing speed and at other times a decrease.

    b. Correlation coefficient produced by Minitab is

Correlations: Ergonomic, Standard

Pearson correlation of Ergonomic and Standard = 0.071

    c. Step 1: The parameter of interest is the population correlation coefficient.

Step 2: H_O: $\rho \leq 0$, H_A: $\rho > 0$

Step 3: $\alpha = 0.05$

Step 4: r = 0.071, using Equation 14-3.

$$t = \frac{r}{\sqrt{\dfrac{1-r^2}{n-2}}} = \frac{0.071}{\sqrt{\dfrac{1-(0.071)^2}{10-2}}} = 0.2013$$

Step 5: For $\alpha = 0.05$ with n -2 = 10 – 2 = 8 degrees of freedom, t = 1.8595. The decision rule is if $t > 1.8595$ reject H_O, otherwise, do not reject the null hypothesis.

Step 6: Because $0.2013 < t = 1.8595$, we fail to reject H_O.

Step 7: There is insufficient evidence to conclude that a positive correlation exists between administrative assistants using ergonomic and standard keyboards

14.59

a.

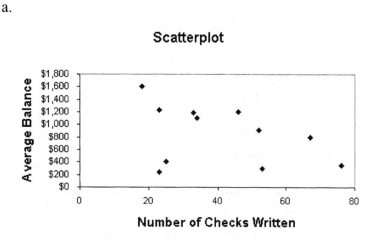

b.

SUMMARY OUTPUT

Regression Statistics	
Multiple R	0.378864769
R Square	0.143538513
Adjusted R Square	0.048376126
Standard Error	453.9233193
Observations	11

ANOVA

	df	SS	MS	F	Significance F
Regression	1	310790.7635	310791	1.5083534	0.250539111
Residual	9	1854417.418	206046		
Total	10	2165208.182			

	Coefficients	Standard Error	t Stat	P-value	Lower 90.0%	Upper 90.0%
Intercept	1219.803532	333.178933	3.66111	0.0052265	609.0486136	1830.558451
Checks Written	-9.119641901	7.425508984	-1.2282	0.2505391	-22.73144531	4.492161507

The regression model is $\hat{y} = 1219.8035 + (-9.1196)(x)$

c. To find the confidence interval for the change in the number of checks, we need to find the confidence interval for the slope coefficient and then multiply it by 25. The interval is found in the output.

Lower 90%: 25 x –22.7314 = -568.285; Upper 90%: 25 x 4.4922 = 112.305

d. H_0: $\beta_1 = 0$
    H_A: $\beta_1 \neq 0$

SUMMARY OUTPUT

Regression Statistics	
Multiple R	0.378864769
R Square	0.143538513
Adjusted R Square	0.048376126
Standard Error	453.9233193
Observations	11

ANOVA

	df	SS	MS	F
Regression	1	310790.7635	310790.8	1.508353
Residual	9	1854417.418	206046.4	
Total	10	2165208.182		

Decision Rule:
If F > 5.117 reject H_0, otherwise do not reject H_0.
Since 1.5 < 5.117 do not reject H_0 and conclude that the overall model is not significant so that an increase in the number of checks written by an individual cannot be used to predict the checking account balance of that individual.

14.61

a.

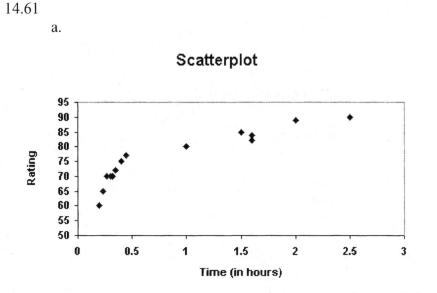

Scatterplot

There appears to be a possible positive linear relationship between time (in hours) and rating.

b.

SUMMARY OUTPUT

Regression Statistics	
Multiple R	0.915504887
R Square	0.838149199
Adjusted R Square	0.824661632
Standard Error	3.786842178
Observations	14

ANOVA

	df	SS	MS	F
Regression	1	891.1322016	891.1322	62.14236
Residual	12	172.0820842	14.34017	
Total	13	1063.214286		

	Coefficients	Standard Error	t Stat	P-value
Intercept	66.71114789	1.587951365	42.01083	2.15E-14
Time (x)	10.61666113	1.346772042	7.883042	4.37E-06

$\hat{y} = 66.7111 + 10.6167(x)$

Student reports will vary but they should include a test to determine if the model is significant. Since F=62.14236 students should conclude that the overall model is significant at the .10 level. They should also comment on what the R^2 is and what this means to the model.

Chapter 14

14.63
   a.   Minitab output:

Regression Analysis: 05JAVJ versus 05JMJ

```
The regression equation is
05JAVJ = 165537 + 0.525 05JMJ


Predictor    Coef   SE Coef     T      P
Constant    165537     36049   4.59   0.006
05JMJ       0.5246    0.1598   3.28   0.022


S = 4472.48   R-Sq = 68.3%   R-Sq(adj) = 62.0%


Analysis of Variance

Source          DF         SS          MS       F      P
Regression       1   215498715   215498715   10.77   0.022
Residual Error   5   100015570    20003114
Total            6   315514286
```

The regression equation is $\hat{y} = 165537 + 0.525x$

   b. Step 1: The independent variable is the average selling prices for houses during the period January to July of 2005.

Step 2: The scatter plot is

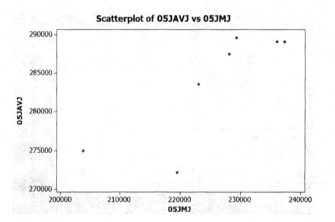

Step 3: From Minitab:

Correlations: 05JAVJ, 05JMJ

```
Pearson correlation of 05JAVJ and 05JMJ = 0.826
```

Step 4: The Minitab output is in part a.
The regression equation is $\hat{y} = 165537 + 0.525x$ and the coefficient of determination as $R^2 = 68.3\%$

Step 5: H_O: $\beta_1 = 0$,
H_A: $\beta_1 \neq 0$;
$\alpha = 0.05$,
the p-value $= 0.022$ with the degrees of freedom $= 7 - 2 = 5$.

Step 6: The p-value $= 0.022 < \alpha = 0.05$. Therefore, we reject the null hypothesis.

Step 7: There does exist enough evidence to indicate that the average selling prices during the period January to July of 2005 are linearly related to the median selling prices during that same period.

c.

Step 1: Define the y (dependent) and x (independent) variables.
The dependent variable is the average selling price of homes in the period 1995 to 2004, and the independent variable is the median selling price of homes in that same period.

Step 2: Obtain the sample data.
The experiment consists of average selling prices and corresponding median selling prices of home for a sample of 10 years.

Step 3: Compute the regression equation and the standard error of the estimate. Minitab output:

```
The regression equation is
95AVO4 = - 22194 + 1.35 95M04


Predictor      Coef  SE Coef        T      P
Constant     -22194     4839    -4.59  0.002
95M04       1.35049  0.02845    47.47  0.000


S = 2327.92   R-Sq = 99.6%   R-Sq(adj) = 99.6%


Analysis of Variance

Source           DF           SS           MS        F      P
Regression        1  12210351200  12210351200  2253.15  0.000
Residual Error    8     43353800      5419225
Total             9  12253705000

Predicted Values for New Observations

New
Obs    Fit  SE Fit       90% CI             90% PI
  1  241151    1061  (239177, 243125)   (236393, 245909)
```

The regression equation is $\hat{y} = -22194 + 1.35x$ and the estimate of the standard error of the estimate is 2327.92.

Step 4: Construct and interpret the confidence interval estimate of the average dependent variable for the given independent variable.
In step 3, the confidence interval was given as ($239177, $243,125). This indicates that, using a 90% confidence interval, the estimated average selling price during a year in which the median selling price for homes was $195,000 is somewhere between $239177 and $243,125.

14.65

a.

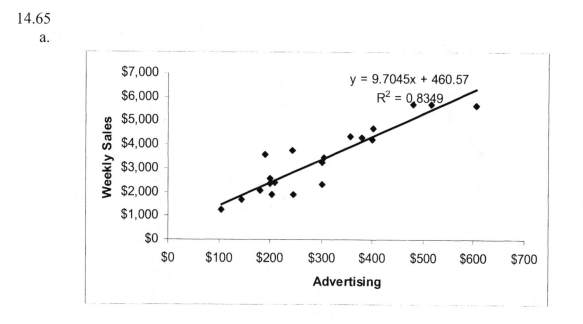

b. The 95% confidence interval for the increase in sales if found by finding the 95% confidence interval for the slope coefficient in the regression model and multiplying it by 50. The interval can be found in the shown output.

	Coefficients	Standard Error	t Stat	P-value	Lower 95%	Upper 95%
Intercept	460.567578	330.389599	1.394014	0.180285	-233.55575	1154.69091
Advertising	9.70447122	1.017240888	9.539993	1.83E-08	7.5673258	11.8416167

Lower 95%: 50 x 7.5673 = 378.365   Upper 95%: 50 x 11.8416 = 592.08
A $50 increase in advertising will result in an increase in sales of $378.365 to $592.08.

c. No it is not appropriate in this case. It is appropriate if the value 0 is in the range of x values in the sample.

d.

For Average Predicted Y (YHat)	
Interval Half Width	286.0036653
Confidence Interval Lower Limit	2115.458156
Confidence Interval Upper Limit	2687.465486

e. The conclusions and inferences made from a regression line are statistically valid only over the range of the data contained in the sample used to develop the regression line. The $100 is outside of the range of the sample.

Chapter 15 Solutions

When applicable, selected problems in each section will be done following the appropriate step-by-step procedures outlined in the corresponding sections of the chapter. Other problems will provide key points and the answers to the questions, but all answers can be arrived at using the appropriate steps.

Section 15-1 Exercises

15.1

    a. $b_1 = 4.14$. This implies that, holding x_2 constant and increasing x_1 by one unit, the average y is estimated to increase by 4.14 units. $b_2 = 8.72$. This implies that, holding x_1 constant and increasing x_2 by one unit, the average y is estimated to increase by 4.14 units.

    b. $\hat{y} = 12.67 + 4.14(4) + 8.72(9) = 107.71$

15.3

    a. $\hat{y} = 87.7897 - 0.9705x_1 + 0.0023x_2 - 8.7233x_3$

    b. $F = 5.3276 > F_{0.05} = 3.0725$ (Using Excel's FINV) Also, p-value $= .00689 <$ any reasonable alpha. . Therefore, reject H_0: $\beta_1 = \beta_2 = \beta_3 = 0$. At least some part of the model is statistically significant.

    c. $R^2 = \dfrac{SSR}{SST} = \dfrac{16646.09124}{38517.76} = 0.432167$

    d. X_1 (p-value $= 0.1126 > \alpha = 0.05$ ➔ fail to reject H_0: $\beta_1 = 0$) and x_3 (p-value $= 0.2576 > \alpha = 0.05$ ➔ fail to reject H_0: $\beta_3 = 0$) are not significant.

    e. $b_2 = 0.0023$ ➔ $\hat{y}$ increases 0.0023 for each one unit increase of x_2.
        $b_3 = -8.7233$ ➔ $\hat{y}$ decreases 8.7233 for each one unit increase of x_3.

    f. The confidence intervals for β_1 and β_3 contain 0, This indicates that x_1 and x_3 are not statistically significantly different than 0 in this model.

15.5

a. Minitab output:

Regression Analysis: yi versus x1, x2

The regression equation is
yi = 5.05 - 0.051 x1 + 0.888 x2

Predictor	Coef	SE Coef	T	P	VIF
Constant	5.045	8.698	0.58	0.580	
x1	-0.0513	0.2413	-0.21	0.838	1.1
x2	0.8880	0.1475	6.02	0.001	1.1

S = 6.82197   R-Sq = 84.5%   R-Sq(adj) = 80.1%

Analysis of Variance

Source	DF	SS	MS	F	P
Regression	2	1775.12	887.56	19.07	0.001
Residual Error	7	325.78	46.54		
Total	9	2100.90			

The estimated regression equation is $\hat{y} = 5.05 - 0.0513x_1 + 0.888x_2$

b. Minitab output:

Correlations: yi, x1, x2

	yi	x1
x1	0.206	
x2	0.919	0.257

Cell Contents: Pearson correlation

Using the steps from Chapter 14:
Step 1: Define the parameter of interest.
   The parameter of interest is the population correlation coefficient between y and x_1, ρ;

Step 2: Formulate the appropriate null and alternative hypotheses.
   $H_O: \rho = 0$ $H_A: \rho \neq 0$

Step 3: Specify the level of significance.
   $\alpha = 0.05$

Step 4: Compute the test statistic.

$$t = \frac{r}{\sqrt{\dfrac{1-r^2}{n-2}}} = \frac{0.206}{\sqrt{\dfrac{1-0.206^2}{10-2}}} = 0.5954$$

Step 5: Construct the rejection region.

The degrees of freedom are n – 2 = 8; the critical values are ± 2.306.

Step 6: Reach a decision.

Since -2.306 < t = 0.5954 < 2.306; we fail to reject H_O.

Step 7: Draw a conclusion.

The correlation with the dependent variable is not significant.

c. Step 1: The parameters of interest are the population coefficients of x_1 and x_2,

Step 2: H_O: $\beta_1 = \beta_2 = 0$, H_A: at least one $\beta_i \neq 0$

Step 3: $\alpha = 0.05$

$$\text{Step 4: } F = \frac{\dfrac{SSR}{k}}{\dfrac{SSE}{n-k-1}} = \frac{\dfrac{1775.12}{2}}{\dfrac{325.78}{10-2-1}} = 19.07$$

Step 5: The numerator degrees of freedom are k = 2 and the denominator degrees of freedom are n – k – 1 = 10 – 2 – 1 = 7; the critical value = 4.737.

Step 6: Since F = 19.07 > 4.737, reject H_O.;

Step 7: The overall model is significant.

d. Minitab output:

Predictor	Coef	SE Coef	T	P	VIF
Constant	5.045	8.698	0.58	0.580	
x1	-0.0513	0.2413	-0.21	0.838	1.1
x2	0.8880	0.1475	6.02	0.001	1.1

S = 6.82197 R-Sq = 84.5% R-Sq(adj) = 80.1%

A VIF < 5 for a given independent variable indicates that this independent variable is not correlated with the remaining independent variables in the model. Both x_1 and x_2 have VIFs equal to 1.1. Therefore, neither of the independent variable is correlated with the other independent variable. Multicollinearity does not exist between the two independent variables.

15.7

a. Minitab output:

Correlations: Sales, Sales Increa, Return on Ca, Market Value, Stock Price

	Sales	Sales Increa	Return on Ca	Market Value
Sales Increa	0.157			
Return on Ca	-0.037	-0.122		
Market Value	0.910	0.158	0.028	
Stock Price	0.397	0.018	-0.087	0.430

b. Minitab output:

Regression Analysis: Stock Price versus Sales, Market Value

The regression equation is
Stock Price = 32.1 + 0.0037 Sales + 0.00587 Market Value

Predictor	Coef	SE Coef	T	P
Constant	32.11	10.80	2.97	0.009
Sales	0.00374	0.06498	0.06	0.955
Market Value	0.005873	0.007692	0.76	0.456

S = 27.7683 R-Sq = 18.5% R-Sq(adj) = 8.9%

Analysis of Variance

Source	DF	SS	MS	F	P
Regression	2	2981.8	1490.9	1.93	0.175
Residual Error	17	13108.4	771.1		
Total	19	16090.2			

The estimated regression equation is $\hat{y} = 32.1 + 0.0037x_1 + 0.00587x_2$

c. Using the steps from chapter 14:
Step 1: Define the parameter of interest.
The parameters of interest are the population coefficients of x_1 and x_2.

Step 2: Formulate the appropriate null and alternative hypotheses.
H_O: $\beta_1 = \beta_2 = 0$,
H_A: at least one $\beta_i \neq 0$

Step 3: Specify the level of significance.
$\alpha = 0.10$

Step 4: Compute the test statistic.
The test statistic provided by Minitab is $F = 1.93$

Step 5: Construct the rejection region.
The numerator degrees of freedom are $k = 2$ and the denominator degrees of freedom are $n - k - 1 = 20 - 2 - 1 = 17$; the critical value provide by Minitab is 2.64464.

Step 6: Reach a decision.
Since $F = 1.93 < 2.64464$, fail to reject H_O.

Step 7: Draw a conclusion.
The overall model is not significant.

d. The coefficient of determination equals 18.5% and the adjusted coefficient of determination equals 8.9%. This is a difference of 9.6% which is substantial. This suggests that at least one of the variables might be removed.

e. Minitab output:

Regression Analysis: Stock Price versus Market Value

```
The regression equation is
Stock Price = 32.5 + 0.00628 Market Value


Predictor         Coef    SE Coef      T      P
Constant        32.517      7.859   4.14   0.001
Market Value  0.006276   0.003103   2.02   0.058


S = 26.9886    R-Sq = 18.5%    R-Sq(adj) = 14.0%


Analysis of Variance

Source            DF        SS       MS      F      P
Regression         1    2979.3   2979.3   4.09   0.058
Residual Error    18   13110.9    728.4
Total             19   16090.2
```

Step 1: The parameter of interest is the population coefficient of x_1

Step 2: H_O: $\beta_1 = 0$, H_A: $\beta_1 \neq 0$

Step 3: $\alpha = 0.10$

Step 4: The p-value is 0.058

Step 5: If the p-value is less than α, reject the null hypothesis; otherwise fail to reject the null hypothesis.

Step 6: Since the p-value = $0.058 < 0.10$, reject H_O.

Step 7: There is sufficient evidence to conclude that the market value is a significant predictor of the stock price.

15.9

a. Minitab output:

Regression Analysis: Market Value versus 52WK HI, P- E

```
The regression equation is
Market Value = - 977 + 11.2 52WK HI + 118 P- E


Predictor      Coef    SE Coef        T        P    VIF
Constant     -977.1      664.0    -1.47    0.159
52WK HI       11.20      12.57     0.89    0.385    1.0
P- E         117.72      13.27     8.87    0.000    1.0


S = 933.549    R-Sq = 82.4%    R-Sq(adj) = 80.3%


Analysis of Variance

Source           DF          SS          MS        F        P
Regression        2    69367140    34683570    39.80    0.000
Residual Error   17    14815723      871513
Total            19    84182863
```

The estimated regression equation is $\hat{y} = -977.1 + 11.252$WK HI $+ 117.72$P-E

b. Step 1: The parameters of interest are the population coefficients of x_1 and x_2,

Step 2: H_O: $\beta_1 = \beta_2 = 0$, H_A: at least one $\beta_i \neq 0$

Step 3: $\alpha = 0.05$

Step 4: The test statistic provided by Minitab is $F = 39.36$

Step 5: The numerator degrees of freedom are $k = 2$ and the denominator degrees of freedom are $n - k - 1 = 20 - 2 - 1 = 17$; the critical value is 3.592.,

Step 6: Since $F = 39.80 > 3.592$, we reject H_O

Step 7: The overall model is significant.

c. Minitab output:

```
Predicted Values for New Observations

New
Obs    Fit   SE Fit      95% CI         95% PI
 1    1607      268   (1041, 2173)  (-443, 3656)


Values of Predictors for New Observations

New
Obs   52WK HI   P- E
 1      31.0    19.0
```

The estimated market value is $\hat{y} = 1607$

15.11

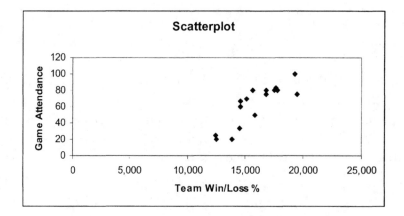

There appears to be a positive linear relationship between team win/loss percentage and game attendance.

Scatterplot

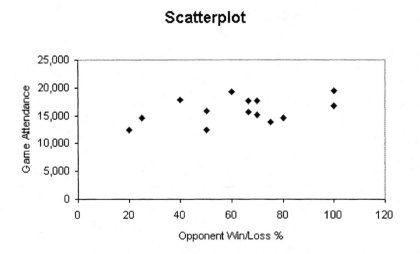

There appears to be a positive linear relationship between opponent win/loss percentage and game attendance.

Scatterplot

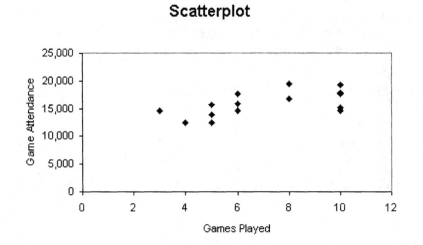

There appears to be a positive linear relationship between games played and game attendance.

Scatterplot

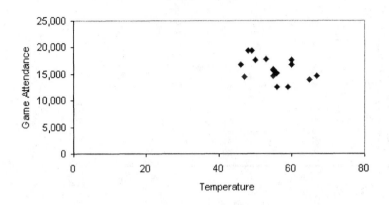

There does not appear to be any relationship between temperature and game attendance.

b.

	Game Attendance	Team Win/Loss %	Opponent Win/Loss %	Games Played	Temperature
Game Attendance	1				
Team Win/Loss %	0.848748849	1			
Opponent Win/Loss %	0.414250332	0.286749997	1		
Games Played	0.599214835	0.577958172	0.403593506	1	
Temperature	-0.476186226	-0.330096097	-0.446949168	-0.550083219	1

No alpha level was specified. Students will select their own. We have selected .05.

Critical t = ± 2.1448

t for game attendance and team win/loss % = $0.8487/\sqrt{(1-0.8487^2)/(16-2)} = 6.0043$

t for game attendance and opponent win/loss % = $0.4143/\sqrt{(1-0.4143^2)/(16-2)} = 1.7032$

t for game attendance and games played = $0.5992/\sqrt{(1-0.5992^2)/(16-2)} = 2.8004$

t for game attendance and temperature = $-0.4762/\sqrt{(1-(-0.4762)^2)/(16-2)} = -2.0263$

There is a significant relationship between game attendance and team win/loss % and games played. Therefore a multiple regression model could be effective.

c. Multiple regression equation using x_1, x_2, x_3, x_4 as independent variables to predict y

Regression Analysis

Regression Statistics	
Multiple R	0.880534596
R Square	0.775341175
Adjusted R Square	0.693647057
Standard Error	1184.124723
Observations	16

ANOVA

	df	SS	MS	F	Significance F
Regression	4	53230058.97	13307514.74	9.490783318	0.001427993
Residual	11	15423664.97	1402151.361		
Total	15	68653723.94			

	Coefficients	Standard Error	t Stat	P-value	Lower 95%
Intercept	14122.24086	4335.791765	3.257130790	0.0076378234	4579.222699
Team Win/Loss %	63.15325348	14.93880137	4.227464568	0.0014184533	30.27315672
Opponent Win/Loss %	10.09582009	14.31396102	0.705312811	0.495280282	-1.40901163
Games Played	31.50621796	177.1297820	0.177870811	0.862057676	-358.3540008
Temperature	-55.4609057	62.09372861	-0.893180470	0.390882768	-192.12835

d. $R^2 = 0.7753$ so 77.53% is explained.

e. $H_0: \beta_1 = \beta_2 = \beta_3 = \beta_4 = 0$
   H_A: at least one β_i does not equal 0

   Decision Rule:
   If p-value $< \alpha$, , reject H_o, otherwise do not reject H_o
   Since p-value (Significance F) = .00143 reject H_o and conclude that the overall model is significant.

f. For team win/loss % the p-value = 0.0014 < 0.08 so this variable is significant
   For opponent win/loss % the p-value = 0.4953 > 0.08 so this variable is not significant
   For games played the p-value = 0.8621 > 0.08 so this variable is not significant
   For temperature the p-value = 0.3909 > 0.08 so this variable is not significant

g. The standard error of the estimate is 1184.1274. Practical significance is a decision made based on whether an interval of $\pm 2(1184.1274)$ is small enough to add value to the value being estimated. .

h. Multicollinearity is present when the independent variables are correlated with one another.   This is indicated if the VIF for pairs of variables is greater than 5. The VIF for the variables in this problem are:

	VIF
Team Win/Loss Percentage and all other X	1.569962033
Temperature and all other X	1.963520336
Games Played and all other X	1.31428258
Opponent Win/Loss Percentage and all other X	1.50934547

The low VIF values indicate multicollinearity is not a problem since no VIF is greater than 5.

i.

	Coefficients	Standard Error	t Stat	P-value	Lower 95%	Upper 95%
Intercept	14122.24086	4335.791765	3.25713079	0.007637823	4579.222699	23665.25902
Team Win/Loss %	63.15325348	14.93880137	4.227464568	0.001418453	30.27315672	96.03335024
Opponent Win/Loss %	10.09582009	14.31396102	0.705312811	0.49528028	-21.40901163	41.6006518
Games Played	31.50621796	177.129782	0.177870811	0.862057676	-358.3540008	421.3664367
Temperature	-55.4609057	62.09372861	-0.89318047	0.390882768	-192.12835	81.20653863

Because the confidence intervals for Opponent win/loss %, games played, and temperature all include the value 0 it is indicating the same thing as the t-tests in that these variables are not significantly different from 0. The interpretation of the intercept would not be relevant since none of the predictor variables is likely to be zero.

Section 15-2 Exercises

15.13

a. The number of dummy variables = number of levels $-1 = 4 - 1 = 3$.

b. $y = \beta_0 + \beta_1 x_1 + \beta_2 x_2 + \beta_3 x_3 + \beta_4 x_4 + \varepsilon$; $x_1 = \{1$ for level 1, 0 otherwise$\}$, $x_2 = \{1$ for level 2, 0 otherwise$\}$, $x_3 = \{1$ for level 3, 0 otherwise$\}$

c. $\beta_0 =$ the average value of y for the fourth level of the categorical variable and when $x_4 = 0$.

$\beta_i =$ the difference in the average value of y when the categorical variable at level i is changed from level i to level four while holding x_4 constant, i = 1, 2, and 3.

$\beta_4 =$ the amount of change in the average value of y when x_4 is increased by one unit while holding all other x_i constant.

15.15

a. Since the apartment is in the town center, $x_2 = 1$ which implies $\hat{y} = 145 + 1.2(1500) + 300(1) = 2245$.

b. Since the apartment is not in the town center, $x_2 = 0$ which implies $\hat{y} = 145 + 1.2(1500) + 300(0) = 1945$.

c. The difference between the answers in part a. and b. (2245 -1945 = 300) equals the value of b_2. Therefore, b_2 indicates the average premium paid for living in the city's town center.

15.17

a. As the vehicle weight increases by 1 pound, the average highway mileage rating would decrease by 0.003 for a specified type of transmission.

b. If the car has standard transmission the highway mileage rating will increase by 4.56 holding the weight constant.

c. $\hat{y} = 34.2 - 0.003x_1 + 4.56(1) = 38.76 - 0.003x_1$

d. $\hat{y} = 34.2 - 0.003(4394) + 4.56(0) = 21.02$

e. Incorporating the dummy variable essentially gives two regression equations with the same slope but different intercepts depending upon whether the automobile as an automatic or standard transmission. The regression model for an automatic transmission is $E(y) = \beta_0 + \beta_1x_1$; if the automobile has a standard transmission the equation becomes $E(y) = (\beta_0 + \beta_2) + \beta_1x_1$

Chapter 15

15.19

a. Minitab output:

Regression Analysis: PP100 versus X1, X2

```
The regression equation is
PP100 = 197 - 43.6 X1 - 51.0 X2


Predictor     Coef   SE Coef      T      P
Constant    196.57     12.95  15.18  0.000
X1          -43.57     18.31  -2.38  0.029
X2          -51.00     18.31  -2.79  0.012


S = 34.2535   R-Sq = 33.5%   R-Sq(adj) = 26.1%


Analysis of Variance

Source           DF     SS     MS     F      P
Regression        2  10628   5314  4.53  0.026
Residual Error   18  21119   1173
Total            20  31747
```

$$\hat{y} = 197 - 43.6x_1 - 51x_2$$

b. When $x_1 = 0$ and $x_2 = 0$, the model becomes $y_i = \beta_0 + \varepsilon$. Therefore, $\beta_0 =$ the average PP100 of the Korean-branded vehicles. When $x_1 = 1$ and $x_2 = 0$, the model becomes $y_i = \beta_0 + \beta_1 + \varepsilon$ which represents the average PP100 for Domestic vehicles. Therefore, $\beta_1 =$ the difference in the average PP100 between Domestic and Korean vehicles. When $x_1 = 0$ and $x_2 = 1$, the model becomes $y_i = \beta_0 + \beta_2 + \varepsilon$ which represents the average PP100 for European vehicles. Therefore, $\beta_2 =$ the difference in the average PP100 between European and Korean vehicles.

c. Step 1: The parameters of interest is the population coefficients of x_1 and x_2. In order for the averages to be equal, it must be true that $\beta_1 = \beta_2 = 0$

Step 2: H_0: $\beta_1 = \beta_2 = 0$,
   H_A: at least one $\beta_i \neq 0$

Step 3: $\alpha = 0.05$

Step 4: The test statistic provided by Minitab is $F = 4.53$

Step 5: The numerator degrees of freedom are $k = 2$ and the denominator degrees of freedom are $n - k - 1 = 21 - 2 - 1 = 18$; the critical value is 3.555

Step 6: Since $F = 4.53 > 3.555$, we reject H_0

Step 7: There is sufficient evidence to conclude that the average PP100 is the not same for the three international automobile production regions

15.21

a. You will need two dummy variables for the type of client

$x_2 = 1$ if manufacturing, 0 otherwise

$x_3 = 1$ if service, 0 otherwise

Regression Analysis

Regression Statistics	
Multiple R	0.835474124
R Square	0.698017012
Adjusted R Square	0.568595732
Standard Error	975.3064045
Observations	11

ANOVA

	df	SS	MS	F
Regression	3	15390889.56	5130296.519	5.393371239
Residual	7	6658558.078	951222.5826	
Total	10	22049447.64		

	Coefficients	Standard Error	t Stat	P-value
Intercept	-586.2555597	974.2029083	-0.601779727	0.566292865
Hours (x1)	22.86106295	29.33445824	0.779324532	0.461318736
Manufacturing (x2)	2302.267018	895.0615733	2.572188425	0.036889988
Service (x3)	1869.813042	764.538844	2.445674352	0.044387958

$$\hat{y} = -586.2556 + 22.8611(x_1) + 2302.2670(x_2) + 1869.8130(x_3)$$

b. F critical at the 5% significance level would be 4.347. Since F = 5.3934 > 4.347 conclude that the overall model is significant and the model would be useful in predicting the net profit earned by the client.

c. The p-value for hours is 0.4613 so you would conclude that the hours spent working with a client is not useful in this model in predicting the net profit.

d.

Regression Analysis

Regression Statistics	
Multiple R	0.819643712
R Square	0.671815815
Adjusted R Square	0.589769769
Standard Error	951.0704495
Observations	11

ANOVA

	df	SS	MS	F
Regression	2	14813167.64	7406583.818	8.188277754
Residual	8	7236280	904535	
Total	10	22049447.64		

	Coefficients	Standard Error	t Stat	P-value
Intercept	71	475.5352248	0.149305448	0.885007898
Manufacturing (x2)	2689	726.3920544	3.701857673	0.006026483
Service (x3)	2127	672.5083643	3.162785941	0.013338842

$$\hat{y} = 71 + 2689(x_2) + 2127(x_3)$$

e. Manufacturing: 2760

Government: 71

The difference, 2689, is b_2

$(2760 - 71) \pm 2.3060(951.07)$; 495.8326 ----- 4882.1674

15.23

a. Minitab output:

Regression Analysis: MathSAT versus Gender, VerbalSAT

```
The regression equation is
MathSAT = 390 - 37.0 Gender + 0.263 VerbalSAT


Predictor      Coef  SE Coef       T      P
Constant     390.00    35.97   10.84  0.000
Gender      -36.966    1.807  -20.45  0.000
VerbalSAT   0.26338  0.06998    3.76  0.000


S = 7.77253   R-Sq = 86.8%   R-Sq(adj) = 86.4%


Analysis of Variance

Source          DF     SS     MS       F      P
Regression       2  29779  14889  246.46  0.000
Residual Error  75   4531     60
Total           77  34310
```

The regression equation is $\hat{y} = 390 - 37.0x_1 + 0.263x_2$

b. While implausible, β_0 = the average math SAT score for females who score 0 on the verbal portion of the SAT examination. β_1 = the difference in the average math SAT scores between males and females for those who score a specific average value on the verbal portion of the SAT examination. β_2 = the amount the average math SAT score changes as the average verbal SAT score increase by one point given the specific gender of the student taking the examination.

c. Step 1: The parameter of interest is the population coefficient of x_1

Step 2: H_O: $\beta_1 = 0$, H_A: $\beta_1 \neq 0$

Step 3: $\alpha = 0.05$

Step 4: The test statistic provided by Minitab in part a. is $t = -20.45$

Step 5: The numerator degrees of freedom are n-k-1 = 78 – 2 – 1 = 75 the lower critical value provide by Minitab is -1.9921

Step 6: Since t = -20.45< -1.9921, we reject H_O

Step 7: There is sufficient evidence to conclude that the gender of the student taking the SAT examination is a significant predictor of the students' average math SAT score for a given verbal SAT score.

d. $\hat{y} = 390 - 37.0x_1 + 0.263x_2 = 390 - 37.0(1) + 0.263(500) = 484.5 \approx 485$.

Section 15-3 Exercises

15.25

  a.

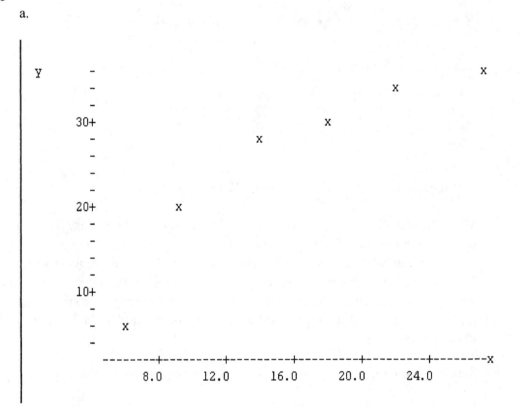

b. $\hat{y} = 4.937 + 1.2643x$

Predictor	Coef	SE Coef	T	P
Constant	4.937	5.448	0.91	0.416
x	1.2643	0.3102	4.08	0.015

$S = 5.498$ R-Sq = 80.6%   R-Sq(adj) = 75.7%

Analysis of Variance

Source	DF	SS	MS	F	P
Regression	1	501.94	501.94	16.61	0.015
Residual Error	4	120.89	30.22		
Total	5	622.83			

The p-value = 0.015 < α = 0.05. Therefore, reject H_0 and conclude that there is a linear relationship between the dependent and independent variables.

c. $\hat{y} = -25.155 + 18.983 \ln x$

Predictor	Coef	SE Coef	T	P
Constant	-25.155	6.917	-3.64	0.022
lnx	18.983	2.561	7.41	0.002

$S = 3.251$ R-Sq = 93.2%   R-Sq(adj) = 91.5%

Analysis of Variance

Source	DF	SS	MS	F	P
Regression	1	580.57	580.57	54.95	0.002
Residual Error	4	42.27	10.57		
Total	5	622.83			

The adjusted R^2 (91.5%) for the curvilinear model exceeds the R^2 of the simple linear model. The model's variance estimate is smaller for the curvilinear model and the F-test has a smaller p-value. It appears that the logarithmic model provides a better fit of the data.

15.27

   a. Minitab scatterplot:

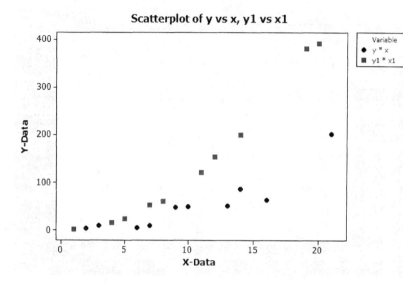

   b. The scatter plot indicates that there are two quadratic models. Since the two models are not equal distance from each other, this indicates that there is interaction between x_2 and the quadratic relationship between y and x_2.

```
The regression equation is
y = 4.9 - 3.58 x1 - 0.014 x1sq + 1.42 x1x2 + 0.528 x1sqx2


Predictor      Coef  SE Coef      T       P
Constant       4.90    10.84   0.45   0.658
x1           -3.580     3.671  -0.98   0.345
x1sq        -0.0140     0.2067 -0.07   0.947
x1x2          1.424     2.002   0.71   0.488
x1sqx2       0.5276     0.1231  4.29   0.001


S = 15.0083   R-Sq = 98.7%   R-Sq(adj) = 98.3%


Analysis of Variance

Source          DF       SS      MS       F       P
Regression       4   255018   63755  283.04   0.000
Residual Error  15     3379     225
Total           19   258397
```

The equation is $\hat{y}_i = 4.9 - 3.58x_1 - 0.014x_1^2 + 1.42x_1x_2 + 0.528x_1^2x_2$.

c. The two interaction turns are $\beta_3 x_1 x_2$ and $\beta_4 x_1^2 x_2$. So you must conduct two hypothesis tests:

(i) To determine if there is interaction between x_2 and the linear relationship between x_1 and y, we must test to determine if $\beta_3 = 0$.

Step 1: The parameter of interest is the population coefficient of $x_1 x_2$

Step 2: H_O: $\beta_3 = 0$, H_A: $\beta_3 \neq 0$

Step 3: $\alpha = 0.05$

Step 4: The p-value is 0.488

Step 5: If the p-value is less than α, reject the null hypothesis; otherwise fail to reject the null hypothesis

Step 6: Since the p-value = 0.488 > 0.05, we fail to reject H_O

Step 7: There is not sufficient evidence to conclude that there is interaction between x_2 and the linear relationship between x_1 and y.

(ii) To determine if there is interaction between x_2 and the quadratic relationship between x_1 and y, we must test to determine if $\beta_4 = 0$. The p-value for $\beta_4 = 0.001$, there is sufficient evidence to conclude that there is interaction between x_2 and the quadratic relationship between x_1 and y.

d. The second hypothesis indicated that there was sufficient evidence to conclude that there is interaction between x_2 and the quadratic relationship between x_1 and y.

15.29

a.

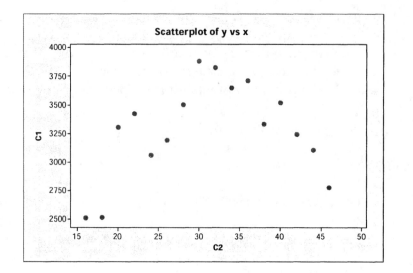

SUMMARY OUTPUT SIMPLE LINEAR REGRESSION

Regression Statistics	
Multiple R	0.279123232
R Square	0.077909779
Adjusted R Square	0.012046191
Standard Error	415.8160232
Observations	16

ANOVA

	df	SS	MS	F
Regression	1	204526.2382	204526.2382	1.182896072
Residual	14	2420641.512	172902.9651	
Total	15	2625167.75		

	Coefficients	Standard Error	t Stat	P-value
Intercept	2902.964706	364.6679609	7.960569661	1.45046E-06
Days	12.26323529	11.27539503	1.087610257	0.295137486

SUMMARY OUTPUT – 2ND ORDER MODEL

Regression Statistics	
Multiple R	0.891151457
R Square	0.794150919
Adjusted R Square	0.76248183
Standard Error	203.883143
Observations	16

ANOVA

	df	SS	MS	F
Regression	2	2084779.382	1042389.691	25.07653158
Residual	13	540388.3682	41568.33602	
Total	15	2625167.75		

	Coefficients	Standard Error	t Stat	P-value
Intercept	-1070.397689	617.2526804	-1.734132104	0.106527339
Days	293.4829482	42.17763668	6.958259668	9.94294E-06
Days2	-4.535801821	0.674415013	-6.725535071	1.41423E-05

b. For the simple linear model F = 1.1829 < 4.6001 so conclude that the simple linear model is not a significant model.
For the 2nd Order Model F = 25.0765 > 3.8056 so conclude that the 2nd order model is a significant model.

c. The 2nd Order model with a squared term would be preferred to the simple linear model. As stated in part b the simple linear model is not significant, p-value 0.295 > .05 and has an R^2 of 0.0779. The 2nd order model is significant, p-value ≈ 0 < .05 and has an R^2 of 0.7942.

d. Charles should use the 2nd order model with days squared for the reasons stated in parts b and c above.

Chapter 15

15.31
    a.

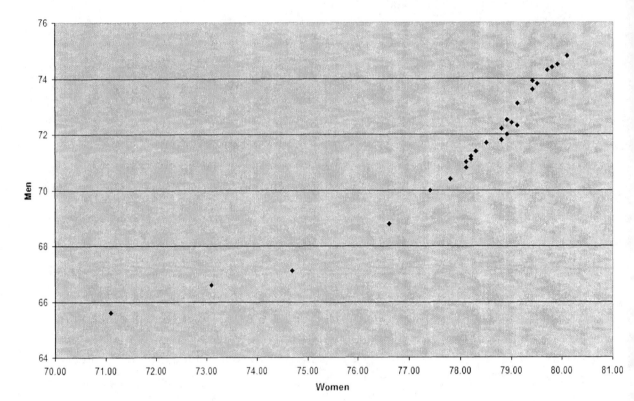

b. There appears to be one curve in the sample data. Therefore, a second-order polynomial seems to be the correct model.

SUMMARY OUTPUT

Regression Statistics	
Multiple R	0.9940
R Square	0.9880
Adjusted R Square	0.9871
Standard Error	0.2659
Observations	28

ANOVA

	df	SS	MS	F	Significance F
Regression	2	145.6974	72.8487	1030.737	9.58492E-25
Residual	25	1.7669	0.0707		
Total	27	147.4643			

	Coefficients	Standard Error	t Stat	P-value	Lower 95%	Upper 95%
Intercept	758.0664	56.5385	13.4080	6.43E-13	641.6232	874.5095
Women	-19.2549	1.4901	-12.9221	1.45E-12	-22.3238	-16.1861
Women Sq	0.1339	0.0098	13.6548	4.29E-13	0.1137	0.1541

The regression equation is:
Men = 758.0664 – 19.2549Women + 0.1339Women Sq

c. Step 1: The parameters of interest is the population coefficients of x and x^2. In order for the averages to be equal, it must be true that $\beta_1 = \beta_2 = 0$

Step 2: H_O: $\beta_1 = \beta_2 = 0$, H_A: at least one $\beta_i \neq 0$

Step 3: $\alpha = 0.05$

Step 4: The test statistic is F = 1030.737

Step 5: The numerator degrees of freedom are k = 2 and the denominator degrees of freedom are n – k – 1 = 28 – 2 – 1 = 25; the critical value is 3.3852.

Step 6: Since F = 1030.737 > 3.3852, we reject H_O.

Step 7: There is sufficient evidence to conclude that women's average life expectancy can be used in a second-order polynomial to predict the average life expectancy of men.

d. The predicted value is $\hat{y} = 758.0664 - 19.2549(100) + 0.1339(100)^2 = 171.58$. Such an answer has little or not validity. An examination of the past data indicates that the average length of life of women has always been larger than that for man. This is an example of how unwise it is to extrapolate when using regression models.

15.33

a. Minitab scatter plot:

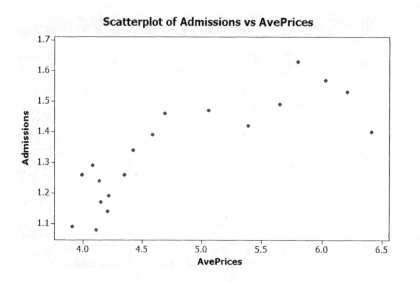

b. There appears to be three "curves." This would suggest a fourth order polynomial.

c. Minitab output:

Regression Analysis: Admissions versus AvePrices, AP2, AP3, AP4

```
The regression equation is
Admissions = - 30.0 + 24.5 AvePrices - 7.3 AP2 + 0.98 AP3 - 0.0499 AP4


Predictor      Coef   SE Coef       T      P
Constant     -30.00     56.96   -0.53  0.607
AvePrices     24.49     45.55    0.54  0.599
AP2           -7.31     13.54   -0.54  0.598
AP3           0.984     1.772    0.56  0.588
AP4        -0.04990   0.08621   -0.58  0.572


S = 0.0772561   R-Sq = 82.8%   R-Sq(adj) = 77.9%


Analysis of Variance

Source           DF       SS       MS      F      P
Regression        4  0.40256  0.10064  16.86  0.000
Residual Error   14  0.08356  0.00597
Total            18  0.48612
```

Note that the F-test has a p-value of 0.000. However, the individual t-tests all have very large p-values. There is also a substantial difference in the adjusted and unadjusted coefficient of determination. This suggests that there may be some components that are redundant and should be removed from the model.

d. To determine if the fourth order components should be removed we must determine if $\beta_4 = 0$. We test the hypothesis $\beta_4 = 0$. Since its the p-value = .572 > 0.05, we fail to reject H_O; there is sufficient evidence to remove the fourth order component.

(ii)   Minitab output:

Regression Analysis: Admissions versus AvePrices, AP2, AP3

```
The regression equation is
Admissions = 2.71 - 1.76 AvePrices + 0.510 AP2 - 0.0414 AP3


Predictor        Coef  SE Coef       T       P
Constant        2.709    6.990    0.39   0.704
AvePrices      -1.764    4.173   -0.42   0.679
AP2            0.5098   0.8205    0.62   0.544
AP3          -0.04141  0.05317   -0.78   0.448
```

To determine if the third order components should be removed we must determine if $\beta_3 = 0$. Since its p-value = 0.488 > 0.05, there is sufficient evidence to remove the third order component.

Minitab output:

```
The regression equation is
Admissions = - 2.68 + 1.47 AvePrices - 0.129 AP2


Predictor        Coef  SE Coef       T       P
Constant      -2.6842   0.9447   -2.84   0.012
AvePrices      1.4722   0.3800    3.87   0.001
AP2          -0.12856  0.03723   -3.45   0.003


S = 0.0745897   R-Sq = 81.7%   R-Sq(adj) = 79.4%


Analysis of Variance

Source          DF       SS       MS       F       P
Regression       2  0.39710  0.19855   35.69   0.000
Residual Error  16  0.08902  0.00556
Total           18  0.48612
```

To determine if the second order components should be removed we must determine if $\beta_2 = 0$. Since its p-value = 0.000 < 0.05, there is sufficient evidence to retain the second order component.

The resulting equation is $\hat{y}_i = -2.68 + 1.47x_1 - 0.129x_1^2$

Section 15-4 Exercises

15.35

a.

```
              y        x1       x2
x1         0.582
           0.047

x2         0.645    0.709
           0.024    0.010

x3         0.985    0.578    0.640
           0.000    0.049    0.025

Cell Contents: Pearson correlation
                  P-Value
```

x_3 is the most highly correlated with the dependent variable. It should enter the model first.

b.

Stepwise Regression: y versus x1, x2, x3

```
  Alpha-to-Enter: 0.25   Alpha-to-Remove: 0.25

Response is y on 3 predictors, with N = 12

Step               1
Constant       -3.097

x3              0.973
T-Value         18.12
P-Value         0.000

S                2.08
R-Sq            97.04
R-Sq(adj)       96.75
Mallows C-p      0.1
```

The estimated equation is $\hat{y} = -3.097 + 0.973x_3$.

c.

```
The regression equation is
y = - 3.84 + 0.053 x1 + 0.0032 x2 + 0.956 x3

Predictor        Coef      SE Coef         T         P
Constant       -3.842        4.083     -0.94     0.374
x1             0.0531       0.5437      0.10     0.925
x2            0.00320      0.01529      0.21     0.840
x3            0.95618      0.07976     11.99     0.000


S = 2.308       R-Sq = 97.1%      R-Sq(adj) = 96.0%

Analysis of Variance

Source           DF           SS          MS         F        P
Regression        3      1419.04      473.01     88.77    0.000
Residual Error    8        42.63        5.33
Total            11      1461.67
```

The difference between the two models is that the full model has two additional independent variables. Viewing the p-values and the adjusted R^2, however, it appears that x_1 and x_2 are not significant additions to the model. Using the adjusted R^2, it is apparent that the equation developed used Standard Selection explains the most variation in the dependent variable adjusting for the number of independent variables in the model.

15.37

a. x_2 and x_4 were the only variables to enter the model because x1 and x3 did not have high enough coefficients of partial determination to add significantly to the model.

b. The stepwise model and the "full" model with the same variables would be identical. Stepwise regression is just a variable selection procedure. After the variables have been selected, the method of least squares is used to obtain estimates of the parameters for both the full model and stepwise regression. This results in the same estimates for both procedures.

c. Stepwise regression cannot have a larger R^2 than the full model since R^2 is increased every time a new variable is added. So the full model will have an R^2 at least as large as the Stepwise model. This off course assumes the same pool of independent variables is used for both procedures.

15.39

  a. Minitab output:

Stepwise Regression: y versus x1, x2, x3, x4

```
   Alpha-to-Enter: 0.15   Alpha-to-Remove: 0.15


Response is y on 4 predictors, with N = 10


Step              1      2      3
Constant      80.19  47.99  32.08

x3             -8.7   -7.1   -5.0
T-Value       -4.72  -4.90  -2.98
P-Value       0.001  0.002  0.025

x1                    0.91   0.76
T-Value               2.91   2.68
P-Value              0.023  0.037

x4                           0.95
T-Value                      1.83
P-Value                     0.117

S              9.85   7.09   6.13
R-Sq          73.60  88.05  92.34
R-Sq(adj)     70.30  84.64  88.51
Mallows C-p    13.3    4.7    3.6
```

The resulting equation is $\hat{y} = 32.08 + 0.76x_1 - 5x_3 + 0.95x_4$

Minitab output:

Stepwise Regression: y versus x1, x2, x3, x4

Forward selection. Alpha-to-Enter: 0.25

Response is y on 4 predictors, with N = 10

Step	1	2	3
Constant	80.19	47.99	32.08
x3	-8.7	-7.1	-5.0
T-Value	-4.72	-4.90	-2.98
P-Value	0.001	0.002	0.025
x1		0.91	0.76
T-Value		2.91	2.68
P-Value		0.023	0.037
x4			0.95
T-Value			1.83
P-Value			0.117
S	9.85	7.09	6.13
R-Sq	73.60	88.05	92.34
R-Sq(adj)	70.30	84.64	88.51
Mallows C-p	13.3	4.7	3.6

The resulting equation is $\hat{y} = 32.08 + 0.76x_1 - 5x_3 + 0.95x_4$

b. Minitab output:

Stepwise Regression: y versus x1, x2, x3, x4

```
Backward elimination.  Alpha-to-Remove: 0.1

Response is y on 4 predictors, with N = 10

Step            1      2      3
Constant     32.80  32.08  47.99

x1            0.47   0.76   0.91
T-Value       0.98   2.68   2.91
P-Value      0.373  0.037  0.023

x2            0.55
T-Value       0.77
P-Value      0.478

x3           -4.8   -5.0   -7.1
T-Value      -2.69  -2.98  -4.90
P-Value      0.043  0.025  0.002

x4            0.93   0.95
T-Value       1.74   1.83
P-Value      0.143  0.117

S             6.35   6.13   7.09
R-Sq         93.14  92.34  88.05
R-Sq(adj)    87.66  88.51  84.64
Mallows C-p   5.0    3.6    4.7
```

The resulting equation is $\hat{y} = 32.08 + 0.76x_1 - 5x_3 + 0.95x_4$

Note: This is the model from step 2, it is chosen because of the higher adjusted R square value.

c. Minitab output:

Best Subsets Regression: y versus x1, x2, x3, x4

Response is y

```
                        Mallows       x x x x
Vars  R-Sq  R-Sq(adj)     C-p     S  1 2 3 4
   1  73.6       70.3    13.3  9.8544    X
   1  70.1       66.3    15.8 10.492         X
   2  88.1       84.6     4.7  7.0872  X   X
   2  86.9       83.1     5.6  7.4255    X X
   3  92.3       88.5     3.6  6.1293  X   X X
   3  91.8       87.7     4.0  6.3288    X X X
   4  93.1       87.7     5.0  6.3517  X X X X
```

Using adjusted R^2 as the criterion, the resulting equation is $\hat{y} = 32.08 + 0.76x_1 - 5x_3 + 0.95x_4$.

15.41
  a.

	Ads Placed Previous Week	Calls Received the Previous Week	Airline Bookings	Calls Received
Ads Place Previous Week	1			
Calls Received the Previous Week	0.70901747	1		
Airline Bookings	0.3606948	0.219988054	1	
Calls Received	0.58435892	0.654482969	0.533973	1

You would expect the variables that are most highly correlated with the dependent variable to enter the model first. Based on that expectation, the expected order would be Calls Received the Previous Week, Ads Placed the Previous Week and then Airline Bookings.

b.

Western State Tourist
Association
Table of Results for Forward Selection

Calls Received the Previous Week entered.

	df	SS	MS	F
Regression	1	62251.059	62251.059	7.493158862
Residual	10	83077.191	8307.7191	
Total	11	145328.25		

	Coefficients	Standard Error	t Stat	P-value
Intercept	-18.32798293	155.8801498	- 0.117577401	0.908730578
Calls Received the Previous Week	1.067908547	0.390123033	2.737363487	0.020927236

No other variables could be entered into the model. Stepwise ends.

Calls Received the Previous Week was the first variable to enter the model and it was significant at the 0.05 significance level and no other variables entered the model.

c. The two models developed are identical since the only significant variable was entered into both models. Both procedures produce the same exact model. So for this data neither procedure is preferred over the other.

15.43

  a. Minitab scatter plot:

    (1)

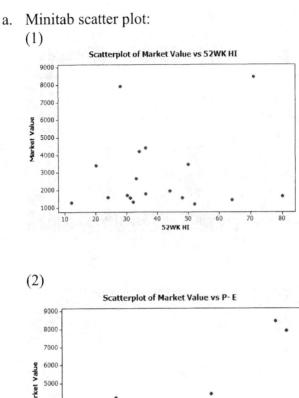

    (2)

Examining the first scatter plot, it would appear that there are two outliers. However, the slope on the regression equation seems to almost equal 0 with no curves. The second scatter plot seems to have a slight concave curvature, supporting the analyst's decision to produce a second-order polynomial.

b. Minitab output:

Stepwise Regression: Market Value versus 52WK HI, P- E, HISq, PESq, HIPE

Forward selection. Alpha-to-Enter: 0.25

Response is Market Value on 5 predictors, with N = 20

```
Step             1
Constant       1110

PESq           1.60
T-Value       11.48
P-Value       0.000

S               750
R-Sq          87.99
R-Sq(adj)     87.32
Mallows C-p    -0.3
```

The equation is $\hat{y} = 1110 + 1.60x_2^2$

c. The forward selection stepwise regression agrees with the analyst's decision to produce a second-order polynomial since the square of the P-E ratio is in the resulting regression equation. The fact that the p-value = 0.000 provides inferential support to this statement.

15.45

a. Minitab output:

Stepwise Regression: CPI versus Gas Price, Heat Oil, Diesel, Crude Oil

Backward elimination. Alpha-to-Remove: 0.1

Response is CPI on 4 predictors, with N = 15

* ERROR * X-matrix is (nearly) singular.

The message indicates that there is multicollinearity among the predictor variables.

b. Minitab output:

Correlations: CPI, Gas Price, Heat Oil, Diesel, Crude Oil

	CPI	Gas Price	Heat Oil	Diesel
Gas Price	0.507			
	0.054			
Heat Oil	0.858	0.703		
	0.000	0.003		
Diesel	0.582	0.867	0.834	
	0.023	0.000	0.000	
Crude Oil	0.582	0.867	0.834	1.000
	0.023	0.000	0.000	*

Cell Contents: Pearson correlation
                P-Value

Either crude oil or diesel prices should be removed since they have the same correlation coefficient with the dependent variable and a correlation coefficient with each other of 1.

c. Crude oil prices were removed for the following stepwise procedure.
Minitab output:

Stepwise Regression: CPI versus Gas Price, Heat Oil, Diesel

```
Backward elimination.  Alpha-to-Remove: 0.1


Response is CPI on 3 predictors, with N = 15


Step                    1          2
Constant           0.8739     0.8741

Gas Price          0.00005
T-Value               0.41
P-Value              0.689

Heat Oil           0.00089    0.00089
T-Value               4.97       5.14
P-Value              0.000      0.000

Diesel            -0.00029   -0.00023
T-Value              -1.53      -1.84
P-Value              0.154      0.091

S                  0.00639    0.00616
R-Sq                 79.65      79.33
R-Sq(adj)            74.09      75.89
Mallows C-p            4.0        2.2
```

The resulting equation is $\hat{y} = 0.8741 + 0.00089x_2 - 0.00023x_3$

Chapter 15

Section 15-5 Exercises

15.47

a.

The regression equation is
$$\hat{y} = -16.02 + 2.1277x$$

b.

$H_0 : B_1 = 0.0$

$H_A : B_1 \neq 0.0$

Predictor	Coef	SE Coef	T	P
Constant	-16.02	10.22	-1.57	0.156
x	2.1277	0.2658	8.00	0.000

$S = 18.54$ R-Sq = 88.9%   R-Sq(adj) = 87.5%

Analysis of Variance

Source	DF	SS	MS	F	P
Regression	1	22013	22013	64.07	0.000
Residual Error	8	2749	344		
Total	9	24762			

The p-value equals 0.000 which is smaller than the significance level = 0.05. Thus, the regression equation is found to be significant.

c. Note, the solution was done using Minitab. The Minitab standardized residuals will be slightly different than those computed in Excel (Minitab uses Studentized Standardized Residuals). The plots will still provide the same general conclusions.

RESI1	SRES1
8.2567	0.50886
16.8735	1.02038
14.2350	0.83940
-7.2759	-0.42265
-3.7867	-0.21760
-10.4253	-0.59423
-22.1916	-1.26229
-30.3627	-1.79839
18.2325	1.15838
16.4445	1.24124

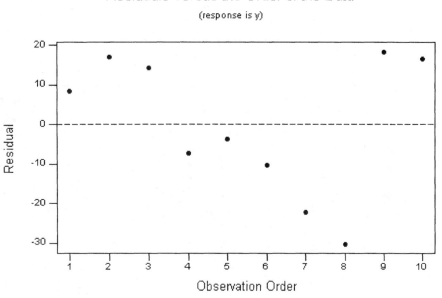

Residuals Versus the Order of the Data
(response is y)

This graph indicates that the error terms are not independent of each other. Some "time" related factor is influencing the randomness of the residuals.

No evidence is available to refute the assumption that the residuals have equal variances at each value of the independent variable.

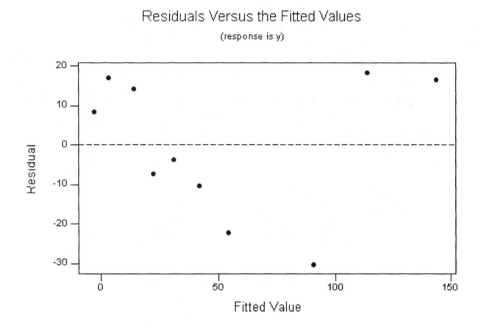

Residuals Versus the Fitted Values
(response is y)

The residuals are positive for small values, negative for the intermediate values, and positive again for the large values of the fitted values. This indicates that, perhaps, a 2nd order term be placed into the model.

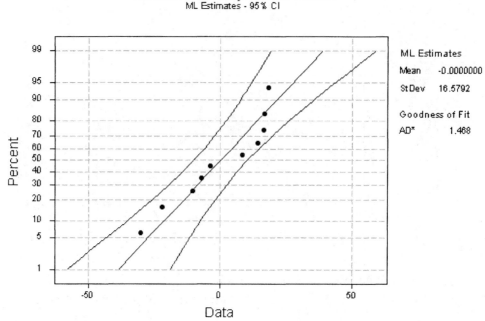

Normal Probability Plot for RESI1
ML Estimates - 95% CI

ML Estimates
Mean   -0.0000000
StDev   16.5792

Goodness of Fit
AD*   1.468

The normal probability plot indicates that the assumption that the residuals possess a normal distribution cannot be rejected.

15.49

a. Minitab output:

Regression Analysis: y versus x1, x2

```
The regression equation is
y = 17.0 + 1.54 x1 - 0.119 x2


Predictor      Coef   SE Coef       T       P
Constant     17.010     6.199    2.74   0.029
x1           1.5416    0.2811    5.48   0.001
x2          -0.1193    0.2811   -0.42   0.684


S = 8.50528   R-Sq = 85.8%   R-Sq(adj) = 81.8%
```

The equation is $\hat{y} = 17.0 + 1.54x_1 - 0.119x_2$

b.

e_i	r_i
3.2646	0.53825
10.8786	1.59564
-10.1214	-1.48457
-5.7773	-0.87248
-2.9528	-0.48684
-11.5668	-1.43995
5.3218	0.68149
3.3218	0.42538
7.7253	0.98443
-0.0939	-0.01356

c. The appropriate residual plot to determine if the linear function is the appropriate regression function is a plot of the residuals versus the independent variable (x) or the fitted value ($\hat{y}_i$).

Minitab plot:

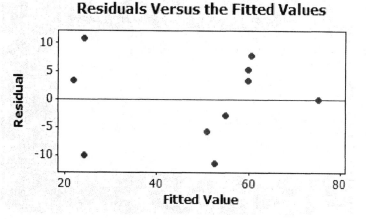

This residual plot shows the residuals scattered about 0. The residual plot supports the choice of the linear model.

d. The appropriate residual plot to determine if the residuals have a constant variance is a plot of the residuals versus the independent variable (x) or the fitted value ($\hat{y}_i$).

Minitab plot:

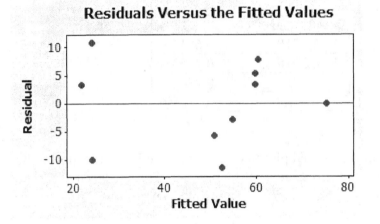

The residual plot does not display any non-random pattern. This indicates that the residuals do have a constant variance.

e. The appropriate residual plot to determine if the residuals are independent is a plot of the residuals versus a "time" variable.

Minitab plot:

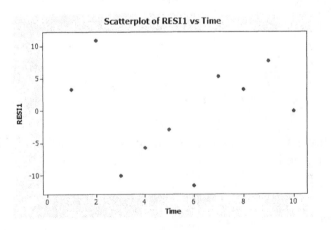

This residual plot shows positive residuals early in the experiment. In the middle of the experiment, the residuals are negative, and at the end they are positive again.

f. Minitab probability plot:

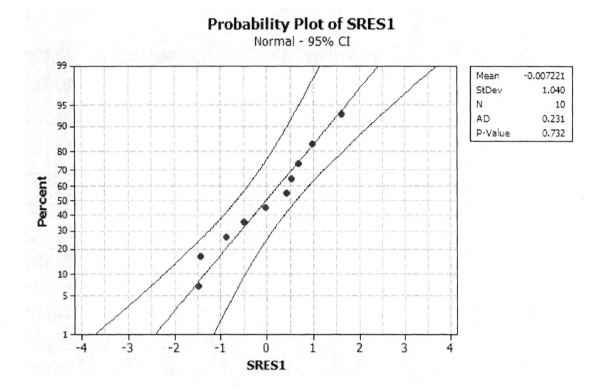

The probability plot shows all of the standardized residuals within the confidence bounds. This indicates that the error terms are normally distributed.

Chapter 15

15.51

a.

SUMMARY OUTPUT

Regression Statistics	
Multiple R	0.880534596
R Square	0.775341175
Adjusted R Square	0.693647057
Standard Error	1184.124723
Observations	16

ANOVA

	df	SS	MS	F	Significance F
Regression	4	53230058.97	13307514.74	9.4907833	0.001427993
Residual	11	15423664.97	1402151.361		
Total	15	68653723.94			

	Coefficients	Standard Error	t Stat	P-value	Lower 95%
Intercept	14122.24086	4335.791765	3.25713079	0.0076378	4579.222699
Team Win/Loss Percentage	63.15325348	14.93880137	4.227464568	0.0014185	30.27315672
Opponent Win/Loss Percentage	10.09582009	14.31396102	0.705312811	0.4952803	-21.40901163
Games Played	31.50621796	177.129782	0.177870811	0.8620577	-358.3540008
Temperature	-55.4609057	62.09372861	-0.89318047	0.3908828	-192.12835

Students should recognize that the overall model is significant by looking at the F and Significance F and should recognize that only team win/loss percentage variable is significant. Students can determine this by looking at the p-values of all the independent variables.

b.

RESIDUAL OUTPUT

Observation	Predicted Game Attendance	Residuals	Standard Residuals
1	14615.28455	-113.2845461	-0.111717834
2	13226.07735	-767.0773523	-0.756468762
3	16954.06403	-1354.064031	-1.335337483
4	16792.71228	-12.71227981	-0.01253647
5	15983.81404	-1383.81404	-1.364676053
6	18640.79321	659.2067879	0.650090035
7	14959.28101	-356.2810143	-0.351353689
8	14923.38203	865.617969	0.853646573
9	16953.96812	846.0318821	0.83433136
10	17458.24315	1991.756852	1.964211086
11	12695.06465	1194.935346	1.178409529
12	16458.92747	-1361.927469	-1.34309217
13	16916.67146	749.3285431	0.738965417
14	12472.55998	27.44001682	0.027060525
15	17884.93123	-1104.931227	-1.089650157
16	17423.22544	119.7745624	0.118118094
Average Residuals		0.00	

The residuals are the difference between the actual values and the predicted values from the model. The mean of this is 0 so you would expect the average of the residuals to be 0.

c.

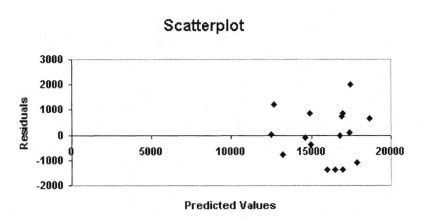

The plot of residuals does not appear to have a pattern, therefore the constant variance assumption has apparently not been violated.

d.

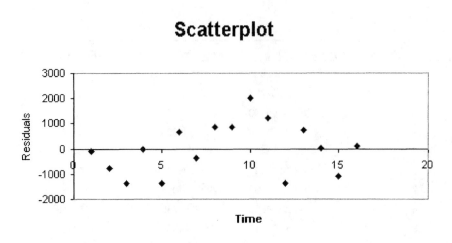

The plot of the residuals against time shows a systematic variation about zero, indicating that the residuals are dependent. However, this plot assumes that the observations are collected in time-series order. If not, then this check for independence should not be performed.

e.

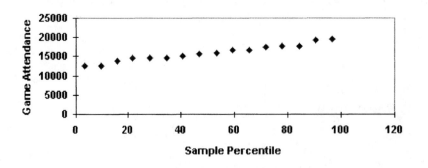

Based upon the normal probability plot which is almost a straight line we can assume the model error terms are approximately normally distributed.

15.53

a. Minitab output:

Regression Analysis: CPI versus Heat Oil, Diesel

```
The regression equation is
CPI = 0.874 + 0.000887 Heat Oil - 0.000235 Diesel


Predictor         Coef     SE Coef       T       P
Constant       0.87406     0.02134   40.95   0.000
Heat Oil     0.0008873   0.0001728    5.14   0.000
Diesel      -0.0002347   0.0001279   -1.84   0.091


S = 0.00616296   R-Sq = 79.3%   R-Sq(adj) = 75.9%
```

$$\hat{y} = 0.874 + 0.000887x_1 - 0.000235x_2$$

b. The appropriate residual plot to determine if the linear function is the appropriate regression function is a plot of the residuals versus the independent variable (x) or the fitted value ($\hat{y}_i$).

Minitab plot:

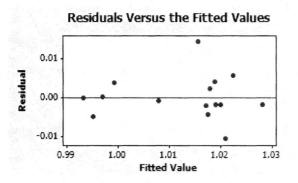

This residual plot shows the residuals scattered about 0. The residual plot supports the choice of the linear model.

c. The appropriate residual plot to determine if the residuals have a constant variance is a plot of the residuals versus the independent variable (x) or the fitted value ($\hat{y}_i$).

Minitab plot:

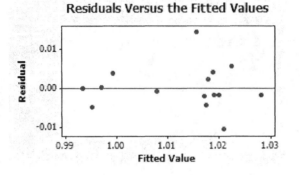

The residual plot seems to indicate that the dispersion gets larger for larger fitted values. This indicates that the residuals do not have constant variances.

d. The appropriate residual plot to determine if the residuals are independent is a plot of the residuals versus a "time" variable.

Minitab plot:

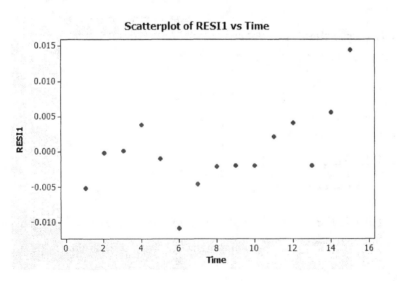

This residual plot shows the residuals scattered about 0. The residuals, however, follow a pattern of being negative, positive, negative, and positive. The linear model appears to be insufficient.

e. Minitab probability plot:

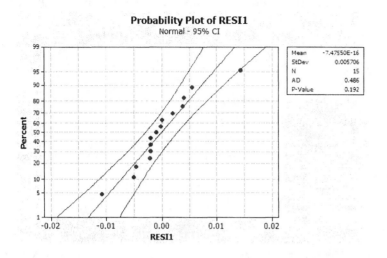

The probability plot shows all of the standardized residuals within the confidence bounds. This indicates that the error terms are normally distributed.

15.55

a. Minitab output:

Regression Analysis: Grosses versus Admissions, AvePrices, Total Screens

```
The regression equation is
Grosses = - 6.81 + 5.29 Admissions + 1.51 AvePrices - 0.000033 Total Screens


Predictor           Coef     SE Coef        T      P
Constant         -6.8099      0.1834   -37.13  0.000
Admissions        5.2878      0.2731    19.36  0.000
AvePrices        1.51364     0.05053    29.95  0.000
Total Screens -0.00003251  0.00001011   -3.22  0.006


S = 0.0788179   R-Sq = 99.9%   R-Sq(adj) = 99.8%
```

The equation is $\hat{y} = - 6.81 + 5.29x_1 + 1.51x_2 - 0.000033x_3$

b. The appropriate residual plot to determine if the linear function is the appropriate regression function is a plot of the residuals versus the independent variable (x) or the fitted value ($\hat{y}_i$).

Minitab plot:

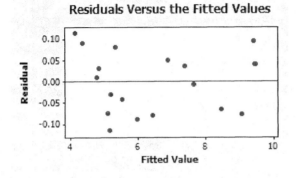

Residuals Versus the Fitted Values

This residual plot shows the residuals scattered about 0. The residuals, however, follow a pattern of being positive, negative, positive, and positive. The residual plot indicates that a higher order model may be in order.

c. Minitab output:

Regression Analysis: Grosses versus Admissions, AvePrices, ...

```
The regression equation is
Grosses = 0.97 - 3.20 Admissions + 0.285 AvePrices + 0.000029 Total Screens
            + 3.12 AdmissSq + 0.103 AvePriceSq - 0.000000 TScrenSq


Predictor            Coef      SE Coef       T       P
Constant            0.966        1.404    0.69   0.505
Admissions         -3.205        1.394   -2.30   0.040
AvePrices          0.2852       0.4254    0.67   0.515
Total Screens  0.00002897  0.00004661    0.62   0.546
AdmissSq           3.1217       0.5025    6.21   0.000
AvePriceSq        0.10307      0.03814    2.70   0.019
TScrenSq       -0.00000000  0.00000000   -0.69   0.503


S = 0.0413482   R-Sq = 100.0%   R-Sq(adj) = 100.0%
```

The equation is $\hat{y} = 0.97 - 3.20x_1 + 0.285x_2 + 0.000029x_3 + 3.12x_1^2 + 0.103x_2^2 + 0.000000x_3^2$

d. Minitab plot:

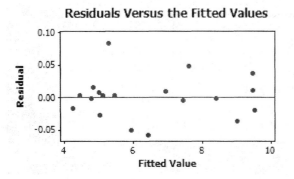

The residual plot does not display any non-random pattern. This indicates that the addition of the quadratic terms have alleviated the non-randomness with the residuals.

e. Minitab probability plot:

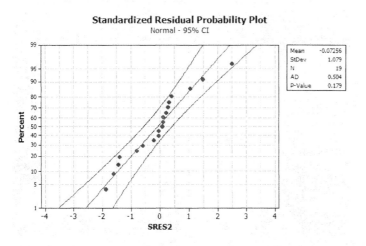

The probability plot shows all of the standardized residuals within the confidence bands. This indicates that the error terms are normally distributed.

End of Chapter Exercises

15.57

The least squares objective is the same for both simple linear and multiple linear regression. We wish to minimize the sum of the squared differences between the observed y values and the expected y values.

15.59

A model is apt if it satisfies the regression assumptions.

15.61

a. The coefficient of x_1 indicates that the average y increases by three units *holding x_2 constant*.

b. The interpretation provided in part a. true regardless of the value of x_2 since x_2 only affects the y-intercept of this model.

c. When $x_2 = 1$, $E(y) = 5 + 3x_1 + 5(1) + 4x_1(1) = 10 + 7x_1$. Note that the coefficient of x_1 actually equals 7 when $x_2 = 1$. Therefore, the interpretation is that the coefficient of x_1 indicates that the average y increases by 7 units *when $x_2 = 1$*.

d. When $x_2 = 2$, $E(y) = 5 + 3x_1 + 5(2) + 4x_1(2) = 15 + 11x_1$. Note that now the coefficient of x_1 actually equals 11 when $x_2 = 2$. Therefore, the interpretation is that the coefficient of x_1 indicates that the average y increases by 11 units when $x_2 = 1$. For this model, the interpretation in part a is no longer true.

e. When interaction terms exist in the model, those coefficients affected by the interaction terms have conditional interpretations.

15.63

Regression Statistics	
Multiple R	0.919126442
R Square	0.844793416
Adjusted R Square	0.782710783
Standard Error	23849.68125
Observations	15

ANOVA

	df	SS	MS	F	Significance F
Regression	4	30960327043	7740081761	13.60756414	0.000470491
Residual	10	5688072957	568807295.7		
Total	14	36648400000			

	Coefficients	Standard Error	t Stat	P-value	Lower 95%	Upper 95%
Intercept	-125307.8062	31082.09519	-4.031510921	0.002393684	-194563.0421	-56052.6
Pages X1	175.8963214	39.76976966	4.422864977	0.001288354	87.28373715	264.5089
Competing Books X2	-1573.777885	1995.851361	-0.788524595	0.448679286	-6020.812614	2873.257
Advertising Budget X3	1.591706487	0.444463005	3.581190042	0.005001797	0.601381026	2.582032
Age of Author X4	1613.747496	625.0234231	2.581899232	0.027327123	221.1082826	3006.387

a. $R^2 = 0.8448$; F critical would be 3.4780; since $F = 13.6076 > 3.4780$ conclude that the overall model is significant.

b.

	Coefficients	Lower 95%	Upper 95%
Intercept	-125307.8062	-194563.0421	-56052.6
Pages X1	175.8963214	87.28373715	264.5089
Competing Books X2	-1573.777885	-6020.812614	2873.257
Advertising Budget X3	1.591706487	0.601381026	2.582032
Age of Author X4	1613.747496	221.1082826	3006.387

The confidence intervals indicate the range of values by which the dependent variable may change for a one unit change in the corresponding independent variable, all other independent variables being held constant. If the confidence interval contains zero it also indicates the independent variable is not statistically significant in the regression model.

c. The critical t-value would be ± 2.2281

	Coefficients	Standard Error	t Stat	P-value
Intercept	-125307.8062	31082.09519	-4.031510921	0.002393684
Pages X1	175.8963214	39.76976966	4.422864977	0.001288354
Competing Books X2	-1573.777885	1995.851361	-0.788524595	0.448679286
Advertising Budget X3	1.591706487	0.444463005	3.581190042	0.005001797
Age of Author X4	1613.747496	625.0234231	2.581899232	0.027327123

Pages – t = 4.4229 > 2.2281 conclude pages is significant
Competing Books – t = -0.7885 > -2.2281 conclude competing books is insignificant.
Advertising Budget - t = 3.5812 > 2.2281 conclude advertising budget is significant
Age of Author – t = 2.5819 > 2.2281 conclude age of author is significant.

d. The interval is found as follows: 175.8963 $\pm$ 2.2281(39.7698)
        87.2852 ------ 264.5074

e.

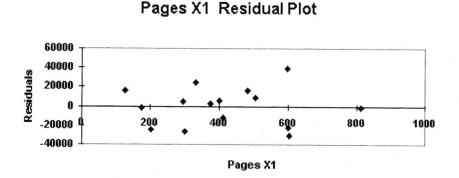

Pages X1 Residual Plot

The plot appears to be linear since the model bands around 0

Competing Books X2 Residual Plot

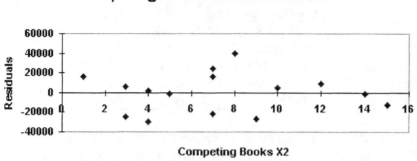

The plot appears to have a non-linear trend.

Advertising Budget X3 Residual Plot

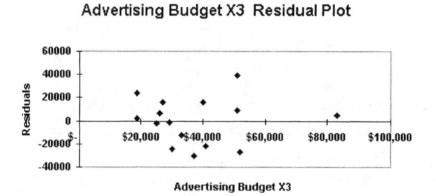

The plot appears to be linear since the model bands around 0

Age of Author X4 Residual Plot

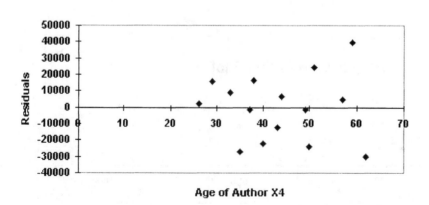

The plot appears to have a non-uniform (funnel) appearance.

Scatterplot

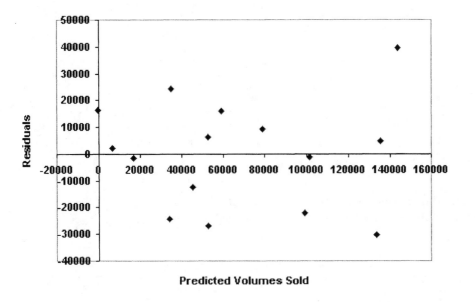

It appears the assumption of constant variance might have been violated

Scatterplot

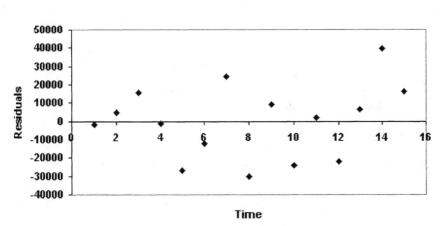

The alternating up and down pattern suggests the residuals are not independent.

Normal Probability Plot

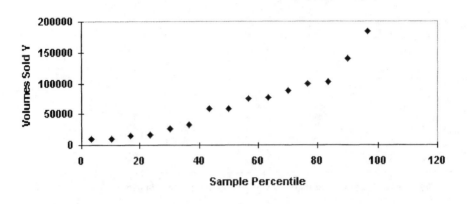

It appears the residuals are normally distributed.
Based upon the previous plots it appears that the model is not apt.

15.65

Scatterplot

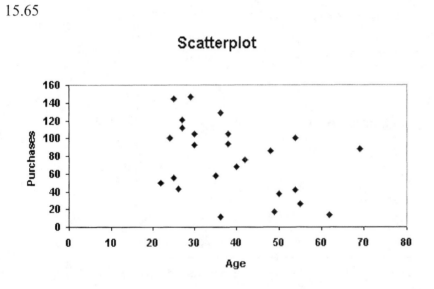

There appears to be a negative linear relationship between age and purchases.

Scatterplot

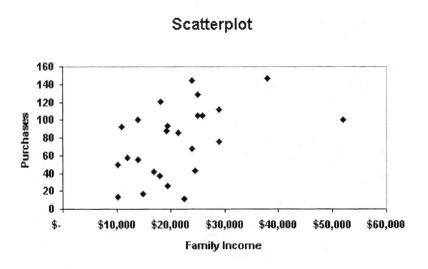

There appears to be a slight positive linear relationship between purchases and family income.

Scatterplot

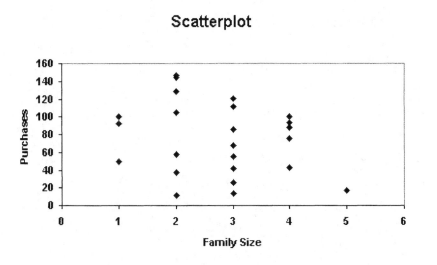

Based on the scatter plot it is difficult to detect any pattern of relationship between family size and purchases.

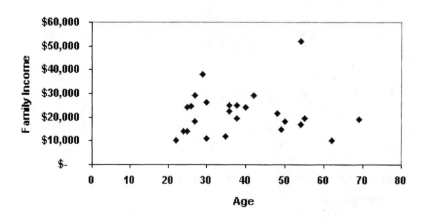

There does not appear to be any relationship between age and family income.

There appears to be a slightly positive linear relationship between age and family size.

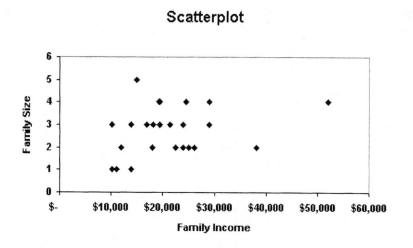

There seems to be little correlation between income and family size.

15.67

Family income was brought into the model because it had the highest correlation with average monthly purchases.

Using PHStat:

J.J. McCracken
Table of Results for Forward Selection

Family Income X2 entered.

	df	SS	MS	F	Significance F
Regression	1	8118.480548	8118.480548	6.14241706	0.020968538
Residual	23	30399.27945	1321.707802		
Total	24	38517.76			

	Coefficients	Standard Error	t Stat	P-value	Lower 95%	Upper 95%
Intercept	33.7553515	18.76904387	1.798458765	0.08524316	-5.07132112	72.5820241
Family Income X2	0.0019913	0.000803465	2.478390013	0.02096854	0.000329208	0.00365339

15.69

Using the Excel printout from problem 15.68 the interval is: 0.000329 – 0.003653. This interval indicates that as income increases, families spend more money at McCracken, and the average per dollar increase in purchasing is in the range indicated.

15.71

There are several issues to address when deciding whether to add a new variable to the regression model. Among these are:

1. Did the adjusted R^2 increase? In this case, the answer is yes, from 0.2108 to 0.3905.

2. Did the standard error decrease? Yes, from 36.3553 to 32.5313. Note that when the adjusted R^2 increases, the SSE will also decrease.

3. For a model that will be used for forecasting purposes, is the added variable significant? In this case the critical t value is equal to ± 2.074. Since the calculated t = -2.593 < -2.074 we conclude the variable is significant.

4. Does the introduction of the new variable into the model introduce a high level of multicollinearity? In this case, age, is negatively correlated with the dependent variable. This is consistent with the resulting sign on the regression coefficient when age is entered. The low correlation between x_1 and x_2 is an indication that the addition of x_1 will not introduce much multicollinearity problem.

15.73

For reasonable levels of alpha, only two variables will enter the model. In order for the variable, Family Size, to enter, the significance level would have to be larger than .25. Thus, the model will be cut-off at two variables.

Possible points to consider in the report are:
Relatively low R^2 compared to 1.0
The relatively large standard error given the size of the dependent variable.
The fact that there are many other variables that could have been included in the model but no data were collected.

15.75

a. Minitab scatter plot:

There is one pronounced "turn" in the scatter plot. This suggests that the polynomial should be a second order polynomial

b. Minitab output:

Regression Analysis: Income/loss versus Sales, SalesSq

```
The regression equation is
Income/loss = 35 - 0.443 Sales + 0.000078 SalesSq


Predictor         Coef      SE Coef      T      P
Constant          34.6        199.9    0.17   0.867
Sales          -0.4427       0.1642   -2.70   0.031
SalesSq      0.00007783   0.00002512   3.10   0.017


S = 373.295   R-Sq = 59.3%   R-Sq(adj) = 47.7%


Analysis of Variance

Source          DF       SS       MS      F      P
Regression       2   1420900   710450   5.10   0.043
Residual Error   7    975444   139349
Total            9   2396343
```

The equation is $\hat{y} = 35 - 0.443x + 0.000078x^2$

c. The parameters of interest are the population coefficients of x and x^2. The test statistic provided by Minitab is F = 5.10. The numerator degrees of freedom are k = 2 and the denominator degrees of freedom are n – k – 1 = 10 – 2 – 1 = 7; giving a critical value of 3.257 (Using Excel's FINV option), since F = 5.10 > 3.257, conclude the overall model is significant.

d. The parameter of interest is the population coefficient of x^2 since x^2 furnishes the curvature for the model. The test statistic provided by Minitab in part b. is t = 3.10. The degrees of freedom are n – k - 1 = 10 – 2 – 1 = 7 giving an upper critical value of 2.9979. Since t = 3.10 > 2.9979, there is sufficient evidence to conclude that curvature exists in the model that predicts Amazon's net income/loss using sales figures.

15.77
a. Minitab output:

Regression Analysis: Market Value versus 52WK HI, P- E, HISq, PESq, HIPE

```
The regression equation is
Market Value = 2857 - 26.4 52WK HI - 80.6 P- E + 0.115 HISq + 2.31 PESq
             + 0.542 HIPE


Predictor    Coef  SE Coef      T      P
Constant     2857     1674   1.71  0.110
52WK HI    -26.36    51.02  -0.52  0.613
P- E       -80.63    69.80  -1.16  0.267
HISq       0.1151   0.5240   0.22  0.829
PESq       2.3133   0.8019   2.88  0.012
HIPE       0.5421   0.6228   0.87  0.399


S = 803.423   R-Sq = 89.3%   R-Sq(adj) = 85.4%


Analysis of Variance

Source          DF        SS        MS      F      P
Regression       5  75146023  15029205  23.28  0.000
Residual Error  14   9036840    645489
Total           19  84182863
```

The estimated regression equation is

$$\hat{y} = 2857 - 26.4x_1 - 80.6x_2 + 0.115x_1^2 + 2.31x_2^2 + 0.542x_1x_2$$

b. The appropriate residual plot to determine if the linear function is the appropriate regression function is a plot of the residuals versus the independent variable (x) or the fitted value ($\hat{y}_i$).

Minitab plot:

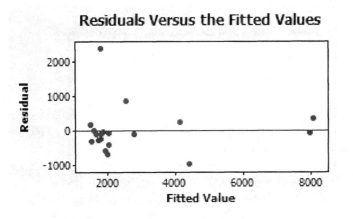

Residuals Versus the Fitted Values

This residual plot shows the residuals scattered about 0 in a band. The residual plot supports the choice of the linear model.

c. The appropriate residual plot to determine if the residuals have a constant variance is a plot of the residuals versus the independent variable (x) or the fitted value ($\hat{y}_i$).

Minitab plot:

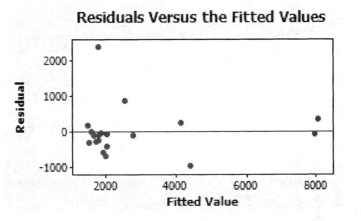

Residuals Versus the Fitted Values

With the exception of what might be an outlier, the residual plot indicates that the dispersion is constant for any given fitted value taking in to account that the residuals are samples. This indicates that the residuals do have constant variances.

d. The appropriate residual plot to determine if the residuals are independent is a plot of the residuals versus a "time" variable.
    Minitab plot:

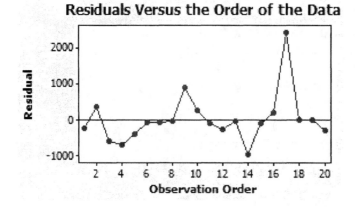

Residuals Versus the Order of the Data

This residual plot shows the residuals exhibit a "wave form." The linear model appears to be insufficient. The addition of an independent variable representing time is indicated.

e. Minitab probability plot:

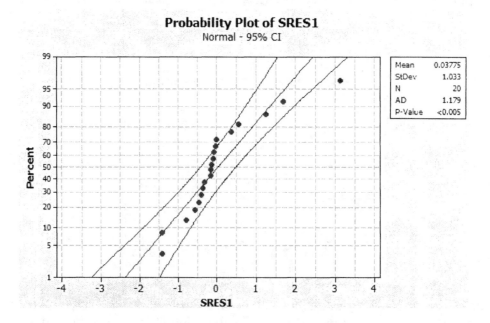

Probability Plot of SRES1
Normal - 95% CI

The probability plot shows two of the standardized residuals beyond the confidence bounds. This indicates that the error terms are not normally distributed. A transformation of the independent or dependent variables is required.

15.79

To deal with the categorical variables, we will recode the data, using dummy variables, as follows:

Driver Sex: Male = 1   Female = 0

Seat belt status:	D1	D2	D3
Not observed	0	0	0
Wearing	1	0	0
Not wearing	0	1	0
Not required	0	0	1

Knowledge of seat belt law	D4	D5	D6
No response	0	0	0
Aware	1	0	0
Not aware	0	1	0
Uncertain	0	0	1

Employment Status	D7	D8	D9
No response	0	0	0
Employed	1	0	0
Unemployed	0	1	0
Retired	0	0	1

Insurance Certificate	D10	D11	D12
Not observed	0	0	0
In vehicle	1	0	0
Not in vehicle	0	1	0
Other	0	0	1

Because D9 and D12 have no entries, they must be eliminated before the correlation matrix is determined. The correlation matrix becomes:

Chapter 15

	Driv Citat	Vehil Year	Sex	Age	D1	D2	D3	D4	D5	D6	D7	D8	Year In State	Regis Vehic	Years Ed	D10	D11	Ins Status
Driv Citat	1																	
Vehic Year	0.030071	1																
Sex	0.257473	-0.25833	1															
Year	0.290971	0.116277	-0.04182	1														
D1	0.017898	0.155711	-0.12042	0.064997	1													
D2	0.012496	-0.06634	0.052132	-0.08079	-0.907	1												
D3	0.016939	-0.24442	0.129048	-0.01959	-0.107	-0.262	1											
D4	0.103341	0.189027	0.045194	-0.06644	0.1669	-0.099	-0.182	1										
D5	-0.08893	0.073879	-0.11676	-0.00231	-0.107	0.118	-0.031	-0.641	1									
D6	-0.00774	-0.22917	0.104828	0.181912	-0.087	-0.059	0.3936	-0.521	-0.0251	1								
D7	0.134696	-0.09875	0.192186	-0.30686	-0.107	0.083	0.0098	0.0392	0.0098	-0.1905	1							
D8	0.134696	0.098752	-0.19219	0.306856	0.107	-0.083	-0.01	-0.039	-0.0098	0.1905	-1	1						
Year in State	0.174276	0.12232	0.088115	0.610012	-0.113	0.092	-0.05	0.0234	-0.0856	0.0744	-0.039	0.0391	1					
No. Veh	0.176535	-0.04777	0.136736	0.330033	0.1512	-0.129	0.0028	0.0265	-0.0433	0.0584	-0.012	0.0118	0.285945	1				
Years Edu	0.005358	0.247238	-0.13712	0.048782	0.2284	-0.206	-0.116	0.1549	0.0024	-0.287	-0.059	0.0593	0.055306	0.108400	1			
D10	0.067598	0.070845	-0.02452	0.034299	-0.004	0.035	-0.001	0.2242	-0.0012	-0.2036	0.1382	-0.138	0.103962	0.189502	-0.1026	1		
D11	0.067597	-0.07084	0.024523	-0.0343	0.0043	-0.035	0.0012	-0.224	0.0012	0.2036	-0.138	0.1382	-0.10396	0.189502	0.1026	-1	1	
Ins Stat	0.002831	0.060221	0.127365	0.046721	-0.098	0.07	0.0482	0.0783	-0.1815	0.0392	-0.042	0.0425	0.166711	0.149672	-0.0169	0.1409	-0.141	1

Because of the large number of independent variables neither Excel or the PHStat programs will handle this problem. Using the stepwise option in Minitab we find:

Stepwise Regression: Vehicle Year versus Driving Cita, Driver Sex, ...

```
  Alpha-to-Enter: 0.15  Alpha-to-Remove: 0.15


Response is Vehicle Year on 17 predictors, with N = 100


Step                    1      2      3
Constant            90.57  71.45  73.18

Driver Sex          -11.4  -10.1   -9.1
T-Value             -2.65  -2.37  -2.16
P-Value             0.009  0.020  0.034

Years Education            1.53   1.39
T-Value                    2.24   2.06
P-Value                    0.028  0.043

D3                                 -24
T-Value                          -2.04
P-Value                          0.044

S                    20.5   20.1   19.8
R-Sq                 6.67  11.25  14.95
R-Sq(adj)            5.72   9.42  12.29
```

So only the drivers' gender (male or female), years education and the dummy variable associated with not being required to wear a seat belt are significant in the model. However, only 14.959% of the variation in the year of the vehicle can be explained by the available data.

Chapter 16 Solutions

When applicable, selected problems in each section will be done following the appropriate step-by-step procedures outlined in the corresponding sections of the chapter. Other problems will provide key points and the answers to the questions, but all answers can be arrived at using the appropriate steps.

Section 16-1 Exercises

16.1

Generally, quantitative forecasting techniques can be used whenever historical data related to the variable of interest exist, the historical data can be quantified and the past is prologue to the future. That is to say, we believe that the historical patterns will continue into the future. Whenever these conditions do not exist, for example, when a new product is introduced for which there is no historical data, then a qualitative technique, which relies on expert opinion, market surveys, or managerial judgment, must be used for forecasting the product's demand.

16.3

Past measurement of the variable of interest measured at successive points in time is a good definition of time series data. Examples of time series data are the quarterly revenues of a publicly traded company, temperatures taken hourly, the daily patient population count of a local hospital, the number of houses sold every month. Any past measurement of the variable of interest taken at successive points in time is time series data.

16.5

The trend component is one of four generally recognized components of time series data. These components are the trend, the seasonal, the cyclical, and the random. Not every time series exhibits all of these components, but every time series will exhibit at least one of these components.

The trend is the long-term increase or decrease in a variable being measured over time. Trends can be classified as either linear or nonlinear, depending on whether their rate of change is relatively constant or not. A good way to identify whether or not a trend component is present in a time series is to use a time series plot.

16.7

    a. The forecasting horizon is the lead time: the number of periods between when the forecast is made and time period to which it applies. Here the forecast is made in March and is applicable in September. There are six time periods (months) between March and September. Therefore, the forecasting horizon is 6 months.

    b. The medium term forecast has a forecasting horizon of three months to two years. Since this forecasting horizon is six months, it would be considered to me a medium term forecast.

    c. The forecasting period is the unit of time for which forecasts are to be made. Here that unit of time is a month.

    d. The forecasting interval is the frequency with which new forecasts are prepared. Here a forecast is made each year (every 12 months). Therefore, the forecasting interval is 12months.

16.9

    a. This part of the exercise is done using Equation 16-1 following the steps shown in Example 16-1. Radio advertising has a base value of 300 and newspaper advertising has a base value of 400.

Year	Radio advertising	Index	Newspaper Ad	Index
1	300	100.00	400	100
2	310	103.33	420	105
3	330	110.00	460	115
4	346	115.33	520	130
5	362	120.67	580	145
6	380	126.67	640	160
7	496	165.33	660	165

    b. The unweighted aggregate index is found using Equation 16-2 following the steps shown in Example 16-2.

Year	Radio advertising	Newspaper Ad	Sum	Index
1	300	400	700	100.00
2	310	420	730	104.29
3	330	460	790	112.86
4	346	520	866	123.71
5	362	580	942	134.57
6	380	640	1020	145.71
7	496	660	1156	165.14

c. The Laspreyres Index is found using Equation 16-4 following Example 16-4.

Year	Radio	% radio	Newspaper	Laspeyres
1	300	0.3	400	100
2	310	0.42	420	104.59
3	330	0.42	460	113.78
4	346	0.4	520	126.43
5	362	0.38	580	139.08
6	380	0.37	640	151.89
7	496	0.43	660	165.08

d. The Paasche Index is constructed using Equation 16-3 following Example 16-3.

Year	Radio	% radio	Newspaper	Paasche
1	300	0.3	400	100
2	310	0.42	420	104.41
3	330	0.42	460	113.22
4	346	0.4	520	124.77
5	362	0.38	580	136.33
6	380	0.37	640	148.12
7	496	0.43	660	165.12

16.11

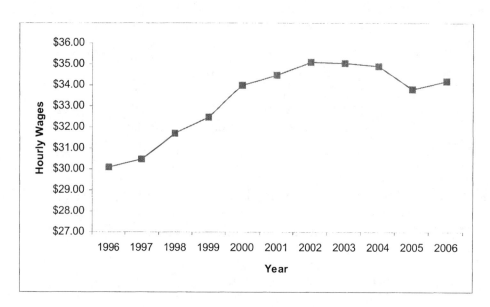

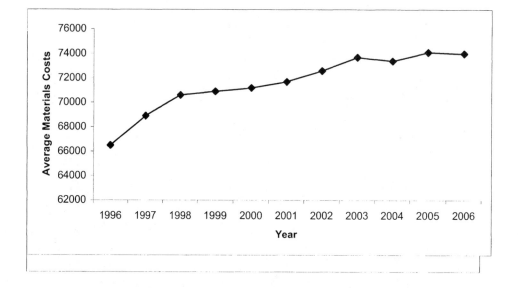

Both graphs show an upward trend with random components. The average material cost time series exhibits a cyclical component with a recurrence period of five years. The hourly wages time series may be indicating a cyclical component with a recurrence period of nine years. However, there is not enough data to determine if this pattern will repeat.

16.13

This exercise should be done using Equation 16-4 following the steps shown in Example 16-4. However, first we must convert hourly wages to reflect their impact on the cost of a house. So, in 1996:

$$.6(\text{cost of a house}) = \$66500$$
$$\text{Cost of a house} = \$110833$$
$$\text{Labor cost} = \$110833 - 66500 = \$44333$$

Year	Labor Costs	Materials Costs	% Materials	% Labor	Laspeyres Index
1996	44333	66500	60	40	100.00
1997	49893	68900	58	42	106.36
1998	57764	70600	55	45	113.59
1999	58009	70900	55	45	114.07
2000	55943	71200	56	44	112.95
2001	61078	71700	54	46	117.03
2002	67015	72600	52	48	122.09
2003	73700	73700	50	50	127.88
2004	67754	73400	52	48	123.44
2005	74100	74100	50	50	128.57
2006	83447	74000	47	53	134.95

16.15

a. Minitab Time Series Plot:

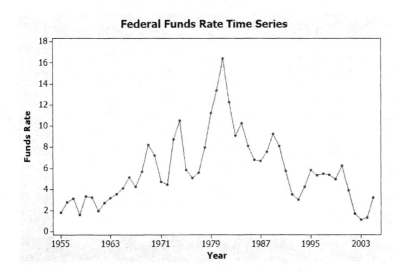

b. There are two distinct areas exhibiting a linear trend. In the time period 1955 – 1980 the trend is positive. In the time period 1981 – 2005 the trend is negative. A cyclical component is evidenced by the wave form which re-occurs approximately every five years. Finally, random components are evident throughout the time series indicated by the random deviations from a "smooth" wave form.

    c. The wave form repeats itself approximately every five years. Thus, the recurrence period is 5 years.

16.17

    a. The Laspeyres Index (for instance) for the 1st Qtr of 2000 is calculated as

$$I_t = \frac{\sum q_o p_t}{\sum q_o p_o} = \frac{736784(0.994) + 5838(0.006)}{720122(0.994) + (4615)(0.006)}(100) = 1.31.$$

The other indices are

Quarter	Total Sales	E-Commerce	% E-C	I_t
2006 Q_1	950892	25218	2.6	132.06
2005 Q_4	922500	23569	2.5	128.12
2005 Q_3	920884	22656	2.4	127.89
2005 Q_2	901813	21410	2.3	125.24
2005 Q_1	882446	20118	2.2	122.55
2004 Q_4	872468	19146	2.1	121.17
2004 Q_3	852892	18024	2.1	118.45
2004 Q_2	838525	17091	2.0	116.45
2004 Q_1	831010	16407	1.9	115.41
2003 Q_4	814969	15372	1.9	113.18
2003 Q_3	814198	14630	1.8	113.07
2003 Q_2	791446	13679	1.7	109.91
2003 Q_1	787291	12772	1.6	109.33
2002 Q_4	779680	12317	1.6	108.28
2002 Q_3	778522	11559	1.5	108.12
2002 Q_2	768926	10835	1.4	106.78
2002 Q_1	763071	10094	1.3	105.97
2001 Q_4	776493	9419	1.2	107.83
2001 Q_3	751150	8314	1.1	104.31
2001 Q_2	757004	8394	1.1	105.12
2001 Q_1	748652	8254	1.1	103.96
2000 Q_4	745258	7876	1.0	103.49
2000 Q_3	740730	7353	1.0	102.86
2000 Q_2	734915	6495	0.9	102.06
2000 Q_1	736784	5838	0.8	102.31
1999 Q_4	720122	4615	0.6	100.00

b. The Laspeyres Index for 1st Qtr of 2004 is 115.41 This means that the actual percentage change in the retail sales for the period of the 4th Qtr 1999 to the 1st Qtr of 2004 is 15.41%.

c. The Laspeyres Index for 1st Qtr of 2004 is 115.41. Therefore, to determine the actual percentage change in the retail sales for the period of the 1st Qtr 2004 to the 1st Qtr of 2006 is, the calculation is

$$\frac{132.06-115.41}{115.41}100 = 14.43\%.$$

Section 16-2 Exercises

16.19   This exercise follows the procedure outlined in Figures 16-19 and 16-20.

Month	Sales	12-Period Moving Average	Centered Moving Average	Ratio to MA
1	23500			
2	21700			
3	18750			
4	22000			
5	23000			
6	26200	28337.500		
7	27300	28337.500	28337.500	0.963
8	29300	28479.167	28408.333	1.031
9	31200	28700.000	28589.583	1.091
10	34200	28883.333	28791.667	1.188
11	39500	29208.333	29045.833	1.360
12	43400	29500.000	29354.167	1.478
13	23500	29816.667	29658.333	0.792
14	23400	30075.000	29945.833	0.781
15	21400	30350.000	30212.500	0.708
16	24200	30475.000	30412.500	0.796
17	26900	30683.333	30579.167	0.880
18	29700	30616.667	30650.000	0.969
19	31100	31241.667	30929.167	1.006
20	32400	31825.000	31533.333	1.027
21	34500	32525.000	32175.000	1.072
22	35700	33216.667	32870.833	1.086
23	42000	33850.000	33533.333	1.252
24	42600	34191.667	34020.833	1.252
25	31000	34450.000	34320.833	0.903
26	30400	34808.333	34629.167	0.878
27	29800	35241.667	35025.000	0.851
28	32500	35800.000	35520.833	0.915
29	34500	35933.333	35866.667	0.962
30	33800	36333.333	36133.333	0.935
31	34200	36450.000	36391.667	0.940
32	36700	36883.333	36666.667	1.001
33	39700	37000.000	36941.667	1.075
34	42400	37175.000	37087.500	1.143
35	43600	37366.667	37270.833	1.170
36	47400	37525.000	37445.833	1.266
37	32400	37800.000	37662.500	0.860
38	35600	38075.000	37937.500	0.938
39	31200	38366.667	38220.833	0.816
40	34600	38725.000	38545.833	0.898
41	36800	39266.667	38995.833	0.944
42	35700	39658.333	39462.500	0.905
43	37500			
44	40000			
45	43200			
46	46700			
47	50100			
48	52100			

16.21

The individual ratio to moving average values are shown below, along with the normalized values.

	Ratio to MA Values			Total	Seasonal Index	Normalized Index
January	0.792	0.903	0.860	2.556	0.852	0.849
February	0.781	0.878	0.938	2.598	0.866	0.863
March	0.708	0.851	0.816	2.375	0.792	0.789
April	0.796	0.915	0.898	2.608	0.869	0.866
May	0.880	0.962	0.944	2.785	0.928	0.925
June	0.969	0.935	0.905	2.809	0.936	0.933
July	0.963	1.006	0.940	2.909	0.970	0.966
August	1.031	1.027	1.001	3.060	1.020	1.016
September	1.091	1.072	1.075	3.238	1.079	1.075
October	1.188	1.086	1.143	3.417	1.139	1.135
November	1.360	1.252	1.170	3.782	1.261	1.256
December	1.478	1.252	1.266	3.996	1.332	1.327
				Sum =	12.045	

The normalized index for January, .849, compared to July, .966, indicates that both months have sales below the average trend value for the year, but January's are lower than July's.

16.23

This exercise is completed using the procedures outlined in Figure 16-18 through 16-24.

a.

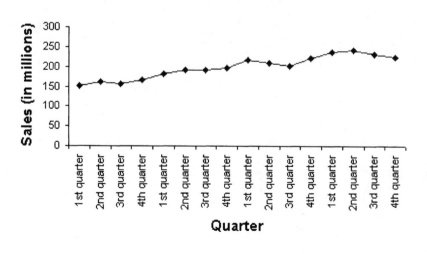

There appears to be an upward linear trend but you also see a seasonal component as a slight drop in the 3rd quarter.

b.

Year	Quarter	Period	Actual Sales	4 Period Moving Average	Centered Moving Average	Ratio to MA	Deseasonalized Sales
2003	1st quarter	1	152				146.858
	2nd quarter	2	162	159.5			158.684
	3rd quarter	3	157	167	163.250	0.962	163.553
	4th quarter	4	167	174.5	170.750	0.978	169.689
2004	1st quarter	5	182	183	178.750	1.018	175.843
	2nd quarter	6	192	190.5	186.750	1.028	188.070
	3rd quarter	7	191	199.25	194.875	0.980	198.972
	4th quarter	8	197	203.5	201.375	0.978	200.172
2005	1st quarter	9	217	206.25	204.875	1.059	209.659
	2nd quarter	10	209	212.25	209.250	0.999	204.722
	3rd quarter	11	202	217	214.625	0.941	210.431
	4th quarter	12	221	225.25	221.125	0.999	224.558
2006	1st quarter	13	236	232.5	228.875	1.031	228.016
	2nd quarter	14	242	233.25	232.875	1.039	237.046
	3rd quarter	15	231				240.642
	4th quarter	16	224				227.607

Because the seasonal index numbers do not add to 4, we normalize them by multiplying each by 4/4.00445 to get the following values:

Quarter	Seasonal Index
1	1.035013
2	1.020898
3	0.959934
4	0.984154

c.

SUMMARY OUTPUT					
Regression Statistics					
Multiple R	0.977				
R Square	0.954				
Adjusted R Square	0.951				
Standard Error	6.499				
Observations	16.000				

ANOVA					
	df	*SS*	*MS*	*F*	*Significance F*
Regression	1	12297.687	12297.687	291.180	9.14188E-11
Residual	14	591.276	42.234		
Total	15	12888.963			

	Coefficients	*Standard Error*	*t Stat*	*P-value*	
Intercept	147.913	3.408	43.402	2.5E-16	
Period	6.014	0.352	17.064	9.14E-11	

RESIDUAL OUTPUT

Observation	Predicted Deseasonalized Sales	Residuals	Squared Residuals	Absolute Value	
1	153.927	-7.069	49.966	7.069	
2	159.941	-1.257	1.580	1.257	
3	165.955	-2.402	5.770	2.402	
4	171.969	-2.280	5.199	2.280	
5	177.983	-2.140	4.580	2.140	
6	183.997	4.072	16.585	4.072	
7	190.011	8.961	80.292	8.961	
8	196.026	4.146	17.192	4.146	
9	202.040	7.620	58.057	7.620	
10	208.054	-3.332	11.103	3.332	
11	214.068	-3.637	13.226	3.637	
12	220.082	4.476	20.037	4.476	
13	226.096	1.920	3.688	1.920	
14	232.110	4.936	24.363	4.936	
15	238.124	2.517	6.336	2.517	
16	244.139	-16.532	273.303	16.532	
			MSE	MAD	
			36.955	4.831	

Values of the MSE and MAD are best used to compare two or more forecasting models. For this model the MAD, for instance indicates the average forecasting error is less than five (million). For the final period of data this is about 2%, which might be considered acceptable.

d. and e.

Quarter	Period	Seasonally Unadjusted Forecast	Seasonal Index	Seasonally Adjusted Forecast
Quarter 1 2007	17	250.15	1.0350	258.91
Quarter 2 2007	18	256.17	1.0209	261.52
Quarter 3 2007	19	262.18	0.9599	251.68
Quarter 4 2007	20	268.20	0.9842	263.95

16.25

a. As an example, the first moving averages is calculated as:

$$\frac{2+12+23+20}{4} = 14.25.$$

Minitab output:

t	Yt	MA
1	2	*
2	12	14.25
3	23	18.25
4	20	23.25
5	18	29.50
6	32	34.75
7	48	39.00
8	41	44.00
9	35	51.75
10	52	57.25
11	79	*
12	63	*

b. The centered moving average is the average of each adjacent pair of moving averages. As an example, the moving average for time period 2 =

$$\frac{14.25 + 18.25}{2} = 16.25$$

Minitab output:

t	Yt	MA	Centered MA
1	2	*	*
2	12	14.25	*
3	23	18.25	16.250
4	20	23.25	20.750
5	18	29.50	26.375
6	32	34.75	32.125
7	48	39.00	36.875
8	41	44.00	41.500
9	35	51.75	47.875
10	52	57.25	54.500
11	79	*	*
12	63	*	*

c. To calculate the ratio-to-moving-averages, each time series value is divided by the corresponding centered moving average. As an example, the first ratio-to-moving-average is calculated as 23/16.25 = 1.41538. The ratio-to-moving-averages are:

t	Yt	MA	Centered MA	Ratio
1	2	*	*	*
2	12	14.25	*	*
3	23	18.25	16.250	1.41538
4	20	23.25	20.750	0.96386
5	18	29.50	26.375	0.68246
6	32	34.75	32.125	0.99611
7	48	39.00	36.875	1.30169
8	41	44.00	41.500	0.98795
9	35	51.75	47.875	0.73107
10	52	57.25	54.500	0.95413
11	79	*	*	*
12	63	*	*	*

d. To calculate the seasonal indexes, the average of the ratio-to-moving-averages are calculated for each quarter. As an example, the seasonal index for the first quarter is calculated as $\dfrac{0.68246 + 0.73107}{2} = 0.70676$; the second quarter $= 0.97512$; the third quarter $= 1.35854$; and the fourth quarter $= 0.97590$. The sum of the seasonal indexes $= 4.01632$. The indexes are adjusted by dividing each by the sum of the seasonal indexes and multiplying the result by 4 (for quarterly data). Thus, the first $= [0.70676/4.01632]4 = 0.70389$, the second 0.97116, the third 1.35302, and the fourth 0.97194.

e. We deseasonalize the data by dividing the actual data by the appropriate seasonal index. As example, the first observation is deseasonalized by $2/0.70389 = 2.84135$.

Minitab output:

t	Yt	Deseasonalized
1	2	2.8414
2	12	12.3564
3	23	16.9990
4	20	20.5774
5	18	25.5722
6	32	32.9503
7	48	35.4762
8	41	42.1837
9	35	49.7237
10	52	53.5442
11	79	58.3879
12	63	64.8188

f. The trend line is produced using Minitab

Minitab output:

Regression Analysis: Deseasonalized versus t

```
The regression equation is
Deseasonalized = - 0.607 + 5.42 t

Predictor      Coef   SE Coef      I      P
Constant    -0.6067    0.8505   -0.71  0.492
t            5.4194    0.1156   46.90  0.000

S = 1.38186   R-Sq = 99.5%   R-Sq(adj) = 99.5%

Analysis of Variance

Source          DF      SS      MS       F      P
Regression       1  4199.9  4199.9  2199.40  0.000
Residual Error  10    19.1     1.9
Total           11  4219.0

Predicted Values for New Observations

New
Obs    Fit  SE Fit        95% CI             95% PI
  1  69.845   0.850  (67.950, 71.740)  (66.230, 73.461)
  2  75.265   0.954  (73.139, 77.390)  (71.523, 79.006)
  3  80.684   1.060  (78.322, 83.046)  (76.803, 84.565)X
  4  86.103   1.168  (83.501, 88.706)  (82.072, 90.135)X
```

The equation is $\hat{y}_t = -0.607 + 5.42t$

g. The unadjusted forecasts are produced, as an example, by $\hat{y}_{13} = -0.607 + 5.42(13) = 69.845$, $\hat{y}_{14} = 75.265$, $\hat{y}_{15} = 80.684$, and $\hat{y}_{16} = 86.103$. To provide the seasonalized adjusted forecasts, the unadjusted forecasts are multiplied by the appropriate seasonal index. So $\hat{y}_{13} = 0.70389(69.845) = 49.1632$, $\hat{y}_{14} = 0.97116(75.265) = 73.0944$, $\hat{y}_{15} = 1.35302(80.684) = 109.1671$, and $\hat{y}_{16} = 0.97194(86.103) = 83.6870$.

16.27

a. Minitab scatter plot:

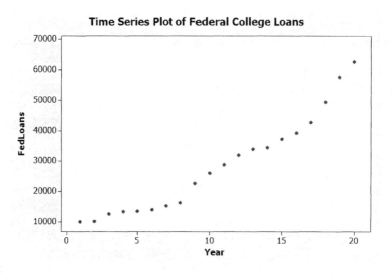

There appears to be a linear trend evidenced by the slope from low to high values. Randomness is exhibited since not all of the data points would lie on a straight line.

b. Minitab output:

Regression Analysis: FedLoans versus Year

```
The regression equation is
FedLoans = 990 + 2623 Year

Predictor    Coef   SE Coef      T       P
Constant      990      1932    0.51   0.615
Year       2622.8     161.3   16.26   0.000

S = 4159.83   R-Sq = 93.6%   R-Sq(adj) = 93.3%

Analysis of Variance

Source           DF          SS            MS        F        P
Regression        1  4574695629    4574695629   264.37   0.000
Residual Error   18   311474937      17304163
Total            19  4886170566
```

The regression equation is $\hat{y} = 990 + 2623t$ and the coefficient of determination is $R^2 = 93.6\%$. To determine if a linear trend exists, we test that the slope is equal to zero: H_O: $\beta_1 = 0$, H_A: $\beta_1 \neq 0$; $\alpha = 0.10$, Minitab lists the p-value as 0.000. Therefore, reject the null hypothesis. There does exist enough evidence to indicate that there exists a linear trend in this data

c. The school year 2010-11 is year 26. Therefore, we produce a 90% prediction interval for the loan amount in year 26.

Minitab output:

```
Predicted Values for New Observations

New
Obs    Fit  SE Fit        90% CI           90% PI
  1  69183    2668  (64557, 73809)  (60614, 77752)
```

Thus, the prediction interval is (60614, 77752) in $ millions.

16.29

This exercise is completed using the procedures outlined in Figure 16-18 through 16-24.

a.

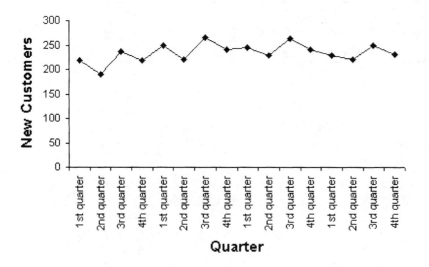

The graph indicates a seasonal component to the data.

b.

Regression analysis can be used to find the linear model needed to make forecasts for periods 13 – 16.

SUMMARY OUTPUT

Regression Statistics	
Multiple R	0.59044058
R Square	0.34862008
Adjusted R Square	0.28348208
Standard Error	17.9108678
Observations	12

ANOVA

	df	SS	MS	F	Significance F
Regression	1	1716.924825	1716.925	5.352024	0.043253006
Residual	10	3207.991841	320.7992		
Total	11	4924.916667			

	Coefficients	Standard Error	t Stat	P-value
Intercept	211.893939	11.02337709	19.22223	3.16E-09
Period	3.46503497	1.497782006	2.313444	0.043253

2001	Period	Forecast	Actual	Forecast Error	Forecast Error Squared	Absolute Error
Qtr. 1	13	256.9393939	229	-27.93939394	780.6097337	27.93939394
Qtr. 2	14	260.4044289	221	-39.4044289	1552.709017	39.4044289
Qtr. 3	15	263.8694639	248	-15.86946387	251.8398835	15.86946387
Qtr. 4	16	267.3344988	231	-36.33449883	1320.195806	36.33449883

MSE	MAD
976.33861	29.88694639

Values of the MSE and MAD are best used to compare two or more forecasting models. For this model the MAD, for instance indicates the average forecasting error is about 30. This is better than 10% of data values. The firm might decide this level of average error is too high.

c.

Quarter		1	2	3	4
		1.0655	0.9124	1.0752	0.9593
		0.9990	0.9349	1.0894	0.9897
Total		*2.0645*	*1.8473*	*2.1646*	*1.9490*
Seasonal Index		1.0323	0.9236	1.0823	0.9745

Since the index values do not add to 4, we normalize them by multiplying each one by 4/4.0127.

Quarter	Index
1	1.0290
2	0.9207
3	1.0789
4	0.9714

d. Run the regression model based upon the deseasonalized sales

2001	Period	Forecast
Qtr. 1	13	256.5620033
Qtr. 2	14	260.0884382
Qtr. 3	15	263.614873
Qtr. 4	16	267.1413079

e.

Period	Forecast	Seasonal Index	Adjusted Forecast	Actual	Differences	Difference Squared	Absolute Differences
13	256.562	1.0290	264.0107	229	-35.0107	1225.7504	35.0107
14	260.0884	0.9207	239.4574	221	-18.4574	340.6745	18.4574
15	263.6149	1.0789	284.4074	248	-36.4074	1325.4997	36.4074
16	267.1413	0.9714	259.5053	231	-28.5053	812.5503	28.5053
						MSE	*MAD*
						926.1187	*29.5952*

f. The adjusted model has a lower MSE and MAD so I would recommend the deseasonalized data model.

16.31

This exercise combines the linear model components developed in the Taft Ice Cream example with the nonlinear elements in the Harrison Equipment example.

a.

Regression
Analysis

Regression Statistics	
Multiple R	0.931912269
R Square	0.868460477
Adjusted R Square	0.858342052
Standard Error	19.63573031
Observations	15

ANOVA

	df	SS	MS	F	Significance F
Regression	1	33092.62857	33092.62857	85.8296117	4.33333E-07
Residual	13	5012.304762	385.5619048		
Total	14	38104.93333			

	Coefficients	Standard Error	t Stat	P-value	Lower 95%
Intercept	36.0952381	10.66923438	3.383114176	0.004898727	13.04576299
Month	10.87142857	1.173459332	9.264427219	4.33333E-07	8.336324301

Forecast for period 16 without transformation = 36.0952 + 10.8714(16) = 210.0376

Regression
Analysis

Regression Statistics	
Multiple R	0.98563659
R Square	0.971479488
Adjusted R Square	0.969285603
Standard Error	9.143186599
Observations	15

ANOVA

	df	SS	MS	F	Significance F
Regression	1	37018.16114	37018.16114	442.8122994	1.99795E-11
Residual	13	1086.772195	83.59786119		
Total	14	38104.93333			

	Coefficients	Standard Error	t Stat	P-value	Lower 95%
Intercept	65.29858233	3.620698469	18.03480265	1.39488E-10	57.47654036
Month^2	0.698807472	0.03320838	21.04310575	1.99795E-11	0.62706514

Forecast for period 16 with transformation $= 65.2986 + 0.6988(16)^2 =$ 244.1914

Actual cash balance for Month 16 was 305. The transformed model had a smaller error than the model without the transformation. Based on this analysis and the analysis from problem 16-30 students should prefer the transformed model.

b. Model without transformation:

For Individual Response Y	
Interval Half Width	48.27804189
Prediction Interval Lower Limit	161.7600534
Prediction Interval Upper Limit	258.3161371

Model with transformation:

For Individual Response Y	
Interval Half Width	23.89550188
Prediction Interval Lower Limit	220.29634337
Prediction Interval Upper Limit	268.08734713

The model without the transformation has the wider interval so based on this you should select the model with the transformation.

16.33

   a. Minitab scatter plot:

      There appears to be a linear trend evidenced by the slope from small to large values. Randomness is exhibited since not all of the data points would lie on a straight line.

   b. Minitab output:

Regression Analysis: E-Commerce versus Quarter

```
The regression equation is
E-Commerce = 3141 + 769 Quarter


Predictor    Coef   SE Coef      T      P
Constant   3141.1     378.3   8.30  0.000
Quarter    768.62     24.49  31.38  0.000


S = 936.666   R-Sq = 97.6%   R-Sq(adj) = 97.5%


Analysis of Variance

Source          DF          SS         MS       F      P
Regression       1   864009009  864009009  984.80  0.000
Residual Error  24    21056224     877343
Total           25   885065232
```

      The regression equation is $\hat{y} = 3141 + 769t$ and the coefficient of determination is $R^2 = 97.6\%$. To determine if a linear trend exists, we test that the slope is equal to zero: H_O: $\beta_1 = 0$, H_A: $\beta_1 \neq 0$; $\alpha = 0.10$, Minitab lists the p-value as 0.000. Therefore, reject the null hypothesis. There does exist enough evidence to indicate that there exists a linear trend in this data

c. Minitab output:

```
Predicted Values for New Observations

New
Obs    Fit  SE Fit      95% CI          95% PI
  1  23894     378  (23113, 24675)  (21809, 25979)
  2  24662     400  (23837, 25488)  (22561, 26764)
  3  25431     422  (24561, 26302)  (23311, 27551)
  4  26200     444  (25284, 27116)  (24060, 28339)
```

The fitted values are $F_{27} = 23894$, $F_{28} = 24662$, $F_{29} = 25431$, and $F_{30} = 26200$

d. The forecast bias is calculated as

$$\frac{\sum(y_t - F_t)}{n} =$$

$$\frac{(25916 - (23894)) \ + (26432 - (24662)) \ + (25096 - (25431)) \ + (26807 - (26200))}{4} = \frac{4064}{4}$$

$= 1016$. This says that, on average, the model over forecasts the e-commerce retail sales by $1016 million.

Section 16-3 Exercises

16.35

a.

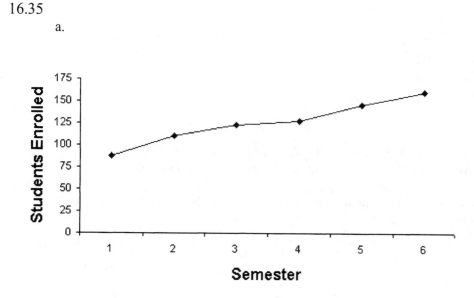

b. Yes it does appear that trend is present.

c. Equation 16-16 is used for this part of the exercise following Example 16-6.

Semester	Actual Enrollment	Forecast Enrollment	Forecast Error	Alsolute Forecast Error
1	87	90	-3.00	3.00
2	110	88.95	21.05	21.05
3	123	96.32	26.68	26.68
4	127	105.66	21.34	21.34
5	145	113.13	31.87	31.87
6	160	124.28	35.72	35.72
7		136.78		
			Sum	139.67
Alpha	0.35			
MAD	23.278			

d. Equations 16-18, 19 and 20 are used here following Example 16-7.

Semester	Actual Enrollment	Constant	Trend	Forecast Enrollment	Forecast Error	Absolute Forecast Error
Initial Values		80	10			
1	87	89.4	9.85	90	-3	3
2	110	101.4	10.39	99.25	10.75	10.75
3	123	114.03	10.95	111.79	11.21	11.21
4	127	125.38	11.05	124.98	2.02	2.02
5	145	138.15	11.48	136.43	8.57	8.57
6	160	151.7	12	149.62	10.38	10.38
7				163.69		
					Sum	45.93
Alpha	0.2					
Beta	0.25					
MAD	7.655					

e. The MAD for the single exponential smoothing forecast was 23.278
    The MAD for the double exponential smoothing forecast was 7.655

    The double exponential smoothing forecast appears to be doing the better job of forecasting course enrollment.

16.37

    a. Minitab scatter plot:

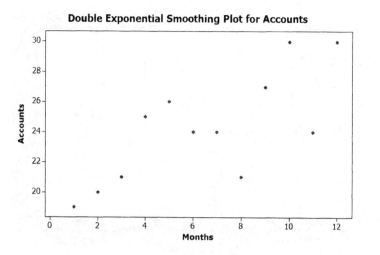

The time series contains a strong upward trend, so a double exponential smoothing model is selected.

    b. Minitab output:

Regression Analysis: Accounts versus Months

```
The regression equation is
Accounts = 19.4 + 0.752 Months


Predictor    Coef   SE Coef      T      P
Constant   19.364     1.550  12.49  0.000
Months     0.7517    0.2106   3.57  0.005


S = 2.51867   R-Sq = 56.0%   R-Sq(adj) = 51.6%


Analysis of Variance

Source           DF       SS      MS      F      P
Regression        1   80.813  80.813  12.74  0.005
Residual Error   10   63.437   6.344
Total            11  144.250
```

The equation is $\hat{y}_t = 19.364 + 0.7517t$. Since $C_0 = b_0$, $C_0 = 19.364$. $T_0 = b_1 = 0.7517$.

c. $F_1 = C_o + T_o = 19.3644 + 0.7517 = 20.1154$

$C_1 = \alpha y_1 + (1 - \alpha)(C_o + T_o) = 0.15(19) + (1 - 0.15)(20.1154) = 19.9481$

$T_1 = \beta(C_1 - C_o) + (1 - \beta)T_o = 0.25(19.948 - 19.3644) + 0.75(0.7517) = 0.7099$

$F_2 = C_1 + T_1 = 19.9483 + 0.7098 = 20.6580$

Calculations proceed in a similar way to produce:

Months	Accounts	Ct	Tt	Ft
1	19	19.9481	0.709921	20.1154
2	20	20.5593	0.685246	20.6580
3	21	21.2079	0.676076	21.2445
4	25	22.3513	0.792928	21.8839
5	26	23.5726	0.900018	23.1443
6	24	24.4018	0.882293	24.4727
7	24	25.0914	0.834142	25.2840
8	21	25.1867	0.649432	25.9256
9	27	26.0108	0.693076	25.8362
10	30	27.1983	0.816682	26.7038
11	24	27.4127	0.666122	28.0149
12	30	28.3670	0.738166	28.0788

The forecast is given by Minitab:

```
Forecasts

Period  Forecast    Lower    Upper
13       29.1052  23.9872  34.2231
```

d. MAD as calculated by Minitab:

```
Accuracy Measures

MAPE  8.58150
MAD   2.08901
MSD   6.48044
```

16.39

a.

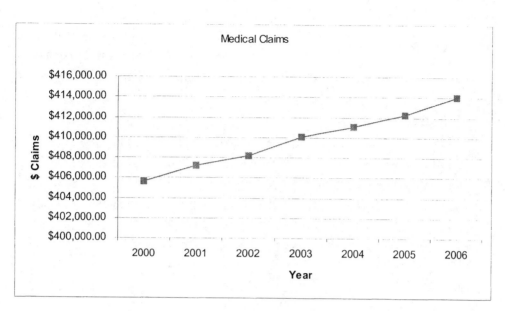

b. Use Equation 16-18, 19 and 20 and follow the steps in Example 16-7 using Regression coefficients for initial Constant and Trend.

```
The regression equation is

Medical Claims = 404331 + 1362 Year

Predictor       Coef   SE Coef        T       P
Constant      404331       202  1999.89   0.000
Year         1361.65     45.21    30.12   0.000

S = 239.219   R-Sq = 99.5%   R-Sq(adj) = 99.3%
```

c.

Year	Medical Claims	Constant	Trend	Forecast Claims	Forecast Error	Absolute Forecast Error
Initial Values		$404,331.00	$1,361.65			
2000	$405,642.43	$405,680.10	$1,359.77	$405,692.65	$50.22	$50.22
2001	$407,180.60	$407,075.05	$1,365.04	$407,039.86	-$140.74	$140.74
2002	$408,203.30	$408,380.89	$1,356.16	$408,440.09	$236.79	$236.79
2003	$410,088.03	$409,824.80	$1,369.33	$409,737.06	-$350.97	$350.97
2004	$411,085.64	$411,167.01	$1,365.26	$411,194.13	$108.49	$108.49
2005	$412,200.39	$412,449.29	$1,352.81	$412,532.26	$331.87	$331.87
2006	$414,043.90	$413,862.56	$1,361.88	$413,802.11	-$241.79	$241.79
				$415,224.44		**MAD**
						$208.70

See MAD calculations in the table in part b.

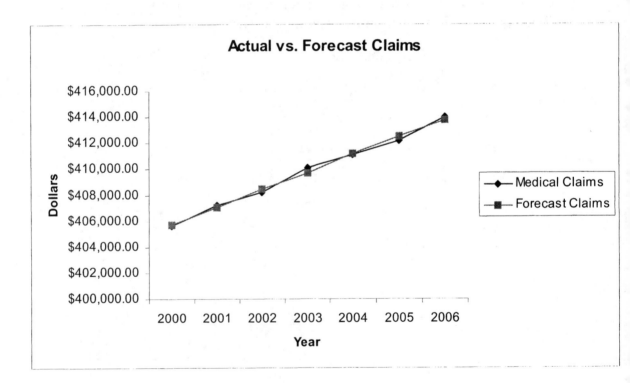

16.41

a. Minitab time series plot:

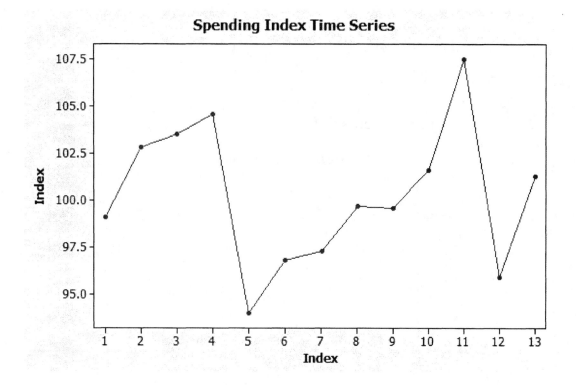

There does not appear to be any trend component in this time series.

b. The forecast is calculated as an example $F_1 = F_2 = 99.1$. Then $F_3 = 0.25y_2 + (1 - 0.25)F_2 = 0.25(102.8) + 0.75(99.1) = 100.025$. The forecasts are given in this Minitab output:

Time	Index	Smooth	Predict	Error
1	99.1	99.100	99.100	0.00000
2	102.8	100.025	99.100	3.70000
3	103.5	100.894	100.025	3.47500
4	104.6	101.820	100.894	3.70625
5	94.0	99.865	101.820	-7.82031
6	96.8	99.099	99.865	-3.06523
7	97.3	98.649	99.099	-1.79893
8	99.7	98.912	98.649	1.05081
9	99.6	99.084	98.912	0.68810
10	101.6	99.713	99.084	2.51608
11	107.5	101.660	99.713	7.78706
12	95.9	100.220	101.660	-5.75971
13	101.3	100.490	100.220	1.08022

c. $\text{MAD} = \dfrac{\sum |y_t - F_t|}{n} = \dfrac{42.4476}{13} = 3.2652$

d. $F_{14} = 0.25y_{13} + (1 - 0.25)F_{13} = 0.25(101.3) + 0.75(100.22) = 100.49$

16.43

a. Minitab time series plot:

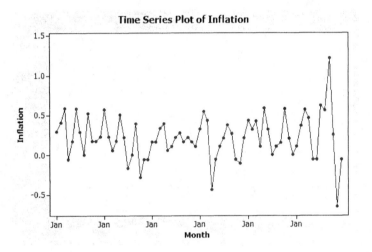

The time series does not exhibit a trend, so a single exponential smoothing model is selected.

There does not appear to be any trend component in this time series.

b. The forecast is calculated as an example $F_1 = F_2 = 0.296$. Then $F_3 = 0.15y_2 + (1 - 0.15)F_2 = 0.15(0.413) + 0.85(0.296) = 0.3136$.
The forecasts are given in this Minitab output:

Year	Month	Inflation (%)	Forecast	Absolute Value (Actual - Forecast)
2000	1	0.296	0.296	0.000
2000	2	0.413	0.296	0.117
2000	3	0.588	0.314	0.274
2000	4	-0.058	0.355	0.413
2000	5	0.176	0.293	0.117
2000	6	0.584	0.275	0.309
2000	7	0.290	0.322	0.032
2000	8	0.000	0.317	0.317
2000	9	0.521	0.269	0.252
2000	10	0.173	0.307	0.134
2000	11	0.173	0.287	0.114
2000	12	0.230	0.270	0.040
2001	1	0.573	0.264	0.309
2001	2	0.228	0.310	0.082
2001	3	0.057	0.298	0.241
2001	4	0.170	0.262	0.092
2001	5	0.510	0.248	0.262
2001	6	0.226	0.287	0.061
2001	7	-0.169	0.278	0.447
2001	8	0.000	0.211	0.211
2001	9	0.395	0.179	0.216
2001	10	-0.281	0.212	0.493
2001	11	-0.056	0.138	0.194
2001	12	-0.056	0.109	0.165
2002	1	0.169	0.084	0.085
2002	2	0.169	0.097	0.072
2002	3	0.337	0.108	0.229
2002	4	0.392	0.142	0.250
2002	5	0.056	0.180	0.124
2002	6	0.111	0.161	0.050
2002	7	0.223	0.153	0.070
2002	8	0.278	0.164	0.114
2002	9	0.166	0.181	0.015
2002	10	0.221	0.179	0.042
2002	11	0.166	0.185	0.019
2002	12	0.110	0.182	0.072

(Table continues on next page…)

(Continuation of Table from Page 559)

Year	Month	Inflation (%)	Forecast	Absolute Value (Actual - Forecast)
2003	1	0.330	0.171	0.159
2003	2	0.549	0.195	0.354
2003	3	0.436	0.248	0.188
2003	4	-0.435	0.276	0.711
2003	5	-0.055	0.170	0.225
2003	6	0.109	0.136	0.027
2003	7	0.218	0.132	0.086
2003	8	0.381	0.145	0.236
2003	9	0.271	0.180	0.091
2003	10	-0.054	0.194	0.248
2003	11	-0.108	0.157	0.265
2003	12	0.217	0.117	0.100
2004	1	0.432	0.132	0.300
2004	2	0.323	0.177	0.146
2004	3	0.429	0.199	0.230
2004	4	0.107	0.233	0.126
2004	5	0.587	0.214	0.373
2004	6	0.318	0.270	0.048
2004	7	0.000	0.277	0.277
2004	8	0.106	0.236	0.130
2004	9	0.158	0.216	0.058
2004	10	0.580	0.208	0.372
2004	11	0.210	0.263	0.053
2004	12	0.000	0.255	0.255
2005	1	0.105	0.217	0.112
2005	2	0.366	0.200	0.166
2005	3	0.573	0.225	0.348
2005	4	0.466	0.277	0.189
2005	5	-0.052	0.306	0.358
2005	6	-0.052	0.252	0.304
2005	7	0.619	0.206	0.413
2005	8	0.564	0.268	0.296
2005	9	1.223	0.313	0.910
2005	10	0.252	0.449	0.197
2005	11	-0.653	0.420	1.073
2005	12	-0.051	0.259	0.310
			0.212	Sum = 15.765

c. MAD = 15.765/71 = 0.222

d. $F_{73} = 0.15y_{72} + (1 - 0.15)F_{72} = 0.15(-0.051) + 0.85(0.259) = 0.212$

16.45

a. The time-series plot of the data indicates an upward trend over time. A forecasting model that can explicitly incorporate this trend effect is needed. The double exponential smoothing model will incorporate the trend effect.

b.   Use Equations 16-18, 19 and 20 and follow Example 16-7.

Month	Actual Shirts Sold	Constant	Trend	Forecast Shirts Sold	Absolute Forecast Error	MAD
Initial Values		28848.00	2488.96			
1	37630	32595.57	2866.54	31336.96	6293.04	6293.04
2	34780	35325.69	2825.62	35462.11	682.11	3487.58
3	35150	37551.04	2645.54	38151.30	3001.30	3325.48
4	45990	41355.26	2993.14	40196.58	5793.42	3942.47
5	36130	42704.73	2500.04	44348.41	8218.41	4797.66
6	47090	45581.81	2613.15	45204.76	1885.24	4312.25
7	37220	45999.97	1954.65	48194.96	10974.96	5264.07
8	49180	48199.70	2028.18	47954.63	1225.37	4759.23
9	40010	48184.30	1415.10	50227.88	10217.88	5365.75
10	50720	49823.53	1482.34	49599.41	1120.59	4941.23
11	63560	53756.69	2217.59	51305.87	12254.13	5606.04
12	48470	54473.42	1767.33	55974.28	7504.28	5764.23
13	64350	57862.60	2253.89	56240.76	8109.24	5944.61
14	69590	62011.19	2822.30	60116.49	9473.51	6196.68
15	69000	65666.79	3072.29	64833.49	4166.51	6061.33
16	71196	69230.46	3219.70	68739.08	2456.92	5836.06
17				72450.17		
Alpha	0.2					
Beta	0.3					

SUMMARY OUTPUT

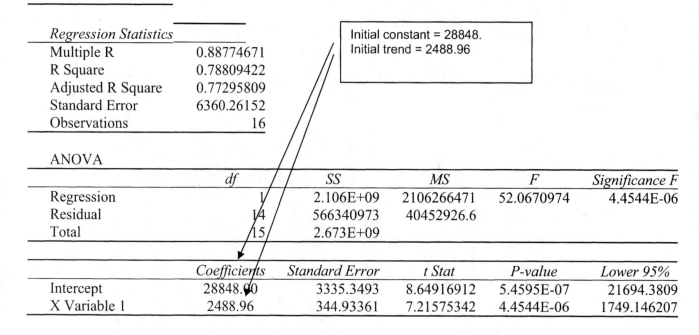

Regression Statistics	
Multiple R	0.88774671
R Square	0.78809422
Adjusted R Square	0.77295809
Standard Error	6360.26152
Observations	16

Initial constant = 28848.
Initial trend = 2488.96

ANOVA

	df	SS	MS	F	Significance F
Regression	1	2.106E+09	2106266471	52.0670974	4.4544E-06
Residual	14	566340973	40452926.6		
Total	15	2.673E+09			

	Coefficients	Standard Error	t Stat	P-value	Lower 95%
Intercept	28848.00	3335.3493	8.64916912	5.4595E-07	21694.3809
X Variable 1	2488.96	344.93361	7.21575342	4.4544E-06	1749.146207

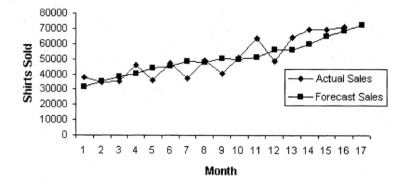

The MAD produced by the double exponential smoothing model at the end of month 16 is smaller than the MAD produced by the single exponential smoothing model. This is due to the fact that the double exponential smoothing model explicitly incorporates the trend effect that is present in the time series, thus, producing a more accurate forecast.

c.

Beta Values 5136.51	Alpha Values							
	0.05	0.1	0.15	0.2	0.25	0.3	0.35	0.4
0.05	5136.51	5259.61	5338.25	5410.42	5538.97	5664.36	5779.94	5893.95
0.1	5161.78	5314.37	5413.38	5490.21	5636.92	5756.44	5863.68	5969.74
0.15	5190.25	5373.74	5489.53	5587.58	5728.26	5835.69	5929.96	6055.09
0.2	5221.54	5435.98	5563.39	5680.04	5807.55	5897.36	5975.45	6140.21
0.25	5258.63	5499.53	5632.25	5763.76	5871.37	5939.32	6053.73	6213.94
0.3	5304.15	5563.03	5693.97	5836.06	5917.96	5961.39	6121.89	6284.81
0.35	5351.00	5631.84	5746.89	5895.15	5946.77	6024.47	6178.71	6394.69
0.4	5398.88	5697.43	5817.68	5940.06	5958.25	6080.76	6226.07	6497.20
0.45	5447.51	5758.44	5883.23	5970.43	5971.96	6126.74	6325.85	6591.03
0.5	5496.65	5814.14	5939.24	5986.43	6023.34	6162.71	6417.80	6675.50
0.55	5546.03	5866.59	5985.16	5988.63	6065.82	6218.98	6501.02	6750.50
0.6	5595.43	5913.91	6020.70	5977.92	6099.54	6305.10	6575.09	6816.40
0.65	5644.63	5954.43	6045.79	5985.32	6124.84	6383.23	6639.99	6873.95
0.7	5693.43	5987.86	6060.56	6024.76	6144.13	6452.95	6696.06	6924.16
0.75	5741.63	6013.98	6065.31	6057.17	6223.13	6514.11	6743.92	6968.24
0.8	5789.07	6032.66	6060.45	6082.70	6295.19	6566.84	6784.40	7007.50
0.85	5835.56	6066.82	6046.53	6101.58	6359.94	6611.48	6818.49	7043.24
0.9	5880.96	6098.20	6024.14	6114.14	6417.20	6648.56	6847.27	7076.77
0.95	5925.12	6127.30	6004.03	6126.16	6466.98	6678.76	6871.87	7109.26

d.&e. Student reports will vary but could include comments such as: The data table shows the MAD values for different combinations of alpha and beta values. Of the combinations considered the minimum MAD at the end of month 16 occurs when alpha = 0.05 and beta = 0.05. The forecast for month 17 with alpha = 0.05 and beta = 0.05 is 71,128.45.

End of Chapter Exercises

16.47

A seasonal component is one that is repeated throughout a time series and has a recurrence period of at most one year. A cyclical component is one that is represented by wavelike fluctuations that has a recurrence period of more than one year. Seasonal components are more predictable.

16.49

    a. Since the recurrence period is less than one year, a seasonal component exists in the time series.

    b. The pattern is linear with a positive slope. This indicates that a linear trend component exists.

    c. Since the recurrence period is more than one year, a cyclical component exists in the time series.

    d. The time series is exhibiting changes in time with no other components. Therefore, the time series is exhibiting a random component.

    e. The steady decrease indicates a linear trend component. The "wave-like" shape with recurrence period of 10 years indicates that a cyclical component also exists.

16.51

    a. This problem should be solved using the steps outlined in the Taft Ice Cream example of section 16-2.

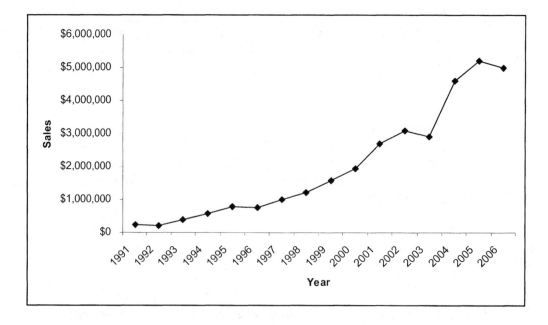

There does appear to be an upward linear trend

b.

SUMMARY OUTPUT						
Regression Statistics						
Multiple R	0.9479					
R Square	0.8985					
Adjusted R Square	0.8913					
Standard Error	567012.9456					
Observations	16					
ANOVA						
	df	*SS*	*MS*	*F*	*Significance F*	
Regression	1	3.98574E+13	3.99E+13	123.9719	2.43055E-08	
Residual	14	4.50105E+12	3.22E+11			
Total	15	4.43585E+13				
	Coefficients	*Standard Error*	*t Stat*	*P-value*	*Lower 95%*	*Upper 95%*
Intercept	-682238010.3021	61455226.5311	-11.1014	2.52E-08	-814046479.3	-5.5E+08
Year	342385.2941	30750.5945	11.1343	2.43E-08	276431.7698	408338.8

It is expected that as time increases by one year the sales are expected to increase by $342,385.2941. There is a fairly strong relationship since the correlation coefficient is 0.9479. Since 123.9719 > 4.6001 you would conclude that there is a significant relationship.

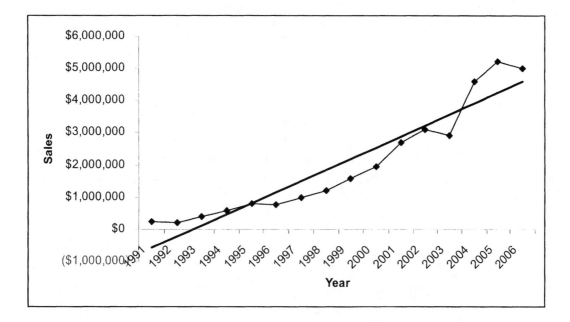

c.

Observation	Predicted Sales	Residuals	Absolute Residual
1	(548,889.7059)	788,889.7059	788,889.7059
2	(206,504.4118)	424,504.4118	424,504.4118
3	135,880.8823	269,119.1177	269,119.1177
4	478,266.1764	108,733.8236	108,733.8236
5	820,651.4706	(25,651.4706)	25,651.4706
6	1,163,036.7647	(401,036.7647)	401,036.7647
7	1,505,422.0588	(507,422.0588)	507,422.0588
8	1,847,807.3529	(630,807.3529)	630,807.3529
9	2,190,192.6471	(620,192.6471)	620,192.6471
10	2,532,577.9412	(585,577.9412)	585,577.9412
11	2,874,963.2353	(163,963.2353)	163,963.2353
12	3,217,348.5294	(113,348.5294)	113,348.5294
13	3,559,733.8236	(641,733.8236)	641,733.8236
14	3,902,119.1177	703,880.8823	703,880.8823
15	4,244,504.4118	971,495.5882	971,495.5882
16	4,586,889.7059	423,110.2941	423,110.2941
		MAD =	461,216.7279

d.

Year	Forecast
2007	4,929,275.00
2008	5,271,660.29
2009	5,614,045.59
2010	5,956,430.88
2011	6,298,816.18

e.

For Individual Response Y	
Interval Half Width	1232095.322
Prediction Interval Lower Limit	5066720.854
Prediction Interval Upper Limit	7530911.499

16.53

Use Equations 16-18, 19, 20 and follow the steps outlined in Example 15-7.

a.

The starting values (-891,275,11) and (342,385.29) for this model are determined using simple linear regression with the time defined as 1, 2, . . . 16

0.2	
0.4	
$ (891,275.00)	
$ 342,385.29	

Period	Year	Sales	Constant	Trend	Forecast	Error	Absolute Error
1	1901	$240,000.00	$(391,111.76)	$405,496.47	$(548,889.71)	$788,889.71	$788,889.71
2	1992	$218,000.00	$55,107.76	$421,785.69	$14,384.71	$203,615.29	$203,615.29
3	1993	$405,000.00	$462,514.77	$416,034.22	$476,893.46	$(71,893.46)	$71,893.46
4	1994	$587,000.00	$820,239.19	$392,710.30	$878,548.98	$(291,548.98)	$291,548.98
5	1995	$795,000.00	$1,129,359.59	$359,274.34	$1,212,949.49	$(417,949.49)	$417,949.49
6	1996	$762,000.00	$1,343,307.14	$301,143.63	$1,488,633.93	$(726,633.93)	$726,633.93
7	1997	$998,000.00	$1,515,160.61	$249,427.56	$1,644,450.77	$(646,450.77)	$646,450.77
8	1998	$1,217,000.00	$1,655,070.54	$205,620.51	$1,764,588.18	$(547,588.18)	$547,588.18
9	1999	$1,570,000.00	$1,802,552.84	$182,365.23	$1,860,691.05	$(290,691.05)	$290,691.05
10	2000	$1,947,000.00	$1,977,334.45	$179,331.78	$1,984,918.07	$(37,918.07)	$37,918.07
11	2001	$2,711,000.00	$2,267,532.99	$223,678.48	$2,156,666.23	$554,333.77	$554,333.77
12	2002	$3,104,000.00	$2,613,769.17	$272,701.56	$2,491,211.47	$612,788.53	$612,788.53
13	2003	$2,918,000.00	$2,892,776.59	$275,223.90	$2,886,470.74	$31,529.26	$31,529.26
14	2004	$4,606,000.00	$3,455,600.40	$390,263.87	$3,168,000.50	$1,437,999.50	$1,437,999.50
15	2005	$5,216,000.00	$4,119,891.41	$499,874.72	$3,845,864.26	$1,370,135.74	$1,370,135.74
16	2006	$5,010,000.00	$4,697,812.91	$531,093.43	$4,619,766.13	$390,233.87	$390,233.87
17	2007				$5,228,906.34		
					MAD		$526,262.47

b.

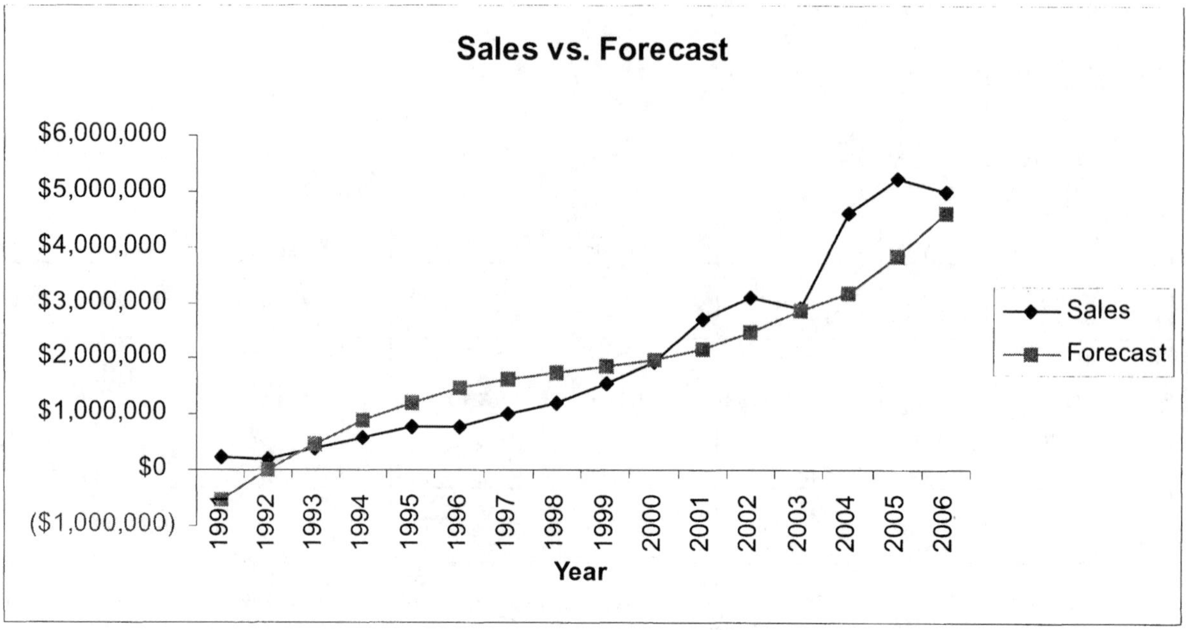

c.

$ 526,262.47	Beta Values 0.5	0.4	0.3	0.2
Alpha Values 0.1	$568,793.54	$547,728.21	$523,915.68	$498,375.36
0.2	$538,592.87	$526,262.47	$515,577.21	$497,639.06
0.3	$481,539.18	$466,164.76	$459,595.63	$452,681.23
0.4	$454,803.56	$449,962.38	$436,850.70	$421,877.56

Different combinations of alpha and beta, including the initial values of 0.2 and 0.4, were evaluated using Excel's data table feature. Note that the combination of alpha = 0.4 and Beta = 0.2 produced the smallest MAD of the alpha/beta combinations evaluated.

16.55

a.
Minitab scatter plot:

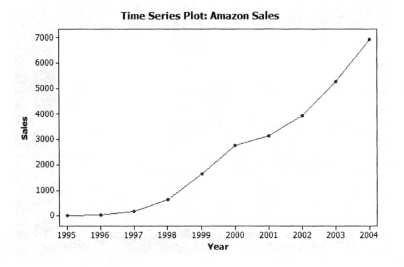

The time series contains a strong upward trend, so a double exponential smoothing model is selected.

b.
Minitab output:

Regression Analysis: Yt versus t

```
The regression equation is
Yt = - 1779 + 767 t


Predictor      Coef  SE Coef      T      P
Constant    -1778.7    442.1  -4.02  0.004
t            767.33    71.25  10.77  0.000


S = 647.119   R-Sq = 93.5%   R-Sq(adj) = 92.7%


Analysis of Variance

Source           DF        SS        MS       F      P
Regression        1  48575116  48575116  116.00  0.000
Residual Error    8   3350102    418763
Total             9  51925218
```

The equation is $\hat{y}_t = -1778.7 + 767.33t$.
Since $C_o = b_o$, $C_o = -1778.7$. $T_o = b_1 = 767.33$.

c.

$$F_1 = C_o + T_o = -1778.7 + 767.33 = -1011.37$$

$$C_1 = \alpha y_1 + (1 - \alpha)(C_o + T_o) = 0.10(0.5) + (1 - 0.10)(-1011.37) = -910.183$$

$$T_1 = \beta(C_1 - C_o) + (1 - \beta)T_o = 0.20(-910.183 - (-1778.7)) + 0.80(767.33) = 787.567$$

$$F_2 = C_1 + T_1 = -910.183 + 787.567 = -122.6156$$

Calculations proceed in a similar way to produce

Year	AvePrice	Ct	Tt	Ft
1	0.5	-910.18	787.563	-
2	15.7	-108.79	790.330	-122.62
3	147.7	628.16	779.653	681.54
4	609.8	1328.01	763.693	1407.81
5	1639.8	2046.51	754.655	2091.70
6	2761.9	2797.24	753.869	2801.17
7	3122.9	3508.29	745.305	3551.11
8	3932.9	4221.52	738.891	4253.59
9	5263.7	4990.74	744.957	4960.42
10	6921.1	5854.24	768.665	5735.70

$$F_{2005} = 5854.24 + 768.665 = \$6622.91$$

d.

MAD as calculated by Minitab:

```
Accuracy Measures

MAPE    20382
MAD       521
MSD    395394
```

16.57

This exercise is completed using the procedures outlined in Figure 16-18 through 16-24.

a.

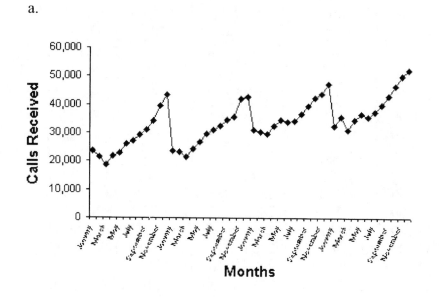

There appears to be a slight linear trend as well as a seasonal trend.

b.

Month	Period	Calls Received	12 Period Moving Average	Centered Moving Average	Ratio to MA	Deseasonalized Data
January	1	23,500				27685.13302
February	2	21,700				25154.19025
March	3	18,750				23768.62844
April	4	22,000				25399.2792
May	5	23,000				24866.29326
June	6	26,200	28337.5			28083.95273
July	7	27,300	28337.5	28337.5	0.9634	28261.05611
August	8	29,300	28479.1667	28408.3333	1.0314	28835.55904
September	9	31,200	28700	28589.5833	1.0913	29012.859
October	10	34,200	28883.3333	28791.6667	1.1878	30135.79141
November	11	39,500	29208.3333	29045.8333	1.3599	31448.77185
December	12	43,400	29500	29354.1667	1.4785	32699.31442
January	13	23,500	29816.6667	29658.3333	0.7924	27685.13302
February	14	23,400	30075	29945.8333	0.7814	27124.79501
March	15	21,400	30350	30212.5	0.7083	27127.92793
April	16	24,200	30475	30412.5	0.7957	27939.20712
May	17	26,900	30683.3333	30579.1667	0.8797	29082.75169
June	18	29,700	30616.6667	30650	0.969	31835.6258
July	19	31,100	31241.6667	30929.1667	1.0055	32194.82948
August	20	32,400	31825	31533.3333	1.0275	31886.42024
September	21	34,500	32525	32175	1.0723	32081.52677
October	22	35,700	33216.6667	32870.8333	1.0861	31457.53665
November	23	42,000	33850	33533.3333	1.2525	33439.20044
December	24	42,600	34191.6667	34020.8333	1.2522	32096.56208

(Table continues on next page…)

(Continuation of Table from Page 572.)

Month	Period	Calls Received	12 Period Moving Average	Centered Moving Average	Ratio to MA	Deseasonalized Data
January	25	31,000	34450	34320.8333	0.9032	36520.81377
February	26	30,400	34808.3333	34629.1667	0.8779	35239.04993
March	27	29,800	35241.6667	35025	0.8508	37776.27347
April	28	32,500	35800	35520.8333	0.915	37521.66245
May	29	34,500	35933.3333	35866.6667	0.9619	37299.4399
June	30	33,800	36333.3333	36133.3333	0.9354	36230.44283
July	31	34,200	36450	36391.6667	0.9398	35403.9604
August	32	36,700	36883.3333	36666.6667	1.0009	36118.25996
September	33	39,700	37000	36941.6667	1.0747	36917.00327
October	34	42,400	37175	37087.5	1.1432	37361.33205
November	35	43,600	37366.6667	37270.8333	1.1698	34713.07475
December	36	47,400	37525	37445.8333	1.2658	35713.07611
January	37	32,400	37800	37662.5	0.8603	38170.14085
February	38	35,600	38075	37937.5	0.9384	41266.78215
March	39	31,200	38366.6667	38220.8333	0.8163	39550.99773
April	40	34,600	38725	38545.8333	0.8976	39946.1391
May	41	36,800	39266.6667	38995.8333	0.9437	39786.06922
June	42	35,700	39658.3333	39462.5	0.9047	38267.06536
July	43	37,500				38820.13201
August	44	40,000				39365.95091
September	45	43,200				40171.65092
October	46	46,700				41150.33506
November	47	50,100				39888.1891
December	48	52,100				39254.24611

Since the index values do not add to 12, we will normalize them by multiplying each by 12/12.0448 to find the following values:

The seasonal index for August is 1.0161 which means that calls in August are 1.61% higher than the average for the year.

c. See part b for the deseasonalized data.

SUMMARY OUTPUT

Regression Statistics	
Multiple R	0.938916529
R Square	0.881564249
Adjusted R Square	0.878989559
Standard Error	1763.399426
Observations	48

ANOVA

	df	SS	MS	F	Significance F
Regression	1	1064707645	1.065E+09	342.3962	6.08795E-23
Residual	46	143040566.6	3109577.5		
Total	47	1207748211			

	Coefficients	Standard Error	t Stat	P-value
Intercept	25248.99786	517.1088997	48.827235	2.79E-41
Period	339.9681419	18.37273159	18.503952	6.09E-23

RESIDUAL OUTPUT

Observation	Predicted Deasonalized Data	Residuals	Absolute Residuals
1	25588.96601	2096.167014	2096.167
2	25928.93415	-774.7439033	774.7439
3	26268.90229	-2500.273849	2500.2738
4	26608.87043	-1209.591236	1209.5912
5	26948.83857	-2082.54531	2082.5453
6	27288.80672	795.1460107	795.14601
7	27628.77486	632.2812477	632.28125
8	27968.743	866.816042	866.81604
9	28308.71114	704.1478541	704.14785
10	28648.67928	1487.112131	1487.1121
11	28988.64743	2460.124421	2460.1244
12	29328.61557	3370.69885	3370.6989
13	29668.58371	-1983.450689	1983.4507
14	30008.55185	-2883.75684	2883.7568
15	30348.51999	-3220.592065	3220.5921
16	30688.48813	-2749.281019	2749.281
17	31028.45628	-1945.704589	1945.7046
18	31368.42442	467.2013825	467.20138
19	31708.39256	486.4369227	486.43692
20	32048.3607	-161.9404649	161.94046
21	32388.32884	-306.8020699	306.80207
22	32728.29699	-1270.760334	1270.7603
23	33068.26513	370.9353164	370.93532
24	33408.23327	-1311.671192	1311.6712

(Table continues on next page…)

(Continuation of Table from Page 575)

Observation	Predicted Deasonalized Data	Residuals	Absolute Residuals
25	33748.20141	2772.61236	2772.6124
26	34088.16955	1150.880375	1150.8804
27	34428.1377	3348.135775	3348.1358
28	34768.10584	2753.556612	2753.5566
29	35108.07398	2191.365918	2191.3659
30	35448.04212	782.4007099	782.40071
31	35788.01026	-384.0498666	384.04987
32	36127.9784	-9.718444423	9.7184444
33	36467.94655	449.056727	449.05673
34	36807.91469	553.4173575	553.41736
35	37147.88283	-2434.808083	2434.8081
36	37487.85097	-1774.774857	1774.7749
37	37827.81911	342.3217312	342.32173
38	38167.78726	3098.994898	3098.9949
39	38507.7554	1043.242329	1043.2423
40	38847.72354	1098.41556	1098.4156
41	39187.69168	598.3775417	598.37754
42	39527.65982	-1260.594467	1260.5945
43	39867.62797	-1047.495952	1047.496
44	40207.59611	-841.6451967	841.6452
45	40547.56425	-375.9133316	375.91333
46	40887.53239	262.8026692	262.80267
47	41227.50053	-1339.311431	1339.3114
48	41567.46867	-2313.222565	2313.2226

	MAD
	1424.277

d.

Month	Period	Forecast
January	49	41907.4368
February	50	42247.4050
March	51	42587.3731
April	52	42927.3412
May	53	43267.3072
June	54	43607.2753
July	55	43947.2434
August	56	44287.2115
September	57	44627.1796
October	58	44967.1477
November	59	45307.1157
December	60	45647.0837

e. Deseasonalizing the data has increased the R^2 and decreased the MAD.

Month	Period	Unadjusted Forecast	Seasonal Index	Adjusted Forecast
January	49	41907.4368	0.8488	35572.333
February	50	42247.4050	0.8627	36445.963
March	51	42587.3731	0.7889	33595.260
April	52	42927.3412	0.8662	37182.217

16.59

   a. Use Equations 16-18, 19, 20 and follow Example 16-7.

Beta	0.2
Initial Constant Value	23424.5567
Initial Trend Value	420.89

	Month Number	Calls Received	Constant	Trend	Forecast Calls	Error	Absolute Error
				407.075915			
Jan	1	23,500	23776.361	5	23845.45068	-345.45	345.45
				307.738457			
	2	21,700	23686.749	1	24183.43646	-2,483.44	2,483.44
				97.9589520			
	3	18,750	22945.59	9	23994.48762	-5,244.49	5,244.49
				56.2169900			
	4	22,000	22834.839	1	23043.54905	-1,043.55	1,043.55
				60.5747407			
	5	23,000	22912.845	5	22891.05623	108.94	108.94
				189.637951			
	6	26,200	23618.736	7	22973.41973	3,226.58	3,226.58
				329.303002			
	7	27,300	24506.699	4	23808.37373	3,491.63	3,491.63
				507.862922			
	8	29,300	25728.802	9	24836.00199	4,464.00	4,464.00
				706.396342			
	9	31,200	27229.332	3	26236.66451	4,963.34	4,963.34
				956.967224			
	10	34,200	29188.582	2	27935.72795	6,264.27	6,264.27
				1331.14524			
	11	39,500	32016.44	1	30145.54959	9,354.45	9,354.45
				1733.24184			
	12	43,400	35358.068	4	33347.58491	10,052.42	10,052.42

(Continuation of Table on Page 578)

	Month Number	Calls Received	Constant	Trend	Forecast Calls	Error	Absolute Error
Jan	13	23,500	34373.048	1189.589453	37091.30977	-13,591.31	13,591.31
	14	23,400	33130.11	703.0839626	35562.63727	-12,162.64	12,162.64
	15	21,400	31346.555	205.7562114	33833.19378	-12,433.19	12,433.19
	16	24,200	30081.849	-88.33623802	31552.31124	-7,352.31	7,352.31
	17	26,900	29374.81	-212.076748	29993.51275	-3,093.51	3,093.51
	18	29,700	29270.187	-190.5860861	29162.73345	537.27	537.27
	19	31,100	29483.681	-109.7701131	29079.60068	2,020.40	2,020.40
	20	32,400	29979.128	11.27346978	29373.91043	3,026.09	3,026.09
	21	34,500	30892.321	191.6573973	29990.40181	4,509.60	4,509.60
	22	35,700	32007.183	376.2982435	31083.97885	4,616.02	4,616.02
	23	42,000	34306.785	760.9589906	32383.48132	9,616.52	9,616.52
	24	42,600	36574.195	1062.249229	35067.74405	7,532.26	7,532.26
Jan	25	31,000	36309.156	796.7914501	37636.44447	-6,636.44	6,636.44
	26	30,400	35764.758	528.5535691	37105.94702	-6,705.95	6,705.95
	27	29,800	34994.649	268.8211216	36293.31119	-6,493.31	6,493.31
	28	32,500	34710.776	158.2823188	35263.47007	-2,763.47	2,763.47
	29	34,500	34795.247	143.5199837	34869.05838	-369.06	369.06
	30	33,800	34711.013	97.96931632	34938.76668	-1,138.77	1,138.77
	31	34,200	34687.186	73.61000976	34808.98266	-608.98	608.98
	32	36,700	35148.637	151.1781641	34760.79614	1,939.20	1,939.20
	33	39,700	36179.852	327.185561	35299.81508	4,400.18	4,400.18
	34	42,400	37685.63	562.9040561	36507.03762	5,892.96	5,892.96
	35	43,600	39318.827	776.96269	38248.53415	5,351.47	5,351.47
	36	47,400	41556.632	1069.131089	40095.79001	7,304.21	7,304.21

(Continuation of Table on page 579)

	Month Number	Calls Received	Constant	Trend	Forecast Calls	Error	Absolute Error
Jan	37	32,400	40580.61	660.1005654	42625.7631	10,225.76	10,225.76
	38	35,600	40112.569	434.4721236	41240.71105	-5,640.71	5,640.71
	39	31,200	38677.633	60.59048521	40547.04096	-9,347.04	9,347.04
	40	34,600	37910.579	-104.9384449	38738.22325	-4,138.22	4,138.22
	41	36,800	37604.512	-145.1640512	37805.64016	-1,005.64	1,005.64
	42	35,700	37107.478	-215.5379742	37459.34807	-1,759.35	1,759.35
	43	37,500	37013.552	-191.2155937	36891.94049	608.06	608.06
	44	40,000	37457.869	-64.10906545	36822.33679	3,177.66	3,177.66
	45	43,200	38555.008	168.1405197	37393.76037	5,806.24	5,806.24
	46	46,700	40318.519	487.2145671	38723.14882	7,976.85	7,976.85
	47	50,100	42664.587	858.9852223	40805.73362	9,294.27	9,294.27
	48	52,100	45238.858	1202.042338	43523.57	8,576.43	8,576.43
	49				46440.90		
						MAD	5,181.12

b.

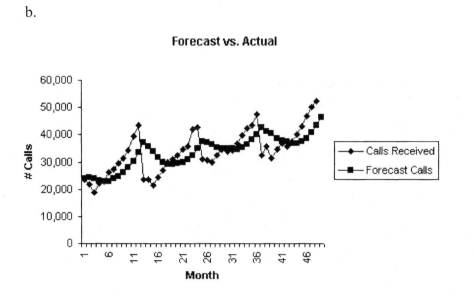

c. The double exponential explicitly models the trend effect. By developing the linear trend model on deseasonalized data you are able to adjust for both trend and seasonality. The MAD for the double exponential model is 5181.12. The MAD for the linear trend model based on deseasonalized data is 1,419.1298. I would recommend the linear trend model.

d.

Alpha	Beta 0.3	0.25	0.2	0.1
0.1	5190.35	5101.89	5013.90	4823.45
0.15	5397.24	5258.43	5130.99	4892.37
0.2	5538.02	5354.95	5181.12	4872.93
0.3	5374.41	5192.38	5019.96	4709.27

The data table above shows the MAD for various combinations of alpha and beta. Of the combinations considered, the values of alpha = 0.30 and beta = 0.10 provide the lowest MAD.

16.61
a.
Minitab time series plot

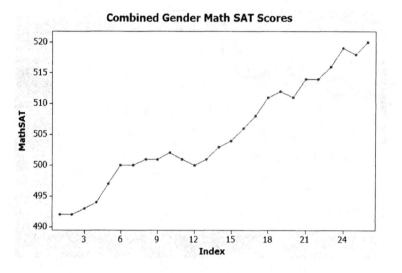

Combined Gender Math SAT Scores

b. Minitab output:

Regression Analysis: MathSAT versus Years

```
The regression equation is
MathSAT = 490 + 1.09 Years


Predictor     Coef  SE Coef       T      P
Constant   490.249    0.728  673.64  0.000
Years      1.09265  0.04712   23.19  0.000


S = 1.80215   R-Sq = 95.7%   R-Sq(adj) = 95.5%


Analysis of Variance

Source            DF     SS      MS       F      P
Regression         1  1746.1  1746.1  537.62  0.000
Residual Error    24    77.9     3.2
Total             25  1824.0
```

Using 1980 = year 1, the estimated regression equation is
$\hat{y}_t = 490.249 + 1.09265t$ and the coefficient of determination is $R^2 = 95.7\%$.

H_O: $\beta_1 \leq 0$,
H_A: $\beta_1 > 0$;
$\alpha = 0.10$,

the test statistic is $t = \dfrac{b_1 - \beta_1}{S_{b_1}} == 23.19$

the degrees of freedom $= n - 2 = 26 - 2 = 24$ and the critical value is $t_{0.10} =$ 1.3178, (6) The t test statistic of 23.19 is larger than the upper t-critical value of 1.3178. Therefore, reject the null hypothesis. There is sufficient evidence to indicate that the average SAT Math scores of students continue to increase during this period.

c. The year 2010 is represented by the time value $= 31$. Therefore, the forecast is $\hat{y}_t = 490.249 + 1.09265(31) = 524.1212$.

d. Time series forecasts are based on the assumption that the structure tha has occurred in the past will continue to occur in the future. Since the SAT math examination was changed in March 2005, it is quite dubious that the historical structure will repeat itself in the future. Making a forecast, as in part c., is an example of the regression concept of extrapolation.

Chapter 17 Solutions

When applicable, selected problems in each section will be done following the appropriate step-by-step procedures outlined in the corresponding sections of the chapter. Other problems will provide key points and the answers to the questions, but all answers can be arrived at using the appropriate steps.

Section 17-1 Exercises

17.1

The hypotheses are: H_O: $\tilde{\mu} \leq 10$

H_A: $\tilde{\mu} > 10$

W is found as follows:

Values	Difference	Absolute Difference	Rank	R+	R-
10.21	0.21	0.21	1	1	
13.65	3.65	3.65	9	9	
12.30	2.30	2.30	6	6	
9.51	-0.49	0.49	2		2
11.32	1.32	1.32	3	3	
12.77	2.77	2.77	8	8	
6.16	-3.84	3.84	10		10
8.55	-1.45	1.45	4		4
11.78	1.78	1.78	5	5	
12.32	2.32	2.32	7	7	
				W = 39	

Since this is an upper tail test, and n = 10, letting $\alpha = .05$, we reject if W > 45. Therefore, there is not enough evidence to reject the null hypothesis.

17.3

The hypotheses are: H_O: $\tilde{\mu} \geq 14$

H_A: $\tilde{\mu} < 14$

W is found as follows:

Values	Difference	Absolute Differences	Rank	R+	R-
9	-5	5	10		10
15.6	1.6	1.6	4	4	
21.1	7.1	7.1	11	11	
11.1	-2.9	2.9	6		6
13.5	-0.5	0.5	2		2
9.2	-4.8	4.8	8		8
13.6	-0.4	0.4	1		1
15.8	1.8	1.8	5	5	
12.5	-1.5	1.5	3		3
18.7	4.7	4.7	7	7	
18.9	4.9	4.9	9	9	
				W = 36	

Since this is an lower tail test, and n = 11, letting α = .05, we reject if W < 13. Therefore, there is not enough evidence to reject the null hypothesis.

17.5

a. The hypotheses are: H_0 : $\tilde{\mu} \leq 4000$

H_A : $\tilde{\mu} > 4000$

b. Using the Wilcoxon Signed Rank test we find W as follows:

Life	Difference	Absolute Difference	Rank	R+	R-
1973	-2027	2027	12		12
4459	459	459	3	3	
4838	838	838	9	9	
4098	98	98	1	1	
3805	-195	195	2		2
4722	722	722	6	6	
4494	494	494	4	4	
5894	1894	1894	11	11	
4738	738	738	7	7	
3322	-678	678	5		5
5249	1249	1249	10	10	
4800	800	800	8	8	
				W = 59	

Since this is an upper tail test and n = 12, letting α = .05, sum the positive ranks and reject if W > 61. Therefore, there is not enough evidence to reject the null hypothesis and the manager cannot conclude the median time is greater than 4000 hours.

17.7

By agreeing the mean weight is 11 ounces, but also claiming that more than 50% of the tubes contain less than 11 ounces, the consumer group is stating the distribution is skewed to the right and the median is less than 11 ounces. Putting the claim in the alternative hypothesis we are testing:

$$H_O: \quad \tilde{\mu} \geq 11$$
$$H_A: \quad \tilde{\mu} < 11$$

Using the Wilcoxon Signed Rank test we find W as follows:

Ounces	Difference	Absolute Differences	Rank	R+	R-
10.9	-0.1	0.1	1.5		1.5
11.7	0.7	0.7	15	15	
10.5	-0.5	0.5	12		12
11.8	0.8	0.8	17	17	
10.2	-0.8	0.8	17		17
11.5	0.5	0.5	12	12	
10.8	-0.2	0.2	4.5		4.5
11.2	0.2	0.2	4.5	4.5	
11.8	0.8	0.8	17	17	
10.7	-0.3	0.3	8		8
10.6	-0.4	0.4	10		10
10.9	-0.1	0.1	1.5		1.5
11.6	0.6	0.6	14	14	
11.2	0.2	0.2	4.5	4.5	
11	0	0			
10.7	-0.3	0.3	8		8
10.8	-0.2	0.2	4.5		4.5
10.5	-0.5	0.5	12		12
11.3	0.3	0.3	8	8	
10.1	-0.9	0.9	19		19
				W = 92	

Since one of the differences equaled 0, we only rank 19 values. This is a lower tail test with n = 19 and α = .05. We reject if W < 53. Therefore, there is not enough evidence to support the consumer group's claim.

17.9

Since we are interested in differences both above and below 30, this should be a two tailed test. The appropriate hypotheses are:

$$H_O: \quad \tilde{\mu} = 30$$
$$H_A: \quad \tilde{\mu} \neq 30$$

Using the Wilcoxon Signed Rank test we find W as follows:

Ounces	Difference	Absolute Differences	Rank	R+	R-
25	-5	5	10.5		10.5
24	-6	6	14.5		14.5
21	-9	9	17		17
35	5	5	10.5	10.5	
25	-5	5	10.5		10.5
25	-5	5	10.5		10.5
35	5	5	10.5	10.5	
38	8	8	16	16	
32	2	2	4	4	
36	6	6	14.5	14.5	
35	5	5	10.5	10.5	
29	-1	1	1.5		1.5
30	0	0			
27	-3	3	6.5		6.5
28	-2	2	4		4
27	-3	3	6.5		6.5
31	1	1	1.5	1.5	
32	2	2	4	4	
30	0	0			
30	0	0			
				W = 71.5	W = 81.5

Because some of the differences are 0, n = 17. From Appendix P, the upper and lower values for the Wilcoxon test are 34 and 119 for $\alpha = .05$. We do not reject the hypothesis.

Chapter 17

17.11

This problem is done following the steps outlined in Example 17.1.

a. The chi-square table will vary depending on how students construct the data classes, but using data classes one standard deviation wide, with the data mean of 7.6306 and a standard deviation of .2218, we find the following table and chi-square value.

e	o	$(o-e)^2/e$	
14.9440	21	2.45417	
32.4278	31	0.06287	
32.4278	27	0.90851	
14.9440	16	0.07462	sum = 3.5002

Testing at the $\alpha = .05$ level, $\chi_\alpha^2 = 5.9915$. Since the calculated $\chi^2 = 3.5002$ we do not reject the hypothesis the data come from a normal distribution.

b. Since we concluded the data come from a normal distribution we test the following:

$$H_O: \ \mu \geq 7.4$$
$$H_A: \ \mu < 7.4$$

Decision Rule: If $z < -1.645$, reject H_0, otherwise do not reject.

$$z = \frac{7.6306 - 7.4}{\frac{.2218}{\sqrt{95}}} = 10.13$$

Therefore, we do not reject the null hypothesis and conclude the average pH level is at least 7.4.

Section 17-2 Exercises

17.13

a. Use U_2, reject if $U \leq 11$.

b. Use U_1, reject if $U \leq 55$.

c. Use smallest of U_1 or U_2, reject if $U \leq 64$.

d. Use z value from Equation 17-8. Reject if $z < -1.645$

e. Use z value from Equation 17-8. Reject if $z < -1.28$ or $z > 1.28$.

17.15

This exercise can be done following the steps shown in the Blaine County Highway District Example.

a. Statistical evidence is associated with rejecting the null hypothesis, therefore the hypotheses are.

$$H_0: \tilde{\mu}_1 - \tilde{\mu}_2 \leq 0$$
$$H_A: \tilde{\mu}_1 - \tilde{\mu}_2 > 0$$

b. Constructing the table of ranks we find:

Sample 1	Rank (Sample 1)	Sample 2	Rank (Sample 2)
4.4	15.5	3.7	11
2.7	5	3.5	9.5
1	1	4	12
3.5	9.5	4.9	17
2.8	6.5	3.1	8
2.6	4	4.2	13
2.4	3	5.2	18
2	2	4.4	15.5
2.8	6.5	4.3	14
	Sum of Ranks = 53		Sum of Ranks = 118

Since the alternate hypothesis indicates population 1 has the larger median, we use U_1 as the test statistic.

$$U_1 = n_1 n_2 + \frac{n_1(n_1 + 1)}{2} - \sum R_1 = 9(9) + \frac{9(9+1)}{2} - 53 = 73$$

Using Appendix L with $n_1 = 9$ and $n_2 = 9$, the decision rule becomes:

Reject if $U \leq 21$

Since $U = 73$, we cannot reject the null hypothesis. We cannot conclude that the first population median exceeds the second population mean.

17.17

The hypotheses to test are:

$$H_0: \quad \tilde{\mu}_1 - \tilde{\mu}_2 = 0$$
$$H_A: \quad \tilde{\mu}_1 - \tilde{\mu}_2 \neq 0$$

This problem can be solved using Minitab.

Mann-Whitney Test and CI: C1, C2

C1   N = 40   Median =   481.50
C2   N = 35   Median =   505.00

Point estimate for ETA1-ETA2 is   -25.00

95.1 Percent CI for ETA1-ETA2 is (-62.00,9.00)

W = 1384.0

Test of ETA1 = ETA2 vs ETA1 not = ETA2 is significant at 0.1502

The test is significant at 0.1501 (adjusted for ties)

Cannot reject at alpha = 0.05

17.19

This exercise can be done following the steps shown in Example 17-2.

The hypotheses to test are:

$$H_0: \quad \tilde{\mu}_1 - \tilde{\mu}_2 = 0$$
$$H_A: \quad \tilde{\mu}_1 - \tilde{\mu}_2 \neq 0$$

Using Appendix N, with n = 10, the decision rule is:

Reject if $T \leq 8$

The following table is found. Note, the table shows the sum of the positive ranks because this gives a smaller sum than the sum of the negative ranks. In a two-tailed test, you always use the smallest sum to calculate T.

Item	Sample 1	Sample 2	d	Rank of d	Rank with smallest sum
1	19.6	21.3	-1.7	-7	
2	22.1	17.4	4.7	10	10
3	19.5	19	0.5	1	1
4	20	21.2	-1.2	-4.5	
5	21.5	20.1	1.4	6	6
6	20.2	23.5	-3.3	-9	
7	17.9	18.9	-1	-3	
8	23	22.4	0.6	2	2
9	12.5	14.3	-1.8	-8	
10	19	17.8	1.2	4.5	4.5
					T = 23.5

Since T = 23.5, we do not reject the null hypothesis.

17.21

This exercise can be done following the steps shown in Example 17-2.

The hypotheses to test are:
$$H_0: \quad \tilde{\mu}_1 - \tilde{\mu}_2 = 0$$
$$H_A: \quad \tilde{\mu}_1 - \tilde{\mu}_2 \neq 0$$

Using Appendix N, with $n = 7$, the decision rule is:

$$\text{Reject if } T \leq 2$$

The following table is found:

Sample 1	Sample 2	d	Rank of d	Rank with smallest sum
1004	1045	-41	-2	2
1245	1145	100	4.5	
1360	1400	-40	-1	1
1150	1000	150	6	
1300	1350	-50	-3	3
1450	1350	100	4.5	
900	1140	-240	-7	7
				T = 13

Since $T = 13$, we do not reject the null hypothesis.

17.23

This exercise can be done following the steps shown in Example 17-2.

H_0: $\tilde{\mu}_2 = \tilde{\mu}_1$
H_A: $\tilde{\mu}_2 \neq \tilde{\mu}_1$

Sample 1	Sample 2	d	Rank	Ranks with smallest sum
234	245	-11	-5	
221	224	-3	-2	
196	194	2	1	1
245	267	-22	-6	
234	230	4	3	3
204	198	6	4	4
				T = 8

If $T \leq 0$ reject H_0, otherwise do not reject H_0
Since $8 > 0$ do not reject H_0 and conclude that the medians are the same.

17.25

H_0: $\tilde{\mu}_P = \tilde{\mu}_H$
H_A: $\tilde{\mu}_P \neq \tilde{\mu}_H$

$U1 = (10)(8) + (10)(10+1)/2 - 92 = 43$

$U2 = (10)(8) + (8)(8+1)/2 - 79 = 37$

Decision Rule:

If $U \leq 13$ reject H_0, otherwise do not reject H_0
Since $37 > 13$ do not reject Ho and conclude that the produce would receive the same median ranking from each group

17.27

H_0: $\tilde{\mu}_S - \tilde{\mu}_J = 0$

H_A: $\tilde{\mu}_S - \tilde{\mu}_J \neq 0$

U1 = (6)(8) + (6)(6+1)/2 – 43 = 26

U2 = (6)(8) + (8)(8+1)/2 – 62 = 22

Utest = 22

The p-value = 0.426 do not reject Ho and conclude that there is no difference in median deductions taken for charitable contributions depending on whether the tax return was filed as a single or joint return.

17.31

This exercise can be done following the steps shown in Example 17-2.

a. Want to use a paired-t test

H_0: $\mu_d \geq 0$

H_A: $\mu_d < 0$

Old Material	New Material	d
45.5	47.0	-1.5
50.0	51.0	-1.0
43.0	42.0	1.0
45.5	46.0	-0.5
58.5	58.0	0.5
49.0	50.5	-1.5
29.5	39.0	-9.5
52.0	53.0	-1.0
48.0	48.0	0.0
57.5	61.0	-3.5
	Average	-1.7
	Std. Dev.	3.011091

$$t = (-1.7)/(3.011091/\sqrt{10}) = -1.785$$

Since –1.785 > t critical = -2.2622 do not reject H_0 and conclude that the soles made from the new material do not have a longer mean lifetime than those made from the old material.

b. H_0: $\tilde{\mu}_O \geq \tilde{\mu}_N$

H_A: $\tilde{\mu}_O < \tilde{\mu}_N$

Old Material	New Material	d	Rank d	Ranks with smallest expected sum
45.5	47.0	-1.5	-6.5	
50.0	51.0	-1.0	-4	
43.0	42.0	1.0	4	4.0
45.5	46.0	-0.5	-1.5	
58.5	58.0	0.5	1.5	1.5
49.0	50.5	-1.5	-6.5	
29.5	39.0	-9.5	-9	
52.0	53.0	-1.0	-4	
57.5	61.0	-3.5	-8	
			T=	5.5

One observation was removed because the difference was 0. Using $\alpha = 0.025$ the decision rule becomes:

If $T \leq 6$ reject H_0, otherwise do not reject H_0

Since $5.5 < 6$ reject H_0 and conclude that the medians are not the same.

c. Because you cannot assume the underlying populations are normal you must use the technique from part b.

17.33

This exercise can be done following the steps shown in the Future Vision Example.

a. H_0: $\tilde{\mu}_O \geq \tilde{\mu}_C$

H_A: $\tilde{\mu}_O < \tilde{\mu}_C$

See table on next page...

California Cars	Rank California	Out-of-State Cars	Rank Out-of-State
66	135.5	63	104
66	135.5	54	24.5
58	55	59	65.5
68	154	58	55
63	104	59	65.5
63	104	70	174
63	104	69	164.5
63	104	50	8.5
70	174	41	1
76	199.5	57	46
69	164.5	69	164.5
54	24.5	51	10.5
70	174	62	90
62	90	52	14.5
80	210.5	70	174
61	80	53	19
65	126.5	80	210.5
61	80	56	37
47	3	61	80
77	203.5	62	90
75	194	60	73.5
52	14.5	63	104
77	203.5	61	80
86	215	51	10.5
58	55	58	55
53	19	59	65.5
74	190	65	126.5
54	24.5	54	24.5
58	55	59	65.5
62	90	58	55
78	205.5	64	117.5
81	212.5	64	117.5
67	144.5	78	205.5
54	24.5	75	194
68	154	63	104
54	24.5	71	180.5
54	24.5	61	80
76	199.5	60	73.5
65	126.5	56	37
62	90	49	6
69	164.5	68	154
56	37	66	135.5
66	135.5	52	14.5
58	55	61	80
70	174	57	46

(Continuation of Table on Page 598)

57	46	63	104
48	4	55	30.5
74	190	79	208
52	14.5	60	73.5
49	6	49	6
79	208	73	188
70	174	57	46
71	180.5	67	144.5
63	104	59	65.5
67	144.5	72	185
68	154	67	144.5
68	154	58	55
65	126.5	55	30.5
63	104	68	154
61	80	75	194
56	37	59	65.5
68	154	62	90
69	164.5	66	135.5
68	154	63	104
72	185	70	174
68	154	64	117.5
57	46	64	117.5
52	14.5	57	46
66	135.5	69	164.5
63	104	76	199.5
57	46	64	117.5
65	126.5	52	14.5
56	37	64	117.5
71	180.5	72	185
55	30.5	59	65.5
64	117.5		7147

(Continuation of Table on Page 599)

62	90
76	199.5
66	135.5
62	90
64	117.5
59	65.5
72	185
54	24.5
75	194
63	104
59	65.5
42	2
64	117.5
65	126.5
70	174
55	30.5
63	104
58	55
63	104
69	164.5
66	135.5
65	126.5
62	90
66	135.5
56	37
66	135.5
67	144.5
79	208
74	190
67	144.5
68	154

(Continuation of Table on Page 600)

57	46
75	194
76	199.5
59	65.5
60	73.5
64	117.5
59	65.5
69	164.5
69	164.5
76	199.5
82	214
68	154
56	37
59	65.5
62	90
53	19
57	46
65	126.5
56	37
69	164.5
61	80
70	174
56	37
72	185
62	90
81	212.5
71	180.5
67	144.5
50	8.5
63	104
67	144.5
63	104
61	80
	16073

$$U1 = (140)(75) + (140)(140+1)/2 - 16073 = 4,297$$
$$U2 = (140)(75) + (75)(75+1)/2 - 7147 = 6,203$$

$$\mu = 140(75)/2 = 5,250$$

$$\sigma = \sqrt{140(75)(140+75+1)/12} = 434.7413$$

$$z = (4297-5250)/434.7413 = -2.19$$

$$\text{p-value} = 0.5 - 0.4857 = 0.0143$$

Since $0.0143 < 0.10$ reject H_o and conclude that California drivers do have a higher median driving speed than out-of-state drivers.

b. A type I error is rejecting a true null hypothesis. Since we rejected that out-of-state drivers drive at least as fast as California drivers we could be concluding that California drivers drive faster when in fact they do not.

17.35

This exercise can be done following the steps shown in Example 17-2.

a. Since the typists are rating the software systems, the data are ordinal

b. No, because the data is not at least interval; the median would be the best measure

c. H_0: $\tilde{\mu}_1 = \tilde{\mu}_2$
H_A: $\tilde{\mu}_1 \neq \tilde{\mu}_2$

Typist	System 1	System 2	d	Rank of d	Ranks with smallest sum
1	82	75	7	4.5	
2	76	80	-4	-2.5	2.5
3	90	70	20	8	
4	55	58	-3	-1	1
5	49	53	-4	-2.5	2.5
6	82	75	7	4.5	
7	90	80	10	6.5	
9	70	80	-10	-6.5	6.5
				T=	12.5

One observation was removed because the difference was 0. Using $\alpha = .01$, the decision rule is:

If $T \leq 2$ reject H_o, otherwise do not reject H_o

Since $12.5 > 2$ do not reject H_o and conclude that the medians are the same for both types of word processing systems

d. Since there is no significant difference in the measures of central tendency the decision could be made based on some other factor, such a cost..

Section 17-3 Exercises

17.37

This exercise can be done following the steps shown in Example 17-3.

a. H_0: $\tilde{\mu}_1 = \tilde{\mu}_2 = \tilde{\mu}_3$
H_A: Not all population medians are equal

b.

Level of Significance	0.05
Group 1	
Sum of Ranks	118.5
Sample Size	8
Group 2	
Sum of Ranks	62
Sample Size	8
Group 3	
Sum of Ranks	119.5
Sample Size	8
Sum of Squared Ranks/Sample Size	4020.813
Sum of Sample Sizes	24
Number of groups	3
H Test Statistic	5.41625
Critical Value	5.991476
p-Value	0.066662

Do not reject the null hypothesis

c. H_o: $\mu_1 = \mu_2 = \mu_3$
H_a: Not all population means are equal

Anova: Single Factor

SUMMARY

Groups	Count	Sum	Average	Variance
Group 1	8	236	29.5	32.57143
Group 2	8	173	21.625	47.125
Group 3	8	237	29.625	66.55357

ANOVA

Source of Variation	SS	df	MS	F	P-value	F crit
Between Groups	336.0833	2	168.0417	3.447009	0.05075	3.466795
Within Groups	1023.75	21	48.75			
Total	1359.833	23				

Since $3.447 < 3.4668$ do not reject H_o and conclude that all population means are equal.

d. Because you cannot assume normal populations you should use the Kruskal-Wallis test.

17.39

a. H_0: $\tilde{\mu}_1 = \tilde{\mu}_2 = \tilde{\mu}_3 = \tilde{\mu}_4$

H_A: Not all population medians are equal

b. Using Equation 17-10.

$$H = \frac{12}{N(N+1)} \sum_{i=1}^{k} \frac{R_i^2}{n_i} - 3(N+1) =$$

$$\frac{12}{80(80+1)}\left(\frac{409600}{20} + \frac{608400}{20} + \frac{211600}{20} + \frac{1849600}{20}\right) - 3(81) = 42.11$$

Selecting $\alpha = .05$, $\chi_\alpha^2 = 7.8147$, since $H = 42.11$, we reject the null hypothesis of equal medians.

17.41

a. No

b. It is not necessary because the adjustment is only necessary when the null hypothesis is not rejected and the null hypothesis was rejected.

17.43

This exercise can be done following the steps shown in Example 17-3.

H_0: $\tilde{\mu}_1 = \tilde{\mu}_2 = \tilde{\mu}_3 = \tilde{\mu}_4$

H_A: Not all population medians are equal

Using PHStat:

Level of Significance	0.01
Group 1	
Sum of Ranks	26
Sample Size	4
Group 2	
Sum of Ranks	58
Sample Size	4
Group 3	
Sum of Ranks	37
Sample Size	4
Group 4	
Sum of Ranks	15
Sample Size	4
Sum of Squared Ranks/Sample Size	1408.5
Sum of Sample Sizes	16
Number of groups	4
H Test Statistic	11.13971
Critical Value	11.34488
p-Value	0.010994

Do not reject the null hypothesis

Adjusting for ties, the test statistic is 11.21 which is smaller than the critical value (11.34488). Therefore the null hypothesis is not rejected.

17.45

H_0: $\tilde{\mu}_1 = \tilde{\mu}_2 = \tilde{\mu}_3$

H_A: Not all population medians are equal

Constructing a table like that shown in Table 17-4, find the following values.

Rank Car 1	Rank Car 2	Rank Car 3
85.5	25.5	120

$H = [12/(21)(21+1)][(85.5^2/8) + (25.5^2/6) + (120^2/7)] - 3(21+1) = 13.9818$

Testing at $\alpha = .05$, $\chi_\alpha^2 = 5.9915$

Since $13.9818 > 5.9915$ reject H_0 and conclude that not all population medians are equal.

End of Chapter Exercises

17.47

The Kruskal-Wallis one-way analysis of variance is the nonparametric counterpart to the analysis of variance procedure and is used if the decision makers are not willing to assume normally distributed populations. It is applicable any time the variable has a continuous distribution, the data are at least ordinal, the samples are independent, and the samples come from populations whose only possible difference is that at least one may have a different central location than the others. Examples will vary.

17.49

Student answers will vary depending upon the organization selected.

17.51

a & b

Possible Sets	Sum of Ranks	Probability
none	-	1/16
1	1	1/16
2	2	1/16
3	3	1/16
4	4	1/16
1,2	3	1/16
1,3	4	1/16
1,4	5	1/16
2,3	5	1/16
2,4	6	1/16
3,4	7	1/16
1,2,3	6	1/16
1,2,4	7	1/16
1,3,4	8	1/16
2,3,4	9	1/16
1,2,3,4	10	1/16

c.

T	0	1	2	3	4	5	6	7	8	9	10
P(T)	1/16	1/16	1/16	2/16	2/16	2/16	2/16	2/16	1/16	1/16	1/16

17.53

a. H_0: $\tilde{\mu}_1 - \tilde{\mu}_2 = 0$

H_A: $\tilde{\mu}_1 - \tilde{\mu}_2 \neq 0$

Company 1	Rank 1	Company 2	Rank 2
246	5	300	8
211	2	305	9
235	3	308	10
270	6	325	14
411	18	340	16
310	11	295	7
450	19	320	13
502	20	330	15
311	12	240	4
200	1	360	17
	97		113

$$U1 = (10)(10) + (10)(10+1)/2 - 97 = 58$$
$$U2 = (10)(10) + (10)(10+1)/2 - 113 = 42$$

$$Utest = 42$$

If $\alpha = .10$, $U_\alpha = 27$

Since $42 > 27$ do not reject H_0 and conclude that the medians are not different.

b. H_0: $\mu_1 - \mu_2 = 0$
H_A: $\mu_1 - \mu_2 \neq 0$

	Company 1	Company 2
Mean	314.60	312.30
Std. Dev.	105.2386	32.1906

Testing to see if the variances are equal:

$$F = (105.2386)^2/(32.1906)^2 = 10.6879$$
$$F_{0.05} = 3.179$$

Reject hypothesis of equal variances. Thus, we are required to utilize the t-test for unequal variances. This test requires the calculation of the degrees of freedom as follows:

$$\frac{\left(105.2386^2/10 + 32.1906^2/10\right)^2}{\left(\left(\frac{\left(105.2386^2/10\right)^2}{10-1}\right) + \left(\frac{\left(32.1906^2/10\right)^2}{10-1}\right)\right)} = 10.67 \rightarrow 10 \text{ degrees of freedom}$$

Decision Rule:
If $t > 1.8125$ or $t < -1.8125$ reject H_o, otherwise do not reject H_o

$$t = (314.60 - 312.30)/\sqrt{\frac{105.2386^2}{10} + \frac{32.1906^2}{10}} = 0.0661$$

Since $0.0661 < 1.8125$ do not reject H_o and conclude that the means are not different.

We must assume normal populations and independence in sampling.

17.55

a.

H_0: $\tilde{\mu}_1 - \tilde{\mu}_2 = 0$

H_A: $\tilde{\mu}_1 - \tilde{\mu}_2 \neq 0$

Urban	Rank Urban	Rural	Rank Rural
76	12	55	7
90	19	80	14
86	18	94	21
60	9	40	4
43	5	85	17
96	22	92	20
50	6	77	13
20	1	68	10
30	2	35	3
82	15	59	8
75	11		
84	16		
	136		117

$U1 = (12)(10) + (12)(12+1)/2 - 136 = 62$

$U2 = (12)(10) + (10)(10+1)/2 - 117 = 58$

$Utest = 58$

If $\alpha = .02$, $U_\alpha = 24$

Since $58 > 24$ do not reject H_0 and conclude that the medians are not different.

b. H_0: $\mu_1 - \mu_2 = 0$

H_A: $\mu_1 - \mu_2 \neq 0$

	Urban	Rural
Mean	66	68.5
Std. Dev.	24.9909	20.7806

Testing for equal variances:

$F = 24.9909^2/20.7806^2 = 1.4463$

$F_\alpha = 5.178$ at $\alpha = .01$

Accept hypothesis of equal variances.

Decision Rule:
If t > 2.5280 or t < -2.5280 reject H$_o$, otherwise do not reject H$_0$

$$S_{pooled} = \sqrt{(12-1)24.9909^2 + (10-1)20.7806^2 /(12+10-2)} = 23.1911$$

$$t = (66 - 68.5)/(23.1911)(\sqrt{(1/12)+(1/10)}) = -0.2518$$

Since –0.2518 > -2.5280 do not reject H$_o$ and conclude that the means are not different.

We must assume independence when sampling from normal populations with equal variances.

17.57

Putting the claim in the alternate hypothesis we find the following:

H_0: $\tilde{\mu} \leq 6$
H_A: $\tilde{\mu} > 6$

Using the Wilcoxon Signed Rank test we find W as follows:

Errors	Difference	Absolute Differences	Rank	R+	R-
2	-4	4	9.5		
4	-2	2	3.5		
1	-5	5	12		
0	-6	6	13		
6	0	0			
7	1	1	1	1	
4	-2	2	3.5		
2	-4	4	9.5		
9	3	3	6.5	6.5	
4	-2	2	3.5		
3	-3	3	6.5		
6	0	0			
2	-4	4	9.5		
4	-2	2	3.5		
2	-4	4	9.5		
				W = 7.5	

Since two of the differences equaled 0, we only rank 13 values. This is a upper tail test with n = 13. Since the significance level is not given, students will have to make a choice. If α = .05, using Appendix P, we reject if W > 70 Therefore, there is not near enough evidence to conclude the median is greater than 6 errors per page.

17.59

The hypotheses being tested are:

H_0: $\tilde{\mu} = 1989.32$

H_A: $\tilde{\mu} \neq 1989.32$

Using the Wilcoxon Signed Rank test we find W as follows:

Balance	Difference	Absolute Differences	Rank	R+	R-
1827.85	-161.47	161.47	15		15
1992.75	3.43	3.43	1	1	
2012.35	23.03	23.03	7	7	
1955.64	-33.68	33.68	9		9
2023.19	33.87	33.87	10	10	
1998.52	9.2	9.2	3	3	
2003.75	14.43	14.43	6	6	
1752.55	-236.77	236.77	17		17
1865.32	-124	124	13		13
2013.13	23.81	23.81	8	8	
2225.35	236.03	236.03	16	16	
2100.35	111.03	111.03	12	12	
2002.02	12.7	12.7	5	5	
1850.37	-138.95	138.95	14		14
1995.35	6.03	6.03	2	2	
2001.18	11.86	11.86	4	4	
2252.54	263.22	263.22	18	18	
2035.75	46.43	46.43	11	11	
				W = 103	W = 68

This is a two tailed test with n = 18. With $\alpha = .05$, using Appendix P, we reject if $W \leq 40$ or $W > 131$. Looking at the two values in the table we see there is not enough evidence to conclude the median has changed from $1989.32.

17.61

a. The hypotheses to be tested are:

$H_0: \quad \tilde{\mu}_1 = \tilde{\mu}_2$

$H_A: \quad \tilde{\mu}_1 \neq \tilde{\mu}_2$

Constructing the paired difference table:

Student	Test 1	Test 2	d	Rank	Ranks with smallest sum
1	42	34	8	12.5	
2	36	34	2	3	
3	44	45	-1	-1	1
4	27	30	-3	-6	6
5	40	45	-5	-9.5	9.5
6	34	32	2	3	0
8	50	44	6	11	0
9	29	32	-3	-6	6
10	43	40	3	6	0
11	42	34	8	12.5	0
12	22	32	-10	-14	14
13	26	30	-4	-8	8
14	45	40	5	9.5	0
15	41	39	2	3	0
				T=	44.5

Using Appendix N, with $\alpha = .05$, Reject if $T \leq 21$ or if $T \geq 84$

Since $44.5 > 21$ do not reject H_0 and conclude that the medians are the same.

b. A Type II error is the probability of accepting a false null hypothesis. In this case a Type II error would mean we accepted the null hypothesis that the medians of the two tests are the same when, in fact, they are not the same.

17.63

    a. They should use the Wilcoxon Matched-Pairs Signed Rank test since the problem does not say you can assume a normal distribution and because you are using matched pairs.

    b Putting the claim in the alternate hypothesis:

$$H_0: \tilde{\mu}_{w/oA} \geq \tilde{\mu}_A$$
$$H_A: \tilde{\mu}_{w/oA} < \tilde{\mu}_A .$$

Automobile	Without Additive	With Additive	d	rank of d	Ranks with smallest expected sum
1	28	28.5	-0.5	-1	
2	25	26	-1	-3	
4	22	21	1	3	3
5	24	26	-2	-6	
6	19	21	-2	-6	
7	26	25	1	3	3
8	27	29	-2	-6	
				T =	6

Using $\alpha = .025$, $T_\alpha = 4$

    c. Since $6 > 4$ do not reject H_0 and conclude the additive does not improve the mileage. The claim is not supported.

Chapter 18 Solutions

When applicable, selected problems in each section will be done following the appropriate step-by-step procedures outlined in the corresponding sections of the chapter. Other problems will provide key points and the answers to the questions, but all answers can be arrived at using the appropriate steps.

Section 18-1 Exercises

18.1

Both Deming and Juran emphasized that quality was the key component to business competitiveness and that the best way to improve quality came from improving the processes and systems that produce products and deliver services. There are, however, some differences in the philosophies of the two quality pioneers. While Juran focused on quality planning and helping businesses drive down costs by eliminating waste from their processes, Deming advocated a philosophy known as total quality management (TQM), which focused on continuous process improvement directed toward customer satisfaction. In his 14 points, Deming emphasized the importance of leadership if a company is to become a world-class organization. Juran is credited with being one of the first to apply the Pareto Principle to quality improvement activities. This principle is designed to focus management attention on the vital few quality problems that exist in the organization. A primary difference between Deming and Juran is evident in their views regarding goals and targets. While Juran advocated the use of goals and targets in quality improvement activities, Deming argued that goals and targets were detrimental to the constancy of purpose designed to foster a commitment to long-term continuous process improvement activities.

18.3

Student answers will vary. Some students, especially those unfamiliar with the advantage that higher quality can provide a firm, may argue that quality improvement efforts are expensive, since they demand that workers be trained properly and that managers fix quality problems. They may think that these quality improvement costs are never fully recovered by firms in competitive markets. However, others will realize that improving quality can eliminate or reduce rework and scrap. Higher quality may allow a firm to reduce its warranty expense. Also, improved quality translates into greater customer satisfaction and some marketing studies have shown that it is less expensive to keep the customers that you have than it is to try and get new customers. Students who appreciate the strategic importance that high quality can play in an organization will argue that while there are costs to quality, the benefits of having good quality more than make up for any costs incurred in improving the firm's overall product and service quality. Because rework, scrap, and warranty expenses decrease with higher quality, prices for certain high quality goods and services can be competitive.

While student examples will vary, they may cite the experience of electronics manufactures where costs have been declining but quality has increased. Other examples may include automobiles, camping equipment, and personal computers.

18.5

Student answers will vary depending on the process at their school. A simple example would be

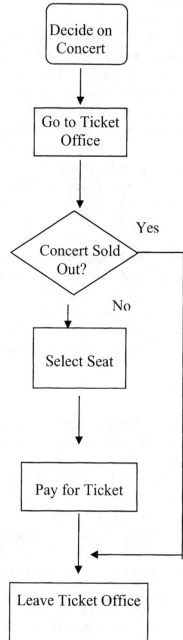

18.7

Student answers will vary depending upon answers to Exercise 18.6.

18.9

Student answers will vary. Some possible causes by category are:

People: Too Few Drivers, High Driver Turnover
Methods: Poor Scheduling, Improper Route Assignments
Equipment: Buses Too Small, Bus Reliability, Too Few Buses
Environment: Weather, Traffic Congestion, Road Construction

Section 18-2 Exercises

18.11

This exercise can be done following the steps shown in the Hilder's Publishing Example.

We first find the centerline as follows:

$$\overline{p} = 270/(30*100) = 0.090$$

Assuming that 3-sigma control chart limits are to be established then

$$UCL = 0.090 + 3 * \sqrt{\frac{0.090 * (1 - 0.090)}{100}} = 0.176$$

$$LCL = 0.090 - 3 * \sqrt{\frac{0.090 * (1 - 0.090)}{100}} = 0.004$$

18.13

Because a process can go out of control rather quickly it is imperative that the control charts be updated as soon as information becomes available. In this way if the process is found to be out of control it can be stopped to determine the assignable cause for the problem.

18.15

a.

	Panel 1	Panel 2	Panel 3	Panel 4	Panel 5	X-Bar	Range
Hour 41	0.764	0.737	0.724	0.716	0.752	0.7386	0.048
Hour 42	0.766	0.785	0.777	0.79	0.799	0.7834	0.033
Hour 43	0.812	0.774	0.767	0.799	0.821	0.7946	0.054

Notice that the subgroup means and subgroup ranges for Hours 41-43 are within the control limits for the control charts constructed in problem 18-14. However, the subgroup mean for Hour 43 is close to the upper control limit for the x-bar chart. Also, the subgroup ranges are all below the centerline. While this is not yet a concern a series of nine consecutive values below the centerline (or above the centerline), or six or more consecutive points moving in the same direction would indicate that the process has lost statistical control. At this time, end of Hour 43, there is no evidence that a special cause of variation is present in the process.

b. Yes. Without the control chart limits it would not be possible for us to see the natural, inherent variation of the process. We need the charts that we developed in problem 18-14 to determine whether evidence of special cause variation is present.

18.17

a.

Period	Mean	Range
31	5.3325	1.05
32	4.7875	1.25
33	4.975	0.84
34	5.4425	0.91
35	4.8525	1.47
36	5.3025	1.16
37	5.3375	0.65
38	5.38	0.61
39	6.08	2.09
40	6.2525	1.17

Looking at the mean values of these observations it appears that the process has gone out of control since all but 2 observations and the 1st 8 in sequence are below the LCL.

b. Note: The differences in the control chart limits shown here and in problem 18-16 are due only to rounding differences reflected in the type of software used.

X-bar Chart

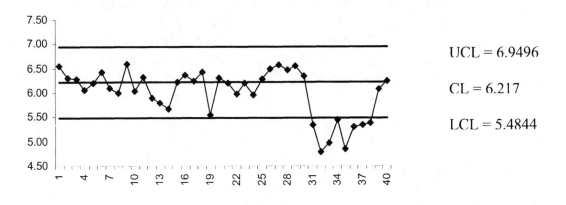

UCL = 6.9496

CL = 6.217

LCL = 5.4844

R-chart

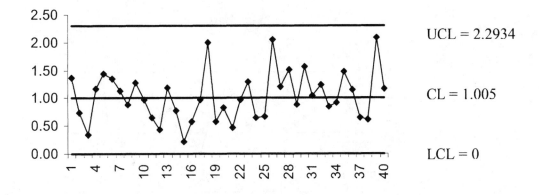

UCL = 2.2934

CL = 1.005

LCL = 0

The report will vary with the student, but should certainly comment on the R-chart being in control but the X-bar chart going out of control in periods 31-38. An assignable cause should be found.

18.19

This exercise can be done following the steps shown in the Hilder's Publishing Example.

a.

The appropriate control chart for this situation is a p-chart. The centerline, p-bar, equals the number of account errors/number of accounts sampled. For the sample consisting of 100 account records for each of the last 30 days we find that p-bar equals 238/(30*100) = 0.0793. The estimated standard error is 0.0270 and is calculated as shown below.

$$\sqrt{\frac{0.0793 * (1 - 0.0793)}{100}} = 0.0270$$

The 3-sigma upper control limit is 0.0793 + (3*0.0270) = 0.1603. The 3-sigma lower control limit is 0.0793 - (3*0.0270) = -0.0017 which is then set equal to 0.0000.

The chart is shown below.

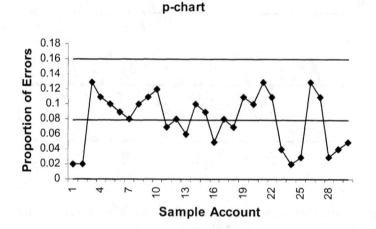

p-chart

b. The process appears to be in control. All of the data points are within the upper and lower control limits and there do not appear to be any runs in the data.

c.

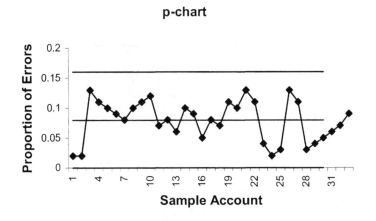

p-chart

The process still appears to be in statistical control. No sample proportions are outside of the control limits. There is a potential for concern if the next sample proportions continue to trend upward. A sustained upward trend would suggest that an assignable cause was present in the process.

18.21

This exercise can be done following the steps shown in the Cattleman's Bar and Grill Example.

a. The x-bar and R-charts are used together to monitor a process where the characteristic of interest is a variable (i.e., a characteristic measured on a continuous scale). Since time is measured, the machine downtime that is being monitored is a variable characteristic and requires that both the x-bar and R-charts be used.

b. The centerline for the x-bar chart is the average of the subgroup means and equals 82.46.

c. The centerline for the R-chart is the average of the subgroup ranges and equals 12.33.

d. UCL = 2.114*12.33 = 26.07   and LCL = 0*12.33 = 0

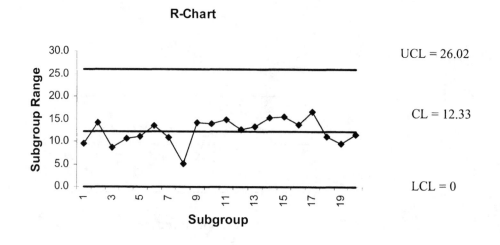

$$UCL = 82.46 + (0.577*12.33) = 89.57. \qquad LCL = 82.46 - (0.577*12.33) = 75.35$$

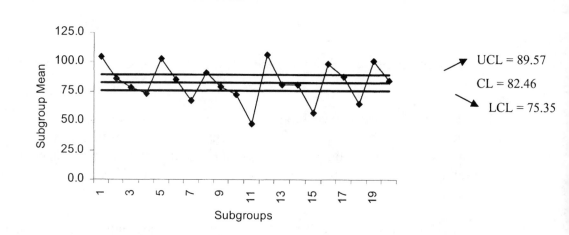

f. While the range chart has no points outside the control chart limits, there is a run of 9 values above the centerline, which indicates a possible loss of statistical control. The x-bar chart exhibits an out of statistical control condition given that there are several subgroup means above the upper control limit and several below the lower control limit. This provides strong evidence that the process was not in statistical control at the time the control chart was developed.

18.23

This exercise can be done following the steps shown in the Cattleman's Bar and Grill Example.

a. UCL = 2.282 * 100.375 = 229.056
    CL = 100.375
    LCL = 0 * 100.375 = 0

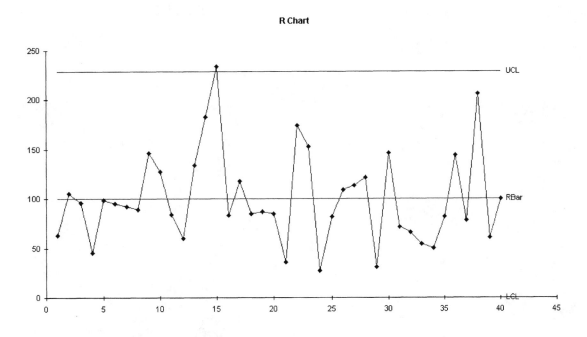

b. UCL = 415.3 + 0.729(100.375) = 488.473
    CL = 415.3
    LCL = 415.3 − 0.729(100.375) = 342.127

XBar Chart

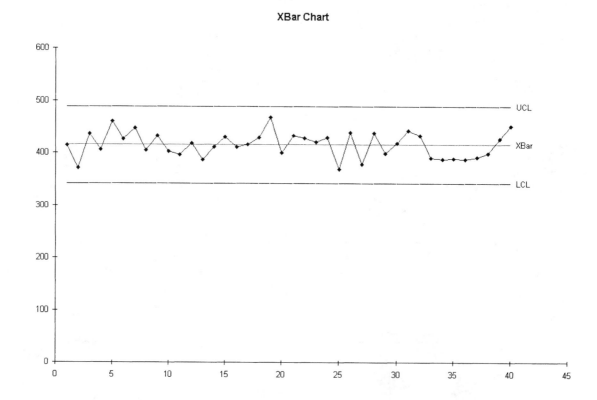

c. The process appears to have lost control with respect to its variability, which is measured by the R-chart. Note that week 15 is above the upper control limit on the R-chart. The range chart measures the dispersion or spread of the process. Ajax should investigate for an assignable cause that could explain the higher variability in week 15. Furthermore, since the range chart shows that the process is out of control, we should question the validity of the x-bar chart. Whenever the range chart reflects an out of control situation, the x-bar chart, which is determined using the average range of the subgroups, is compromised.

18.25

This exercise can be done following the steps shown in the Hilder's Publishing Example.

a. The appropriate control chart for this data is the p-chart.

b. $\bar{p} = 441/(300*50) = 0.0294$

$s = \sqrt{(0.0294)(1-0.0294)/50} = 0.0239$

$UCL = 0.0294 + 3(0.0239) = 0.1011$

$LCL = 0.0294 - 3(0.0239) = -0.0423$ so set to 0

p-chart

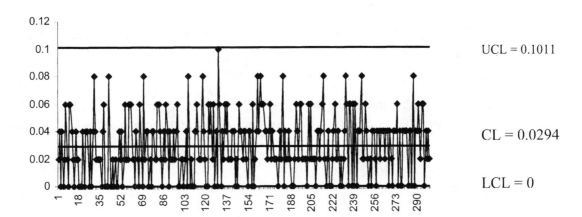

c.

Sample Number	301	302	303
p-bar	0.12	0.18	0.14

p-chart

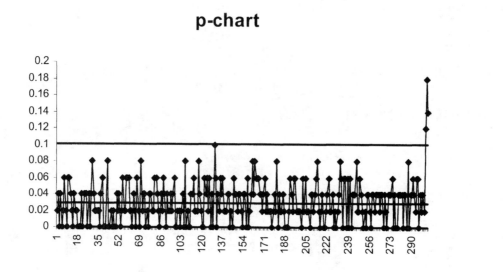

UCL = 0.1011

CL = 0.0294

LCL = 0

All of these points are above the UCL which indicates that the process has gone out of control.

d. The new sample proportion would be 0.28 which is again above the UCL. This suggests that the process is still out of control and getting further out of control.

18.27

This exercise can be done following the steps shown in the Chandler's Tile Example.

a. $\bar{c} = 29.3333$

$$UCL = 29.3333 + 3(\sqrt{29.3333}) = 45.5814$$
$$LCL = 29.3333 - 3(\sqrt{29.3333}) = 13.0852$$

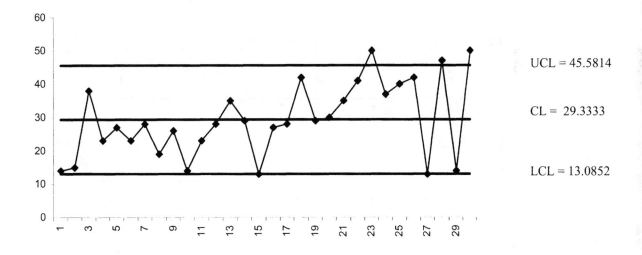

c-chart

UCL = 45.5814

CL = 29.3333

LCL = 13.0852

b.   The process seems to be out of control since several observations are above the UCL or right at the LCL and there seems to be a run (observation 4 – 12) below the center line and observations 27 – 30 seem to be alternating one above or near the upper UCL and the next below the LCL, etc.

c. Need to convert the data to bags per passenger by dividing bags by 40 and then developing a u-chart based upon the explanation in CD-Rom optional topics.

$$CL = 29.333/40 = 0.7333$$

$$UCL = 0.7333 + 3*\sqrt{0.7333/40} = 1.1395$$

$$LCL = 0.7333 - 3*\sqrt{0.7333/40} = 0.3271$$

u-chart

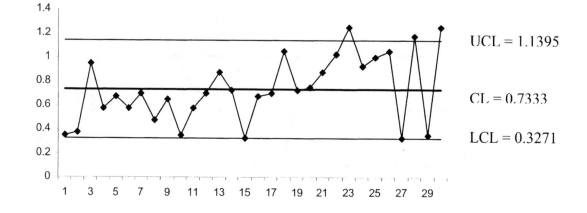

End of Chapter Exercises

18.29

a. The Shewart factor for the x-bar chart with a subgroup size of 3 is A2 = 1.023. The Shewart factors for the range chart are D3 = 0.0 and D4 = 2.575 for the lower and upper control limits, respectively.

b. UCL = 2.575*0.80 = 2.06   LCL = 0*0.80 = 0

c. UCL = 2.33 + (1.023*0.80) = 3.1468   LCL = 2.33 - (1.023*0.80) = 1.512

18.31

The centerline of the control chart is the average proportion of defective = 720/(20*150) = 0.240. For 3-sigma control chart limits we find

$$UCL = 0.240 + 3*\sqrt{\frac{0.240*(1-0.240)}{150}} = 0.345$$

18.33

The appropriate control chart is the p-chart for monitoring the proportion of

$$LCL = 0.240 - 3 * \sqrt{\frac{0.240*(1-0.240)}{150}} = 0.135$$

defectives (in this case we can monitor the proportion of on time shipments). The centerline p-bar is equal to the average of the 21 sample proportions and equals 0.9152. The centerline can also be found by summing the total number of successes (on-time shipments = 1922) and dividing by the total number of samples (21*100 = 2100). The standard error of the subgroup proportions is estimated by the following equation

The 3-sigma control limits are computed as follows:

Lower Control Limit = 0.9152 - 3*0.0279 = 0.8315

Centerline = 0.9152

Upper Control Limit = 0.9152 + 3*0.0279 = 0.9989

The control chart is shown below.

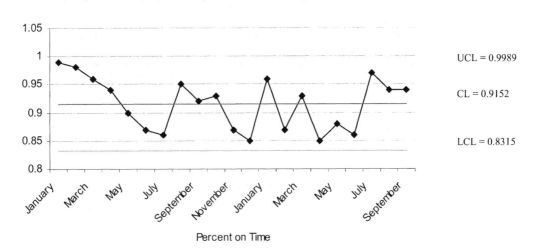

The delivery process appears to be in statistical control. Some concerned might be expressed concerning the first seven sample proportions trending down, which indicates that the proportion of on-time deliveries is falling. There are also some sample proportions close to the lower limit that might be cause for concern and investigation. However, there are no points below the lower control limit.

18.35

The appropriate chart is the p-chart. $\bar{p} = 0.0524$

$$\sqrt{\frac{0.0524 * (1 - 0.0524)}{100}} = 0.0223$$

The 3-sigma control limits are computed as follows:

Lower Control Limit = 0.0524 - 3*0.0223 = -0.0145 so set to 0

Centerline = 0.0524

Upper Control Limit = 0.0524 + 3*0.0223 = 0.1193

The control chart is shown below.

p-chart

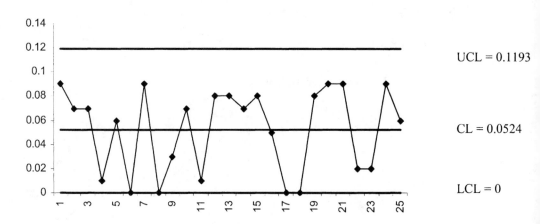

The process appears to be in control.

18.37

a. x-bar chart: CL = 0.7499
   UCL = 0.7499 + (0.577)(0.0115) = 0.7565
   LCL = 0.7499 – (0.577)(0.0115) = 0.7433

   R-chart: CL = 0.0115
   UCL = (0.0115)(2.114) = 0.0243
   LCL = (0.0115)(0) = 0

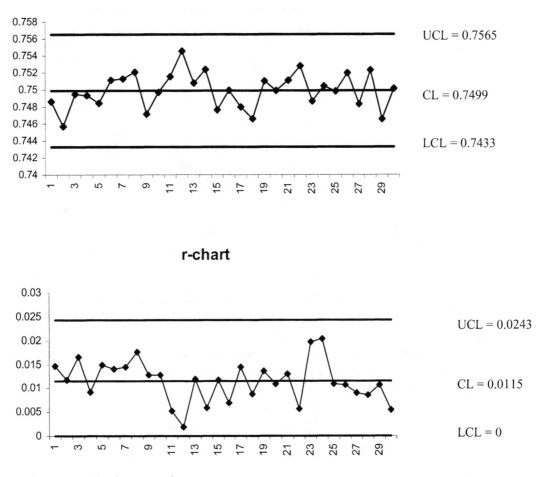

The process appears to be in control.

b.

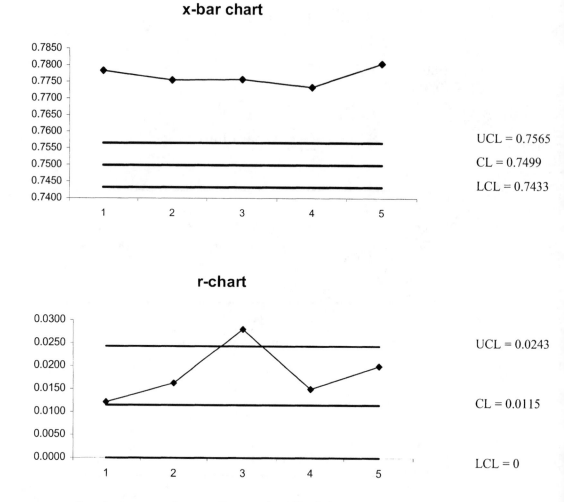

It now appears that the process is out of control. All of the averages are above the UCL and in the range chart one value is above the UCL.

Chapter 19 Solutions

When applicable, selected problems in each section will be done following the appropriate step-by-step procedures outlined in the corresponding sections of the chapter. Other problems will provide key points and the answers to the questions, but all answers can be arrived at using the appropriate steps.

Section 19-1 Exercises

19.1

A good outcome occurs whenever the "best" outcome results, or at the very least, the worst outcome does not occur. There is, however, an important distinction between a good outcome and a good decision. In decision analysis if we have properly used all the information available in making the decision, it was a good decision. It is important, however, that decision makers realize that in an uncertain environment, where they do not have control over the outcomes of their decisions, bad outcomes can, and will, occur. However, in the long run, by making good decisions there should be an increase in the number of good outcomes.

19.3

The decision environment described here is one of certainty. In such an environment the results of selecting each alternative are known before the decision is made. In this problem, Varsity Contracting knows what outcomes will occur in terms of the time required and the costs involved. The following table provides a breakdown of the revenues and expenses for the decision facing Varsity.

Annual Revenues & Costs	Accept Contract	Reject Contract
Annual Revenues	$0.10 * 100,000 * 12 months = $120,000	$0.00
Costs:		
Labor	2 workers @ $8.00 per hour for 8 hours per night for 5 nights per week for 52 weeks = $33,280	$0.00
Supplies	$200 per week for 52 weeks = $10,400	$0.00
Overhead	20% of Labor Cost (0.2*$33,280) = $6,656	$0.00
Total Annual Costs	$50,336	$0.00
Profit	$69,664	$0.00

Given that Varsity will realize an annual profit of $69,664, Varsity should sign the contract.

19.5

Multiplying each state of nature outcome by the appropriate probabilities, we find the following table:

		States of Nature			Expected Values
		S_1	S_2	S_3	
	A_1	150	80	-20	51
Alternatives	A_2	60	40	45	48.5
	A_3	240	70	-10	81
Probabilities		0.3	0.2	0.5	

Select the alternative with the largest expected value, A_3.

19.7

Multiplying each state of nature outcome by the appropriate probabilities, we find the following table:

		States of Nature				Expected Values
		S_1	S_2	S_3	S_4	
	A_1	170	45	-60	100	32.0
Alternatives	A_2	30	190	175	-65	91.5
	A_3	145	-50	120	110	85.5
	A_4	-40	80	10	70	37.0
Probabilities		0.1	0.2	0.4	0.3	

Select the alternative with the largest expected value, A_2.

19.9

a.

	Demand			
Purchase	10,000	15,000	20,000	25,000
10,000	8,500	8,500	8,500	8,500
15,000	5,250	12,750	12,750	12,750
20,000	2,000	9,500	17,000	17,000
25,000	(1,250)	6,250	13,750	21,250

b. 1. The maximum values are 8500, 12750, 17000 and 21250, in order, so purchase 25,000 hotdogs and buns.

2. The minimum values are 8500, 5250, 2000 and –1250, in order, so purchase 10,000 hotdogs and buns.

3.

Opportunity Loss Table				
	Demand			
Purchase	10,000	15,000	20,000	25,000
10,000	-	4,250	8,500	12,750
15,000	3,250	-	4,250	8,500
20,000	6,500	3,250	-	4,250
25,000	9,750	6,500	3,250	-

The maximum regret values are 12750, 8500, 6500, 9750, so purchase 20,000 hotdogs and buns.

19.11

a.

	Demand			
Production	20000	40000	60000	80000
20000	$ 2,800,000.00	$ 2,600,000.00	$ 2,400,000.00	$ 2,200,000.00
40000	$ 1,800,000.00	$ 5,800,000.00	$ 5,600,000.00	$ 5,400,000.00
60000	$ 800,000.00	$ 4,800,000.00	$ 8,800,000.00	$ 8,600,000.00
80000	$ (200,000.00)	$ 3,800,000.00	$ 7,800,000.00	$ 11,800,000.00

Acquisition Cost	$ 200,000.00
Selling Price	$ 250.00
Discount Price	$ 50.00
Coupon (Demand Exceeds Supply)	$ 10.00
Variable Production Cost	$ 100.00

b. Maximin: Max(2200000, 1800000, 800000, -200000) so produce 20,000.
Maximax: Max(2800000, 5800000, 8800000, 11800000) so produce 80,000.

19.13

This problem should be done following the steps shown in Example 19-1.

Purchases	Demand				
	100,000	150,000	200,000	225,000	250,000
100,000	1000000	1000000	1000000	1000000	1000000
150,000	675000	1575000	1575000	1575000	1575000
200,000	350000	1250000	2150000	2150000	2150000
225,000	187500	1087500	1987500	2437500	2437500
250,000	25000	925000	1825000	2275000	2725000

Fixed Cost	150,000				
Variable Cost	5				
Shipping	1.5				
Sales Price	18				

Probabilities	0.1	0.4	0.2	0.2	0.1

Purchases	Expected Value
100,000	1,000,000
150,000	1,485,000
200,000	1,610,000
225,000	1,582,500
250,000	1,465,000

Using the expected value criterion, 200,000 dozen roses should be purchased. The expected profit of purchasing this amount is $1,610,000.

19.15

This problem should be done following the steps shown in Example 19-1.

Probability of Demand	0.15	0.2	0.2	0.3	0.15
			Demand		
Supply	500	1000	2000	4000	7000
500	$ (7,000.00)	$ (7,000.00)	$ (7,000.00)	$ (7,000.00)	$ (7,000.00)
1000	$ (8,500.00)	$ (4,000.00)	$ (4,000.00)	$ (4,000.00)	$ (4,000.00)
2000	$(11,100.00)	$ (6,600.00)	$ 2,400.00	$ 2,400.00	$ 2,400.00
4000	$(16,700.00)	$(12,200.00)	$ (3,200.00)	$ 14,800.00	$14,800.00
7000	$(23,000.00)	$(18,500.00)	$ (9,500.00)	$ 8,500.00	$35,500.00

Supply	Expected Value
500	-7000
1000	-4675
2000	-1425
4000	1075
7000	-1175

Best Expected Value Decision

Supply 4,000 for EV of 1,075

19.17

a.

Revenue per unit $ 600,000
Variable Cost per unit $350,000
Salvage Cost per unit $150,000

	States of Nature (possible successful restaurants)					
Purchase	0	1	2	3	4	5
0	-	-	-	-	-	-
1	(200,000)	250,000	250,000	250,000	250,000	250,000
2	(400,000)	50,000	500,000	500,000	500,000	500,000
3	(600,000)	(150,000)	300,000	750,000	750,000	750,000
4	(800,000)	(350,000)	100,000	550,000	1,000,000	1,000,000
5	(1,000,000)	(550,000)	(100,000)	350,000	800,000	1,250,000

The maximum values for each alternative are 0; 250,000; 500,000; 750,000; 1,000,000; and 1,250,000, so purchase 5 restaurants for a maximum profit of $1,250,000.

b. The minimum values for each alternative are 0; -200,000; -400,000; -600,000; -800,000; and
    -1,000,000, so purchase no restaurants for a profit of $0.

c.

Mall Option:

Revenue per unit $ 500,000
Variable Cost per unit $250,000(includes franchise cost)
Salvage Cost per unit $100,000

| | States of Nature (possible successful restaurants) | | | | | |
Purchase	0	1	2	3	4	5
0	-	-	-	-	-	-
1	(150,000)	250,000	250,000	250,000	250,000	250,000
2	(300,000)	100,000	500,000	500,000	500,000	500,000
3	(450,000)	(50,000)	350,000	750,000	750,000	750,000
4	(600,000)	(200,000)	200,000	600,000	1,000,000	1,000,000
5	(750,000)	(350,000)	50,000	450,000	850,000	1,250,000

Larger Buildings:

Revenue per unit $ 1,000,000
Variable Cost per unit $500,000(includes franchise cost)
Salvage Cost per unit $200,000

| | States of Nature (possible successful restaurants) | | | | | |
Purchase	0	1	2	3	4	5
0	-	-	-	-	-	-
1	(300,000)	500,000	500,000	500,000	500,000	500,000
2	(600,000)	200,000	1,000,000	1,000,000	1,000,000	1,000,000
3	(900,000)	(100,000)	700,000	1,500,000	1,500,000	1,500,000
4	(1,200,000)	(400,000)	400,000	1,200,000	2,000,000	2,000,000
5	(1,500,000)	(700,000)	100,000	900,000	1,700,000	2,500,000

d. Mall Option:
    Maximax: The maximum values for each alternative are 0, 250,000; 500,000;
    750,000; 1,000,000; 1,250,000, so purchase 5 franchises for a maximum profit of
    1,250,000
    Maximin: The minimum values for each alternative are 0; -150,000; -300,000; -
    450,000;
    -600,000; - 750,000, so purchase 0 franchises for a profit of $0.

    Larger Building Option:
    Maximax: The maximum values for each alternative are 0, 500,000; 1,000,000;
    1,500,000; 2,000,000; 2,500,000, so purchase 5 franchises for a maximum profit
    of 2,500,000
    Maximin: The minimum values for each alternative are 0, -300,000; -600,000; -
    900,000;
    -1,200,000; -1,500,000, so purchase 0 franchises for a profit of $0

e.

Purchase	Expected Profit
0	-
1	223,000
2	401,000
3	489,000 Optimal
4	397,000
5	251,000

Mall Option:

Purchase	Expected Profit
0	-
1	230,000
2	420,000
3	550,000
4	580,000 Optimal
5	490,000

Larger Building Option:

Purchase	Expected Profit
0	-
1	428,000
2	736,000
3	844,000 Optimal
4	632,000
5	364,000

Based on the expected value criteria they should purchase 3 franchises with the larger building option for an expected profit of $844,000.

Section 19-2 Exercises

All the problems in this section can be done following the steps shown in Exercise 19-2.

19.19

a.

	Opportunity Loss Table		
	States of Nature		
Probabilities	0.5	0.2	0.3
Alternative	S_1	S_2	S_3
A_1	0	25	40
A_2	15	15	20
A_3	35	0	0

b.

		States of Nature			Expected Values
		S_1	S_2	S_3	
	A_1	145	55	80	107.5
Alternatives	A_2	130	65	100	108.0
	A_3	110	80	120	107.0
Probabilities		0.5	0.2	0.3	

$$EVUC = .5(145) + .2(80) + .3(120) = 124.5$$
$$EVPI = 124.5 - 108.0 = 16.5$$

19.21

Production	Demand 20000	40000	60000	80000	
20000	$ 2,800,000	$ 2,600,000	$ 2,400,000	$ 2,200,000	
40000	$ 1,800,000	$ 5,800,000	$ 5,600,000	$ 5,400,000	
60000	$ 800,000	$ 4,800,000	$ 8,800,000	$ 8,600,000	
80000	$ (200,000)	$ 3,800,000	$ 7,800,000	$ 11,800,000	
Prob.	0.1	0.3	0.4	0.2	EVUC
EVUC	$ 280,000	$ 1,740,000	$ 3,520,000	$ 2,360,000	$7,900,000

Production	Expected Value
20000	$ 2,460,000.00
40000	$ 5,240,000.00
60000	$ 6,760,000.00
80000	$ 6,600,000.00

EVPI = $7,900,000 - $6,760,000 = $1,140,000

19.23

Probability of Demand	0.15	0.2	0.2	0.3	0.15	
	Demand					
Supply	500	1000	2000	4000	7000	
500	$ (7,000.00)	$ (7,000.00)	$ (7,000.00)	$ (7,000.00)	$ (7,000.00)	
1000	$ (8,500.00)	$ (4,000.00)	$ (4,000.00)	$ (4,000.00)	$ (4,000.00)	
2000	$(11,100.00)	$ (6,600.00)	$ 2,400.00	$ 2,400.00	$ 2,400.00	
4000	$(16,700.00)	$(12,200.00)	$ (3,200.00)	$ 14,800.00	$14,800.00	
7000	$(23,000.00)	$(18,500.00)	$ (9,500.00)	$ 8,500.00	$35,500.00	EVUC
EVUC	$ (1,050.00)	$ (800.00)	$ 480.00	$ 4,440.00	$ 5,325.00	$8,395.00

Supply	Expected Value
500	-7000
1000	-4675
2000	-1425
4000	1075
7000	-1175

EVPI = $8,395 - $1,075 = $7,320

Section 19-3 Exercises

19.25

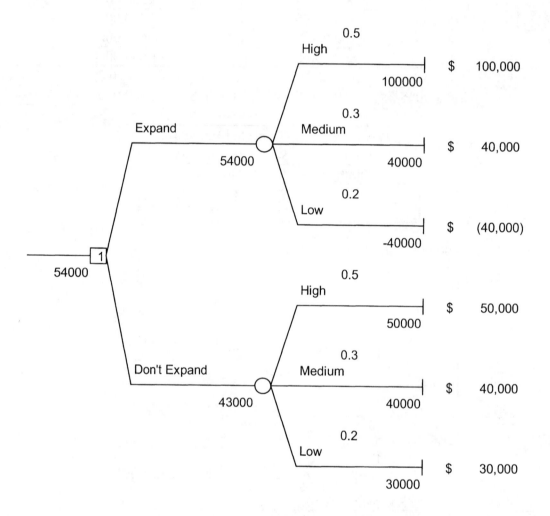

The owners should expand.

19.27

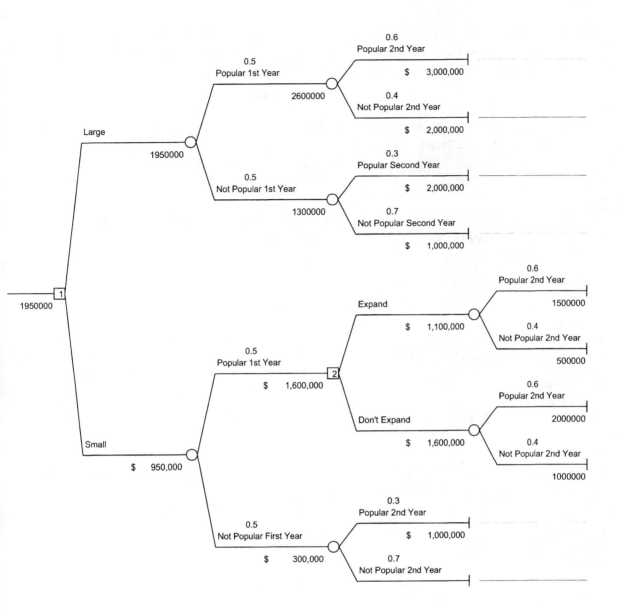

The developer should build the large resort.

Chapter 19

End of Chapter Exercises

19.29 The expected value of the *Do Not Develop* branch on the decision tree is $78 per unit while the expected value of the develop branch is $82. The best decision is to work on the improved model.

19.31 The expected value of the don't contract branch is $82. By evaluating the contract branch of the decision tree we find an expected value of $81. So the best decision is not to sign the contract and develop the improved model.

19.33 Max (-400,000; -800,000; -1,200,000; -1,600,000; -2,000,000) so Max = -400,000 which is associated with build 10

19.35

Variable Land Cost (per block)	200,000
Fixed Construction Cost (per block)	250,000

Variable Construction Cost (Per Unit)	70,000
Selling Price(per unit)	200,000
Auction Value	75,000

			Demand				
Build	0	10	20	30	40	50	EV
10	(400,000)	850,000	850,000	850,000	850,000	850,000	787,500
20	(800,000)	450,000	1,700,000	1,700,000	1,700,000	1,700,000	1,450,000
30	(1,200,000)	50,000	1,300,000	2,550,000	2,550,000	2,550,000	1,800,000
40	(1,600,000)	(350,000)	900,000	2,150,000	3,400,000	3,400,000	1,837,500
50	(2,000,000)	(750,000)	500,000	1,750,000	3,000,000	4,250,000	1,625,000
Probabilities	0.05	0.10	0.25	0.25	0.20	0.15	

Optimal decision based on expected value would be build 40 at an expected profit of $1,837,50

19.37

Decision	Failure	Successful	EV
Don't Market	-	-	-
Market	(20,000,000)	50,000,000	22,000,000
Probabilities	0.4	0.6	

Based on the expected value the company should market the product.

19.39

Decision	Exellent	Good	Fair	Poor	EV
Don't Market	-	-	-	-	0
Market	70,000,000	50,000,000	10,000,000	(20,000,000)	31,000,000
Probabilities	0.3	0.3	0.1	0.3	

Based on the expected value the company should market the product.

19.41

		Demand						
Prepare		3	4	5	6	7	8	EV
	3	10.5	7	3.5	0	-3.5	-7	3.325
	4	8.5	14	10.5	7	3.5	0	9.425
	5	6.5	12	17.5	14	10.5	7	12.825
	6	4.5	10	15.5	21	17.5	14	13.975
	7	2.5	8	13.5	19	24.5	21	13.325
	8	0.5	6	11.5	17	22.5	28	11.775
Probabilities		0.1	0.3	0.25	0.2	0.1	0.05	

Based on the expected value they should prepare 6 orders for an expected value of $13.975

19.43

Opportunity Loss
Table:

Build			Demand				
Build	0	10	20	30	40	50	EOL
10	-	-	850,000	1,700,000	2,550,000	3,400,000	1,657,500
20	400,000	400,000	-	850,000	1,700,000	2,550,000	995,000
30	800,000	800,000	400,000	-	850,000	1,700,000	645,000
40	1,200,000	1,200,000	800,000	400,000	-	850,000	607,500
50	1,600,000	1,600,000	1,200,000	800,000	400,000	-	820,000
Probabilities	0.05	0.10	0.25	0.25	0.20	0.15	

To minimize the EOL you would build 40 units for an expected opportunity loss of $607,500. This is the EVPI. The $607,500 is the most you would pay for perfect information so if someone is willing to sell it to you for $10,000 you would definitely purchase it.

19.45

The following decision tree represents the decision faced by Graciela Grimm and the Grimm Group.

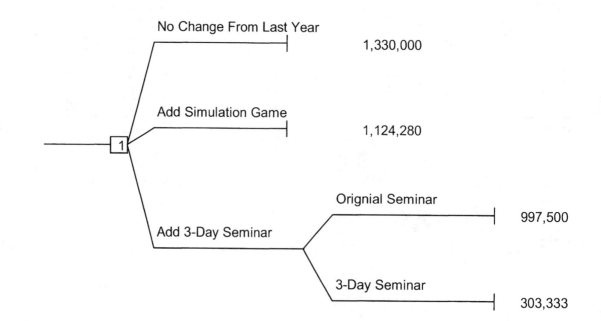

19.47

If the original margins can be maintained, then the revenues and costs become (use new demand values in calculating revenues):

Seminar	Revenues	Costs	Profits
Quality	$1,320,000	$792,000	$528,000
Material	$1,035,000	$621,000	$414,000
JIT	$1,609,800	$1,046,370	$563,430

The total profit is $1,505,430 if margins can be maintained.

The decision tree with the new information becomes:

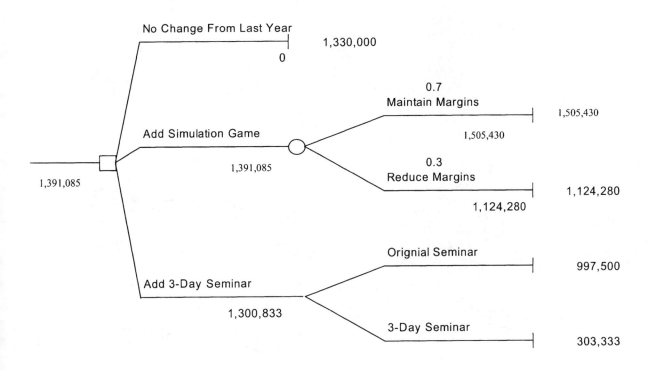

As can be seen from the tree, the best decision now is to add the simulation game.

19.49

NOTE: The solution below is based upon a correction that needs to be made to the textbook problem. On problem 19.48, in the table entitled "League Race" the Yes/No column needs to be reversed. The table should be as follows:

League Race		
Player Strike	*Tight*	*Not Tight*
No	$5.00	$2.50
	p = 0.42	p = 0.28
Yes	$4.00	$2.00
	p = 0.18	p = 0.12

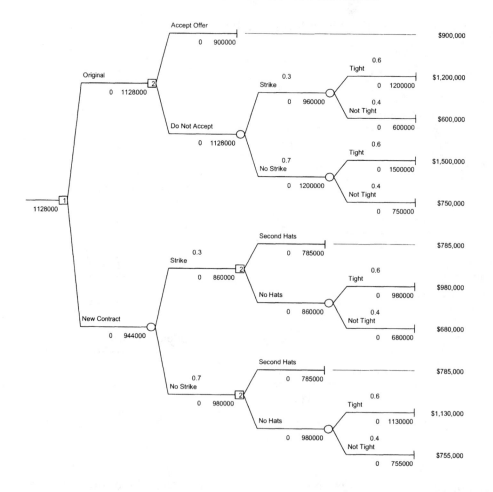

19.51

The expected cost to you for the above proposal is $944,000. The expected cost of buying them on the open market is $1,128,000. In this case since we are discussing cost you would accept the proposal if you were the purchasing manager.

19.53

The decision tree for the Gregston Corporation is shown below. By folding back the decision tree the expected values for the various alternatives are determined. Based on expected profits, Gregston should Not Test and Drill.

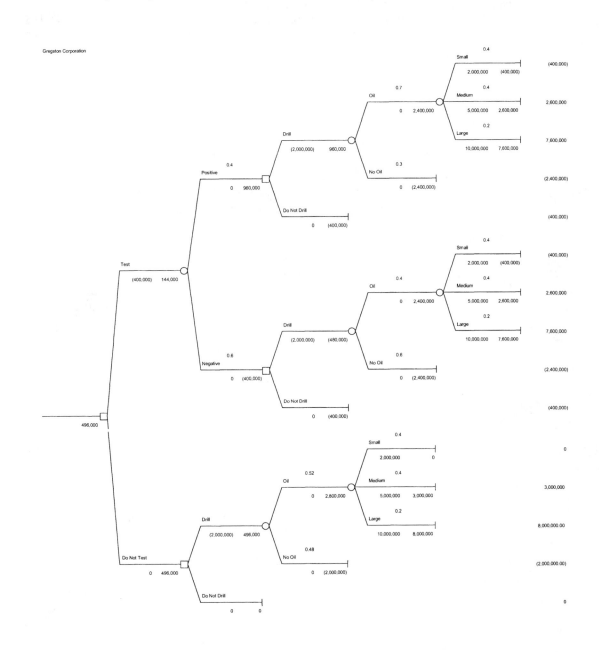

Note: the probabilities associated with the branches No Test –Drill are based on the probability the test has been positive in this area and the probabilities of finding oil when the test is both positive and when the test is negative as follows:

$(0.7*0.4) + (0.6*0.4) = 0.52$ = probability of Oil. $1-0.52 = 0.48$ = probability of No Oil.

19.55

For the decision to change, the expected value of the Test branch will have to be greater than the expected value of the Do Not Test branch.
$(x)(960,000) + (1-x)(-400,000) \geq 496,000; x \geq 0.66$